MANDATE FOR LEADERSHIP III:
POLICY STRATEGIES FOR THE 1990s

Charles L. Heatherly is Vice President for Academic Affairs at The Heritage Foundation. He served in the Reagan Administration as Director of the White House Fellowships Program, Deputy Administrator and Acting Administrator of the U.S. Small Business Administration and Deputy Under Secretary for Management at the U.S. Department of Education. He edited sections One and Four and served as project director for the *Mandate III* volume.

Burton Yale Pines is Senior Vice President and Director of Research at The Heritage Foundation. Formerly a foreign correspondent and associate editor at *Time* magazine, Pines is the author of *Back to Basics* and a three-time winner of the New York Newspaper Guild's Page One Award. He is Chairman of the National Center for Public Policy Research and Vice-Chairman of the Center for Peace and Freedom. He edited sections Two and Three.

MANDATE FOR LEADERSHIP III:
POLICY STRATEGIES FOR THE 1990s

CHARLES L. HEATHERLY
and
BURTON YALE PINES
Co-Editors

STUART M. BUTLER
GEORGE NESTERCZUK
W. BRUCE WEINROD
Section Editors

and

MARK B. LIEDL
Contributing Editor

Copyright © 1989 by The Heritage Foundation
214 Massachusetts Avenue, N.E.
Washington, D.C. 20002

Distributed by arrangement with
National Book Network
4720 Boston Way
Lanham, MD 20706

Library of Congress Cataloging-in-Publication Data

Mandate for leadership III : policy strategies for the 1990s
/ Charles L. Heatherly, Burton Yale Pines, editors.
p. cm.
Includes index.
1. Administrative agencies—United States. 2. United States—
Executive departments. 3. Political planning—United States.
4. Presidents—United States. I. Heatherly, Charles L. II. Pines,
Burton Yale.
JK421.M3433   1989
353'.072—dc 19   88–39730 CIP
ISBN 0–89195–045–1 (alk. paper)
ISBN 0–89195–046–X (pbk. : alk. paper)

Table of Contents

Foreword

by
Edwin J. Feulner, Jr.
President, The Heritage Foundation

Mandate III is the Heritage Foundation's most ambitious project ever. It enlisted some 400 participants, most with experience in the Reagan Administration. That suggests the key way in which it differs from *Mandate I* (1980) and *Mandate II* (1984), both of which had enormous impact during the Reagan era.

Think of it this way: The first two *Mandates* diagnosed the federal government's afflictions, e.g., obesity and arthritis, and prescribed the appropriate cures, e.g. deregulation and reduced spending. For *Mandate III* we were able to call on hundreds of those who have had hands-on experience trying to administer those cures.

In some cases they were successful. In others, the detailed policy information in the previous *Mandate* volumes at the very least helped focus the debate.

The Heritage Foundation has always been more than just a "think tank." Heritage is not an ivory tower where ideas and research are ends in themselves. Its mission is to help translate sound ideas into public policy. *Mandate III* goes further in that direction than anything yet published.

Clearly an action plan for 1989 must differ from those offered four and eight years ago, but the principles guiding our recommendations are unchanged. We want public policy to reflect and strengthen the ideals of individual liberty, limited government, free enterprise, and strong national defense.

"Conservative," too, can be a misnomer if construed to mean hostility to change and a desire to "conserve" the status quo. What

Heritage seeks to conserve and strengthen is America's moral, cultural, and intellectual heritage. But, far from seeking to roll back the clock, we seek change that is practical and achievable in today's political and cultural contexts.

We still want more economic growth through less bureaucracy, fewer regulations, lower taxes, and less government spending. We still want the private sector, where competitive pressures and consumer choice lead to quality, to assume as many as possible of the functions Washington performs poorly, inefficiently, and often counterproductively. And we still want state and local governments to take over much of what Washington has spent the better part of this century usurping, for they can be far more sensitive, innovative, and flexible than the remote, muscle-bound federal bureaucracy.

As for defense and foreign policy, we still want the forces of democratic capitalism to do more than merely contain totalitarian expansion. They should stay on the march begun by the Reagan Administration, for that offers the only hope for oppressed and impoverished Third World nations.

We still want to move toward development and deployment of a strategic defense system. Heritage played a key role in developing the President's Strategic Defense Initiative.

I mention, of course, only a few items. These and others are detailed in the following pages. Hundreds of specific policy proposals were spelled out in our *Issues '88,* published last spring. *Mandate III* builds on and expands the proposals in that three-volume publication.

How different today's battleground is from the ground we were contesting just a few years ago. Eight years ago, the battle was still over fundamentals. How would the debate be framed?

Would we debate how to expand the welfare state or how to contain it? How to tax and regulate Americans even more, or how to lighten these burdens? How to contain communist expansion and negotiate more "arms-control" deals, or how to put democratic capitalism on the offensive and move from mutual assured destruction to a strategic-defense system?

We've won that battle. The intellectual debate has been framed in our terms.

Indeed, what history will find remarkable about the 1980s is how far and fast we've advanced. In many ways, the dreadful 1970s have been repealed. We've taken what, ten years ago, was called unthinkable and shown that it's *workable*—when given a chance. Just as the New Deal revolution of the 1930s laid the foundation for the Great Society of the

1960s, the intellectual battles we've won over the last decade have established the premises for formulating public policy well into the next century.

However, with that battle won, the need for more action intensifies, and we must not underestimate the enormity of the task. Face it: We knew long before Ronald Reagan got to the Oval Office that the Washington elephant would be hard to rein in, let alone steer in our direction, but we did not foresee *how* hard.

In the heady days following the tax and spending cuts of 1981, we fell to putting too much faith in the power of ideas to effect change by themselves, unaided by the unglamorous work needed to build coalitions and genuine grass-roots organizations.

We underestimated the stamina of liberalism, forgetting that its intellectual bankruptcy hadn't diminished the entrenched power of its institutions. Liberalism's key bastion is, of course, Congress, but by no means its only one. Indeed, virtually the entire federal government can be viewed as a self-perpetuating preserve of obsolete liberal nostrums.

Today's challenge, then, as the following pages make clear, is to sharpen the political skills that translate principles into policies. As we do so, of course, we must not forsake principles for the technocratic ideal of mere "competence." The authors that follow offer a wealth of practical advice, but they know above all that the monstrosity called the federal government needs far more than competent management; it needs fundamental change by men and women of vision and principle. *Mandate III* is dedicated to those courageous individuals, the veterans of the Reagan Revolution and volunteers in tomorrow's call to duty.

Acknowledgments

Mandate III is the product of not only the 400 authors and contributors listed in the text but of many other individuals who helped keep the project on course and on schedule. The editors are greatly indebted to contributing editor Mark B. Liedl, who managed the efficient flow of mountains of paper between project team chairmen, contributors, and editors for parts Two and Three; to editorial assistant Mark Pietrzyk, who contributed his considerable skills to the fifteen chapters of parts One and Four and supervised the preparation of the index; and to Roger A. Brooks, Director of the Asian Studies Center, who supervised the section on Asia.

Many individuals served as outside readers to give the editors the benefit of their extensive experience in policy areas and management issues. Michael Sanera, Robert E. Moffit, Jeanne Sclater and Timothy N. Hunter offered helpful suggestions on several chapters. Our colleagues at The Heritage Foundation, especially Phillip N. Truluck and Gordon S. Jones, offered many valuable insights and suggestions.

We are much indebted to Richard Odermatt and Jean Savage for their diligent copyediting, to Joan Seivwright for typing the chapters of part Four, and to Don Hall for supervising the typing of parts Two and Three.

CLH
BYP
SMB
GN
WBW

The Heritage Foundation

The Heritage Foundation was established in 1973 as a nonpartisan, tax-exempt policy research institute dedicated to the principles of free competitive enterprise, limited government, individual liberty, and a strong national defense. The Foundation's research and study programs are designed to make the voices of responsible conservatism heard in Washington, D.C., throughout the United States, and in the capitals of the world.

Heritage publishes its research in a variety of formats for the benefit of policymakers, the communications media, the academic, business and financial communities, and the public at large. Over the past five years alone The Heritage Foundation has published more than 900 books, monographs, and studies, ranging in size from the 564-page government blueprint, *Mandate for Leadership II: Continuing the Conservative Revolution,* to more frequent "Critical Issues" monographs and the topical "Backgrounders" and "Issue Bulletins" of a dozen pages. At the start of 1981, Heritage published the 1,093-page *Mandate for Leadership: Policy Management in a Conservative Administration.* Heritage's other regular publications include the monthly *National Security Record* and the quarterlies *Education Update* and *Policy Review.*

In addition to the printed word, Heritage regularly brings together national and international opinion leaders and policymakers to discuss issues and ideas in a continuing series of seminars, lectures, debates, and briefings.

Heritage is classified as a Section 501(c)(3) organization under the Internal Revenue Code of 1954, and is recognized as a publicly supported organization described in Section 509(a)(1) and 170(b)(1)(A)(vi) of the Code. Individuals, corporations, companies, associations, and foundations are eligible to support the work of The Heritage Foundation through tax-deductible gifts.

Note: Nothing written here is to be construed as necessarily reflecting the views of The Heritage Foundation or as an attempt to aid or hinder the passage of any bill before Congress.

The Heritage Foundation
214 Massachusetts Avenue, N.E.
Washington, D.C. 20002
U.S.A.
202/546-4400

Contributors

Wayne A. Abernathy is a legislative assistant for Senator Phil Gramm, specializing in economic security issues. He previously served on the staff of the Subcommittee on International Finance and Monetary Policy of the Senate Banking Committee where he advised Committee Chairman Jake Garn on strategic trade issues.

Leon Aron is the Salvatori Fellow in Soviet Studies at The Heritage Foundation and was formerly a Senior Project Director with the Newspaper Advertising Bureau, Inc. He earned his B.A. from the Moscow State Pedagogical Institute and his Ph.D. from the Graduate School of Arts and Sciences of Columbia University.

Marshall J. Breger is Chairman of the Administrative Conference of the United States and a member of the Department of State Advisory Committee on International Law. A former Visiting Fellow at the Heritage Foundation, he holds a B.A., M.A., and J.D. from the University of Pennsylvania and a B.Phil. degree from Oriel College, Oxford University.

Roger A. Brooks is Director of the Asian Studies Center at The Heritage Foundation and served as Director of the Policy Planning Staff in the State Department's Bureau of International Organization Affairs (1985–1987). A former Army Intelligence Officer, Brooks is a graduate of Harvard University and the Fletcher School of Law and Diplomacy.

Jim Burnley is Secretary of the U.S. Department of Transportation and former Director of the Volunteers in Service to America (VISTA) program. Mr. Burnley is a graduate of Yale and received his law degree from Harvard Law School.

Henry N. Butler is Associate Professor at George Mason University School of Law where he teaches law & economics and banking regulation. He earned his M.A. and Ph.D. in economics from Virginia Polytechnic Institute and State University and his law degree from Miami School of Law.

Stuart M. Butler is Director of Domestic Studies and the Roe Institute for Economic Policy Studies at The Heritage Foundation. Co-author of *Out of the Poverty Trap: A Conservative Strategy for Welfare Reform*, Dr. Butler has taught at Hillsdale College in Michigan and holds a Ph.D. in economic history from St. Andrews University in Scotland.

Nolan Clark is the Director of Policy Development at the Federal Trade Commission. He also served as Associate Administrator for Policy and Resource Management of the U.S. Environmental Protection Agency at the beginning of the Reagan Administration.

Ray S. Cline is currently the Chairman of the U.S. Global Strategy Council and Professor of International Relations at Georgetown University. Formerly the Director of the Bureau of Intelligence and Research at the Department of State, he holds B.A., M.A., and Ph.D. degrees from Harvard University.

Milton R. Copulos is currently serving as a consultant to the National Critical Materials Council. Former Director of Energy Studies and Senior Analyst in Science, Technology, and Natural Resources at The Heritage Foundation, he holds undergraduate and graduate degrees from The American University.

Louis J. Cordia is Director of Executive Branch Liaison at The Heritage Foundation and Director of the Washington Executive Bank—Heritage's talent bank service. He is a member of the Reagan Alumni Board and has served as a special assistant to the Administrator of the Environmental Protection Agency. He was educated at Hamilton College.

Donald J. Devine is President of Donald Devine Company and Chairman of Citizens for America. A former Director of the Office of

Personnel Management, he received his Ph.D. from Syracuse University.

Ronald F. Docksai is Vice President for Government Relations for Merrell Dow Pharmaceuticals, Inc., and was formerly the Assistant Secretary for Legislation at the U.S. Department of Health and Human Services. He was educated at St. John's College, New York, holds an M.A. and M.P.A. from New York University, and a Ph.D. from Georgetown University.

Nicholas N. Eberstadt is a Visiting Scholar at the American Enterprise Institute and a Visiting Fellow at the Center for Population Studies at Harvard University. He holds an A.B. from Harvard College, an M.Sc. from the London School of Economics, and an M.P.A. from the Kennedy School of Government at Harvard University.

Jeffrey A. Eisenach is President of the Washington Policy Group and a Visiting Fellow at the Heritage Foundation. He served in the Reagan Administration as executive assistant to James C. Miller III at the Federal Trade Commission and at the Office of Management and Budget. He holds a Ph.D. in economics from the University of Virginia.

Charles H. Fairbanks, Jr., is Research Professor of International Relations at the Johns Hopkins School of Advanced International Studies and directs the Foreign Policy Institute's Program in Soviet and American National Security Policymaking. Formerly the Deputy Assistant Secretary of State for Human Rights at the State Department, Mr. Fairbanks received his doctorate from the University of Chicago.

Peter J. Ferrara is Associate Professor of Law at the George Mason University School of Law and a John M. Olin Distinguished Fellow in Political Economy at The Heritage Foundation. He was a former Senior Staff Member of the White House Office of Policy Development. He holds a J.D. from Harvard Law School and A.B. in economics from Harvard College.

William J. Gribbin served as Deputy Director of the Office of Legislative Affairs during the first year of the Reagan Administration and as editor-in-chief of the Republican Party platform in 1984 and 1988. He received his doctorate in American history from the Catholic University of America.

Charles Grizzle is Assistant Administrator of the Office of Administration and Resources Management at the Environmental Protection Agency. He formerly served as Deputy Assistant Secretary for Administration at the U.S. Department of Agriculture. He earned his B.A. from the University of Kentucky at Lexington and completed the Senior Managers in Government program at the Kennedy School of Government at Harvard University.

James T. Hackett was Acting Director of the U.S. Arms Control and Disarmament Agency early in the Reagan Administration and currently is editor of *National Security Record* at The Heritage Foundation.

Francis P. Hoeber is President of Hoeber Corporation, Arlington, Virginia. He is also a member of the President's General Advisory Committee on Arms Control and is an Adjunct Professor of National Security Studies at Georgetown University.

Kim R. Holmes is Deputy Director of Defense Studies at The Heritage Foundation and an Adjunct Professor at Georgetown University. He is a former senior fellow at the Institute for Foreign Policy Analysis, which is associated with the Fletcher School of Law and Diplomacy. He has a Ph.D and masters degree from Georgetown University and a B.A. from the University of Central Florida.

Thomas M. Humbert is Special Assistant to the Associate Director of the Office of Management and Budget. The author of numerous publications on fiscal and monetary policy, he was previously Walker Fellow in Economics and Senior Policy Analyst at The Heritage Foundation. He earned his bachelor's degree from the University of Virginia and holds an MBA from the University of Chicago.

Timothy N. Hunter is a management strategist employed with the Interior Department and is special assistant to the President's Council on Management Improvement. He was director of the Midwestern regional office at the Intercollegiate Studies Institute for five years. Mr. Hunter graduated with honors from the University of New Mexico.

Fred Ikle is a Distinguished Fellow at the Center for Strategic and International Studies. Former Undersecretary of Defense for Policy, he served as Co-Chairman of the Commission on Integrated Long-Term Strategy. During the Nixon and Ford Administrations, he was

Director of the U.S. Arms Control and Disarmament Agency. Ikle received his Ph.D from the University of Chicago.

Gordon S. Jones is a Senior Fellow at The Heritage Foundation and has worked for Senator Jake Garn, Senator Paula Hawkins, the Senate Republican Policy Committee, the Department of Interior and the EPA. He has degrees from Columbia University, Stanford University and George Washington University.

David Jordan is a Professor of Government at the University of Virginia. A former U.S. Ambassador to Peru, he holds a B.A. from Harvard University and a Ph.D. from the University of Pennsylvania.

Alan L. Keyes is a resident scholar at the American Enterprise Institute in Washington, D.C., and is a former Assistant Secretary of State for International Organization Affairs. He holds a Ph.D. and A.B. from Harvard University.

C. Ronald Kimberling is the Executive Director of the Ronald Reagan Presidential Foundation and a former Assistant Secretary for Post-Secondary Education at the U.S. Department of Education. He received his Ph.D. from the University of Southern California, holds three masters degrees, and completed his undergraduate education from California State University, Northridge.

Jay P. Kosminsky is a Defense Policy analyst at The Heritage Foundation and formerly was a research and teaching fellow at Harvard University's Center for Science and International Affairs. He earned his BSFS from Georgetown University and currently is a doctoral candidate at the Fletcher School of Law and Diplomacy.

James V. Lacy is General Counsel for the U.S. Consumer Product Safety Commission. He formerly served as Director of the Office of Export Trading Company Affairs at the International Trade Administration of the U.S. Department of Commerce. He received his B.A. from the University of Southern California and his law degree from Pepperdine University School of Law.

Thomas M. Lenard is Vice President of Heiden Associates, an economics consulting firm. Previously he served with the Office of Management and Budget as an Adviser on Economic Policy, and at the Federal

Trade Commission. He was an Assistant Professor of Economics at the University of California at Davis.

Charles M. Lichenstein is a Distinguished Fellow at The Heritage Foundation and served as Deputy U.S. Ambassador to the United Nations (1981–1984). He holds a degree in political science from Yale University.

Mark B. Liedl is a Washington political and public policy analyst. He is editor of *Issues '88: A Platform for America* and has served as Research Director of the National Republican Senatorial Committee.

H. Joachim Maitre is Dean of the College of Communication and Director of the Center for Defense Journalism at Boston University. He was formerly the Editor-in-Chief and Axel Springer Publishing General Manager of Ullstein/Propylaein Books, Berlin. He earned his Ph.D. in literature from McGill University.

John Marshall is Manager of the Federal Crop Insurance Corporation at the U.S. Department of Agriculture. Previously he has worked at the Office of Management and Budget and the Department of Education. He received his B.A. and MBA degrees from the University of Virginia.

David H. Martin practices law in Washington D.C. He was Director of the U.S. Office of Government Ethics from 1983 to 1987 and a former Chief Counsel to the U.S. Secret Service. He holds a law degree from George Washington University.

J. William Middendorf, II, is a Heritage Foundation trustee and Chairman of Middendorf Anasary & Co., Inc. of Washington, D.C. Formerly U.S. Ambassador to the European Economic Community (1985–1987) and U.S. Ambassador to the Organization of American States (1981–1985), he holds an A.B. from Harvard University and an MBA from New York University.

Robert E. Moffit is Deputy Assistant Secretary for Legislation at the U.S. Department of Health and Human Services. Previously he has worked for the Office of Personnel Management and served as a Senior Legislative Assistant to Congressman Robert K. Dornan. Mr. Moffit is a graduate of LaSalle College in Philadelphia and holds a doctorate in political theory from the University of Arizona.

Stephen Moore is a Grover M. Hermann Fellow in Budgetary Affairs at The Heritage Foundation and co-editor of *Privatization: A Strategy for Taming the Federal Budget*. He has served the Reagan Administration as the Research Coordinator for the President's Commission on Privatization. He is a graduate of the University of Illinois.

Joseph A. Morris is General Counsel and Chief Executive Officer of the Mid-America Legal Foundation in Chicago. He has served as General Counsel of the Office of Personnel Management, Chief of Staff and General Counsel of the U.S. Information Agency, and Director of the Office of Liaison Services of the Department of Justice. He received his undergraduate and law degrees at the University of Chicago.

George Nesterczuk is President of Nesterczuk & Associates, a Management Consulting Firm in Alexandria, Virginia, and former Executive Associate Director of the U.S. Office of Personnel Management. Mr. Nesterczuk has held executive positions in the Department of Defense, Department of Transportation and in private industry. He holds a B.A. from Cornell University and an M.S. from the University of Maryland.

Mackubin T. Owens, Jr., is currently a Professor of Defense Economics at the U.S. Naval War College in Newport, Rhode Island. He served formerly as Adjunct Professor at the Marine Corps Command and Staff College and a consultant for the Center for Naval Analyses. He earned his Ph.D. from the Claremont Graduate School.

Jeffrey Pahre has worked with USX Corporation (formerly U.S. Steel) for 18 years in a variety of financial assignments. He served as USX representative to the President's Commission on Executive Exchange from September 1984 to July 1985. Mr. Pahre holds an MBA from the University of Chicago and a B.A. from the University of Washington.

William H. Peterson is an Adjunct Scholar at The Heritage Foundation and a Burrows T. and Mabel L. Lundy Professor of Business Philosophy at Campbell University. He formerly served as Chief Economist for U.S. Steel.

Daniel Pipes is Director of the Foreign Policy Research Institute and Editor of *Orbis*, its quarterly journal of international affairs. He has taught at the University of Chicago, Harvard University, and the U.S.

Naval War College. He received both his B.A. and Ph.D. from Harvard University.

Richard Pipes is the Baird Professor of History at Harvard University's Russian Research Center and served as Director of European and Soviet Affairs on the National Security Council (1981–1983). He earned an A.B. from Cornell University and a Ph.D. from Harvard University.

Robin R. Ranger is a Visiting Fellow with the U.S. Institute for Peace and a former Professor of International Relations at the University of Southern California. He was a Bradley Resident Scholar at The Heritage Foundation and is author of *Arms and Politics, 1958–1978: Arms Control in a Changing Political Context*.

James R. Richards is Inspector General at the U.S. Department of Interior. Previously he worked at the Department of Energy, Department of Justice, and on Capitol Hill. He holds a B.A. from Western State College and a law degree from the University of Colorado.

David B. Rivkin, Jr., is an attorney with the Office of Vice-President George Bush. He holds degrees in international relations and Soviet studies at Georgetown University and a law degree from Columbia University.

Roger W. Robinson, Jr., former Senior Director for International Economic Affairs at the National Security Council, is currently President of RWR, Inc., a Washington-based consulting firm dealing in international business. Prior to joining the NSC, Mr. Robinson was a vice president in the International Department of the Chase Manhattan Bank, N.A., where he had responsibilities for USSR, Eastern Europe, and Yugoslavia for a five-year period.

William A. Russell, Jr., is President of William Russell and Associates, Inc. He served in the Reagan Administration as Director of the Office of Congressional and Public Affairs at the Federal Communications Commission. He is a graduate of the University of Tennessee.

William Schneider, Jr., is Chairman, the President's General Advisory Committee on Arms Control and Disarmament, also President of International Planning Services, Inc., and Vice President of Schneider-Sohn and Associates, Inc. Formerly Undersecretary of State for Security Assistance, Science, and Technology at the State Department, he earned his Ph.D. from New York University.

Ralph L. Stanley is Chief Executive Officer and Co-Chairman of the Municipal Development Corporation in New York City. Formerly the Administrator of the Urban Mass Transportation Administration, he holds degrees from Princeton University and the Georgetown University Law Center.

Richard Stone is a former U.S. Senator from Florida and is currently the Vice Chairman of Capital Bank in California and a member of the Board of Directors of Capital Bank in Miami. He also served as Presidential Special Envoy for Central American Affairs and Ambassador-at-Large (1983–1984).

Richard Teske, Deputy Assistant Secretary for Public Affairs at the Department of Health and Human Services, received the Secretary's first special service award as the department's strategist and chief communicator. He represented the Reagan Administration at the United Nations and International Health Conferences. He graduated from the University of Minnesota summa cum laude in 1971.

Michael M. Uhlmann is a partner at the law firm of Pepper, Hamilton and Scheetz of Washington, D.C., former Special Assistant to President Reagan for Policy Development, and former Assistant Attorney General in the Ford Administration. Educated at Yale, Mr. Uhlmann also has a law degree from the University of Virginia and a doctorate from the Claremont Graduate School in California.

Wayne H. Valis is a former Special Assistant to President Reagan for Public Liaison and is currently President of Valis Associates of Washington, D.C. He previously served in the Nixon and Ford White House and at the American Enterprise Institute and Intercollegiate Studies Institute.

W. Bruce Weinrod is Director of Foreign Policy and Defense Studies at The Heritage Foundation. A former Capitol Hill and White House staffer, he is a member of the International Institute for Strategic Studies. Weinrod has an M.A. from the University of Pennsylvania and a J.D. from Georgetown Law School. He is an Ex Officio member of all *Mandate for Leadership III* foreign policy and defense task forces.

Jack Wheeler is Director of the Freedom Research Foundation in La Jolla, California. He holds a Ph.D. in philosophy from the University of Southern California. Wheeler has worked extensively with anticommunist resistance movements around the world and was one of the founding fathers of the Reagan Doctrine.

Carol P. Whitten served in the Reagan Administration in the Department of Education as Director of the Office of Bilingual Education and Minority Affairs. She was appointed by President Reagan to the National Advisory Council on Educational Research in June of 1988. She received her B.S. and M.S. degrees from Barry College in Miami, Florida.

Bruce Yandle is Alumni Professor of Economics at Clemson University. A former Executive Director of the Federal Trade Commission, he is the author of numerous books and articles on regulation. He received his MBA and Ph.D. degrees from Georgia State University.

Dov S. Zakheim is Chief Executive Officer and President of Systems Planning Corporation, Inc., and an Adjunct Scholar of The Heritage Foundation. He formerly served as Deputy Undersecretary of Defense for Planning and Resources. He earned his B.A. from Columbia University and his doctorate from St. Antony's College at the University of Oxford.

PART ONE

THE WHITE HOUSE AND POLICY LEADERSHIP

The White House and Policy Leadership

by
Charles L. Heatherly

Part One of this volume addresses the organization and operation of the policy-related offices of the White House and the management of policy initiatives in two vital areas, budget reform and deregulation. It also proposes a political strategy for transforming the President's electoral majority into a "governing majority," a majority coalition capable of gaining control of Congress as well as the White House.

The President is the chief executive of a vast policy-making and policy-coordinating entity called the Executive Office of the President with nearly 2,000 employees (counting OMB, NSC, CEA and all the other units). The President's top aides and advisors are each responsible for some aspect of presidential decision-making, with the chief of staff responsible for the coordination of the aparatus while also serving on frequent occasions as the President's principal adviser. Yet the President himself has responsibility for the key decisions that set this political machine in motion and give it direction. He chooses his top staff, determines their relationships to the Cabinet, and defines the policy goals and themes they will pursue. What principles and political considerations guide a new President in making these decisions? How do these decisions affect the policy framework and thereby the policy outcomes of the White House?

Many important matters are the province of the chief of staff, who must organize people, paperflow procedures, and communications systems to serve the President's needs. Such items as titles and reporting relationships, physical location of offices, size and frequency of staff meetings, the handling of letters and calls from Members of Congress, the scheduling of the President's time and the frequency and timing of media briefings and press conferences—all are within his domain. How many of the President's decisions are self-executing, and what needs to be done to assure implementation? Who should take the lead in an ad hoc coordinating group and who should be its members?

To most citizens the answers to such "administrative" questions may not appear to have a direct bearing on the level of farm price supports, the budget for the SDI program, and other policy issues. They do matter, however, to White House staff, who know that the *process* of policy-making is intimately related to its substance. If it is true that "policy is people," it is also true that policy is process, for process directs people. Control over the ideas, information, and people entering the Oval Office is not a mere administrative detail; it is real power. Who speaks to the President, when and under what circumstances, and who gets the last word (in person or on a decision document) can often be decisive to the outcome.

The importance of these administrative structures should be obvious: the organization and operation of the White House and its various staff functions (for example, presidential personnel selections, the priorities of the public liaison effort, the tasks assigned to the congressional relations staff) have a direct bearing on the policy decisions, priorities, and general character of the presidency. If the President and his senior advisers do not think these things through and set up a structure and decision-making procedures that meet the President's needs, others will fill the vacuum and make those decisions for them.

The authors of these chapters are veterans of the Reagan Administration, five having served within the Executive Office of the President. The other two served in executive branch agencies and private sector positions that brought them into frequent contact with senior White House staff. All have witnessed White House operations up close over many years.

A veteran of the Ford and Reagan Administrations, Michael M. Uhlmann, gives a tour of the recent history and present topography of the White House policy-making apparatus. The chapter is presented in the form of a memo to the President "in order to emphasize the personal responsibility of the President for the organization and direction of his principal staff, his 'official family.' "

Uhlmann discusses from both an historical and functional perspective the missions and working relationships of the three principal policy-making units of the Executive Office of the President—OMB, the Office of Policy Development, and the National Security Council. Regarding the pivotal role of OMB, he is even-handed in assessing the debits and credits on the OMB ledger but issues a warning that policy-making by "number-crunching" has its limits: "Budget-driven policy tends to produce government-by-adding-machine, which . . . does not carry much potential for inspiring presidential leadership. . . ." The domestic policy staff should not try to direct the total policy-making apparatus of the executive branch; the great bulk of the policy development work can and should be done by the policy staffs in the agencies. What it can do, however, is to "play an honest broker's role in seeing to it that issues are properly vetted and that their formulation takes into account the full range of considerations required of presidential decisions." It can also "provide policy perspective to the activities of congressional affairs, political affairs, speech-writing, and the personnel offices of the White House."

The role of *The White House Office of Legislative Affairs* is described in great detail by William J. Gribbin, a long-time congressional staffer and alumnus of the Max Friedersdorf shop of the early Reagan years. Every facet of the Office's operations is examined, from the handling of mail from Members of Congress to preparations for congressional leadership meetings with the President.

The strengths and weaknesses of the OLA are assessed in the light of two models, the "Nixonian" and the "Johnsonian," which approach congressional relations from different assumptions:

> In the Johnsonian model, *the President must win* . . . . He and those who work for him understand that there is no substitute for ultimate victory. . . . He rewards allies and punishes opponents. He strives for a majority of power, not a consensus of sentiment.
>
> In the Nixonian model, by contrast, *the President must be on the winning side*. What matters are triumphs, even if they are borrowed.

Gribbin illustrates how the Reagan White House vacillated between these two approaches, being somewhat "Johnsonian" in the early years but definitely more "Nixonian" in the second term. He also sheds light on the lackluster performance of the Administration in the legislative arena after the first two years, ascribing most of the responsibility for the poor scorecard to attitudes and decisions imposed from above:

The most crippling blow against the Office's effectiveness on the Hill was the decision of Administration strategists to part company with the President's Republican base in the House of Representatives on several key issues, especially taxes. Once congressional Republicans realized the White House had no permanent alliance with them, they would have no permanent interest in the Administration.

The Office of Public Liaison is put under the microscope and found to have important strategic value to a President interested in building relationships with new constituencies. The origins of OPL in the Nixon Administration are described, as well as its organization and activities under Presidents Ford, Carter, and Reagan. Wayne Valis, who was on the staff of OPL under three Presidents and directed the business liaison activities of the Office under Elizabeth Dole, classifies the three functions of OPL as:

◆ *constituency-building*—the strategic goal of OPL;
◆ *policy advocacy*—the promotion of public understanding of specific policy initiatives, such as the tax cuts or the President's Central America proposals;
◆ *policy facilitation*—the providing of various "services," including access to policymakers.

The three functions are related. "The trick," says Valis, "is to make sure the myriad day-to-day activities in the 'servicing' and advocacy realms support the long-term goals in the realm of constituency-building."

Stephen Moore frames his discussion of *Managing the Federal Budget* with a depressing summary of recent failures and a dire warning: "Gaining control of the budget . . . while resisting calls for new taxes, looms as perhaps the most critical domestic policy challenge confronting the new Administration." Yet we should not despair, counsels Moore: "The budget *can* be tamed." But how? That is the subject of his extensive survey of the causes and possible cures of the budget mess. One hint: he does not think the bipartisan National Economic Commission will cut the Gordian knot created by an unworkable budget process. The solution is not to raise new taxes that will only perpetuate the spending habits of Congress. The solution is to change the budget process to build in effective incentives for budget discipline.

Moore offers a comprehensive, ten-point plan for reforming the budget process and the ground rules that now make a balanced budget a fiscal impossibility:

◆ A Balanced Budget Amendment to the Constitution
◆ Presidential Line-Item Veto
◆ Strengthened Rescission Authority
◆ Abandonment of the "Current Services Budget"
◆ A Two-Year Budget Cycle
◆ Effective Penalties against Continuing Resolutions
◆ Comprehensive Credit Reform
◆ Prohibition against "Off-Budget" Spending
◆ Long-Term Budget Impact Statements for New Spending Programs
◆ Redefinition of Entitlement Programs

But Moore does more than just throw out good ideas; he presents six concrete proposals for marketing the President's budget reform plan. He then concludes with a "four-year deficit reduction strategy" that could help keep spending under control if the Congress doesn't adopt the more comprehensive reforms that are really needed.

Jeffrey A. Eisenach offers a sobering review of the condition of the deregulation movement at the end of the Reagan Administration. His findings are not encouraging. For the next Administration he proposes a new strategy for reducing the burdens of government regulations by a more direct, confrontational approach. "When one looks at the overall impact of regulation on the economy," says Eisenach, "there is little evidence of a general decline in regulatory costs. Indeed, the overall trend in the second Reagan term has been toward a resumption of regulatory growth."

Eisenach describes the roles played by Congress and the courts in obstructing and frustrating regulatory reform and imposing costly new regulatory burdens. To deal with the micromanagement incursions of Congress, Eisenach advocates an aggressive counterattack, beginning with a presidential statement of the policy objectives for his Administration's deregulation initiatives: "The President should issue a new Executive Order that contains a clear statement of objectives, one that doesn't tiptoe around the *substantive* definitions needed to keep deregulation on track in executive branch agencies." The President must assert control over executive branch regulatory *outcomes*. This will be highly controversial and the President should be prepared for a protracted contest in Congress and the courts.

The People Factor: Managing Presidential Personnel outlines a plan for establishing presidential control over political appointments within the Administration to assure policy consistency in all appointments. The author, The Heritage Foundation's director of executive branch liaison Louis J. Cordia, gives the recent history of the Presidential Personnel Office (PPO), including a summary of its salient features during the Reagan years.

Cordia challenges the White House to fill the top 1,000 policy positions by March 1, 1989. He also calls for legislation to increase the number of non-career (i.e., political) positions in the Senior Executive Service in order to give the President and his agency heads greater control over the management of the agencies. Also recommended is a two-tiered training program for all political appointees to improve their effectiveness as managers and help maintain their commitment to the President's policy agenda in the face of competing pressures in their agency environment. Key to the success of the President's personnel operation, Cordia believes, is strong support from the chief of staff and the President himself. The President must take a personal interest in the appointments and insist that high standards of competence, character and commitment be enforced.

These chapters provide a blueprint for the development of an effective White House policy operation, supported by a loyal team of political executives throughout the executive branch. Policy leadership must come from the top, but policy coordination and implementation efforts are equally important. Each occupant of the Oval Office brings a different management style and personal predilections to the job, and no handbook can offer solutions in advance to the myriad daily problems that will confront him.

The role of personalities, personal biases, jealousies and other human factors can never be exorcised from the policy-making process. Nevertheless, adherence to a policy framework and a strategic plan can help minimize the effects of these intrusions. Similarly, there are principles and axioms to be followed in the implementation and marketing of the President's policy goals and legislative initiatives. These essays are an attempt to point the way to policy leadership and coordination within the White House and to energetic and sophisticated policy marketing by the President's team.

1

The Politics of Presidential Leadership

by
Charles L. Heatherly*

The President who walks into the Oval Office on January 20, 1989 will have the supreme advantage of having followed Ronald Reagan instead of Jimmy Carter. By this good fortune he will have the opportunity to set an agenda for his presidency instead of having his agenda shaped by the economic and foreign policy disasters left him by a predecessor.

The new President and his party should view the peace and prosperity of the Reagan years not only as a magnificent achievement but as an unparalled opportunity—the foundation on which to build a lasting political coalition capable of gaining control of the total policy-making machinery of government, not just the White House. The opportunity is there, but with it comes a challenge, a challenge as formidable as any encountered by any President in modern times.

Seldom has there been a greater need for presidential leadership, but seldom have there been so many obstacles to its successful assertion. These obstacles are rooted in two separate but related features of contemporary American politics. The first is the aggressive insistence by Congress that large areas of authority traditionally thought to be within the province of the President must now be subjected to formal or informal legislative control. On the domestic front Congress has approved—indeed, celebrated—the creation of the modern administrative state, which for reasons both of efficiency and accountability requires a powerful, energetic executive. Yet while

*The author is grateful to Michael M. Uhlmann for his valuable contributions to the preparation of this paper. The recent works of Charles Kesler, John Marini, and John Wettergreen were also important to the development of these ideas. The paper itself is, of course, entirely the author's responsibility.

Congress lacks the capacity to administer this vast bureaucratic machinery of government, it has with increasing boldness sought to prohibit or limit the exercise of presidential control. The result has been a loss of accountability and coherence, which in domestic affairs is serious enough, but in the realm of foreign affairs and national security is proving dangerous and potentially disastrous.

Recent disputes between the President and Congress are in part a disagreement on the level of principle, the inevitable consequence of a constitutional structure which invites the two political branches to struggle for control of the nation's policy agenda. But the disagreement is also an increasingly partisan dispute arising from the fact that Congress and the White House have been controlled by opposing political parties for the great majority of the past forty years. As a result, there is a growing tendency for the Democrats to think of themselves as the Congressional Party, who must replicate within the legislature the authority and machinery necessary to running the government. This would seem to be an impossible task, but Congress persists nonetheless. There may be a temporary partisan pleasure in frustrating Republican Presidents, but Congress runs the risk of permanently debilitating not only the presidency but the nation's capacity for self-government as well. Even a Democratic President might well have great difficulty in coping with this new imperial Congress, which increasingly sees presidential authority as something merely delegated to the President and subject to recall when differences arise—as if Congress were the nation's elected board of directors and the President its chief executive officer.

The second feature of the contemporary political scene which adversely affects the capacity of Presidents to exercise leadership is the sheer size of the government itself. Every President at least since Truman has lamented his inability to control the government bureaucracy. All have tried—at times *with* congressional cooperation—to effect greater managerial direction. All have left office believing the goal to be impossible of achievement.

With the growth of government has come an exaggerated sense of expectancy attached to the occupant of the Oval Office. As head-of-government, the President is looked upon as the Solver-in-Chief of every problem under the sun. The President is expected to be familiar with the most remote and arcane features of hundreds of federal programs. This expectancy is massively reinforced and purveyed by television, which implies presidential accountability for every nut and bolt of the governmental machinery. This brings thousands of problems and demands to the White House, which in turn has produced a White House bureaucracy whose growth has paralleled the government at large.

With nearly 2,000 personnel and a plethora of minibureaucracies whose proprietors are acutely conscious of "turf," the Executive Office of the President (EOP) has become a major managerial enterprise. While no President could survive without a large staff, the management of that staff has become a measure of presidential leadership. This challenge is made especially difficult precisely because the ends of government—the policy goals that supposedly guide day-to-day decision-making—are themselves the subject of dispute and controversy. Indeed, the very process of decision-making is subject to "leaks" and the intensive scrutiny of the media, not to mention retrospective soul-searching and image-polishing by former staff.

Whoever takes the Oath of Office on January 20, 1989, in short, will find it difficult to exercise the authority requisite to the effective management of the welfare state and to the maintenance of America's role as leader of the free world. Confronted by a bureaucracy resistant to direction and control, by a Congress insistent on circumscribing and second-guessing his decisions, and by an EOP staff intent on managing *him*, the President has to struggle mightily to assert the truth of *The Federalist*'s observation that "energy in the Executive is the leading character in the definition of good government." Yet, while the task of reasserting presidential leadership is daunting, it is not impossible. The Constitution's grant of executive power is considerable. But the mere existence of legal authority to act is only the raw material of leadership; the *willingness* to act is its animating force. Without that willingness, the finest staff, the best organization, the most sophisticated decision-making procedures, and the most farsighted policies will be insufficient to achieve success.

———————————◇———————————

POLITICS AND GOVERNANCE

A President-elect's advisers and staff might well think, not without justification, that presidential leadership is simply an extension of the leadership traits and abilities that won the election. After all, the presidency is the greatest prize in the game of politics, and the person who succeeds in that quest has demonstrated his leadership skills very convincingly. Is not leading the nation as President a simple continuation of the same grand enterprise as winning the public's support on election day? Is not governing the country much like achieving popular support at the polls? This conventional, pragmatic view is true but misleading. It is true in the sense that governing is much like waging a continuous political campaign. But it is misleading in one decisive respect. Governing means exercising the *powers* of government, not merely occupying the office; it means harnessing public opinion on behalf of policy goals and not merely measuring the public pulse by means of polls. If the President wishes to do more than preside over the nation as head of state, he must convert his electoral majority into a governing majority. In our system of divided powers that means producing victories in the legislative arena. It is in this latter respect that recent Presidents—including the most consistently popular President in recent memory, Ronald Reagan—have been frustrated and largely unsuccessful.

Presidential leadership does require many of the same skills needed to win electoral victory, but whereas election campaigns necessarily treat issues as mere means to an end—a vote for the candidate—the politics of governing reverses this relationship: the personality and character of the President are used as means to generate support for the program. Presidents who are now thought of as successful leaders were those who left a legacy of programmatic achievement, not a saga of favorable public opinion polls. This point should be so obvious as not to require a reminder, but our era is so enamored of charisma and personality that we easily forget that those leaders who gained a "page in history" were those who changed the direction of government, and in so doing, changed the character and identity of our political parties as well.

The Reagan Legacy and the Conservative Opportunity

The great legacy of Ronald Reagan is that he changed the terms of political debate and the framework within which policy alternatives are considered. That legacy will shape political discourse for many years to come. President Reagan's success in changing the terms of policy debate is an historic achievement, and it presents his successor with an historic opportunity—the opportunity to build on that foundation by *institutionalizing* the conservative policy agenda and thereby consolidating the governing coalition that made it possible.

The next President will be judged on his ability to consolidate and build upon Ronald Reagan's achievements. That consolidation and institutionalization will require a different kind of leadership—a different management style, a different form of persuasion, and at times a more confrontational political approach in dealing with adversaries in Congress.

The 1984 election was a tragic case of excluding the politics of governance from the politics of elections. After the losses in the 1982 election spooked White House strategists, they lost faith in the power of ideas and the promise of a "Reagan Revolution" as the formula for victory in the upcoming presidential election. They turned instead to something they thought was more reliable than policy blueprints or the vagaries of the economy—the personal popularity of the President. This conscious rejection of an issue-based campaign that might have improved his party's position in Congress was the de facto white flag of the Reagan Revolution. The 1984 campaign should have been used as an opportunity to regain the initiative and revalidate the 1980 mandate. Instead, it produced only a personal triumph at the expense of political opportunities that would not come again in the Reagan presidency.

As a result of the 1984 re-election strategy, President Reagan won a second term but not a second beginning. Ronald Reagan would be President for four more years, but he had little in the way of a policy mandate. Moreover, he had distanced himself from his allies and key supporters in Congress, which further crippled his ability to enact his program.

The Administration's limited *programmatic* success, especially on domestic spending and social issues but also in Nicaragua, illustrates that even a popular President re-elected in a landslide can score only partial, intermittent successes against the entrenched fiefdoms of liberal orthodoxy. These fiefdoms have strong defenses and tend not to respond to the *rhetoric* of presidential initiatives; they respond only to the exercise of *presidential power*.

The few decisive victories of the Reagan Administration on the domestic front—victory in the tangible sense of actually enacting a fundamental policy change—were achieved only by the mobilization of massive public support, support that had to be focused on a specific decision point at a critical moment. Such ad hoc coalition campaigns were dependent on the President's visible personal involvement and his skills as the "Great Communicator." Since White House strategists were understandably reluctant to roll out this cannon too often, such mobilizations were infrequent (and even then not always successful). Presidential power that depends so heavily on such ad hoc mobilizations is a paper tiger because these coalitions cannot be kept on "war alert" for eight years. By contrast, the forces that opposed the President's initiatives were there on the battlefield every day in a state of permanent readiness. They remain so today.

Each new President confronts this same dilemma: high expectations and a broad agenda, but little power actually to change the direction of the government. If Ronald Reagan and his "Reaganauts" could only *slow down* the growth of federal spending, not reverse it or eliminate wasteful programs, what hope is there for any other conservative President who wants to challenge the entrenched orthodoxies of the modern liberal welfare state?

———————————◇———————————

A NEW STRATEGY FOR PRESIDENTIAL LEADERSHIP

An ad hoc presidency which draws its power from a series of gerry-built coalitions is no match for the permanent power and hardball politics of the liberal coalition that still controls the machinery of American government. What is needed is a presidency committed to altering this unfavorable balance of power through an ambitious and aggressive "politics of governance," a politics that seeks nothing less than control of the policy apparatus at both ends of Pennsylvania Avenue.

What would be different about a presidency committed to the politics of governance? It would go about the serious business of government in a serious way; that is, *it would undertake a long-term program aimed at winning majority control of Congress* as the key to governance. Unless conservatives wish to accept the status of a permanent "opposition party," they must adopt the goal of building a governing coalition. A party that does not aim at institutionalizing its gains will always be an opposition party, never a governing party.

The President shares law-making power with Congress in our separation of powers system. But whereas the politics of governance is second nature to the leaders of Congress, it does not come naturally to the thinking of White House strategists. This is not surprising. There is little incentive—political, moral or institutional—for White House political strategists to think in long-range terms. Under the Constitution as amended in 1947, Presidents have only *one* election to be concerned with: their own re-election—which is an all-or-nothing, one-time event. If the President's re-election chances and the size of his election victory can be increased by focusing exclusively on that one contest, separating it from the fate of his party's congressional seats, why not do so? Both Richard Nixon in 1972 and Ronald Reagan in 1984 ran for re-election as though Congress were a neighboring country, and not as though the fate of supporters running for Congress had something to do with the fate of their presidencies. It is ironic that the decline of presidential power has occurred as a result of this preoccupation with the personal popularity of the President.

This combination of historical, institutional and political forces has produced a paradigm of presidential power that is myopic and insular: it does not understand or support the kind of *sustained political effort* needed to strengthen the President's ability to govern the country. Congress, on the other hand, has developed a finely tuned sense of its own institutional interests and seeks continually to expand its power. More significantly, it does not need or seek any political mandate to do this: Congress *as an institution* is beyond the control of the American people because of the nature of congressional pork barrel politics.[1] The 435 separate congressional elections are not decided primarily on national issues of any kind, let alone an issue as remote as usurpation of presidential authority. Thus, individual Members of Congress are largely free of accountability for the actions taken by Congress as an institution.

The result of these converging forces has been a steady shift in the balance of power from the executive branch to the legislative branch. A more traditional balance of power must be restored before any President can hope to implement a program of change mandated by his election.

Surveying this political minefield, a new President should make a commitment to reverse this trend and to build a governing coalition that can support his presidency and his party's political program. We call the political strategy that aims to do this the "politics of governance." This strategy requires, first and foremost, a commitment to *party government* as distinct from government by personality. A strong political party is the only possible vehicle for organizing and sustaining a viable governing majority. Ad hoc coalitions and personality-based organizations that ebb and flow with the fate of individuals will not suffice. A party is itself a coalition of coalitions, but it is united by principles that constrain and meliorate the economic interests and passions that motivate much human endeavor.

This new politics would require party leaders and party technicians to apply their political and organizational skills to *strategic* plans and operations as readily and systematically as they now do to purely tactical matters. For the White House it would require a different approach to congressional relations, based on the goal of building a congressional majority within the President's own party by running election and re-election campaigns on a common platform. This in turn would require different tactics in dealing with the liberal leadership of Congress and a greater willingness to accept temporary defeats as a means of dramatizing the differences between the parties as the best strategy for gaining popular support.

Such a strategy would promote a party realignment. By focusing the spotlight of political debate on the differences between the two parties *at the level of principle*, the different agendas of the two major parties would become clear. There would be no permanent "congressional party" opposed by a permanent "presidential party": each of the two major parties would vie for control of the White House *and* Congress. The American people's interest in politics would be reawakened: the results of elections would actually affect the policies being carried out by the vast bureaucracy that pervades our lives.

The President who forged such a coalition would earn more than one page in the history books. His legacy would be one of impressive achievement in policy and program. But his most important legacy would be a truly competitive two-party system all across the American political landscape, beginning with the 95 percent of House of Representatives districts now considered to be safe for incumbents.

The most important political questions confronting the new President are precisely these seminal political decisions. Should the President in 1989 not worry about the shape of the political system in 1999? Should he not care about the prospects for restoring the balance of power with an imperial Congress? Presidential success can be enhanced by considering the varied issues and opportunities in a larger context—the need for an energetic and principled "politics of governance" that can build and sustain a governing majority for a generation.

————————◇————————

PRESIDENTIAL INITIATIVES:
A CONSTITUTIONAL MANDATE

A comprehensive policy blueprint for all domestic and foreign policy institutions of the government is presented in the policy chapters of this volume. Some of the President's first initiatives will be obvious, such as gaining control of the budget. What will be suggested here is not a list of the "ten most urgent" or "five most critical" initiatives the President should address in his first weeks and months. Instead, what is suggested is a way of thinking about the problems and issues already on his plate, a way of sorting them out.

There are, first of all, the issues that absolutely must be dealt with because of pressing national security interests (such as Nicaragua) or inescapable fiscal choices (federal spending). At the other end of the spectrum are issues he may choose to tackle because of deeply held personal beliefs. In between, there are dozens of issues that advisers will think are urgent or important in varying degrees. These should be examined in the light of four criteria:

1) How important is the issue intrinsically in terms of the President's philosophy and convictions? Is it really something that is basic to his deepest values and priorities?

2) Does the issue need to be addressed *now*? Timing is all important in politics, and some matters must be addressed in the first weeks of a presidency if they are to be tackled at all.

3) Can the issue be delegated to a Cabinet member for the time being, with presidential involvement at a later, critical stage?

4) How does the proposed initiative support long-term goals and add to the strength of the governing majority needed for across-the-board progress on the broad policy agenda? Some very tough battles— even battles that cannot be won in one or two years—serve to energize and mobilize forces that add to the President's coalition over the long haul.

Looking at possible presidential initiatives in the light of these criteria may help sort out the many alternative themes and proposals that will be presented. Any proposal that meets *all* of the above tests should be at the top of the list of presidential initiatives.

There are some initiatives that meet the above tests and are essential to the long-term success of the Administration. The initiatives recommended below address both the constitutional and political dimensions of the problem of the imperial Congress. They will require a considerable investment of energy and political will, but they will pay enormous dividends:

1) The President should propose repeal of the constitutional amendment limiting a President to two terms in office. This measure was passed hastily in 1946 by a Republican Congress eager to strike back at the FDR legacy: they shot themselves in the foot and seriously weakened our separation of powers system. It was a mistake and is long overdue for repeal.

2) The President should seek outright repeal of the War Powers Act.

It is an unconstitutional infringement on his authority as Commander-in-Chief and he should say so.

3) The President should declare that he will not sign omnibus appropriations bills and that he will seek authority to veto individual titles of such bills.

4) The President should reassert his authority over his own executive branch, starting with a challenge to the legal status of "guidance" language placed in "conference reports" but never voted on and passed by the two Houses of the Congress. Such language is only advisory; it is not binding on executive departments and agencies but they generally behave as if it were. The President should instruct his agency heads that it is not binding and should ask his Attorney General to prepare to defend his Cabinet officers if challenged in court.

5) The President should propose legislation that would extend the coverage of the provisions of the Ethics in Government Act and the many civil rights laws to the Members of Congress and their employees. It is intolerable that Congress has exempted itself from these laws; it's time to challenge that arrogance.

6) The President should direct his agency heads, with assistance from OMB, to establish a system for cataloging and reporting the full extent and costs of executive branch responses to congressional inquiries about and involvement in specific grant awards, contract awards, construction projects, feasibility studies, and university research grants. Congressional involvement in the purely administrative processes of federal agencies should not be tolerated: the way to stop it is to publicize it, and each agency can compete in developing innovative ways to do so. The media will love it.

These initiatives would put the liberal leaders of Congress on notice that the President does not intend to play Ring-around-the-Rosey while they continue their assault on the powers of the executive branch. This battle must be carried to the public—and it can be won there.

What is suggested by these recommendations is a new approach to the so-called honeymoon period, the first few months of a new President's term. The conventional wisdom calls for the newly inaugurated President to pick two or three of his most urgent legislative proposals and push hard for their adoption, thus using this honeymoon period to get off to a fast start. Any honeymoon with Congress will indeed be short-lived. For this very reason, the President should announce to the American people that he will not be satisfied with a short honeymoon followed by three and half years of business as usual. He should tell

Congress that his program will come in waves, not in raindrops, and that he will make liberal control of Congress the primary issue in 1990 and 1992 if his proposals are rejected by a Congress out of step with the American people.

———————————◇———————————

THE CHARACTER OF LEADERSHIP

In developing the policy agenda for the first year of his presidency, the President should try to infuse his policy-making machinery with a few basic principles:

First, consistency of principle and constancy of purpose are the bedrock essentials for all policy development: the President must be known as a man of conviction, integrity and high moral standards. His policies must be based on well-articulated principles, and when policy changes and compromises occur—as they inevitably will—they must be explained in terms of pragmatic steps toward policy objectives that remain unchanged.

Second, while it will be necessary at the beginning of the term to focus presidential attention on a handful of high priority policy initiatives—in the legislative message and the budget reform package, for example—it is critical that the broad policy agenda articulated in the party platform and in campaign pledges also be given impetus and active support through Executive Orders and specific initiatives. Some of his first initiatives should set in motion policy changes and processes that will take time to reach their "critical mass" in terms of public support and political feasibility, but nonetheless must be launched in the first days and weeks of the presidency.

Third, there should be a conscious effort to appoint to positions in the Administration only those individuals who meet the criteria for a position of public trust and political accountability—the "three C's" of *commitment, competence,* and *character.* Commitment must be understood to mean commitment to the policy agenda, not simply an identification with a political campaign or a political pedigree. Persons appointed to sub-Cabinet positions as undersecretaries and assistant secretaries must meet these tests and must think of themselves as members of the President's team, committed to his principles and policies. With the right people in those jobs the President has a fighting chance to move his programs forward. Without them, all the presidential speeches and Executive Orders in the world will not change the landscape of official Washington.

Fourth, progress in transforming the President's electoral majority into a governing majority will require a different calculus of political risks and rewards, a new sophistication in the collaboration with friends and coalitions in Congress, and a bold outreach to new constituencies now ripe for recruitment into the conservative orbit. The new calculus of political risks will tell an astute President that short-term losses in Congress are tactical devices to dramatize issues and keep the liberals in Congress on the defensive. New constituencies of middle-class blacks, Hispanics, Asians and other ethnics will gravitate to his party and its congressional candidates as they begin to identify their values and their children's futures with the President's program. Success in this realm will require a visionary party leadership that amounts to statesmanship, but nothing less will suffice to bring about the realignment of party loyalties that is the prerequisite for a new governing coalition.

———————————◇———————————

LEADERSHIP: THE MORAL DIMENSION

In setting a theme for his presidency, the President must animate the public's moral imagination and give people a challenging vision of the future. Most political agendas are dry as dust, and amount to little more than appeals to economic self-interest. That is politics-as-usual, and no President can afford to be entirely above it. But as man does not live by bread alone, politics, too, must transcend mere "getting and spending." The President should remind the nation that our future will be determined as much by our moral character as by the size of our checkbook balance and the number of income transfer programs carried in our national accounts. One way to do that is to place before the public proposals calculated to respond to their genuine moral concerns.

The public is now receptive to appeals of this sort on at least two major issues: the reform of our educational institutions and the elimination of widespread narcotics abuse. Significant progress has already been made on the former front, although there is a long way yet to go. As to the latter, the public is already aroused, and the issue demands specifically moral leadership. The tendency of most politicians is to treat both in the usual manner: create new agencies, rearrange bureaucratic boxes, and throw more money at them. But budgetary parsimony is not the essence of the difficulty in either area, and (although more money may have to be spent) budgetary generosity is not the essence of the cure. Both problems, at bottom, are moral problems requiring moral solutions.

Our nation's educational system is in dire need of a major overhaul, and only the President can focus the public's attention with sufficient clarity and force to achieve lasting results. First, we have allowed curricula to depart from what used to be called "the basics"—a thorough grounding in math and science, English language and literature, history, geography, and civics. Second, we have forgotten that a sound education has to do with the formation of character no less than with the training of intellect. Third, our educational system seems designed to avoid accountability; many of its managers appear to regard parental concerns as a kind of intrusion. Have they forgotten that their mission is to serve, not to rule?

The public mood is ripe for capturing by a President who will go forward with these proposals: a return to basics, the restoration of character-building, and the restoration of accountability by way of increased parental choice. So defined, the "education issue" transcends the capacity of bureaucrats to impose their narrow agendas, limits the ability of Congress to "solve" the problem merely by throwing more money at it, and reminds the public of what true leadership is all about.

The problem of narcotics abuse has a similar character. Some additional resources may be necessary on the law enforcement side, but there is a limit on the amount and efficacy of more spending in that area. The real problem exists on the so-called "demand" side: it is fundamentally a problem of public opinion and public morality.

The public is concerned, even frightened, and when they are in such a mood the people will insist on more government of almost any kind. But they should not be deluded into thinking that greater spending, more police, or more drug counselors will cure the problem without active public involvement. Their passions against narcotics abuse must be constructively aroused and directed to those areas where they can have the most beneficial use—in their homes, in their schools and neighborhoods, even in popular entertainments.

No President can be a bystander to such an issue. He must get into the thick of it, not just as the chief executive of the government, but as a moral teacher. He need not, and should not, sound like a fire-and-brimstone preacher, but he should not shy away from describing the fate that will befall us, as individuals and as a nation, if the plague of narcotics is not defeated. The public expects him to lead, and he must answer the call. If he succeeds in mobilizing the nation's will and resourcefulness to defeat this deadly menace, the people will be eternally grateful.

These two issues are ripe for presidential leadership. They have been discussed at some length as examples of the interplay between ideas, institutions, politics and statesmanship.

————————————◇————————————

CONCLUSION

A strategy of presidential leadership that takes ideas and issues seriously will build a governing coalition based on the universal principles of the American Constitution and the shared values of the American people. That coalition will be cemented by the success of the politics of governance in achieving sustained economic growth, expanded opportunities for Americans of all races and backgrounds, and renewed confidence in the future of freedom at home and abroad. Such a strategy will require the reassertion of presidential powers and prerogatives that have been eroded through congressional usurpation and political neglect, and it will require aggressive and sustained policy advocacy on the part of the President's entire team. A President with the vision to pursue such a strategy will not have to worry about his page in history. He will have written it himself.

————————————◇————————————

NOTES

1. For an extended analysis of the historical and political basis of this problem, see *The Imperial Congress: Crisis in the Separation of Powers* (New York: Pharos Books, 1989), Gordon S. Jones and John Marini, editors.

2

Organizing for Policy Leadership: A Memo to the President

by
Michael M. Uhlmann*

There is no one "best" way to organize the White House, only a series of more or less undesirable ways, each with compensating virtues and vices. A pyramidal staffing structure with you and the chief of staff at the pinnacle may appear at first glance to be highly efficient, but it is likely to be too rigid in the joints and may isolate you to a dangerous extent. By contrast, a less rigidly hierarchical structure may prove too loose and make you the victim of others' agendas. As with much else in government, balance is necessary, and it is a measure of the difficulties facing the modern presidency that every President since the 1950s has had to reorganize his staff (sometimes more than once) in an effort to achieve it. In the end, you should have a staffing structure that makes you feel comfortable and that performs the major tasks required of the modern presidency. The difficulty is that the performance of all those tasks is bound to make you feel *un*comfortable.

$$\diamond$$

THE WHITE HOUSE STAFF

The central function of the White House staff is to keep you informed about all matters essential to the governance of the

---

*This contribution is presented in the form of a memo to the newly elected President in order to emphasize the personal responsibility of the President for the organization and direction of his principal staff, his "official family." Gary Bauer, Carnes Lord, and Robert Searby contributed ideas to the development of this paper. The views expressed are, however, entirely the responsibility of the author.

nation, and in particular about matters essential to the execution of your policy program. That imposes upon them both a positive and a negative duty: to *bring in* what is important and to *keep out* that which is not. The effective performance of that duty requires a secretariat system for channeling paper into and out of your office and, more critically, the exercise of judgment. If those who seek to influence you—which includes virtually everyone you come in contact with— get the idea that you open your own mail, your in-box will soon resemble Santa's mail box in December. On the other hand, if you depend entirely on the judgment of the chief of staff and the staff secretary as to what you should read and not read, they will end up making decisions that properly speaking should be yours alone to make. A good deal of trial-and-error will be necessary before some sort of happy medium is struck between having too little and too much information. In finding that magical balance, there is no substitute for keeping your chief and his subordinates apprised of what you do and don't consider important.

Presumably, the directors of the various White House offices will be skilled professionals who are personally dedicated to your agenda. But human nature being what it is, the very talents which brought them to your attention may also cause them to invest considerable pride in the maintenance of their own bureaucratic turf. As there are only so many hours in a day, only so many people you can personally manage, and only so many issues you can or should be intimately acquainted with, large segments of the Executive Office of the President (EOP) necessarily have to work in the dark, both as to what your wishes may be, and as to what other staff units and executive branch departments may be doing. That feeling of isolation, which is inevitable in the modern White House, only serves to reinforce turf-consciousness.

There is an upper limit on the extent to which the problems of isolation and turf-consciousness can be cured in any bureaucracy, but there are two things you can do to address them. The first is to insist that the major office heads have occasional access to you over and above the formal paper flow which emanates from their offices. The purpose of such access is twofold: 1) to make them feel that they are valued members of your team and, by so doing, reinforce their loyalty while obtaining from them useful information which may otherwise be filtered out by your staff secretariat; and 2) to remind them about your priorities and how their activities relate to those priorities.

The second thing you can do is to insist that the major components of the EOP are brought together with each other on a regular basis to discuss progress (or the lack of it) on your major agenda items. Such meetings need not require your presence except episodically, but you should let it be known that it is important for them to meet and that you wish to be apprised of what happens at those meetings. Given the natural tendency of bureaucratic components to lead a life of their own, you will be well advised to break down the artificial barriers which tend to encourage members of your official family to operate at cross-purposes. Make clear to your chief of staff that you understand such barriers to be inevitable but that you expect them to be kept at a minimum. That will simultaneously indicate to him that he will be judged in part by the success with which he eliminates those barriers, ensure that the secretariat is not unduly restricting information which you ought to possess, and increase morale among those who are there to serve you. Most importantly, it will remind everyone that you do not intend to be a mere creature of your staff system and that, whatever the system may be, its operations will be guided by *your* priorities.

―――――――――◇―――――――――

CABINET AFFAIRS

An analogous strategy should apply to relations with your Cabinet officers. Despite the lip-service paid to the concept of "Cabinet government" (a slippery term which means different things to different people), the Cabinet cannot operate as an effective deliberative body. It is, for one thing, too large (and growing larger), and the skills and interests of its members too varied to serve as a true policy-making unit. Furthermore, there is an inherent inequality in the members' rank. State, Defense, Treasury, Justice, and in these days, OMB, are by the nature of the functions they perform essential to the nation's governance. The principal officers of these departments can make or break your reputation, and their active cooperation is vital to the execution of your policies. Other departments rise and fall in importance depending on the significance and timing of particular issues; but on a day-in, day-out basis what they do or fail to do will not determine the fate of your Administration. Of necessity, therefore, the better part of your time will be taken up with affairs of the major departments.

What, then, is to be done with the rest of the Cabinet members and with the Cabinet as a whole?

The same tendencies which afflict major players in the EOP—isolation from one another and from the main lines of your policy program, and undue turf-consciousness—afflict Cabinet officers and major non-Cabinet agency heads, only more so. Over time, government agencies are acted upon by a variety of centrifugal forces, chief of which are the pressures brought to bear by Congress. Only slightly lesser in importance are the activities of the permanent bureaucracies and of interest groups affected by a particular agency's policies. Finally, the agency heads themselves are inclined to view the world through the tunnel vision of their personal agendas, which may or may not coincide with your own. Harold Ickes may have overstated the case with his famous remark that Cabinet officers are "the natural enemies" of the President, but he pointed to an important truth which lies at the heart of every Administration.

You will have at your disposal three tools to control an Administration whose natural tendency is to fly apart: the power to appoint and remove, the power to command, and the power to persuade. Each has virtues and limits; all must be employed.

Personnel policy is discussed at length elsewhere in this volume, but it goes without saying that the appointment of agency heads at once capable and loyal to you is vital. Even the most capable and loyal agency head, however, will feel enormous pressure from Congress, interest groups, and the bureaucracy to part company from you on many issues. The trick is to employ as many counterweights as possible. But in some cases you may have no choice but to remove a recalcitrant official. That is easier said than done in the case of agency heads, because they are often political figures in their own right. Even so, you may have to resort to removal, either through the rarely employed method of a formal firing, or through the more commonly employed method of "easing out." Either way, it will not be a cost-free exercise; but you should not shrink from doing what needs to be done. Fear of displeasing the President is as often, if not more often, as strong an incentive as the desire to please him, and the sure knowledge that you will, if necessary, remove a senior officer will act as a salutary incentive to keep others in line.

The power to command, like the power to remove, is rarely employed in a formal sense except when the President is acting in a military capacity as Commander-in-Chief. Most often, his command authority is conveyed implicitly, that is, by the mere fact of choosing Policy Option A as opposed to Policy Option B. It is in consequence of that decision that the actors necessary to implement the chosen policy are supposed to fall into line. Whether they do so is a function of many factors other than a President's ability to command. It is rare, for example, for an agency head to be so opposed to a particular policy that he will be moved to resign. But he has a great many other means at his disposal to deflect a presidential policy decision away from its intended course. A well-timed leak to a member of Congress or journalist, or the passive encouragement of interest-group opposition may be sufficient. And there are a dozen other techniques—delay being one of the most frequently employed—whereby a reluctant agency head can alter presidential policy without appearing to be disloyal.

Finally, it must be noted that most domestic policy issues seldom have an "either/or" character to them, especially in the early stages of their consideration. Would-be policymakers throughout the Administration have multiple opportunities during the decision-making process to make their views known, and the final decision usually has something to make them content even if it is less than what they want. It is rare, therefore, when a President actually has to command an agency to behave in a particular way; by the time it is necessary to do so, the damage to the presidential decision has already been done.

The power to persuade remains the most potent (and certainly the most frequently used) power at your disposal. It comes in endless varieties, formal and informal, be it an address to the nation, a message to Congress, a phone conversation with a recalcitrant senator, a Cabinet meeting, or a pep-rally speech to a group of supporters; and it can be as different as a carrot is from a stick. All forms are necessary; all will be used at one point or another during your tenure in office. Different appeals are necessary to move different subordinates in your direction, and it is the highest form of political art to know which appeal to employ, when, and with whom.

In dealing with members of your Administration, you can in most cases count on their willingness to cooperate, at least at the outset. Whether they will remain so in the long run depends in large part on your taking actions to remind them that they are part of a team, *your* team. In this regard, you would do well to emulate some of the institutional devices used by President Reagan. His "Cabinet Council" system derived in part from a collegial decision-making process he followed while governor of California; it was, in short, a system he felt comfortable with. But it derived also from opinions he received from Cabinet officers in prior Republican Administrations (some of whom served in his Cabinet as well), in which they lamented their isolation and the interposition of an overly aggressive and turf-conscious White House staff. Reagan took pains to correct these defects by establishing a series of Cabinet Councils (each with a series of interagency working groups reporting to them) in which the major policy decisions of his Administration would be debated. The Councils proved too many and too cumbersome for most genuinely deliberative undertakings and their number was reduced in the second term. But they did serve the indispensable function of making the members feel that they were part of something larger and more important than their own agency's agenda. They offered the additional advantage of exposing the White House staff on a regular basis to the nature and quality of departmental work.

The opportunities for persuasion afforded President Reagan in the numerous meetings of his Cabinet and Cabinet Councils were used to great advantage, even when the formal decision was deferred (as it often was) to another time with a smaller group. And Cabinet officers (especially those from the lesser departments) were pleased by having at least some small-group access to the President on a fairly regular basis. One of the most underestimated devices for keeping an Administration together is the simple technique of providing regular forums for senior officials to learn and re-learn what *you* consider important and why. A Cabinet Council system, or something like it, is a splendid device for accomplishing that purpose.

―――――――――――◇―――――――――――

OFFICE OF MANAGEMENT AND BUDGET

No discussion of controlling the executive branch would be complete without reference to the role of the Office of Management and Budget. Here is the place—perhaps the only place—where the day-to-day activities of the entire government can be routinely monitored and rendered reasonably accountable. OMB has a number of advantages in this respect which cannot be easily replicated elsewhere. In the first place, it has a large, experienced, and hard-working professional staff. Second, the cyclical regularity of the budget cycle brings before OMB the hard factual data which are prerequisite to many important presidential decisions. Third, because OMB is armed with the power to clear legislation and major regulations and to set spending and personnel levels, agencies cannot safely ignore its directions. Further, because its staff is often as familiar with agency programs as are the program managers themselves, it is difficult for agencies to "fudge" their performance records before an OMB audience. In short, when OMB speaks, agencies listen. Fourth, while OMB is responsible to the President, it is institutionally separate from the White House Office and thereby creates a useful layer of insulation between the President and the often politically unpopular decisions OMB has to make. Finally, OMB's formal role in reviewing legislative and regulatory proposals enables a President to impose consistency on his Administration's legislative program and at least some measure of control over the rabbit-like multiplication of *Federal Register* pages.

What this adds up to is that a President and his immediate staff can use OMB as a kind of ongoing detective agency to find out what's happening in the departments and agencies, and to police budgetary and policy "misbehavior." A President need not, and should not, involve himself on a regular basis in OMB's business, other than on those dozen or so occasions during the course of a budget cycle when he must make a major political decision. But he can and should make use of the information gathered by OMB and its institutional power to check the natural centrifugal tendencies of government agencies.

The potential liabilities of OMB to a President are the inverse of its assets. Its very size, skill, power, information base, and institutional independence tend to make it a creature unto itself and its director a potent political figure in his own right. OMB, in short, bears watching even as its considerable assets are employed on your behalf. "Get to know your Budget Director" is the only safe rule to follow— and, preferably, *before* you appoint him. Like other major Cabinet officers, he too must be persuaded that, for all his institutional power and independence, he remains first and last a member of *your* Administration. As an added piece of insurance, you should appoint to your senior staff someone who is well versed in budgetary matters. He need not and should not interfere with the OMB director, but he can provide you with valuable second opinions.

In these days of trillion-dollar federal budgets, many major policy decisions are made by budget trade-offs; it is a complicated poker game involving the White House, Congress, the agencies, and affected interest groups. But it is important to remember that budget-driven policy can distort one's vision by reducing the art of governing to the mere administration of things. Budget-driven policy tends to produce government-by-adding-machine, which is fine and necessary as far as it goes, but it does not carry much potential for inspiring presidential leadership in either domestic or foreign policy. That defect must be remedied by separate institutional components of the White House, specifically, your domestic policy and national security staffs.

THE DOMESTIC POLICY STAFF

The domestic policy staff function has in recent years been something of a poor stepchild in White House operations, a casualty of policy increasingly driven by macroeconomic considerations. Back in the days when government was, by contemporary standards, a relatively simple affair, the formulation of domestic policy initiatives was entrusted primarily to departments and agencies. The White House policy staff was often little more than a single aide, assisted by a handful of analysts from the Bureau of the Budget, who would consult with agency officers and diverse outside advisers and present ideas for the President's consideration. This largely informal process began to assume more formal shape when Joseph Califano became a free-wheeling, all-purpose domestic policy "czar" for President Johnson, but it was not until the early 1970s that the idea of a domestic policy staff acquired full institutional status. It has retained that status in various forms and under various names ever since and will no doubt remain a permanent feature of the modern presidency.

How best to use your domestic policy staff is, however, a problem, one that every President since Nixon (who created the first formal staff unit) has struggled with. In addressing this problem, you will need to weigh a number of critical factors. First, it is likely, given the experience of your predecessors over the past half-century, that you will spend by far the greater part of your time on foreign affairs. Absent special circumstances, that leaves little time for the detailed consideration of domestic policy proposals. Second, the domestic affairs side of your presidency is more likely to be made or broken by macroeconomic forces, which are primarily and properly the focus of attention of Treasury, OMB, and your economic advisors. And, third, absent specific presidential emphasis (and sometimes, even with it), departments and agencies are adept at resisting what they consider to be undue control from White House policy experts. They possess, in that regard, a distinctive advantage which they employ to great effect against all but the most able and experienced members of the White House policy staff, namely detailed knowledge of the legal and factual data base of programs under their supervision. The size of the policy portfolios typically assigned to domestic policy aides makes it difficult for them to devote more than a limited amount of time and attention to any one part, and they are heavily dependent upon the data and analyses supplied by the agencies. Bad faith is not to be presumed in agency dealings with the White House, but no President can disregard the strong proprietary interest which agencies take in controlling policy issues without "interference" from White House aides. Finally, even when the White House does succeed in imposing its design on the formulation of a major domestic policy, its control diminishes as the policy moves through the implementation stage.

Merely to describe the problem is to understand why Presidents of the past 20 years have had difficulty defining just what it is that a domestic policy staff can or should do. It cannot displace the institutional role of or hope to compete in detailed expertise with OMB, the Council of Economic Advisers, or with any of the other major institutional components of the EOP. Nor can it do so with departments and agencies of the executive branch in general.

What the domestic policy staff can do, however, is to play an honest broker's role in seeing to it that issues are properly vetted and that their formulation takes into account the full range of considerations requisite to a presidential decision—on everything from consistency with your overall program to political and social impact. The staff can gather critical intelligence from many sources, private as well as public; generate ideas in a wider context than any agency of government is typically capable of doing; work closely with OMB to police and analyze the effectiveness of agency performance; and provide policy perspective to the activities of the congressional affairs, political affairs, speech-writing, public liaison, and personnel offices of the White House.

Above all, the domestic policy office should be the one place where a distinctively *presidential* perspective is brought to domestic affairs, one that transcends the often parochial or institutionally self-interested view which prevails almost everywhere else in government. It is on this point that recent Presidents have failed, with certain exceptions, to consider how best to make use of their domestic policy staffs. The tendency has been to demand too much or too little, either by trying to run the government from the White House, or by merely allowing domestic advisers to pick up matters no one else was interested in doing. The first, however, is impossible, as more than a few Presidents have discovered; and the latter is the waste of talent and the loss of an important opportunity.

The opportunity lies precisely in concentrating domestic policy staff efforts on those issues on which you wish to leave your stamp. The trick here is to have a limited agenda. The government as a whole will resist major reorientation, but for all its resistance there is nevertheless a certain deference to presidential initiative which can be seized upon and turned to political advantage—provided you select your targets carefully, make clear that you intend to achieve them, and are prepared to generate political support on their behalf. These need not, and in most cases should not, involve major new expenditures, but there are any number of issues which are crying out for political definition, for which Congress is incapable of providing direction, and for which the public would vigorously applaud presidential leadership.

Once you draw up a short list of issues which concern you most, structure your domestic policy staff in such a way as to make clear to everyone—in government and out—that you are serious about achieving results. Once you have settled upon your short list of presidential priorities, a particular person should be charged with the overall management of each issue—from the definition of the problem to the design of a solution. Invest him with sufficient authority to accomplish the task, and hold him accountable for the results. Make clear to him and to everyone else—departmental officials, OMB, the speechwriting, political affairs, congressional relations staffs, and other units of the EOP and the executive branch whose cooperation is necessary—that he is the honest broker of the policy process on that issue. The designated aide should be held responsible for vetting the issue fully with relevant agencies, for seeing to it that the views of affected constituencies (both those in favor as well as those opposed) are solicited, for obtaining the necessary budgetary and economic analyses, and for formulating a communications plan to sell it to the public and a legislative plan to sell it to Congress. Most of this work will have to be done by professionals outside the domestic policy staff, but unless a member of that staff is charged with coordinating their work, you will run the risk of losing a distinctively presidential perspective on the issue. Predictable lamentations will be heard from predictable quarters that such an investment of responsibility "interferes" with someone else's precious turf, but in truth there is ample opportunity for these complaining others to contribute their relevant expertise to the plan. You can, in any event, mollify a good deal of such carping by making clear that the final proposal will be thoroughly debated before approval by you.

You will not be able to do this on more than a few issues, but you can and should do so on those which matter to you and on which you are prepared to stake some portion of your reputation. Once you make clear that you are personally dedicated to a particular issue and that one of your aides has been delegated the authority to develop it for you, most of the Administration will fall into line.

A final word of caution: investing a domestic policy staff member with power to coordinate the policy process on selected issues should not be read by him or anyone else as an invitation to supplant the role of department, agency, or EOP office heads. He must be empowered to coordinate and to task others pursuant to your instructions, but there is a difference between that and becoming a self-appointed, self-important policy czar who tries to run the government from a staff seat in the White House.

———————————◇———————————

THE NATIONAL SECURITY COUNCIL

There remains to be discussed, in this necessarily broad overview of presidential policy management, the role of the National Security Council. In the effort to assert presidential control over the government, perhaps nowhere else are the difficulties and dangers more dramatically revealed. Unclear delegations of authority, bureaucratic lethargy, warfare between White House and agency staffs or between agencies themselves, interference by Congress, leaks to the news media—all these things can deflect or derail presidential success in domestic policy, but the failure will seldom prove fatal to a President or the nation. The same defects in national security affairs, however, can ruin both a President as well as the presidency while inflicting damage on America's vital national interests. The margin for error is less, in short, and the public will forgive or forget mistakes less easily.

It is a measure of both the importance of international affairs and the difficulty of harnessing a huge bureaucratic apparatus to conduct them that all Presidents since Truman have found it necessary to rearrange their staff organization and the process by which State, Defense, and the intelligence community are subjected to presidential control. No President has been particularly happy with any set of arrangements, but some, clearly, have been more successful than others.

The 40-year history of the NSC is in a sense a continuing replication of the forces which led to its creation. Originally conceived by the Defense Department and its allies in Congress as a means for inducing greater cooperation among military and foreign affairs agencies and for ensuring that those agencies would have a voice in White House councils, the NSC was quickly converted by Truman into a mechanism for consolidating presidential control over those who sought to exercise control over him. He did so both because he was acutely sensitive to the necessity of maintaining presidential prerogative in foreign affairs and because he was able to repose unusual trust and responsibility in his Secretaries of State. The NSC staff was kept small, its function being little more than that of a secretariat, and State was responsible for generating policy initiatives and analyses and for coordinating the activities of relevant government agencies. Much the same approach was taken by Eisenhower, for much the same reasons. Consistent with the military staff system he was comfortable with, however, Eisenhower greatly formalized and expanded the NSC staff, and subdivided its activities into separate planning and operations units.

K ennedy believed the Eisenhower system was too bureaucratic and inflexible and too prone to protect self-serving, parochial departmental interests. He abolished most of the Eisenhower apparatus but, unlike Truman and Eisenhower, his State Department was unwilling or unable to generate creative ideas or to coordinate the major units of government. Over time, that work devolved by default upon the NSC staff, with decidedly mixed results. While the role of NSC shifted gradually from that of a secretariat to that of a policymaker, NSC policy-making under Kennedy remained ad hoc and was oriented heavily toward crisis management.

Lyndon Johnson, as in most things, preferred to be his own national security adviser and bypassed the NSC staff. Major policy decisions were made in a small informal weekly gathering of Johnson, the Secretaries of State and Defense, and the Director of Central Intelligence. Other than the national security adviser, no other staff was present. No formal records were kept, and much of the foreign policy/defense bureaucracies were kept in the dark.

Nixon came to office with an already developed foreign policy agenda and was determined to bend the national security apparatus to his ends. He realized the value of thorough analysis and reanalysis which had been the hallmark of Eisenhower's system, but shared Kennedy's beliefs about its tendency toward self-serving bureaucratic rigidity. At the same time, he felt that the Kennedy-Johnson approach was driven excessively by ad hoc decision-making without reference to overarching foreign policy goals. His national security adviser, Henry Kissinger, was a serious student of world affairs, and Nixon himself was both an experienced practitioner and thoughtful analyst of international politics. Policy ideas and analyses were generated in the first instance by departments and agencies, but their work was subjected to continual reanalysis by the NSC staff. Important as that work was, it was incidental to the main lines of Nixon's foreign policy, which he and Kissinger forged by themselves from the White House.

Upon his promotion to Secretary of State, Kissinger designed and conducted foreign policy from Foggy Bottom, and the NSC staff reverted to a secretariat role.

President Carter sought to use the NSC staff as an idea-creating institution, which suited the background and disposition of his National Security Adviser. The departments and agencies, principally State, were to analyze NSC-generated ideas in the light of their own institutional experience. Such a system was almost bound to result in ineffective stalemate, exacerbated by personality and policy conflicts between the national security adviser and the Secretary of State. In frustration, Carter devolved greater responsibility upon his security adviser, who in turn became an increasingly public figure, much to the chagrin of the Secretary of State, who finally resigned.

Reagan came to office with a conscious design to "deimperialize" the presidency, and, accordingly, the NSC staff was significantly downgraded in contrast to what it had been under Nixon and Carter. The President had general ideas about the reorientation of American foreign and defense policy but little in the way of practical experience to guide implementation. That, combined with his penchant for collegial decision-making and passive rather than active direction of the government, invited departmental and agency bureaucracies to dominate the policy process. It is a measure of their triumph that Reagan had six different national security advisers over the course of seven years.

This brief survey of presidential efforts to direct the government's foreign policy bureaucracies suggests a number of ideas that you should consider in establishing your own system.

First, Presidents impose or adopt procedures which they feel comfortable with. Despite all the textbooks with their handy bureaucratic charts, the presidency remains a highly personal office that will sooner or later reflect the style, work habits, opinions, and character of the man in the Oval Office. A bureaucratic design fitted to A will not, for good or ill, work for B. When it comes to bureaucratic structures, Presidents will get pretty much what they want—and what they deserve.

Second, what Presidents think they want, or what makes them feel comfortable, is not necessarily what they need or what the conduct of foreign policy may require.

Third, it is as much an error to believe that you can use the NSC to replicate the experience, analytical capability, or factual data possessed by departments and agencies as it is to believe that you can rely on departments and agencies to transcend their parochial interests.

Fourth, there is no institutional surrogate for the absence of hands-on presidential leadership. Providing leadership, especially to talented, ambitious men with ideas and interests of their own, is a far more difficult task than arranging and rearranging boxes on paper. The most perfectly designed bureaucratic flow chart will not supplant the need for thoughtful ideas. In the end, it is the compelling idea which inspires the behavior of bureaucratic actors. A badly designed bureaucratic system can frustrate even the best ideas, to be sure, but a good idea is itself one of the means by which bureaucratic systems are molded to produce efficacious results—provided a President has the wit to know a good idea when he sees it.

Whatever the structure you ultimately put in place, presidential leadership must begin with the direct and personal supervision of the principal actors—your NSC director, the Secretaries of State and Defense, and the Director of Central Intelligence. You should not attempt to assert control over the many details of their everyday activities. What you should do, and employ your NSC staff to do, is to rearrange important agency agendas not just by frequent personal contact with and management of the agency heads, but by imposing a conceptual framework on their activities. Whatever might be said about the effectiveness of the foreign policy establishment at the microlevel, it is at the macrolevel that our most conspicuous failures have occurred.

The most frequently underestimated tool of management in international relations policy-making is the articulation of a coherent set of principles to guide particular actions. Tactical capacity abounds in the foreign affairs establishment, but only you can provide the strategic framework which should guide both planning and operations. A well-developed sense of where you wish to go is in fact the first and most important step in getting you there; to the extent you are unsure at the strategic level, a vacuum is created, and the bureaucracy will be quick to fill it with ideas of its own, which are more likely to serve permanent institutional interests than any goal of yours.

The present decision-making process suffers from severe fragmentation, and granting the impossibility of perfection, it will have to be put back together again. The warfare among State, Defense, CIA, and NSC—aside from the political embarrassment and tactical failures it can lead to—tends to produce ideas that are thought to be safe rather than sound. They are notable more for satisfying the criteria of bureaucratic compromise than for advancing the national interest. The interagency process in recent years particularly has been incapable of articulating coherent national goals, which is in a sense not surprising. Only a President can provide the vision to drive the process and supply the political support necessary to sustain it. The military establishment which believes that no one else knows anything about warfare, the intelligence establishment which believes that its officers alone know how the world really works, and the diplomatic establishment which believes that only career FSOs can conduct international relations—all will resist, but, in the end, will succumb to a coherently articulated statement of national purpose.

Among other things, you ought to use your NSC staff as the principal source of inspiration for your own strategic articulation of American policy. You and they should consult with thoughtful observers within and outside the government, but the final articulation should remain within your control. For that reason, the preparation of your major foreign policy statements should remain within the province of the NSC staff.

Second, the staff should be authorized to exercise greater clearance authority than they now do over policy speeches and testimony delivered by departments and agencies. Again, detailed control is neither necessary nor desirable, but departmental statements should be carefully scrutinized for consistency with your overall approach.

Third, senior NSC staff should be invested with the chairmanship of key interagency committees. The number and makeup of these committees may vary with circumstance, but at a minimum you will need to deal separately with such diverse subjects as operations coordination, long-term planning, policy development, crisis management, covert action, and defense policy. NSC chairmanship of these committees should be intended less to exert detailed control over their members' activities and opinions than to make clear that you are ultimately responsible for policy and that your staff is there to prod and guide the process toward *your* objectives.

Finally, you ought to give serious consideration to asserting greater presidential control over the State Department with two principal objectives in mind: the reconstitution of an intellectually fertile policy planning staff, and the expansion of the number of policy-making positions subject to your direct appointment.

CONCLUSION

None of the steps discussed in this chapter alone will suffice, but together they form at least a skeletal framework from which you can assert the requisite degree of presidential control. Even if all these revisions are undertaken, there will still be plenty of "give" in the joints, and multiple opportunities for would-be policymakers from diverse bailiwicks to have their say. It is not a closed system that you wish to establish, with policy made in the dark by you and a few well-chosen aides, but rather an open system, one which gives everyone his say but at the same time makes clear that you, and not the bureaucracy, are in charge. That is why we have presidential elections. In the end, presidential leadership means presidential accountability; without that leadership, no one is accountable.

3

The President and the Congress: The Office of Legislative Affairs

by
William J. Gribbin

The Office of Legislative Affairs (OLA) should be approached with the conservative maxim: if it ain't broke, don't fix it. It needs no major overhaul of its operations. The Office's tradition of competent and committed personnel must continue. But there is no magic formula that will transform the Office into the legislative dynamo it seemed to be during the first year of the Reagan presidency.

Changes are needed indeed, but they must be effected at other levels within the White House. The new President must determine at the outset whether he will run a Johnsonian or Nixonian system of congressional relations. His choice in that regard will be critical to the performance of the Office, as will be his willingness to curb Cabinet government, raise the general level of competence in the White House staff, and bolster the proficiency of the Office with a strategic framework that gives long-range direction to its activities.

Recommendations for the Office are, in effect, recommendations for the President's overall relationship to the Congress and to his supporters and opponents there. The suggested improvements must be carried out immediately if they are to be achieved at all, for their success depends on a consistent legislative approach based on clear policy objectives and personal commitment from the President—and that approach and those objectives must be determined at the outset.

◇

BUDGET AND STAFF LEVELS

Staffing levels remained fairly constant during the Reagan years: a director, deputy director, office manager or executive assistant,

staff assistants to the director and deputy, four Senate lobbyists and
four or five counterparts for the House, each of whom has a staff
assistant, and two to four persons specializing in congressional mail
(and, as part thereof, agency liaison). There is an optimum size for any
legislative affairs operation, especially in the White House, where the
flow of paperwork from a larger staff would outpace the decision-
making ability of those who receive it. With the proper hands, a
professional staff of a dozen should be ample. With poorly selected
staff, twice that number will not suffice.

The Office's true personnel strength depends in part upon its relationship to its counterpart offices in departments, agencies, and
bureaus. When there is a strong, mutually supportive relationship
between the White House center and the dozens of outlying congressional relations operations in government, then the White House team
becomes the point of a much larger flying wedge.

But the converse must be true as well. The legislative affairs shops
throughout government must see in the White House Office a role
model, an advisor, and a protector against opponents both on the Hill
and in their own agencies. The assistant secretaries of legislative affairs
and their lesser counterparts in commissions and bureaus must find in
the White House Office someone to take their side, to give them what
amounts to orders, to assure them of high-level aid in their agencies'
internal policy struggles. Without that, legislative offices in the executive branch agencies come to see the White House legislative office as
a demanding nuisance, bossy and a busybody, but no help when their
own going gets rough. Under those circumstances, to whom would
they be loyal? To Cabinet secretaries and agency chiefs, of course.
When the White House fails to make departmental congressional
relations workers full partners in a common enterprise, one can hardly
blame those staffs for making friends closer to home.

———————————◇———————————

FUNCTIONS OF OLA

The Office of Legislative Affairs handles all dealings between the
President and Congress. (Well, not quite all: OMB's legislative
office bears quite a bit of the load.) The director of the Office is the
President's chief liaison with Congress. This should be someone
widely known and trusted on the Hill. This person, rather than a chief
of staff or other official, should be the one who presents the President

with legislative strategy and who poses the difficult decisions for him to make.

Because the director's role is a more than full-time job, the deputy director should be someone of sufficient weight to handle the internal paperwork—memos, speech clearances, policy option papers, and so forth—that demand both prompt and decisive handling. The deputy also serves as the contact point for departmental and agency legislative affairs offices. For at least part of the Reagan years, the deputy was the policy component of the Office, working closely with the Office of Policy Development and attending all Cabinet Council meetings, as well as OMB legislative strategy sessions, and representing the Office on virtually all internal task forces, study groups, and so forth.

It is a jocular maxim that the White House does not "lobby," inasmuch as the use of public funds for any lobbying is prohibited by law. So the President's lobbyists—or whatever they be called—represent his interests on the Hill, act as troubleshooters between the President and the members, explain congressional interests within the White House, and try, in ways too numerous to list, to advance the Administration's legislative agenda.

That can mean being browbeaten by a peevish member because some third-level departmental official failed to return his call. It can mean using the President's box at the Kennedy Center to spend an evening with some members of Congress, to whom personal access will probably be easier in the future. It means being alert for opportunities to do legitimate favors for members. It means endless detail work that might pay off in the future, when the Administration will desperately need that particular vote. It also means close attention to the human side of life in official Washington: arranging for a presidential call to a hospitalized member, sending presidential condolences and congratulations, and getting to know members as real people with real problems.

The Office recommends for or against congressional meetings with the President and arranges their details. In addition, the Office handles those presidential nominations of special interest to the White House, whether by itself or in tandem with the relevant department.

The Office handles all congressional mail in a small unit of two to four persons, whose patience and capabilities cannot be sufficiently praised. A huge percentage of it is routine, but much is substantive and thoughtful. Issue mail is routinely referred to the departments for the drafting of replies by those officials responsible for the particular subject. The Administration's response is then sent to the member(s) over the signature of the Office director or, in rare cases, that of the President or the chief of staff. So if a member writes the President to complain about a certain Cabinet officer, that letter is likely to be answered by a departmental underling who works for the very person faulted by the letter. The same holds true on policy questions. The shortcoming of this system is obvious.

On a more dramatic level, the Office is supposed to round up the votes for enactment of the President's legislative initiatives, or at least those which are not spun off to the departments. The percentage so delegated will vary from Administration to Administration. During the Reagan years, almost everything was left to the agencies, with at best cursory White House participation. This was not neglect of work by the Office, however. It was a pattern set from above.

There is some justification for this pattern. After all, the Office is rather small. It is not humanly possible for its personnel to honcho more than a few of the President's issues. That won't change. Most of the new Administration's agenda will be carried by the departments, but they can be made to carry it more energetically and more effectively.

Whatever the legislative goals assigned to the Office, it does not work toward them unaided. Indeed, in any major showdown with Congress, the Office must rely upon the resources of the Public Liaison Office and the Political Affairs Office. Those offices have the connections and wherewithal to bring interest group, constituent, and party pressure upon wavering or undecided Members of Congress. Their heroic efforts on behalf of President Reagan's economic package in 1981 were central to the success of the Legislative Affairs team.

It should be said that a major function of the Office of Legislative Affairs is nitpicking. By which gate will members enter the grounds? Singly or together? In what order? In what room will they be made to wait, and for how long, perhaps so that a Cabinet officer can drop by unexpectedly to give them good news about matters of particular interest to their constituents, thereby softening them up before their session with the President? Will the President receive them in the Oval Office or in one of the private rooms in "the Mansion," an especially intimidating experience for most members? Will spouses be invited to an early evening reception, in order to ensure that the members not bring up unpleasant subjects with the President? Will the opening minutes of the meeting be choreographed by the White House staff, to leave little time for spontaneous give-and-take, during which the President might hear or say something not intended by his subordinates?

Will one or more senior members of the President's party be included in a delegation of junior members, to put a damper on the group if it tends to get too candid or critical?

These questions reflect standard operating procedure in an Administration in which congressional interaction with the President has been orchestrated to perfection. Whether it is desirable to continue in that mode is for the new President to decide.

There is no congressional oversight or micromanagement of OLA's affairs. The important restraints on the Office—and they are necessary ones—are internal. There is a built-in tension between the Office and the President's policy shop. The latter's role is to advance policy ideas; OLA's job is to get them accepted by the Congress. It is easy for a policy office to reject compromise, but difficult for a legislative office to prevail without it. On the other hand, there is a natural tendency for those who work directly with Congress to emphasize its institutional point of view, to become, in effect, ambassadors from the Hill to the White House rather than the other way around. Among the symptoms of this malaise is the temptation to urge a compromise solution prematurely, before the full impact of the Administration's efforts can be felt—or, more frequently, to counsel against a presidential initiative because Hill leaders will not be enthusiastic about it and success will be problematical. While keen sensitivity to Hill attitudes is part of the Office's mission, the tendency to accept these attitudes as "gospel" must be resisted.

---◇---

THE NIXONIAN AND JOHNSONIAN MODELS

The most important factor affecting OLA's operations is the attitude or inclination of the President toward congressional relations. To oversimplify, there are two models, the Johnsonian and the Nixonian.

In the Johnsonian model, the President is personally familiar with Capitol Hill and its players. He has been, or quickly makes himself, part of the system. He thus recognizes the inevitability of congressional impositions and resolves to deal with Congress as the key to his success. In a Nixonian model, on the other hand, the President is not at ease with congressmen individually or with Congress institutionally. He remains aloof either by choice or ineptness. He lacks personal connections on the Hill and has few real friends there. He sees it as simply another obstacle to the accomplishment of his goals, but is unwilling to take the problem as one requiring adjustments or tactics not already familiar to him.

In the Johnsonian model, *the President must win.* Perhaps not this time around, but eventually. He and those who work for him understand that there is no substitute for ultimate victory. And because he is not interested in compromises, except of a temporary and superficial sort, a Johnsonian President recognizes he has real friends and real enemies in Congress. He rewards allies and punishes opponents. He strives for a majority of power, not a consensus of sentiment.

In the Nixonian model, by contrast, the President *must be on the winning side.* What matters are triumphs, even if they are borrowed. The problem with this approach is that it is possible for the President to be always on the winning side only if he is always open to the possibility of changing his position. Thus, a Nixonian President hedges his bets. So do those who work for him: Why, after all, should they stick their necks out ahead of his? Accordingly, the President lacks permanent friends in Congress—indeed, within his own Administration—for those who agree with him today never know when he might abandon them to deal with their opponents. One can hardly imagine a better summary of the last years of the Nixon Administration.

In the early years of Ronald Reagan's term in office, he seemed to have a Johnsonian relationship with the Congress. Though not part of the Hill's old chum network, he was certainly part of the nation's political establishment. As two-term Governor of California, he was no outrider. A party loyalist, gregarious and outgoing, he seemed the best arm-twister since LBJ. He also seemed determined to win.

Most of that was illusion, though it took time for the realities to sink into the collective awareness of Congress. In fact, President Reagan was as distant personally from members as was his predecessor. On the one hand, he was adamant (in a Johnsonian mode) about his fundamental principles, without which more tax increases would have succeeded. On the other, he acquiesced (in a Nixonian mode) in the efforts of others to impose tremendous new Social Security taxes and other "revenue enhancements," and frequently followed the path of seeking a "bipartisan solution" which undercut the morale and effectiveness of his staunchest allies.

In short, congressional relations in the Reagan White House had aspects of both Johnsonian and Nixonian operations. Perhaps that is the case in most Administrations. But this should give pause to the new President. His long-run success or failure may be determined, not by one or another clever strategy or bold initiative, but by certain assumptions and attitudes on his part and among his advisors that will make his relationship with Congress Johnsonian or Nixonian.

—————————◇—————————

ACHIEVEMENTS AND FAILURES DURING THE REAGAN YEARS

To be both accurate and fair, we should put the Office's legislative win/loss record in the context of the way the Reagan White House functioned. Imagine the difficulty of conducting successful congressional relations on behalf of, and often directed by, a senior staff one or more of whose members:

◆ Opposed including in a presidential visit to New York City one of the two New York senators because "New York City's not in his district."

◆ Discovering the racial composition of Grenada several days after its liberation, exclaimed, "You mean we invaded a black country?"

◆ Asserted that certain senators could not be pro-life because they were Democrats.

◆ Decided to announce Mr. Reagan's opposition to an antibusing rider, for the vetoing of which he had publicly criticized Mr. Carter only a few months earlier.

That mere sampling is not meant to be either gossipy or petty. But one must cite such specifics adequately to convey the hindrances with which the Office of Legislative Affairs had to deal throughout the Reagan years. Take the matter of five-minute congressional quickies: members introduce the President to Miss Sweet Potato or bring by a boy scout who saved someone's life or present the President with handicrafts from the folks back home. These photo opportunities matter greatly to the members, boost their popularity, and make them more amenable the next time the White House lobbyists come by to ask for their votes. But when the person controlling the President's schedule scorns them, preferring to reserve office time for events like an exchange of birthday gifts with an earringed Elton John, the legislative affairs staff is lucky to get its toe in the Oval Office door. (The event with Mr. John was never made public, but photos do exist.)

There was a certain mind-set brought from Sacramento. To many of the Californians, the national legislature was simply a more annoying version of the institution they had faced in Sacramento. It was remarkable that none of them had ever been a member of their state legisla-

ture, had never even run for elective office. They knew little about a
legislative view of process and prerogatives.

It is no wonder that personal disputes between the Reagan White
House and Republican members of Congress were a recurrent headache for the Legislative Affairs Office. For example, a remarkable
package of endorsements from leading Republican senators and congressmen on behalf of the Hill's foremost expert on the FTC brought
only a pro forma interview at the Office of Presidential Personnel,
where the interviewer had already reserved the FTC vacancy *for
himself.* In another instance, the endorsement by virtually all Senate
Republicans of one of the Hill's most respected GOP women was not
enough to get her seriously considered for a seat on the Federal
Elections Commission. Such instances have been legion, and each one
has made it a bit harder for the Office to succeed in its overall mission.
This is not to say that the President should have yielded jobs in the
executive branch to whomever members wanted therein. But congressional interest in these matters should have been taken far more
seriously.

Against that backdrop, the achievements of the Legislative Affairs
Office have been all the more creditable. In the first place, by hard
work and reliability, the staff restored White House-congressional
relations after their virtual collapse during the Carter years. Officials
throughout the Administration and in the White House itself would
have been wise to follow their example: returning every phone call, no
matter how late at night; ignoring no request, even if the answer must
be a polite negative; putting up with impositions of all sorts in order to
advance the President's chances of winning on the Hill.

It helped mightily that the Reagan Administration entrusted the
formation of the Office to a well-known, widely trusted veteran of
Nixon-Ford congressional affairs, Max Friedersdorf. It helped that he
was given a lead role in selecting the heads of major congressional
relations offices around government, thus imprinting a pattern of
loyalty to the White House agenda in departments which might need a
reminder in that regard. It helped that the Office had a policy anchor
in the deputy's role as an internal troubleshooter, minimizing problems
with the Hill that might be caused or exacerbated by other offices. It
helped too that the Office was willing to make life extremely difficult
for departmental offices which were slow to adjust to the fact of Ronald
Reagan in the Oval Office. Certain DOD personnel intended to continue their practice of giving Democratic members notice about appointments to the military academies ahead of Republican members.

Officials at the Centers for Disease Control intended to present pro-abortion papers at a Planned Parenthood meeting as part of their official duties. A USDA official assured the press he wouldn't let the Reagan White House dictate his management of certain nutrition programs. In these and other cases, frivolous or profound, it was important for the Legislative Affairs Office to show the Hill that Reagan policy was being enforced.

In all these ways and others, the Office quickly established its reputation as the best White House legislative shop in memory. On the other hand, when a ship runs aground, the rowers down below are the first to get blamed. That explains the "failures" of the Legislative Office in the later years of the Reagan Administration, most of which involved the inability of the Office to compensate for the mistakes that were accumulating elsewhere.

A major cause of "failure" in the Office was the unwillingness of the White House to discipline Cabinet members. The flagrant autonomy of most Cabinet chiefs eroded both the credibility of the Legislative Affairs Office on the Hill and its ability to insist upon a clear policy line there.

The most crippling blow against the Office's effectiveness on the Hill was the decision of Administration strategists to part company with the President's Republican base in the House of Representatives on several key issues, especially taxes. Once congressional Republicans realized the White House had no permanent alliance with them, they would have no permanent interest in the Administration.

There were some mistakes within OLA as well. One serious one was the tendency to foster an unrealistic attitude toward the President's hardened enemies in Congress. This was partly out of habit, for congressional relations folk are understandably reluctant to offend a member with whom they might have to deal in the future. Extraordinary care was taken not to anger members who, under the best of circumstances, would remain mortal enemies to everything the President stood for—and would *never* vote with the President on a major issue. And so, the Office had the President engage in jolly public interaction with his chief Hill opponents. President Reagan later paid the price for such PR mistakes. How could he convince the public in his televised addresses that Hill opponents of Contra aid were dangerous schemers when he himself had all along confirmed them in their role of the "loyal opposition"?

This is in part the result of the failure by Legislative Affairs to realize, from the outset, that there could be no accommodation with the President's ideological opponents; the congressional Left could behave despicably toward Mr. Reagan, but he was institutionally inhibited from striking back in kind. *Reversing that situation is probably the most urgent mission for the Legislative Affairs Office in the next Administration.*

––––––––––––––––––––⟡––––––––––––––––––––

RECOMMENDATIONS

The following recommendations are based on the assumption that the President wants to be successful in enacting his legislative program and that he realizes that this will take more then a business-as-usual approach to congressional relations. If the new President is serious about *winning*—as distinct from merely being on the winning side—he should make legislative affairs his primary theater of operation. Some of these recommendations may seem trivial or superficial, but successful congressional relations depend heavily on symbolic actions, gestures, and the creative direction of public affairs.

The President should keep in mind that no matter what the specific audience or circumstance he is addressing, he is really speaking to the American people. When they respond, Congress listens. That should be remembered in assessing and implementing these proposals:

1) Restore the constitutional role of the Vice President as the presiding officer of the Senate. In that capacity, the Vice President should be responsible for much of the high-level dealings between the White House and the Congress. This will inevitably make him a powerful figure in his own right, but a strong President should welcome that prospect. If his Vice President is a former senator, all the more auspicious!

2) Be President of all the people, but don't try to be a colleague of all the Congress. Each President has real enemies, not just opponents—and both they and the public should know that *he* knows and will treat members accordingly.

3) Do not tacitly legitimate corrupt power structures by appearing on network television joking and backslapping with members of Congress who are hostile to your policies and dangerous to the country's future. If a President signals to the American people that his adversaries are just "regular guys," then politics is just a game and it doesn't matter who wins. Why should anyone else care, and why should they

ever get mad at their congressman just because he obstructs the President's policies?

4) Keep the Legislative Affairs offices at least as close to the Oval Office as they now are.

5) Hire as director of the Office someone with sufficient personal prestige that he cannot be intimidated by other advisers. Only someone who is in a position to walk off the job in protest can do it as well as it needs to be done.

6) Assure the director of the Office personal access—easy, informal, unscheduled, frequent access—to the President.

7) Explain to the director, and make sure the explanation is relayed to the Office staff, that the President is interested in legislative victories over the long term rather than being on the winning side in the short term. It's the total record that counts, not winning every roll call.

8) Appoint as deputy director someone who is respected as a policy analyst as well as a legislative affairs hand, so that the legitimate interests of congressional affairs—which often means nothing more than placating powerful or threatening members of Congress—will be counterbalanced by commitment on the issues.

9) Solidify the political base—in a hurry. Immediately consolidate a one-third-plus-one margin in the House and Senate. The veto will be the only trump card in a game where the stakes are the nation's future. That means, from the outset, paying extraordinary attention to ideological friends on the Hill, for in the final analysis, all the others will let him down. That sounds radical, but it is nonetheless true.

10) Issue veto threats only in the President's name, not from aides. The formula used by the Reagan Administration—"the President's senior advisors would recommend a veto"—became a joke on the Hill.

11) Ensure that all appointive congressional relations positions throughout government are awarded by the White House, through the Office of Legislative Affairs. Throughout the entire executive branch, legislative offices should form a network of loyalty to the President's program, with their jobs dependent upon the White House legislative director as much as the agency head.

12) Give a grown-up State of the Union Address. Make it short and make it businesslike. The President should surprise the American people with a mature speech that lets them—and the Members—know he is not going to conduct "politics as usual."

13) Fire somebody, anybody, for not staying in line with Administration policies. The best way to show official Washington that the President will not be a legislative patsy is to fire the first departmen-

tal—or White House—official who contravenes or undercuts his position.

14) Hold all legislative strategy meetings in the Oval Office. The formation of a Legislative Strategy Group without presidential participation early in the Reagan Administration was an important part of an unprecedented abdication of presidential power.

15) Regain control of the President's daily schedule by resisting the seizure of his schedule by the Department of State. The incredible impositions of time made by that Department upon the President's workday would not be tolerated coming from any other segment of the government. The President's priority in terms of time should be Congress and his legislative program, foreign and domestic.

16) Socialize with members of Congress. Most do not bite. That means more than maintaining a ceremonial friendship with a key figure or two. The informal dimension of congressional relations is invaluable for a chief executive who really wants to be a player on Capitol Hill.

17) Insist upon a certain degree of spontaneity in relations with members of Congress. The President does not really need a script to call a member, ask for a vote, inquire about the family, register a complaint, or extend a thank-you for a vote that may have been particularly difficult.

18) Read a healthy sampling of incoming congressional mail, including all items from key leaders. There is no telling what the President may learn about his own Administration.

4

Public Liaison and Coalition Building

by
Wayne H. Valis*

ORIGINS OF THE OFFICE
OF PUBLIC LIAISON

In the congressional elections of 1958, the Democrats solidified their hold on both the United States Senate and House of Representatives. An aging Republican President confronted his final two years in office with the prospect of an increasingly partisan Congress that would obstruct his legislative program in an attempt to prepare for the election of a Democrat in the 1960 presidential campaign. Flying over the United States after this election, President Eisenhower and his aide Bryce Harlow discussed how they would deal with the looming legislative logjam. Ike wondered whether he could engender a sense of enthusiasm throughout the country for his program. Harlow suggested that the President make every effort to revitalize the grassroots that had propelled Ike to the presidency in the first place. As the two men continued their flight across the American heartland, they decided to organize an office in the White House to communicate with many of the key organizations and groups that give America its pluralist character. They assigned Robert Keith Gray, a bright, energetic Nebraskan, to organize the new effort. Thus was established, in embryonic

*Morton Blackwell, Linda Chavez, Robert K. Gray, Mark Klugman, William Marumoto, Lawrence F. O'Brien, Sr., Robert R. Reilly, Donald F. Rogers, Alexander Trowbridge, and Mildred Webber made contributions to this paper. The author is especially indebted to the late Bryce Harlow, who was a source of insight and inspiration over many years. The views and opinions expressed here are, however, entirely the responsibility of the author.

form, the precursor of the Office of Public Liaison (OPL), "a home for broad interest groups at the White House," in the words of Harlow.

Since these early years, OPL has grown and changed shape, reflecting the various Presidents and their staffs. Harlow intended it to permit organized groups to bring "their spectrum of issues and concerns to the President, but within a symbiotic relationship, emphasizing mutuality, wherein the President had a mechanism to use to ask the groups for their help."

The election of 1960 brought an end to the fledgling OPL. Interest group and political functions were now included in the domain of Special Assistant to the President Lawrence F. O'Brien, who headed up a reorganized congressional relations and Cabinet affairs unit. O'Brien relied on about 40 key people in the various departments who reported on pending legislation every Monday afternoon. O'Brien and his staff refined and compressed these reports and presented them to President Kennedy (and later President Johnson) to prepare him for the weekly Tuesday congressional leadership breakfast. "As part of this," O'Brien noted, "we retained all interest group activity. There was no separate shop [for public liaison]." The primary special interest group activities were with the Meanys and Reuthers, AFL-CIO and organized labor. During the battle on Medicare, for example, O'Brien et. al. mobilized senior citizens organizations to do battle with the AMA.

Relations with the business community were somewhat chilly. The New Frontier and Great Society were largely concerned with social programs, and usually the business community was neutral or opposed. Of the business community, O'Brien said, "we didn't have daily contact, although there were many occasions for meetings and drop-bys. Henry Ford dropped by often, as did some others. . . . The one exception was in 1962 when the Reciprocal Trade Act was expiring. We had to decide whether or not to go for a new bill, or just a simple extension. We decided to go for a new bill, and created a task force to work with the media and business. We worked closely with the Chamber of Commerce, with whom we generally had little contact, and other business groups." The result was a smashing success for President Kennedy and O'Brien.

The system continued in effect throughout the Johnson years, even after O'Brien departed the White House in 1965 to become Postmaster General. Alexander Trowbridge, Commerce Secretary under President Johnson, recalls that policy head Joseph Califano also dealt with interest groups. Under LBJ there was a policy grouping (i.e., economics, labor, civil rights, education), and each policy director was expected to coordinate with the appropriate interest groups in that particular area of responsibility. Both O'Brien and Trowbridge believed that this arrangement and integration of function particularly suited the operating styles of Presidents Johnson and Kennedy.

After the election of Richard Nixon to the presidency in 1968, Bryce Harlow again played a key role in the rebirth of OPL. As head of the Nixon congressional relations operation, Harlow well knew the value of lobbying support by the private sector. Thus, OPL was reestablished in 1969, and Charles Colson soon became its director. Constituency building and providing support services (appointments, access to policymakers, courtesy meetings, etc.) were the main goals for the Colson operation, which were seen as a vital part of Nixon's re-election campaign strategy.

Colson recruited a talented team, including Donald F. Rodgers, Michael P. Balzano, William A. Marumoto, and Henry Cashen, who worked to organize the "silent majority." For the first time, significant elements of organized labor massively supported a Republican candidate for President. The famous "hard hat" marches on Wall Street and in New York were a major part of this effort. Roman Catholics, ethnic Americans (especially of Italian and Polish descent), blue-collar workers: all were gathered into the 1972 campaign. By 1973 it appeared that the work of the Colson operation had helped reshape the American political landscape. Unfortunately, the Watergate-related activities of Colson shattered his office and by 1974 completely overshadowed the accomplishments of the earlier period.

Under President Ford the Office of Public Liaison received its present name and was radically restructured by William J. Baroody, Jr. During the two years of the Ford presidency, OPL was designed to provide access between citizens and their organized groups on the one hand, and the President and the government's policymakers on the other. Two-way communications and services were provided to citizen groups through a wide array of sophisticated approaches. Pursuing President Ford's goal of putting an end to "the long nightmare of Watergate," which had severely eroded public trust in government, Baroody sought to foster dialogue and a feeling of open access to the White House. Through a series of "town hall" forums across the country and other aggressive communications programs, as well as a myriad of small group meetings in the White House, OPL made a major contribution to the President's overall program of reestablishing confidence in the presidency.

Under President Carter, OPL was decentralized and divided into six
or seven units. The number of staff performing OPL functions increased from about 28 to almost 60. Although new functions were
grafted on, there was little attempt at coordination and each unit
performed independently. Carter's OPL director, Anne Wexler, understood the need to combine politics with policy—that is, the need to put
politics at the service of policy to the extent possible. Thus the
frequent meetings she arranged between policy chief Stuart Eizenstat
and leading chief executive officers of major companies led to a
surprising degree of business support for an administration not often
in political harmony with the business community. This integrated
approach provides a clear lesson for those carrying out a liaison role.

President Reagan's first OPL director, Elizabeth Dole, assisted by
her deputy Red Caveney, organized the unit in a highly centralized
and structured manner, emphasizing tight control, maximum coordination, and "zero defect" operation. Much of 1981 was spent in
drafting detailed constituency strategy plans and reaching out to diverse groups. The most important function of OPL in this early period
of Reagan's first term was to organize grassroots coalition activity
behind the President's economic recovery program and other (primarily domestic) legislative initiatives. OPL was instrumental in gaining
passage of the budget cuts of 1981 and 1982, the Economic Recovery
Tax Act of 1981, the TEFRA package of 1982 and the sale of AWACS
aircraft to Saudi Arabia in 1982, the latter being OPL's first-ever
significant venture into the foreign policy arena.

In order to succeed with these initiatives, it was necessary to defeat
the Democratic House leadership on a series of rules votes, a truly
formidable task. Recognizing the difficulty of the task, Chief of Staff
Jim Baker orchestrated a campaign to overwhelm the Democratic
House of Representatives with convincing demonstrations of support
for the President's program. This was accomplished by mobilizing over
one thousand organizations, a grand coalition of special interest groups
that veteran "pols" would have thought impossible six months earlier.
House Speaker Thomas P. O'Neill was awed by the literally millions of
mailgrams and phone calls that swamped congressional offices on
behalf of the President's budget and tax cuts. He called it "a telephone
blitz like this nation has never seen."

This period was the high watermark not only of OPL, but of the
policy achievements of the Reagan Administration. Under its second
director, Ambassador Faith Ryan Whittlesey, OPL turned its attention
to building public support for the President's proposals for aid to the

Contra freedom fighters in Nicaragua and many of the social issues so devoutly supported by conservatives. Through the new "Outreach Working Group on Central America," OPL held a series of intensive briefings and distributed White House digests of information, thereby playing a major role in the mobilization of public support for democracy in Central America and the Nicaraguan freedom fighters in particular. OPL also established strong working relationships with broad coalitions formed around social issues such as school prayer, tuition tax credits, and abortion.

In January 1985, despite abundant evidence of the success of OPL over the previous four years, new chief-of-staff Donald Regan mysteriously downgraded OPL, reducing its new director Linda Chavez to Deputy Assistant to the President and adding a new level of bureaucracy to the structure, thereby diminishing her role and access to the Oval Office. Chavez coped with the staff reductions and other changes by closing the Central America outreach effort and streamlining all constituency operations. This was in line with the chief of staff's directive to focus all resources on galvanizing private sector support for the massive tax revision of 1986—which turned out to be the last major success of OPL. Under these circumstances it is not surprising that the office declined in importance.

Under its last two directors, Mari Maseng and Rebecca Range, OPL reflected the Administration's less ambitious agenda in the last years of the Reagan presidency. Unable to mount any major political or legislative offenses, OPL had to struggle to help the President sustain vetoes and wage largely defensive battles—all with the smallest staff and fewest resources of its twenty-year history.

———————————◇———————————

ROLE OF OPL

The necessity for public liaison activities should be likened to the role of other White House liaison units. The White House has a press office to serve as liaison to the "fourth estate," a Congressional Relations Office as liaison to the Congress, and an Intergovernmental Relations Office as liaison to state and local government. There must be some institutional White House structure to deal with the enormous number and variety of constituency groups that now play an important role in our political system.

As political parties have disintegrated, congressional leadership has fragmented, and the influence of the media has increased, special interest and public interest citizen groups have become extremely sophisticated and effective in influencing the Congress and in using litigation and the courts to shape public policy. These groups have developed enormously elaborate communications networks and large interlocking systems of committees and task forces to generate reports, proposals, and analyses of legislation and industry trends. The White House must have the capability of communicating with these entities. Having such a capability gives the President important additional tools for gaining public understanding and support for his policy initiatives—and for building lasting coalitions that can have enormous electoral significance.

It might also be argued, as its founders in the Nixon-Ford Administrations believed, that equity and fairness are served by providing a mechanism for organized groups of diverse stripe to seek redress of grievances and get a hearing—outside the formal atmosphere of the federal bureaucracy—for their ideas, complaints and requests, and their aspirations or prayers directed at the President, with some hope of more than a form-letter response from the White House.

Moreover, a function not to be belittled is the role OPL can play in sensitizing the White House staff to the real world outside (in both positive and negative terms), thereby reducing somewhat the isolation and bunker mentality that inevitable afflict the courtiers of every White House regime.

———————————◇———————————

STRATEGIC AND OPERATIONAL FUNCTIONS

It is important for everyone on the President's staff—and in his Administration generally—to understand the goals and functions of OPL in both strategic and operational terms. OPL's activities support the President's policy agenda by broadening and strengthening his relationships with organized groups that are major "players" in the political arena.

There are three dimensions to the OPL mission, and all three are important to the overall success of the President's program:

1) **Constituency-building** is the strategic goal of OPL, and must be based on a well conceived plan focused on the President's natural allies and those constituencies that can be brought into the fold.

2) **Policy advocacy** is the second goal of OPL and is the one that is

most readily understood: generating public understanding and support for particular policy initatives.

3) **Policy facilitation** is the third goal and encompasses most of the activities usually referred to as "services" and "access."

OPL must strive to perform all three functions effectively. Otherwise OPL can degenerate into merely providing a friendly "point of access" to the Administration for an ever-increasing number of special interest groups. To advance on all three fronts the White House must have a strategic sense of its vital interests, must know its primary constituencies (actual and potential) and be willing to differentiate among groups on the basis of their usefulness, but at the same time maintain a cordial and "proper" relationship with major groups of immense diversity and power.

OPL can mobilize important constituency elements in ways available to no other government unit outside the White House. Among the most effective activities are small-group meetings with the President in the Oval Office, the Roosevelt Room, or the Cabinet Room. Larger gatherings in the Family Theater, Old Executive Office Building (the Indian Treaty Room or the auditorium) or the Rose Garden are also effective. The citizens involved in such meetings can be genuine "grassroots leaders" of local organizations or the seasoned (and sometimes jaded) representatives of Washington-headquartered associations.

In terms of policy advocacy, OPL is an important supplement to the White House communications or "surrogate" operation. The effect of this kind of concentrated attention can be enormously effective if coordinated with other White House and Administration units. This is an area in which the Reagan White House was seriously deficient.

It should be emphasized that these large organizations possess extensive internal communications systems, each independent of the national media and many the equivalent of highly effective direct mail networks. The Reagan White House operation failed to utilize these networks on a consistent, sustained level, although there were sporadic successes and some new networks developed, particularly among organizations concerned with the social issues. The networks used so effectively in the great budget and tax battles of 1981–82 were hardly tapped at all in the second term.

OPL facilitates policy-making by 1) gathering intelligence from all major private sector groups in intimate ways often not otherwise available, 2) gathering ideas, approaches, and data from the private sector's enormous analytic networks (task forces, study groups, etc.),

3) identifying people and human resources to fill government jobs, carry out special duties and informal missions, etc., and 4) acting as troubleshooter or ombudsman to prevent crises or conflict, and at times providing a "traffic control" function for interest groups.

The specific trouble-shooting work of a liaison office can be wide-ranging. During a major 1982 legislative battle, the author conducted arduous negotiations with one trade association executive, attempting to persuade him to end his association's oppostion to the President's proposal. After numerous offers and counteroffers and weeks of effort, the executive advised me that his board was adamant and had decided to oppose the legislative initiative; the association would be sending mass mailgrams to the Congress. After much pleading, and more negotiations, the executive called once more, saying, "Sorry, but the mailgrams go out. I'll do one thing, though. They won't be mailed until the day before the vote. And you know how the mails are." (Such is the power of the Washington staffs of "grassroots" organizations: when timing is everything, policy is set as much by the seemingly technical decisions of the staff as by the resolutions passed by boards or annual meetings.)

Activities that produce "deals" and subtle agreements with powerful organizations can be of great assistance to the White House Congressional Relations Office, Presidential Personnel Office, and Office of Policy Development, but coordination with these offices has ranged at times from excellent to almost nonexistent.

———————◇———————

OPL SERVICES

Many of the services OPL provides to groups are obvious or have already been discussed. OPL works with groups on issues of mutual concern, seeking their views and advice on 1) general issues, 2) legislative initiatives, 3) personnel appointments, 4) political action, and 5) agency regulations (OPL acted as an important adjunct to the Reagan regulatory reform program in this respect). All of these services should be offered, in theory, in time to make a difference, before White House actions are finally decided or implemented. Thus, OPL relies heavily on inclusion in a sound White House staffing system in order to function effectively.

In addition to these substantive services, OPL is generally responsible for creating a "warm feeling," the necessary, if not always accurate belief that good friends will not be forgotten. This personal equation is established by showing genuine concern and by working on such diverse services as presidential proclamations, commendations, letters of appreciation, state dinner invitations, possible trips to Camp David or Camp Hoover, rides on Air Force One or Marine One, autographed photos, invitations to the home of the VP, the opportunity to represent the President at important events; down to such apparently trivial items as gifts. These include presidential cuff links, tie clips, pens, stick pins, and many more. These may sound trivial, but these small tokens are warmly received when recipients know they were given sincerely and invariably are highly prized. Over the course of its eight years, the Reagan White House provided fewer tokens of this nature than any in recent memory, with a predictable effect on political operations.

———————◇———————

CONSTITUENCY GROUPS: IMPORTANT DISTINCTIONS

Identifying and differentiating between organized groups is vitally important to the success of OPL, but more importantly, to the success of any presidency. The chief of staff, counsellor, pollster and other major presidential political strategists must help guide OPL in deciding on which constituency groups it must concentrate. There are literally thousands of groups, of which several hundred are national organizations with highly sophisticated Washington operations.

The key policy question is: are all constituency groups to be treated equally? The answer to his question goes to the heart of the entire operation. Will a permanent political majority be created by broad, equal treatment or by efforts to build particular combinations? The answer is obvious, but there is a natural tendency in practice to blur distinctions and seek friendly relations with everyone. This diffuses the focus of the operation and wastes resources. It is, of course, necessary to be civil to all groups and avoid unnecessary friction. But it is vital to establish some highly refined, politically attuned operating procedures to afford different treatment, access and services to different types of groups. For example, during the Ford Administration, some distinctions that should have been made occasionally were not. This sometimes led to misallocation of resources, alienation of friends, and in a few instances, to political embarrassment. In one case, offering a helping hand and hearty welcome to Ralph Nader resulted in a lawsuit.

Another important political question concerns whether OPL will service Washington-based groups almost exclusively, or will reach out to grassroots organizations that may not appear "on the charts." For example, the NEA and AFL-CIO were implacably opposed to the Reagan coalition, yet substantial elements of the rank and file of both groups voted for President Reagan, as well as for GOP legislators. The political question is how to deal with these, or similar groups. Does OPL deal only with the Washington leadership, or does it work with politically supportive local leaders? This becomes complicated, yet it is important for OPL's success.

THE STRUCTURE OF OPL

The structure of any Office of Public Liaison will depend upon its mission and environment. Depending on whether OPL is designed to 1) develop voter blocs, 2) organize legislative coalitions, 3) service constituency groups, or 4) be an ombudsman, different structures will be necessary. No mode should be adopted until the primary mission of OPL is clarified.

The most common structure has been to assign almost all major interest groups a "particular" special assistant. This was the mode under Ford/Baroody and Carter/Wexler, and eventually under the Reagan OPL models. The pressure from each interest group to have a designated special assistant is enormous and has usually proven irresistible. This mode works best in terms of servicing constituency groups and fulfilling the ombudsman role. The good news with this mode is that it "covers the waterfront." The bad news is that it often squanders precious resources and energy on some constituencies with which there is little chance of any pay-off in terms of support for the President's program.

Another structure, which was partly attempted by Dole at the outset, is to organize around broad governmental functions (e.g., human resources, trade and commerce). Under this mode, each special assistant would cover several constituencies, reporting through "super special assistants" or deputy assistants. In this system there needs to be a "strategic reserve" of resources to be used as situations require. One virtue of this structure is its similarity to the organizing principles of other White House offices—OMB, the Office of Presidential Personnel, and the Office of Policy Development, for example. Working relationships with these offices is greatly facilitated if they have similar staffing structures. The main disadvantage is that many powerful interest groups clamor for more personalized attention than this structure can deliver.

Yet another mode would be to assign a deputy assistant or "super special assistant" to each of three areas: 1) voter bloc development; 2) legislative coalition-building; and 3) general servicing work. This variation would permit a very vigorous and offensive deployment of resources. This aggressive approach maximizes a rifle shot approach to political coalition building, but it is short on the "two-way communication" and "access to government" roles. It requires very close coordination with the policy staff and the political staff.

—————————◇—————————

CONCLUSION

The three functions of the Office of Public Liaison can be carried out in any one of several structures; there is no one best way to do it. What is important is that all three functions —constituency building, policy advocacy and "services"—are built into the plan from the beginning. Second, there must be a resolute commitment to maintaining the strategic element (constituency building based on some well-conceived plan for expanding the base of the President's political coalition) in the face of the daily pressures for more short-term goals. The trick is to make sure the myriad day-to-day activities in the "servicing" and advocacy realms support the long-term goals in the realm of constituency building.

A third important element of a successful OPL operation is professionalism: the staff must be experienced in political affairs, committed to the President's philosophy and program, and able to work in a pressure-cooker environment. Staffers must be reminded occasionally that they work for the President and not the interest groups with which they interact: "capture" by an outside group—no matter how friendly the group may be—must be avoided, and if detected it must be dealt with firmly.

The director of OPL must be someone who is widely known and respected among the President's staff, who can represent the President effectively in any public forum or negotiating session, and who is afforded full access and standing as a senior member of the President's staff. The director must work closely with colleagues in the West Wing, particularly the policy and legislative directors, and must have the full confidence of the chief of staff. It is vital that the OPL director's position not be treated as the "woman's" slot in the West Wing, as this kind of tokenism will severely diminish its effectiveness as part of the President's "inner Cabinet." Capable women can be found for *any* position in the White House, not just OPL.

Finally, the management team in OPL must be committed to a creative and innovative approach to building public understanding and support for the President's program. They should look beyond the Washington Beltway to the heart of America and find new ways to inform and energize citizens who share the President's goals and will support his program. Providing services and access to the recognized leaders of powerful national organizations located in Washington is the "bread and butter" of the OPL operation. But the meat and potatoes is coalition-building for policy advocacy. Coalition-building pays off not only in tangible support for specific policy initiatives but in long-term strengthening of the President's base of suppport. Those are goals necessary both to any successful White House management plan and to the political future of the President and his party.

5

Managing the Federal Budget

by
Stephen Moore*

For both Congress and the President, balancing the federal budget has proven to be an onerous exercise in futility. In every year but one since 1960 the federal government has spent more than it has collected in tax revenues. Despite his pledge in 1980 to balance the budget, Ronald Reagan was frustrated repeatedly in his battles against Washington's prospending juggernaut. Reagan left the White House with the budget deficit about twice as high as when he was first elected. This explosion of national indebtedness stands as a conspicuous blemish on the Reagan economic record. Gaining control of the budget, therefore, while resisting calls for new tax hikes, looms as perhaps the most critical domestic policy challenge confronting the new Administration.

Notwithstanding past failures, the budget *can* be tamed. The deficit appears to be shrinking finally, from its 1986 peak of $220 billion. Contrary to popular belief, the path to a balanced budget by 1993 as prescribed by the Gramm-Rudman-Hollings Deficit Reduction Law, will not necessitate new tax increases or painful cuts in spending. Balancing the budget over the next four years requires a three-tiered presidential fiscal policy agenda: 1) maintaining steady economic growth as a means of reducing federal entitlement outlays and raising federal tax receipts; 2) holding the *growth rate* of total spending to between three and four percent annually; and 3) blocking the passage of new spending initiatives that would increase the deficit.

Just as important to winning the war on the deficit, however, is for the President to assert leadership in calling for a new budget act. The

*The author wishes to thank Martha Phillips, Margaret Davis, Dan Mitchell, Carol Crawford, Ken Quartermain, Jim Mietus, and Robert Rector for their contributions to this chapter. The views and opinions expressed here are, however, entirely the responsibility of the author.

congressional budget process has broken down entirely and imposes no fiscal discipline upon individual lawmakers. Congress's recent dismal budgetary track record has made a convincing case for procedural reforms. Between 1976 and 1987—a period spanning three presidencies—Congress spent an average of $30 billion per year more than the President requested. Worse yet, almost every year that Ronald Reagan held the White House, Congress sent to him an eleventh-hour, catch-all "continuing resolution." In November 1987 Congress did not pass the $1 trillion budget until almost three months after the fiscal year had begun, and even then it had to wrap $600 billion of spending into a single massive bill weighing fifteen pounds. This budget blackmail ploy forced the President either to sign the most expensive piece of legislation in history, or close down the entire U.S. government. To discourage such irresponsible budget packaging and to restore the President's proper leadership role in the nation's fiscal affairs, the congressional budget process must be fundamentally revamped.

––––––––––––––––$\Diamond$––––––––––––––––

REVIEWING THE REAGAN RECORD

In spite of the growth of the budget deficit, the Reagan Administration's fiscal policy was successful in three areas.

1) *Tax Cuts Promoted Economic Growth*

Reagan slashed the average American worker's income tax bill by more than 25 percent in 1981. These income tax rate reductions played a significant role in pulling the American economy out of the worst national recession since the 1930s and triggering over 70 straight months of economic expansion—shattering the record for sustained peacetime economic expansion. Unfortunately, subsequent tax increases have eroded most of the gains made in 1981.

2) *National Defense Spending Restored to Traditional Levels*

Ronald Reagan reestablished traditional spending priorities within the federal budget. The share of the federal budget devoted to national defense expanded over the Reagan years from the all-time low of 23 percent during Jimmy Carter's term in office up to about 28 percent. (Even after the Reagan defense build-up, however, the 28 percent share of the budget spent on defense was quite low in historical terms; as recently as 1960—before the Vietnam War—over half of the federal budget was spent on national defense.)

3) *Creation of New Spending Programs Halted*

With the exception of federal catastrophic health insurance legislation enacted in Reagan's last months, no major domestic spending programs were launched during the Reagan years. This was a significant accomplishment: Ronald Reagan brought to a close an era of unprecedented federal programmatic expansion, beginning with Lyndon Johnson's Great Society agenda and carrying over through the 1970s.

The Reagan Years and the Budget Deficit

The source of the triple digit budget deficits of the 1980s—Reagan's glaring fiscal failure—is an issue of continuing confusion. Blame often has been directed at the Reagan tax cuts and defense buildup. The facts contradict such an assessment. Over the Reagan years, federal tax collections climbed by over $300 billion in current dollars. These increased tax revenues were enough to finance the entire Reagan defense build-up, leaving $175 billion to pay for domestic program expansions and deficit reduction. Even as a percentage of total output taxes remain high; in 1988 federal taxes consumed 19.3 percent of the gross national product (GNP); only five times in the last 40 years have Americans been taxed this heavily. The deficit is therefore not attributable to insufficient revenues.

The Reagan national defense build-up has been equally misinterpreted. To be sure, the Pentagon budget has risen by $125 billion in current dollars and $75 billion in constant dollars since 1981. Yet, the extent of this spending build-up has been grossly overstated by being compared with the spending levels during the previous five years of U.S. military neglect. From 1975 through 1979 Congress "defunded" national defense to fund a massive expansion in entitlements. In fact, even the Carter Administration's last budget set in motion the process of reversing this detrimental policy of robbing the defense budget to pay for domestic program expansions. Carter's last budget envisioned a five-year Pentagon spending plan that closely paralleled the defense outlay pattern that actually emerged under President Reagan's leadership.

Moreover, those who would point the budget knife exclusively at the Pentagon budget fail to recognize that the Reagan defense build-up ended in 1986. In each of the past three federal budget cycles defense programs have taken a real cut in spending levels. Further, today's defense spending levels are low, not high in historical terms. The United States now devotes 6.1 percent of GNP to national defense, as compared to an average of 8.4 percent between 1950 and 1980.

The primary source of the budget deficit has been continued growth in domestic spending. In fact, if the domestic budget had been simply frozen at 1981 levels—even without cutting a single program—the budget would be balanced today. But programs expanded. The major culprit was federal entitlement programs, which expanded by over $175 billion during Reagan's two terms—or 40 percent greater than the dollar increase in defense spending. As a percentage of GNP, domestic spending is today about twice as high as it was in 1960.

———————————◇———————————

NEEDED: A NEW BUDGET ACT

The budget deficit crisis first captured public alarm in the early 1980s, when the annual deficit first rose to the unprecedented level of $100 billion in 1982 and to over $200 billion the following year. Yet the roots of the crisis that generated those huge budget deficits can be traced directly to an event occurring almost a decade earlier: the passage of the 1974 Budget and Impoundment Control Act.

The 1974 Budget Act was passed in the wake of the Watergate scandal, when regard for the institution of the presidency had reached its lowest ebb. The 1974 Act stripped the President of his authority to impound funds—that is, to refuse to spend excessive program funding appropriated by Congress. This was an executive branch budgetary power that had been routinely exercised by such popular chief executives as Thomas Jefferson, Franklin Roosevelt, and John Kennedy. In fact, Presidents Kennedy, Johnson, and Nixon reduced federal appropriations by between five and eight percent each year by making liberal use of the impoundment power. If Ronald Reagan had been empowered with this same budget cutting tool, and had used it to an equal extent as his recent predecessors, the budget deficit would have been about $50 billion lower each year. By repealing the President's impoundment authority, Congress endowed itself with virtually complete and unchecked control of the federal purse strings.

The 1974 Budget Act also failed to provide political incentive for lawmakers to "just say no" to spending. Because the cost of funding the federal government's 1,052 assistance programs is widely disbursed to all taxpayers, while the benefits are narrowly focused to specific program beneficiaries, the political payoff from preserving or expanding funding levels almost always exceeds the reward from reducing any program's budget. Consequently, Washington's pro-spending coalitions have built a political fortress around all existing spending programs—regardless of how obsolete or wasteful—shielding them from even minor cuts. Ronald Reagan repeatedly recommended about thirty program terminations in his budgets, yet all survived with the exception of general revenue sharing and a few other very small programs.

It is no historical accident that each year since the Budget Act took full effect federal spending has rapidly escalated. Between 1975 and 1988 the federal budget tripled in size. In the late 1970s this massive spending build-up was financed primarily through the highest federal taxes in U.S. history; in the 1980s the uninterrupted spending binge was financed through deficit spending. The average annual federal budget deficit between 1950 and 1975 equaled 0.8 percent of GNP. Since the Budget Act's passage, and despite record high revenues, the average annual budget deficit has been 3.8 percent of GNP—or almost five times higher.

Clearly Congress's ineffective budgetary procedures have profoundly influenced fiscal outcomes. When the next President presents his first budget, he should also send to Congress proposals for reforming the 1974 Budget Act. His plan should contain the following provisions:

1) *Balanced Budget Amendment to the Constitution*

The national debt has risen to over $2.5 trillion—two and a half times its level just ten years ago. Each year the federal government devotes over 14 percent of the federal budget—or almost $140 billion each year—to finance annual interest payments on the national debt. Yet, every attempt by Congress and the President to reduce deficit spending has failed. Budget summits have produced temporary spending slowdowns at best. The Gramm-Rudman-Hollings Deficit Reduction Law, although a step in the right direction, has been violated by Congress whenever convenient.

Lawmakers cannot disobey the United States Constitution, however. Only an enforceable balanced budget amendment—as is contained in virtually every state constitution—will permanently end deficit spending. The amendment should take effect in 1993—the date that Congress is scheduled to reach a balanced budget under Gramm-Rudman-Hollings. This amendment should forbid Congress from increasing the national debt ceiling unless three-fourths of the members of both chambers vote to do so.

To collect support for this initiative, the White House should draw upon the experiences in the states and cities with balanced budget requirements. Virtually every state and local government in the United States has some type of statutory balanced budget requirement and these have worked extremely well. A study by the federal Advisory Commission on Intergovernmental Relations on fiscal discipline in the states finds that those 44 states with balanced budget requirements "tend to have lower deficits or larger surpluses, and also tend to have lower levels of state government spending" than those six without such laws. Based upon these findings, ACIR concludes: "The experience of the states is relevant to the fiscal problems of the federal government. . . . The Commission thus urges Congress to consider proposing a balanced budget amendment to the United States Constitution so as to ensure a level of fiscal discipline comparable to that found in the states."

2) *Presidential Line-Item Veto*

One method of restoring the proper balance of power between the legislative and executive branches would be to provide the President with a line item veto. This would permit the President to veto specific items in a spending bill, while approving the remainder of the legislation.

The line-item veto is a particularly urgent reform now that Congress has adopted the routine convention of passing continuing resolutions which may contain funding for the entire budget in a single bill. The President's regular veto power is perceived as toothless against such end-of-the-year, catch-all spending bills, because a veto would close down the government. Presidents are unwilling to force such a budget showdown except under extreme circumstances. As a result the President is often forced to swallow billions of dollars of wasteful spending each year. A line-item veto is an appropriate and effective antidote.

Forty-three states have granted their governors line item veto authority. Several economic studies have found that the version that works best on the state level is the "item reduction veto"—as was used by Governors Ronald Reagan in California and Michael Dukakis in Massachusetts. This empowers the chief executive to veto any amount of a program's spending level, rather than taking all-or-nothing. The growth of spending in states with the item reduction veto has been found to be over 2 percent lower each year, on average, than in states without it.

3) *Strengthened Rescission Authority*

If the line item veto remains unacceptable to Congress, a compromise would be to enhance the President's rescission authority. The President was given the rescission authority as a weak substitute to the impoundment power. When the President issues a rescission request, Congress must vote to approve the spending reductions within 40 days. If legislators ignore the rescission, spending remains at the appropriated level. Between 1986 and 1988 President Reagan issued over 400 rescission requests with potential budget savings of $18 billion. Congress did not even vote on a single one.

The enhanced rescission power would place the burden on Congress to vote down a rescission. Unlike a line item veto, which requires a two-thirds vote in each house to be overridden, a simple majority vote in each house would block a rescission. This would not therefore constitute a dramatic shift in budget power toward the executive branch. If program funding cannot win support from a simple majority of members in each house, the spending is not justified.

4) *Abandonment of the Current Services Budget*

The current services budget is an estimate of how much the government would spend to adjust all programs for inflation, react to demographic changes, and meet commitments in previously enacted legislation. As a result, the current services budget automatically projects government spending will be considerably higher in the next fiscal year than it was in the previous fiscal year. Such information can serve a very useful accounting purpose. But the concept of current services has been largely distorted by members of Congress and special interest groups to increase spending levels.

The current services concept explains why it has been possible for the federal budget to grow by almost 60 percent during the Reagan years, and yet for Congress to hoodwink the public into believing that the federal budget has been the victim of savage cuts. For example, in response to President Reagan's FY 1988 budget request, a *Washington Post* story carried the chilling headline: "Administration Proposes Massive Cuts in Medicare." Yet the President's budget in reality called for a level of spending higher than the prior year. But under current services, a budget "cut" is any reduction from what Congress intends to spend, not what it spent last year. This is quite different from the way a household or business defines a budget cut and thus frames the budget debate in rhetoric that is extremely favorable to those who wish to raise spending.

The same principle also applies to the revenue side of the federal ledger. If tax rates are lowered, and revenues increase, but not as rapidly as they might have under the old tax code, this translates into a tax "cut." Hence, although federal revenues have grown by over 70 percent since Reagan became President, the budget has reported that tax revenues have declined. In short, the current services budget framework conceals rather than reveals information about the budget.

The current services budget concept should be replaced by a spending freeze baseline. The current year's spending and revenues would automatically become the baseline to measure the growth or reduction in the next year's spending levels and tax collections. A budget cut would then be defined as any reduction from the preceding year's spending level. Both Congress and the President should be required to present their budgets within this budget scorekeeping framework.

5) *Two-Year Budget Cycle*

In seven of the last eight years Congress proved itself incapable of completing its annual budget responsibilities in twelve months. This chronic budget tardiness has resulted in routine reliance on eleventh hour catch-all spending bills containing billions of dollars in wasteful spending. To prevent this irresponsible budget-packaging, Congress should switch to a biennial budgeting system. In the first year of each new Congress, the legislature would construct a budget authorizing and appropriating program spending levels for two years.

This budgeting approach—though by no means a panacea for Congress's fiscal failings—would have several advantages over the status quo. First, it would minimize opportunities for election-year budget politicking, a practice which inflates spending significantly, because budgets would always be crafted in nonelection years. Second, a two-year budget would place Congress under substantial political pressure to honor its deficit reduction promises. Under annual budgeting, lawmakers frequently pass budgets with ambitious spending cuts in future fiscal years ("out years") for which the budget does not apply. These budget cuts rarely materialize. For instance, twice in the past five years Congress pledged to sell the Naval Petroleum Reserves, yet the oil fields are still owned by Uncle Sam.

Finally, two-year budgeting would improve the management of federal agencies. Federal agency heads would be given greater lead time to absorb budget cuts, thus ensuring minimal service disruptions of the kind that have been recently experienced at the Coast Guard and the Postal Service. The Defense Department would benefit in particular, as two-year budgeting would improve its long-term planning capabilities and foster multiyear contracts for procurement items that are far more economical.

6) *Effective Penalties Against Continuing Resolutions*

Congressional reliance on continuing resolutions has been universally condemned as irresponsible and wasteful. Yet Congress passes these mammoth budget packages—rather than the 13 individual appropriations bills as it is supposed to do—because they render the President defenseless against the billions of dollars of parochial spending that these bills typically contain. Furthermore, there is nothing to discourage the practice except public disapproval, which tends to be short-lived.

A new budget act should statutorily forbid Congress from combining more than one appropriation bill into any single piece of legislation. Or other impediments could be established. If Congress does not give the President a general line-item veto, an automatic line-item veto should become effective anytime Congress sends the White House a continuing resolution. This would be an appropriate delegation of authority to the President, since these budget bills are otherwise virtually vetoproof because of their size. In addition, program funding levels in any C.R. should be limited by law to the previous year's outlays. This would be in keeping with the original intent of C.R.s, which was that spending would be "continued" at the previous year's amount until a regular appropriation bill was passed. Disallowing spending hikes for all programs contained in continuing resolutions would strongly deter their use.

7) *Comprehensive Credit Reform*

The federal government lends more money each year than any other financial institution in the world. Its $250 billion loan portfolio exceeds in value the combined loan assets held by the nation's two largest commercial banks. The federal government also currently guarantees $450 billion worth of outstanding loans issued by private lenders. The delinquency rate on federal loans is almost three times the rate on privately originated loans.

The current federal "cash flow" accounting system is ill-suited to measure the real budgetary cost of the government's massive lending program. When the federal government makes a direct loan—to a farmer, a student, or a veteran, for instance—the entire face value of the loan is treated as an asset. This unbusiness-like budgeting convention fails to measure or even acknowledge the subsidy to the borrower through low interest rates, generous payback provisions, etc. And, of course, many of the government's loans will never be paid back.

Treatment of federal guaranteed loans is even more misleading. Since no cash outlay occurs at the time of the guarantee, loan guarantees are treated in the budget as if they imposed no cost on the taxpayer. Yet each year defaulted guaranteed loans cost the federal Treasury approximately $8 billion.

This improper accounting treatment of loan programs has provided lawmakers with an incentive to divert federal resources into the credit portion of the budget, where the immediate costs can be hidden. In fiscal 1986, for instance, while Congress cut back spending slightly to comply with Gramm-Rudman-Hollings deficit targets, it issued a record $160 billion worth of loan guarantees. A *Washington Post* story noted: "What the right hand taketh in budget cuts, the left hand giveth in loans."

Any serious effort to recapture control of the budget will require more accurate accounting treatment of loan programs. The objective of credit reform is to capitalize the cost of direct loans and loan guarantees in the year they are issued—so that the timing of benefits and costs coincide. All direct loans should be sold through government auctions in the year the agency makes the loan. The difference between the face value of the loans and the cash received when they are sold would then represent their cost to the Treasury. Federal lending agencies should also be required immediately to purchase reinsurance for their loan guarantees. The expense of acquiring this reinsurance would constitute the taxpayer subsidy to the borrower.

The virtue of credit reform is that it requires federal lending agencies to obtain appropriations for the loans they make during the upcoming fiscal year. This would force Congress to recognize explicitly the taxpayer cost of all new loan commitments and remove the bias in the current budgetary process whereby agencies purportedly reduce the budget deficit by shifting government subsidies into the credit portion of the budget. Credit reform would place loan programs on an equal budget status with direct spending programs and give policymakers objective information to determine whether a loan or a direct subsidy is the more efficient form of subsidy.

8) *Prohibition Against "Off-Budget" Spending*

"Off-budget spending" is a budgeting ploy invented by Congress to disguise the fiscal impact of favored programs. In 1987 almost 20 percent of all federal spending was technically "off-budget." Worse yet, Congress wishes to shield several other major programs from the budget knife through this budgetary ruse. Many lawmakers wish to move the federal highway program, the Federal Aviation Administration, the Postal Service, and even Social Security—both the outlays and the revenues from the social insurance tax—off-budget so that these programs no longer affect the official calculation of the budget deficit.

This accounting tactic is budgeting with blindfolds. It creates distortions in measuring the impact of federal spending on the economy—since "off-budget" federal revenues and receipts have precisely the same economic impact as "on-budget" programs. "Off-budget spending" also directly impedes policymakers' efforts to prioritize spending. The "off-budget" distinction should be abolished. Until then, no new programs should be taken off-budget.

9) *Long-Term Budget Impact Statements for New Spending Programs*

In 1988 Congress proposed over one dozen new spending programs, including day care subsidies, welfare "reform," long-term health care, and antidrug programs. The first year cost of these programs was minimal so as not to breach Gramm-Rudman-Hollings deficit targets; yet the five-year cost was over $100 billion, and their ten-year cost was undetermined. This was an example of the time-worn congressional budget gimmick of hooking the taxpayer on the low downpayment of new spending, while camouflaging the massive balance due. The passage of such new spending programs severely disrupts any long-term budget balancing strategy and insures huge budget deficits in future years.

To counteract this budgeting tactic, the Congressional Budget Office should be required to perform one-, five- and ten-year budget impact estimates for all new spending. These estimates will give Congress and the public improved foresight to balance the long-term costs versus benefits of new spending commitments.

In addition, congressional points-of-order should be imposed against any new program that would increase deficit spending, not just in the first year of the program's life, but for five years. If CBO found a new program not to be deficit neutral, it should be prohibited from consideration on the House or Senate floor unless more than three-fifths of the members vote to override a point-of-order against it. This will prevent Congress from hastily enacting long-term budget busters without fully considering the fiscal implications of their actions.

10) *Redefinition of Entitlement Programs*

The media and the public have been led to believe, incorrectly, that the primary beneficiaries of entitlement programs are low-income needy families and that any cuts in entitlements would necessarily slash funding for basic safety net programs. This widespread misconception allows Congress to treat all entitlements as untouchable budget items.

By definition, an entitlement is any direct payment from the federal government to an individual. Entitlement funds go to individuals and families of all income levels. Fully 80 percent of entitlement funds are for "non-means tested" programs—i.e., the income of the recipient is not a condition of eligibility. Only 20 percent of these nonmeans tested entitlement dollars go to poor families or individuals.

Social Security, the largest entitlement program, is indicative of the general problem with entitlements. Social Security distributes over $200 billion to the elderly each year, yet only $15 billion of these payments, or less than 8 percent of the total, assists elderly with incomes below the poverty level. Furthermore, although the recipients of Social Security have made payments into the system during their working years, the typical retiree receives back his or her full contribution to the Social Security trust fund within about four years of retirement. All payments beyond the first four years of retirement are purely a generational transfer from the young to the old, funded by current workers' payroll taxes. For the past two decades, middle-class entitlement programs, like Social Security, have been exempted from budget restraint, largely because they are conveniently lumped together with those antipoverty programs that comprise the basic federal safety net.

Entitlement programs should be redefined in such a way as to assist federal policymakers and the public in distinguishing poverty abatement programs from middle- and upper-income entitlements. The simplest way to do this would be to create a category of federal spending called "welfare" which would consist of all programs that make payments to individuals where eligibility is based upon a needs assessment. This would include such programs as Aid for Families with Dependent Children (AFDC) and food stamps. All other programs which provide benefits directly to individuals, *but are not principally targeted to the poor*, would be classified as "entitlements." This simple reclassification would alter fundamentally the political dynamics that have made it so difficult to reduce the explosive growth of entitlement spending. Congress could adopt meaningful entitlement reforms while holding intact the basic set of safety net programs.

◇

STRENGTHENING THE GRAMM-RUDMAN-HOLLINGS DEFICIT REDUCTION ACT

The most significant triumph of the past ten years with respect to the budget was the passage in 1985 of the Gramm-Rudman-Hollings Deficit Reduction Act (GRH). GRH requires Congress to cut the budget deficit by approximately $36 billion in each of the next four years to achieve a balanced budget by FY 1993. The budget law is equipped with a blunt enforcement mechanism: if Congress fails to reach the GRH deficit ceiling, automatic across-the-board spending reductions, known as "sequestration," will be invoked to force the deficit down to the targeted level.

Although GRH has not worked as effectively as originally envisioned, it has made two significant contributions to the congressional budget-making process. First, by erecting inflexible deficit reduction ceilings, Congress is now held to an objective annual budget performance standard. The mere existence of these ceilings, along with the threat of sequestration, has forced Congress to be more cost-conscious. Lawmakers concede, for instance, that they would never have abolished general revenue sharing had it not been for the spending discipline imposed by GRH deficit ceilings. The overall annual growth rate of spending in the five years prior to Gramm-Rudman-Hollings was 8.7 percent, but has been trimmed to 3.3 percent since the new budget law's enactment.

Second, the budget law has established the important principle of "deficit neutrality" in federal budgeting. New spending measures can only be enacted if lawmakers raise federal revenues to pay for them, or cut spending of existing programs by an equal amount. This "pay-as-you-go" concept has forced Congress to make unpleasant budgetary trade-offs and thus is beginning to curb spending growth.

To insure that Congress remains on the GRH balanced budget path, the Administration must adopt the following strategy:

1) *Hold Congress to the GRH Annual Deficit Ceilings*

The President must declare to Congress his intention fully to enforce GRH over the next four years. The President's budget proposal must fully conform to GRH deficit reduction targets. The President should then declare in each of his annual budget messages that he intends fully to enforce the budget law by 1) vetoing spending bills that would violate the law's ceilings, 2) refusing to permit the ceilings to be revised, and 3) enforcing the budget law by allowing sequestration to be invoked if Congress neglects to set spending priorities responsibly. By convincing Congress of his willingness to allow across-the-board spending cuts, the President can gain a strategic bargaining position on budget matters. Lawmakers have demonstrated in the past that they desperately wish to avert a sequester, which would fall on many of their favored programs.

2) *Make All Programs Eligible for Across-the-Board Spending Cuts*

Congress has exempted almost 40 percent of the federal budget, including most entitlement programs, from the automatic spending cuts of GRH. Because of these sweeping exemptions, some lawmakers acknowledge that they have little to lose from a sequester, thus reducing the effectiveness of this enforcement mechanism. Furthermore, programs that remain unprotected receive sharp reductions in the case of a sequester inconsistent with their overall impact on the budget. Defense constitutes only 31 percent of the budget (excluding interest on the debt), but receives 50 percent of GRH cuts. The President should lobby for placing all programs—from the Navy to foodstamps—under the GRH knife, and for a formula whereby each program receives an equal percentage cut in its budget. With this formula, a GRH sequester would be genuinely "across-the-board" in impact and entirely conform to the spending priorities established by Congress.

--------------------◇--------------------

MARKETING THE PRESIDENT'S BUDGET

The President's annual budget plan, which is released each February, is the single most important document the executive branch produces. It is the principal device for formally conveying to the Congress and the American public the Administration's budget priorities. This budget document must be effectively marketed if it is to influence substantially the budgetary priorities of the legislative branch, which actually appropriates program funding. Effective marketing of the President's budget requires the following:

1) *Market the Budget As "The President's Budget"*

The Office of Management and Budget is charged with the responsibilities of preparing and overseeing the Administration's budget. Yet this document is the President's budget; it is not the OMB budget. The Reagan Administration's budgetary effectiveness was curtailed by the common perception that its yearly budget more closely reflected the priorities of OMB Director David Stockman and then later James Miller than those of Ronald Reagan. OMB was placed in the position of "whipping boy" for Congress and the press. White House detachment from its own budget impeded the Administration's ability to translate Reagan's electoral victories into a mandate on budget priorities.

To avoid these past problems, formal presentation of the budget should be made by the President—rather than the director of OMB. A major prime-time presidential press conference should be held for the budget's unveiling. Furthermore, responsibility for promoting the budget should be shared by the President's domestic policy staff and NSC staff—not foisted onto OMB alone to make it responsible for carrying "bad news." If it is truly the "President's Budget," the White House staff must shoulder responsibility for selling it to the public and Congress. The director of OMB should appoint a special assistant to work as a liaison between his office and the West Wing to ensure coordination of all executive branch budget marketing efforts.

2) *Maximize Agency Support for the President's Budget*

During the Reagan years, agency heads were often in open rebellion to the "OMB budget," or simply distanced themselves from it. Agency heads quickly recognized that funding denied in the President's budget could be recaptured during the congressional budget process. For instance, in 1985 the director of the Small Business Administration lobbied on Capitol Hill for retention of his agency only months after the President's budget had called for its abolition. When the President's budget can not even win the unanimous and enthusiastic support of his own hand-picked appointees, it stands little chance of serious consideration in Congress.

To assure unified support from Cabinet secretaries and other agency heads, the White House must assert direct control over the budget pass-back process. The White House should not act as a referee between the OMB and the executive branch agencies, as it typically has in the past. Rather, the original spending "targets" sent to the agencies should be cleared through the White House. In keeping with the movement away from a current services budgeting concept, the budget baseline should be last year's spending level, with agencies required to justify to the White House any increases over that amount. This will preempt the common complaint of Cabinet officials that OMB robbed their agency's budget.

Ultimately, the President must insist on the loyalty of his Cabinet to maximize the effectiveness of his budget blueprint. There are several specific steps the President can take directly to keep the executive branch in line with official Administration budget policy. An informal system of rewards and punishments should be established for agency heads. For instance, at the end of each budget cycle, the President might formally honor the three Cabinet officials most effective in cutting their budgets.

3) *Increase the Number of Political Appointees Within OMB*

Few agencies have a more direct executive branch policy formulation role than the Office of Management and Budget. Yet curiously, the agency is composed of only about 20 political appointees in an agency of 550 employees. OMB, therefore, is an agency staffed almost entirely with career staff members who have assumed a de facto role as principal spokesmen across the government for the Administration on budgetary priorities.

There is little question that OMB career staff have a high level of expertise, which it will be esential for the new Administration to draw upon. Moreover, the OMB staff's diligence in cutting government spending has generally exceeded the efforts of the average Reagan political appointee within the federal agencies. Nonetheless, the current low ratio of political appointees to career staff is problematic for two reasons. First, although OMB career employees are very dedicated to the agency mission of weeding out waste in government and controlling federal spending, it is inappropriate to expect them vigorously to promote the President's specific policy orientation and priorities. That is the primary function of political appointees. Second, many high level political appointees in other federal agencies are typically resentful of being relegated to the position of functional subordinates to OMB career staff who have no real political or ideological affiliation with the President. This resentment impedes uniform executive branch support for the President's budget.

To resolve these problems, the number of political appointees in OMB should be increased by at least 50 percent. This would enable OMB political staff more fully to monitor OMB operations and would enhance the new President's ability to rely on OMB as an extension of the White House's authority over the activities of executive branch agencies.

4) *Issue a "Freeze Budget" Rather than a Current Services Budget*

By releasing its budget within the current services framework, the Reagan Administration portrayed its priorities in the worst possible light. The proposed budget cutbacks for individual programs were reported in newspapers as being deep and painful. This raised public alarm needlessly, and allowed the spending coalitions in Congress to win the rhetorical war over the budget.

This public relations blunder can be avoided. The President is now required by law to issue a current services budget. But this does not prohibit the President from unilaterally releasing a freeze budget (as described earlier), which defines budget cuts and increases in language that the American people can understand. The President should issue a freeze budget as his main budget document in February, whether Congress formally scraps the current services concept or not. This will virtually force the media to report proposed program cuts and increases within the context of the previous year's budget. In order to satisfy the law that requires a current services budget, OMB should release a second document later in the budget cycle. Alternatively, the current services budget numbers could be contained in an appendix to the budget and come out simultaneously with the main document.

5) *Release the Major Themes of the Budget with the Main Budget Document*

The President's budget consists of several volumes. One of the most valuable of these is the Major Policy Initiatives—an invention of the Reagan Administration. This major themes document highlights the major budget priorities contained within the main budget volume and the justifications for substantial increases or cutbacks in program funding levels. Unfortunately this valuable report has limited impact on the budget debate if it is released weeks after the main budget, as was often the case under Reagan. By then the press and many in Congress had already fully passed judgment on the President's budget.

In politics timing is everything. The Major Policy Initiatives should be continued but it should be presented in conjunction with the main budget document.

6) *Revive the "Waste, Fraud, and Abuse" Budget Theme*

After eight years of Ronald Reagan, much of the public believes that all of the fat has been shaved from the budget. This misperception has slowed much of the political momentum for budget cuts. The President can build support for his proposed budgetary cutbacks by convincing the public and media that the bureaucracy still wastes billions of dollars of funds each year. Recent history demonstrates that "waste, fraud, and abuse" can be a strong selling point for slowing down government spending. When the media learned in the early 1980s that the Pentagon had purchased coffee pots for $7,000 and hammers for $400, the incidents captured national headlines, raised public outrage that the Pentagon was spending too much, and ignited a movement to reform DOD procurement policy.

To reignite the "waste, fraud, and abuse" issue, every six months the President should release a "Pork List" at a White House press conference containing dozens of specific examples of blatant incidents of federal agencies wasting taxpayer money. These examples should be similar to the Pentagon's $7,000 hammer. In addition, every week a "Golden Fleece" award for wasteful government spending should be awarded by OMB. This award—which was the brainchild of recently retired Wisconsin Senator William Proxmire—has been an extraordinarily effective public affairs device and should be carried on by the executive branch.

———————————————◇———————————————

A FOUR-YEAR DEFICIT REDUCTION STRATEGY

As was the case in the Reagan years, the focus of the budget debate over the next four years will center on the question of whether the budget should be balanced through tax increases or spending restraint. There are several compelling reasons why new taxes should be deemed a nonoption for fighting the deficit. First, taxes are already at record high levels and are scheduled to continue to rise to new heights.

Congress has already built into the tax code a hike in the Social Security payroll tax in 1990 that will cause federal revenues to climb by over $7 billion a year. Second, a large tax increase is a prescription for slower economic growth and less expansive job creation. Since the economy drives the budget (rather than the budget driving the economy), an economically unsettling tax hike may paradoxically make it more not less difficult to achieve a balanced budget.

Most importantly, the Gramm-Rudman-Hollings deficit reduction schedule insures that a tax increase will only increase spending levels and cannot reduce the deficit. The reason for this is that GRH acts as a de facto cap on spending. Spending is capped at a level equal to the sum of projected revenues plus the allowable GRH deficit ceiling. Hence, Congress can spend more without busting GRH only by raising revenues. This also means that every dollar in new taxes raised will automatically translate into one dollar of increased spending; the deficit would remain unaltered.

The spending ceilings imposed on Congress over the next four years are not excessively stringent. In 1993 federal revenues are projected to be $1.26 trillion—without changes in the tax code. If overall spending can be held to between 3 and 4 percent nominal growth, the deficit will be very close to zero in that year. (Passage of a recently proposed federal bail-out of the savings and loan industry, which could cost up to $80 billion, would require a more ambitious spending reduction formula, of course.) Therefore, the centerpiece of the President's four-year fiscal policy plan should be to restrain the overall growth rate of government spending, while ensuring that excessive growth in any particular program be offset by program reductions elsewhere in the budget. The President should adopt the following strategy to limit spending growth:

1) *Appoint a Commission on Entitlements*

A *New York Times* editorial recently summarized the budget deficit problem concisely: "No equitable fix will be possible until Americans of good will face the issue: everyone can't be entitled." Indeed, 40 percent of the federal budget—or $400 billion a year—is devoted to direct government payments to individuals. In constant dollars, entitlement growth has tripled since 1970. Therein lies the major source of the budget deficit.

Because of the political popularity of the major entitlement programs—including Social Security, Medicare, veterans benefits, and welfare—Congress and the President have been unwilling to address the issue in a responsible manner. Neither party is willing to take the political heat in calling for entitlement reform. In a rare moment of openness, one senator insisted recently that cutting entitlement benefits is regarded on Capitol Hill as "the political equivalent to touching the third rail."

Only a bipartisan commission on entitlements can break this political gridlock. Reagan Administration commissions such as the Social Security Commission, the Greenspan Commission, and the Kissinger Commission all effectively defused explosive political issues and became the springboard for legislative action. The President should appoint a commission for entitlements and request in its charter that it:

—Examine the purpose of entitlements.

—Specify how entitlement policy goals can be reached most efficiently.

—Define the proper entitlement responsibilities among the various levels of government.

—Determine the extent to which entitlement programs foster American values, including individual freedom, social responsibility, and the work ethic.

—Suggest program consolidations to reduce bureaucratic costs.

2) Establish A Follow-Up Grace Commission

The new President should immediately appoint a follow-up task force to the 1984 Grace Commission. That commission's report identified over 2,000 ways to "eliminate waste, inefficiency, and mismanagement in the federal government." Grace recommendations have already saved the taxpayer an estimated $39 billion per year, yet over 600 of its major reforms with potential savings of $70 billion have yet to be implemented. The follow-up commission should be assigned three principal tasks in its mandate: 1) identify recommendations of Grace I where no action has been taken and where potential budgetary savings are still achievable, 2) investigate why no action has been taken to implement these reforms, and 3) recommend strategies to overcome the political obstacles to reform. As with the original study, "Grace II" should consist of distinguished business leaders and should be entirely privately funded if possible. The chairman should be an individual with both the skill and courage to tackle the political constraints that have hindered the implementation of Grace cost cutting measures.

3) *Adopt an Aggressive Veto Strategy*

Powerful Presidents have tended to make heavy use of the veto power. Franklin Roosevelt, Harry Truman, and Dwight Eisenhower are recent Presidents who used the veto extensively to conform Congress's spending priorities with their own. The veto is also the President's best defense against excessive spending and tax increases.

The importance of an aggressive veto strategy is best illustrated by examining Ronald Reagan's sparing use of this budget tool. Reagan has vetoed 64 bills, or 8 per year—far below the historical norm for presidencies. His reluctance to veto large spending bills and force budget showdowns has impaired his effectiveness in controlling federal outlays. Perhaps more importantly, because Reagan signed almost all spending bills that crossed his desk, he formally endorsed an eight-year congressional agenda of domestic program expansion—an expansion that was directly contrary to his own initial budget priorities. The Reagan White House was therefore never capable of making a convincing case to the American public that Congress is principally responsible for the budget deficit.

To hold Congress to Gramm-Rudman and immediately to establish his proper leadership position over all federal fiscal policy matters, the President should veto any legislation that exceeds the spending levels contained in his budget request. He should announce far in advance his intention to veto such legislation, even if this requires a temporary closing of the government. Continuing resolutions should not be exempted from the presidential veto; rather they should be identified as primary targets. By declaring early in the legislative process his intention to veto, the President will be laying the essential political groundwork of coalition building necessary to insure that the vetoes are sustained.

4) *Use Every Vehicle for Budget Reform*

Despite the paramount importance of budget process reform, Congress is unlikely voluntarily to agree to new rules that would make spending more difficult. The President in concert with congressional allies must begin to investigate every piece of budget legislation as a potential vehicle for budget reform. Gramm-Rudman-Hollings, for instance, was passed as an amendment to the 1985 Debt Ceiling Extension. Budget reform measures should be attached to continuing resolutions, debt ceiling bills, and large authorization bills. Only by holding such vital legislation hostage will lawmakers consent to fundamental budget-making rule changes. For this strategy to be effective, the President must be willing to engage in high stakes showdowns with Congress that may lead to a temporary closing of the federal government.

In addition, the President should advertise the need for a line item veto by issuing a list of all the items he would veto out of every spending bill that is sent to him. This should include a tally of the total savings foregone simply because the President lacks this budget tool.

5) *Establish a Pay-As-You-Go Principle for All New Spending*

In 1988 Congress introduced over a dozen new spending items, ranging from federal day care legislation to Japanese-American Internment compensation, with a combined five-year price tag of over $100 billion. This pent-up congressional spending is perhaps the most serious threat to a realistic deficit reduction plan.

The President must immediately declare the introduction of a "pay-as-you-go" principle with regard to the federal budget. The White House should announce that all new spending programs must be deficit neutral, or they will be vetoed. This means that lawmakers will be forced to announce the off-setting spending cuts or the specific revenue sources to pay for new programs. The budget crisis will be brought to a close only when firm presidential leadership convinces Congress that the deficit finance option has been permanently ended.

6) *Explore Opportunities for Privatization of Federal Goods and Services.*

The nation's states and cities have relied heavily on privatization strategies to maintain balanced budgets without raising taxes substantially or impairing government services. In fact, local governments have increased the dollar amount of contracts with the private sector from $22 billion in 1972 to over $100 billion in 1987. The federal government, however, even under Ronald Reagan's presidency, has made very little progress in the area of privatization.

Several forms of privatization could relieve the federal budget deficit and should be aggressively pursued over the next four years. The federal government owns more assets than any other financial institution or business in the world. A recent study by the California-based Reason Foundation has identified over $300 billion worth of federal assets that could be put to more efficient use in the private sector, while increasing federal revenues. Similarly, the General Accounting Office and the Congressional Budget Office have identified potential savings of $4 billion to $6 billion a year if the federal government were to require competitive contracting for thousands of commercial services. Finally, the federal government should further promote the concept of "vouchers," which allow recipients of federal services to choose the service providers of their choice. In areas such as public housing, vouchers have proven to be popular with program recipients while costing about one-third less than new construction of public housing.

In late 1987 President Reagan created a new position within OMB—the Director of Privatization. This office should be retained and given broad authority within the budget process to promote privatization alternatives.

———————————◇———————————

CONCLUSION

After ten years of rising levels of federal red ink, the budget deficit is finally beginning slowly to recede. If the President can hold Congress to the Gramm-Rudman-Hollings track, the budget will be balanced by the next presidential election.

This will require a continuing healthy economy and a cap on federal spending growth. Living within even a modest cap on spending growth, however, depends on several White House actions. The prospending bias of the current budget process must be corrected immediately. The President must also assume his traditional leadership role in federal fiscal affairs. By improving the marketing of his budget he can insure that that document sets the parameters for the federal fiscal agenda. And by making liberal use of his veto power the President can enforce the spending priorities that his budget envisions.

6

A White House Strategy for Deregulation

by
Jeffrey A. Eisenach*

The Reagan Administration's battle against excessive government regulation proved to be even more difficult than expected. Certainly the early Reagan deregulators recognized that they faced tough substantive and political challenges, but they could not have imagined some of the obstacles that would be thrown into their path by Congress and the courts. And they certainly hoped for a more impressive showing than they got from some key regulatory appointees.

While there have been notable successes in deregulation, the overall costs of government regulation have not diminished substantially from the late 1970s. As in so many areas, the Administration must be content with a legacy of stopping or slowing government growth, rather than reducing the government's role.

There would appear to be little prospect for the next President to accomplish substantial overall reductions in government regulation. Nevertheless, continued incremental improvements in regulatory policy can be accomplished. More importantly, in the long run, steps can be taken to rebuild the public consensus for more sensible regulation and to focus attention on the increasingly counterproductive role of congressional and court intervention in the regulatory process.

Specifically, the next President must assert leadership in three areas of regulatory policy. First, he must indicate clearly his objectives for regulatory policy. The most important indicator will be in the form of regulatory appointments, which provide the most tangible indication

---

*The author wishes to thank Jim Tozzi, Dan Oliver, Jeffrey Trout, James Gattuso, and Howard Beales for their contributions to this chapter. The views and opinions expressed here are, however, entirely the responsibility of the author.

of the President's views. Also important, however, is a clear statement of regulatory priorities, which recent Administrations have chosen to issue in the form of presidential executive orders.

Second, he must indicate to Congress and the courts that he takes seriously the constitutional duties of the office of the President and is willing to incur costs, if necessary, to defend the integrity of his office. Recent incursions into the President's authority to study policy changes, appoint his own people within the Executive Office of the President (EOP), and exercise control over regulatory decisions, must be attacked before they become so deeply embedded in precedent and process as to be beyond challenge. In addition, it is time to challenge the independence of the so-called "independent regulatory agencies."

Third, the President should initiate a review of the total costs of government regulation and establish a ceiling on the overall (gross) burden imposed on the economy. The review should be designed to provide a baseline for measuring the overall impact of regulation on the economy, and thus begin the process of educating the public about the effects of government regulatory burdens. The ceiling, which might be permitted to increase over time, should take the form of a "regulatory budget"— i.e., an overall ceiling on the amount of new burdens imposed by each regulatory agency.

―――――――――――◇―――――――――――

THE REAGAN RECORD

President Reagan campaigned aggressively against government overregulation. As a long-time opponent of the excesses of government waste, he carried with him a long list of anecdotes about OSHA-designed toilet seats and polluting trees. If there was any doubt about the Republican Party's intentions, it should have been put to rest by the 1980 platform, which stated that "The Republican Party declares war on government overregulation."

The Administration indicated from the outset that it placed high priority on deregulation, so much so that "regulatory relief" was one of the four components of the President's February 1981 "Program for Economic Recovery." (The others were cutting taxes, reducing government spending, and stabilizing monetary policy.)

The early results of the Reagan effort were impressive. Within a matter of weeks, Reagan issued a moratorium on new regulations, decontrolled oil prices, eliminated the Council on Wage and Price Stability, and identified a set of existing regulations to be changed. On

February 17, 1981, just three and a half weeks into his term, the President issued Executive Order 12291. E.O. 12291 stated the Administration's regulatory principles, implemented a program of centralized review through the Office of Information and Regulatory Affairs (OIRA) at the Office of Management and Budget (OMB), and required regulatory agencies to perform benefit-cost analyses of new regulations. In April 1981, OMB announced a list of 34 specific deregulatory actions designed to help the U.S. auto industry.

However, these administrative steps were not matched by a clear strategy on either the personnel or the legislative fronts. Indeed, the Administration appeared to make a conscious decision to concentrate solely on actions that could be accomplished without changes in legislation. Thus, the Administration's early victories in cutting taxes and federal spending were not matched by legislative victories—or even initiatives—in the area of government regulation.

On the personnel front, key positions remained vacant for months. At the Environmental Protection Agency, for example, several unsuccessful candidates were "run up the flagpole" before the appointment was finally given to Anne Gorsuch (later, of course, Anne Gorsuch Burford) after a delay of more than six months.

Ms. Gorsuch's late arrival and unfamiliarity with the agency, combined with the White House decision to forego legislative initiatives, resulted in one of the greatest missed opportunities of the Administration: the chance to take the offensive on the Clean Air Act, one of the biggest regulatory statutes ever created, which was at that time up before Congress for reauthorization. Most observers believed there was a real chance for changes in the law in favor of benefit-cost analysis and incentive-based reforms, and expected the Administration to take the lead in pushing the legislative agenda. When no action was forthcoming, the consensus quickly dissipated. As a result, no action was taken during the past eight years.

In retrospect, it can also be argued that the Administration was mistaken in its emphasis on regulatory *relief* rather than regulatory *reform*. The former term implied a presumption in favor of "big business," thereby opening the Administration to charges of favoritism.

Long before the end of the first term, the Administration's opportunity to achieve long-lasting structural reforms had dissipated. By the end of 1982, embroiled in controversies at EPA and the Department of the Interior, the Administration found itself on the political defensive— a posture which, due to the nation's deteriorating economy, prevailed across the board.

Looking back on the Reagan Administration's accomplishments, it is clear that there were individual success stories. The Occupational Safety and Health Administration began selecting for enforcement those companies with the worst safety records. The Environmental Protection Agency made some progress in implementing the "bubble" concept. The Federal Trade Commission backed away from the use of "unfairness" as a criteria for pursuing counterproductive advertising regulation. Economic analysis became standard in antitrust law. These are meaningful accomplishments, not to be minimized or dismissed. When one looks at the overall impact of regulation on the economy, however, there is little evidence of a general decline in regulatory costs.

Measuring the impact of regulation is a difficult task, and some measures of regulatory activity have been justly criticized as focusing too much on the quantity of activity and not enough on content. For example, noting that regulatory agency spending has risen in real terms since 1980, or that the number of pages in the *Federal Register* has fallen (both true), provides relatively little information about the impact of regulation. However, some indices of regulatory activity do appear to provide some qualitative insight. In particular, OIRA now keeps track of the number of new regulations that impose new burdens, as distinguished from those that remove burdens. As shown in Table 6-1, in 1982 (the first year this statistic was compiled) the Reagan

Table 6-1   Selected Measures of Regulatory Activity

	1981	1982	1983	1984	1985	1986	1987
Rules Imposing New Requirements	N/A	294	248	260	358	366	451
Rules Eliminating Requirements	N/A	299	217	162	177	142	85
Major Regulations	38	51	39	25	38	47	30
Hours of Paperwork Burden	1.50	1.27	2.02*	1.98	1.89	1.74	1.88

Source: Office of Management and Budget.
*A change in accounting procedures precludes comparison with pre-1983 figures.

Administration issued five more regulations eliminating requirements than regulations imposing new requirements. By 1985, however, the number of new burdens was double the number of burden reductions, and in 1987 the Administration issued more than five times as many new regulatory requirements as it eliminated.

A second qualitative measure of regulatory activity is the number of new major regulations, defined by Executive Order 12291 as those with "an annual [burden] on the economy of $100 million or more." While this measure shows a decline in the number of new rules in 1987, the overall trend was virtually flat.

A third measure of regulatory burdens is the number of hours of federal paperwork requirements, compiled by OIRA pursuant to the Paperwork Reduction Act of 1980. While a change in accounting procedures precludes comparison of pre–1983 with later figures, the paperwork burden declined by roughly 7 percent between 1983 and 1987, despite a slight increase between 1986 and 1987.

In sum, the available measures of regulatory activity and burden clearly refute any claims that regulation has been severely cut back or reduced. Indeed, the overall trend in the second Reagan term has been toward a resumption of regulatory growth.

To a large extent, the Administration's failure to achieve more in the way of a general rollback in regulation can be attributed to roadblocks erected by Congress and the courts. For example, in 1983 Congress was successful in forcing the Administration to issue requirements for workplace labelling of hazardous chemicals. In 1987, a federal appellate court demanded that the standard be extended to all employers, rather than just to manufacturers. Now, in 1988, Congress is actively considering new legislation to require *ex-post* notification of all employees who might have worked in the vicinity of hazardous chemicals.

A number of court decisions worked against the Administration's efforts, including the 1981 "cotton dust" decision limiting use of benefit-cost analysis. Perhaps most egregious, however, was the D.C. Circuit's decision overruling the National Highway Traffic Safety Administration's decision to revoke airbag requirements for automobiles. While admitting that there was no evidence the rule could pass a benefit-cost test, the court found that the agency had not produced sufficient evidence to overturn its earlier finding that air bags should be required and, indeed, that a higher burden of proof was required to overturn a rule than to issue it in the first place.

At times, there seems to have been no limits on congressional and court interference in regulatory matters. Congress has even prohibited

the executive branch from *analyzing* some regulatory policy alternatives. Appropriations riders, for example, have prohibited both OMB
and the Federal Trade Commission from studying proposals to eliminate agricultural marketing orders.

―――――――――――――◇―――――――――――――

REGULATORY REFORM: THE NEED
FOR A CLEAR STATEMENT OF OBJECTIVES

Executive Order 12291 (February 17, 1981), which has formed the
basis for the Reagan Administration's regulatory efforts, is best
known for the regulatory review process it establishes through the
Office of Management and Budget. The review process requires,
among other things, that regulations be approved by OMB prior to
being published in the *Federal Register* and that "Regulatory Impact
Analyses" be performed on regulations with an annual economic
impact of $100 million or more. Supplemented by procedures for
review of paperwork and record keeping requirements under the Paperwork Reduction Act, and by the "Regulatory Planning Process"
procedures established by Executive Order 12498 (January 4, 1985),
the E.O. 12291 regulatory review process establishes a mechanism for
presidential control of agency rule-making.

Procedures, however, are of little value unless *substantive* objectives
are clearly understood. E.O. 12291, in addition to setting out procedural requirements, offers a set of substantive standards to be applied
in evaluating regulations, stating that "regulatory action shall not be
taken unless the potential benefits to society for the regulation outweigh the potential costs" (the "benefit-cost test"), that "regulatory
objectives shall be chosen to maximize the net benefits to society"
(the "social welfare test"), and that "among alternative approaches to
any given regulatory objective, the alternative involving the least cost
to society shall be chosen" (the "cost-effectiveness test").

These requirements seem innocuous enough, but liberals have been
quick to look for a hidden agenda. Their arguments have taken two
main forms. First, they have argued that the standards described above
cannot practically be met due to the unavailability of data. Thus,
requiring regulations to pass a benefit-cost test is equivalent to prohibiting regulation altogether. Second, liberals have suggested that the
substantive standards are simply empty words, designed as a shield for
a politically motivated effort to control regulation from the White
House.

The first criticism—that a benefit-cost analysis requirement would vastly reduce regulatory activity—seems to have been disproved by events: as discussed above, regulatory activity has hardly ground to a halt since imposition of the benefit-cost test in 1981.

As for the "politicization" argument, the Reagan Administration has responded by falling back on the "technical" and procedural aspects of its policy, arguing that the E.O. 12291 process simply formalizes the historical practice of effective White House control and, by doing so, actually makes it more difficult to exercise political influence. Indeed, they point out, the E.O. 12291 process has for the first time imposed strict rules for *ex parte* communications during White House review of regulations, thus insuring that regulatory decisions are made solely on the basis of information contained in the public record.

While narrowly correct, the Administration's defensive response to the politicization argument has taken it off the moral high ground and, arguably, actually made it more difficult to control regulatory agencies. Those familiar with benefit-cost analysis generally, and especially those with hands-on experience in analyzing government regulations, understand that evaluation of regulatory activity is invariably a subjective exercise. What value is society to place on preserving a rare species—the "snail darter" for example? For some individuals, the value is very high, for others nonexistent. Benefit-cost analysis can illuminate the choice by providing an estimate of the direct and indirect costs of the activity involved, but the final choice, whether to build the dam or save the snail darter, is subjective—and therefore inevitably a political choice.

In 1981, of course, with Ronald Reagan's antigovernment campaign rhetoric still fresh in mind, there could be little doubt that the objective of the regulatory review process was to reduce regulatory burdens. The choice, it was understood, should be to build the dam. In 1988, however, policy objectives became less clear, and E.O. 12291 offers very little explicit guidance for the exercise of subjective judgment. Indeed, the order only briefly mentions the goal of "reduc[ing] the burdens of existing and future regulations," and then only in the context of a long list of other goals such as "minimiz[ing] duplication."

This "technocratic" approach to regulatory issues has not contributed to a clear sense of policy priorities and direction among the public nor, importantly, among the 100,000 or so regulatory agency employees who write regulations. Today it is not possible, as it was in the early days of the Administration, for OMB regulatory reviewers to assert a clearly-defined "Reagan agenda" as justification for deregula-

tory positions taken in interagency disputes. Instead, the 75 employees
of the Office of Information and Regulatory Affairs—outnumbered
more than 1,000-to-one—must fight every battle mainly on "technical"
grounds.

To restore effective, centralized control over the regulatory process,
the President should work to establish a shared understanding among
his appointees of his goals for regulatory policy. Since regulatory
policy will not play a significant role in the campaign, it will be
necessary to establish that understanding after the election. Presidents
Ford, Carter, and Reagan have all used Executive Orders as a vehicle
for implementing regulatory policy. The next President should rely on
this well-understood method not only to implement policy but also to
state his regulatory goals and objectives.

In issuing a new executive order, the President should keep in mind
the natural bureaucratic and political tendencies that produced the
regulatory explosion of the 1970s and presently hinder the effectiveness of efforts to cut regulation in the 1980s. No recent President has
found a need to encourage regulatory agencies to be more active, or to
propose stricter regulations than they are inclined to do on their own.
Thus, at a minimum, the President should restate and endorse the
three "technical" principles embodied in E.O. 12291, and give increased emphasis to a discussion of the need to limit and eventually
reduce the burden of government regulation.

Congressional Regulation of the Private Sector

It is also important to keep in mind the pressure for increased
regulation created by the budget deficit, especially the incentive for
Congress to achieve political objectives by mandating the use of private
sector resources.

Congressionally mandated requirements are especially important in
the liberal agenda for social welfare policy. Health care benefits,
parental leave, more extensive pension options, higher minimum wages
and plant-closing notification are among the huge new regulatory
burdens that make up this agenda.

Because these new requirements are imposed directly by Congress,
they may appear to fall outside E.O. 12291's definition of "regulation"
as "an *agency* statement of general applicability and future effect
designed to implement, interpret or prescribe law or policy. . . ." At a
minimum, this ambiguity creates the potential for misplaced emphasis
on minor regulatory issues and/or inadequate attention to "congressional rulemaking." To avoid this problem, the President should state

clearly that he will apply the same analytical framework to all government-imposed burdens on the private sector, regardless of whether it is carried out by regulation or imposed directly by statute.

———————◇———————

REGULATORY APPOINTMENTS

In addition to issuing a clear statement of his regulatory objectives, the President should make his views clear through his appointments to the regulatory agencies. The Reagan experience has shown clearly how important appointments are to implementing the President's objectives.

The Federal Trade Commission is a good case in point: Under deregulator James C. Miller III, the commission made significant progress towards loosening its grip on commercial speech and reversing its counterproductive merger policy. Recent appointments, however, have created a proregulatory majority at the commission, forcing Chairman Dan Oliver—also a committed deregulator—to vote in the minority in unsuccessful efforts to prevent reregulation.

One appointment, the administrator of the Office of Information and Regulatory Affairs at OMB, will say more about the next President's regulatory philosophy than anything else. Under recently passed legislation, this position is now subject to confirmation by the Senate, and the new administrator's confirmation hearings will be taken as a significant indicator of the President's views. Early appointment of a well-known advocate of the free market is therefore crucial.

———————◇———————

RETAKING CONTROL FROM CONGRESS

Increasing congressional encroachment on presidential authority is a phenomenon that affects virtually every area of federal policy, from foreign policy to the budget process. Nowhere, however, has Congress been more effective or insidious in usurping executive branch authority than it has with respect to regulatory policy.

Some forms of legislative control over regulatory policy are entirely appropriate under the Constitution. Whether or not one agrees with particular policy outcomes, for example, it clearly is within the authority of Congress to pass regulatory statutes that impose costs on the private sector. Furthermore, there is no presumption against specific requirements that limit executive discretion in carrying out statutes. These matters of statutory content are part of the intended interplay between the congressional and executive branches of government, and the President is well armed—with the veto among other tools—to play his part in that interplay.

However, in recent years, Congress has found a number of ways *in addition to passing laws* to impose its will on the regulatory process. These tools, including appropriations riders, abuse of investigatory authority, delegation of rulemaking authority directly to agency heads rather than the President, increased reliance on "independent" regulatory bodies, and requirements for Senate confirmation of key regulatory staff, all have the effect of limiting the President's ability to control regulation and to carry out his constitutional duty to "faithfully execute the laws."

A second effect of these developments is to strengthen the ability of individual congressmen, congressional committees, and congressional staff to influence regulatory policy outside the legislative process. From a "public choice" point of view, of course, Congress desires such changes because they permit congressmen to provide constituent favors (in the form of intervention in the regulatory process) without incurring the responsibility attendant to voting on legislation. From a regulatory policy perspective, these developments transform regulation into a tool for directly rewarding special interests, and make it practically impossible for the kinds of rational policy standards laid out in E.O. 12291 to be implemented.

On a broader level, continued presidential acquiescence to congressional and court usurpations of executive power pose a grave threat to our constitutional system of government. In an era in which congressional staff outnumber executive policy-making staff in a number of key policy areas—including regulatory policy and the budget—the prospect for "government by men" as opposed to "government by laws" is frighteningly real.

Retaking control from Congress will require a multifaceted strategy of administrative, legislative, and court actions. Some of the steps that should be taken include:

1) Make presidential control over executive branch regulators explicit in a revised Executive Order. E.O. 12291 currently skirts the issue of presidential control over agency regulatory decisions. While it gives the OMB director authority to review regulations essentially *ad infinitum*, it does not specifically assert presidential regulatory authority. Thus, it preserves and recognizes the principle that Congress may delegate regulatory authority to agency heads, bypassing the President.

In reissuing E.O. 12291, the President should squarely assert his authority—and the authority of his immediate staff when acting on his behalf—to exercise ultimate control, within the scope permitted by the authorizing statutes, over the content of all government regulations. Naturally, this change will provoke litigation, and should only be undertaken in conjunction with the development of a strategy to maximize the likelihood of a favorable outcome.

2) Extend presidential control to the "independent" regulatory agencies. The Supreme Court's recent decision in *Morrison v. Olson*, upholding the constitutionality of the independent counsel statute, appears to give support to the concept of "independent" regulatory agencies. Specifically, *Morrison* appears to support the Court's 1935 decision in *Humphrey's Executor*, which permits Congress, in some circumstances, to limit the President's authority to remove officials from office.

While *Morrison* appears to comment favorably on *Humphrey's Executor*, it also arguably leaves room for distinguishing between the regulatory agency statutes and the independent counsel statute the court upheld. Because of the importance of this issue to the President's ability to "faithfully execute the laws," the President should seek a set of favorable conditions to test *Humphrey's Executor* by dismissing a commissioner of an independent agency purely on policy grounds.

In addition, the President should assert his authority with respect to independent agency decisions in precisely the same manner as with executive branch agencies, bringing their regulatory decisions directly under the provisions of a revised and strengthened E.O. 12291.

Again, these actions will certainly provoke court challenges. However, by seeking out challenges, the President should be able to choose the battleground most favorable to his cause.

3) Eliminate the "independent" agencies. As an alternative, or in addition to the steps taken above, the President might pursue a strategy of eliminating the independent agencies. This could be accomplished through consolidation, by bringing the Federal Trade Commission into the Justice Department, the Securities and Exchange Commission into the Treasury Department, and so forth. Alternatively, the agencies could be eliminated simply by failing to appoint new members and allowing the terms of existing members to run out. (Indeed, this situation is very near to occurring presently at the Federal Energy

Regulatory Commission, where an impasse between the White House and some members of Congress has prevented the confirmation of new members and threatened to leave the agency without a quorum.)

4) Develop a comprehensive litigation strategy for reasserting presidential control. A high-level litigation task force, consisting of the general counsel of OMB, the assistant attorney general for legal counsel (or the Solicitor General), the general counsels of the key regulatory agencies, and chaired by the administrator of OIRA should be formed to manage regulatory litigation throughout the next Administration. The task force should concentrate on devising and executing a comprehensive strategy for a) defending the President's assertion of control over regulatory decisions, b) challenging precedents that prevent rational decision-making or weaken presidential authority, and c) assuring that all significant filings by or on behalf of regulatory agencies are consistent in asserting the President's authority and defending his objectives.

5) Streamline the regulatory review process. The "regulatory planning process" embodied in E.O. 12498, combined with the various other processes run through OIRA, appears to be a case of procedural overkill. OIRA staff spend so much time "running the process" that they have difficulty concentrating on key policy issues. Even at the policy level, process sometimes dominates substance, with too much focus on the number of rules reviewed, the average review time, etc.

One side-effect of this overemphasis on process is to exacerbate the natural tendency for agencies to see OMB as an adversary, in much the same way as business sees government regulators as adversaries. To the agencies, OMB seems out of touch and inflexible, wedded to a set of rules that must be followed whether or not they make sense in a particular case. Rather than an ally in the executive branch battle against congressional micromanagement, agencies may actually see OMB as just another enemy to be overcome. Indeed, Congress may sometimes seem the more attractive ally in a battle where the real enemy is OMB.

While the dynamics of this relationship can never be completely suppressed, the issuance of a new executive order provides an opportunity to review the current process and make adjustments. Buttressed by the President's clear assertion of ultimate rule-making authority, it should be possible to replace the current emphasis on process with greater emphasis on policy. Resources now devoted to relatively minor paperwork or regulatory reviews should be redirected to more intensive involvement in significant policy issues. OIRA staff should organize task forces on key issues, make White House resources (e.g., presidential statements and other press support, congressional relations assistance) available to agencies, and encourage agency heads and key agency staff to see OMB as an ally in their fight against congressional meddling. (See also the discussion of development of a regulatory budget, below.)

6) Undertake a high-profile review of agricultural marketing orders within OMB. As indicated above, congressional appropriations riders currently prohibit OMB from even studying agricultural marketing orders, a type of restriction which potentially could further eviscerate the President's ability to manage the executive branch. While the Reagan Administration's authority to challenge these provisions is hindered by the fact that President Reagan signed the bills containing the riders, the next President will not be so disadvantaged. He should directly challenge this dangerous precedent by ordering OMB to violate the appropriations rider and study agricultural marketing orders. In formulating his request, the President would do well to refer directly to his constitutional authority to "require the opinion, in writing," of his Cabinet officers.

IMPLEMENTING A REGULATORY BUDGET

One key reform not pursued aggressively by the Reagan Administration is the regulatory budget. While there are good reasons for the Administration's decision, including the technical difficulties of implementing a regulatory budget, this reform could do more than any other to limit excessive regulatory growth.

The regulatory budget concept is a simple one. Each year, agencies would be given a single figure, in dollars, representing the net addition in annual regulatory costs they could impose on the private sector during the coming year. Once an agency used up its quota, it would have to balance new regulatory burdens with deregulatory actions of equal effect or, if not, to wait until it received new "budget authority" next year.

In operation, of course, a regulatory budget would be very complex, involving most of the difficulties attendant to the current fiscal budget process and many others unique to regulatory policy. On the other hand, most observers would agree that for all its problems, the fiscal

budget process imposes irreplacable discipline on federal spending and
is well worth the effort. Similarly, the inability to develop a perfect
regulatory budget process should not stop us from attempting to
develop some such process.

Ideally, development of a regulatory budget would follow the model
of the existing Paperwork Budget. It would begin with a baseline
estimate of the total costs of all regulation, which would serve as the
basis for agency budgets. Each year, agencies would be allocated an
amount of increased gross regulatory costs to be imposed on the
economy during the coming year, with the total (government-wide)
cost permitted to grow at some acceptable level (e.g., 1 percent below
the rate of growth of real GNP).

While development of a baseline is not necessary (budgets could
be allocated purely in terms of incremental costs, with current
costs taken as given), it would have the very desirable effect of
providing an estimate of the overall impact of government on the
economy. Such an estimate would give the public a means of gauging
the cumulative impact of individual regulatory actions—each of which
may appear desirable in isolation—on individual freedom. Thus, a
regulatory budget could help raise public concern and restore the
public consensus against overregulation.

A regulatory budget would also be desirable in identifying the
sources of regulatory growth. Because it would include estimates of
both administrative and statutorily imposed regulatory costs, it would
provide a monitor of congressional regulatory activity, thereby increasing government accountability.

While the expertise to develop a regulatory budget exists, the
resources (staff, etc.) do not. One key to freeing up the requisite
resources is to reduce the number of process-oriented "exercises" run
every year by the OIRA staff. Currently, OIRA is responsible for
producing one "Regulatory Program," two "Regulatory Agendas,"
and one "Paperwork Budget" every year. By combining all of these
exercises into a single "regulatory budget," it should be possible to
achieve significant efficiencies. (To do so, however, might require a
legislative change, since the "Regulatory Agenda" is required by
statute to be published twice each year.)

A second way to secure the needed resources to develop a regulatory
budget is to involve all of the major regulatory agencies in the development process. Because this project is clearly relevant to the missions
of the individual agencies, and because the development process is by
nature temporary, it would be appropriate to detail the necessary

resources from the agencies to some regulatory budget task group. Indeed, the "Regulatory Council" created by President Carter would be an appropriate organizational model for such a task force.

◇

CONCLUSION

Regulatory policy will present difficult challenges for the next President. Interest groups continue to clamor for an increasing government role; regulatory agencies remain biased in favor of activist policies; and recent congressional and court actions have weakened presidential authority over the agencies. Public sensitivity to excessive government is perhaps at the lowest level in more than a decade.

However, regulatory policy also presents opportunities. By clearly stating his priorities and exerting his authority, the President can win back control of the regulatory process from Congress and the courts. By moving to develop a regulatory budget, he can begin the process of reminding the public of the aggregate costs of regulation and, for the first time, impose an overall limit on the growth of regulatory control of the economy.

☎

7

The People Factor: Managing Presidential Personnel

by
Louis J. Cordia*

" "People are policy" is the maxim that should guide the President's management of the White House and the departments and agencies throughout the Administration. The success (or failure) of an Administration lies with the people who implement the President's program.

From the Kennedy Administration to the Reagan Administration, the proper management of presidential personnel increasingly has been deemed crucial to the successful implementation of the President's programs. Various means to this end have been tried, with varying degrees of success. There is a remarkable degree of unanimity across partisan and ideological lines regarding the fundamental requirements and procedures for assuring presidential control of the political appointments process.

Ted Sorensen, a top aide in the Kennedy White House, believes that personnel is "clearly the highest priority. You can't spend too much time on personnel . . . the key is getting the right people in office. That will overcome many errors in organization and getting to know the Congress."[1] President Richard Nixon stated of his Administration, "I

---

*I am indebted to more than 100 members of the following Administration groups who meet monthly to discuss, among other issues, personnel management in the executive branch: 1) Administration Personnel Placement Group, 2) Administration Congressional Relations Group, 3) Administration Public Relations Group, and 4) Lawyers in Government Group, as well as a special personnel advisory group which provided guiding principles to this chapter. I am also indebted to my staff and summer interns for their research.

regretted that during the first term we had done a very poor job in the most basic business of every new Administration of either party: we had failed to fit all key posts in the departments and agencies with people who were loyal to the President and his programs. Without this kind of leadership in appointive positions, there is no way for the President to make any impact on the bureaucracy."² President Jimmy Carter commented: "I have learned in my first two and a half weeks why Abraham Lincoln and some of the older Presidents almost went home when they first got to the White House. The handling of personnel appointments, trying to get the right person in the right position at the right time, is a very difficult question."³ "The appointments process is absolutely vital to the success of any Administration because government is nothing more than people," stated Stuart Eizenstat, former domestic policy advisor to President Carter. "A good Administration means the right people in the right places, a bad Administration the wrong people in the wrong places, or the right people in the wrong places."⁴ Robert Tuttle, Director of Presidential Personnel in the final years of Reagan's term, put it succinctly: "After all, personnel is policy."⁵

Establishing the framework for personnel operations immediately after election day is vitally important. For the key post of top personnel adviser, the President-elect should select one of his closest of confidants, a person in whom he has complete confidence and who will have direct access to him through the chief of staff. Then he should clearly articulate policy goals and establish a guiding timetable to achieve these objectives. Without clear goals and criteria, old-fashioned patronage drives personnel selections. In turn, the Administration becomes constituency-based and special interest-driven, with appointees representing others and not the President. That is a sure recipe for failure.

With confidants in place and policy goals identified, a talent bank and selection criteria must be established. Thousands of resumes will flood into the White House. The challenge to the President's personnel team is to find the right combination of politically committed and technically competent people who are willing to serve in the Administration.

The President needs to focus personally on both policy and personnel decisions—and especially the relationship between the two, which is always acknowledged in principle but often unappreciated in practice.

This chapter will provide an overview of presidential staffing patterns from the Kennedy Administration to the Reagan Administration, and will conclude with recommendations for managing presidential personnel.

———————————————◇———————————————

LESSONS FROM RECENT HISTORY

In order better to understand the management of the White House Personnel Office, a 30-year review of the last six Administrations should provide insight and lessons from which future Administrations can benefit. Starting with the Kennedy Administration, certain personnel practices were tried and abandoned, and others were later developed into sophisticated management tools in the Reagan Administration. No personnel system is perfect, but each could learn from the other, and employ those parts which suit the personal interests of the President.

Kennedy Administration

John F. Kennedy distanced himself from personnel selections during his transition and presidency. When objections about the politics of a possible Cabinet appointee were voiced to President-elect Kennedy, he retorted, "Oh, I don't care about those things. All I want to know is: is he able? And will he go along with the program?"[6] Kennedy, like FDR, was uninterested in organizational charts or procedural methods. His interest in personnel appointments was selective and sporadic.

In mid-1961, the first year of the Kennedy Administration, Dan Fenn, a member of the Harvard Business School faculty, was brought in to run the personnel office. "There was nothing there, we had an empty blackboard," Fenn recalled. "At the time, people were only vaguely aware there was a personnel office. I don't think we called it anything. There were only three people in the office, including myself . . . I decided we would not get into Schedule C or presidential commission positions—only presidential appointments. Second, we would not set up a real recruiting program until later. We got together with the Brookings Institution and ran three private seminars around the country, in Chicago, Houston, and San Francisco, talking to scholars and former presidential appointees."[7]

The Kennedy Administration's personnel problems were due to lack of interest on the President's part, resulting in the systematic circumvention of his personnel chief. But the Kennedy Administration pioneered a handy management tool for future personnel operations: tapping like-minded outside groups to help recruit talent to serve in the Administration.

Johnson Administration

While circumvention was a major problem for the Kennedy Personnel Office, it played little part in the Johnson Administration. LBJ was personally involved in personnel selection. If fact, few Presidents kept more control over the process or had their fingers on as many parts of the government as LBJ.

Johnson was the first to develop a computer tracking system, called "Weeder." Weeder stored basic information on potential candidates for Administration positions and permitted the personnel staff to match names with vacancies. The computer was also programmed to supply a list of presidential positions and the incumbents, along with such data as the expiration dates of their appointed terms. It was an ingenious idea, but far ahead of its time. The newness of Weeder and its quality control led to major problems. Despite the problems, Weeder helped identify people quickly, enabling far more personal interviews than were held in the Kennedy Administration.

Johnson also relied on a team of close confidants, whom he often consulted on major appointments. They included outside advisers such as Clark Clifford (who subsequently became his Secretary of Defense), attorney Abe Fortas, CBS President Frank Stanton, and business executive Donald Cook, as well as some of his senior staff, including Joe Califano, Horace Busby, Bill Moyers, Harry MacPherson, and Jack Valenti.[8]

Nixon Administration

Not learning from LBJ's improvement over the JFK personnel operation, President Nixon distanced himself from personnel concerns, preferring to delegate the responsibility to staff members. From the beginning of Nixon's first term, the appointments function was disorganized and fragmented among several White House aides. In fact, even before he took office, Nixon had personnel problems. During the transition, his personnel chief Harry Flemming was responsible for an embarrassing gaffe when he sent letters to every name listed in *Who's Who in America*, requesting recommendations of possible appointees.

Fred Malek was hired by President Nixon to take better control of presidential appointments. Malek was able to review and clear all major political appointments, including staff assistants to top appointees. He also worked closely with Cabinet members to identify candidates for high posts. Previously, the appointment of sub-Cabinet officials had been left to the total discretion of the secretaries. That prerogative was subsequently retrieved. By the end of President Nixon's first term, the strong Cabinet model had been abandoned. "They will know who hired them," maintained a White House aide. "In effect, they will carry commissions from the President, not the secretary. Regardless of who announces it, they'll see something hanging on their walls with Richard M. Nixon on it. There will be no more assistant secretaries saying, 'I don't work for Nixon; I work for the secretary.' If he's hired, he will know why and by whom. There will be less disloyalty and more direction and guidance."[9]

Nixon took too long, a full term, to learn how to manage personnel in his Administration effectively. He did employ LBJ's tool of close confidants who reviewed personnel recommendations for their policy consistency.

Ford Administration

Following a brief transition, Ford moved cautiously, declining to purge the Nixon holdovers he had inherited. He was urged to make changes in the White House and in the Cabinet, but was reluctant. He did not want people to think all Nixon's appointees were bad for government. He was trying to preserve some degree of stability and integrity in the office of the President. "Coming off Watergate, we were very cautious," White House Chief of Staff Dick Cheney commented. "The last thing we wanted to do was to send some 'turkey' up on the Hill for confirmation."[10]

Ford's director of personnel, William Walker, had access to the President, but was not much involved in the high-level appointments. He was chiefly confined to sub-Cabinet and commission appointments. In a symbolic step, Walker restructured the staff, shifting it from the professional recruiters employed by Malek to knowledgeable Washington generalists. "We wanted to get away from simple headhunters and go with a staff that knew Washington and how it worked and were politically sensitive," Walker explained.[11] Furthermore, Walker felt that the best recruiters were not professional recruiters, but those who knew the job qualifications through experience—those who had been in government.

Top selections were made in meetings with the President, who usually knew which people he wanted in which positions. This helped to avoid circumvention of the personnel process.

The Ford Administration underscored one important facet of presidential personnel—the need for experienced people. However, it failed to focus on executive branch experience and the importance of coupling it with political commitment to the President.

Carter Administration

Jimmy Carter was the first presidential candidate to invest a significant amount of money and staff in preparation for a possible transition to the presidency. The personnel portion of the operation was known as the Talent Inventory Process (TIP). In charge of TIP was Jack Watson, who assembled names and collected resumes for possible positions in the Carter Administration.

Once Carter won the election, Watson moved TIP to Washington and promptly became locked in a power struggle over dominance in the appointments area with Hamilton Jordan, the President-elect's campaign director and principal aide. "We had two groups; the problem was how to merge them," Watson explained.[12]

Like JFK and Nixon in his first term, Carter chose to stay away from the appointments process. His first personnel director, James King, lacked the resources, expertise, and authority to deal with the overflow of resumes and requests. Contributing to the disarray was Carter's insistence on giving the Cabinet secretaries a blank check in choosing their subordinates and managing their departments without interference from the White House. He often stated, "There will never be an instance while I am President where the members of the White House staff dominate or act in a superior position to the members of our Cabinet."

It soon became clear to the President's top lieutenants—and only later to Carter himself—that he had made a major mistake in giving the agency heads carte blanche authority to hand-pick their assistants. "One of the failings of the Carter Administration was not being more involved in the appointments process and letting it be taken over by the Cabinet," maintained Stuart Eizenstat. "As a result, we ended up with people who did not share the President's views on certain policy issues and regulatory reform."[13]

It was not until September 1978—18 months into the President's term—that Arnie Miller was hired to reorganize the personnel office and to help the Carter forces gain a grip on the appointments process. "I had to restructure the operation and build an internal capacity,"

Miller said. "I brought people from OMB and others from around town who had a feel of government from the inside, like Harley Frankel, my deputy who came from HEW. Before, those in the office came from the campaign with little government experience . . . Little by little we moved out people."[14] Despite these improvements, Miller's personnel operation never really gained control. Carter never got personally involved. Miller was subsequently left without the force of the President behind him. The office's credibility was further jeopardized when other White House offices made it a practice to call departments and agencies with their own recommendations.

Carter's disinterest in appointments and the fragmented personnel operation resulted in the worst management of presidential personnel in the last 30 years.

Reagan Administration

Ronald Reagan was the second presidential candidate to begin before his nomination to plan in a significant way for a possible takeover of the government by his party. A full year before the election, in November 1979, Edwin Meese asked Pendleton James, then a West Coast "headhunter," to put together a plan for a personnel operation in preparation for a possible Reagan presidency. In April 1980 he was asked to implement the plan, and in late summer he set up operations in a Washington suburb. The personnel operation was clearly subordinate to Meese, who was in charge of the transition from beginning to end and who also played a major role in the campaign.

Calvin MacKenzie has characterized the Reagan personnel operation as tighter than any other. The Reagan Administration "undertook transition personnel selection with more forethought, with a larger commitment of resources, and with more systematic attention to detail than any Administration in the post-war period, perhaps more than any Administration ever."[15]

Targeted appointive positions were first identified which matched Reagan's policy objectives. These were the positions deemed most important in caring out the President's goals. An in-depth analysis was conducted looking into functions, scope and the kind of background that the candidates needed for these positions: the top 100, and then the next 100. The project was divided into functional areas: law, finance, transportation, labor, health, engineering, science, agriculture, and international affairs, among others.

Despite advance planning, the Cabinet was named weeks later than in previous transition periods, the last Cabinet member, Terrel Bell, being named on January 7, a full two months after election day. This delay was due in part to the tremendous amount of time and paperwork it took to comply with newly enacted government ethics laws regarding financial disclosures and conflicts of interest (passed in 1978). The Reagan Administration was the first subjected to these stringent new requirements. All the gray areas had to be identified and the lawyers had to determine how requirements were to be met.

Access to the President by the head of personnel was all important. On a daily basis, Pen James met with Meese, Baker and Deaver to review each candidate after he had passed all the prior checkpoints. Twice a week, James met with the President to present recommendations. The last step in the process was to have the head of White House congressional liaison run the names of prospective nominees by senators on the respective committee overseeing the nomination. This step was taken out of courtesy, and to ensure there would be no surprises.

President Reagan adopted the five criteria for personnel selection recommended by Meese and Pen James: 1) commitment to Reagan's policy objectives, 2) integrity, 3) technical competence, 4) teamwork, and 5) toughness. Holding decisions to these criteria was always difficult. Those who worked in Reagan's personnel office found themselves fighting four forces: 1) personal relationships and recommendations from influential figures close to the President and top White House staff; 2) the Republican Members of Congress and their fondness for trading votes for patronage, 3) the unwillingness of some individuals to serve, and 4) the inherent unpredictability of personnel selection.

Reagan's personnel team underestimated the entrenched power of the status quo in Washington. They discovered that gaining control in Washington is as difficult a battle as winning the election. To battle these forces, Reagan gave his personnel chief unprecedented authority over political appointments at all levels. It was a highly centralized process where recruitment and selection was initiated and controlled from the White House. The Presidential Personnel Office (PPO) had to approve appointees to all political positions at all levels, right down to private secretaries. After initial agreement was reached between PPO and the agency head, the candidate still had to pass a rigorous political clearance that could yield surprises: on occasion, a name that had originated in a list sent to an agency head by PPO was later rejected by the PPO clearance office after a more rigorous background check.

One way that loyalty to the White House was assured was by laying out the ground rules for appointments to Cabinet members very early and with no uncertainty. Pendleton James described the ground rules thus: "When we appointed the Cabinet . . . I sat down with the Cabinet officer along with Ed Meese and Jim Baker and informed him of the role of the presidential personnel operation . . . if you had somebody that you wanted in an office, it would have to go through the White House presidential personnel office because everything in the appointment process went into the Oval Office through the presidential personnel office. We clearly established control at the beginning."[16] While the President encouraged departmental secretaries to develop lists of names to consider, the ultimate approval was that of the President—and the President required all names to be submitted through PPO. This was the most centralized and disciplined system for selection of sub-Cabinet appointees ever established. Amazingly, it worked most of the time.

In several respects, James broadened the horizons of the presidential personnel office. His long relationship with the "California crowd" and his access to Reagan and the President's inner circle guaranteed that his voice would be heard. He was accorded senior staff status and assigned an office in the West Wing of the White House, a visible and highly coveted symbol of the importance attached to the appointments process. Previously, the personnel office was given second-class lodging in the Old Executive Office building. During the Administration's critical start-up period, he had an estimated 100 people on his staff, including volunteers.

As he had planned, James resigned after eighteen months in the White House to return to his private business. He was succeeded by Helene von Damm, a long-time personal assistant to Reagan. She, in turn, was followed by John S. Herrington, another long-time friend from California.

Bob Tuttle, a California native and son of Reagan Kitchen Cabinet member Holmes Tuttle, served the longest tenure in the position, from Herrington's departure in 1985 to the end of Reagan's term. Tuttle worked closely with Cabinet secretaries in making departmental appointments but became aware that over time agency heads acquired broader leeway in selecting their subordinates. Secretary of State George P. Shultz insisted on hand-picking appointees and withstood objections—and threats of retaliation—by conservative Republican senators who claimed that their ideological brethren were being overlooked.

Tuttle instituted several operational changes. He placed considerable emphasis on "referencing"—checking with people whom the candidate had worked for and with, other than those listed on the job resume. It also became standard procedure during personal interviews to ask each candidate if he or she had ever written or said anything potentially embarrassing to the President. Tuttle made a specific point of seeking to place young, conservative Republicans in appointive slots throughout the federal bureaucracy and then promote them to higher positions before the end of the Administration. His plan was to give them government experience and allow them to work in higher, more influential positions in future Republican Administrations.

As is always the case, more could have been done, and there were instances when the system broke down or was short-circuited by powerful figures. But for all its shortcomings, the Reagan Administration was the best in 30 years at managing presidential personnel. There's no reason each successive Administration shouldn't also be better than its predecessors. The principles and procedures needed to select both competent and committed appointees are not difficult to understand; they are, however, often difficult to follow consistently.

-------------------◇-------------------

RECOMMENDATIONS

The heralded "first hundred days" of any new Administration is actually Act Two of the new play; Act One is the ten weeks between election day and inauguration day known as "the transition." Most of the critical decisions that will shape the President's personnel selection process and determine the political texture of his Administration are made in this period. Indeed, the President-elect has probably formulated some basic (if tentative) decisions on key personnel slots even before election day, and has had a small, separate team hard at work on "transition plans." In the first few days following the election victory, these tentative decisions and plans must be refined into firm directions and hard decisions.

Making decisions about key White House staff appointments and Cabinet officers will be the first order of business, and there will be no shortage of candidates eager to surrender the quiet and anonymity of private life for the sacrifices of public service. The President-elect must of necessity establish a few easily understood basic principles to guide his key staff in their recommendations for top-level appointments. An "inner circle" of the President's closest confidants will serve as his advisers on both policy and personnel matters.

His transition planning staff will have identified and prepared briefing books for the top positions he needs to fill quickly—over 1,000 positions in all: PAS positions (Presidential Appointments requiring Senate confirmation), PA positions (not requiring Senate confirmation), and some DAS slots (Deputy Assistant Secretarial positions in the major agencies). These top 1,000 management positions will need to be filled as soon as possible, and no later than by March 1. About 25 key posts—the Cabinet and top White House jobs—will have to be filled in the first month of the transition if the President-elect is to have a team in place to take full advantage of the opportunities available to a new Administration.

While it is easy to fall into a largely ad hoc approach to personnel decisions, the more systematic the approach, the fewer problems will crop up later as appointees assume their duties and begin to experience the cross-pressures and turf battles that go with the territory.

It would be presumptuous to attempt to lay out in great detail the timetable and sequence of every decision that must be taken in the critical days of the transition period and the first months after inauguration. Yet there are a few basic tasks that should be accomplished to give the President-elect a fighting chance actually to control his own Administration—something that does not follow automatically or effortlessly from the election to office. These basic tasks fall into four categories: policy direction, personnel criteria, the timetable for personnel selections, and "ground rules" for appointees.

Policy Direction

One of the primary tasks of the transition team will be to assemble from assorted speeches, the party platform, and other sources, the basic policy objectives of the new Administration organized into both broad policy themes and departmental/agency goals. These themes and goals should be assembled and disseminated quickly to key transition staff who are working on specific projects—the FY 1990 budget, the Inaugural Address, and major domestic and foreign policy initiatives. But equally important is their function as a roadmap for the staff responsible for recommending people for top appointments. Commitment to the policy goals of the Administration is universally acknowledged as an absolutely essential criterion for any political appointment; the more specific and concrete the content of that commitment, the stronger will be the commitment to the President's program.

Personnel Criteria

The three essential qualifications for any position of trust in any new Administration are the "three C's": commitment, competence, and character. The specific standards for ascertaining a strong political commitment to the President should be determined in large part by a shared, firmly-held belief in ideological principles, a longtime personal working relationship, extensive campaign work, and/or an important indirect connection that led to his victory. The level of technical competence to manage the President's objectives should be determined in most instances by executive branch experience. Most top positions will require prior executive branch experience, but it would be a mistake to shut out talented and experienced people who have demonstrated the required dexterity for political combat despite not having prior experience in the federal government.

The level of high moral character needed for political jobs is harder to measure and verify; it is more intangible than the other two C's. However, given the Ethics in Government Act, appointees must pass the tests presented by FBI clearances, financial disclosure, and conflicts of interest standards. Should a prospective appointee be deemed "controversial," the merits of the case should be reviewed to determine if the "controversy" is politically motivated and how it would affect both confirmation and performance on the job. At that point, the President should decide whether to hold firm or defer to political sensitivities that must be accommodated.

The dynamics of Washington politics are such that any Administration needs politically compatible government experts to manage the President's initiatives through the Washington maze. Appointees must be tough, resourceful, and totally dedicated in order to implement the President's program in the face of recalcitrant bureaucracy, congressional opponents, media criticism, and special interest pressure politics.

Timetable for Personnel Selection

The following timetable is both realistic and feasible if the President-elect establishes it as one of his priorities. Meeting its targets will give him "assets-in-place" to help accomplish his goals.

First Month of Transition

1) Appoint top White House staff (chief of staff, legislative affairs office, OMB, political and intergovernmental affairs, NSC, etc.) and the majority of Cabinet officers.

2) Make one of the first appointments—ideally in the first week— the person responsible for recommending people to staff the remainder of the government—the over 3,000 positions subject to the President's

direct appointment or appointment by his agency heads. This person
is the Director of the Office of Presidential Personnel and should have
the rank of Assistant to the President and be located in the West Wing.
He must be on an equal stature with all the President's senior aides
and must have solid rapport with the chief of staff.

3) Implement a plan for personnel recruitment and selection incorporating a) a set of selection criteria to be used in all appointments,
criteria that clearly define the principles of commitment, competence,
and character; b) a presidential directive announcing that while recommendations are invited from Members of Congress, national committee
and state party officials, and others, all appointments will come
through PPO and must have its approval; c) an ambitious timetable for
filling all PAS positions. Obviously, the staff of PPO must themselves
understand and support the policy goals of the Administration, as well
as possess the needed executive branch background and expertise in
personnel recruitment.

4) Establish a set of informal but well-understood "ground rules"
for all Cabinet officers and agency heads, rules that everyone will
follow in personnel and policy matters. The rules are a simple distilla-
tion of the wisdom of seasoned political veterans:

Rule One: Your loyalty to the President must take priority over
loyalties to constituencies and programs; advancing the President's
policy agenda is your primary duty.

Rule Two: There will be ample opportunity to bring new ideas and
proposals to the President, but once the President makes a decision
on a policy or budget issue, you and your staff will be expected to
support it fully.

Rule Three: Your appointees must be people who meet the President's standards of commitment, competence, and character, and
the Presidential Personnel Office will have full authority to manage
the personnel selection process.

Each person offered an appointed position in the new Administration
will be informed of the "rules" at the time the offer of appointment is
made: they are part of the package, not an afterthought. Cabinet
officers must accept certain basic rules if the team is to function
effectively. Anyone who balks at accepting them should be removed
from consideration.

5) Complete the organization and staffing of the Presidential Person-

nel Office, with special attention to a) the management of a computer-based Talent Bank pool of candidates, b) agency liaison and coordination, and c) a deputy for operations. The head of the PPO should focus on overall direction and communication with colleagues in the West Wing and the Cabinet officers. The Assistant to the President for Presidential Personnel must be willing to do battle to enforce consistent adherence to the policy goals and selection criteria established by the President.

6) Establish an efficient PPO clearance system that involves White House senior aides so that major appointments (generally the PAS positions) are given a thorough policy review prior to selection. This clearance system should involve the policy offices—NSC, OMB, policy development, and political affairs, to help assure policy consistency among appointments. When a controversial appointment is made, it should be the result of a conscious decision to change policy direction, not a mistake caused by inattention to the policy views of the nominee.

By Inauguration Day

1) Complete selection of the top 300 PA and PAS appointees.

2) Collect and disseminate the various "transition reports" prepared by the transition teams assigned to agencies as well as various task force reports targeted to priority initiatives.

3) In conjunction with other offices, PPO should establish a program of management training for all sub-Cabinet appointees, consisting of two parts:

Orientation training for all new appointees within 30 days of selection (and before confirmation).

Management development training during the first six months aimed at enhancing appointees' ability to manage policy and program initiatives and deal with the political environment.

By March 1

The President's PPO team should aim to complete the selection of the top 1,000 political appointments by this date. That will include all the remaining PAS and PA positions (except, of course, those term appointments not yet vacant) as well as key non-career Senior Executive Service and deputy assistant secretary positions.

A second area of personnel planning requires early presidential action through new legislation—the expansion of the number of management positions in the executive departments and agencies that are subject to political appointment. At present the number of senior management positions open to presidential appointment is less than in

1968, while the need for political direction and leadership in program management is greater than ever. The President should seek legislation amending the Civil Service Reform Act to raise the current ceilings on political appointees in the SES from 10 percent to 12.5 percent government-wide and from 25 percent to 30 percent in a single agency. Also, by instruction to his Cabinet and agency heads, he should assure that each agency has a minimum of 10 percent political appointees in the SES.

The case of the State Department will require special attention. A joint PPO-OPM-State Department task force should be set up to find ways to augment the ranks of the career Foreign Service Officers with capable political appointees drawn from the foreign policy think tanks and other private sector repositories of foreign policy expertise. No President has ever made a serious, sustained attempt at bringing the State Department under political control. The only way to achieve control is through the expansion of the number of appointees.

These increases in the numbers of political appointees in the SES and FSO ranks should be phased in over three or four years, relying mainly on attrition.

A President needs the capacity to bring in a political team that will assist him in implementing new policies throughout the executive branch. It is unrealistic to expect career officials to be fully responsive and energetic in carrying out new policies with which they may disagree.

These increases in the number of line management positions held by political appointees will result in a proportionate increase in the number of "Schedule C" positions, but this will not require a change in the law since there is no statutory limit. However, Schedule C positions have a natural limit derived from the number of line management positions held by political appointees. It is the number of line management positions held by political appointees—bureau heads, program directors, and division chiefs—that needs to be expanded in order to give the President and his agency heads greater control over the federal workforce.

This legislation will require strong presidential support and consistent advocacy from his Cabinet and staff. It will be a hard fight, but the benefits sought are worth it. Future Presidents of both parties will be the principal beneficiaries, but the federal bureaucracy must be brought under the control of the people's elected government.

The First Year

1) The White House must expand and refine the PPO's Talent Bank of people who can serve as either Administration officials or as outside

coalition-builders (including serving on advisory commissions and task forces). A network of former political appointees should be set up for advice and recommendations (which is exactly what the Kennedy Administration did through the Brookings Institution, and the Reagan Administration did to a degree through the Reagan Appointees Alumni Association).

2) Policy briefing updates should be offered to political appointees on a regular basis. These briefings are vital to ensure that the appointees keep the President's policy agenda first and foremost on their minds.

3) The White House should institute a system of personnel incentives and rewards based on performance. This system should be coordinated by PPO and the policy office but should have frequent presidential involvement. The system will have two parts—*recognition* for exemplary performance by sub-Cabinet officials (undersecretaries and below) and *removal* for officials who fail to meet any one of the performance standards of commitment, competence, and character.

Recognition can take many forms, from a simple presidential citation to an invitation to a state dinner or other prestigious event, or a ride on Air Force One when the President journeys to an appointee's home state or delivers a speech to an important out-of-town meeting. Seats in the President's Box at the Kennedy Center need not be allotted only to White House staff; they can be given out occasionally to sub-Cabinet officials who have done yeoman service or been put through a particularly grueling congressional hearing. Such gestures by the White House will yield large dividends in appointee morale and lasting loyalty.

———————◇———————

CONCLUSION

By implementing these recommendations the President can establish high standards that can produce top-grade officials for his Administration. There will be no need to "ad hoc" every personnel decision if the system in place is responsive and sensitive to political and policy considerations. When the Office of Presidential Personnel is functioning efficiently, the new Administration is being transfused with the talent, ideas, and commitment necessary to carry out policy initiatives. Bringing direction and control to a system that inherently tends toward fragmentation and disintegration is a challenge worthy of the most capable and intelligent of leaders. Shrinking from the challenge could well prove fatal to the President's program.

---◇---

NOTES

1. James P. Pfiffner, "Nine Enemies and One Ingrate: Political Appointments During Presidential Transitions," in G. Calvin MacKenzie, ed., *The In-and-Outers* (Baltimore: Johns Hopkins University Press, 1987), p. 62.

2. Richard M. Nixon, *RN: The Memoirs of Richard Nixon*; Vol. II (New York: Warner Books, 1978), p.284.

3. Jimmy Carter, Presidential Press Conference, February 8, 1977.

4. Stuart E. Eizenstat, interview with Dom Bonafede, May 7, 1985.

5. *Conservative Digest*, July 1986, p. 48.

6. Dom Bonafede, "The White House Personnel Office from Roosevelt to Reagan," in G. Calvin MacKenzie, ed. , *The In-and Outers* (Baltimore: Johns Hopkins University Press, 1987), p.36.

7. Bonafede, p.37.

8. Bonafede, p.38.

9. Bonafede, pp.41–42.

10. Bonafede, p.44.

11. Bonafede, pp.43–44.

12. Bonafede, p.45.

13. Bonafede, pp.45–46.

14. Bonafede, p.47.

15. Bonafede, p.58.

16. Pfiffner, p.73.

PART TWO

DOMESTIC POLICY

Domestic Policy Overview

by
Stuart M. Butler

THE REAGAN LEGACY

A merica is a very different nation today than when Ronald Reagan first entered the White House. Gone is the self-doubt of the late 1970s. Gone is the specter of permanent high inflation and double-digit unemployment. Gone too is the obsessive fear that the nation is running out of its basic resources, from energy to entrepreneurs. And gone is the notion, which haunted Americans in the twilight of the Carter Administration, that the presidency simply is too big a job for one man.

America by autumn 1988 is completing its sixth year of economic expansion, with 17 million jobs created since 1982 and the lowest unemployment rate in 14 years. In the 1970s, the Europeans feared the stagnating U.S. economy would undermine world prosperity; today they hail "Reaganomics" and the "American Miracle," and are copying Reagan's policies of deregulation and tax rate reductions.

The Reagan years, moreover, have led to a profound change in the way Americans look at problems and their solution. In the malaise preceding Reagan, the assumption all too often was that problems resulted from the shortcomings of ordinary Americans: gas lines occurred because Americans were "energy hogs"; falling education standards were due to the inability of young Americans to keep up with students in other lands; economic stagnation was due a decline in the spirit of enterprise. Today America recognizes that problems result more often from failed laws and programs than from the innate failings of its citizens. Thus Americans now look to tax incentives to unshackle enterprise, they seek to improve the quality of teachers and schools to unlock the full potential of students, and they support changes in the welfare system to create incentives for work and family responsibility.

Ronald Reagan has helped achieve this transformation because he entered the White House with clear goals and with a set of broad principles to guide his decisions. When complex questions needed to be resolved, he avoided the temptation to become entangled in the details of the issue—unlike his predecessor—and instead has drawn on his beliefs and principles to help formulate a decision.

Four central principles have underpinned the Reagan domestic policy agenda. First, there is the assumption that in most areas of their lives, ordinary Americans, poor as well as rich, are better able than government to judge what is in their interests. Thus Reagan has supported policies ranging from parental choice in education to allowing public housing tenants to manage their own projects. Second is the belief that free enterprise, spurred by a tax system which provides incentives for work and risk-taking, will improve the economic condition of Americans far more rapidly than any government program. Hence his strong support for deregulation and tax reductions, and his opposition to economic development grants. Third is the fear that freedom and economic growth are jeopardized by burgeoning government. Thus Reagan consistently has pressed for federal budget reductions. And fourth is the belief that collective action is best undertaken by those institutions, private and public, that are closest to the people. Thus Reagan urged policies that would strengthen the family and that would breathe new life into state and local government.

Reagan's Successes

With this broad vision to guide his political actions, Reagan has sought to revive the U.S. economy, by changing the framework of taxes and regulations influencing economic decisions, and to reduce federal intrusion into the lives of Americans. In pursuing this objective, Reagan has enjoyed significant successes. Among them:

Reforming America's tax system. Within months of entering office, Reagan scored a legislative triumph with the passage of the Economic Recovery Tax Act. The Act was an early and major step toward Reagan's goals of reducing substantially the marginal rate of income tax levied on Americans, ending inflationdriven "bracket creep," and simplifying the tax code. And by establishing a tax environment far more conducive to capital formation and risk taking, the Act helped jolt America out of the deep recession caused by a decade of high inflation, irresponsible monetary policy, and a tax code which penalized enterprise. Thanks to the 1981 Act, and to the 1986 Tax Reform Act, Americans will enter 1989 with marginal tax rates about half those prevailing in 1980.

Resisting the pressure to increase spending. Reagan has refused to be blown off course by the deficit. With the exception of 1982, when he agreed to a major tax hike, Reagan has been willing to let the red ink grow rather than cave in to the pressure to raise taxes. He has been right to do so. High tax rates and government spending are far more damaging to an economy than is a deficit. Reagan's determination to hold the line on taxes has had important implications for the politics of government spending. By making it near political suicide for a politician to advocate a tax hike, Reagan has forced proponents of expanded government onto the defensive, at least temporarily. The new Administration thus has a political opportunity to build political support for more permanent constraints on spending growth.

Strengthening federalism. The Reagan Administration has breathed new life into the federal system. States no longer are the backwaters of American government; they once again are on the cutting edge of policymaking. From the presidency of Lyndon Johnson to that of Jimmy Carter, state governments were little more than administrators of federal programs. But now they are policy entrepreneurs, experimenting with new approaches to problems and opportunities, from welfare reform to choice in education to privatization. They are breaking the new ground and Washington is following.

This burst of state policy entrepreneurship, like most enterprise in business, was induced by a combination of crisis and opportunity. The crisis was the assumption among state officials that Reagan's 1981 budget victory meant a drastic cutback in federal aid. In fact, this concern was greatly exaggerated. Nevertheless, the perception of crisis encouraged state officials to consider innovative, less costly alternatives to traditional policies. The opportunity, also created by Reagan's early budget victories, was the greater flexibility allowed state officials through the consolidation of dozens of categorical grants into a series of block grants with reduced regulations. Thus Ronald Reagan will leave office with this vital component of the federal system stronger than ever, able to tackle many of the domestic problems that frustrate the national government.

Reagan's Failures

Despite these successes, Ronald Reagan met with several damaging failures. In some cases these were due to a political balance on an issue that was tipped against him. Frequently his policies failed simply because throughout his presidency, liberals controlled the House of Representatives. But in too many cases failure resulted from strategic blunders or other White House shortcomings. The more serious failures will weaken Reagan's legacy and require the next President to take decisive action if many of the accomplishments of the Reagan Administration are to be preserved. Among the most serious failures:

No clear vision in many key domestic policy areas. Ronald Reagan has been able to command strong popular support for his strategy of holding the line on taxes because he took pains to explain to the American people both the economics and politics of taxing and spending. In other areas, however, he failed either to articulate a coherent vision himself, or to choose officials who could paint a sufficiently clear picture, and thus was unable to rally political support. For instance, by allowing welfare policy to be discussed almost entirely in terms of the budget, he sounded hard-hearted and insensitive to the poor; he lost the initiative to his opponents. By picking Otis Bowen to be Secretary of Health and Human Services, he played into the hands of liberals seeking to expand Medicare. By choosing disastrous appointees at the Environmental Protection Agency, he dissipated the consensus of the late 1970s that it was necessary to strike a proper balance between costly pollution controls and economic growth.

No long-term political strategy for budget control. Since the dramatic budget victories of his first two years in office, Reagan has failed to develop a political strategy to roll back federal spending. He has been curiously reluctant to use his veto firmly and consistently, causing confusion and political damage for his allies in Congress. He also has failed to provide strong support for tactics aimed at creating constituencies for alternatives to direct government spending, such as privatization. And he has not used the power of the presidency to mount an effective challenge to the process by which Congress deals with the budget, the driving force behind spending growth. To the extent there has been budget control, it has been due mainly to concern about the deficit. Yet because Reagan did not develop a comprehensive strategy for changing the political dynamics of spending, as economic growth reduced the size and political impact of the deficit, there has been little to constrain the future expansion of the federal budget.

No strategy to control middle-class social insurance entitlements. Reagan has failed to address runaway middle-class entitlements, especially the Social Security pension program and Medicare. Indeed, he has fumbled almost every opportunity presented to him to take the initiative on this sensitive issue. By not preparing the political ground adequately in 1982, when it was generally agreed that Social Security was in crisis, his reform proposals caused a political catastrophe for the Administration and for Republican candidates that November. The commission he appointed to "save" Social Security rejected all innovative proposals to restructure the system. Worst of all was Reagan's disastrous appointment of Otis Bowen as Secretary of Health and Human Services. With rising public concern over catastrophic health care costs, Reagan could have built support for a comprehensive proposal based on private insurance. Instead he allowed Bowen to commit him to a massive new expansion of Medicare, giving liberals an unexpected opportunity to ignite another surge in social insurance.

———————◇———————

THE CHALLENGE FACING THE NEW PRESIDENT

The Administration of Ronald Reagan has strengthened America's economic base and federal system, and restored the confidence of the American people. The challenge facing the new Administration is to build on Reagan's accomplishments while addressing the weaknesses in his legacy. Just as Franklin Roosevelt's New Deal set the political agenda for two generations, culminating in Lyndon Johnson's Great Society, wise actions by the next President will insure that the "Reagan Revolution" leads in time to an equally historic political transformation.

The following pages detail a domestic policy blueprint with which the next President can build on Reagan's legacy. The chapters contain specific recommendations for each issue area, arranged according to the federal department or agency with primary jurisdiction. And just as Ronald Reagan's agenda has been guided by a set of clear goals, the recommendations below emphasize six broad themes:

1) *Maintain economic growth as the top priority.*

Continued economic expansion is essential to achieving America's most fundamental policy goals. The lives of poorer Americans cannot

be improved without economic growth. Jobs cannot be created for
each new generation of workers without growth. America cannot
maintain its defenses without growth.

The next Administration thus must take steps to prolong the Reagan
economic expansion and avoid actions that would cause the economy
to slow down or stumble. That means, as the following pages recommend, the next President should veto any bill to increase taxes and
should support legislation to reduce further the taxes paid by Americans.

It means holding the line on protectionism. Foreign trade leads to
cheaper goods for Americans, leaving them more of their income for
investment, while international competition forces U.S. firms to be
more efficient. The President thus should take steps to dismantle trade
barriers, such as negotiating a worldwide elimination of restrictions on
trade in goods and services. He must also continue Reagan's policy of
relaxing the antitrust laws, to permit U.S. firms to pool resources to
compete more effectively in world markets. The goal of strong economic growth also means the new President must focus on eliminating
unnecessary federal spending programs. The President must point out
that excessive federal spending, whether financed by borrowing the
dollars of Americans or taking those dollars as taxes, "crowds out"
the private sector and restrains growth.

2) *Address the underlying dynamics of federal spending*.

The new Administration must deal with the political dynamics that
lead Americans to press for federal programs, when other approaches
would be far less expensive and for more effective. As the Nobel prize-
winning "Public Choice" school of economists points out, the principal reason why even grossly inefficient federal spending is hard to
constrain, let alone cut, is that small groups which benefit greatly from
federal spending have the incentive to campaign vigorously for specific
programs, while the impact on each taxpayer is too small to provoke
strong resistance to demands for spending. Liberals as well as conservatives have cause to be concerned about this lopsided balance of
power: wasteful spending means less money for liberal programs as
well as for conservative tax cuts.

The following pages contain proposals to enable the next President
to deal with the political dynamics of federal spending. One of these is
to confront the budget process head-on. Part One of this volume
presents a strategy for reforming the congressional budget process.
This would make the process less prone to special-interest pressure.

The next President must force a public debate on the budget process, to build political pressure for implementing a new budget act.

A second strategy involves privatization. Privatization means using the private sector to provide a service previously delivered by government. Government might contract with private firms to supply a service, for example, or it might provide tax and regulatory incentives to encourage Americans to purchase services from the private sector, rather than seeking them from government. This saves money because the competitive private sector has the commercial incentive to find less and less costly ways of delivering services. Moreover, when it chooses privatization, the government does not renege on its responsibility to provide essential services. It retains that obligation, and it simply uses the private sector to deliver those services with greater efficiency.

Privatization has been used extensively by liberal and conservative governments abroad, and at the state and local level in the United States, to deliver services more efficiently and to build strong coalitions for private alternatives to government. While the Reagan Administration has taken some important steps to introduce privatization, progress at the federal level remains moderate.

The next President must adopt a comprehensive program of privatization. The following pages call, for instance, for more use of private firms to provide government services. Here all Washington has to do is mimic the privatization successes of the states and localities. Recommendations in the following pages propose tax incentives encouraging Americans to purchase retirement medical insurance, and to "opt out" of Social Security in favor of private retirement annuities. Not only would having this choice mean a better financial deal for Americans, but making Americans less dependent on Social Security also would lessen political resistance to structural reform of the system. And among many other privatization proposals, the next President is urged to draw on the lessons of Britain's highly successful privatization program by using employee ownership plans to reduce public employee resistance to the privatization of the Postal Service and Amtrak.

A third approach is to propose fundamental restructuring of a program, or occasionally even recommending a new program, to deal with a new, yet reasonable, demand for federal action, rather than to expand eligibility for an existing program. The advantage of restructuring is that when a program designed for one purpose is expanded to meet a very different need, it does so often by raising benefits for many groups other than the one needing help.

This strategy is best illustrated by a proposal concerning AIDS. Some lawmakers argue that the best way to provide sufferers of this disease with the expensive medical and nursing care they need would be to ease the eligibility requirements for Medicaid and Medicare. Yet Medicaid is designed for the destitute, and Medicare for the elderly and long-term disabled; neither is designed for young, middle-income Americans struck down with a fatal illness of relatively short duration. Expanding the eligibility requirements of Medicaid and Medicare sufficiently to include typical AIDS sufferers would result in including many other groups, at enormous cost, who are best protected with private insurance. Thus the next President is urged to create a new federal program specifically for AIDs victims.

3) *Stress the importance of choice and competition.*

Americans well understand that the freedom to make choices among competing suppliers of services is key to the efficiency and creativity of the American economic system. The next President should invoke this universally accepted premise to build support for a number of policy initiatives.

One is the policy of contracting with the private sector to provide government services. The President should argue that allowing private firms to bid on delivering government services introduces the benefits of competition into what is now a monopoly. In the following pages, the next President is urged to use this argument to build pressure on Congress to remove many legislated impediments to contracting.

The new Administration should stress the importance of competition and choice in proposing reforms in education, by giving strong backing for education vouchers—especially for the low-income inner city families most ensnared by the public school monopoly. Housing vouchers should replace virtually all federally sponsored housing construction and management programs, to introduce greater competition and efficiency and to give low-income Americans greater freedom to choose where they wish to live.

The same appeal to choice and competition should undergird the next President's alternatives to several pending legislative proposals for new federal health programs, ranging from long-term care for the elderly to a comprehensive health care system for working Americans, and to day care for children. The next Administration should not support moves on Capitol Hill to establish new social insurance programs to fund long-term care and a national health system. While such programs might seem attractive to some lawmakers, like all government-run insurance, they would restrict the freedom of Americans to choose the services they want, and they would discourage the private sector from developing varied and innovative plans to serve the public.

In the pages below, the next President is urged instead to address the long-term care issue by proposing tax changes to encourage working-age and older Americans to purchase long-term insurance, reserving government help only for those truly in need. Similarly, a proposal for a comprehensive national system of health care would require Americans to purchase basic private health plans for themselves and their dependents, granting them tax relief for doing so and providing federal financial assistance for low-income Americans to buy such protection. This would preserve freedom of choice, while stimulating competition in the health care industry. Moreover, instead of supporting plans to provide funding for federally approved professional day care services, which would restrict the choice of parents, the next President is urged to seek legislation to reduce the tax burden on families with children, so that parents would have more dollars in their pockets and could make their own child care decisions.

4) *Further strengthen federalism.*

During the Reagan Administration, states have been given new powers and responsibilities, and they have responded with an explosion of innovative policies, from privatization to welfare reform. Being closer to the people than the federal government, and better able to take account of local constraints and opportunities, states have made government more responsive and creative. Moreover, with 50 states experimenting with different approaches to difficult issues, like welfare dependency, and learning from each other's successes and failures, the process of policy improvement has accelerated.

Several proposals below indicate how the new President could expand further the role of state government. One recommendation is for the next Administration to continue the Reagan Administration's efforts to win passage of legislation to give broad powers to the executive branch to grant states relief—or waivers—from certain federal regulations concerning the management of welfare programs. In this way, states would have greater freedom to develop innovative welfare strategies, while still being required to maintain their obligation to assist the poor.

Another recommendation calls for an overhaul of the system of federal aid to the states. Currently such aid is given to all states, with scant regard to the fiscal condition of the state. The new Administration

is urged to support changes in aid formulas to direct virtually all
federal aid to the poorer states, so they would have more resources to
finance programs. Several other proposals, such as those concerning
Medicaid reforms and urban development, would mean giving states
greater or exclusive responsibility for programs carried out at the
federal level.

5) *Instill a stronger sense of personal responsibility, empowering Americans to control their own lives.*

In recent decades, the expansion of government has reduced the
power of Americans to control their own lives. Simultaneously, the
increasing federal presence has led many Americans to evade responsibility for their own conduct, allowing them to call on the federal
government to bail them out whenever they need it. This has led to
some disturbing social and economic effects, and to increasing pressure for the federal government to step in where private action would
be more appropriate and less costly.

Many Americans are frustrated by their loss of power. Parents
seeking better schooling for their children, for instance, feel trapped
within the public school monopoly. Self-help groups within inner cities
find red tape suffocates their attempts to provide services to their own
communities. Other Americans not only accept dependency on government, but have come to expect the government to provide for them
with money taken from other Americans. Some fathers, for instance,
believe they have no duty to support their children, that the welfare
system has that obligation. Many relatively affluent Americans, nearing retirement, see no reason why they should use their own savings
and income to pay for nursing care and health costs, and demand
financial support from younger, less affluent taxpayers.

The next Administration can reduce welfare dependency and explod-
ing middle-class entitlement spending only if the President challenges
Americans to accept greater responsibility for their own well-being,
and takes steps to empower lower-income Americans to exercise
greater control over their lives. He should stress that government has
an obligation to ensure that those Americans who need assistance do
receive help from private or public sources, but that citizens also have
an obligation to take steps to provide for their own needs and those of
their families, to the extent that they are able to do so.

The President thus is urged in the following pages to take actions
and propose legislation which would foster empowerment and responsibility. One proposal calls for the Federal Trade Commission to

examine those regulations at all government levels that prevent neighborhood organizations from delivering social services to their community. Another would accelerate resident management and ownership of public housing projects. Another proposal urges tougher penalties for drug users, recognizing that a market will exist for drugs as long as otherwise responsible Americans flout the law. Yet another would crack down on absent fathers who evade child support payments. And throughout this book, the new Administration is encouraged to support a number of legislative proposals to spur middle-class Americans to take greater financial responsibility for their lives. Among these: tax incentives for health insurance and retirement health care, and freedom for workers to opt out of Social Security in favor of an expanded Individual Retirement Account system.

6) *Strengthen family and community.*

Throughout his Administration, Reagan has stressed that government is only one instrument by which a society can achieve its objectives. Between government and citizens stand institutions that enable Americans, collectively, to address their needs. In many instances, these institutions are far more effective than government at dealing with those needs. The two most important of these institutions are the family and the community.

More than any other institution, strong families preserve the culture and customs of America's diverse people. Among lower income Americans, intact families are a bastion against persistent poverty, while broken families are an invitation to welfare dependency. And the educational and social interests of all children are best served by stable and active families.

The American family, unfortunately, has been under enormous pressure in recent decades. In part this is due to cultural changes that have loosened family bonds. But government policy also has been a key factor. In lower- and moderate-income families, for instance, rising payroll and income taxes have strained family finances and forced many spouses into the workforce. Similarly, the welfare system, by channeling most assistance to broken families, has discouraged families from remaining intact. And by increasing the power of government and professional service providers, at the expense of parental choice, in such areas as education and day care, regulation has weakened the power of parents to determine how their children will be raised.

The new President should declare his commitment to an agenda to strengthen the American family. Such a theme runs through many of the recommendations already cited. Among these: introducing education vouchers to increase parental choice, taking tough action on child support to prevent fathers from evading their responsibilities, and increasing substantially the personal tax deduction for dependents, to reduce the tax code's bias against families with children.

Community is the second most important social institution. By acting together, in local organizations like a neighborhood watch committee, a parents' association or a church, Americans traditionally have addressed the problems and opportunities they face. Such groups, by definition, are designed to use local resources most effectively to deal with local issues. Government generally is less flexible, and less attuned to local conditions. And unfortunately, government programs often suffocate community institutions, rather than supplement them.

The next Administration must build on Reagan's legacy of fostering nongovernment institutions as a central feature of American society. This is particularly important in poor communities, where such institutions are vital to reversing the spiral of poverty and welfare dependency. The following pages recommend several steps the new President should take. For example, he should unleash neighborhood organizations to tackle many urban problems by revising federal rules that currently deny federal funds to many groups successfully dealing with local concerns. He should urge states to remove similar restrictions on state support for neighborhood groups providing social services. In addition, the new President should speed up the introduction of resident management and ownership in public housing projects.

—————————————◇—————————————

BUILDING COALITIONS FOR REFORM

The new President will be unable to reach his goals if he does not pay careful attention to the need to build political coalitions to win passage of key legislation. In his first term, Ronald Reagan used his remarkable ability to communicate with Americans to bring together powerful coalitions to pressure Congress to enact tax reduction and the defense buildup. It has been his general failure to build such coalitions during his second term that has denied him success on such proposals as education vouchers and a conservative version of welfare reform. This failure also has prevented him from blocking several liberal proposals, such as a major expansion of Medicare and numerous protectionist trade measures.

Coalitions are a fundamental part of the American system of government. Coalitions are required to elect a wise President and to enact a much-needed bill. But they also can gang up to block useful legislation and obtain unfair and unnecessary benefits for the few at the expense of the many. These less benign features of coalitions have come to dominate the political process in recent years. Thus the agenda of the next President must include a detailed strategy to undermine selfish coalitions and to build or strengthen coalitions to achieve reform. The themes of empowerment and choice, for instance, should appeal strongly to minority urban Americans who currently have little control over their lives. Thus the new Administration should seek ways of building political support for proposals among blacks and Hispanic organizations. Similarly, privatization means business for private sector firms. Thus the new President might secure the lobbying support of such firms for his privatization initiatives.

The recommendations below are crafted to appeal to such broad constituencies, and in many instances to constituencies normally assumed hostile to the objective being sought. Proposals to contract out government services and to privatize Amtrak and the Postal Service, for instance, involve giving employees a substantial ownership stake in the privatized corporations. In this way public employees would have a strong financial incentive to support the policy. Similarly, several housing and welfare proposals which would reduce the scope of government are designed to appeal to inner city neighborhood organizations. For instance, the proposal to encourage wider use of tenant management in public housing would build tenant support for a reduction in bureaucratic control over inner city public housing.

REKINDLING THE SPIRIT OF AMERICA

After many dark years of economic stagnation and self-criticism in the 1970s, the presidency of Ronald Reagan has helped the nation to emerge into an era of economic strength and confidence. America once again exhibits the characteristics which captured the attention of foreign observers and drew millions of immigrants to its shores. It is once again a country in which freedom, diversity, and opportunity are not only rights enjoyed by all citizens, but are recognized as essential conditions for economic growth and for creative solutions to the country's social problems. America is a country which trusts its people, more than its government, to determine the shape of society.

And it is a country in which the strong take seriously their obligations to the weak.

Reagan has begun the process of restructuring the political institutions and policies of the federal government to reflect these rekindled qualities of America. The pages below contain an agenda that would complete that task. This agenda would result in a set of laws and institutions conforming to the new spirit of America. The proposals recognize that collective action has always been a tradition of America, but they revive the notion that collective action is not necessarily the same as government action. And thus they seek to strengthen those private institutions that are better able than government to achieve the goals of the American people. This underscores the fact, well understood by most Americans today and by the architects of the nation, that when government is the best vehicle to secure the needs of Americans, it is necessary to place checks on its potential excesses. Thus the proposals call for steps to restrain the taxing and spending powers of government.

The agenda also recognizes that while the decentralization of government offers diversity and creativity, it raises the dangers of fragmentation and the more offensive features of "states' rights." Thus the following pages do not call for a return to the federal system of the 1950s, but instead to a modern system in which there are national goals, set by the federal government but fulfilled by the states, that emphasize wide discretion and inventiveness. And the agenda reflects the view of most Americans that while government, together with other institutions, has a clear obligation to help the needy, it should not be a permanent crutch for the able-bodied, nor should it be an open cash register for the greedy. Thus the proposals would create a system of government assistance that acts as a ladder out of dependency, and would end the role of government as a vehicle of enrichment for the affluent.

This agenda would not recreate a society that has long since disappeared. It does not deny that Americans today differ from previous generations in their lifestyles and many of their values. But it recognizes that there are certain features of America and Americans that are constant. The new President also must recognize this as he begins his central task of fashioning a program of policies to prepare America for the next century. The following pages provide him with a blueprint for that task.

8

The Department of Agriculture

Charles Grizzle*
Task Force Chairman

The Department of Agriculture's primary responsibility is the administration of the federal government's farm programs, including agricultural subsidies, price supports, and credit programs. In addition, the Department administers several nutritional programs for the poor, such as the food stamp program, and manages the national forests.

The Reagan Administration's record in agricultural programs has been a mixed blessing for both farmers and the American taxpayer. The 1985 farm bill, the second major farm legislation during Reagan's term, wisely moved farm programs toward a more market-based orientation and has allowed the prices of United States food commodities to become competitive in world markets. Yet the 1985 farm bill failed to make farmers more independent of Washington and allowed federal outlays for agriculture to skyrocket. Delivery of food and nutrition assistance to the poor has been improved, but the rate of error in payments remains too high. Conservation programs have been strengthened, leading to better use of the nation's public lands, but the system still ignores market incentives.

Much needs to be done during the next Administration. Further reform must place the agricultural economy on an even more market-oriented and less subsidized basis. Key to this would be to "decouple" farm subsidy programs from production requirements, thereby allowing farmers to make production decisions based on market factors

---

*Commenting and contributing generously to this chapter were *Mandate III* Task Force Members John Campbell, Robert Chambers, Floyd Gaibler, Stuart Hardy, Christopher Hicks, Anna Kondratas, Kathleen Lawrence, Eric Mondres and Hyde Murray. They do not necessarily endorse all of its views and recommendations.

Task Force Deputy Chairman: Heritage McKenna Senior Policy Analyst James Gattuso.

BUDGET AND PERSONNEL

Secretaries

Richard E. Lyng	1986–present
John R. Block	1981–1986

Personnel

March 1988	109,522
April 1980	123,081
April 1970	106,089

Budget Outlays

Fiscal Year	Total (billions)
1989 Estimate	$48.3
1988 Estimate	$50.7
1987 Actual	$50.4
1986 Actual	$58.7
1985 Actual	$55.5
1980 Actual	$34.8
1970 Actual	$ 8.4

rather than on what Washington dictates. At the same time, the new Administration must work to end the international agricultural trade war, through a multinational agreement restricting farm subsidies and trade barriers. It also must work to reduce federal credit programs for agriculture, minimizing the distortion of investment in rural areas.

In other areas, federal policies which discourage soil and water conservation should be eliminated, and efforts must be strengthened to make best use of Forest Service lands, consistent with the goal of conservation. Major reform of food programs is also needed, in order to increase their effectiveness and ensure that aid is targeted to those who need it most.

———————◇———————

SUMMARY OF AGENCY FUNCTIONS

The United States Department of Agriculture (USDA) was established in 1862. In his first message justifying the creation of a federal role in agriculture, President Abraham Lincoln dubbed the USDA the "people's department," reflecting farming's long domination of American life and economy. At that time, over 40 percent of the U.S. population lived on farms; today, barely 2 percent do. Nevertheless, USDA still could be called the people's department in view of its direct impact on the lives of all Americans, as its programs affect and often control the price and the amount of much of the food they consume.

Among the major functions of USDA are administration of:

◆ *Federal subsidies to farmers and federal crop price support programs*, through the Agricultural Stabilization and Conservation Service and the Commodity Credit Corporation.

◆ *Federal food assistance programs*, such as the Food Stamp and Women, Infants, and Children (WIC) programs, whose office also includes the Food and Nutrition Service.

◆ *Federal crop "marketing orders,"* which regulate the quality and quantity of certain crops through the Agricultural Marketing Service.

◆ *Programs to inspect livestock and crops, and foods sold to the public*, through the Animal and Plant Health Inspection Service and the Food Safety and Inspection Service.

◆ *Federally owned forests*, through the Forest Service.

◆ *Programs to assist and educate farmers in soil conservation*, through the Soil Conservation Service.

◆ *Loan programs for farms and for rural development*, through the Farmers Home Administration and the Rural Electrification Administration.

◆ *Federal crop insurance programs*, through the Federal Crop Insurance Corporation.

◆ *Federal export and foreign aid programs,* administered by the Foreign Agriculture Service.

◆ *Research and educational activities,* carried out by such agencies as the Agricultural Research Service and the Extension Service.

———————◇———————

INSTITUTIONAL CONSTRAINTS

Agriculture policy is watched closely by some of Washington's most powerful interest groups, reflecting almost every facet of agriculture, ranging from organizations representing broad farm interests, such as the American Farm Bureau and the National Farmers Union, to specialized interest groups, like the Fertilizer Institute and the

National Milk Producers Federation. These organizations exercise an enormous influence over policy not only because of the millions of voters they represent, but also because their interests are so directly affected by USDA actions. Efforts to change existing policies thus are strongly opposed by many of these groups. Like most of its predecessors, the Reagan Administration has not been very effective at countering their influence. Plans by any new administration to reform agriculture policy require skilled handling of interest groups on all sides of the issues. All legislative strategies must include plans to work with those groups supporting the Administration and plans to neutralize those groups opposing it.

Congress poses another constraint on USDA policy. Members from farm states or districts understandably feel heat from their agricultural constituencies. Congress's almost uncontrollable urge to micromanage agricultural issues is especially acute concerning agriculture policy. When statutory policy is not carried out precisely as Congress or even a single powerful member envisages, legislative procedures can be used by skilled lawmakers to force a change.

Differences within the executive branch also will constrain the new Administration in developing sound agricultural policy. The Secretaries of State and Treasury, the Director of the Office of Management and Budget (OMB), and the U.S. Trade Representative often play as important a role in deciding issues affecting agriculture as does the Secretary of Agriculture. Yet these officials often have failed to work together toward common goals. USDA also faces internal constraints stemming from its diverse mission and its decentralized structure. This allows groups within the Department to confuse or thwart good policy. To overcome this, the Department must consolidate policymaking responsibilities to keep its policies focused and moving in the right direction.

THE REAGAN ADMINISTRATION RECORD

When the Reagan Administration came into office, American agriculture had been enjoying a nearly decade-long period of unprecedented prosperity. Yet the seeds of a serious downturn—high interest rates and high price support levels (made even higher by the 1981 farm bill)—were already there. When the Reagan Administration succeeded in reducing inflation and foreign competition stiffened, farmers were squeezed by unsupportable debt loads and uncompetitive export prices. The Administration was then faced with the challenge of reforming agriculture so it could adjust to a world of low inflation and international competition. This meant reducing guaranteed commodity prices and subsidies to farmers to make American agriculture more sensitive to market conditions.

While agriculture has come a long way toward this goal, the first farm bill passed during the Reagan Administration, the Agriculture and Food Act of 1981, or the 1981 farm bill, ignored potential changes in world economic conditions and their impact on U.S. agriculture. Following a decade of record growth in world food demand, most policymakers in 1981 felt that the key issue facing U.S. agriculture would be how to produce enough food and how to protect farmers in a world of double-digit inflation and a prime interest rate of over 20 percent. Thus, the farm bill of that year mandated escalating levels of price and income supports. The bill soon proved unworkable, when inflation subsided and interest rates dropped. High support levels then priced U.S. farmers out of world markets, while escalating subsidies prompted dramatic overproduction of crops.

By 1985, it had become evident that these farm policies were not serving the interests of either the taxpayer or American farmers. Thus, the 1985 farm bill, the Food Security Act, significantly reduced price supports. This legislation also began the process of phasing out direct credit programs, which encourage excess investment, and replacing them with private loans guaranteed by the federal government. Perhaps most important in the long run, the Reagan Administration since 1987 has worked to ensure a freer international market for agricultural goods by actively seeking an international agreement to eliminate agricultural trade barriers and subsidies.

Unfortunately, the 1985 farm bill also maintained artificially high direct subsidies, or "target prices," to protect farmers' income. As a result, when net cash income to farmers in 1987 soared to a record $57 billion, federal payments accounted for half. To prevent subsidies from encouraging excessive production, the 1985 bill removed large amounts of acreage from production each year—totaling nearly 75 million acres in the 1987 crop year. These high subsidies and consequent acreage retirement programs are major shortcomings of the 1985 bill. Forcing more U.S. acreage out of production allowed foreign competitors to capture some of America's markets. These high direct subsidies, coupled with large acreage set-asides, have hindered U.S. efforts to be competitive internationally, diluting the positive effects of lower price support levels.

Outside of commodity programs, the Reagan Administration has established a long-term Conservation Reserve Program (CRP) to take fragile farmlands out of production, adopted a balanced policy of public lands, management, and reduced the error rates and abuses in nutrition programs.

————————————◇————————————

THE NEXT FOUR YEARS

As he develops his farm policy, the new President should keep in mind one overriding goal: the establishment of an agricultural economy free of government control and of government subsidy. In the long term, agriculture should operate as do most other industries: with producers using market signals, rather than government directives, to determine and fulfill the needs of consumers. Ultimately, it should operate without direct assistance from the American taxpayer. Policymakers can move toward this goal through such steps as decoupling farm production from subsidies and negotiating an international agreement on farm subsidies. The same general goals of fostering market processes and reducing taxpayer burdens should similarly be pursued by USDA's nonfarm activities, such as forest management and the food stamp program.

Streamlining the Organizational Structure of USDA

USDA has 105,000 employees at 15,000 locations. This does not include the tens of thousands of county-based employees of the Cooperative Extension Service employed by the various land grant universities or the county employees of the Agricultural Stabilization and Conservation Service employed by the Commodity Credit Corporation. Four USDA agencies, the Extension Service, Agricultural Stabilization and Conservation Service (ASCS), Soil Conservation Service (SCS), and the Farmers Home Administration (FmHA), each have offices in almost every U.S. county. Each of these four agencies reports to a different Agriculture Department official in Washington. This structure cripples program efficiency and is an inherent obstacle in the fight to reduce the federal presence in American agriculture.

The new President should consolidate, at least partially, the four agencies which primarily provide services directly to agricultural producers. Specifically, a single agency should be created to handle the activities now performed by ASCS, the Extension Service, the producer-oriented (in contrast to environmental) activities of the Soil Conservation Service, and the producer loan (in contrast to general rural development) activities of FmHA. They should also be placed under the policy guidance of one USDA Undersecretary or Assistant Secretary.

Reforming Farm Subsidy Programs

Farmers and ranchers generally are neither poor nor disadvantaged. Yet many of the largest and most successful of them enjoy enormous benefits, in the form of subsidies, from the taxpayer. Federal farm programs that give blanket support to the agricultural industry amount to little more than corporate welfare. And as with most welfare programs, the government program tends to foster dependency. The result: what once was a strong and independent industry is now a quasi-nationalized industry dependent on federal handouts. Many American farmers today effectively work for the government, with their "profits" and paychecks paid for by the taxpayer.

Despite the media portrayal of the typical farmer as hard-pressed, farm families have had higher incomes than the median American family in every year since 1980. More important, the net worth of farm families far exceeds that of the average American family. Even during the recent economic stress in the agricultural sector, with foreclosures featured regularly on the evening newscasts, the vast majority of farm businesses were quite stable.

With few exceptions, farmers and farm bankers who went broke in the early 1980s, or remain under financial stress today, are those who borrowed and invested heavily in the "get-rich-quick" speculative fever of the 1970s. They bet on rapidly inflating land values—and bet wrong. It is unfair to force the taxpayers to pick up the tab. Yet this precisely is what has happened. From 1980 through 1987, the taxpayer cost of commodity programs skyrocketed 950 percent—much faster than any other item of the federal budget. During this period, taxpayers contributed $112 billion to farm income. Only since the passage of the 1985 Food Security Act has this cost begun to decline.

It is ironic that these policies not only transfer money from the relatively poor to the relatively rich, but they also have hastened the demise of the family farmer—supposedly the prime beneficiary of the multibillion-dollar programs. This is because acreage expansion, the use of labor saving equipment, and increased borrowing have been encouraged, all of which is more difficult for family farmers. Moreover, under current programs, the more farmers produce, the more price and income subsidies they receive, aiding large farming operations and encouraging excess production.

It is hard to imagine a set of policies more likely to invite runaway costs, or more likely to undermine the independence of an industry. Like other welfare programs, farm policies have created a cycle of dependence. Farmers get hooked on subsidies and tailor their operations around the government "fix." And while many farmers would like to end their subsidy "habit," they believe the risk is too great and the short-term penalty for dependency minimal.

The new President must help American farmers break out of their cycle of dependency. To do this, he should propose a program that decouples subsidies from production requirements so that farmers no longer would be required to grow a particular crop to qualify for income support from the federal government. Instead, farmers would receive a flat subsidy payment, calculated perhaps as a percentage of the average payments received in prior years. Planting decisions would then be based on market signals—consumer demand for a product— rather than on what is required by Washington. Farmers no longer would be encouraged to produce goods already in oversupply, and could instead produce crops which are in more demand, or use their land for other purposes. The subsidies, moreover, would be explicit, direct payments to farmers and not be disguised as economic regulations. In the long run, perhaps ten to 15 years, even these remaining subsidies should be phased out, leaving agriculture in a completely free market. Ideally, the decoupling strategy should be adopted multilaterally by the key agriculture exporting nations. But the U.S. should not wait for an international agreement before accepting this sensible policy; it should decouple its own subsidies from production requirements as soon as possible.

In addition, the Administration should take steps to encourage farmers to protect themselves from drought and other natural disasters. Federal programs so far do little more for farmers than make them turn to the U.S. Treasury when disaster strikes. Thus when a natural disaster occurs, the American taxpayer foots the bill. The new Administration must work with Congress to encourage the farmers to make better use of market mechanisms to protect themselves from such disasters. Specifically, the Administration should consider legislation requiring farmers who participate in federal farm programs, or who receive federal farm loans, to obtain either federal or private crop insurance.

Expanding Trade in Agricultural Products

A strong American agricultural economy requires a high volume of export sales, not only to traditional markets, but to the growing markets in developing nations. This strongly suggests that the potential for increased U.S. farm exports depends heavily on free and open markets and on Third World economic growth.

In September 1986, signatory states of the General Agreement on Tariffs and Trade (GATT) met in Punta del Este, Uruguay, to launch the Uruguay Round of multilateral trade negotiations. GATT members placed agriculture prominently on their agenda, called for a rollback of export subsidies and import barriers, and agreed to take steps to harmonize agricultural health and sanitary regulations. The Reagan Administration urged that by the year 2000 GATT totally bar trade distorting subsidies (including domestic subsidies that encourage excess production) and import barriers. Though America's trade partners may not accept this sweeping proposal in its current form, the bold plan nevertheless has focused attention on the root cause of a major trade problem: domestic crop price supports that induce growers to produce more than is needed. As their domestic surplus stocks build, governments traditionally have responded by erecting import barriers and dumping their own products on world markets at subsidized prices.

The Uruguay Round offers governments the opportunity to begin reducing subsidies and trade restrictions. It is significant that the U.S. proposal calls only for the elimination of domestic subsidies that distort trade. Governments still would be permitted to subsidize the income of growers if those payments were decoupled from production requirements. Under a decoupled system, subsidies to farmers would not be based on the amount or type of crop grown. They would then provide no direct incentive to farmers to increase production. Developing countries could be granted a longer transition period before they must end trade distorting subsidies.

The new President should stick with the Reagan Administration's negotiating posture in the Uruguay Round, keeping the focus of the new GATT Round on fundamental reform of domestic policies that distort trade. In addition, the new administration should use the new export subsidy initiatives (principally the Export Enhancement Program and Targeted Export Assistance) of the 1985 farm bill as bargaining chips to press America's competitors to negotiate in good faith by making it more difficult for other nations to increase their exports through subsidy programs. At the same time, the administration must make clear that these export subsidies, like other subsidies, are not in themselves good policy. These and other direct subsidy initiatives should not be institutionalized as permanent features of U.S. farm export policy. In addition, the next Administration should refrain from using food exports as a foreign policy tool unless they would be effective in advancing national security. Prior embargoes caused great hardship to farmers, while failing to advance U.S. interests. Finally, the Administration should use U.S. food aid and economic development programs to encourage indigenous Third World private enterprise in a manner that will promote economic growth. The pilot Food for Progress program, for instance, provides food aid to nations that reduce government intervention in their economies and increase the role of the market.

Reducing Farmer Dependency on Federal Credit

In the early and mid–1980s, U.S. agriculture faced a financial crisis. Though the farm sector as a whole no longer does, the earlier hard times demonstrated that farmers and rural communities should diversify their sources of income and avoid an overdependence on credit. Yet federal credit programs encourage individuals to continue and expand their farming activities and finance this activity through debt. Thus these programs discourage diversification and sound financial practices.

The federal government in the long term should be removed from private credit markets. In the short term, direct lending programs, in which the government itself lends money, should be terminated and replaced, where appropriate, with loan guarantee programs, so as to encourage development of private-sector credit sources. At the same time, because loan guarantees still cost taxpayers' money, policymakers should make sure that this cost is reflected in the USDA budget. To do this, USDA could purchase private reinsurance to cover the risks the government assumes through the guarantees. In this way, the loans would be made through private firms, while the cost of the guarantees to the taxpayers would be made explicit.

◆ *Farmers Home Administration (FmHA) loans.* In fiscal 1987, the level of farm loans guaranteed by FmHA for the first time exceeded the level of direct lending. The new President should continue shifting FmHA to loan guarantees.

Through its Water and Sewer Facility and Community Facility program, FmHA makes loans and grants to rural communities for water and sewer systems and other public facilities. Over time, these two programs should be eliminated, leaving the cost of such investments to the communities benefiting from them. In the short term, the programs should be shifted from direct lending to loan guarantees. This would allow FmHA to use its funds more effectively by leveraging its resources, as well as to foster development of private sector credit.

The FmHA also operates the Business and Industry Loan Guarantee programs, intended to stimulate economic investment in small towns and rural communities. Money under this program, however, too often goes to enterprises which have an inordinately high cost per job created. Moreover, much of the funding goes to large businesses, although smaller enterprises tend to create the most jobs. The new Administration thus should target the program's loans to small-scale enterprises, which produce the most jobs per federal dollar, especially in areas where farmers are attempting to move to nonfarm employment. The FmHA rural housing loan and grant programs for rural housing should be phased out; the Department of Housing and Urban Development is a much more appropriate source of housing assistance.

◆ *Rural Electrification Administration (REA).* REA makes direct loans and guarantees loans made by the Federal Financing Bank, at heavily subsidized rates, to cooperatives and companies that retail electric and telephone service. REA was established in 1936 to give rural America access to electric and telephone service. This mission has been accomplished, yet the subsidies continue. To begin the process of reducing these subsidies, the new President should start privatizing REA's functions. As a first step, REA should shift from direct lending to a program of guarantees of private-sector loans. Eligibility should be tightened, so that such well-off borrowers as subsidiaries of large telecommunication companies no longer qualify. Existing REA borrowers should be encouraged to prepay outstanding loans by giving them discounts for paying off the loans, while eliminating prepayment premiums and penalties. Coupled with these inducements should be a prohibition on the borrowers from seeking further subsidized federal government loans. Then, REA should seek authority to sell its loan portfolio to the private sector.

◆ *Loan asset sales.* In 1987, the Farmers Home Administration raised nearly $4 billion by selling part of its loan asset portfolio to private investors. Not only did this raise money for the federal government, but it forced FmHA to review and upgrade the management of its loan portfolios. Congress, however, has limited future USDA loan asset sales. The new President should press Congress to authorize further sales. If USDA fails to win approval of its proposal to end its direct lending programs, it should seek authority to sell newly originated loans to the private sector.

Improving the Incentives for Land Conservation

A major responsibility of USDA is conservation of the nation's soil and water resources and the management of some 200 million acres of public lands for multiple uses. It shares responsibility for public land management with the Interior Department. Interior is responsible for the national park system and special recreation and fish and wildlife areas, as well other vast public domain areas. USDA's principal responsibilities include programs and activities to cover 1) privately owned farmland, pasture, rangeland, and woodland resources generally used for agricultural and timber production; and, 2) government-owned public lands managed by the Forest Service. As is the case with Interior, USDA activities are designed to protect and improve the environment, with a special emphasis on efforts to increase the productive capacity of natural resources.

Debate over USDA's proper role in managing natural resources reflects the general intense discussion of the subject. This is reflected in the clash between two fundamentally different philosophies. One holds that natural resources are essentially static, fragile, and inherently diminishing in quality and quantity. Proponents of this view argue that regulatory and other policies should be used to protect and preserve these resources from human presence and use as much as possible. Adherents of this school of thought like to call themselves "conservationists."

The other school of thought maintains that natural resources are dynamic, resilient, often renewable, and can be enhanced and improved even as they are used and prudently managed. Proponents of this position tend to promote the use of natural resources for the general benefit of society through a balance of development and good stewardship. In most respects, they are truly conservationists, as they wish to conserve and protect resources for future generations through careful management, while allowing those resources to fulfill the needs of the current generation.

For more than 125 years, USDA generally has followed this second philosophy. The Reagan Administration has continued this and has focused much attention on soil and water conservation and public land management which encourages prudent economic use of these lands.

◆ *Soil and water conservation.* Congress has designed farm price and income support programs that, in practice, encourage farmers to cultivate marginal lands and to use agronomic practices that are neither environmentally nor economically sustainable. In both 1981 and 1985, the Reagan Administration attempted to reduce the incentives for farmers to degrade and deplete soil and water resources, and achieved a measure of success. Federal payments are disallowed for farmers who cultivate fragile lands. A "Conservation Reserve Program," meanwhile, has been created to allow farmers to rent highly erodible and other sensitive lands to the government for ten years, during which time the farmer is required to plant a permanent conserving cover crop.

While these measures represent progress, farm programs still endanger fragile lands. The farm income supports are still distributed on the basis of how many bushels, bales, or hundredweights a farmer produces. This is an almost irresistible incentive to use fragile lands and nonconserving practices. This is another reason to decouple subsidies from production requirements.

A priority for the new President should be to end the connection between farm subsidies and the amount of crop a farmer produces. This decoupling not only would make farm income more efficient, as discussed earlier, but would help improve soil and water condition. The new administration should use USDA's extensive technical capacity to encourage farmers to diversify their farming methods and try what are popularly referred to as alternative agricultural practices.

◆ *Multiple use of public lands.* The National Forest lands under the management of USDA's Forest Service are essentially "working forests," which the law provides shall be managed for economic opportunities and activities. The Reagan Administration's Forest Service has stressed multiple use, with emphasis on obtaining the greatest value possible in a realistic mix by the private sector for timber, oil, gas, and mineral development, and use for rangeland, watershed, wildlife, and recreation. The new President should continue this multiple use policy. Because many different interests seek to use public lands, the Forest Service and the administration must decide what constitutes the optimum balance of uses for these lands. Controversies abound, but most clashes stem from the two differing philosophies of natural resources—between preservationists, who really prefer to see no use and development at all, and conservationists, who believe that the resources can be both used and generally improved.

Another concern is whether the federal government should operate as owner and manager of such assets in the first place. Many argue that these lands should be owned or managed privately. They point out that even the best and most able administrators can rarely make the best decisions on the use of land without the signals and incentives provided by the marketplace. Sometimes the result is too little utilization of the land, as valuable resources go untapped. Other times the result is too much use, as short-term leases lack the property owner's incentive to protect the land from harm. The next Administration could add much to the understanding of the best ways to handle these issues by encouraging pilot projects allowing for nonfederal or nongovernmental management arrangements. To minimize political opposition, this management could be performed by environmentalist organizations, which would have a desire to protect the land but the incentive to allow valuable resources to be utilized where possible. (See Chapter 15.)

Targeting Assistance Programs to the Needy

Begun in the 1930s, federal food assistance programs were aimed originally at bolstering the farm industry and providing funds necessary to distribute surplus crops to the general population. During the 1960s, under Lyndon Johnson's "Great Society," the focus of the programs was shifted from disposal of surpluses to provision of nutritious foods to needy Americans. Today USDA's Food and Nutrition Service manages 13 separate assistance programs, many of which have overlapping goals and target groups. The cost is large by any standard. From 1980 through 1987, nearly $150 billion was spent through these programs. In 1987 alone, total spending topped $20 billion. Among the more important of these programs are:

◆ *The Food Stamp Program.* This costs more than $12 billion annually, and serves some 20 million Americans, two-thirds of whom are children, elderly, or disabled. Because of complex eligibility requirements, the food stamp program long has been plagued by large errors in payments to recipients. Management of the program has improved sharply during the Reagan years, with overpayments falling 18 percent between 1981 and 1986, saving about $700 million. Yet, total food stamp errors still cost taxpayers approximately $800 million every year.

This program lost some of its nutrition focus in 1979 with the elimination of the "purchase requirement," under which recipients had been required to spend up to one-third of their disposable income to purchase a full month's supply of food stamps. Today, a recipient pays nothing for stamps, but receives only enough of them to cover a portion of food costs. The rest of the food cost is paid out of his or her own income. This changed the nature of the program; a full month's nutrition was no longer automatically provided, but left to individual discretion. The Food Stamp Program thus now operates as a simple income supplement rather than a guarantee of adequate nutrition. In addition, stamps can be used to buy nonnutritional goods, such as ice cubes, soft drinks, and candy, further eroding the nutritional benefits the program could provide.

The new President should acknowledge that food stamps today have little to do with nutrition, or even food. He thus should propose that the program be "cashed out" so that recipients receive simple cash payments. This would save printing and administrative costs. Many states (through which stamps are distributed) would be eager to administer cash-out demonstration projects, such as the one in Washington State. Unless accompanied by broad welfare reform, however, any attempt to cash out the Food Stamp Program nationally would meet with stiff political opposition from many advocacy groups and members of Congress. Food stamp policy ought to be evaluated and reformed as part of a major welfare reform initiative. (See Welfare section of Chapter 13.)

◆ *Supplemental food programs.* One of the Department's largest programs is the Special Supplemental Food program for Women, Infants and Children (WIC). A similar program, the Commodity Supplemental Food Program, serves essentially the same group, as well as providing benefits to certain elderly Americans. The WIC program is large and has grown rapidly. Since 1980, the number of people receiving benefits from the program has increased about 80 percent, while funding has more than doubled, from $746 million to more than $1.7 billion. Unlike the Food Stamp Program, WIC is intended to serve health, as well as nutritional purposes. Eligibility is structured to give preference to those with the greatest need, such as infants and pregnant and breastfeeding women. One of every four babies born in the U.S. now receives WIC benefits. So do many other Americans with incomes below and up to 185 percent of the poverty line.

Because the WIC program is very popular politically, there is pressure to increase its funding. This, however, would only permit increased participation by less needy participants for whom the effectiveness of WIC is not clear. The new President should resist funding increases. Instead, he should reduce costs as many states are now doing. Income verification procedures should be improved and enforcement procedures toughened to crack down on abuses by retailers providing WIC goods.

◆ *Commodity distribution programs.* USDA distributes directly to the public some of the commodities it purchases from farmers. Thus food typically is donated to schools and charitable institutions. The Temporary Emergency Food Assistance Program (TEFAP), for example, at its peak in 1985 and 1986, distributed over 80 million pounds of commodities per month; over 40 percent of this was cheese. Over 5 billion pounds of surplus commodities, worth more than $5 billion, have been distributed since the program was established in 1981.

Surpluses of such commodities are declining, partially as a result of recent reductions in farm price supports, and to a lesser extent, increased exports. The surpluses were depleted most, however, by the unprecedented scope of the TEFAP giveaway. By mid–1988, some commodities, particularly cheese, had dwindled significantly. The new President should press Congress to terminate TEFAP entirely. USDA will continue to have the authority to distribute surplus commodities outside traditional commodity distribution channels if they are available and needed.

◆ *School lunch and child care programs.* The National School Lunch Program is America's largest child nutrition program, subsidizing meals for elementary through high school children. It is available to 98 percent of public school children and more than 90 percent of all school children. Other programs provide similar benefits, including the School Breakfast program, Special Milk program, Child Care Food program, and the Summer Food Service program. Together, these programs cost over $4 billion each year.

Under the School Lunch program, base-level financial assistance is provided to schools for all meals for every student buying a school lunch, no matter what the income level of the student's family. Over 50 percent of the students participating in the school lunch program come from families with incomes exceeding 185 percent of the poverty line. The federal government should not subsidize meals for children whose families·have incomes so greatly exceeding poverty income levels. The School Lunch program should be reformed to prevent this, making more federal funds available to meet the needs of children from low-income families.

--------------------◇--------------------

INITIATIVES FOR 1989

1) Reorganize USDA agencies to reduce costs. USDA includes four agencies, the Agricultural Extension Service, the Agricultural Stabilization and Conservation Service, the Soil Conservation Service, and the Farmers Home Administration, each of which has agents in almost every U.S. county. Each of these agencies operates independently, reporting to different officials in Washington. The result is wasteful duplication of effort and conflicting policies. The new President should consolidate these agencies into a single branch of the USDA to reduce policy conflict and costs.

2) Seek a multinational consensus in the new GATT round for reductions in agriculture subsidies and trade restrictions. Many countries, including the United States, currently subsidize agricultural exports and place restrictions on agricultural imports. Such policies reduce world trade in agriculture, hurting both consumers and farmers. Members of the General Agreement on Tariffs and Trade (GATT), the multilateral organization to promote free trade, recognize the need to eliminate these subsidizes and barriers and have placed agriculture on the agenda for the Uruguay Round of multilateral trade negotiations. An international agreement to guarantee free world trade in agriculture and an end to the agricultural trade wars could be one of the most important achievements of the next administration. While no agreement is likely to be finished in 1989, the new President should try to forge an international consensus on the principles of such an agreement.

3) Propose decoupling farm production requirements from subsidies. The new President should propose major changes in the current farm legislation before it expires in 1990. He should use his first year to attempt the decoupling of agricultural subsidies from production requirements.

4) End the prohibition on loan asset sales by FmHA. In 1987, the Farmers Home Administration sold nearly $3 billion in loans to private sector firms, not only raising cash for the federal government, but making the loan management process more efficient. Since then, however, Congress has barred FmHA from selling certain additional loans. This prohibition should be removed, and FmHA should make further sales of loan portfolios.

5) Abolish the Temporary Emergency Food Assistance Program (TEFAP). Under this program, created in 1981, over 5 billion pounds of surplus dairy products have been distributed to schools and charitable institutions. Its job is now complete, as federal stores of surplus dairy products have dwindled significantly. Congress must act now to ensure this temporary program does not become permanent.

9

The Department of Commerce and the U.S. Trade Representative's Office

James V. Lacy*
Task Force Chairman

The Department of Commerce is charged with promoting United States business activities and international trade and protecting patents and trademarks. Trade negotiations are handled by the U.S. Trade Representative's Office, part of the Executive Office of the President.

The Reagan years have seen a record U.S. peacetime economic expansion with low inflation and unemployment. The Administration signed Free Trade Area agreements with Israel and Canada, further opening markets to U.S. exports. It has vetoed two protectionist trade bills passed by Congress, attempts to create central planning under the guise of national industrial policy. Among other notable achievements have been efforts to promote commercial space activities by ending U.S. government subsidies to NASA for launching commercial payloads that undercut private launching companies.

Record U.S. trade deficits, however, have caused much concern among policymakers about America's competitive position in the world. The Reagan Administration has failed to define clearly what competitiveness means and to offer a detailed free-market competitiveness agenda. Instead, it has erected many new trade barriers, arguing

---

*Commenting and contributing generously to this chapter were *Mandate III* Task Force Members Mary Alexander, James Gattuso, Michael Kelley, John Misroch, and Bretton G. Sciaroni. They do not necessarily endorse all of its views and recommendations.

Task Force Deputy Chairman: Heritage Center for International Economic Growth Director Edward L. Hudgins.

BUDGET AND PERSONNEL

Secretaries

C. William Verity	1987–present
Malcolm Baldrige	1981–1987

Personnel

March 1988	36,720
April 1978	40,140
April 1968	38,511

Budget Outlays

Fiscal Year	Total (billions)
1989 Estimate	$2.6
1988 Estimate	$2.5
1987 Actual	$2.1
1986 Actual	$2.1
1985 Actual	$2.1
1980 Actual	$3.1
1970 Actual	$0.8

that they are needed to head off worse measures by Congress. These new trade restrictions have proved enormously costly to the U.S. consumer and many American businesses, and have impaired U.S. international competitiveness. It also has made it more difficult for the U.S. to argue for free trade with its allies.

The new President must articulate his vision of a competitive economy. The Commerce Department and U.S. Trade Representative's Office then must translate this vision into a policy whose success must be judged in terms of whether it increases: 1) living standards and economic growth; 2) consumer choice; and 3) job opportunities. An economy is competitive, the new President must emphasize, only if it gives entrepreneurs maximum flexibility to start up, manage, and shut down their businesses as they see fit and gives producers the freedom to distribute the factors of production in the most timely and efficient manner.

To promote greater competition and trade liberalization, the new Administration should start Free Trade Area negotiations with interested countries to open further foreign markets to U.S. goods. It should also begin to remove America's own trade barriers—to imports of steel and automobiles, for example, and to U.S. exports of natural gas and timber.

The new Administration must do more than its predecessor to protect U.S. patents. This is important because without the assurance that new discoveries and inventions will not be stolen by competitors, there would be little incentive for innovation. The computerization of the Patent Office in the Commerce Department should be completed. Laws protecting American patents against abuse by overseas businesses should be tightened. The new Administration should continue easing or abolishing regulations such as antitrust laws that place American businesses at a disadvantage in the face of foreign competition. And special emphasis should be given to commercial activities in space through a Space Enterprise Zone.

SUMMARY OF AGENCY FUNCTIONS

The U.S. Department of Commerce was established in 1903 as the Department of Commerce and Labor; it lost its labor responsibilities ten years later. Commerce is concerned with three major goals: 1) to promote domestic economic growth, productivity, and competitiveness; 2) to promote international trade and U.S. exports, while controlling the export of items that may be of strategic or military use to the enemies of the U.S.; and 3) to provide a variety of information on such topics as population, business productivity, and even the weather. Commerce also protects patents and trademarks.

The principal offices within the Department are:

◆ *The Bureau of the Census,* which is the federal government's largest statistical agency.

◆ *The Bureau of Economic Analysis,* which develops and interprets U.S. economic data.

◆ *The National Bureau of Standards,* which is concerned with the uniformity and accuracy of physical and technical measures for length, weight, temperature, time, electricity, and so forth.

◆ *The National Oceanic and Atmospheric Administration,* which establishes policy for the nation's oceanic, coastal, and atmospheric resources.

◆ *The Patent and Trademark Office,* which protects inventions, discoveries, and trademarks for the exclusive use of their creators or owners; nearly 87,000 patent applications were filed in 1987.

◆ *The Office of Economic Affairs,* which analyzes such economic developments as U.S. competitiveness in international markets, the supply and demand for strategic minerals, industrial policy, and business capital investment.

◆ *The Office of Productivity, Technology, and Innovation,* which identifies and seeks to eliminate barriers to productivity growth, provides business information to the private sector, and seeks ways to increase incentives for the commercialization of federally funded basic and applied research.

◆ *The Economic Development Administration,* which was created in 1965 to generate jobs, help protect existing jobs in economically depressed areas, and enhance the capacities of states and localities to plan and conduct economic development programs.

◆ *The Minority Business Development Agency,* which seeks to promote and expand the activities of minority businesses.

◆ *The International Trade Administration,* which promotes exports, administers trade adjustment assistance, collects and analyzes statistical data on international trade, and monitors international trade agreements.

◆ *The United States Travel and Tourism Administration,* which promotes travel to the U.S. by foreign tourists, producing promotional literature and information.

The Office of the U.S. Trade Representative (USTR) is a special unit in the Executive Office of the President. Established in 1963 as the Office of the Special Representative for Trade Negotiations, USTR is responsible for negotiating trade agreements with other countries. The chief U.S. Trade Representative has the title of Ambassador, and is a Cabinet-rank official appointed by the President with the advice and consent of the Senate. With only about 140 employees and a budget of $13.5 million, USTR typically relies on other departments to provide basic economic information.

————————————◇————————————

INSTITUTIONAL CONSTRAINTS

Free trade is opposed by interest groups with incentives to keep America's market closed to imports. Among the most powerful are the leaders of organized labor. To protect their power, union leaders seek to preserve jobs or protect high wages in inefficient U.S. industries, no matter what the ultimate costs to the American economy. Traditional industries such as autos, steel, and textiles also have a vested interest in trade protectionism. If these industries can keep out foreign competitors, they need not restructure to make themselves more competitive.

Officials in states with high union membership in traditional industries tend to back protectionist trade policies. This allows politicians to claim that they are truly compassionate and concerned about jobs. This ignores, of course, the well-recognized fact that even in regions with traditional industries, protectionism simply slows economic adjustment, preventing the creation of more productive industries and exacerbating the unemployment and displacement often associated with economic restructuring.

The nature of the Commerce Department makes it particularly susceptible to protectionist lobbying. The reason: Commerce not only is in charge of promoting trade, but also of monitoring and enforcing trade restrictions. While protectionists lobby incessantly and aggressively, free trade advocates seldom do. For one thing, the biggest beneficiary of free trade is the American consumer—a group too huge and diffuse to be an effective lobby on an issue as specialized as trade. For another, the U.S. firms that benefit from open markets are often young and dynamic, with little time for political lobbying. They tend to concentrate their efforts on developing their businesses and thus not to counter the protectionist pressure exerted on politicians by many older industries.

————————◇————————

THE REAGAN ADMINISTRATION RECORD

When Ronald Reagan took office, the U.S. was in very shaky economic condition and heading for a recession. Inflation in 1980 was 13.5 percent and unemployment was 7 percent. Interest rates averaged a towering 15 percent, that by mid–1981 had soared to 20 percent. In 1980 America exported $224 billion in merchandise and imported $250 billion. The recession, which began in 1979, paused for about a year and then resurged in late 1981, lasting through 1982. This was a period of painful, but necessary, economic restructuring. The basis for sustained economic growth, meanwhile, had been set by the Reagan 1981 tax cut. This has allowed businesses to keep more of their earnings, which has made available more funds for investment. Consumers have been allowed to keep more of their income, which means more money for purchases. In addition, the Reagan Administration began to ease federal business and economic regulations.

The result: the longest peacetime economic expansion in U.S. history, more than six years. By mid–1988, some 17 million net new jobs had been added to the economy since Reagan took office. By contrast most European countries continue to suffer double-digit unemployment and have created virtually no new jobs over the last decade.

During the Reagan years, the issues of the trade deficit and America's competitive position in the world have been major concerns of policymakers. Trade deficits have been seen as indicators that America is becoming noncompetitive and "deindustrialized." Some have argued that manufacturing jobs in such industries as automobiles, steel, and textiles are moving to other countries, especially to Japan. Ostensibly, this was perceived to be the result of two factors: 1) American industries have become less productive; and 2) other countries unfairly have kept their markets closed to U.S. goods and have provided subsidies for their own industries.

These appraisals are largely imaginary. Though the U.S. economy had faltered badly in the late 1970s, from 1981 through 1987 manufacturing productivity surged ahead at a healthy 4.2 percent annually. Manufacturing output grew 38.5 percent between 1983 and 1987. Manufacturing as a percentage of Gross National Product (GNP) has remained constant since 1960 at around 20 percent. The U.S. thus is hardly becoming deindustrialized. The actual number of manufacturing jobs has remained about the same for the last several decades. What has declined is merely manufacturing jobs as a share of the work force, slipping from 25 percent in 1960 to around 16 percent today. This indicates that the manufacturing sector has grown more efficient, producing the same proportion of the GNP with a smaller percentage of the workforce.

The Commerce Department and U.S. Trade Representative's Office can take credit for a number of trade policy achievements. Most important have been the Free Trade Area (FTA) agreements with Israel and Canada. By these, the U.S. and each partner country agree to drop all tariffs and many nontariff barriers to each other's goods and services. Another market opening trade action has been the initiation of a new round of negotiations under the General Agreement on Tariffs and Trade (GATT). The GATT is the international system of trade rules that have helped liberalize world trade since 1947. The current negotiations are known as the Uruguay Round because they began with a meeting in Montevideo, Uruguay. These talks seek to reduce further tariffs between countries and address such nontariff barriers as agricultural subsidies, trade in services, and trade in high technology products. This will open markets in sectors in which the U.S. is especially efficient and stands to increase sales considerably.

In a series of what experts call market-opening sector-specific (MOSS) negotiations, the Reagan Administration has forced Japan, South Korea, and Western Europe to open their markets a bit wider to various U.S. goods. Example: Tokyo agreed to reduce barriers to imports of American beef and to phase out entirely quota limits on certain U.S. citrus fruits. Example: Taipei has liberalized its market for alcohol and tobacco imports.

The Reagan Administration also successfully countered liberal proposals for national industrial planning by which the federal government would give some sectors and industries subsidies, tax breaks, and loan guarantees. Rather than the free market picking economic winners and losers, advocates of what is called National Industrial Policy want the federal government to become partners with big business and labor unions to guide the economy. In Western Europe such partnerships have led to high unemployment and hindered development of new industries.

The Reagan Administration countered national industrial policy by focusing attention on regulatory and tax policies that harm America's competitiveness. The President's Commission on Industrial Competitiveness, chaired by Hewlett-Packard president John Young, helped spark a national discussion on how to increase economic productivity. The late Malcolm Baldrige, Commerce Secretary from 1981 to 1987, led the fight for reform of America's antitrust laws. With some 70 percent of U.S. manufactured goods subject to direct foreign competition, it makes little sense to prohibit American businesses from cooperating with one another. The Export Trading Company Act of 1982 allows businesses to work together when seeking to market their goods overseas. The Administration also successfully established a process by which exemptions from antitrust laws can be secured by businesses wishing to cooperate in joint research and development projects. Since such cooperation is common among America's foreign competitors, this exemption from federal government prosecution under antitrust laws puts America on a more even international footing.

The Reagan Administration has pursued sensible policies for outer space, particularly following the January 1986 *Challenger* shuttle disaster. The Administration ended the massive subsidies for businesses to send cargo into space on the shuttles. As a result, private launch companies now have a fair chance to compete for such cargo. The National Aeronautics and Space Administration (NASA), moreover, was ordered to stop competing with private businesses for commercial cargos. The result has been increased activities by private space-related businesses and plans for the expanded commercial use of space.

Despite its battle for free trade, the Reagan Administration has made a number of serious retreats. As a means of blunting Congress's call for trade protectionism, for example, the Administration has erected or accepted new trade barriers. Current import quota restrictions on automobiles alone add about $5 billion annually to what Americans pay for cars. President Reagan vetoed a protectionist omnibus trade bill in 1988, basing his opposition rather narrowly on the inclusion of a requirement for advance notification by business of plant closings and layoffs. When Congress removed this provision, which it passed separately, Reagan signed the protectionist bill.

In its final years, the Reagan Administration has failed to articulate clearly its competitiveness policy and push it in Congress. In part this failure has been due to the lack of a clear definition of competitiveness. The Administration also has failed to carry through on its plan to abolish the Small Business Administration (SBA). This independent agency, which ostensibly provides loans and loan guarantees to small enterprises, aids only two-tenths of one percent of America's small businesses, most of which are retail outlets where market entry is relatively easy.

———————————◇———————————

THE NEXT FOUR YEARS

The new President inherits a healthy economy, with high job creation, rising productivity, and low inflation. To sustain this, the Commerce Department and the U.S. Trade Representative's Office must pursue policies to increase U.S. competitiveness. These policies should define the goals of competitiveness as:

◆ *Increased national standards of living and economic growth.* In a competitive economy, citizens are able to acquire more goods and services for their dollars. After buying such basics as food, clothing, and shelter, they have more money for consumption of additional goods and services.

◆ *Increased consumer choice.* A competitive economy makes a wide choice of goods and services available. The quality and durability of goods increase to meet consumer demands. New products, like microwave ovens or home computers, quickly become available at prices that increasing numbers of consumers can afford. And new services, add to consumer choices and the quality of life. The final judgment on whether a product is competitive is made by the consumer, who votes with his or her dollars in the marketplace. The competition between countries therefore might be judged in terms of which society makes the widest variety of affordable goods available to consumers.

◆ *Expanded opportunities for productive employment.* A competitive economy offers more job opportunities and an increasing share of jobs at increasing real wage levels. It is because U.S. firms generally employ labor more efficiently than businesses in other countries that they can pay high wages, allowing workers to share the prosperity. In a competitive economy, new job creation is high. Additional population thus is an asset, not a burden. And, the quality of jobs improves. Example: more efficient production techniques mean fewer workers on dangerous, dirty assembly lines.

By defining these as the goals of economic policy designed to spur U.S. competitiveness, the new President will expose flaws in other policies. Trade protectionism, for example, limits consumer choice and requires a larger proportion of income to be spent on the protected goods, thus lowering standards of living. Trade protectionism also "saves" few, if any jobs, for it eliminates jobs in other sectors and raises consumer costs. It is estimated that a 1986 bill to restrict textile and apparel imports would have "saved" each $15,000 salaried job at a cost of $4 million each. Reagan vetoed the bill.

America's ability to sell more overseas and purchase more from other countries depends on increased U.S. productivity. More efficient production techniques in businesses can be achieved through new technology, better methods of industrial organization, cheaper sources of capital goods, or more efficient labor. Through increased productivity, standards of living rise, consumer choice increases, and more opportunities for well-paying jobs become available.

At any given time, some foreign industries may be growing more competitive than their U.S. counterparts. For the U.S. as a nation to be competitive, however, it is not required that all U.S. companies remain competitive in all areas. It does mean that U.S. businesses and entrepreneurs must be able to take advantage of opportunities offered by economic developments in other countries to move into higher-valued product lines or to use cheaper foreign goods to their own advantage. Example: if foreigners produce less costly computer chips, American computer systems manufacturers can use these chips to produce less costly computer systems. If foreigners produce less costly computers, American firms can supply the software packages that make owning a computer worthwhile.

To be competitive with other countries, the American system must retain the maximum economic flexibility to permit the factors of production to be redistributed by entrepreneurs quickly and efficiently from less-valued to higher-valued economic functions. Success in international economic competition means staying on the cutting edge of economic progress. Only a flexible system, free of unnecessary government interference, can remain productive and competitive.

The new President must articulate clearly this vision of an economy with ever-increasing living standards, consumer choices, and employment opportunities, based on increased productivity that results from economic flexibility and entrepreneurial activity.

Establishing Free Trade Areas

Since the end of World War II, international trade has been liberalized somewhat by various rounds of the General Agreement on Tariffs and Trade (GATT) negotiations. While this has yielded important results, it is nevertheless slow and requires agreement by the more than 90 members. If two countries wish complete free trade between one another, they need not endure the slow GATT process, but instead can establish a Free Trade Area. Under such an arrangement, both countries remove all tariffs and many nontariff barriers.

The Free Trade Areas (FTAs) negotiated by the U.S. with Israel in 1985 and Canada in 1988 are pioneering new means of opening markets for U.S. goods. FTAs also encourage countries not party to the agreements to seek trade liberalization. If, for example, the U.S. and Japan were both selling a certain product in a country with which the U.S. had an FTA, the Japanese products would be subject to tariffs while the American goods would not. This would place the Japanese goods at a disadvantage, creating an incentive for Japan to seek better trade terms. There are a number of countries, including the Republic of China on Taiwan, Singapore, and Thailand that want FTAs with the U.S. The new Administration should initiate negotiations with any country seeking complete free trade with the U.S.

USTR officials say privately that they do not have the staff to negotiate more than one FTA at a time. If market-opening FTAs are to be extended to many other countries, more staff may be required, especially for the extensive background work necessary for successful negotiations. The U.S. Trade Representative should determine the manpower needs necessary to negotiate new FTAs and should seek new personnel or borrow personnel from other departments, something the USTR often does.

Removing Import Restrictions

U.S. restrictions on imports, such as quotas on automobiles and steel, cost the American consumer dearly and add to the costs of American businesses using imported raw materials and components. Such restrictions undercut U.S. attempts to open other markets and expose as hypocritical American claims that it favors free and fair trade. The new Administration should act to remove such restrictions.

Since the steel quotas set up by the Reagan Administration are due to expire in September 1989, a first act by the new President should be to declare these restrictions on steel imports will end on schedule. The new President then should declare that quotas neither help the U.S. economy nor force overseas markets to open to U.S. goods. As such, the new President should pledge not to use quotas or cartels as trade measures.

The USTR must better inform policymakers of the true costs of trade protectionism to the U.S. economy. Currently, the USTR office is required by Congress to issue an annual report on foreign trade barriers to U.S. goods. This report provides valuable information on the difficulties faced by U.S. businesses in exporting their goods and on the progress made by the U.S. in dealing with these problems. The trouble is that the report gives a one-sided view of the international trade situation. It fails to examine U.S. barriers to foreign goods.

To remedy this, the USTR should evaluate the nature and costs of U.S. protectionism just as it evaluates the costs of other nations' protectionism. The costs of U.S. tariffs and estimates or the costs of U.S. quotas to U.S. consumers should be listed. Nontariff barriers such as cargo preference rules that require many American exporters to use expensive American ships or domestic content provisions for public construction projects should be exposed.

Removing Export Restrictions

The new Administration should remove restrictions on America's own exports. Current law restricts the export of U.S. natural gas, oil, and timber harvested on federal lands. Natural gas is in such abundance in Alaska that it is pumped back into the oil wells from which it comes. This natural gas could be liquefied and perhaps $5 billion sold annually to Japan. Timber harvested on U.S. public lands also would find markets in Japan. Further, the Jones Act of 1920 requires that half of America's agricultural exports shipped overseas be carried on U.S. vessels. The very high labor and financing cost of these vessels, compared to that of foreign ships, adds to the price of U.S. exports and depresses sales. Such self-imposed restrictions should be removed.

Protecting Property Rights

At the basis of American liberty and the free market system is the right to private property. Protection of property is one of the government's fundamental tasks. Of special economic importance is the right to one's own ideas and the ability to reap the gains of one's inventions. The protection of patents is specifically listed in the U.S. Constitution as one of the powers of Congress. The Commerce Department has the duty of enforcing patent and other intellectual property laws. The incentive provided by these intellectual property rights is crucial to America's continuing industrial and technological progress.

Acquiring patent approval, however, is often very time consuming. To quicken the process, the Reagan Administration ordered the old file-card type of registration system replaced by a computerized system. But this important reform has bogged down. The new Secretary of Commerce personally should supervise installation of the computerized patent system as soon as possible.

The protection of U.S. patent rights against violations by foreigners is a primary function of the International Trade Commission (ITC). A loophole in America's trade laws allows foreigners to use patented U.S. production processes without the approval of the American patentholder; the foreigner then can sell the goods manufactured with this process in the U.S. This loophole should be closed and American process patents afforded the same protection against theft by foreigners as they have against domestic abuse. Section 337 of the 1974 Trade Act should be amended to allow the ITC to act against such abuses.

The Freedom of Information Act (FOIA) of 1974 was meant to ensure Americans access to information about themselves that the federal government might have. As it has turned out, however, the vast majority of those obtaining information under FOIA are not private citizens or even public interest groups or journalists. They are frequently businesses, including many foreign companies, and even communist countries, seeking the trade secrets of U.S. companies. Because of the Act, American businesses dealing with the federal government or complying with federal regulations often are required to turn over proprietary information to a federal agency. This information may become available under the FOIA. This allows foreign companies, often in countries where enforcement of patent rights is lax, to acquire U.S. business secrets, then counterfeit U.S. products and sell them cheaply around the world. This, of course, cuts the demand for the genuine U.S.-made goods. And it penalizes U.S. firms that spend large sums on research and development.

To reduce such theft and counterfeiting, without undermining the intent of the FOIA, Congress could amend the Act to restrict the types of information that government agencies can demand from firms to satisfy regulatory functions, restrict the information that government agencies can release in order to protect trade secrets, and give firms providing information the legal right to challenge the release of information by the government.

Encouraging Commercial Use of Space

Commercial uses of space literally are the next frontier of American industry. Reagan Administration deregulation and privatization efforts have spurred increased private-sector space-related activities. Further efforts by the new President are necessary if the U.S. is to lead in space.

As with any pioneering endeavor, space business is extremely risky. To exploit fully the economic potential of space, business must be able to operate within a recognizable, flexible regulatory environment conducive to business. Space-related businesses by their nature will often operate in several states. Command-and-control, launching, and tracking facilities are likely to be spread throughout the country as in space itself. Jurisdictional questions concerning taxation and regulation of this new sector are likely to arise, creating economic uncertainty. Further uncertainty is caused by antitrust laws. The extraordinary degree of cooperation probably needed between private firms to meet the costly and risky challenges of commercial space activities could lead to prosecution under federal antitrust laws.

Many of the problems involving commercial space activities can be dealt with if the new Administration establishes a Space Enterprise Zone. Such a zone would be a designated volume of space between 50 and 50,000 miles above earth, an area referred to as "near earth orbit." This is the region in which most satellites and commercial space stations would orbit. Businesses with operations in this zone would be exempt from antitrust laws and other regulations that could deter commercial space activities. Further, the federal government could develop a commercial code to clarify questions concerning interstate commercial space activities.

Another potential barrier to space commercial activities is the jurisdictional disputes within the federal government itself. The National Aeronautics and Space Administration (NASA) fought the Commerce Department's attempts to strip NASA of its subsidies and commercial space activities. NASA still is dragging its feet on carrying out the free-market reforms ordered by the Reagan White House. The Department of Transportation, which was recently assigned the job of licensing private space launches, also has begun interfering in commercial space issues.

The potential for continued federal bureaucratic infighting and red tape is clear. To prevent this, the new President should order a restructuring of NASA that stops it from delaying commercial space development. The more the private sector launches and operates in space, the more NASA's budget can be used for such traditional NASA projects as basic research into biological and environmental problems of living in space and probes to the planets.

Several international barriers impede America's commercial space efforts. Intelsat Corporation, for example, is governed by a 1973 treaty between 114 governments to maintain an international satellite telecommunications network. Subscriber governments are shareholders in Intelsat and agree to apply the regulations established by the agreement to their own agencies or businesses engaged in such activities. One provision of this agreement, Article 14D, requires private firms wishing to engage in international satellite telecommunications to consult with Intelsat to assure that the private competitor does not cause substantial economic harm to Intelsat. This is an anticompetitive, government-enforced cartel arrangement. Already it has prevented American businesses from entering the international satellite telecommunications field.

If space enterprise is to be opened fully to the private sector, such monopoly arrangements must be abandoned. As the largest shareholder in Intelsat, the U.S. government should begin negotiations immediately to remove this market closing clause from the Intelsat agreement.

Reorganizing the International Trade Administration

The International Trade Administration and the Office of Trade Administration perform functions important to American business, including the collection of national economic and business statistics, staging international trade shows, providing information on business and investment concerning foreign countries, and maintaining offices across the U.S. to help ease the political problems of international business transactions. Yet there is much overlap and waste in these sections of the Commerce Department.

The U.S. Foreign and Commercial Service (USFCS) maintains staff in all major U.S. embassies worldwide and in 47 states, with computer links to help U.S. businesses and overseas customers and partners to do business and deal with one another's political and economic systems. Yet USFCS maintains a large export promotion staff in Washington. Export promotion is the primary mission of the Office of Trade Development (OTD). This Office also is responsible for putting on trade shows, a function that USFCS also performs on occasions. Interagency turf battles consume time and limited resources that should go to aiding U.S. businesses. There is also too much bureaucracy in Trade Development. It maintains eleven deputy assistant secretaries, more than most Pentagon offices. This creates a layer of bureaucracy that makes the operation of Commerce less efficient.

The International Economic Policy office is in charge of collecting information on business and economic conditions in other countries, doing general analytical work on trade issues, and making trade policy recommendations. Yet the Deputy Assistant Secretary for Trade Information and Analysis, who accumulates American trade statistics, is found in the Office of Trade Development.

The new Secretary of Commerce should issue clear guidelines restricting the U.S. Foreign and Commercial Services, International Trade Policy, and Office of Trade Development to their designated functions. If need be, these units should be reorganized to end duplication of functions. Perhaps 100 positions could be cut in this manner. Further, the new Secretary should examine the possibility of eliminating a layer of the Commerce Department by reducing the number of deputy assistant secretaries when office directors can do the job just as well.

Eliminating Unnecessary Offices

Over the years, a number of offices and programs were established in Commerce that now are of little use to the American economy. To streamline the Department and free up resources for more useful programs, the useless operations should be eliminated.

The Economic Development Administration (EDA), for example, is a Great Society agency meant to promote economic growth in depressed areas of the country through loans and loan guarantees to state governments and businesses. In large part, the jobs created by EDA have been public-sector make-work jobs or jobs for institutes receiving EDA grants. There is little evidence that the economy in general has been helped by this agency. The Reagan Administration has reduced EDA's functions significantly. The new President should abolish EDA altogether.

The U.S. Travel and Tourism Administration (USTTA), which distributes tourist information in a number of Western industrialized countries, also should be eliminated. It duplicates the efforts of airlines, tourist agencies, and the 50 American states, which promote tourism very efficiently. It has had little measurable effect on promoting tourism to America. The $5 million spent on USTTA wastes taxpayer money.

The Trade Adjustment Assistance program, which is under the International Trade Administration, spends $25 million a year, purportedly to help regions and industries affected by imports. Since there is little indication that trade adjustment assistance actually helps the adjustment process, this program should be eliminated.

The Small Business Administration (SBA), an independent agency outside of the Commerce Department, provides loans and loan guarantees to small businesses that initially cannot secure loans from regular banks. Yet the market has done an excellent job of providing capital for such businesses. Only two-tenths of one percent of small businesses receive SBA assistance. SBA, at an administrative cost of $1.5 billion per year, is a pork-barrel program that the new President should abolish.

INITIATIVES FOR 1989

1) Seek fast track negotiating authority from Congress for future Free Trade Areas (FTAs). Trade agreements are painstakingly negotiated over years. And they must be renegotiated if the legislature of just one signatory country amends the agreement. To prevent a long process of renegotiation, Congress usually is asked to vote simply for or against a trade pact without adding amendments. To speed the negotiation of new Free Trade Areas, the new President should ask Congress for fast track negotiating authority so that it can negotiate FTAs and have Congress vote them up or down without amendments.

2) Seek additional staff for the U.S. Trade Representative's Office to negotiate more FTAs. The USTR needs more staff to negotiate Free Trade Area agreements. The new Administration should shift personnel from other federal agencies to do important background work for future FTAs or, if necessary, ask Congress to authorize additional staff.

3) Require the U.S. Trade Representative's Office to issue annual reports on U.S. trade restrictions. The current USTR report on overseas trade barriers to American products does not provide the full international trade picture. To do so and to provide data for fully informed debate on trade issues, USTR should include a review of the cost to Americans of U.S. restrictions on trade, including the costs of tariffs and quota restrictions.

4) Ease U.S. import restrictions. American consumers and businesses suffer from U.S. trade barriers to such imports as automobiles, sugar, and textiles. These restrictions on foreign trade in the long run harm America's competitiveness by reducing the incentive to be more efficient. Moreover, these U.S. barriers make it difficult for Washington to call for the removal of other countries' trade barriers. The new President thus should oppose protectionism and support legislation to liberalize America's market.

5) Seek repeal of export restrictions on U.S. products that are not related to national security. In light of the high U.S. trade deficits, the U.S. should not be restricting or prohibiting the export of such goods as timber or natural gas. The new President should seek repeal of these bans.

6) Protect process patents against theft by foreigners. Patented production processes are protected under American law against theft within the U.S., but not against foreign theft. Process patents should be afforded protection against all abuses with new legislation. When a foreigner uses a stolen U.S. patent to produce counterfeit goods, the act of theft itself should allow action against the thief. The extent of injury should not determine guilt or innocence. The law should be changed to protect American patents without qualification.

7) Amend the Freedom of Information Act to protect U.S. business trade secrets. The Freedom of Information Act allows U.S. citizens and foreigners to obtain certain information from government records.

Since several federal agencies, including the Environmental Protection Agency, require U.S. firms to supply proprietary information, foreign firms, communist governments, and U.S. companies can exploit the Freedom of Information Act to learn the trade secrets of American businesses. The Act should be amended to prevent such abuse.

8) Create a Space Enterprise Zone. Regulations such as antitrust laws currently hinder the commercial development of space by U.S. firms. The new Administration should propose legislation to establish a Space Enterprise Zone, in which various regulations would be suspended. This would encourage businesses to cooperate and take the risks necessary for commercial space activities. Jurisdictional questions between states that would complicate space-related business, such as tax laws and business regulations, would need to be resolved in the legislation.

9) Reorganize NASA so that it will focus on basic research and not hinder private commercial space activities. NASA has attempted to slow the private commercial use of space. Recent reforms bar NASA from commercial activities and allow it to concentrate on basic research. Yet the agency still has the same organization geared to the tasks of 25 years ago, when private commercial space activities were not envisioned and when NASA, for example, launched all communications and weather satellites. The new President should propose to reorganize NASA to allow it to spend most of its funds on basic research and development.

10) Negotiate an amendment to the 1973 Intelsat Agreement to allow free market entry for private companies providing international satellite telecommunication services. Intelsat is a corporation owned by several governments, which operates an international satellite network and regulates all international commercial satellite communications. In practice, the corporation is an American-supported cartel that hinders private entry into space telecommunications. The U.S. should negotiate an end to this monopoly.

11) Seek to abolish the U.S. Travel and Tourism Administration. Airlines, travel agents, and the states themselves already provide tourist services. This is not a job for the federal government. The new Administration should close down this redundant agency.

12) Seek to abolish Trade Adjustment Assistance. Trade Adjustment Assistance provides financial help to industries adversely affected by imports. The purpose of the program is to help firms to ease the transition from one industry to another. But there is little evidence to suggest that the program has any significant impact. And there seems to be little reason to single out those allegedly displaced by imports for special assistance above that received by other unemployed persons.

13) Seek to abolish the Economic Development Administration (EDA). The Economic Development Administration distributes funds for local public works projects. It duplicates other programs within the federal government and it is a federal intrusion into an area of policy that should be reserved to the states. This agency should be abolished.

14) Seek to abolish the Small Business Administration (SBA). The SBA provides loans and loan guarantees to small businesses that cannot secure loans from a bank. Yet it has virtually no impact on the rate of small business formation in America. The new Administration would help small businesses far more by abolishing the SBA and using the saved funds to help reduce taxes on small firms.

10

The Department of Education

C. Ronald Kimberling*
Task Force Chairman

The state of education in the United States is depressing. This first-rate nation cannot compete with third-rate countries in standard indicators of academic achievement. This is not to say that the Reagan Administration has done nothing to remedy this dismal situation. Indeed it has—it stemmed what the National Commission on Excellence in Education called the "rising tide of mediocrity" long enough to allow the nation to look at itself and conclude that something must be done.

It is not, however, the federal government that can reform education fundamentally. Real reform comes from the people. The countless Great Society and 1970s-style education laws and programs increased federal authority and concomitantly decreased local control over education. Teachers' unions became overly strong and began to advocate teachers' rights over what is good for the student. Suddenly, inner cities and suburbs alike were faced with authoritarian teachers and administrators who denied parents their proper role in education.

During the time the Department of Education has been in existence, countless reports have been issued from within and without confirming these facts. The areas of the country that have attempted to bring the community back into the decision-making role have yielded real achievement. Even areas like New York City's Spanish Harlem are demonstrating progress, despite the government's intrusion.

Though the nation's pupils, teachers, and schools do not need a federal Department of Education and surely would benefit from its abolition, the Department nonetheless exists. The new President must

---

*Commenting and contributing generously to this chapter were *Mandate III* Task Force Members Patrick Fagan, Joseph McHugh, and Carol Pendas Whitten. They do not necessarily endorse all of its views and recommendations.

Task Force Deputy Chairman: Heritage *Education Update* Editor Jeanne Allen.

BUDGET AND PERSONNEL

Secretaries

Lauro F. Cavazos	1988–present
William J. Bennett	1985–1988
Terrel H. Bell	1981–1985

Personnel

March 1988	4,789
May 1980	7,385
April 1970	N.A.

Budget Outlays

Fiscal Year	Total (billions)
1989 Estimate	$22.7
1988 Estimate	$18.8
1987 Actual	$16.8
1986 Actual	$17.7
1985 Actual	$16.7
1980 Actual	$14.8
1970 Actual	$ 4.7

---

accept this fact and then instruct his Secretary of Education to use the Department's bully pulpit to bring to light problems and solutions for education reform. The Secretary thus should continue to utilize the Department's research and statistics- gathering capabilities to provide the public with accurate information by which to judge and act upon educational improvements.

The new President should continue to push for reform of the growing education budget. He should seek such reforms as restructuring vocational training programs and ensuring that federal support for postsecondary education goes only to the needy and academically deserving. A top education priority should be to halt federal government encroachment upon communities. Removing many of the spending requirements of Chapters 1 and 2 elementary/secondary education funds, for instance, would allow communities to implement programs responsive to their students' needs without government oversight.

Because of the cumbersome technical aspects of program administration, committed Department appointees tend to get bogged down by routine matters, leaving themselves too little time to push for real reforms. While ineffective programs can be abolished, and others improved, it takes a consistent, concerted effort and it takes the already growing support of the American people.

––––––––––––––––◇––––––––––––––––

SUMMARY OF AGENCY FUNCTIONS

The Department of Education was created in 1979 and drew together into one Cabinet-level department programs that had been housed within what was then the Department of Health, Education and Welfare and is now the Department of Health and Human Services. The Department of Education's principal program offices, in order of size and budget, are:

◆ *The Office of Postsecondary Education (OPE),* which administers assistance to postsecondary students and institutions. OPE has authority over nearly half of the Department's budget.

◆ *The Office of Elementary and Secondary Education (OESE),* which provides federal assistance to local and state agencies for schooling younger children.

◆ *The Office of Special Education and Rehabilitative Services (OSERS),* which deals exclusively with education of the handicapped and adult rehabilitation. A small portion of its budget is allocated for research projects.

◆ *The Office of Vocational and Adult Education (OVAE),* which provides states with funding and technical assistance to train youth and adults for work and to help adults obtain a high school diploma or its equivalent.

◆ *The Office of Bilingual Education and Minority Language Affairs (OBEMLA),* which assists local school districts in improving the English-speaking ability of Limited English Proficient students through support of bilingual education programs.

Among the Department of Education's most important administrative support offices are the Office for Civil Rights (OCR) and the Office of Educational Research and Improvement (OERI), which includes the National Center for Education Statistics.

––––––––––––––––◇––––––––––––––––

INSTITUTIONAL CONSTRAINTS

The new Administration's ability to shape national education policy will be limited by a number of factors. Washington, for example, wields a relatively small stick in making policy because education spending remains almost exclusively the responsibility of state and local governments and the private sector. Of the $328 billion the U.S. will spend on education in the 1988–1989 school year, less than 7 percent will come from the federal government. Not only do states control much of what happens in the schools within their borders, but also they are a strong force in muscling Washington for continued support. The states and localities make themselves heard through groups like the National League of Cities and the National Council of State Legislatures.

Washington also is lobbied intensively by "private" groups with an interest in specific federal policy, such as the National Education Association (NEA), the National Association of State Universities and Land Grant Colleges, and the Council of Chief State School Officers, for new programs or for more money to expand the old ones. Then there are the National School Boards Association (NSBA) and the National Association of Student Financial Aid Administrators (NAS-FAA), which strenuously oppose any budget cuts or reforms in education. About the only constituents not heard in Washington are parents.

B ecause the Reagan Administration has resisted them, the lobbyists have bypassed the Education Department and have concentrated on the liberal-dominated congressional committees, particularly during the budget process. The result: year after year, even flawed education programs have been reauthorized and expanded.

Education programs fall under the jurisdiction of the House Education and Labor Committee, chaired by Augustus Hawkins (D-Ca) and the Senate Labor and Human Resources Committee, chaired by Edward Kennedy (D-Ma). Both committees are dominated by those determined to expand federal programs. Responsive to or allied with professional education groups and associations, these committees effectively have run the Department's programs and set its policies. They refuse to give serious consideration to proposals, such as education vouchers and tuition tax credits, opposed by their clients. Reagan Administration appearances before congressional committees, requiring hours of preparation and staff time, barely are taken into account by the committee members and their staffs when drafting education budgets or program legislation.

The courts too have made it increasingly difficult for the executive and legislative branches to grapple with problems of education. Federal court decisions, for instance, prevent local authorities from providing appropriate education for bilingual children, those with physical or mental impairments, and racial minorities in "at risk" groups. Communities with such sensitive problems as racial tension or an influx of non-English speaking immigrants are powerless in addressing them because the courts have determined policy and centralized policy-making at the federal level for educating children of differing backgrounds and abilities. The root of this federal court intrusion is the 1947 *Everson* decision, in which the Supreme Court supported federal over local control of schools. Though the *Everson* case mainly concerned religion's place in the classroom, the decision in effect set precedent for a string of decisions giving courts a right to meddle in education, sometimes by taking over the authority of the executive branch. Courts have run school systems (Boston), allocated monies from the Secretary's discretionary fund (Chicago), and even determined that teachers do not have a right to defend themselves against violence (Newark).

As policy has been increasingly determined by the courts, the Administration and Congress have been forbidden to deal with a growing number of issues. Civil rights rulings in cases of treatment of the handicapped, racial minorities, and even learning-disabled students and those lacking English proficiency have restricted the ability of communities to address these issues. Instead, courts have imposed their own views of appropriate solutions with little regard to cost. Nonetheless, organizations representing minority interests still are frustrated by the government's inability to remedy educational ills. And parents and teachers find themselves on opposite sides over what is permissible, resulting in distrust and, consequently, a severely weakened parent-teacher partnership.

Courts also prevent Washington from giving more control of education to the states by requiring the federal government to monitor all civil rights compliance. This oversight wrests control away from the states making local policy inferior to federal policy.

Effective policy-making is impeded too by the organizational structure and bureaucratic traditions inherited by the Department of Education from the old Department of Health, Education, and Welfare (HEW). HEW was a centrally managed bureaucratic behemoth; when the Department of Education was established, its organizational structure was modeled on HEW's centralized bureaucracy. For example, the Department's Office of Planning, Budget, and Evaluation has exercised considerable control over program policy. Mid-level careerists often are involved in budget policy formulation while presidential appointees are kept in the dark. The result: Reagan-appointed Assistant Secretaries of Education have been able to make little policy and have found themselves relegated to being operations managers.

THE REAGAN ADMINISTRATION RECORD

A t the beginning of 1981, American education was suffering from years of loosely designed curricula, which had eroded student performance in basic subjects. Scholastic Aptitude Test (SAT) scores had been slipping since the mid–1960s. American students were falling behind their European and Japanese counterparts in international tests, while minorities were being bused long distances to supposedly superior schools that featured teachers on strike and "dumbed-down" textbooks. The result: the first generation in America to receive an education inferior to that received by their parents. Meanwhile, the National Education Association was celebrating its political victory in forcing the creation of a Cabinet-level Department of Education.

The Reagan Administration has scored notable education victories. Most important has been the grass-roots education reform movement stimulated by the Department. The National Commission on Excellence in Education's April 1983 report, *A Nation at Risk*, captured the average American's dismay and frustration with the direction of American education. It set the compass for the state and local reforms that have followed. This populist reform movement, perhaps more than anything else, has helped reverse the test score decline and has reinvigorated the curriculum.

The *A Nation at Risk* report was but one of several initiatives that demonstrated how effective the Department can be in stimulating local and private action by means other than direct funding or control. The secret here, of course, has been the Department's exploitation of its "bully pulpit." So effectively did Secretary Bennett use it to make the case for traditional education values and practices that liberals almost certainly began to regret their having created the Department. Under Bennett, the Department began publishing its "What Works" series of books, providing practical information to educators on such topics as ridding schools of drugs and highlighting good teaching techniques. Bennett delighted in shaking up the educational establishment by attacking sacred cows like soaring college tuition and sparking debate on his education reforms.

Spurred by Bennett, parents and reform-minded school officials were encouraged to demand teacher accountability and reforms to improve teaching standards. Outside Washington, at least, Bennett forced the education lobbies onto the defensive. Behind the scenes, Bennett encouraged Chester Finn, Assistant Secretary for Educational

Research and Improvement, to repair the nation's statistical database for education, which had become dangerously unreliable in some areas. Inside Washington, Bennett accomplished little to make reforms part of the legislative framework. He preferred the bully pulpit to negotiating on the Hill.

The Reagan Administration's major legislative victory in education was achieved in the first few months of 1981, when more than two dozen categorical grant programs in elementary and secondary education were consolidated into the new Chapter 2 block grant. A block grant is a preferable means to distribute federal funds because it gives states and localities flexibility in using the money. Categorical grants require the recipient to spend the federal money in a specific way, say, administering incentive programs for disadvantaged students. With a block grant, federal money is given to states to distribute as they see fit within very broad general guidelines. This allows states to be more responsive to local authorities. Thanks to this flexibility, block grants also reduce costs and the administrative burden on states and local agencies.

The Reagan Administration scored another, though more modest, victory in 1986 when Congress bowed to years of White House pressure and agreed to require all recipients of guaranteed student loans to demonstrate financial need. A victory too was won on bilingual education. Here Congress in 1988 gave local school districts greater flexibility to institute their own curricula according to the needs of individual students. Privatization also struck a chord, as the Education Department and the Department of Agriculture were the first federal agencies to sell part of their loan portfolios to private investors in 1987. The sale of college housing loans at market value rates enabled the Department to liquidate some two-thirds of its college housing loan portfolio, raising nearly $1 billion.

The biggest education policy disappointment of the Reagan Administration, of course, was its failure to keep or even seriously pursue its election campaign vow to abolish the Department. Had the Administration made a specific legislative proposal, and had it been strongly endorsed by Secretary Terrel Bell within 100 days of taking office, Congress might have concurred, albeit reluctantly. But the White House was preoccupied with other issues during that time, while Bell personally was committed to preserving the Department.

A bigger disappointment in the long term may be the Administration's failure to secure passage of any voucher or tuition tax credit legislation. A voucher is a certificate of a certain value provided to parents, who can then use the voucher as cash, to help pay for the education of their children at either a public or private school. The school then "cashes in" the voucher with the government. While most vouchers would be used for public schools, a voucher also would provide some financial assistance to parents who could not otherwise afford to send their child to a private school. The money that normally would be received by a public school on behalf of the child would instead be given to the parent to offset part of the cost of private school tuition. By giving lower-income parents the opportunity to send their children to private schools, vouchers introduce competition into the public school system. If the public school does not provide a good education, it loses the child and the cash value of the voucher to the private sector. The Reagan agenda for education correctly endorsed the voucher proposal as a means of improving schools through competition and giving the needy alternatives.

Tuition tax credits, meanwhile, offer modest relief for the double taxation imposed on those who pay local taxes for public schools and, in addition, pay tuition to attend private schools. While still paying local taxes to support public schools, these families would be able to recover up to half the cost of each child's tuition through a tax credit on their yearly income tax return. Although the Senate passed a tuition tax credit bill in 1982, the House rejected the measure. In Reagan's second term, despite Secretary Bennett's arguments for vouchers, congressional liberals and public education lobbyists remained firmly opposed. The Department should have, but did not, make vouchers a litmus test on poverty policy. Although Bennett argued correctly that vouchers would give poor Americans a chance to influence the quality of their schools, the Department did little to marshal the support of those inner-city minorities who would benefit most from vouchers.

The Administration also has not shaped legislation when Congress was reauthorizing education programs. Consistently, the Department has been late in offering its own proposals during the reauthorization process. The result: the Administration has missed opportunities to influence the course of vocational, postsecondary, and special education. A major mistake was the Department's centralization in 1981 of budget and program policy responsibilities in the Office of Planning, Budget, and Evaluation. This has focused attention on the budget process, giving much lower priority to devising a strategy to effect legislative policy changes. Such otherwise credible proposals as reducing excessive subsidies to banks for making student loans or eliminating complicated special funding for vocational education, which might have found bipartisan support, too frequently have been sent to Capitol Hill in the form of a budget that was deemed "dead on arrival." The Reagan Administration has seemed ignorant of the fact that key program policy proposals should be handled separately from budget formulation.

————————◇————————

THE NEXT FOUR YEARS

Given the poor state of American education, the new Administration must seek a complete restructuring of the American educational system. Tinkering will not work; fundamental reform is necessary. There is little chance that the public education system will reform itself. It is this system, after all, that has created most of the problems.

The next President must point out to the American people that a major cause of education's problems lies in the shift in financing from local to state control. Since the 1971 *Serrano* decision by the California Supreme Court mandated that per-pupil expenditures be virtually equal throughout the state's school districts, local school boards have been losing authority to state legislatures. As a result, parents have lost much of the voice they had traditionally concerning the education of their children. The shift in financing ultimately has spawned huge, powerful, and distant bureaucracies.

America cannot afford a similar shift of power from the state to the federal level. The new President should seek immediately to make states responsible for all aspects of education. This is accomplished by removing federal oversight authority from federal money for specific programs, and instead, giving solid amounts of money to the states to distribute as they see fit. States can best respond to the unique needs of their citizens. Federal strings need to be detached to restore parental authority and involvement to the nation's public schools. To help parents improve the nation's schools, they should be given a choice as to where their education tax dollars should be spent. By stimulating competition, schools will be immediately forced to improve or suffer the consequences. Vouchers and tuition tax credits empower the parent, as do state- and community-sponsored open enrollment plans for public schools of choice.

Such proposals can be translated into policy through a strategy that involves parents and school officials. Effective coalitions of minorities and disgruntled teachers who do not have options available to them because of their financial standing or place of residence can convince

Congress to approve federal vouchers and tax credits, and they can convince their legislatures to open up all public school enrollments. The new Administration must publicize the countless success stories of minority, inner-city schools that have excelled because of parental choice and involvement, and reward those responsible for their efforts.

Encouraging Equity and Choice

The new President should recognize that the key to reforming the American educational system is to reinstate parental control through choice and decentralization. It is, of course, impossible to turn back the clock and reinstate the neighborhood school system that encouraged parents to take an active interest in their children's schooling. Yet parents still can be empowered by having a choice of public schools and through education vouchers and tax credits.

Vouchers and tax credits make parents into consumers and allow them to choose where and how their child will be educated. As such, they force the schools to compete with one another for students. Schools offering the best education will attract the most students and thus get the most funds from the state; those failing to attract students will have to improve or shut their doors for lack of customers. It is not ideology that recommends open-enrollment plans, vouchers, and tax credits; it is the proved, common-sense notion that giving consumers the ability to decide how to spend their money makes providers of goods and services more responsive than they are under today's centrally administered education system. Competition works in the economy; the new President should restore it to education.

The new Administration should recognize that polls find that voters like vouchers. Significantly, a majority of voter groups, representing both Democratic and Republican strongholds, favor the personal choice that vouchers provide. There is strong support for vouchers among urban minorities, the Americans most disadvantaged by the public school monopoly. States, in fact, already have begun taking matters into their own hands by initiating systems of public schools of choice. Recent Minnesota legislation establishes America's most ambitious open enrollment plan: any child may attend any school in the state. And New York City's Spanish Harlem boasts the nation's most successful magnet school project.

The next Secretary of Education should use his bully pulpit to encourage states to promote greater educational choice through open enrollment plans and other means. The Secretary should advocate educational choice reforms every time federal program legislation comes up for renewal, and on behalf of parents, take proconsumer stands that encourage state and local experimentation and initiative. State programs will alert large numbers of Americans to the benefits of competition and create a nationwide constituency for a federal voucher.

Restoring Excellence to Elementary/Secondary Education

Reforming elementary/secondary education may be the greatest education challenge awaiting the new President. Bloated bureaucracies, hidebound policies, and weak curricula and discipline have guaranteed educational failure for tens of millions of America's children. In its most extreme manifestations, such as the Chicago public school system, learning literally has come to a halt. Reviving the public school systems requires four steps: 1) restoring local control over school districts; 2) providing parents with choice in selecting a school; 3) establishing alternative routes to teacher certification; and 4) imposing classroom discipline.

To help localities regain control over their schools, the new Administration should lend moral support to local groups and encourage varied local experiments. Federal budget proposals should change the way educational funds are distributed. Funds should be provided as block grants to local authorities for programs that are currently administered at the federal level, such as bilingual education, handicapped services, dropout prevention, and programs for teaching gifted students. The federal government can also strengthen the role of parents by reducing its oversight of the administration of the Chapter 1 program, which provides financial assistance to states and communities to improve opportunities for disadvantaged children. Finally, the Secretary can use the bully pulpit to identify state practices that tend to overregulate local education.

Teacher certification rules in most states are little more than cartels operated by teachers' unions and colleges of education to enforce monopolies in what amounts to restraint of trade. For years, teacher education colleges have convinced state legislatures to require those seeking to obtain teaching certificates to take increasing numbers of courses about teaching—rather than about the subjects to be taught. This almost surely has impaired quality of teaching in the classroom and has prevented excellent but uncredentialed individuals from teaching. The new Secretary should seek legislation barring federal funds for any school programs where existing certification requirements prevent certification of competent teachers. The new Secretary also should oppose efforts to nationalize or centralize teacher-credentialing standards. This would merely create a national cartel to protect incompetent teachers from competition.

To back local school administrators who crack down on drugs, gangs, and violence, the new Secretary should work with the Justice Department in filing *amicus* briefs on behalf of school officials who encounter legal difficulties when trying to take tough disciplinary actions to make their schools safe. In this context, the new Administration should view the drug problem as a part of the educational crisis. Thus the new Secretary should endorse harsh minimum sentencing laws at the state and federal level for those convicted of selling drugs to children.

Reforming Vocational Education and Training

Vocational programs are the most fragmented and poorly designed of all education efforts. Federal vocational education and employment training programs, for example, are scattered throughout the Departments of Education and Labor and a number of other agencies. Across the nation, some 8,000 private, for-profit, accredited postsecondary trade schools receive billions of federal dollars in student aid and funds from the Job Training Partnership Act programs. Billions more are spent in training and retraining workers, often because these individuals have been ill-served by the formal education system.

The challenge for the new Administration is to gain better, measurable results from this enormous public and private investment in vocational education and training. The new President will have an opportunity to do so in 1989 with the scheduled reauthorization of the Perkins Vocational Act, which governs the major federal vocational programs, including formula grants to the states and adult basic education programs and several small categorical grant programs. The new President should direct the Secretaries of Education, Labor, and Health and Human Services to develop a vocational education reform plan by August 1, 1989. Such a plan should streamline federal vocational education programs without increasing expenditures, while expanding individual choice in vocational training.

As part of this plan, the federal government should return to the states complete responsibility for public vocational education through high school. As such, the federal government should repeal its $848 million vocational education grant program, which currently gives the state $1 for every $9 spent by the state on vocational education. The bulk of the funds are spent at the secondary level. Instead, the new Administration should propose that states be responsible for high school vocational training.

Those who seek vocational training for entry-level work generally receive funds from such federal student financial assistance programs as Pell Grants or Stafford Student Loans or the Department of Labor's Job Corps or Job Training and Partnership Act programs. The new Administration should eliminate duplication of benefits and program inefficiency by coordinating these programs.

To expand personal choice and to enable workers to obtain training to meet the changing needs of the economy, the new Administration should propose a program to permit individuals and employers to establish tax-free Individual Education and Training Accounts. These IETAs would be similar to the popular Individual Retirement Accounts (IRAs). IETA funds could pay for the retraining of dislocated workers or allow workers with jobs to train for positions of increased responsibility. These accounts would give workers greater control and choice in their own training. Similar to IRAs, workers would be allowed to contribute up to $2,000 annually, with complete tax deductibility for lower-income wage earners and deductibility of interest earnings only for upper-income earners. Executives at the TRW Corporation have been advocating a form of IETA for several years.

To encourage continued private sector support of vocational education, the new Administration should support legislation to reinstate the employee tax deductions for employer-paid tuition. Until the 1986 tax reform, employees could not only deduct the expenses of work-related education, but also exclude from income any tuition paid by the employer. The tax benefit was to be renewed in 1987, but Congress let it expire, closing a tax provision under which employers could provide up to $5,250 in tax-free tuition benefits to employees. The new President should back proposals introduced in 1988 to reinstate this deduction. These incentives encourage workers to improve their skills and knowledge without the direct aid of the federal government.

Improving Financial Accountability for Higher Education

The federal government supports postsecondary education chiefly through student financial assistance programs. The Pell Grant program in 1988 gave a total of $4.4 billion in individual grants to financially needy students for tuition to attend any accredited college, university, or trade school. Stafford Student Loans (formerly Guaranteed Student

Loans) and Supplemental Loans for Students (SLS loans), amounting
to some $10 billion each year, are federally subsidized and guaranteed
loans made available by financial institutions to middle class as well as
poorer students.

The new Administration should learn from the Reagan Administration's failed attempts to redirect grants and loans to the needy.
Reagan Administration proposals attempted to give student financial
assistance primarily to the neediest students. Its proposed cuts, however, made any reform seem like a rationalization for cutting the
program's budget. Attempts to cut federal student aid to middle and
upper class students thus encountered fierce opposition and were
blocked. The lesson here for the new Administration is to separate
legislative proposals from the budget process. Real reforms in program
direction should be proposed and fought for at other points throughout
the year when the Administration is able to devote resources to trying
to win its battles.

The new Administration should seek legislation to link student loans
to degree completion. Each year, some students obtaining federal
grants or subsidized loans drop out of college, even though eligibility
for such aid ostensibly requires the recipients to demonstrate "satisfactory academic progress." It is only fair to the taxpayer to require
those receiving federal grants and loans to earn them in the classroom.
To encourage students to complete their education, the new Administration should propose a program providing small, incremental rewards
to students who successfully attain their academic goals. For example,
college juniors and seniors would receive an increase of $100 to $200
in the maximum grant award available. Perhaps some small loan
forgiveness—say 5 percent to 10 percent of the amount borrowed—
could be awarded upon degree completion. This would create an
incentive for students who receive federal support to study, and it
would give the taxpayer a better return on the investment.

The new Administration should encourage more private-sector support for financing college costs. As a start, the Administration should
urge restoration of the tax deduction that employers, before 1987, were
able to take for college tuition paid on behalf of their employees. This
encouraged workers to take college-level courses and created a more
highly skilled work force for the employer. Employers also should be
given a partial tax credit for hiring students in cooperative education
programs. These programs are partnerships between colleges and
businesses in which students work in a professional position related to
their major field and can earn credit toward graduation. The revenues

that this credit may cost the Treasury could be offset by eliminating the Department of Education's cooperative education grant program, which pays universities directly to administer cooperative education programs.

The new Administration must be more successful than its predecessor in reducing the cost of the loan programs without reducing aid to students. This could be achieved by restructuring the costly Stafford Student Loan Program. This program gives banks lending to students a federal guarantee that the principal and interest will be paid in the event of default. In addition, the federal government subsidizes the interest rate charged to the students by banks, so that the student pays a fixed rate of only 8 percent. The federal government thus pays lending institutions to make loans available.

To lower costs, this federal interest rate subsidy should be eliminated after the fourth year of repayment. Currently, the borrower enjoys a subsidy for ten years after graduation. Moreover, banks should be guaranteed a profit based on long-term, rather than short-term, Treasury bills. This change would make future program costs predictable.

Clarifying Civil Rights Legislation

The Civil Rights Restoration Act of 1988 threatens all private educational institutions. Under the Act's terms, any establishment receiving federal funds directly or indirectly is subject to all federal civil rights regulations. Nearly every educational institution thus faces a myriad of possible lawsuits challenging everything from lack of physical access for the handicapped to sex discrimination in the classroom. Even a school's annual Christmas pageant can be challenged for the religious content of the songs sung and the decorations displayed. The Education Department's Office for Civil Rights already has been inundated with what formerly would have been dismissed as trivial or spurious complaints about private institutions. Such complaints may reduce the ability of Office for Civil Rights to deal with more substantive cases of discrimination.

The new Administration must submit to Congress technical amendments to the Civil Rights Restoration Act of 1988 to clarify federal authority over the private affairs of individuals as a result of being affiliated with a school or facility that benefits from federal funds. Without such action, U.S. courts will be flooded by suits invoking the 1988 Act in a way that subjects all individuals to poor interpretations of existing statutes that promote one set of views over another.

INITIATIVES FOR 1989

1) Restructure the Department of Education. To improve efficiency and restore proper authority to program offices, the new Administration should trim the size and authority of the Department's staff offices, which provide support services for all offices. The "Management Improvement Service (MIS)," established ostensibly to serve as an "in-house" management consulting service for program offices, should be abolished; it is unnecessary. Program managers have access to training and information government-wide if they need help in solving management problems. Routine personnel actions now handled by the Office of Management for the entire Department, which take weeks to process, could be handled more easily and quickly by each office. These and other administrative activities should be decentralized, as they are in a number of other federal departments. The small enforcement staff in the Office for Civil Rights should be transferred to the Justice Department to emphasize that, while the Department of Education should have an investigative role, it should not serve as a federal law enforcement agency. Justice's Civil Rights Division is well equipped to handle enforcement of civil rights laws. The budget development process must be reformed to strengthen the role of presidentially appointed assistant secretaries.

2) Enhance the role of the Secretary of Education. Several federal departments currently have responsibility for education programs. This results in a lack of coordination and confusion regarding federal objectives. The new President should issue an executive order formally granting the Secretary of Education authority for planning and coordinating education programs throughout the government. If Education is to remain a Cabinet-level agency, its chief should be the Administration's top policymaker in education. A more coordinated federal policy will yield more effective programs and legislative successes.

3) Increase privatization efforts. The Department of Education was among the first federal agencies to sell part of its loan portfolio to the private sector, when in 1987 it began to privatize its college housing loans. From then until early 1988 sales yielded almost $1 billion. Congress then barred the Department from selling any more of its loans. The new Administration should seek immediately to overturn the legislative ban against completing the sale of the remaining $250 million worth of Academic Facilities and College Housing loans. Doing so would complete the liquidation of these portfolios. The Department also should expand its efforts to contract with private-sector firms to provide the Department's basic administrative services, such as the distribution of funds and accounting for vocational and special education programs.

The Department also should privatize partially the Fund for the Improvement of Postsecondary Education (FIPSE), the National Center for Education Statistics (NCES), and the National Diffusion Network (NDN). They should be restructured as federally chartered, tax-exempt foundations, free from most agency regulations and from civil service rules. FIPSE, which awards grants for research in higher education, should be given an annual "challenge match" appropriation from Congress, equal to about half its current $11.6 million appropriation, and encouraged to seek private donations for the rest of its program budget. This would reduce the federal obligation to the program and encourage private support. NCES and NDN sell products—education statistics and model programs, respectively. As quasi-private institutions, they would have the freedom and incentive to become more entrepreneurial, thereby supplying new and innovative information without being stifled by cumbersome and outdated federal requirements.

4) Create tax-free College Savings Accounts. College tuition costs have been rising rapidly in recent years, making it difficult for many Americans to afford college education. The new President should press Congress to enact legislation allowing low- and middle-income families to establish tax-deferred savings accounts to meet their future college costs. Ultimately, these accounts could reduce demand for direct federal student aid funds and, of course, significantly increase the pool of private savings.

5) Establish a means test for noneducational services for the disabled. Federal dollars to support the goals of PL-94-142 (the Education for All Handicapped Children Act of 1976, as amended) provide for educational and such noneducational services as room and board for full-time resident students. These services are widely available to families of all income brackets with handicapped children. The limited funds available to help the handicapped would go farther if upper-income families were required to pay a reasonable share of the non-educational costs. In this way educational services could be expanded for poorer families with disabled children without increasing appropriations. Upper-income families, therefore, should be means tested to determine their contribution.

6) Modify the "ability to benefit" provision in student aid. High school dropouts now may receive federal student aid grants and loans if they are deemed by postsecondary institutions to have the "ability to benefit" from a particular program of education or training. While many schools and colleges have established praiseworthy remedial programs to help these students, some institutions provide minimal counseling and screening. Abuses are widespread among proprietary (trade) schools, such as admitting unqualified students and keeping their student aid when they drop out. Some "schools" actually go to unemployment lines to recruit "students" by promising to get them federal financial aid. To prevent abuses of student aid and help ensure that students can benefit from the programs, the new Administration should press for legislation limiting student aid for non-high school graduates to a period of one year or until completion of postsecondary training, whichever comes first. The one-year limit would allow deserving students access to a school but would prevent students who drop out or fail to attain high school equivalence in their first year from receiving further federal aid. This would allow high school dropouts to enroll in further education, but would stop many abuses by poor quality schools.

7) Expand the magnet school program. Magnet schools are centers of specialized instruction capable of attracting large numbers of minority students. Two or three magnet schools often are established in place of one school, and may emphasize science, art, or literature. Magnet schools have been highly successful in motivating students, reducing dropout rates, and creating parental involvement by existing as an option to other public schools. The next Secretary of Education should publicize the magnet school program by visiting magnet schools around the nation, giving awards for special or innovative achievement, and pointing out the particular successes of these schools in communities with high concentrations of disadvantaged and minority students. The Administration could help expand magnet schools by reducing the requirements on how federal education funds are spent and encouraging states to allow school districts to utilize existing federal support for creating new magnets and experimenting with similar choice options.

8) Repeal several small, low-priority programs. Small categorical programs often live far beyond their usefulness. The Education Department has a long list of tiny programs that should be retired—gracefully—to free funds for more important activities. Those deserving immediate repeal are:

◆ All special grants authorized for individual colleges and universities ($15.4 million in fiscal 1988).

◆ FIPSE Community Service grants, which provide grants to colleges to administer community service programs, in which students perform work in exchange for having their financial obligations offset ($1.4 million).

◆ Graduate Assistance in Areas of National Need, which provides scholarships to encourage individuals to make academic/career decisions in areas identified by the Department to be a national need ($7.7 million).

◆ Impact Aid, Part B Payments, which provides grants to localities to compensate them when federal activities result in increased enrollments or loss of local revenues ("B" children either live on federal property or have parents who work on federal property and have little impact upon their school districts) ($134 million).

◆ Library Services and Construction Programs, which provide funds to make public library services available to every community ($101.6 million).

◆ Law School Clinical Experience Grants, which provide funds to stimulate the creation of clinical experience programs in law schools (virtually every law school has its own such programs) ($3.8 million).

◆ Patricia Roberts Harris Public Service Fellowships, which provide fellowships to encourage graduate students in public, service-related fields because of a perceived shortage that no longer exists ($3.2 million).

◆ Special Programs for the Disadvantaged Training Grants, used to train staff to administer TRIO programs which help students from disadvantaged backgrounds to complete college ($1.2 million).

◆ Veterans Educational Outreach Programs (VEOP), which provide assistance to postsecondary institutions for tutoring and counseling programs initiated in response to the special needs of Vietnam-era veterans ($2.94 million).

◆ The Women's Educational Equity Act (WEEA), which provides grants to individuals and organizations to promote educational equity for women in response to feminist groups' concerns of the 1970s ($3.4 million).

Most of these programs began as efforts to address some real or perceived inequity or to promote innovative models. At one time or another, some may have been useful to the nation. In 1965, for example, when only 25 percent of all Americans lived within five miles of a public library, the Library Services Program may have made some sense. The program helped establish library programs in communities. Today, however, some 95 percent of Americans are within 5 miles of a library. As such, the program clearly is an anachronism.

The new Administration should engage in appropriate "housecleaning," urging Congress to end small programs that have outlived their usefulness.

☎

11

The Department of Energy

Milton R. Copulos*
Task Force Chairman

The Department of Energy was established in 1977 to oversee federal energy programs. Under the Carter Administration, DOE concentrated on administering the cumbersome price and allocation regulations for crude oil imposed by Congress following the 1973 OPEC embargo, and on a variety of subsidy programs for new forms of energy. The philosophy underlying the Carter approach toward energy policy emphasized market intervention, regulation, and conservation.

Although DOE has not been abolished, as Ronald Reagan pledged when running for the presidency, his Administration has shifted the Department's direction dramatically. It now emphasizes market mechanisms rather than regulation, and spurring supply rather than artificially constraining demand. The result has been lower prices to consumers, markets more sensitive to the changing needs of the economy, and energy sources that are more secure.

Despite this progress, the new Administration will face a number of important issues. Among the most pressing: building the new nuclear reactors to produce plutonium and tritium for the nation's strategic arsenal; reorganizing the Nuclear Regulatory Commission; and securing access to the Arctic National Wildlife Refuge for oil and gas drilling. Also important will be the establishment of a nuclear waste repository, the reform of the tax code to provide fair treatment for energy development, and the privatization of the nation's uranium enrichment enterprise through the creation of a United States Enrichment Corporation.

---

*Commenting and contributing generously to this chapter were *Mandate III* Task Force Members Scott Campbell, Michael German, Nelson Hay, William Martin, Lyle Reed, H. B. "Bud" Scoggins, Margaret Sibley, and Sharon Wilson. They do not necessarily endorse all of its views and recommendations.

Task Force Deputy Chairman: Heritage Policy Analyst Kent Jeffreys.

BUDGET AND PERSONNEL

Secretaries

John S. Herrington	1985–present
Donald Hodel	1982–1985
James Edwards	1981–1982

Personnel

March 1988	16,657
April 1980	21,421
April 1970	N.A.

Budget Outlays

Fiscal Year	Total (billions)
1989 Estimate	$11.8
1988 Estimate	$10.5
1987 Actual	$10.7
1986 Actual	$11.0
1985 Actual	$10.6
1980 Actual	$ 6.5
1970 Actual	$ 2.4

Over the longer term, DOE will have to address such issues as how to improve environmental quality in a cost-effective manner through such methods as easing controls to permit the wider use of natural gas; the development of a new smaller reactor design for a second generation of civilian nuclear power plants; and the completion of the development of the advanced laser isotope separation technology for uranium enrichment. In addition, the new Administration should seek legislation to merge the Department of Energy with the Department of the Interior. Above all, the new Administration must continue the Reagan commitment to market forces which has yielded very positive results.

————————————◇————————————

SUMMARY OF AGENCY FUNCTIONS

The Department of Energy, established in the shadow of the oil crisis, was created to coordinate and enforce federal regulations affecting the nation's energy markets and supplies. In addition, it has responsibility for the production of nuclear materials for the Department of Defense and for civilian nuclear reactors. The programs of the Department can be divided into two broad areas:

◆ *Nuclear materials production for the Defense Department,* which requires managing the design and production of the nation's nuclear warheads. This includes the production of weapons-grade material and operation of the necessary reactors.

◆ *Civilian energy programs,* which consist of various fossil fuels programs (primarily coal research and synthetic fuels programs, but including the Strategic Petroleum Reserve), the civilian nuclear programs (involving nuclear fuel reprocessing, radioactive waste disposal, and reactor design), and conservation and renewable energy programs.

———————————◇———————————

INSTITUTIONAL CONSTRAINTS

Since DOE was established, the debate over energy policy has been dominated by two conflicting and highly polarized camps. One is comprised of individuals from the environmentalist and consumerist movements, together with the advocates of national economic planning. They hide neither their personal antipathy for energy producers nor their enthusiasm for a highly intrusive, centrally planned approach to energy policies. The second camp, drawing its strength from the private sector, seeks market-based policies with a minimum of governmental involvement.

Under the Carter Administration, DOE was run largely by central planning advocates. This shaped energy policymaking, leading to a progression of "National Energy Plans" calling for huge federal spending, comprehensive regulation, and punitive taxes on energy producers. Though the Reagan Administration has done much to reverse the antiproducer bias, self-styled "public interest" groups continue to pressure the agency and Congress to adopt nonmarket policies and programs.

DOE has been one of the most closely monitored federal agencies. Congressional oversight hearings are frequent, and Congress rarely hesitates to alter DOE budget requests and impose new requirements on the agency. Congressional scrutiny has been particularly close in the House of Representatives, where the Energy and Commerce Committee and its subcommittees have used oversight and regulatory powers to frustrate such Reagan Administration initiatives as full decontrol of natural gas prices and the privatization of the federally

owned Power Marketing Administrations (PMAs). The House committee, for instance, even barred the Department from studying possible
privatization of the PMAs.

DOE also has been beset by its own internal conflicts and turf
battles, especially in its early years. In large part, this internal tension
stemmed from an organizational structure that had overlapping authorities for broad programmatic areas, and no clear reporting structure.
These battles have quieted since the Department's reorganization
during Secretary Donald P. Hodel's tenure. This has streamlined the
agency greatly, increased efficiency, and alleviated many of the internal conflicts. Hodel meanwhile improved DOE's image among its client
groups, including environmental organizations, through an open-door
policy that made him among the most accessible of the Reagan Cabinet
officers.

Another internal problem has been the systematic undermining of
Administration initiatives by career DOE employees. Selling the Power
Marketing Administration, for instance, has been stymied by program
managers as well as by the special interest groups outside the agency.
Similarly, the selection of a technology for the new reactor to produce
plutonium and tritium to replace the aging facilities located at Hanford,
Washington, and Savannah River, South Carolina, has had a fair
consideration of alternative designs delayed by bureaucratic maneuvering.

—————————————◇—————————————

THE REAGAN ADMINISTRATION RECORD

DOE, on balance, is a largely unheralded Reagan Administration
success story. The President made clear in his earliest days in
office his intent to redirect federal energy policy. One of his first acts
in office was the elimination of the last vestiges of the price and
allocation controls on crude oil imposed by Congress in the 1970s. The
Administration then streamlined the activities of the Department and
eliminated such wasteful or ineffective controls and programs as those
setting the price and allocation of crude oil and refined petroleum
products. In particular, it trimmed the regulatory staff of the Economic
Regulatory Administration by 90 percent, from 2,000 to just 200. It
also abolished the Synthetic Fuels Corporation, the costly program to
develop alternative but inefficient energy sources, and relaxed regulations which had been causing independent oil producers to abandon
low-producing stripper wells (wells that produce ten barrels per day or

less) on federal lands. Although each well's output is relatively small, in aggregate they account for a substantial portion of U.S. production.

One of DOE's most important accomplishments was the publication of the 1987 *Energy Security* report. This 335–page volume makes a compelling case for market-oriented solutions to energy concerns. *Energy Security*, moreover, has given DOE credibility in producing such reports, making the Department a bully pulpit for market-oriented energy policies. The Department's natural gas initiative, announced early in 1988, typifies this.

Despite these achievements, the Reagan Administration has failed to win support for the complete elimination of the regulations that long have hampered U.S. energy development. While congressional intransigence is largely at fault, resistance within the White House is also to blame. An example is the White House's abrupt withdrawal of a proposal to decontrol natural gas prices, earmarked for late 1982. Department officials had prepared congressional supporters for the announcement, and chances for enactment appeared better than ever. Yet senior White House staff members, at the last moment, convinced the President to reverse his decision. This weakened DOE effectiveness in future campaigns to win Hill backing for the Reagan energy agenda.

Congress bears the full blame, however, for the derailed effort to sell the Power Marketing Administrations. These were established in the 1930s to sell electricity generated by federal dams. Though the full cost of their operation is supposed to be recovered through customer charges, they are heavily taxpayer-subsidized.

$$\diamond$$

THE NEXT FOUR YEARS

The new President's energy policies must continue to rely on market forces. They are the most efficient allocator of resources, and demonstrably provide the lowest energy costs to consumers. Therefore, government impediments to the operation of a free market in energy must be removed. At the same time, all departments of the government, especially Treasury, must recognize the unique features of energy exploration and production when they develop regulations and enact tax changes.

The issues facing the new Administration fall into four broad categories: 1) supply enhancement, 2) removal of market impediments, 3) environmental concerns, and 4) security issues.

In the first category are tax and regulatory policies that inhibit domestic resource production. These include such issues as restrictions on access to federal lands and the tax code bias against extractive industries. The second category includes such regulations that distort or impede the market's operations as controls on natural gas, subsidies to specific energy resources, and environmental regulations biased for or against specific types of energy use. The third category concerns the interrelationship between energy and environmental issues. Among these are the greenhouse effect (the warming of the Earth's atmosphere that some scientists attribute to the burning of fossil fuels), lagging local compliance with the National Ambient Air Quality Standards for automotive fuels, and the continuing battle over nuclear waste disposal. The fourth category involves areas where defense and security considerations are paramount, like the Strategic Petroleum Reserve and U.S. dependence on oil imports.

An immediate task of the next Administration is to identify areas where, through changing circumstances or through unanticipated results of policy decisions, the government retards energy production or conservation. In the past, well-intended actions have harmed the nation's energy security. The 1986 tax reform typifies this. In attempting to avoid favoring specific industries, the law inadvertently penalizes the oil and gas industry severely. Treasury officials erroneously accepted the claim that tax provisions that had taken into account the oil industry's unique circumstances were tax breaks and should thus be eliminated. As a result, the depletion allowance was severely curbed by the 1986 law. This was a serious mistake. The depletion allowance is merely the mineral industry's form of depreciation—a business tax deduction widely recognized as legitimate. Without it, U.S. oil producers cannot recover their capital as it is consumed, as would a manufacturer as its equipment wears out. By curbing the depletion allowance, the amount of money available for domestic energy development has been reduced sharply.

The new Administration also must restore balance between energy and environmental considerations. There is broad public and congressional support for environmental regulation, but little understanding of how this regulation affects the economy. Regulation, like restricting access to federal lands, reduces America's ability to make full use of its vast domestic energy potential. Therefore the goals of resource development and environmental preservation are viewed as conflicting. But with advances in technology, this need not be the case. The new Administration thus must convince Americans, through a campaign of public information, that they can have plentiful energy along with a protected environment.

Another priority for the new Administration, of course, should be America's energy security. To reduce the threat of disruption by boycotts or merely changes in the world oil market, the Administration should urge Congress to remove barriers to domestic energy production and conservation. The recent growth of U.S. oil imports to levels unseen in a decade are a warning that another energy crisis could cripple both the U.S. and its policy in the Middle East. Secure energy supplies require an end to regulations and discriminatory taxes that discourage domestic oil and gas production.

Upgrading the Production of Nuclear Materials

The U.S. has produced nuclear materials for the nuclear weapons program since the World War II Manhattan Project. The principal weapons materials are plutonium and tritium. Until recently, U.S. supplies of these substances were produced at federal nuclear reactors at Hanford, Washington, and Savannah River, South Carolina. After a safety review following the nuclear accident at Chernobyl, in the Soviet Union, a decision was made to mothball the Hanford reactor and to reduce the activity of the Savannah River reactor by 60 percent.

Serious safety concerns make replacement of the two plants an urgent priority. The critical need is a continuing supply of tritium, an essential component of the triggers of nuclear weapons. This material deteriorates after about twelve years; therefore, a decline in production threatens to leave the U.S. without an adequate nuclear arsenal.

Replacing these aging nuclear weapons reactors is complicated because Congress has decided that their replacements must be licensed by the Nuclear Regulatory Commission (NRC), as are commercial plants. Congress has taken this position because of safety concerns revealed during reviews of the units by the National Academy of Sciences. Since the NRC licensing procedure is open to obstruction by antinuclear groups, the potential exists for severe and dangerous delays in replacing the nuclear reactors. Therefore, a key consideration in choosing a design for the new weapons reactors must be that it can be licensed easily and quickly.

Given this constraint, the Secretary of Energy approved the development of two new production facilities: a heavy water reactor will be built at Savannah River, and four High-Temperature Gas-Cooled Reactor (MHTGR) modules will be built in Idaho. Congress must appropriate the funds for these. This decision addresses virtually all the issues regarding replacement of the existing facilities. While there is some concern that the heavy water design might encounter licensing difficulties and delays, since no reactors of this kind have been built in the U.S. for several decades, selecting a MHTGR unit, in addition to the heavy water reactor, provides an alternative should there be licensing problems. The MHTGR was found to be the safest design available by a DOE review panel examining potential designs.

The next Administration should move quickly to execute the Secretary's decisions. It should seek immediate congressional approval for funding the project and complete construction as quickly as possible.

Reviving the Nuclear Industry

In addition to addressing the problems associated with producing nuclear materials for America's arsenal, the new Administration also should take steps to reinvigorate America's nuclear industry.

◆ *Uranium enrichment.* The U.S. government owns uranium enrichment facilities in Kentucky, Ohio, and Tennessee, which produce fuel for the domestic and much of the foreign nuclear power industry. Until the mid–1970s, the U.S. was the world's sole producer of enriched uranium. But U.S. actions to reduce the proliferation of nuclear weapons, combined with changes in the U.S. nuclear energy market, gave the Soviet Union and European firms a chance to enter the world market. The U.S. has since lost 60 percent of its foreign customers, and domestic sales have fallen.

Despite this shrinking market, DOE's three enrichment facilities continue to price their product at levels far above the going market rate, behaving like any government-run enterprise. DOE could correct this by establishing a semi-independent enrichment corporation whose pricing policies would be determined by normal business factors. This federal corporation would keep tight government control of enrichment technologies and yet allow much greater responsiveness to market forces. The new President should press for legislation creating the U.S. Enrichment Corporation.

Over the long term, to remain competitive in the world enrichment market, the U.S. must acquire a technological alternative to the energy-intensive gaseous diffusion plants currently in use for uranium enrichment. The reason is that electricity costs, which are a major portion of the cost of operating an enrichment plant, are expected to rise substantially. A less energy-intensive alternative technology therefore is needed for the U.S. enrichment industry to remain competitive. The Advanced Laser Isotope Separation (AVLIS) system has been under development in the U.S. since 1973 and meets that requirement. Currently the U.S. has a lead of between four and six years in developing important nuclear technology. By 1992, the U.S. could move on to production-scale AVLIS operations. The next Administration should continue the AVLIS research program to maintain America's competitive edge.

◆ *The civilian nuclear industry.* New electric power plants must be constructed if regional brownouts and blackouts are to be avoided. While electricity can be generated from almost any fuel, the ideal source of future electrical energy is nuclear power. For one thing, the U.S. has large domestic uranium deposits, reducing the need to import oil. For another, nuclear power does not pollute the atmosphere—an important characteristic in light of growing concern over acid rain. In addition, mining uranium ore for nuclear fuel disrupts the environment far less than mining for coal.

Thanks to public opposition, no new U.S. nuclear plants have been ordered in a decade. One way of defusing the opposition would be to develop a new standardized design for commercial plants that answer current public concerns. This would help reduce regulatory delays and permit preapproval for most new plants. The nuclear industry practice has been to build custom-designed plants for each customer. This has meant that the major components in each new plant have had to go through the entire process of regulatory scrutiny, leading inevitably to approval delays caused by nuclear power opponents. Standardization would reduce these delays and permit smaller, modular power plants to be used. Components for these "off-the-shelf" plants could be manufactured in a factory and assembled on the site. Such standardized techniques would reduce costs. The most promising candidate for a civilian program of standardized plants is the same technology that would fit America's defense needs—the Modular High Temperature Gas-Cooled Reactor (MHTGR).

◆ *Nuclear waste.* Scientists long have agreed that nuclear waste can be disposed of safely. The Department of Energy currently is seeking sites for depositing such wastes. However, local public opposition arises each time a site is selected. As a result, electric utilities using nuclear power must store their used fuel at the reactor sites where available space is rapidly becoming scarce. Unless nuclear waste repositories can be developed, some nuclear plants will be forced to close. The new Secretary of Energy should select and win approval for a permanent site as quickly as possible. If necessary, the Secretary should seek congressional approval to locate the waste repository on federal lands without obtaining approval from local authorities.

◆ *The Nuclear Regulatory Commission.* The Nuclear Regulatory Commission (NRC) was established in January 1975 as the successor to the Atomic Energy Commission. It regulates the civilian nuclear power industry, issuing licenses governing all aspects of civilian nuclear activities, including the certification of the components, construction, and operation of nuclear power plants, and the export of nuclear materials and equipment. Over the years, the licensing and regulatory process of nuclear matters has become legalistic and adversarial, thanks in large part to the opposition of antinuclear groups. As a result, licenses are delayed interminably by litigation. The nation's economic well-being is not being served by the current regulatory practices of the NRC.

Legislation currently before Congress would convert the NRC from a multimember Commission, where internal disputes are common, to an executive agency headed by one official. It would also streamline the regulatory process. This would allow a more balanced and speedy system of licensing. If enacted, the new Administration should move to carry out the reforms. If the legislation still has not been passed when the new Administration takes office, the Department should lobby vigorously for reintroduction and passage of the measure.

Establishing Stronger Incentives to Improve Domestic Oil and Natural Gas Production

The U.S. oil and natural gas industry is going through a painful transition. The decline of world oil prices has forced the oil industry to become more efficient. Yet this has not stopped U.S. crude oil production from falling and imports from soaring. The U.S. in mid–1988 was importing more oil, in absolute terms and as a percentage of domestic consumption, than before the 1973 OPEC oil embargo. At the same time, congressional actions restricting oil exploration have made it increasingly difficult for U.S. producers to develop the nation's considerable oil and natural gas reserves. These actions include adverse changes in the tax code and restrictions on access to federal lands. The new Administration must act quickly to eliminate these impediments.

◆ *Tax incentives.* Some lawmakers and independent oil producers call for an oil import fee, a tax placed on each barrel of imported crude oil or refined petroleum products. The aim of such a fee would be to make foreign oil more expensive than domestic oil, and therefore less attractive to U.S. purchasers. Higher priced imported oil also would allow domestic producers to raise prices, improving industry revenues and providing money for new investment. Yet to have a significant impact, the fee would have to be relatively high. This then would harm the rest of the economy very seriously. The new President should continue the Reagan Administration's opposition to such a fee, and instead press to restore oil exploration incentives that have been eliminated by Congress. The new President also should press Congress to relax access to federal lands to give the U.S. oil industry more access to domestic oil reserves.

The new President should propose six tax incentives to spur U.S. oil production to offset the imports from the Arab members of OPEC. These would not raise prices to consumers, but would raise sufficient new revenues for the federal Treasury, through income taxes paid by workers employed in the oil fields and by federal royalty payments, to offset totally the initial revenue losses resulting from the tax changes.

1) The transfer rule. The transfer rule prohibits the purchaser of an oil well who is eligible for the depletion allowance from retaining that tax benefit. Allowing purchasers to be eligible for the allowance would make wells more attractive and would increase the capital available to drillers to invest in exploration. According to official estimates, repealing the rule would cost the Treasury $23.4 million annually in lost tax revenues. In return, this would spur sufficient new exploration to add 55,000 barrels per day to domestic oil production, which in mid–1988 totaled 8.2 million barrels per day. The resultant tax loss to the Treasury would be the equivalent of $1.17 for each new barrel per day of extra productive capacity. By comparison, purchasing oil on the open market at current prices would cost around $13.00 per barrel. Moreover, additional domestic production reduces the need to store oil in case of an interruption of foreign supplies. Strategic Petroleum Reserve storage costs currently are about $1 per barrel annually. Repealing the transfer rule therefore is a far less expensive way of securing supplies than stockpiling foreign oil.

2) The net income limitation. The total tax deduction an oil producer can take for depletion cannot exceed 50 percent of the producer's income. Repeal of this rule would cost the treasury $47.2 million annually, but would increase U.S. oil production by 58,000 barrels per day, at a cost of just $2.23 in lost revenue per barrel of new production added.

3) Recovery of geophysical and geological outlays. Business generally is allowed two types of deductions for money it spends on

operations. One type of outlay is known as an expense, such as labor costs or materials consumed in the course of business. The full amount of an expense can be deducted from an individual or business's earnings in the year in which it occurs. The other type of deduction is for capital expenditures, such as plant and equipment. The deduction for these expenditures must be spread over a period of years. Expensing of expenditures obviously is advantageous, since it allows the tax savings to be realized immediately. Currently, the costs of geologic mapping, gathering seismic data, and other work that precedes oil drilling cannot be expensed. This rule should be changed. This would cost the Treasury $260 million, but would result in 200,000 barrels per day of new production, at a cost in lost revenue of $3.56 per barrel.

4) A tax credit for exploration and development. A 5 percent tax credit for oil exploration and development would reduce Treasury revenue about $740 million annually, but would stimulate 325,000 barrels per day in new production. The tax loss would be equivalent to $6.24 per barrel.

5) The depletion allowance for independent oil firms. The depletion allowance has been reduced steadily since 1969. It should be restored to the full 27.5 percent which was in effect for 40 years prior to 1969. It would cost the Treasury $680 million annually, but would add 280,000 barrels per day of new production. The revenue cost per barrel would be $6.65.

6) Integrated oil companies and the depletion allowance for new production. Integrated oil companies currently are not permitted to take the depletion allowance. Allowing them to do so would mean a $2 billion loss to the Treasury, but it would stimulate 370,000 barrels per day of new production. This action would provide capital for exploration offshore, in Alaska, and other frontiers where integrated companies are the principal operators. Its cost per barrel of new production added would be $14.81.

When all six of the items are totaled, they at first would reduce Treasury collections by $3.75 billion annually. In return, they would stimulate production of 1.288 million new barrels of oil daily, at an average additional cost per barrel of $7.98 (this figure is adjusted to eliminate double counting). In mid–1988, the U.S. imported 1.243 million barrels per day from OPEC members. According to the Department of Energy's estimate of the workforce additions that would be required to seek out, drill, and operate the new oil wells, these tax changes would create an additional 175,000 jobs in the oil industry, and two to three times that number in secondary employment. The tax revenues on the wages and royalties generated by new employment alone would top $3 billion. Thus the six tax changes would benefit the taxpayer and improve American energy security.

Currently, the oil and natural gas industry is among the most heavily taxed sectors of the economy. It suffers under very discriminatory taxes, including the Superfund Tax and the tax on Intangible Drilling Costs. Even under normal conditions, these taxes would be unjustified. Given the depressed state of prices on the world oil market, the high U.S. production costs caused in part by these taxes, and the security threat posed by dependance on imports, the taxes are especially damaging. The new President should push for their repeal.

◆ *Access to federal lands.* Many of the most promising areas for new U.S. oil and natural gas discoveries lie within the boundaries of land controlled by the federal government or in offshore areas under federal control. Restrictions imposed by Congress, however, have closed huge portions of these lands to exploration for oil and natural gas. Without more access to these reserves, the U.S. is destined to become increasingly dependent on foreign sources of oil, as existing domestic deposits are consumed and cannot be replaced. To prevent this, access to onshore and offshore areas of the public domain should be eased. Although jurisdiction over access lies with the Department of the Interior, subject to congressional constraints, the Secretary of Energy must use his bully pulpit to foster a political environment in which eased access is recognized as important to domestic energy security.

The most immediate and important area that should be granted easier access is the Arctic National Wildlife Refuge (ANWR). Only 1.5 million acres of this 19 million acre tract would be open to exploration. It is thought to hold the last super-giant oil field, rivaling Alaska's Prudhoe Bay. Yet environmental groups threaten to block attempts even to determine if an oil field actually exists in the ANWR, let alone develop it. The Secretary of Energy should make access to ANWR the highest legislative priority of his congressional liaison staff, and should work closely with the Secretary of the Interior to assure congressional approval for access to ANWR at the earliest possible date.

Using Natural Gas and Alcohol Fuels to Improve the Environment

Many environmental concerns associated with oil and coal could be solved, at far lower costs than those incurred today, by eliminating barriers to the wider use of natural gas. Yet federal regulations, which often mandate specific technologies for meeting emission standards, limit the flexibility of firms to use natural gas as a pollution reduction technique. Natural gas is among the most abundant domestic fuels, and poses far less of a threat to the environment than coal or fuel oil, its principal competitors. Use of natural gas in conjunction with other fuels, such as coal, can reduce pollution emissions with savings of from 20 percent to 90 percent in emission control costs. The new President should push for changes in environmental rules to encourage the use of natural gas or fuel mixtures that include natural gas. Rules also should be altered to encourage the use by electric utilities of "combined cycle" turbines, which burn natural gas. The new Administration, in addition, should seek changes in environmental regulations that currently subject facilities burning natural gas to far stricter emission standards than those burning coal or oil.

Rationalizing Federal Energy Regulatory Commission Rules

The Federal Energy Regulatory Commission regulates the interstate sale of natural gas and electricity and licenses hydroelectric plants. It was established when DOE was created. While nominally under DOE's authority, FERC is for all practical purposes an independent body. The price controls administered by FERC still are the primary obstruction to the smooth operation of the natural gas market. Under the Reagan Administration, FERC has made major progress in deregulating the gas market, and began deregulating the electricity market as well. FERC has reduced the so-called take or pay obligations, which required many pipelines to pay for natural gas whether they used it or not. And it helped release more gas to the market by eliminating or raising the price ceiling for some categories of natural gas, and by making it easier for gas producers without long-term transportation contracts to send their gas through interstate pipelines when space was available.

The new President should urge FERC, as an early priority, to revise remaining regulations that impede the market. Among the needed revisions:

◆ *Gas inventory rules.* Pipelines currently are required to maintain certain levels of gas reserves. They cannot, however, pass on to customers the costs associated with storing these gas supplies. They should be permitted to do so.

◆ *Service obligations.* As a condition of licensing, pipelines must provide transportation to those customers who contract with them. But after the contract expires, the pipelines still are obliged to provide transportation services, on demand, to these companies under the original contract on a year-to-year basis. This enables the customer to shop around for the best deal, while the pipeline company must be available to supply that customer. This leads to costly uncertainties for pipelines. The rule should be changed so that pipeline companies are not locked into such one-sided agreements.

◆ *Pipeline centralization rules.* Pipeline centralization rules were established to prevent overbuilding of pipelines when the industry was expanding. These rules are now out of date and hold back the construction of needed pipelines. They should be revised to permit faster licensing of pipelines when demand is high.

Deregulating the Electric Utility Industry

The new President should seek to deregulate the electric utility industry by separating generation from transmission. The electric utility industry for the most part consists of integrated local companies that both generate and transmit electricity. Because local utilities have a responsibility to assure continuity of power, they are regulated locally, a practice that results in inefficiencies. The reason for this is that, because utilities earn their profits through the rate of return on investment permitted by the local regulatory body, their profits are not based on the efficient sale of electricity, but on the amount they spend on capital investment. As a result, utilities have an incentive to spend more than is necessary on capital investment, in the end raising costs to the consumer and introducing inefficiencies into each integrated company.

This inefficiency could be reduced by a separation of generation and transmission, in effect dividing utilities into two companies, one selling electricity to retail customers, and the second selling electricity to the transmission company. Each would have an incentive to seek the lowest costs. The consumer would benefit. Moreover, small generating companies could more easily enter the market as suppliers.

This separation could be accomplished by permitting companies wishing to divide into separate generation and transmission units to choose to be regulated for a transition period by FERC. Once the separation was complete, the transmission company would continue to exist as a regulated utility under FERC jurisdiction, because it would continue to have a local monopoly, but the generating company would be deregulated. The effect of this change would be sharply increased competition in power production, and therefore lower costs to the consumer.

Merging the Departments of Energy and Interior

Federal responsibility for energy matters is split between the Departments of Energy and Interior. There are many common issues affecting both energy and nonfuel minerals that fall under the jurisdiction of both agencies. Moreover, most of DOE's nondefense functions concern natural resource questions, such as research into fossil fuel use. A more rational set of policies could be achieved by merging the two agencies into a single Department of Natural Resources. The defense-related activities should be placed within a new, smaller agency, without Cabinet status, linked to the Department of Defense. The new Administration should propose legislation to effect such a reorganization.

—————————————◇—————————————

INITIATIVES FOR 1989

1) Expand the federal alternative fuel program. The new Administration should encourage wider use of alternative fuels. The DOE and the Department of Transportation, in September 1988, instituted pilot programs to encourage wider use of alternative fuels. These would help reduce the nation's vulnerability to import disruptions, and would help improve air quality. Such programs also could potentially lower fuel costs for federal vehicles. The purchase by the federal government of vehicles capable of using natural gas or alcohol fuels has the added benefit of providing an incentive for automobile manufacturers to establish production lines that could manufacture such vehicles for civilian use. The time tables for these programs should be accelerated and market incentives for alternative fuels should be encouraged.

2) Win passage of the six tax reforms needed to reduce America's dangerous dependence on imported oil. Several tax law changes in recent years have discouraged the domestic production of oil, leaving America dangerously dependent on imported oil. The new Administration should submit a package of energy security tax reforms to restore incentives for domestic production, comprising: repeal of the transfer rule; repeal of the net income limitation; the expensing of geologic and geophysical costs; a 5 percent tax credit for exploration and development; the full depletion allowance for independent oil firms; and availability of the depletion allowance on new production to integrated oil companies. These changes would stimulate sufficient domestic production to help offset imports from the Arab members of OPEC and ultimately would generate sufficient new tax and royalty revenues to more than cover the initial revenue losses.

3) Eliminate barriers to the operation of the natural gas market. During the Reagan Administration, many regulations impeding the operation of the national gas market have been reversed, ensuring more supplies to U.S. consumers. Nevertheless, many onerous regulations still remain. Under the new Administration, the Federal Energy Regulatory Commission should fully deregulate the natural gas market.

4) Complete the Strategic Petroleum Reserve. The Strategic Petroleum Reserve (SPR) is intended to hold 750 million barrels of oil to offset the effect of a major disruption. Since this would provide only short-term help, it is not an effective insurance policy. But it is important in two other ways: First, its very existence discourages arbitrary interruptions by those nations seeking to gain some political or economic advantage through an embargo of oil shipments to the U.S., and second, it would provide great psychological benefit in the event of threatened or actual supply disruptions, such as those of the 1970s. It could reduce such market anxiety in the short term. At the moment, the SPR contains approximately 600 million barrels. The 750 million-barrel target should be completed. Due to physical limitations on delivery capacity from the SPR, only about 3 million barrels of oil per day could be removed from storage for the first 100 days of an import cutoff. Still this is sufficient to offset most potential disruptions, since an interruption of oil from such major suppliers as Canada is unlikely.

5) Improve the Free Trade Agreement with Canada. The recent trade agreement with Canada permits the free flow of Canadian gas across the U.S. border. U.S. energy and natural resource firms, however, cannot operate freely in Canada. The new Administration should negotiate to improve the existing pact to assure that energy firms from both nations can operate without restriction across the border. In addition to the economic benefits this would achieve for U.S. businesses, and for consumers on both sides of the border, freer flows of energy would further enhance U.S. energy security.

12

The Environmental Protection Agency*

Nolan Clark*
Task Force Chairman

The Reagan Administration had a rare opportunity to reform America's flawed environmental protection programs. It has squandered this opportunity and perhaps made it impossible for a successor to design a federal system to protect the environment at a cost the nation can afford to pay over the long term.

The process of rebuilding a constituency for sound and responsible environmental reform will be long. To begin this process, the new Administration must make existing Environmental Protection Agency (EPA) programs more efficient and less burdensome. In particular, it should overhaul the agency's monitoring and data-gathering functions to improve the information base from which regulations are made. It should use "alternative dispute resolution mechanisms" to obtain prompt, private cleanup of hazardous waste sites in a manner fair to both the public and the firms responsible for the pollution.

The next Administration should change the terms of debate on the environment by mounting an ambitious campaign to explain the goals and premises of its environmental policy. This is needed to build public support for wider use of market mechanisms that protect the environment while avoiding the unnecessary costs associated with a purely regulatory approach. For this it needs well-publicized studies demonstrating the current regulatory system's poor record in improving the environment, such as in the Superfund program. And as it begins to

---

*Commenting and contributing generously to this chapter were *Mandate III* Task Force Members Barbara Bankoff, Frank Blake, Robert Crandall, Brian Mannix, Steve Steckler, Fred Smith, Jim Tozzi, and Heritage Policy Analyst Kent Jeffreys. They do not necessarily endorse all of its views and recommendations.

Task Force Deputy Chairman: Heritage Grover M. Hermann Fellow Stephen Moore.

BUDGET AND PERSONNEL

Secretaries

Lee M. Thomas	1985–present
William D. Ruckelshaus	1983–1985
Ann M. Burford	1981–1983

Personnel

March 1988	15,367
April 1980	14,703
April 1970	N.A.

Budget Outlays

Fiscal Year	Total (billions)
1989 Estimate	$5.1
1988 Estimate	$4.9
1987 Actual	$4.9
1986 Actual	$4.9
1985 Actual	$4.5
1980 Actual	$5.6
1970 Actual	$0.4

change the terms of the debate, the new Administration should propose legislation to strengthen market mechanisms when major environmental programs, such as the Clear Air Act, are being reauthorized by Congress.

◇

SUMMARY OF AGENCY FUNCTIONS

Created in 1970, the Environmental Protection Agency is primarily a regulatory body, designed to gather federal environmental enforcement programs under one agency roof. The EPA's responsibilities include setting the national standards for air quality that states are required to meet and the technology-based standards to be met by major private emitters of air and water pollution. EPA regulates the testing, use, and disposal of such potentially hazardous substances as pesticides and new chemical products. It sets standards for the disposal of nontoxic and hazardous solid wastes and directs the cleanup of hazardous waste disposal sites.

Although one of the newest federal regulatory agencies, EPA is the largest and most influential federal agency outside the Cabinet. EPA regulations directly affect the availability and cost of most products bought by Americans. Thus, flawed environmental litigation or EPA regulatory programs impose tremendous costs on the economy. In 1986, for example, spending for pollution abatement and control was estimated by the Department of Commerce to be over $80 billion. Conversely, rational and effective EPA programs could increase directly the economy's efficiency while protecting the environment.

―――――――――◇―――――――――

INSTITUTIONAL CONSTRAINTS

Powerful constraints limit the ability of any Administration to protect the environment in a cost-effective manner. Among these constraints are the media. Environmental bad news sells newspapers and TV news shows, while environmental successes do not rate front page news. As a result, the public is told much more about environmental setbacks than gains. To make matters worse, according to authoritative surveys, most of the media assume that government is better able than private markets to deal with environmental issues. Thus, proposals for government controls typically receive a favorable press.

State and local governments also press for federal solutions, although many environmental problems are local. The reason: many state and local governments do not want to take the heat of wrestling with complex environmental matters, preferring to pass the buck to the federal government and the federal Treasury. In this way, Washington can be blamed whenever environmental problems occur and when unpopular, stringent controls are imposed. While some of the professional champions of the environment may be part of the solution, many more are part of the problem. Too many professional environmentalists simply do not understand how markets and incentives work, and thus, assume they play no role in solutions. Some of those who do understand are ideologically hostile to property rights, individual freedom, and technological development.

The business community also has been an obstacle to private mechanisms for dealing effectively with environmental concerns. Given proper incentives, of course, business ingenuity can be used to solve environmental problems. Yet businesses also prefer to shift costs to others and avoid risk and controversy. Thus corporations and trade associations have supported stricter environmental controls if these would burden potential rivals, such as new entrants to a market. Most larger businesses, meanwhile, do not want to be seen as environmental "bad guys," so they support or do not strenuously oppose legislation that raises consumer costs without providing equivalent environmental benefits. Lawmakers usually are similarly disposed. Environmental issues are ready-made for demagoguery and congressional empire building. Supporting a "clean environment" while condemning Big Business wins votes.

For the most part, the EPA career staff provides technically sound research. Unless supervised, however, EPA staff often draws policy implications from these research findings that misallocate economic resources. The EPA staff also generally balks at trying alternative environmental policies. Any political initiative that significantly shifts the focus of meeting environmental standards from government control to private incentives, or from federal to local or state regulation, seems to threaten the careerists and so invites opposition or foot dragging within the agency. It also invites leaks and distorted reports by the bureaucracy to the press and Congress.

———————————◇———————————

THE REAGAN ADMINISTRATION RECORD

When the Reagan Administration took office, there was a very widespread recognition, albeit some of it reluctant, that the U.S. was suffering from environmental overregulation. Reagan had campaigned on a platform that promised to get the government off the backs of Americans. Business groups had prepared their lists of existing and proposed regulations that they wanted eliminated. Though Americans in 1981 still demanded a clean environment, there was a general feeling that major environmental problems were well on the way toward being solved. Professional analysts, moreover, had become increasingly critical of bureaucratic environmental regulation and were open to notions of using market mechanisms to regulate pollution efficiently. Environmental groups were on the defensive, and Congress was in no mood for legislation-expanding regulations.

The Reagan Administration thus had a rare opportunity to offer an alternative policy model for environmental controls: to place greater emphasis on developing property rights and on other solutions using market incentives. It has failed to do so and has provided absolutely no vision for a tough environmental policy based on market mechanisms. Without this vision and with its ill-chosen appointments at EPA, the Reagan Administration has lost the initiative on environmental issues.

There have been some gains, of course. The Administration has won Supreme Court approval for the "bubble" policy for existing sources of emissions. This policy treats each existing industrial plant as if it were enclosed by a bubble. The aggregate emissions within the bubble are controlled, and decisions on trade-offs between the existing sources of emissions are left to the plant operator. Several states have been authorized to set up their own bubble policies. Federal and state bubble policies are estimated to have saved industry over $435 million with no negative impact on the environment. Commendable too is the Administration's continued use of "banking," often in conjunction with the bubble policy. Banking is the practice of reducing emissions at certain times in exchange for the right to increase emissions at other times. The overall goal is to reduce the total amount of pollution in a given area, while recognizing the need for flexibility in the pace of industrial activity.

While the bubble policy permits internal trading within a single plant, a broader policy of trading rights among various factories has been continued by the Administration. This trading of rights enables new factories to meet the stringent emissions limits imposed on them without always having to use costly technology. Similarly, the Administration has introduced widespread use of cost-benefit analysis in assessing environmental regulation. The Task Force on Regulatory Relief, headed by Vice President George Bush, identified a number of proposed and existing regulations that imposed high costs and provided few environmental benefits. Several of these regulations have been dropped or revised.

The Administration successfully has resisted ill-considered legislation in several important areas. In the debate over the potential threat to the ozone layer posed by chlorofluorocarbons, for instance, the Reagan Administration has argued that this is an international problem and cannot be effectively dealt with solely at the national level. Thus EPA wisely has preempted unilateral congressional action. Similarly, the Administration has avoided hasty acid rain legislation which would impose a much greater cost than demonstrable benefits on the U.S.

These achievements are dwarfed by the Administration's blunders. For one thing, the Reagan Administration has failed dismally to seize the moral high ground to change the course of environmental policy, allowing itself to be depicted as environmentally insensitive. As such, the Administration long ago lost the credibility to deal effectively with Congress or with environmental groups.

For another thing, the White House has failed to paint a broad picture of its alternative to Carter era intrusive regulation. Although the Reagan Administration extolled the virtues of a free market, it has not offered a positive, market-oriented approach to environmental protection as an alternative to the command and control approach that it inherited. Instead of providing a different vision, it has appeared simply to offer lower budgets, federal inaction, and fewer restrictions on polluting industries. When dealing with highly charged political issues with moral and even religious overtones, a philosophy that seems to consist only of doing less cannot compete effectively with statist activism.

The Reagan Administration also has failed to follow through on key elements of its strategy of economic analysis and reliance on markets in addressing environmental issues. Although the Reagan team initially articulated new, market-oriented policies, it was strongly opposed by entrenched bureaucracies and their congressional allies. Soon the Administration resorted to budget cuts as a substitute for reform. This has undercut potential public support for the Administration's market approach. Congress, meanwhile, has passed legislation limiting the ability of EPA to use cost-benefit analysis in establishing regulations. And because of White House failure to articulate the merits of cost-benefit analysis, Americans still tend to believe that no cost is too high to pay for environmental protection.

Similarly, the Reagan Administration has not captured the initiative on the issue of hazardous and toxic waste. As a result, policies have been adopted that will cost scores of billions of dollars, while voluntary cleanup of hazardous waste sites is retarded and innocent corporations are penalized.

The Comprehensive Environmental Response, Compensation, and Liability Act of 1980 (CERCLA or Superfund) and the Resource Conservation and Recovery Act of 1976 (hazardous waste control) were flawed when they were first enacted. Rather than learn from past mistakes, Congress reauthorized CERCLA in 1986 and RCRA in 1984. The Administration has failed to offer an effective alternative to such misguided legislation.

THE NEXT FOUR YEARS

Many existing environmental programs are based upon the assumption that all human impact on the environment can be eliminated. This would require the impossible and the undesirable—humans would have to cease almost all economic activity. Instead of basing policies on an unrealistic standard, society should seek to minimize environmental risks.

There is bipartisan concern for the quality of the environment in the U.S. Agreeing on the goal, however, does not reduce the importance of selecting the best method to attain it. The U.S. does not have to choose between full employment and environmental safety. America need not sacrifice international competitiveness to win a marginal reduction in industrial emissions, although government regulations often present these stark alternatives. To avoid this dilemma, the new Administration must harness the free market to protect the environment through rational economic incentives.

Although the American public wants clean air and clean water, concerns about the federal budget deficit make most Americans resist new spending. Most Americans also complain about restrictive new regulations. The new Administration should mobilize these sound sentiments for a policy that improves the environment without costly new programs. It also can make the credible argument that centralized decision-making cannot be cost-effective. The new Administration should make the case for setting overall limits for pollutants that ensure a clean environment and then establish market mechanisms to induce individual firms to find the most efficient means to stay within the limits.

Fulfilling the Promise of Superfund

Superfund was originally justified as the federal response to the dangers of abandoned hazardous waste sites. Superfund quickly became enlarged by pork-barrel politics and is now EPA's major program. In a June 1988 analysis of the $10 billion program, the Office of Technology Assessment concludes "that Superfund remains largely ineffective and inefficient." Unless the new Administration improves the performance of Superfund, much of its environmental budget will be wasted.

EPA rarely seeks an injunction to force a polluter to clean up a site
because such practice degenerates into years of court battles. In most
instances, EPA proceeds with the necessary cleanup and attempts to
recover costs through litigation at a later date. Cleanup costs can easily
exceed $20 million for a single site. But under current legislation, any
firm that contributed even a fraction of the total waste at a site can be
held liable for the full cost of the cleanup. EPA is not required to bring
suit against all responsible firms, even when they are known. When
EPA enters negotiations, it retains the threat of imposing total liability
on any firm.

The reluctance on the part of responsible parties to expose themselves to this kind of liability is to be expected. Firms should have the
option of seeking independent arbitration for cleanup responsibility
and costs. EPA should be limited to assigning costs proportionate to
each party's share of responsibility if parties agree to binding arbitration of the matter. Once an EPA-supervised cleanup is completed, all
firms that complied with the findings under arbitration should be
released from future private tort liability. Currently, so many conditions are attached to any release of liability that it is practically
worthless to the firm. If the cleanup was properly performed, there
should be no future potential injury. Questions of liability for injuries
incurred prior to the cleanup should be left up to the states.

This approach is more flexible and more equitable than litigation. It
would provide a carrot for firms that agree to binding arbitration, and
a stick for those that do not, by assuring each participating company
that it will not have to pay more than its appropriate share for the
cleanup. Firms refusing to participate could still be sued for the
remaining cost of the cleanup.

For the duration of Superfund's authorization, the new President
should pursue four goals:

1) Encourage the development and demonstration of cost-effective,
permanent cleanup technologies, such as super efficient incinerators.
Too much money is being spent on temporary solutions to hazardous
wastes, such as removal or impoundment. If hazardous wastes are
truly a threat, cleanup must be permanent. If a site is not a major
threat, there is no federal role in the cleanup.

2) Ensure that cleanup costs are consistent from site to site. Studies
show huge price differences between similar cleanups.

3) Develop stronger state-level control measures for cleanup procedures and decisions as a prelude to turning over both funding and operation of Superfund to the states.

4) Most important, publicize the expensive pork barrel that Superfund has become. Without accurate information, the public will continue to accept the claims of those who profit from the waste at EPA.

Using Market Mechanisms to Clean the Air

Comprehensive Clean Air Act amendments have been proposed, but not adopted, several times over the past two years. These present the new Administration with its first, and perhaps best, opportunity to offer a well-designed package of proposals to shift current law toward more market-based approaches.

The new Administration's package should address at least four key elements:

◆ *Ozone and carbon monoxide standards.* EPA should not make ozone or carbon monoxide (CO) standards more stringent than they are now without compelling scientific justification. Setting tougher standards ignores the tremendous improvements being made in the control of ozone and CO. A revision of the methods used to measure ozone and CO levels is needed, as many substandard areas have exceeded the strict standards only for a few hours every three years—and then at only one monitoring site for an entire metropolitan area. Yet failure to comply with federal air quality standards can trigger such punitive sanctions as a loss of federal highway funds and restrictions on industrial expansion. Congressional reluctance to see sanctions imposed on localities has resulted in an extension of several deadlines for improving air quality. The new Administration should eliminate politically timed deadlines and base air quality goals on economic and scientific realities. For example, ozone forms during hot, humid weather. With the unusually hot summers of recent years, sincere efforts to comply with federal ozone standards have been overwhelmed by nature. A more rational and flexible approach would obviate the need for ad hoc exceptions to the standards.

◆ *National Ambient Air Quality Standards (NAAQS).* The 1977 amendments to the Clean Air Act require EPA to review air standards for major pollutants every five years. The new President should announce his intention to veto any bill that would require EPA to impose new legislatively selected standards under an accelerated timetable. Current law is based on careful scientific examination of known and potential risks from pollutants.

◆ *Mobile sources.* Federal technological controls on car and truck emissions have reduced automotive emissions significantly. Hydrocarbon emissions from new model cars are 96 percent lower than precontrol levels. The same is true for carbon monoxide emissions. Without any further action, total "mobile source" emissions will continue to decline. Because of local climate and rapid population growth in such areas as Southern California and Denver, Colorado, federal standards for air quality have not been achieved, even though these states impose emissions controls that are far more restrictive than elsewhere in the nation. The new Administration should not attempt to address these unique local conditions through more stringent national standards. Any further toughening of requirements should be left entirely to the states.

◆ *Acid deposition.* The U.S. spends approximately $30 billion per year on air pollution abatement. As a result, emissions of the chemical components of acid rain have been reduced significantly. The present state of scientific knowledge does not justify massive new reductions in allowable emissions levels. The present standards are already lowering emissions, and proper market incentives, such as trading emission rights, will make them even more effective.

Expanding State and Local Responsibility for Sewage Wastewater Treatment

The 1987 Clean Water Act authorized $18 billion of federal funds to construct new local sewage treatment facilities. The legislation phases out the 15-year-old wastewater treatment grant program in 1991 and replaces it with a temporary federal program, which provides funds to state-run revolving loan programs for localities building new or upgraded sewage facilities. The most important element of the 1987 Act is that it terminates all federal wastewater treatment subsidies in 1994.

The top priority of the new Administration should be to persuade Congress not to reauthorize the wastewater treatment program for a fourth time and extend it beyond 1994. The program has been condemned by Congress's own research arm, the Congressional Budget Office, as being largely ineffective and wasteful. The program has become a multibillion-dollar pork barrel primarily benefiting the Northeast's large urban areas. More important, by requiring federal taxpayers, rather than local polluters, to pay the cost of environmental cleanup, it discourages cities and industries from taking independent steps to prevent pollution of local lakes and streams.

Congress's intent, when it passed the original wastewater treatment grant program in 1972, was for the construction program to be a one-time federal infusion of funds for environmental cleanup. Since then, nearly $52 billion has been spent. The program should be allowed to expire as now scheduled.

In the meantime, the new Administration should ensure that the funds that already have been authorized are spent efficiently on environmentally sensible projects. In past years, the lure of free federal funds has prodded communities to build very expensive treatment plants with capacity far greater than ever could be needed. These oversized facilities saddle local taxpayers with huge operating costs. Currently, the federal government pays 55 percent of the cost of a sewage plant's construction; localities pay only up to 45 percent. Studies by the Congressional Budget Office have found that this generous federal match encourages cities to build uneconomical facilities. The new Administration thus should oppose any attempt by Congress to continue the grant program after its scheduled termination in 1990.

Removing Disincentives to
Privatized Wastewater Treatment

One of the most encouraging developments in water treatment in recent years has been privatization. During the past decade, over 150 communities have contracted with private firms to finance, own, and operate sewage treatment plants. Under this arrangement, the city pays an annual fee to the private owner for wastewater treatment service, then passes the cost on to residents in their monthly water bills. By so doing, cities have cut sewage treatment costs by about 20 percent. One reason privately construted plants are less expensive is that federally funded facilities must comply with 16 regulations, including the Davis-Bacon Act and environmental impact requirements. Although the 1986 Tax Reform Act rescinded some of the tax incentives for privatization, several cities—most recently, Mount Vernon, Illinois—have demonstrated that privatization is still financially attractive.

Current federal regulations, however, restrict the intermingling of federal loan or grant funds with private funds for capital infrastructure, such as a sewage treatment plant. In addition, the rules require any plant constructed with federal funds to be publicly owned. This discourages cities from considering privatization, since they would forfeit federal funds if they chose a private owner and operator for their sewage plants. The new Administration should design a strategy to remove the disincentives to privatized wastewater treatment. EPA should issue a regulation requiring any city applying through the states for any federal funds first to perform a privatization feasibility study and then to solicit bids from private wastewater treatment operators. This would force cities to explore the potential cost savings of privatization before they build a new public facility.

EPA too must ensure that, when the federal government begins to make contributions to state revolving loan funds in 1991, these funds are made available equally to those cities building a public facility and those contracting with private firms. Since both private and public sewage treatment facilities achieve the same environmental objectives, states should be mandated to make the federally subsidized low-interest loans to cities regardless of the ownership structure of the facilities.

To comply with federal regulations prohibiting the intermingling of funds in the new loan program, cities should be permitted to use federal funds to make lease-purchase payments to the private owner, so that after 20 to 30 years the city would own the facility. Alternatively, EPA could require that the city place these funds in an escrow account for 20 years, and at the end of that period, use the funds to purchase the facility in one payment.

Through such initiatives, EPA will spur competitive alternatives to public funding of wastewater treatment projects. Private entrepreneurs already have demonstrated convincingly that they are capable of building and operating cost-efficient plants that comply fully with federal clean water regulations. This private sector involvement in financing environmental facilities should be encouraged since cities will have to attract private funds when federal subsidies are terminated in 1994.

———————————◇———————————

INITIATIVES FOR 1989

1) Prepare a package of market-based environmental legislation. EPA traditionally has focused on regulation to achieve environmental objectives. Yet establishing pollution markets, whereby industries have a market incentive to find the least costly way of reaching environmental goals, can be more efficient than regulation. Thus, EPA should establish a policy that sets overall pollution production limits and then encourages market mechanisms to find the most efficient means to abide by the limits. Mandating technological solutions, as with coal-scrubber laws, is less effective and more costly than such simple alternatives as switching fuels. The White House Office of Policy Development, in consultation with EPA, should prepare a legislative package of market-based environmental statutes that rely on economic incentives and respect for property rights. Such statutes should include Clean Air Act amendments, Wastewater Treatment Grant Program revisions, and an overhaul of Superfund.

2) Freeze existing emissions standards. National levels of emissions are dropping dramatically, and there is no demonstrable need for increasing federal controls. Moreover, such controls can impose unnecessary costs on firms, thereby destroying jobs. The EPA thus should freeze Clean Air Act regulatory standards at their current levels, and the new President should vow to veto any legislation that would make emissions standards more stringent before current efforts take full effect.

3) Recognize that environmental protection is primarily a state responsibility. During the past two decades, the federal government has assumed funding and regulatory responsibility for virtually all environmental issues. This has obscured the local nature of many environmental problems, relieved the states of their obligation for environmental cleanup, and discouraged innovative state approaches to environmental problems. The new President should convene a high-level Administration task force on "Federalism and Environmental Regulation" composed of state governors and representatives from EPA and the Office of Management and Budget. This task force would identify environmental programs and responsibilities to be transferred to the states. A central aim of the task force should be to develop federal incentives for the states to assume new environmental responsibilities.

4) Stress the advantages of a market-based system of environmental protection. To restore the credibility of market solutions to environmental problems and to gain the public support needed to influence legislation, the new EPA aggressively must present the facts on the total costs of environmental legislation. The dollar amounts shown in the federal budget are just the tip of the iceberg. Most Americans, including many lawmakers, know too little about the consequences of the past 15 years of federal environmental regulation. The EPA thus should launch an expanded program of research and program review.

The new Administration must inform the public about which programs have succeeded and which have failed, of the risks that have been reduced and those that remain.

5) Employ cost-benefit analysis for all environmental regulation. As a guide for good policy, the practice of cost-benefit analysis measures the costs of a regulation imposed on workers, businesses, and consumers, and it compares this with the benefits likely to be achieved, such as cleaner air. This is a valuable analytical tool to assess the net impact of a proposed rule, and it should be adopted in all environmental regulation. Thus, the new President should announce his determination to veto new environmental legislation if it prohibits a cost-benefit analysis of environmental cleanup. At the same time, the Administration should require cost-benefit analysis of all current regulations.

6) Require privatization and competition in all wastewater treatment plant construction funds. Current federal regulations restrict the freedom of cities to use federal funds in conjunction with private funds for capital construction projects. This means a city wishing to use federal wastewater treatment loans to finance a less costly private plant may find its loan withdrawn. The restrictions thus encourage many cities to adopt more expensive projects in order to obtain federal support. EPA should ensure that wastewater treatment loans are available to cities that opt for private competitive operations of their facilities. Federal contributions to state revolving loan funds should be made only if the states make loans to cities that seek private financing and ownership of their wastewater facilities. EPA should issue guidelines requiring states receiving federal funds to remove any bias in their revolving loan programs against private financing alternatives.

7) Keep EPA below Cabinet level. Some in Congress have proposed making EPA a Cabinet-level agency. This would only institutionalize and enlarge flawed federal programs. The new Administration should seek to return primary environmental responsibility to the individual states, and the EPA should offer technical assistance, monitoring, and oversight of national goals and programs.

8) Establish a single repository for all information on the current state of the environment. Currently, data are often gathered after the policy decisions have been reached. Such procedures are inappropriate and wasteful. Sensible environmental enforcement and reliance upon market incentives require good monitoring and informaion. Accurate cost-benefit analysis and risk assessment require data obtained from monitoring. Those who prefer a government solution to problems are always helped by the confusion arising from an incomplete or inaccurate data base.

13

The Department of Health and Human Services

The Department of Health and Human Services is the largest domestic Cabinet department. It handles matters ranging from the Social Security system to health care for the poor. Given the wide span of the Department's responsibilities, this chapter is divided into three sections, covering health, welfare, and Social Security.

BUDGET AND PERSONNEL

Secretaries

Otis R. Bowen	1985–present
Margaret M. Heckler	1983–1985
Richard S. Schweiker	1981–1983

Personnel

March 1988	123,580
April 1980	167,400
April 1970	107,910 (HEW figure)

Budgets Outlays

Fiscal Year	Total (billions)
1989 Estimate	$396.8
1988 Estimate	$375.1
1987 Actual	$351.3
1986 Actual	$333.9
1985 Actual	$315.5
1980 Actual	$194.2
1970 Actual	$ 47.7

Health

Ronald F. Docksai*
Task Force Chairman

The new President must take the offensive on health issues by attacking Congress's piecemeal approach to health policy as an inadequate remedy for the serious problems of an outdated and basically unsound system. He must offer the American people a vision of a revitalized health care system that provides incentives for increased quality and technological innovation, while at the same time reducing costs, bureaucracy, and uncertainty. He must advocate reforms that refocus American health care on serving the needs of consumers, not those of providers, bureaucrats, or special interests. And he must offer to all Americans a system that gives them control over health care decisions, while encouraging them to set aside the resources they need to purchase this care.

The new President should vow to achieve sweeping health care reform by the end of his term. The goal should be to overhaul completely America's health care tax policies and to restructure the three major health programs of the federal government—Medicare, Medicaid, and veterans health benefits. To reach this goal, the new President will need to work during his first year to build broad public support for his proposals and then spend the remainder of his term pushing his legislative agenda through Congress.

———————◇———————

SUMMARY OF AGENCY FUNCTIONS

The major health care programs of the federal government are concentrated in three main offices:

---

*Commenting and contributing generously to this chapter were *Mandate III* Task Force Members Judy Boddie, Peter Ferrara, Patricia Jarvis, Sam Kazman, Kevin Moley, and Sara Thomasson. They do not necessarily endorse all of its views and recommendations.

Task Force Deputy Chairman: Heritage Policy Analyst Edmund F. Haislmaier.

◆ *The Health Care Financing Administration*, which was created in 1977, within the Department of Health and Human Services, to oversee the federal government's two biggest health care programs, Medicare and Medicaid. Medicare pays for hospital care and physician services for the elderly and disabled Social Security recipients, and is funded through a combination of payroll taxes, premiums, and general revenues. Medicaid pays for medical services for the poor and medically needy through a system of federal grants to the states. With the Medicare and Medicaid programs, HCFA is responsible for administering the vast majority of federal health spending, a huge sum amounting to roughly one-tenth of the entire federal budget. The Health Care Financing Administration is headed by an administrator appointed by the President.

◆ *The Public Health Service*, which was created by Congress in 1798 as the U.S. Marine Hospital Service, to care for sick and injured seamen. Its current form dates from the establishment of the commissioned corps of the Public Health Service (PHS) in 1889. The PHS now is part of the Department of Health and Human Services and serves as the federal government's principal health agency, to protect and advance the health of the American people. PHS programs include biomedical research, health regulation, communicable disease control, education of health professionals, and the direct provision of health care services to such medically needy populations as migrant workers. The PHS is headed by the Assistant Secretary for Health, who oversees the activities of the surgeon general and seven major operating agencies: the Agency for Toxic Substances and Disease Registry; the Alcohol, Drug Abuse, and Mental Health Administration; the Centers for Disease Control; the Food and Drug Administration; the Health Resources and Services Administration; the Indian Health Service; and the National Institutes of Health. Fiscal 1987 outlays for PHS were almost $10 billion.

◆ *The Veterans Administration*, which is not part of HHS, provides health care to millions of Americans through an extensive network of general and psychiatric hospitals, nursing homes, outpatient clinics, and other facilities. The VA's Department of Medicine and Surgery is headed by the chief medical director and its fiscal 1987 outlays were over $10 billion.

———————◇———————

INSTITUTIONAL CONSTRAINTS

The American health care system is a $500 billion-dollar-a-year industry accounting for over 11 percent of America's gross national product. The federal government was responsible for $142 billion of this amount in 1987, or about 29 percent of all U.S. health care spending. Medicare and Medicaid are, respectively, the second and third largest discrete programs in the entire federal government, eclipsed only by Social Security. And almost every part of the nation's health care system is influenced by federal dollars or federal regulation.

An enormous number of individuals and groups have a stake in the system, and thus are deeply interested in policy governing it. Collectively, they constitute what could be termed a "health industrial complex." Foremost among them is the Washington axis of career government bureaucrats who administer much of the system and the congressmen who view it as a vehicle to power and reelection. The former tend to be committed to an expansion of the federal social insurance system for health care; the latter see promises of subsidized health as paying political dividends.

Other groups with a direct interest include beneficiaries of government programs and their advocates. The beneficiary group with the greatest political clout is the elderly, skillfully mobilized by the American Association of Retired Persons (AARP). Political pressure from the elderly is immense, and directed almost exclusively to expanding federally funded health programs like Medicare.

Suppliers of health services predictably lobby for policies that will expand federal health care. Physicians, hospitals, drug companies, product manufacturers and suppliers, researchers, financial institutions, and a growing army of health care consultants all have a keen interest in health policy and devote millions of dollars to campaigning for policies that serve their interests. The long-standing policy of allowing businesses to deduct from their taxable income their outlays for employee health care, and the increased federal regulation of employee benefits since 1974 have given employers and unions an enormous stake in the structure of the system.

Although the primary goal of these pressure groups tends to be an expansion of the federal government as a purchaser of health services, there are also pressures to put a brake on this expansion. Beneficiaries are beginning to question just how much they gain from a system in which costs are rising so rapidly, yet some of their most basic needs, such as chronic long-term care for the elderly, are largely ignored. And corporations are finding that even their lucrative tax breaks no longer offset the enormous expenses and problems associated with funding and managing health benefits for their employees.

These factors are prompting lawmakers, health care providers, and beneficiaries to look at innovative changes in the design of the health care system. This gives the new President a unique opportunity to outflank the health industrial complex and build a coalition to develop a health care system for Americans that combines sound economic principles with high-quality, accessible care.

◇

THE REAGAN ADMINISTRATION RECORD

Despite the best intentions of the Reagan Administration, the major problems afflicting the U.S. health care system inherited by Ronald Reagan remain unsolved. These problems include: guaranteeing adequate long-term care, better acute-care coverage for the elderly, a shortage of nursing professionals, federal overregulation, health care inflation, and runaway federal health care spending. Added to the list are the new problems caused by the AIDS crisis and growing concerns about medically uninsured citizens. The underlying causes of these problems and concerns stem in large part from the inherent dynamics of the U.S. health care system, and from the institutional constraints which have made many reforms politically impossible. But the Reagan Administration also has been at fault, thanks to the unwise tactics it has used in dealing with the political pressures it has faced.

Still, the Reagan Administration has made some important policy changes. It has encouraged states to play a greater role in government programs, and thus brought innovation to a moribund system. In 1981, the White House won passage of legislation to combine dozens of small categorical health programs into three block grant programs: the Preventive Health and Health Services Block Grant; the Alcohol, Drug Abuse and Mental Health Block Grant; and the Maternal and Child Health Block Grant. These have led to greater flexibility and better local management of program funds and have ensured that more of the money actually was used to meet the needs of the target constituencies.

The Reagan Administration also convinced Congress in 1986 to repeal the Health Planning Program. This program was designed to reduce health care costs by certifying the need for new or expanded facilities or major equipment before they could be built or purchased. But by promoting a regulatory rather than a competitive approach, the program resulted in so much bureaucracy that the cost of compliance at times exceeded the cost of proposed new investments. In addition, the system of Public Health Service hospitals was transferred to local control. There was no longer a reason for maintaining the federal role.

Innovation and price competition also have been enhanced by Administration-sponsored legislation in 1981 that allowed states to use alternative methods for providing health care through Medicaid. Alternative, and more competitive, methods of delivering health care similarly have been encouraged by changes in the Medicare program which took effect in 1985. These allow beneficiaries to sign up with prepaid health plans as long as they cost no more than 95 percent of the average per capita outlays of Medicare. Previously, Medicare would only reimburse patients for services already received. The change allows beneficiaries to "shop around" for the best health care.

The Reagan Administration did succeed in including in the 1983 Social Security amendments a prospective payment system (PPS) for Medicare reimbursements. Under this, Medicare establishes a fixed schedule of fees that it pays hospitals for the treatment of each of 468 diagnostic related groups (DRGs) of illnesses. If the actual cost to the hospital is less than the DRG fee, it keeps the difference; if more, it absorbs the loss. The aim is to spur price consciousness and competition among hospitals. The wisdom of this policy, however, is unclear. While any reform is better than the previous open-ended reimbursement system, which invited physicians and hospitals to charge as much as they could for treating a patient, a price control system such as PPS falls far short of the reforms needed to restore normal market incentives to health care. This is clear from PPS's track record. Like all price controls, PPS simply encourages the health industry to shift costs to activities not covered by the controls. As such, while PPS has slowed the growth of Medicare hospital reimbursements to 7 percent a year, or about the annual rate of overall medical inflation, Medicare's physician reimbursements are growing 16 percent a year.

The Reagan Administration also has reformed the U.S. Food and Drug Administration (FDA). The 1983 Orphan Drug Act boosted research on drugs for rare diseases by offering tax incentives and exclusive marketing rights. In 1984, Congress passed legislation shortening the new drug approval (NDA) process for generic drugs, while extending patent protection of newly developed pharmaceuticals. This has accelerated the availability of generic drugs, while giving firms a strong incentive to develop new drugs. A year later, the FDA issued its NDA rewrite, a series of new regulations aimed at streamlining the approval process. In 1987, responding to the AIDS crisis, the agency issued its "Treatment Use IND" regulations, permitting desperately ill patients to be treated with "investigational new drugs" not yet approved by FDA. And the FDA has approved a record number of products during the past six years. Yet, as FDA officials admit, the drug approval process still needs fundamental reform. Many new U.S.-developed drugs continue to be available abroad long before they are in America, despite actions in July 1988 to ease imports of unapproved drugs for personal use.

These Reagan Administration successes have been offset by failures to win passage of key legislation, ill-considered proposals, and a lack of interest regarding health issues on the part of senior White House officials. Richard Schweiker, President Reagan's first Secretary of HHS, came to office with a definite reform agenda and actually succeeded in passing elements of it, such as combining a number of programs into block grants. But by the beginning of Reagan's second term, his staff had lost all interest in reforming health care entitlement programs. In picking Margaret Heckler to succeed Schweiker, the Administration sought to project a compassionate image and placate interest groups, marking time on fundamental reform. When Heckler at last resigned, the White House tapped Otis Bowen, a doctor and former governor with respectable credentials and proved management skills, yet with no apparent commitment to Reagan's philosophy of curbing the growth of government.

This lack of interest among key White House officials virtually guaranteed legislative setbacks. A major legislative failure was the Administration's unsuccessful 1984 attempt to enact real reforms to slow health care inflation. The proposal included limiting the tax deductibility of employer-provided health insurance; this would have discouraged employers from agreeing to union demands for more costly health benefits. The package also would have required Medicare patients to pay more for short hospital stays in exchange for protection from catastrophic hospital costs. It also would have introduced a Medicare voucher with which beneficiaries could purchase insurance or prepaid health plans. This voucher would have encouraged the elderly to seek better and less costly coverage.

One reason the Administration failed to win passage of this package was that the needs to moderate costs and improve catastrophic protection did not appear as great then as they do today. Another reason was the Administration's flawed political strategy. The Administration underestimated the strength of the business-union coalition opposed to limiting the tax deductibility of group insurance. And the Administration failed to include such provisions that could win popular support as expanding health care deductions in the personal tax code. Given today's increased public attention to catastrophic coverage and to the costs of health care, the new President will have a much greater chance of success with a similar, but improved, reform package.

The most serious policy error of the Reagan Administration may be its support for an expansion of Medicare to provide catastrophic acute care protection for the elderly. Reagan, together with most Americans, correctly believes that the elderly must not be impoverished by a serious or persistent illness. Yet instead of seeking legislation to give private insurance companies an incentive to offer catastrophic hospital and long-term care insurance, Reagan was persuaded by Administration officials and Republican lawmakers to endorse an expansion of Medicare and hence of the federal government. It was a serious blunder. Supporters of a tax-financed national health system seized on the Bowen-Reagan proposal, declaring it a welcome admission by the White House that only the federal government could deal with the problem. Congressmen who favored a private-sector approach to the issue to encourage quality and innovation and to constrain federal spending found themselves undercut by the White House and labeled as "anti-elderly" by their opponents.

The result was the legislation signed by the President in July 1988, which constitutes the biggest expansion of Medicare since it was created in 1965. The legislation provides little more protection than the elderly already receive through Medicare and private Medigap policies, yet it increases Medicare premiums and levies a new tax on senior citizens. The measure does virtually nothing to defray long-term nursing home costs, the biggest financial headache for the elderly. And it eliminates ceilings on the taxpayer-supported Medicare system's commitment, thus promising to ignite an uncontrollable explosion of future spending. By accepting the premises of the measure, Ronald Reagan has given unexpected momentum to lawmakers who seek to create a federally funded national health system in America.

———————————◇———————————

THE NEXT FOUR YEARS

The politics of how the new President deals with health policy issues will be as important as the agenda he pursues. Institutional constraints will make it very difficult, if not impossible, for him to achieve swift reforms. In the short run, he can only make changes that address minor problems while preparing the political ground for more fundamental reform.

The experience of the past two years shows that Congress and many interest groups sense public support and a political opportunity for a major expansion in the federal government's role in health care. Long-term care and mandated benefits legislation almost certainly will be reintroduced at the start of the next Congress, and a whole range of AIDS-related health legislation is likely to follow close behind. Many of these measures will not significantly improve the health care of Americans. All will increase the cost of medical care to patients and taxpayers and enrich the medical industry.

Consequently, the most important short-term objective for the new President is to develop—before taking office—a clear vision of the health care system he wishes to create for Americans, and a political strategy for communicating his vision to the American people. By this he will seize the legislative initiative. The goal should be the achievement of sweeping health care reform by the end of the term.

As he unveils this vision, the new President first should point out the underlying deficiencies of the current system, particularly its inability to adapt to changing needs and technology and its inherently inflationary structure. The current system is not geared to meet the growing need for long-term care and terminal illnesses not suited to hospital care. At the same time, the system provides insufficient incentives for hospitals, physicians, or patients to use new technologies and procedures to reduce the costs of treating less serious illnesses.

The new President should point out that the principal reason for this lack of cost consciousness is because federal policy encourages the reimbursement system in both private insurance and public programs to favor the interests of providers, not consumers. Policies are geared to covering the cost of specific procedures or the services of specific providers, not meeting the consumer's general need for comprehensive health services and protection against high medical costs.

Under this third party payment system, most consumers directly pay only a small portion of their medical bills. The greatest proportion is reimbursed by an insurance company, an employer, or a government agency. This insulates patients and providers from the real costs of their decisions. It thus discourages patients from questioning the need or cost of procedures and encourages providers to increase costs or offer additional services of only marginal benefit. The new President should emphasize that until these incentives are changed, it will be impossible to provide Americans with the health services they need without incurring runaway costs. He must make it clear that health care financing problems are interrelated and can only be solved by comprehensive reform, not by Congress's current piecemeal approach.

Having explained the causes of the deficiencies in America's health care system, the new President should propose reforms that would restructure the entire system to serve the needs of the consumer rather than the health care industry. Specifically, the new President should send to Congress an omnibus health care reform bill as his legislative vehicle for achieving reform.

For political and economic reasons, the centerpiece of the bill must be a set of tax deductions to encourage consumers to purchase health services and insurance directly rather than through the current third party system. The inclusion of a politically popular tax deduction is essential to gaining acceptance for the reform package and to counter politically potent proposals to expand federally supported services. At the same time, these tax policies would introduce effective consumer choice as the primary mechanism for forcing providers to offer quality services at competitive prices, thereby bringing health care inflation under control. Also, by encouraging consumers to purchase routine health care services out of pocket, health insurance companies would have incentives to concentrate on providing policies more suited to the natural function of insurance—coverage for unlikely but very expensive occurrences.

Reducing health care inflation and restructuring health insurance to focus on catastrophic coverage are essential preconditions for successful restructuring of government health programs later in the term, particularly Medicare and veterans health benefits. The government would be able to fulfill its commitments to these groups of beneficiaries more effectively and efficiently by providing them with vouchers. This is a certificate of a certain value which can be used to purchase a service. A voucher for Medicare would encourage the elderly to shop around for the best combination of price and quality in medical insurance or prepaid health plans, leading to better services at lower cost. A voucher system also would give beneficiaries more control over their own health care decisions.

The new President should plan on introducing his omnibus health care reform legislation in 1990, giving him a year to build public support for his proposals and forestall congressional initiatives by campaigning against them as inadequate remedies.

In developing his overall strategy, the new President should consider the grim fact that the AIDS crisis may give him leverage to win support for a regulatory overhaul of the Food and Drug Administration. For the first time, some of the victims of FDA's unnecessarily long and restrictive approval process are highly visible and organized.

The new President then must go over the heads of Congress and the special interests and appeal directly to Americans for their support. Reagan successfully did this with the 1981 tax cuts and the 1986 tax reform. The new President must begin by asking Congress for a very large loaf, expecting full well that he will only get half. But then he must take what Congress gives him and immediately turn around and ask for the rest. In accepting the first part, he must tell the American people that it is a good start, but only a start, and solicit their support for his renewed efforts to finish the job.

Transferring Health Care Tax Deductions from Employers to Individuals

The central feature of an omnibus overhaul of health care would be tax changes to transfer most of the health care tax deductions from the employer to individuals and families. This would spur cost consciousness and create the consumer-sensitive market largely absent from the current system. The transfer would be phased in over a three-year period, and should include the following provisions:

First, Americans would be permitted to deduct fully from their taxable income all out-of-pocket medical expenses, without having to itemize their tax returns. Currently, only taxpayers who itemize can deduct medical expenses, and only those expenses exceeding 7.5 percent of their income. The proposed change would give consumers an incentive to pay directly for more of their own medical care, particularly that which is inexpensive or routine, such as preventive checkups, dental care, prescription drugs, treatment of common injuries or infections, or minor emergency treatments. To encourage the purchase of insurance policies with higher copayment levels, under which the patient pays a larger share of the bill, this deduction should include expenditures on insurance policy deductibles and coinsurance. Out-of-pocket expenses for long-term care and premiums for long-term care insurance should be treated the same as those for acute care under these deductions. Because this is likely to be the provision with the most popular support, and because encouraging consumers to pay directly for less expensive services will lead them to start questioning the cost of all medical care, this provision should be the central element in the reform package.

Second, taxpayers would be allowed to deduct up to 80 percent of the cost of individual health insurance premiums. Currently, such premiums offer most individuals no tax relief, while company-provided plans are deductible by the firm. This provision could be phased in with corresponding reductions in the amounts employers are allowed to deduct for purchasing insurance for their workers. This would be of particular help to workers in smaller firms, which often do not provide company-paid insurance. The main reason for making this deduction separate from that for out-of-pocket medical expenses is that allowing health insurance premiums to be fully deductible might lead to overinsurance, blunting the economic benefits of encouraging consumers to purchase low-cost medical services directly. As with out-of-pocket expenses, taxpayers should be allowed to take this deduction without itemizing.

Third, taxpayers should be allowed to deduct medical expenses for needy relatives without having to meet the dependent support test. Under current law, before a taxpayer can claim a personal exemption or other deduction for a dependent, he must demonstrate that he provided at least 50 percent of that dependent's total support for the year. This change would encourage families to assume more of the health care costs for medically or financially needy relatives, particularly the elderly, the disabled, the unemployed, and low-wage workers. This provision would be particularly helpful in meeting the need for long-term care services and insurance for the present elderly population. It also would help extend coverage to young uninsured workers entering the job market, and provide more flexibility to the parents of disabled children.

Fourth, corporate health care tax deductions should be limited to money spent on preventive health and "wellness" services provided at the workplace. Most of the existing corporate health care tax deductions would be phased out under the tax changes discussed above. This remaining deduction would encourage corporations to target their health benefits where they can do the most good, with firms encouraged to make sure their employees stay healthy. While such services are low in cost, their potential is enormous for reducing later demand for more expensive treatments.

Defusing the Medicare Time Bomb

Medicare faces heavy long-term financing problems which threaten to produce untenable payroll tax burdens for workers or deep benefit reductions for retirees. Based on the federal government's own most recent projections, Part A of the system, which finances hospital coverage through the Medicare payroll tax of 2.9 percent of wages, is likely to run short of funds to pay promised benefits between 1999 and 2006. The cost of Part B, which reimburses physicians' fees, is already increasing rapidly and will rise even faster when the new catastrophic legislation is implemented.

To address these financing problems and the underlying perverse incentives that cause them, the new President's proposed omnibus legislation should include two key amendments concerning Medicare.

First, the surtaxes and new drug benefits contained in the 1988 catastrophic health legislation should be repealed. Under the legislation, elderly couples could face income tax surcharges of as much as $2,000 by 1993. As more of the elderly become aware of the real cost of the catastrophic legislation, repeal will become an increasingly popular action for the new President to advocate.

Second, in exchange for repealing the surtaxes on the elderly, Medicare should be restructured by eliminating the current $564 inpatient hospital deductible and establishing instead a new set of front-end coinsurance rates for both Part A (hospital care) and Part B (outpatient physician services). Coinsurance refers to the share of a medical bill which must be paid by the patient. The new rates should be tapered so that beneficiaries pay a declining share of the bill as their hospital and doctor charges increase. For example, Medicare enrollees would pay, say, 20 percent of the first $2,000 of Medicare-approved medical costs, 15 percent of the next $3,000, 10 percent of the next $5,000, and so forth. The rates should be designed so that no beneficiary would pay more than $2,500 in 1991. Both this cap and the specific coinsurance rates should be indexed to program costs for the years beyond 1991, to keep pace with inflation.

The advantage of this change is that, like the 1988 legislation, it would limit beneficiaries' potential out-of-pocket costs, while protecting those with serious illnesses. But unlike the 1988 law, which does nothing to encourage cost control, requiring beneficiaries to pay more of their front-end costs would spur them to question the need and expense of their treatment for less serious conditions.

These two amendments would defuse the time bomb of Medicare costs.

Other measures are needed to change how the medical care of retirees is funded. These measures should seek two goals: first, they should encourage working Americans to establish private savings to supplement or replace their Medicare coverage, second, they should aim to replace the current Medicare reimbursement system with a voucher program.

Under an "opting out" proposal, workers would be given the option of establishing private savings and insurance accounts during their working years to substitute for part of their Medicare coverage in retirement. Legislation for this was introduced in 1985 by Rep. French Slaughter (R-Va.) This should form the foundation of the new Administration's proposals. Under the Slaughter plan, workers and their employers could contribute to individual health care savings accounts (HCSAs) up to the amount of employee and employer Medicare payroll taxes. Contributors would receive an income tax credit equal to 60 percent of the amount paid into these accounts; and the contributions and investment returns would accumulate tax-free until retirement. To the extent each worker used this option, he or she would receive reduced Medicare coverage for more routine medical expenses in retirement. The accumulated private funds in the account, moreover, would be available to purchase supplementary private health insurance or to pay for expenses directly.

In tandem with legislation to permit this opting out of Medicare, the new Administration should propose Medicare vouchers for those Americans choosing to remain within the system. The certificates would be used by Medicare beneficiaries to purchase insurance or prepaid health plans approved by Medicare. The face value of the voucher would vary according to the health condition of the beneficiary to ensure coverage was available. The vouchers would stimulate innovation and price competition in health care, since recipients would have the incentive to seek the best deal from insurers.

A voucher system can only work well in a functioning and competitive free market, however. The problem with health care today is that regulation and tax policies prevent the private health market from functioning properly. Thus normal market incentives must be restored to health care through changes in the tax code before the government can take full advantage of the potential of health care vouchers.

Restoring Medicaid to Its Original Function

Medicaid originally was intended to finance basic health care services for the poor. But, by default, it has increasingly become a program for financing care for those who are driven into poverty by high medical expenses. Absent major reforms, Medicaid's problems will only grow worse. The projected growth in the elderly population will increase the demand for nursing care. At the same time, the need for catastrophic acute or long-term care is increasingly a problem for the young as much as the old. The costs of caring for younger patients with severe disabilities or terminal illnesses such as AIDS or degenerative neuromuscular diseases can far outstrip those for a retiree spending the last months of his or her life in a nursing home. Having exhausted their resources and run out of other options, more of these younger patients are now ending up on Medicaid rolls.

Blunting the consequences of catastrophic occurrences such as fire, floods, shipwrecks, accidental deaths, and so forth, is precisely what true insurance is designed to do; it does so in every area—except health care. In the long run, using tax incentives to restructure health insurance is the only real solution to financing catastrophic health care. Yet, even if insurance were restructured tomorrow, many patients would still be trapped in the existing system and some portion of the poor would need catastrophic care, such as drug abusers with AIDS.

To respond to these needs, the new President, as part of his omnibus health care legislation, should propose separate programs to fund long-term care for the elderly poor and comprehensive treatment for AIDS patients. Freeing it from the burdens of financing AIDS and long-term care for the elderly is the essential first step in restructuring Medicaid and restoring its original function of providing basic health care services to the poor. The next step is to incorporate Medicaid changes into an overall welfare reform strategy to give states more flexibility in administering programs and to encourage the development of innovative and cost effective methods for delivering services to the poor. (See Welfare section in this chapter.) Medicaid should be a part of this welfare reform, not an exception to it.

In proposing Medicaid reforms, the new President will be able to build on Reagan Administration foundations. The 1981 Omnibus Budget Reconciliation Act gave states more latitude in tailoring their Medicaid programs to meet their particular needs, and the states have accepted the challenge eagerly. States also have been allowed to request waivers from federal regulations governing the way they administer Medicaid; in 1982 more than two-thirds of the states applied for such waivers.

In 1982 the Health Care Financing Administration approved funding for demonstration programs in seven states to test alternative medical delivery systems for Medicaid recipients. The successes and failures of these demonstrations can guide future state experiments. In keeping with an overall welfare reform strategy, the new President should seek legislation to give the states even more flexibility by reducing federal Medicaid regulations and expand the availability of waivers.

Meeting the Need for Long-Term Care

Federal and state governments already spend over $20 billion a year on long-term care for elderly Americans unable to pay for these services themselves. This help is provided primarily through Medicaid. Yet Medicaid is not well designed for dealing with the long-term care financing needs of the elderly. In spite of federal Medicaid waivers giving states more flexibility in providing long-term care, the basic structure and regulations governing the program are geared to providing for the acute-care needs of the nonelderly poor.

The best way to deal with the burdens imposed on Medicaid by retirees needing long-term care would be to separate Medicaid's existing acute-care and long-term care functions. The eligibility criteria and benefits of each program could then be adjusted for two different sets of needs.

The new President should propose legislation to remove all long-term care assistance from Medicaid. Instead, it would be provided through a new, separate, federal/state program. Such assistance should be better designed to cover elderly couples, since nursing home expenses for a disabled individual often can impoverish the spouse. A couple should be allowed to keep substantially more income and assets than under current Medicaid law and still qualify for government aid.

Once the long-term care costs of low-income Americans are taken care of by the government, the remaining issue would be how to deal with cases of moderate-income and affluent Americans hit suddenly with high nursing home costs. The pressure for a massive expansion of federal long-term care assistance comes mainly from moderate-income Americans concerned about nursing home costs draining their finances. Yet this is not really a health policy issue, but an estate planning issue. It does not call for government help. The government should not be asking the taxpayer to preserve substantial private estates. The very fact that the issue is one of protecting available resources demonstrates that the elderly person or couple in this situation can afford private insurance or other private alternatives.

The federal government should encourage Americans to begin buying insurance for long-term care during their working years to reduce the annual cost of premiums. It could do this by extending the same tax policies to long-term care insurance that now apply to life insurance. Thus the income earned on investment reserves for long-term care policies would no longer be taxed, just as life insurance reserves are not taxed. Similarly, the benefits paid by long-term care policies would be made tax exempt, as life insurance benefits are. Moreover, all workers and retirees would be permitted to use vested funds in pension plans, 401(k) plans, Individual Retirement Accounts (IRAs), and other retirement plans to make tax-free purchases of long-term care insurance.

After the tax code has been changed to make catastrophic acute and long-term care insurance more affordable, working Americans should be required to purchase catastrophic health insurance for themselves and their families. There will always be the danger that some individuals who can afford protection will prefer to play Russian roulette with their own and their families' health. Such individuals should not be allowed a free ride on the rest of society, expecting government, charitable organizations, or hospitals to defray or absorb the costs of their lack of foresight. Instead, they should be required by law to purchase protection, at least for their dependents and preferably also for themselves. This would be similar to current policies in many jurisdictions requiring auto owners to have liability insurance.

Financing the Treatment of AIDS

The AIDS (Acquired Immune Deficiency Syndrome) crisis has revealed many of the flaws in America's existing system for financing and delivering health care. As a result of the incentives in existing federal policy, the current structure of private health insurance is geared mainly to meeting acute-care expenses. And because most health insurance is provided by employers, patients who lose their jobs, whether due to their illness or other factors, are left without even this protection. Nor is the existing structure of public assistance programs much better equipped to deal with this problem.

Existing federal programs are geared to meeting the needs of individuals with health problems very different from those of AIDS patients. For both elderly and disabled Social Security recipients, for instance, Medicare is designed primarily to finance occasional hospital and physician care. It is not designed to pay for long-term nursing care for such conditions as Alzheimer's Disease or AIDS. Similarly, disability insurance is designed to provide cash assistance to individuals who, because of some injury, are temporarily or permanently unable to work. Hence there is a waiting period before benefits will be paid, so that Medicare officials can determine whether the beneficiary is going to recover and resume working. It is not designed to fund the support or treatment of the terminally ill.

For most illnesses there are, at best, only a handful of treatment options. Doctors choose the one likely to offer the best results, given the patient's individual physiology and the severity of the illness. But AIDS patients are vulnerable to a wide variety of infections and cancers that can strike suddenly and can occur in numerous combinations. The result is that doctors face a different medical condition in almost every AIDS patient they treat. This means that AIDS patients need a comprehensive range of services, provided by highly trained and costly specialists. And as the disease progresses, AIDS patients may require months of expensive skilled nursing care.

The question is: what is the best way to provide and finance this necessary care and treatment? In a modern, affluent, and compassionate society such as the U.S., citizens expect the cost of treating such expensive and unanticipated illnesses to be spread through the population in some manner. Americans see this as a humane reaction to an unexpected health care catastrophe for which individuals are unprepared.

Costs can be spread in various ways. Some have suggested that private health insurers should be forced to accept AIDS sufferers at normal premium levels, with all premium payers, in effect, picking up the cost for AIDS. This would be a mistake. It would place the cost of treating AIDS sufferers on Americans who had the foresight to obtain health insurance, allowing those without insurance to avoid making any financial contribution. Worse still, forcing insurance companies to pay the tab and pass on the cost to their policyholders could mean dramatic increases in premium costs, encouraging or forcing millions of Americans to drop what will become more costly health insurance.

Similarly, trying to use existing government programs to accommodate the new challenge of AIDS would detract from those programs' original purposes, causing endless problems of duplication and eligibility disputes. Even more important is the danger that an uncoordinated, piecemeal approach to meeting the AIDS crisis will give numerous special interests leverage to expand their favorite government programs or to create new ones. There are always those eager to profit from public crises. In fact, the use of AIDS to justify expanded budgets or new programs already has started.

The new President should propose, as part of his omnibus health reform package, a separate program within the Public Health Service to finance the treatment of Human Immunodeficiency Virus (HIV)-infected individuals. The program would be administered by the states and financed primarily by federal block grants according to the number of cases in each state. Use of the funds would be limited to officially designated treatment centers certified by the states, modeled on existing successful facilities pioneered by several cities. These would provide comprehensive inpatient and outpatient AIDS treatment and care. States would be free to determine which public or private facilities should be treatment centers and to set the compensation or reimbursement levels for doctors and other health care providers working in those centers.

Any American with a confirmed positive diagnosis of HIV infection automatically would be eligible to seek treatment at a center. States should be allowed to charge patients coinsurance to defray part of the cost of their treatment. In the case of patients with spouses or dependents, the charges imposed by states should be restricted by federally established maximum and minimum income and asset levels, to ensure that spouses or dependents are not impoverished. States also should be allowed to prevent patients from sheltering assets by transferring them to others following their diagnosis of HIV infection. This would be similar to the asset transfer restrictions that now apply in the Medicaid program.

The centers would enhance efforts to gather more comprehensive data on the disease itself and conduct clinical research into curing or preventing it. Moreover, while the biggest part of the cost of treating victims would be borne by all Americans, the proposal would correctly require AIDS sufferers to make a reasonable contribution to their treatment, without jeopardizing the economic security of their families.

Speeding the Food and Drug Approval Process

Most Americans believe that insuring the safety of the medicines they use and the food they eat is one of government's appropriate regulatory functions. How the Food and Drug Administration does this, however, needs to be reformed. The FDA regulatory process inflicts an excessive burden on the food and drug industries and ill serves the consumers. The Reagan Administration has tried to reform this important agency, but FDA reforms too often have been blocked by congressmen more concerned with the needs of special interest groups than those of consumers.

The most striking evidence of the need for FDA reform is the way its inordinately long drug review process repeatedly has denied patients with terminal or life-threatening illnesses access to drugs that might save or prolong their lives. The AIDS crisis has been particularly instrumental in focusing public attention on this problem and the need for FDA reform. The new President should take advantage of this opportunity by including in his omnibus health care reform legislation proposals to overhaul the FDA and make it more responsive to the needs of consumers without jeopardizing its mission to protect public safety.

First, the new President should propose amendments to allow patients with terminal or life-threatening illnesses to use unapproved drugs on an informed consent basis and to permit limited domestic production and sale of such drugs for this purpose.

Second, the new President should propose reforms to allow more prescription drugs with proved records of safety and effectiveness to be sold over the counter. There is already a growing trend toward more self-medication using nonprescription drugs and home diagnostic tests, and in recent years FDA has permitted more drugs to be sold without a prescription. The evidence indicates that consumers support these changes and use the medications responsibly.

Third, he should propose a more reasonable standard for FDA approval of food products. Current FDA regulations, based on the 1952 Delaney Amendment to the Food and Drug Act, prohibit the FDA from approving food products containing carcinogens in any amount. In the 35 years since this amendment, the technology for identifying chemical elements has improved dramatically. As a result, trace amounts of carcinogens that in earlier years went undetected can now be identified in many food products, though the risk of their causing cancer is, at most, negligible. To compensate for the effects of improved technology, the FDA in many cases has ignored these regulations and approved products anyway. This leaves the food industry in the difficult position of trying to meet what are in effect arbitrary standards. Consequently, the next Administration should propose a clearer and more reasonable standard for determining acceptable levels of carcinogens in food products.

Improving Health Care for Veterans

While it is not a part of the Department of Health and Human Services, the Department of Medicine and Surgery of the Veterans Administration currently operates 172 hospital centers, 229 out-patient clinics, 120 nursing homes, and 16 domiciliaries which provide less intensive nursing care. In fiscal 1986, this system treated 1.3 million patients in hospitals, 24,000 in nursing homes, and 13,000 in domiciliaries, while recording over 19 million visits to outpatient clinics. This hospital system was established 70 years ago to treat the large number of veterans returning from the First World War.

The original intention of the VA was to compensate veterans for injuries and losses sustained in wartime service. Benefits were later expanded to cover impoverished or sick veterans even if there was no connection between their present condition and their previous military service. Today, however, the whole structure of VA health benefits has become increasingly outdated, redundant, and inefficient. Maintaining a separate federally owned and operated health care system for veterans along with Medicaid and Medicare and private programs leads to wasteful duplication.

The new President should propose a plan to convert veterans health benefits from a system of government hospitals, doctors, and nurses to a reimbursement system like Medicare. The plan should propose privatizing the vast majority of existing VA health care facilities by selling them to private health companies or nonprofit organizations. The plan also should include provisions to provide veterans health benefits in the form of vouchers so they can purchase insurance or health benefits in the private sector. That would satisfy the federal government's obligation to veterans without the wasteful cost of maintaining a separate health care system for these Americans. In designing this voucher system, the focus should be on encouraging veterans to purchase catastrophic acute and long-term care insurance.

―――――――――――――◇―――――――――――――

INITIATIVES FOR 1989

1) Begin a campaign to enact omnibus health care reform legislation. The new President's most important short-term health care initiative is to generate public support for omnibus health care reform legislation. Only by mobilizing public support for reform can he politically outflank the interest groups of the health industrial complex and make major changes later in the term. The ability to mobilize and shape national public opinion on important issues is one of the most important powers of the presidency.

2) Reform the National Institutes of Health extramural grant program to ensure that the maximum amount is devoted to basic research. While NIH is commonly thought of as a federally operated research facility, 70-to-80 percent of its research budget goes as outside grants to universities and hospitals. This extramural grant program has developed a notorious reputation for billing high administrative expenses to NIH by grantees. Institutions receiving NIH money have come to view these grants as a way of funding their overhead costs and expansion projects, at the expense of the basic research that the grants are supposedly designed to support. It is estimated that such charges will consume 30 percent of NIH grant funds this year. The next

Administration should reform this grant program to get more value for the government's research dollars. This would be backed by the researchers themselves, who would like to see more of the money go to basic research.

3) Reform federal laws and regulations concerning medical malpractice and liability and encourage states to enact similar reforms. Malpractice insurance costs have skyrocketted in recent years because liability laws have led to unreasonably high damages awards against physicians. This has caused many very competent physicians to leave the medical profession, leading to serious shortages in some specialties, such as obstetrics. The 1987 Report of the Secretary's Task Force on Medical Liability and Malpractice contains recommendations in the areas of tort reform, alternatives to litigation such as pretrial screening, arbitration and contracts, improved licensing of doctors, and changes in the ways insurance companies underwrite liability insurance policies. These reforms would reduce the volume of costly litigation and lead to more reasonable awards for damages, thereby moderating insurance costs. While most of these reforms must be at the state level, the new President can encourage states to take action.

4) Restore the Alcohol, Drug Abuse, and Mental Health Administration to its original research function. The next Administration should transfer ADAMHA programs funding drug abuse treatment and clinical training for mental health professionals to the Health Resources and Services Administration. This will free ADAMHA to concentrate on its primary mission of researching and evaluating treatments for these disorders.

5) Seek legislation to reduce subsidies for health professions education provided through Health Resources and Services Administration programs. Through a variety of programs administered by HRSA, the federal government provides over $200 million to institutions and students to promote graduate education for physicians, nurses, and public health professionals. In large part these subsidies are unnecessary. The high earning potential of the health professions provides adequate incentives to attract quality personnel. And students pursuing graduate degrees in medicine that will enable them to earn large salaries should finance their own education by borrowing against their future income. While there is currently a shortage of nurses, hospitals and other institutions are already taking steps to improve recruitment and retention by raising salaries, improving working conditions, and offering educational assistance. Since most federal educational funds go directly to schools and hospitals rather than to students, they have little direct effect on the number or types of people studying to be health professionals.

Consequently, support for these programs should be reduced significantly. The remaining funds should be consolidated into a state block grant that targets assistance where it is most justified—paying for the education of minority and disadvantaged students or encouraging doctors to work in such less financially rewarding specialties or areas as primary care or rural communities.

6) Launch an information campaign to encourage Americans to purchase long-term care insurance. The current pressure for federal funding of long-term care exists because few Americans have long-term care insurance. The new Administration should design and launch an aggressive public education program focusing on the risks, costs, and financing options for long-term care and make that information widely available, especially to Social Security beneficiaries.

7) Establish a comprehensive federal long-term care data base. A major concern of private insurers is the lack of solid data to use in designing long-term care insurance policies. More data on the incidence, duration, and costs of long-term care are needed. The federal government should take the lead in developing such a database in consultation with private insurers. This would enable the private market to grow more rapidly.

8) Encourage the use of innovative funding mechanisms for long-term care. The next Administration should review federal and state laws, regulations, and tax policies to determine how they can be changed to make it easier for the elderly to use their home equity to finance long-term health care insurance or services. For example, under a reverse annuity mortgage, permitted now in several states, the elderly homeowner receives a payment each month in return for a mortgage on his or her home. The mortgage is paid off when the home is sold. Under a sale and leaseback arrangement, a variant of this idea, the elderly homeowner actually sells her home but acquires an unlimited right to rent back the property for life at a predetermined rate. Through these mechanisms, the elderly could use their home equity for nursing home care insurance and expenses while retaining occupancy of the home.

Similarly, the next Administration should review laws, regulations, and tax policies to determine if they should be changed to encourage

insurers to offer life insurance policies that are convertible, completely
or partially, into coverage for long-term care when the policyholder
retires.

9) Propose legislation to create a Primary Care Block Grant. The Health
Resources and Services Administration (HRSA) currently funds over
600 community health centers and 140 migrant health centers providing
primary health care services to 6 million poor persons annually. In
1981 the Reagan Administration proposed increasing the program's
efficiency and flexibility by transferring control of these centers to the
states with federal funding provided through a block grant. This was
rejected by Congress, which bowed to heavy lobbying by service
providers. The next Administration should reintroduce this proposal
with adequate funding.

☎

Welfare

Stuart M. Butler*
Task Force Chairman

When the Reagan Administration entered office, the United States poverty rate was increasing rapidly, having moved from 11.4 percent in 1978 to 14.0 percent in 1981. Within eighteen months, the trend of mounting poverty had been reversed, leading to the longest and sharpest decline in the poverty rate since the early 1970s. After climbing to a high of 15.2 percent at the end of the recession, the rate fell to 13.5 percent in 1987.

This cut in the poverty rate has been powered by the U.S. economic expansion. But American poverty could have been reduced more than it has. What is blocking its fall is a welfare system characterized by excessive centralization, antifamily bias, and incentives for dependency. The Reagan Administration has instituted important reforms, but Congress thwarted its efforts to decentralize the system to foster efficiency and policy innovation. This has forced the White House to resort to modest administrative changes to achieve at least a limited decentralization.

The new Administration needs to build on what Ronald Reagan has accomplished in four areas. First, it should seek legislation to transfer the primary responsibility for welfare to the states, allowing them to restructure and consolidate programs. To ensure that poorer states have the resources for appropriate welfare, the system of federal aid to states should be revamped to target aid only to poorer states.

Second, actions should be taken to strengthen the American family. Intact families seem to be the most formidable bulwark against poverty, yet the current welfare system does little to encourage family stability, and much to undermine it. For instance, the rules governing Aid to Families with Dependent Children (AFDC), which provides income support to single mothers, should be changed to discourage

---

*Commenting and contributing generously to this chapter were *Mandate III* Task Force Members Doug Besharov, Peter Germanis, Bill Gribben, Ron Haskins, Anna Kondratas, Kate O'Beirne, Carl Dahlman, and Heritage Policy Analyst Robert Rector. They do not necessarily endorse all of its views and recommendations.

teenage mothers from leaving home. There should be tougher enforcement of child support by absent fathers.

Third, stronger work incentives should discourage dependency. For instance, the Earned Income Tax Credit should be restructured to provide assistance for child care and to improve the earnings of those trying to escape welfare through work. In addition, work requirements should be made a standard feature of welfare programs.

And fourth, the new Administration should aim at "empowering" the poor. The current welfare system tends to provide more money to the middle-class "poverty industry" of service providers than it gives to the poor. This poverty industry opposes self-help strategies and other measures that would reduce the need for its services. Thus the new Administration strongly should endorse vouchers, deregulation of welfare services, and similar consumerist policies that would give the poor the power of choice.

America currently spends about $100 billion each year trying to eradicate poverty. Despite the recent success in reducing the poverty rate, the war on poverty has been going badly for two decades. If the war is to be won, there must be a new strategy based on a hard-headed understanding of human nature and an appreciation of the potential strengths of federalism. Simply pouring more money into welfare benefits and variations of failed Great Society programs will not help the poor.

---◇---

SUMMARY OF AGENCY FUNCTIONS

Although the Department of Health and Human Services has the primary responsibility for managing federal public assistance programs, known generally as welfare, the system of federal public assistance includes over 50 programs operated by several federal departments. The food stamp program, for instance, is run by the Department of Agriculture, but housing assistance is provided by the Department of Housing and Urban Development. In addition, many federal welfare programs, such as Aid to Families with Dependent Children, require a substantial commitment of funds by states.

The principal HHS agencies with jurisdiction over federal welfare programs are:

◆ *The Family Support Administration (FSA)*, which manages state-administered financial assistance and services, primarily for low-income families, FSA programs include Aid to Families with Dependent Children and the Community Services Block Grant.

◆ *The Social Security Administration (SSA)*, which manages the Supplemental Security Income (SSI) program, which provides cash assistance to impoverished elderly, blind, and disabled Americans. (See Social Security section of this chapter.)

◆ *The Office of Human Development Services (HDS)*, which manages the Social Services Block Grant, Head Start, and several small programs for low income families.

------------------◇------------------

INSTITUTIONAL CONSTRAINTS

Welfare policy-making is influenced by many forces. In the background are the media, which set the tone of the debate. Another factor is the array of organizations providing welfare services to the poor. Employees of these organizations depend often totally on federal and state welfare spending for their salaries. In many respects, the members of this middle-class poverty industry are as dependent on welfare spending as are the poor. And not surprisingly, the welfare industry devotes enormous time, money, and effort advocating policies that would increase the level of federal spending, thereby boosting the welfare industry's revenues and strengthening its role in providing services.

Careerists at the Department of Health and Human Services and at other agencies that manage welfare programs, such as the Department of Agriculture, also tend to press for an expansive federal role. Sometimes this is done for narrow financial interests, but more often because they apparently genuinely believe that only an active federal government can protect America's poor. Another strong constraint on policymaking are legislators and their staffs serving on key congressional committees. They work closely with representatives of the poverty industry, and with HHS careerists and the press. Indeed, there is a revolving door among committee staff, the agencies, and the associations for professional service providers, such as the American Public Welfare Association. The result: proposed regulations and barely developed policy ideas conflicting with the conventional wisdom often are ambushed quietly in the paper jungle of HHS and other federal agencies or publicly by attacks in Congress and the press.

THE REAGAN ADMINISTRATION RECORD

The war on poverty was going badly when Ronald Reagan entered office. Though the poverty rate had fallen steadily throughout the 1960s and remained relatively constant through the mid-1970s, it turned up sharply during the last three years of the Carter Administration. Between January 1979 and Inauguration Day 1981, about 5 million more Americans had joined the ranks of the poor, a one-fifth increase in the total number of poor. This dismal situation facing the Reagan Administration had two main causes. One was a stagnating economy with rampant inflation, already sliding into a deep recession. This economic crisis had caused a precipitous decline in median family income and job opportunities. Second was a centralized, bureaucratized welfare system, which encouraged dependency and placed a regulatory straitjacket on state and local efforts to find new solutions to poverty.

The Reagan Administration adopted a four-part strategy to stop the retreat in the battle against poverty: economic expansion, decentralization, better targeting of benefits, and linking benefits more to work effort. Within eighteen months, when the first package of Reagan economic policies had begun to take effect, the four-year poverty rate rise slowed and then reversed, leading to the sharpest and most sustained fall in the poverty rate since the early 1970s. As Reagan correctly argued, sustained economic growth, combined with tax relief for the poor, is the most effective general antipoverty program. The continuing economic expansion has been particularly beneficial to the most impoverished groups.

Reagan tax reforms, meanwhile, have almost eliminated the absurdity, resulting from years of inflation-induced bracket creep, of forcing Americans below the poverty line to pay federal taxes. The 1981 tax legislation began the process of removing these Americans from the tax rolls by indexing tax rates, while the 1986 tax reforms ended the taxation of more than 4 million low-income families.

The Reagan Administration also has made significant headway in reversing excessive centralization of the welfare system. Federal assistance to states had come with thousands of mandates attached. This federal red tape had the effect of micromanaging state and local officials. It discouraged policy innovation and blocked state efforts to use resources more efficiently. In Reagan's first term, two broad changes in the financing of human service programs began a process of decentralization. The first was the consolidation in 1981 of dozens of small, restrictive categorical grants into nine block grants, covering health, education, and welfare programs. Money that previously had been earmarked for only one purpose now could be used by the states for more pressing needs, while streamlined regulations allowed states to be more creative in using both federal money and their own matching funds.

The second change was as much psychological as real. In 1981, the Administration won congressional approval for reductions in the future outlays of many antipoverty programs. In some instances, such as certain job training programs, there were real reductions in outlays. In most instances, however, the cuts actually were merely reductions in the rate at which the programs had been expanding. In fact, there was an almost 10 percent real growth between 1981 and 1987 in 59 major federal antipoverty programs. Nevertheless, the erroneous perception of deep welfare cuts induced a sense of crisis in many state capitals. This growing anxiety fortuitously set entrepreneurial juices flowing, transforming state government. Governors and state legislatures moved swiftly to overhaul their welfare programs, attract higher-quality administrators, and experiment with new approaches. This flowering of state government, recalling an earlier era when states were hailed as laboratories of policy change, has been one of the most important accomplishments of the Reagan Administration.

This process of decentralization was given a further boost with the creation in 1987 of the Interagency Low Income Opportunity Board (ILIOB) as the result of a White House review of welfare policy by Acting Director of the Office of Policy Development Charles Hobbs. The Board is the antidote to Lyndon Johnson's Office of Economic Opportunity (OEO), whose primary mission was to centralize federal action by coordinating funding of different federal agencies. By contrast, ILIOB's primary function is to act as a single point of contact for states wishing to obtain waivers from those federal regulations that frustrate innovative welfare reform at the state and local level. The Board has helped states launch experiments or restructure their welfare systems. Among them: Wisconsin's "learnfare" program, linking Aid to Families with Dependent Children (AFDC) benefits to high school attendance by children in the family; and New Jersey's plan to turn hundreds of welfare beneficiaries into family day care providers, thereby increasing day care services while reducing the welfare rolls.

The Reagan Administration also has taken steps to channel funds more efficiently to Americans in need. This has made it possible to assist the poor while constraining the growth in total welfare spending. For example, significant savings in the AFDC program were achieved by reducing the payment of benefits more sharply when a family obtains earnings from work. Despite critics' warnings, this has not discouraged welfare recipients from accepting jobs. The Administration also has won the intellectual debate over "workfare." The Community Work Experience Program (CWEP), for instance, permits states to require certain welfare beneficiaries to perform some work, while the WIN Demonstrations program gives states greater flexibility in designing work requirements. Nevertheless, Congress did not legislate a national work requirement. The welfare reform legislation of 1988 does establish the principle of linking work and welfare, but in practice it will require very few beneficiaries to take a job. Meanwhile, the legislation triggers yet another expansion of costly and ineffective welfare state programs.

Steps toward a conservative reform of welfare have been marred, however, by several failures of strategy. Perhaps the most damaging is that Ronald Reagan, unlike Lyndon Johnson, has not sketched for the American people the broad vision of the kind of welfare system that he was seeking to construct. Thus Reagan has not generated the same degree of public support for welfare reform as for, say, tax reduction. This has made it easier for his opponents to generate public criticism of Reagan welfare reform.

Especially in Reagan's first term, the driving force behind welfare reform was the Office of Management and Budget (OMB), not HHS. Without a clear picture of the welfare system that he wishes to create, and with budget officials taking the lead on welfare policy, Reagan has fed the perception created by his opponents that he is only interested in cutting government, not in helping the poor. This perception has been reinforced by Reagan's reluctance to confront the middle-class entitlement programs, like Social Security. (See Social Security section of this chapter.)

The political consequences of this public perception have been aggravated by a consistent failure of HHS secretaries to make welfare reform a priority or to debate the issue vigorously. This has proved particularly damaging during the tenure of Otis Bowen, when for the first time in 15 years there was a great opportunity to change the welfare system fundamentally, thanks to the widespread acceptance among liberals that the current system is not working, and to the strong support among Americans for a work requirement in welfare. Yet Bowen, obsessed with expanding the federal government's role in health care, has been virtually silent on welfare, squandering what may have been a unique opportunity to use the enormous political resources of an HHS secretary to build a coalition for reform.

◇

THE NEXT FOUR YEARS

Welfare policy alone cannot conquer poverty, nor can government alone. To rid America of poverty, there must be continued economic growth, elimination of policies that discourage self-improvement, and a stronger focus on education. But there must also be a change of attitudes in poor communities toward such social problems as teenage pregnancy, widespread drug use, family breakup, and the able-bodied living on welfare. Welfare policy thus is but one component of the fight against poverty. But it is an important component. If it is badly structured, it undermines public and private efforts to deal with the root causes of poverty.

The Reagan Administration has begun modestly to restructure America's welfare system and to revive the fortunes of the poor. Reagan has shown that the best welfare system for the able-bodied poor is a growing economy, not handouts. He has encouraged state and local government, which stand closest to the people and thus are most aware of the problems and opportunities facing the poor, to take a much greater role in combating poverty. And he has emphasized the point that government should be soft-hearted but not soft-headed. It should recognize, for instance, the simple truths that well-meaning generosity in welfare benefits fosters permanent welfare dependency, and that telling the poor that they have no obligations in return for help only weakens families and communities.

The task of reforming attitudes and programs is far from complete. While the states now are the leaders in designing welfare policy, laws rooted in the Johnson era constrain the creative power of federalism. Some steps have been taken to move away from the philosophy of one-way "welfare rights" and entitlements, which has helped foster dependency, toward a two-way system of obligations on recipients as well as on society. Yet the proper balance remains elusive. Similarly, the importance of the family in keeping poverty at bay may now be widely accepted, yet many programs still do little to strengthen the family, and some appear to erode it.

Thus the new President still must articulate a clear vision of an American system of welfare and take action to transform this vision

into reality. He should tell Congress and the American people that the
primary goal of his welfare agenda will be to create a welfare system
that tries to make the poor independent of government, not well-cared-
for wards of government. The key to this, he should stress, is a growing
economy that produces jobs and advancement, and welfare programs
that require beneficiaries to take a job. He should add that for those
locked into the underclass of hopelessness in the inner cities, seemingly impervious to the job-creating machine around them, independence will only come by strengthening local private and public institutions. Policy thus should aim to build up self-help organizations,
helping them to attack the crushing culture of welfare dependency
among the underclass as well as its economic problems, and giving
rein to the creativity of state and local government.

Decentralizing the Welfare System

Policy experimentation is needed to solve the problems of poverty
and welfare dependency. No honest politician or scholar, conservative
or liberal, can say with confidence that he or she has the complete
answer to this complex problem. Thus the focus of federal action
should not be to impose some new "solution," but rather to accelerate
the process of discovering real solutions. This means a pluralistic
system in which states have much wider authority to attempt innovative approaches by redesigning existing programs.

The new Administration thus should continue the activities of the
Interagency Low Income Opportunity Board, and seek legislation from
Congress to give the Board wide powers to permit states to redesign
their welfare systems. The Board should be permitted to grant waivers,
or exemptions from federal rules which establish state procedures for
implementing federally supported welfare programs. Such waivers
would allow the states to attempt innovative approaches to the poverty
problem. The existing authority is inadequate. Current law, for instance, forbids states from combining AFDC and food stamps into a
comprehensive income support program. Other limitations similarly
reduce flexibility. The Board should be empowered, among other
things, to shift funds from one major program to another, simplify or
change eligibility rules, and replace services to the poor with cash or
vouchers. To the extent that this saves money while reducing measurable poverty and dependency, the state should be allowed to keep part
or all of the savings for additional antipoverty initiatives.

This would not return welfare policy to a pre-1965 decentralization,
where some states chose to do little—for philosophical or financial

reasons—to address pressing social needs. Decentralization based on waivers requires the state to convince Washington that its proposal has merit. And inaction by a state does not mean no action to help the poor; it means simply that the benchmark federally sponsored welfare system continues to apply within that state.

It would make sense to provide federal financial aid only to poorer states, requiring richer states to pay the full costs of AFDC, Medicaid, and other shared programs. Politically, however, this would be difficult. No member of Congress wants his or her state to lose federal aid. And even if a state is rich, its officials would balk at raising taxes to assume programs now paid for with federal funds. A politically realistic strategy to restructure federal aid for antipoverty programs might combine changes in the distribution of federal dollars favoring poorer states with an across-the-board federal income tax cut. The revenue loss resulting from the tax cut would be offset by a reduction in total aid to the states. Under this combined tax cut and formula change, poor states would be better off, because if they were to raise state taxes dollar for dollar to offset the federal tax reduction, they would have more resources. Though richer states would still appear to lose by this arrangement, since their federal assistance would be cut to channel more aid to poorer states, a federal tax cut would be an immediate and popular benefit to taxpayers, reducing potential resistance to the cutback in federal aid.

Strengthening the Family

Family instability and poverty are inextricably linked. The persistent rise in the number of children in AFDC-supported families is due almost entirely to the breakup or nonformation of intact families among poorer Americans. In effect, the U.S. is experiencing the "maternalization" of poverty. Nearly half of America's poor live in families with no husband present, even though such families are only 16 percent of the population. In 1987, two-parent families had a 6 percent poverty rate, in sharp contrast to 34 percent for female-headed families.

The rise in illegitimate births during the last few decades, especially to teenagers, is one of today's most disturbing social trends. To reverse this requires a change in the social acceptability of teenage pregnancy in the communities where it is rife. This can come only through leadership from schools, churches, community groups, and other institutions, not through regulations from HHS.

Nevertheless, federal and state governments can strengthen families. States, for instance, could make divorce laws more promother and prochild, with judges awarding more family resources and assets to the mother. While the federal government, of course, cannot alter state divorce laws, it can draft a model divorce law for consideration by states just as it has drafted model commercial codes.

The new President should support legislation to make the welfare system explicitly profamily rather than implicitly antifamily. Few teenage women probably become pregnant to qualify for welfare, but the availability of welfare does relieve the pressure on both father and mother to marry and support the child. Welfare permits fathers to escape their financial responsibilities, and gives mothers the option of remaining single and dependent on government. AFDC rules should be revised to require teenage beneficiaries to remain in their family home and in school, rather than using AFDC and other benefits to set up an independent household. Once welfare enables a young mother to leave the family home, she tends to lose child care assistance from relatives and other help that would allow her to enter the workforce. The result: she becomes trapped in long-term welfare dependency.

The welfare system also should aim to substitute earned income for government aid. One direct way to do this would be to crack down on absent fathers who fail to support their children. Currently about 90 percent of children benefiting from AFDC have able-bodied but absent fathers. Not only would a tough child-support policy provide income to poor families, but, more important, it would send the clear message that fathering a child imposes responsibilities that cannot be avoided. The new Administration should seek to withhold AFDC funds from states unless the states do more to identify the fathers of illegitimate children and then force these fathers to pay their share of their children's upkeep. Social Security and IRS data should be used to detect delinquent fathers and to establish a system of automatic wage withholding across state lines, so that money is collected from a father in one state for a court order obtained by the mother in another. Currently the difficulty of obtaining support from fathers who move to another state is a major loophole in state child-support laws. In addition, federal law should allow states to require public-sector work or community action by any deadbeat father who claims he has no source of income, sending fathers to jail if they refuse to comply.

Finally, AFDC should be made an explicitly temporary program. This is not to say, of course, that current long-term AFDC recipients should be left destitute. It is simply to admit that if a family is still dependent on AFDC after, say, five years, the system is not helping that family to become independent. The federal government should phase out its contribution to AFDC for a family after five years, forcing the state to consider other public or private approaches that might end the family's welfare dependency. Allowing such families to remain permanently on AFDC gives state officials little incentive to try more effective alternatives.

Encouraging Work

In those cases where support from the father is not available, steps should be taken to make it easier for mothers to enter the workforce. Rigorous evaluations of state work programs show that well-designed programs can improve the recipients' earnings while reducing dependency. The new Administration should make work requirements a standard feature of federally supported welfare programs. Such work requirements should be based on the existing skills of the welfare recipient and states should have to place a certain percentage of welfare recipients into jobs in order to receive federal job-training funds. The reason for this requirement is that many liberals and some states see work requirements as merely a synonym for expensive job training programs which often do not lead the trainee to permanent employment. The work provisions of the welfare reform package of 1988 reflect the liberal view. Although job training and education programs could supplement work requirements, they are not a substitute for genuine work requirements.

There is a widespread belief, however, that strengthening work incentives or requirements will have only a limited impact in moving families off the welfare rolls because of an alleged shortage of day care services, making it very difficult for mothers to combine work with bringing up a child. This has encouraged many lawmakers to contend that there is no point in imposing work requirements unless the federal government launches a major new program to fund professional day care services.

Yet most day care in America is provided informally and very effectively in the family home or a neighbor's home. Federal funding and regulation of day care at best would substitute high-priced professional care for low-cost informal care, and at worst would reduce the availability of care in very poor communities where good professionals do not choose to work. A federal takeover of day care could do for the quality and availability of inner-city child care services what the public school monopoly has done for inner-city education. There is no evidence, moreover, that a lack of day care assistance is a serious impediment to welfare recipients wishing to work.

The new Administration thus should focus on the need to make entry level jobs more attractive to welfare recipients. Raising the minimum wage is not the way to do this, since about 80 percent of workers in minimum wage jobs are not from poor families. More important, raising the minimum wage hurts, rather than helps, former welfare recipients seeking entry level jobs. The reason for this is that, faced with a higher minimum wage, employers will lay off or not hire individuals with the lowest skills and least experience.

A far better way to make jobs more attractive to welfare recipients would be by increasing and reforming the Earned Income Tax Credit (EITC). The EITC currently provides a credit equal to 14 percent of wages for families, with children, earning below $6,000 per year. The credit is phased out gradually beyond that income, declining to zero for a family earning $17,000. The tax credit also is refundable, meaning it is paid even if it exceeds the family's tax liability. Hence the EITC rewards work, even if the family does not earn enough to pay federal taxes.

The new Administration should propose legislation to increase the EITC. This would raise the after-tax earnings of the lowest paid workers without the adverse side effects of hiking the minimum wage. Further, the Administration should propose amending the EITC to vary the credit according to the number of children in the family, to direct most help to children on the edge of poverty. Finally the Administration should propose converting the credit from a percentage of total annual earnings to a credit based on the worker's hourly wage, with the credit falling as the wage rate rises. Linking the EITC in this way to hours worked means the lowest paid workers employed full time would receive proportionally the most help.

These reforms would help alter the current system of government financial assistance to the poor, where most help is given to those who are not working, to one that encourages work as the best route out of poverty. An enhanced EITC also would encourage welfare mothers to leave welfare by increasing their "take-home" earnings. And it would encourage families to stay together by raising the potential earnings of a low-skilled father, allowing him to support his family and thus replace government as the family's chief breadwinner. With the suggested EITC supplement, a father earning the minimum wage would be able to support a family of four above the poverty level. The revenue cost of the enhanced EITC would be more than offset by the reduced need for means-tested government benefits.

This reform of the EITC should be part of a general reform of the tax code to reduce the bias against all intact, working families with children. This bias results from the steady rise in the Social Security payroll tax, which takes no account of family size. The bias also exists because the effective value of the personal tax exemption for the taxpayer, his or her spouse, and each dependent has fallen during the past four decades. Low-income families are hurt most by the antifamily nature of the tax system. Example: a father supporting a wife and two children on $15,000 per year pays approximately $2,600 in taxes to the federal government (including the employer share of the Social Security payroll tax). Raising these personal exemptions from the current $2,000 to about $6,500 would bring their value into line with income growth during the past four decades. (See Chapter 22.) An alternative, which would partly reduce the tax burden on lower-income families, would be to provide a tax credit of $750 for each young child, refundable against Social Security taxes if there is no federal income tax liability. Such a "toddler tax credit" would grant tax relief to the families under the greatest financial pressure. It would, in particular, provide these families with the money they need to cover day care expenses so that a single mother, or both parents in an intact family, can enter the workforce.

Empowering the Poor

A major political roadblock to fundamental welfare reform is the poverty industry. The Reagan Administration calculates that only 24 percent of the more than $100 billion annually spent by federal and state governments on antipoverty programs actually trickles down to the poor in the form of cash assistance. Too much of the rest pays for tens of thousands of middle-class service providers, ranging from physicians reimbursed by Medicaid to public housing managers paid from housing funds to social workers with salaries financed by block grant funds.

The new Administration must empower poor communities to challenge the domination of the poverty industry. Ironically, empowerment was the slogan of the radical liberal reformers of the 1960s. Yet their version of empowerment has been political in nature; the poor were to have "maximum feasible participation" in organizations to secure access to federal funds. Yet genuine empowerment is economic. It gives the poor maximum control over their lives, maximum choice over who shall help them help themselves, and maximum opportunity to improve their economic condition. Once the poor have a chance to control their own lives, they will have the incentive to challenge the service providers who currently maintain them as dependent clients.

The new Administration can take several actions to foster this empowerment. First, the Federal Trade Commission should review thoroughly federal and state regulations governing the organizations and individuals that may receive government funds to serve the poor. In many instances, these rules block self-help efforts by communities because state or federal funds are denied to "uncredentialed" individuals or organizations. These credentialing rules often merely protect cartels of professional service providers. Rules deemed anticompetitive by the Federal Trade Commission should be eliminated. This would permit local community organizations in many instances to replace outside professionals in the provision of such services as housing management, remedial education, and job training.

Second, the federal government systematically should favor community organizations over professionals as contractors for antipoverty services. For instance, discretionary funds for economic development or remedial education programs in the inner cities should go more to local groups and less to firms or professional organizations outside the community. Organizations within poor communities are consumers as well as providers of their own services, and thus have a vested interest in reducing poverty and dependency. Outside professionals in many instances do not; in fact, they have the reverse incentive because a reduction in poverty reduces the need for the poverty industry. The remarkable success of tenant management in public housing, for instance (see Chapter 14), shows how creative poor people can be when allowed to manage their own affairs. Thus money to combat teenage pregnancy should be provided to those groups within poor communities which have a proven track record in these areas. Housing assistance should be used to foster self-help housing rehabilitation programs, and assistance for anticrime and drug prevention programs should build on the sometimes unorthodox but often highly effective tactics of community groups in poor neighborhoods.

Third, wherever possible, the poor should receive vouchers or cash to obtain the services they wish. In contrast to programs in which the government pays firms or organizations to provide services to the poor, a voucher means that the government gives money directly to the poor in the form of a certificate of a specific value which must be used for a particular service. Food stamps are one example of a voucher currently in use. These vouchers would allow the poor to behave like other consumers: they would be able to "shop around" among competing providers, who would thus have to pay closer attention to their wishes. The new President should advocate vouchers explicitly as a device to give poor Americans the dignity and power of consumer choice. Such action would force the poverty industry to explain why the poor must be denied economic rights viewed by most Americans as basic.

Coordinating Federal Antipoverty Programs

Effective federal action against poverty will be delayed as long as the effort is diffused among dozens of overlapping programs, each with different eligibility requirements, that are managed by several agencies and monitored by many congressional committees. The three major assistance programs, for instance, are administered by three separate Cabinet departments. The Food Stamp program is operated by the Department of Agriculture, AFDC by HHS, and housing by the Department of Housing and Urban Development. Combining the major means-tested support programs into one federal agency may be the best way to streamline, simplify, and coordinate federal antipoverty efforts. But this would be hard to achieve. Agency careerists and even political appointees fiercely resist such consolidation, since many would lose control over pet programs. More important, powerful, turf-conscious congressional committees undoubtedly would block such a move.

Bowing to political reality, the new Administration should not attempt to consolidate the programs, but rather to strengthen the Interagency Low Income Opportunity Board (ILIOB). This would improve program coordination without challenging departmental or committee jurisdiction. To give the Board the necessary authority to obtain rule changes from federal departments, the chairman of the ILIOB should be a top White House official, and the new President should make it clear to Cabinet officials that the chairman has his full support.

Coordination also would be improved if the federal budget clearly identified the antipoverty programs; this would give legislators and the public a more accurate picture of how much is being spent and for what purposes. The Office of Management and Budget should restructure the annual budget to place appropriate programs under a new function termed "Welfare and Antipoverty Expenditures." All 59 major means-tested programs should be included. Grouping these programs in one budget category would allow lawmakers and the public to measure the extent and scope of the federal effort, and lay the foundation for improved policy-making and coordination.

Measuring Poverty More Accurately

It is hard for America to win a successful war on poverty when it is so hard to identify the "enemy." Even leaving aside such complicating notions as "relative" versus "absolute" poverty, the measurement of poverty is a crude process. As a result of this defective measurement, millions of Americans who would not normally be considered poor receive generous assistance, while millions of others who should be considered very poor qualify for little or no help.

The root cause of this defect is that the baseline official poverty rate is a badly flawed measurement of what is generally understood to be poverty. It is based only on reported cash income. Thus unreported— or "underground"—income is not measured, nor are assets taken into account. Moreover, regional cost-of-living differences are scarcely recognized. Excluded from measurement are such in-kind benefits as food stamps, public housing, and Medicaid. Thus billions of taxpayer dollars spent on these programs have no effect whatever on mitigating poverty—according to the official poverty definition. The fact that noncash benefits may make the family far better off is ignored.

The exclusion of in-kind benefits from the poverty rate measurement is no small matter. The Census Bureau has calculated the value of in-kind benefits. For 1987 it found that, if the market value of all in-kind benefits were included in measuring poverty, then the poverty rate would be 8.5 percent (20.4 million individuals) instead of the official rate, based on cash income, of 13.5 percent (32.5 million individuals).

Federal and state governments cannot target aid to the most needy unless they have a more accurate measurement of who the most needy are. To obtain this, the new Administration should revise the benchmark poverty rate data in two ways.

First, it should institute a consumption standard in place of the income standard. Rather than using a specific amount of cash income as the baseline for poverty, the federal government would use the local market value of a basket of necessary goods and services as the threshold for determining of poverty line income. The government would establish the quantity and quality of food, housing, clothing, and other essential items needed to keep a family just above what most Americans would consider a life of poverty. The total cost of obtaining these items locally would then be the benchmark for determining whether the family's income was below the poverty level. In this way the poverty rate would take account of regional variations in the cost of living.

Second, in-kind benefits should be included in the calculation of family income. By including the cash value of such benefits as housing and food assistance, the true condition of the family would be determined more accurately.

The new Administration also should establish an official dependency rate. This would indicate the proportion of the population depending on government welfare to stay above the poverty threshold. Since a major stated goal of antipoverty policy is to turn the poor into independent self-supporting citizens, a dependency rate is important as an index of the success of government policy in achieving that goal. It would indicate how many Americans had escaped poverty only by going on the dole.

———————————◇———————————

INITIATIVES FOR 1989

1) Appoint a high-level White House official with the power to cut red tape for states requesting relief from federal rules regarding welfare programs. The Reagan Administration's Interagency Low Income Opportunity Board enables states to obtain exemptions from red tape, so that innovative welfare experiments can be launched. The new President should continue the Board and choose a top White House official to chair it. This would give the Board authority to arrange waivers of rules from departments.

2) Require states to report more fully on ways in which block grant money is used. One reason Congress prefers to create new categorical grant programs is that often there are no data showing that states are already tackling a particular problem with block grant funds. For example, Congress in 1988 enacted a major new program for the homeless, despite the fact that states can—and many do—use housing block grant money to help the homeless. Lawmakers opposing this new program could not present data to show that it would duplicate existing efforts. By requiring states to report on the use of block grant money, Congress would have more information on the extent of state and local actions to help the poor. This not only would reduce the continuous pressure on Congress to do something, but it would also inform federal lawmakers more fully of the many highly innovative actions being undertaken by state and local government.

3) Change AFDC rules to deny assistance to teenage mothers who do not remain in the family household. When young mothers use Aid to

Families with Dependent Children and other welfare benefits to set up an independent household, often they lose child care help from relatives and find it harder to join the workforce. Thus, their ability to become truly independent diminishes and they tend to stay longer on the welfare system. Making AFDC more restrictive would encourage young mothers to stay in a family environment where they are more likely to obtain the help they need from relatives to free themselves of welfare dependency.

4) Crack down on deadbeat fathers. One reason many women with children are forced onto welfare is that absent fathers do not fulfill their financial responsibilities. The federal government should work with states to improve the collection of child support through such actions as automatic withholding from paychecks of court-ordered child support and requiring unemployed fathers to take available jobs.

5) Establish workfare as a standard feature of federally supported welfare programs. Work requirements should be an integral part of America's welfare system, to encourage independence. The welfare reform legislation of 1988 requires states to enroll a minimum proportion of welfare recipients in education, training, job search, or work programs. But the proportion is too low and should be raised.

6) Establish a Welfare and Antipoverty Expenditures category in the federal budget. Programs designed to relieve poverty currently are included under numerous functional categories in the budget, making it almost impossible to identify the full scope and cost of welfare. Therefore, these programs should be grouped together under a single budget heading in the budget, so that lawmakers and the public can see the full scope and cost of programs, and can more easily determine where there are gaps and overlapping federal actions.

7) Launch a Federal Trade Commission investigation of regulations that inhibit competition in services to the poor. Many state rules, and some federal regulations, prevent uncredentialed individuals or organizations from providing federally supported services to the poor. This restricts competition among social welfare providers by making it illegal for many community groups to deliver services. The effect is to raise the general cost of welfare services, since the range of potential suppliers is reduced, and to eliminate job opportunities for the poor. Therefore the Federal Trade Commission, which investigates activities and rules which reduce competition, should investigate regulations which inhibit competition in welfare services, and issue recommendations for regulatory changes to federal, state, and local governments.

8) Reform the calculation of the poverty rate by introducing a consumption standard and by including in-kind benefits. In measuring the income of a household to determine if it is in poverty, as defined by the official poverty rate, in-kind benefits are not included. Moreover, the rate takes no account of major differences in the cost of living from one place to another. The basis for calculating the poverty rate should be changed. The cash value of benefits received should be added to the cash income of a family to determine total income in calculating program eligibility. The income threshold for determining whether a family is considered poor should be changed from a nationwide income standard to one which reflects the total local cost of the goods and services deemed necessary to avoid poverty.

9) Establish a dependency rate. The aim of welfare policy should be to help the poor to become self-sufficient. Yet the effect of many programs is to make the poor dependent on the government. The federal government thus should measure more accurately the effectiveness of its programs in turning poor Americans into independent citizens by calculating how many Americans would fall below the poverty level if it were not for government support.

The Social Security System

Peter J. Ferrara*
Task Force Chairman

Of all federal programs, Social Security has the most private-sector alternatives available to its beneficiaries. These alternatives include company pensions, Individual Retirement Accounts (IRAs), health insurance, life insurance, and disability insurance. Originally seen as a supplement to private retirement plans, the Social Security program essentially has crowded out private alternatives. In doing so, it restricts the economic freedom of workers to choose among the alternatives and deprives them of an opportunity to accumulate their own stake in the private economy as savers and investors.

Mandated reliance on Social Security is particularly inappropriate for today's young workers, not only because it inhibits their freedom of choice, but also because it serves them very poorly. Social Security taxes now are so high that young workers will receive a low return from Social Security even if all of its currently offered benefits are paid. Black Americans and others who have below average life expectancies get a particularly bad deal from the program. Their earlier deaths mean, on average, that they collect less from Social Security than do whites. Moreover, whether all promised benefits can be paid to today's young workers without enormous tax increases is still quite questionable. Yet the Social Security payroll tax is already far too high, holding down economic growth and limiting job opportunities.

The new Administration must restore the proper balance between public and private pension programs. The payroll tax rate increases in January 1988 and those scheduled for January 1990 are projected to yield more revenue than needed to pay benefits for the next three decades, assuming continued steady economic growth. Yet these tax increases could undermine the economic growth needed to keep Social Security solvent. Consequently, these payroll tax rate increases should be repealed and replaced with a fundamental reform of the system. To

*Commenting and contributing generously to this chapter were *Mandate III* Task Force Members John Goodman and Norman Ture. They do not necessarily endorse all of its views and recommendations.

make the tax reductions permanent and provide for a better retirement pension system for today's young workers, Congress should adopt a new compact between the generations. Today's retirees should be paid all promised benefits in full, while today's workers should be allowed the freedom to choose to rely more on the private sector and less on Social Security.

If the baby boomers begin relying more on private alternatives, the burden on Social Security, when their generation retires, will be reduced sharply, avoiding the need for any tax increases. Indeed, the program's expenditures could be reduced enough to permit payroll taxes to be cut. By strengthening private alternatives, Americans will have greater freedom of choice, pay lower payroll taxes, and enjoy higher retirement benefits.

SUMMARY OF AGENCY FUNCTIONS

Social Security is the largest federal domestic program. In fiscal 1989, total spending on the system's old-age, survivors, disability, and retirement hospital benefits will amount to about $300 billion. This is financed by payroll taxes, known to all working Americans as FICA (from the Federal Insurance Contribution Act, which was the 1939 tax act authorizing the payroll levies). The Social Security program is administered by the Social Security Administration (SSA), which is part of the Department of Health and Human Services.

The main elements of the system are:

◆ *The pension program*, technically still called old-age benefits, which pays cash benefits to retired workers and survivors benefits to widows.

◆ *The disability program*, which pays disability benefits to support workers below age 65 and their families when the worker is not physically capable of working.

◆ *The Medicare program*, which provides hospital insurance and supplementary medical insurance to Americans retired on Social Security or receiving the program's disability benefits for at least two years. (Medicare is discussed in the Health section of this chapter.)

INSTITUTIONAL CONSTRAINTS

Social Security is a minefield for politicians. Perhaps more than any other major program, policy-making for Social Security is subject to powerful constraints. The most potent pressure comes from the beneficiaries of Social Security, currently about 30 million strong. They oppose any significant cuts in the program and are politically well organized and very active. The American Association of Retired Persons (AARP) and similar organizations agitate and mobilize the elderly to support expansion of the system with little regard for what this will cost future generations.

Groups representing the elderly are aided by a deeply ideological old guard of Social Security advocates in the public policy community. Many were once officials of the system. They believe that government-sponsored social insurance is the answer to a multitude of social welfare problems. They view the private sector as interested only in exploiting the elderly for profit, and they view markets as chaotic, arbitrary, and haphazard. This old guard vigorously opposes any fundamental change in Social Security. Politicians who favor big government seek to fan alarm among the elderly by claiming that every promarket, antibig government candidate for office wishes to impoverish senior citizens. Understandably, politicians who favor reform of Social Security fear the electoral force of elderly Americans and often feel compelled to accept the agenda of the Social Security lobby, even when they do not favor the policy.

THE REAGAN ADMINISTRATION RECORD

As Ronald Reagan was taking office, Congress was congratulating itself for having cured the Social Security financing crisis of the mid-1970s, which was caused by a surge in inflation-indexed benefit payouts combined with a recession which stagnated payroll tax revenues. In December 1977, Congress had enacted the largest peacetime tax increase in U.S. history designed, said President Jimmy Carter and Social Security Administration experts, to guarantee the financial soundness of the system "for the rest of this century and well into the next one." Yet, a few months after Reagan entered office, the 1981 Annual Report of the Social Security Board of Trustees concluded that the system likely would be unable to pay promised benefits by late 1982 or early 1983. The continuing combination of indexed benefit expenditures and a sagging economy was pushing the system to collapse.

In May 1981, the Administration responded to the crisis with a package of expenditure reductions to avoid the collapse. The plan was a bold attempt to deal with the crisis quickly and decisively. Reagan had campaigned on a pledge not to reduce Social Security benefits for current retirees, and his 1981 proposals fundamentally kept this pledge. The only element that affected current retirees was a one-time, three-month delay in cost-of-living increases. The proposals would have reduced benefits for those who chose early retirement before age 65, though full benefits would still be available at 65. The formula used to calculate increases in future benefits for current workers would have been changed—but only temporarily—so that, for a period, future benefits would not grow quite as rapidly.

The proposal quickly collided with the institutional constraints to changes in Social Security policy. The ideological old guard vociferously denounced the proposal as anti-elderly. The organizations representing the elderly sought to prove they were on watch in Washington, sounding the alarm that the Reagan Administration was about to smash the financial security of the golden years of U.S. retirees. Reagan's political opponents chimed in with the same message. Republican lawmakers were engulfed in the firestorm and refused to support the Administration proposals. The Senate voted 96–0 on a gratuitous resolution advising the President not even to send his proposals to Capitol Hill. The Administration got the message; its proposals were never sent to Congress.

Instead, the Administration appointed a national commission to devise a bailout scheme for Social Security and defuse the political crisis. With a few exceptions, the commission, chosen by Congress and the President, consisted of unimaginative politicians and bureaucrats, interested not in fundamental reform of the system but merely in a short-term political compromise. This was reflected in the commission's January 1983 proposals: an acceleration of already legislated payroll tax rate increases scheduled through 1990; a one-third increase in payroll taxes on self-employed workers; a permanent, one-time, six-month delay in annual cost-of-living adjustments; federal taxation of one-half of Social Security benefits, formerly tax-exempt, for retirees with incomes above certain thresholds; a requirement that new federal workers and current employees of nonprofit organizations, formerly exempt from Social Security, join the system; and termination of the right of state and local government employees to opt out of the system, unless they already had exercised the right.

Congress adopted the package almost without change, adding a gradual increase in the retirement age, from 65 to 67, commencing in the year 2000, and adjusting the taxation of Social Security benefits.

This package merely tinkered with the basic structure of Social Security. In the process, nearly everyone was hurt. Benefits to the elderly were effectively cut and taxed, FICA taxes on workers were increased and their promised benefits reduced, and the remaining rights of some workers to choose alternatives to the program were eliminated.

Since this politically damaging episode, the Reagan Administration has done nothing more on Social Security. It has not developed a political strategy to deal with the institutional constraints surrounding Social Security policy and to regain the initiative. Worse still, the Administration has destroyed any chance of building a coalition for retirement reform on Capitol Hill by undercutting its own supporters. For instance, when Senate Republicans in 1985 backed a one-year freeze on Social Security COLAs to reduce the budget deficit, the Administration initially went along. But as soon as the political going became rough, the White House retreated, withdrawing its support for the measure.

———————————◇———————————

THE NEXT FOUR YEARS

The retirement system in America has been based on the concept of the "three-legged stool," in which Americans rely on Social Security, employer pensions, and private savings for their retirement needs. Reflecting this triad philosophy, an array of private programs provide many of the benefits of Social Security. Company pensions, IRAs, 401(k) plans, Keoghs, and other retirement savings plans perform in the private sector the basic function of Social Security retirement benefits. Similarly, private life and disability insurance perform the basic functions of Social Security survivors and disability benefits, and private health insurance performs a similar function to Medicare.

Social Security has been usurping the role of the other two legs of the stool. The maximum Social Security tax for an individual worker, including both the employer and employee shares, has grown from $60 in 1949 to $185 in 1958, $348 in 1965, and $6,759 in 1988. By 1990, it will be almost $8,000, continuing to grow thereafter. This heavy mandated reliance on Social Security greatly restricts the economic freedom of Americans and deprives the average worker of a major opportunity to accumulate capital through private alternatives. It displaces a private array of services offered in a competitive market with a highly politicized government monopoly—in effect, socializing a large part of the nation's financial industry.

Overreliance on Social Security makes even less sense now than before because the program is a bad deal for today's young workers. Social Security taxes are so high that, even if these workers receive all the benefits currently offered by the program, they will still be receiving below-market returns on the taxes they and their employers are paying into the system. Indeed, for many workers, the rate of return will be negative. Black Americans and other minorities have below-average life expectancies, and so they tend to receive even lower returns on the taxes they pay. A white male at birth today can expect to receive 50 percent more in retirement benefits than a newly born black male.

The new President should seek to restore the traditional three-legged stool theme of the U.S. retirement system. He should do this by supporting legislation to encourage private retirement savings and to allow working Americans to choose private retirement plans in place of Social Security, thereby returning Social Security to its proper role as a supplement to private pensions.

Cutting Skyrocketing Payroll Taxes

It is questionable whether even the inadequate returns and benefits promised under the system can be paid. Under the Social Security Administration's own most widely cited intermediate assumptions, the payroll tax-financed system will run short of funds to pay promised benefits by 2030, just before young workers entering the workforce today will retire. By 2035, the program's total expenditures will be running almost 50 percent greater than total income. Paying all the benefits promised to today's young workers under these projections would require an increase in the total Social Security payroll tax rate to 23 percent, compared with 15.02 percent today.

Yet the payroll tax is already far too high, severely hampering economic growth and limiting job opportunities for today's young workers. For most workers, the total employee and employer payroll tax burden is greater than the worker's income tax liability. By the end of this decade, total payroll tax revenues will be approaching individual income tax revenues.

During the 1990s, the huge baby boom generation will be in its prime earning years, swelling Social Security tax payments. At the same time, the smaller generation born during the low fertility years of the Great Depression and World War II will be entering retirement, imposing relatively smaller benefit burdens on the system. Because of these factors, the Social Security Administration's intermediate projections show payroll tax revenues substantially exceeding program expenditures each year for the next two decades.

These projections, however, have been subject to substantial confusion regarding their implications for the federal budget deficit and national debt. Some analysts and politicians have suggested that annual Social Security surpluses will eliminate recent federal budget deficits and even pay off the national debt. These statements are based on several errors. They fail to adjust nominal dollar projections many years into the future for inflation and the relative effects of economic growth over time. They fail to consider the large Hospital Insurance trust fund deficits. And they include interest on the Social Security trust fund bonds as income to the federal government, when, since these are federal bonds, the interest is also an expense of the federal government, and it cancels out as an intragovernmental transfer. To be sure, the projected annual payroll tax surpluses are significant, and they must be taken into account by policymakers. But such trust fund surpluses are not nearly sufficient to eliminate recent annual federal deficits, let alone pay off the national debt.

Moreover, without continuation of the extraordinary economic growth of the Reagan years, even these annual payroll tax surpluses will not develop. Under the more pessimistic Social Security Administration projections, which assume a return to the inflation and recession cycles of the 1970s, the entire system will run short of funds to pay promised benefits soon after the turn of the century, despite the favorable demographic trends.

The larger, long-term problem is that, after a couple of decades of even the favorable trends, Social Security will run into demographic windshear, as the trends reverse. The huge baby boom generation will begin retiring, dramatically increasing benefit demands on the system. At the same time, the relatively small generation born during the low fertility baby-dearth years following the baby boom will be in the workforce, producing relatively small amounts of revenue. Under the Social Security Administration's intermediate projections, annual trust fund deficits (excluding interest on the trust fund bonds) start in 2013 and grow close to 3 percent of GNP by 2035, continuing at that level through 2060, when the projections stop. As a percent of GNP, these annual deficits are more than three times as large as the earlier surpluses and would alone create annual federal deficits for each of these years about as large as current deficits. Under the so-called pessimistic projections, these annual Social Security deficits would climb to 7.5 percent of GNP.

The accumulated Social Security trust funds, meanwhile, are a charade. They do not hold real assets. Their holdings are merely government bonds constituting a promise by the Treasury Department to pay the Social Security Administration. So the trust fund "assets" actually are only claims against the federal government, which will have to be financed out of federal revenues or borrowing if they ever have to be cashed in to finance Social Security benefits. As a practical matter, the Social Security trust funds are nothing more than a statement of the legal authority Social Security has to draw from general revenues in the future. There is no money nor investments to be cashed out. In other words, the larger the trust funds, the bigger Social Security's priority claim against future federal tax revenues.

The new President must put a stop to the continuing process of real tax increases to finance phony funds. He has an opportunity to do so. In January 1988, the combined employer and employee payroll tax rate was raised from 14.3 percent to 15.02 percent. In January 1990, another scheduled increase will hike the tax to 15.3 percent. Under the Social Security Administration's intermediate assumptions, Social Security will be able to pay all promised benefits until about 2020—without the 1988 and 1990 tax increases. This is true even if the large projected deficits in the hospital insurance program have to be covered by the projected surpluses.

The new President should call for repeal of the 1988 and 1990 payroll tax rate increases. This would free today's young workers from an unnecessary tax burden and boost economic activity enough to create more than half a million new jobs. Given the changing fiscal and demographic dynamics of the Social Security system, revenue from the 1988 and 1990 tax hikes simply will delay actions needed to resolve the fundamental problems of the system. The short-term surplus also probably would just provide cover for increases in other government spending without having to increase the deficit. The large 1988 and 1990 tax increases actually could undermine the very economic prosperity that is the premise underlying the projections of Social Security surpluses.

Establishing a New Compact between the Generations

With or without the 1988 and 1990 tax increases, payroll taxes eventually will have to be raised to much higher levels to pay Social Security's promised benefits unless fundamental reforms are adopted. To avoid such damaging tax measures and provide a better overall system for today's young workers, the new President should urge

Congress to make a new compact between generations. Today's elderly would be paid all promised benefits in full, while workers would be allowed the freedom to choose to rely more on the private sector and less on Social Security.

As the first half of the compact, the government should provide all current retirees, and all future retirees at the time they retire, with a Social Security bond, contractually entitling them to their promised benefits. This would give Social Security benefits the same legal status as Treasury bonds: cutting Social Security benefits would become as unconstitutional as refusing to repay a U.S. Treasury bond.

For the second half of the compact, workers and their employers should be allowed to contribute to a private investment account up to some limit, in return for income tax credits equal to the amount of such contributions. To the extent a worker exercises this option throughout his career, he would receive proportionately less in Social Security benefits in his retirement, relying on benefits from his private account instead. All workers and their employers would continue to pay Social Security taxes in full, but for those who contributed to the private accounts, the income tax credits in effect would offset a proportionate amount of the Social Security taxes.

This private sector option should be expanded gradually to the full range of Social Security benefits. Workers and their employers should be allowed to contribute additional amounts to private accounts for life insurance, disability insurance, and even retirement medical insurance in return for income tax credits. To the extent such contributions are made, workers would forego similar benefits payable under Social Security. Ultimately, each worker could have the complete freedom to choose how much to rely on the private accounts and how much to rely on Social Security. Those workers who believe Social Security is better than the private alternatives would be completely free to continue to rely on it.

Such a private account option would strengthen Social Security financially, improving the ability of the program to pay promised benefits. Social Security's revenues would be maintained in full, since workers exercising the option would receive credits against income taxes rather than the payroll taxes that finance Social Security. Yet future Social Security Administration expenditures would be reduced over time as increasing numbers of workers relied more on the private accounts and less on Social Security. By the time the baby boom generation retires, those who have switched to the private accounts will have reduced the burden on Social Security sufficiently to eliminate the likely long-term financing gap completely, avoiding any need for payroll tax increases. Indeed, large payroll tax cuts might be possible.

Moreover, those workers who opt for the private accounts could expect much higher returns and benefits. Through the private accounts, workers could tailor their investment and insurance purchases to suit their needs and preferences. The private account option would give blue-collar and lower-income workers their only real chance to accumulate and control substantial capital resources.

The income tax credits for contributions to the private accounts would reduce income tax revenue. This loss could be kept manageable by introducing the option for only a small part of Social Security at first, and slowly expanding it. The revenue loss eventually would be offset completely by the reduced Social Security expenditures, as workers relied more on their private accounts in place of at least part of Social Security. In addition, there would be an increase in private retirement savings at least equal to the temporary net loss in federal tax revenues. So even if the federal government had to borrow to cover the temporary net revenue loss, the additional borrowing would be offset by the increased retirement savings. The new government borrowing thus would be no new net drain on private savings. Such borrowing, in any event, would amount to no more than an explicit recognition of the government's existing but unfunded Social Security liabilities.

This reform would not threaten the interests of the elderly. It would guarantee their benefits, while expanding freedom of choice and opportunity for workers. Consequently, such reform may be able to overcome the institutional constraints that otherwise prevent Social Security policy change. The old guard would certainly object, and the elderly organizations, as usual, would sound the alarm. But the elderly themselves wisely may see no reason to join the attack. Indeed, the reform is consistent with public attitudes regarding Social Security: it would assure benefits to the elderly, which both young and old demand, but it would offer a new and better way to assure retirement security for the future.

Admittedly, this reform involves political risks. But the present course invites political catastrophe, since continuing crises and proposed expansions eventually will force lawmakers to vote for higher taxes and spending or face retribution for being anti-elderly. The Social Security issue cannot just simply be avoided. Similar reforms have been adopted in Britain with considerable political benefits. In 1978,

Britain allowed employers to introduce employer-sponsored pensions on a company wide basis as a substitute for the government's earnings-related pension program. About half of all workers in Britain have already exercised this option. Under further reforms recently adopted by the Thatcher government, British workers will be able to opt out of the earnings-related program this year on an individual basis. Effectively workers will be able to contribute to individual investment accounts in return for substantial tax rebates. In retirement, they will rely on the benefits payable from these accounts in place of half of the public benefits.

Reforming Individual Retirement Accounts

Returns on saving and investment in the U.S. are subject to heavy, multiple taxation through the corporate income tax, the ordinary personal income tax, and the capital gains tax. Individual Retirement Accounts (IRAs) offset some of this harsh, discriminatory tax treatment for Americans trying to set aside additional funds for their retirement. IRAs allow an immediate tax deduction for contributions and defer taxes on investment returns. They do not involve a special interest tax preference, but a sound, fair, rational way to tax returns on savings and investment. Private savings cannot be expected to perform an important role as part of the three-legged stool of national retirement policy unless Americans can use IRAs to offset the discriminatory tax treatment that otherwise applies to savings in the U.S.

Shortsightedly, the 1986 tax reform substantially restricted the IRA deduction, particularly for workers in companies with pension programs. The new President should propose changing the 1986 rules to restore the $2,000 annual deduction for each worker. All spouses should be allowed the $2,000 annual deduction as well. In addition, the $2,000 deduction should be indexed to increase with the rate of growth of wages, as is the Social Security maximum taxable income, so that the relative value of the deduction will not depreciate over time.

The new President should propose that workers be allowed to use their IRA funds to purchase life, long-term care, disability, or retirement health insurance without taxation or other penalty. In this way IRAs could provide the full range of benefits currently provided by Social Security, together with protection against long-term care costs, which Social Security does not provide.

Reforming Corporate Pension Regulations

Company pensions constitute the third leg of the retirement income system. Current regulations on pensions, imposed by the Employment

Retirement Income Security Act (ERISA) of 1974, are enormously complex and burdensome, discouraging businesses from adopting sound programs. The new President should propose that requirements concerning coverage, participation, and distribution of benefits in pension plans be replaced by simple rules mandating that all employees be granted an equivalent bona fide offer to participate in the pension plan. Legislation introduced by Senator David Pryor (D-AR) would begin to relax these regulations for the small businesses most burdened today.

The 1986 tax reform restricts pension alternatives. For example, the annual maximum contribution to a tax-deferred 401(k) plan was slashed from $30,000 to $7,000. Effective early withdrawal restrictions and penalties were imposed for the first time, further limiting the attractiveness of this pension alternative. The new President should propose that these new restrictions and penalties be repealed and that the maximum contribution limits be restored to their pre-1986 levels.

The company pension system should be improved by making pension contributions and rights more "portable" from one job to the next. This could be done by changing ERISA rules to encourage greater reliance on so-called defined contribution plans, where the employer and the employee contribute to an account that goes with the employee from job to job. Such plans avoid such problems as underfunding or company insolvency.

Restructuring the Social Security Administration

The Social Security Administration has a well-deserved reputation for painting as rosy a picture as it can of the Social Security system and its future prospects. This often has misled policymakers and the American people about the true condition of the program. Throughout the 1970s, for instance, projections in each year's *Annual Report of the Board of Trustees of the Federal Old Age and Survivors' Insurance and Disability Insurance Trust Funds* and *Annual Report of the Federal Hospital Insurance Trust Fund* were wildly optimistic regarding short-term finances. Today they are wildly optimistic regarding long-term finances, failing to base projections on realistic assumptions. The Social Security Administration, moreover, wastes millions of taxpayer dollars on advertising campaigns designed solely to build political support for the status quo. Government bureaucrats should not be using taxpayers' funds in this way, intervening on one side of the public debate with a slick, misleading, public relations campaign.

To counter these shortcomings, the U.S. Treasury should be required to hire a different private accounting firm each year to review that year's Social Security Trustee's reports and recommend how they might be improved. The Social Security Administration should be required to cooperate by providing all the information requested by the contracting firm. All funding for Social Security advertising and public relations campaigns should be halted.

———————————◇———————————

INITIATIVES FOR 1989

1) Repeal the 1988 and 1990 payroll tax rate increases. In January 1988, the combined employer and employee Social Security payroll tax rate was raised from 14.3 percent to 15.02 percent. Under current law, this tax is scheduled to rise to 15.3 percent in January 1990. These tax increases impose an unnecessary burden on today's workers and could undermine the economic expansion needed to finance future Social Security benefits. The next President should support legislation to repeal these tax hikes.

2) Restore and expand Individual Retirement Accounts (IRAs). The tax deduction for IRAs was significantly reduced in the Tax Reform Act of 1986. This discourages many Americans from building up a private retirement savings account to help support them during their retirement years. The new Administration should support legislation to restore the deduction for IRA contributions of up to $2,000 each year for all workers, and to expand that deduction to all spouses. The maximum deductible IRA contribution also should be indexed to increase with wages each year. Further, legislation should be enacted to allow workers to use their IRA funds to purchase life, disability, and retirement health insurance, without tax or other penalty.

3) Provide Americans with accurate information about Social Security. All Social Security Administration funding for advertising and public relations campaigns should be halted. These campaigns give Americans a false impression of the financial condition of the system and the rate of return that Americans will receive on their tax contributions. The next President should take steps to provide Americans with a more accurate picture. He should direct the U.S. Treasury Department to contract with a different private firm each year to analyze that year's Social Security annual reports and publish their analyses. In addition, should direct the Labor Department to require that the employer's share of the payroll tax be reported on each worker's paycheck along with the employee's share.

14

The Department of Housing and Urban Development

Peter J. Ferrara*
Task Force Chairman

The goal of the Department of Housing and Urban Development should be to provide housing assistance directly to the poor in an efficient, cost-effective manner that harnesses free-market competition and incentives. HUD should aim broadly at empowering low-income families to take control of their own lives, through enhanced urban economic opportunity, housing vouchers that provide choice and control, and policies to promote tenant management and ownership of public housing.

These have been the policies and vision of HUD Secretary Samuel R. Pierce, Jr., the Reagan Cabinet member who probably most effectively has transformed the Reagan mandate into reality. Pierce has begun to shift federal housing assistance away from subsidizing construction companies to providing rental assistance funds directly to low-income families in the form of housing vouchers. The new Administration should continue Pierce's work by replacing all programs involving construction of new housing with a full voucher program. Vouchers help many more low-income families for a given amount of resources than new construction programs and give poor families the freedom to choose their housing and location.

The Reagan Administration has won passage of landmark legislation giving public housing tenants the right to manage and ultimately buy the properties in which they live. The next Administration should move determinedly to expand resident management and ownership.

---

*Commenting and contributing generously to this chapter were *Mandate III* Task Force Members Ken Beirne, Mark Frazier, Steve Glaude, John Weicher, Bob Woodson, and Susan Woodward. They do not necessarily endorse all of its views and recommendations.

BUDGET AND PERSONNEL

Secretaries

Samuel R. Pierce, Jr.   1981–present

Personnel

April 1970	14,737
April 1980	17,425
March 1988	13,174

Budget Outlays

Fiscal Year	Total (billions)
1989 Estimate	$21.6
1988 Estimate	$18.6
1987 Actual	$15.5
1986 Actual	$14.1
1985 Actual	$28.7*
1980 Actual	$12.7
1970 Actual	$ 2.4

*HUD bought back loans from local housing authorities causing a one-year increase in outlays. These loans were eventually forgiven.

The target should be to have 20 percent of public housing managed or owned by residents within four years.

For its general housing finance programs, the new Administration should shift as many Federal Housing Administration (FHA) and Government National Mortgage Association (GNMA) functions as possible to the private sector. HUD should privatize completely the Federal National Mortgage Association (FNMA) and the Federal Home Loan Mortgage Corporation (FHLMC), eliminating their unfair and unjustified special privileges. The private sector has proved that it can perform these organizations' functions. Funds for HUD's major economic development program, Community Development Block Grants (CDBG), should be shifted to more urgent priorities, such as expanding housing vouchers for the poor, supporting public housing resident management and ownership, and assisting neighborhood groups involved in service delivery. HUD should seek federal tax incentives for the 100 enterprise zones authorized by Congress in 1987 and expand this program, which is consistent with the goal of creating the best conditions for enterprise in America's blighted inner cities.

During the Reagan Administration, HUD's urban policy has been based on promoting urban economic growth, increasing private economic initiative, and giving states and localities responsibility for public services and infrastructure. This policy has improved the living conditions of urban residents and the financial health of America's cities. The new Administration should build on this by promoting policies that will empower lower-income, disadvantaged residents of the nation's cities to participate in the mainstream economy and address directly the problems and needs they face.

SUMMARY OF AGENCY FUNCTIONS

The Department's principal program-related offices are:

◆ *The Office of Public and Indian Housing*, which administers low-income housing programs, including the state-chartered but federally financed Public Housing Authorities' 1.4 million public housing units and the Section 8 Existing Housing program under which certain low-income families receive certificates that oblige the federal government to pay the private landlord the difference between 30 percent of the tenant's income and the area's "fair market rent" (FMR).

◆ *The Federal Housing Administration (FHA)*, which insures home mortgages against default by qualified borrowers.

◆ *The Office of Community Planning and Development*, which gives state and local governments grants for development projects chosen by them.

◆ *The Office of Fair Housing and Equal Opportunity*, which helps to administer civil rights laws intended to eliminate housing discrimination against racial, religious, ethnic, or other minorities.

◆ *The Office of Policy Development and Research*, which conducts research on housing conditions and policies and develops new HUD policy proposals.

INSTITUTIONAL CONSTRAINTS

Housing and urban policy is heavily influenced by organizations and interests that gain directly from housing construction and operation. Private developers and landlords, for instance, lobby for government payments to build and operate new low-income housing units. Consequently, they generally push for construction programs and oppose vouchers and other direct subsidies to families. Similarly, public housing authorities (PHAs), which have overall responsibility for public housing units, oppose vouchers and such innovations as tenant management, since they reduce the need for PHA bureaucracies and sharply limit their power and role. Mobilizing low-income public housing residents in support of tenant management and ownership, however, has been an effective antidote to the PHAs. Pressure from these residents led Congress to approve provisions in 1987 for public housing resident management and ownership.

Liberal pressure groups, usually in the nation's capital, claiming to speak for the poor, often join forces with the construction industry and PHA bureaucrats. In general they want the federal government to construct additional housing directly for low-income Americans and oppose giving those Americans the vouchers or other means to choose their housing. Politicians and politically well-connected business interests, meanwhile, support urban development programs, like Urban Development Action Grants (UDAG). In many respects, UDAG is an urban slush fund, enabling congressmen and local politicians to secure large grants for favored developers, who predictably are always ready to tell Congress how important such programs are.

———————————◇———————————

THE REAGAN ADMINISTRATION RECORD

When Ronald Reagan entered office, HUD was out of control. Spending had almost doubled, from $7.5 billion in fiscal 1975 to $14.0 billion in fiscal 1981. The Department was feverishly signing long-term pork-barrel contracts with private developers to construct and administer costly new housing units. Under the Carter Administration, HUD had created the Urban Development Action Grant (UDAG) program to provide yet more funds to politically influential developers, this time to build hotels and shopping malls of only marginal benefit, if any, for the poor. HUD was imposing costly mandates and regulations on state and local governments, while at the same time encouraging them to look increasingly to the federal government for handouts to address seemingly every local concern.

Reagan's message has been that a strong and growing economy is the key to meeting the nation's housing needs, generating urban development, and helping the poor. Reducing federal spending by eliminating special interest windfalls and targeting funds on the truly needy has been part of Reagan's strategy for economic growth. Under his philosophy of federalism, state and local governments have been given the freedom to address local needs without costly federal restrictions. They also have been given the responsibility to address their local needs.

HUD Secretary Pierce has combined an openness to new ideas with a dogged determination, low-key effectiveness, and widely praised management reforms. The number of HUD-subsidized low-income housing units increased by almost 40 percent from 1980 to 1988, from 3.1 million to 4.3 million, with $15.4 billion to be spent on low-income housing programs in fiscal 1989. More low-income families are receiving federal housing assistance today then ever before.

HUD has been able to cut future commitments and restrain current spending while expanding the number of families receiving housing assistance. It did this primarily by ending subsidies for new housing construction and substituting far less costly housing vouchers, which directly aid low-income families. Today, expensive new construction under HUD programs virtually has ended, except for special units for the elderly, the handicapped, Indians living on reservations, and uncompleted previous construction contracts. At the same time, HUD expanded Section 8 housing certificates 50 percent between fiscal 1980 and fiscal 1988. HUD won passage of legislation making these certificates more like vouchers. Tenants now have the right to use these certificates anywhere within a metropolitan area, not just within the family's local Public Housing Authority district, as had previously been the case. The legislation also allows families effectively to choose any private unit meeting HUD standards within their geographic area.

HUD has targeted housing assistance on the poorest families. When Reagan took office, families with incomes up to 80 percent of the local area median could receive federal housing aid. So many families qualified for this that HUD had funds for only a few of them. To correct this, HUD successfully pressed Congress to tighten the eligibility requirement to 50 percent of median income. This allows HUD to channel assistance to the most needy families.

A landmark HUD achievement has been its policies to promote self-management and ultimately ownership of public housing units by their low-income residents. The Reagan Administration correctly has believed that, given the opportunity to manage and control their homes, poor people will show the same responsibility and initiative as any other group. This contrasts with liberal paternalism, which assumes that the poor must be told by bureaucrats where and how to live. A strong coalition of conservatives and inner-city tenant groups have defeated Public Housing Authority and liberal resistance to tenant management and ownership. Many PHAs felt threatened by tenant management and refused to use the authority they had to contract with private organizations to perform some or all necessary management and maintenance functions for public housing units. In Reagan's first term, HUD pushed local PHAs to do so, particularly for a project's maintenance, security, and rent collection.

In 1986, HUD established procedures making it easier for public housing residents to create tenant management organizations. These tenant groups have improved building management and maintenance, reduced costs, increased project income, cut welfare costs by creating employment opportunities, and provided other important benefits to low-income families. The regulations require PHAs to consult and cooperate with these organizations.

Under pressure from tenant organizations, Congress broadened this policy in the 1987 housing bill. This gives public housing tenants a "right to manage" by allowing them to establish a nonprofit resident management corporation (RMC) explicitly empowered to enter into a management services contract with the local PHA. The legislation further provides that the RMC may keep any savings or increased income resulting from its management performance. These funds can be used to improve the maintenance and operation of the project, to establish business enterprises that employ public housing residents, or to acquire additional low-income housing.

HUD's own economic development initiative has been the enterprise zone. HUD's comprehensive 1981 enterprise zone proposal sought to reduce taxes, regulations, and other government burdens on economic activity in zones designated in the nation's most economically distressed areas. Though the Senate passed the proposed legislation twice, the Democrat-controlled House refused even to consider it. Nevertheless, HUD's enthusiastic promotion of the idea has led 35 states to adopt their own enterprise zones. So far, over $10 billion has been invested in state zones, creating or saving almost 200,000 jobs in neighborhoods that had been declining. In the 1987 housing bill, Congress at last gave HUD authority to designate 100 federal enterprise zones in distressed areas, but refused to grant federal tax relief for such zones.

The Reagan Administration has transformed the debate over federal urban policy. The old approach fostered state and local dependence on the federal government. Reagan and Pierce have emphasized the roles of robust economic growth, private economic initiatives, and the role of state and local governments in addressing urban needs. Reagan federalism policies have sparked creativity as states and localities now emphasize their regional strengths and advantages. Previously, they were encouraged to stress their weaknesses to qualify for federal aid. HUD encourages state and local governments to use private contractors to provide traditionally public services.

HUD's main failures are due in large part to Congress, which has been bullied by developer and Public Housing Authority special interests. In addition to delaying and diluting the federal enterprise zone legislation, Congress has dragged its feet for years on housing vouchers. And despite the federal deficit and strong Administration opposition, Congress has enacted wasteful new spending drains, such as the Nehemiah program, which provides large subsidies for the purchase of homes by those lucky few middle-class Americans who know how to work the bureaucracy.

At times, HUD has failed to present its ideas effectively. The Department, for instance, produced an honest solid study on the number of America's homeless, yet retreated in the face of harsh, unsubstantiated criticism. The result is that the critics' contention that homelessness is a major national problem is now rooted in the public's mind as a major Reagan Administration failure. HUD should have argued that existence of homeless Americans confirms that conventional housing and urban problems have failed and that what is needed are such reforms as housing vouchers, elimination of rent control, and targeting of aid to the truly needy and others. HUD should have pointed to the insensitive actions by many mayors who ordered mental patients to be turned out into the streets, saving their cities health care expenses, but creating homeless "street people." HUD should have counterattacked by advocating mental health policies and drug rehabilitation. And HUD should have pursued vigorously the intellectual battle over the cause and magnitude of the problem.

THE NEXT FOUR YEARS

The cornerstone of successful housing and urban development policies is rapid national and local economic growth. This will not be achieved by rich bounties of government subsidies, or by costly federal regulations on state and local governments and the private sector. It can only be achieved through policies promoting greater reliance on private, free markets and through federal, state, and local tax and spending reduction, deregulation, and privatization. These principles formed the foundation of Reagan Administration policies, which were highly successful in promoting economic growth.

The next Administration should build on this foundation, and complete the fundamental reforms begun under Pierce's leadership. The nation's low-income housing policies must be made to serve the poor, rather than developer and landlord special interests and entrenched PHA bureaucrats. This means providing assistance directly to the poor themselves, in a form that gives them choices and control such as vouchers, rather than providing the funding through new housing construction programs to developers, landlords, and PHAs, in the hope that some will trickle down to the poor. Policy should be aimed more broadly at empowering the poor to meet their needs. Through tenant management and ultimately ownership of public housing, the poor are again directly given greater choice, control, and opportunity to improve their lives. Through Enterprise Zones, new job and economic opportunities are delivered directly to the poor in distressed inner city areas.

State and local governments must be given the freedom and flexibility to determine how best to meet local needs, as they are most familiar with local concerns, preferences, services, and opportunities. At the same time, state and local governments must take the responsibility for financing worthy projects and services, rather than seeking to avoid the duty of raising local financing and wailing that the federal taxpayer somehow has the responsibility to bail them out on a permanent basis.

Empowering the Poor through More Housing Vouchers

The problem for the poor is not the unavailability of housing, but a lack of sufficient funds to pay for quality housing. Vouchers give the poor the funds that make this private housing affordable. The demand for quality housing created by vouchers would stimulate construction of private housing where necessary. As such, vouchers should become the new President's primary program of housing assistance for the poor.

Numerous studies and demonstration projects show that vouchers can deliver superior housing assistance to a low-income family at less than half the cost of constructing a new unit with federal support. This difference is due in part to costly bureaucratic delays and to federal regulations, such as the Davis-Bacon Act, which artificially increase the labor costs of federally supported housing projects. Even when private firms develop and manage properties, as in the Section 8 program, they have little incentive to compete or improve quality because they effectively are guaranteed tenants, rent, and high profits.

In a voucher system, by contrast, private developers and landlords must attract tenants. This competition keeps costs down. And because tenants can keep the difference between the vouchers and the rents they pay, they will shop for the best housing at the lowest price—just as wealthier Americans do. This will create a more competitive housing market, which restrains rents. As a result of vouchers' cost advantage, more than twice as many low-income families can be helped with the same amount of government resources. Vouchers also give low-income families the freedom to choose where to live, rather than being assigned by bureaucrats to a particular building and even apartment. Thus a family can use its housing voucher to move across town or to the suburbs if these offer better job opportunities or schools. Public housing, of course, locks poor families into generally poor neighborhoods where they and their children easily become victims of deterioration, violence, crime, drug dealers, and other social pathologies.

The new HUD Secretary should press immediately to substitute vouchers for all low-income housing programs. HUD should ask Congress to fund 100,000 additional vouchers each year and to end construction of new units completely, except for the elderly and handicapped. In fiscal 1990, the Section 8 Existing Housing Certificate program is up for reauthorization. Instead of extending it, HUD should push to replace it with 900,000 vouchers to the families now using the more restricted Section 8 certificates.

Many contracts for subsidized, privately constructed units under Section 8 and other programs will begin expiring shortly, leaving these units free to be rented to any family at unsubsidized market rates unless the contracts are extended. By 2005, the contracts for all the 1.9 million private subsidized units constructed under HUD programs will have expired. In the 1987 housing bill, Congress sought to delay termination of these contracts pending further consideration. The contracts for these costly older units should be allowed to expire. It would cost a great deal to rehabilitate and operate these old units. As the contracts expire, they should be replaced with less costly vouchers, which tenants could use to continue to rent their same units if they chose. Some or all of the resulting savings should be used to expand assistance to more families than were served under the old programs. HUD, in fact, should attempt to "buy out" its existing Section 8 contracts with private landlords, using savings in monthly rent subsidies to expand vouchers more rapidly.

The new Administration should urge Congress to enact legislation that ultimately will offer vouchers to all public housing tenants. All current operating and modernization subsidies to public housing projects would then be ended. Existing projects would be funded through vouchers, rather than operating subsidies to the Public Housing Authorities. If a project could not raise enough income through vouchers and rent payments to continue operating, it should be sold without restriction. The tenants would then use their vouchers to seek housing elsewhere.

Encouraging Resident Management and Ownership

To improve the management of existing public housing projects and the social and economic conditions of their neighborhoods, the new Administration should continue to promote tenant management and ultimate ownership of public housing by the residents. Turning residents into managers and owners gives them a strong personal stake in the properties and the incentive to improve maintenance and living conditions. It also gives them economic power to benefit themselves and the community. When managing or owning properties, the residents can hire themselves to perform services on the project, generally for less than outsiders. The tenants can then use the savings to improve services, maintenance, and living conditions even more. The tenants can also use these savings for education, job training, or other programs for their families.

Tenant managemant already has been proven successful. Example: Tenants began managing the 464–unit Kenilworth-Parkside project in Washington, D.C., in 1982. The results are documented in a detailed study by the international accounting firm of Coopers & Lybrand. By 1985, rental income had risen 77 percent due to improved collections and a vacancy rate which had dropped to 6 percent, compared with the average 18 percent at other projects in the city. Administrative costs had been slashed by 60 percent. Rather than receiving subsidies, the project was running a surplus.

The Kenilworth-Parkside tenant managers have created over 100 new jobs for residents in maintenance work for the project, a co-op food store, a clothing shop, a beauty parlor, a catering service, a trash collection firm, and a roofing company. Recognizing that the project's ultimate success depends on the residents' economic and social condition, the management group has promoted work and education and discouraged welfare and teenage pregnancy. The result: welfare dependency in the project fell from 85 percent in 1982 to just 2 percent in mid–1988. In the 1970s, the project's high school dropout rate was 80 percent; now 30 percent go to college.

The 1987 housing bill provides a reasonably good start toward tenant management. A major roadblock, however, continues to be the reluctance of local Public Housing Authorities to release control over public housing units. The 1987 bill must be recognized as providing for an enforceable tenant "right to manage". Residents should have the right to appeal to HUD where the Public Housing Authority unreasonably refuses tenant management, and HUD should have powers to enforce their right to manage.

Resident managers should be granted complete control over tenant selection and screening and the right to evict nonpaying or destructive tenants. Resident managers should have great flexibility to hire tenants, set wages, and accept volunteer labor, and should be exempt from Davis-Bacon wage rates and other regulations that artificially raise costs.

The ownership provisions in the 1987 legislation are deeply flawed. The resale price of the unit is sharply restricted, eliminating much of the incentive for a resident to care for and maintain the property. Indeed, the property can only be sold to a Resident Management Corporation, Public Housing Authority, or another low-income family. In fact, the property cannot be sold unless the Public Housing Authority or Resident Management Corporation builds a replacement unit. This provision is unnecessary because the sold unit must remain available to low-income Americans. The new Administration should overhaul the ownership provisions.

A resident management corporation with a three-year record of good management should have a statutory right to buy the entire property as a cooperative on behalf of all the tenants. The sale price should be 30 percent of market value, and the tenant group should have the right to a take-back mortgage from the Public Housing Authority, ensuring needed financing. Those residents not wishing to join the co-op should be given a voucher and allowed to continue to rent in the project. HUD should issue new vouchers to replace public housing units sold to residents, ensuring no reduction in available housing for low-income families.

HUD should convert 20 percent of public housing to resident management or home ownership within the next four years. To speed this transfer, the Department should contract with private firms and organizations to assist and prepare tenant groups to take over management and ownership.

Helping the Homeless

Homeless Americans have been callously manipulated to score political and ideological points against the Reagan Administration, and to leverage funds from the federal government for projects and programs that have only a marginal effect on the deep problems of those sleeping on grates or in shelters. Though there have been claims that 2 million to 3 million Americans are homeless, these figures are not based on a count, study, analysis, or even a serious good-faith guess. A careful, comprehensive 1984 HUD study of the homeless concluded that on any single night there were 250,000 to 350,000 homeless in America. And studies by academic experts suggest that there are fewer than that. A 1986 study by the University of Chicago and the University of Massachusetts-Amherst, for instance, concludes that the nightly homeless population in Chicago totaled 3,000, compared with 20,000 estimated by the 1984 HUD study. Counts in other cities have found homeless populations less than one-third the HUD estimates for those cities.

Numbers are important. A homeless population in the range of 250,000 to 350,000 can be cared for by carefully targeted actions rather than by massive federal programs of the kind demanded by professional advocates for the homeless. The new Administration should point out that the problem is solvable and then move to solve it.

The homeless include two separate groups. The first consists of homeless families with children living in welfare hotels. Their homelessness is caused by maladministration of public resources by welfare bureaucracies. For half a century, the U.S. has had a public commitment to assist low-income families with children; they are eligible for food stamps, Aid to Families with Dependent Children, Medicaid, and other programs, as well as housing assistance. These families each should be given a voucher which could allow them to rent moderate housing of their choice in the private market. Vouchers would solve the problem of homelessness for these families at only a fraction of the expense of keeping them in hotels.

The second group of homeless are single men and women; the majority of them are mentally ill and cannot care for themselves. New public housing, other traditional housing policies, or even more new shelters would be of little help to them. They are on the streets because they have been turned out of mental institutions by the policy of deinstitutionalization adopted by liberal governors and mayors in the 1960s and 1970s. Under this policy, mental patients were released from hospitals if they were not deemed a violent threat to others. The result: the population of America's mental institutions has declined from 500,000 in 1963 to about 125,000 today. Once released, these former patients were simply abandoned to the streets by the same liberal mayors and governors and denied the community facilities and follow-up care originally intended. The mayors and governors responsible for this are these same ones who have been criticizing Ronald Reagan for his Administration's insensitivity to the homeless.

This second group of homeless also includes many suffering from alcohol and drug abuse who consequently cannot care for themselves. A few in this second group are homeless because of a temporary personal crisis, such as domestic violence or eviction, and will soon regain self-sufficiency.

To address effectively the problems of this second group of homeless, state and local governments should establish community mental health facilities and alcohol and drug abuse clinics—as the 1963 Community Mental Health Centers Act prescribed—and assign the homeless suffering from problems to the appropriate facility for treatment. Those assigned can be free to come and go as they choose during the day, but should be required to return to the assigned facility for shelter each night, unless they arrange alternative shelter. Allowing those who are mentally incapable or intoxicated or drugged to "choose" to sleep and freeze on the streets is neither compassion nor freedom.

The streets are not for sleeping or residing, and the government should be able to preserve them for their intended uses of transportation and public meeting and discourse. Consequently, localities ought to be able to ban sleeping on the streets at night. The new Administration should criticize as compassionless those local politicians and cities that fail to provide appropriate community mental health facilities for the noninstitutionalized mentally ill. Such cities should be disqualified from receiving urban development funds.

All of the homeless, whether families or single individuals, have much greater difficulty finding housing on their own because of government policies. In New York City or Los Angeles, for instance, rent control restricts the availability of low-priced standard quality housing, since rent restrictions give owners no reason to maintain their units and developers little reason to build new units. Rent control also spurs individuals or small families to continue to occupy huge apartments, denying the space to larger families. HUD should devise a strategy to eliminate rent control in every city. HUD should fund and publicize studies of the effects of rent control. The federal government should withhold housing assistance to all cities practicing rent control.

Through a number of programs, the federal government grants economic development subsidies to projects that destroy single-room-occupancy hotels and other low-income housing in inner cities. During the 1970s, the U.S. lost about one million single-room-occupancy units—nearly 50 percent of the total and enough to house more than double the number of Americans now homeless. HUD and all other federal agencies should deny project funds when significant numbers of low-income units will be lost.

Spurring Competition in Housing Finance

The Federal Housing Administration (FHA) should insure mortgages for low- and moderate-income home buyers who might not qualify for private mortgage insurance. FHA should be prohibited from insuring loans for second homes, investment property, refinancings, and borrowers earning more than 120 percent of the area median income. These markets can be fully served by private insurance. FHA also should be required to maintain the same kind of insurance reserves as do the private sector. FHA should charge premiums reflecting the likelihood of default and comply with the usual industry standards for loan verification and processing. This would protect federal taxpayers from high default liability and require FHA to compete with private insurers on an equal basis.

The federal budget now reflects the default risk to taxpayers of the guarantees provided by the Government National Mortgage Association. As a result, the GNMA budget has gone from a surplus of $650 million in fiscal 1987 to an estimated deficit of $720 million in fiscal 1989. Rapidly increasing FHA and GNMA costs account for about half of the sharp rise in the total HUD budget since fiscal 1987.

The Federal National Mortgage Association (FNMA) and Federal Home Loan Mortgage Corporation (FHLMC) can perform the secondary market operations for FHA and insured loans now performed by GNMA. Wholly private firms also perform these functions. Consequently, GNMA should leave the operations for such loans to these alternative institutions. GNMA's only other function is insuring pools of mortgages involved in HUD new construction programs. If these programs are replaced with vouchers, as they should be, GNMA would have no function and could be abolished.

FNMA and FHLMC, now owned and operated as private corporations, currently receive substantial federal assistance. The Treasury and Federal Reserve Board trade their securities along with Treasury bonds and other federal securities, creating an aura of federal backing for FNMA and FHLMC securities in the market. This impression is enhanced by federal regulations allowing depository institutions to use these securities as collateral, by U.S. Treasury credit directly available to FNMA and FHLMC, and by other special privileges. These benefits enable FNMA and FHLMC to sell their securities at lower interest rates than can private firms, since such benefits persuade buyers to view the securities as less risky than other securities. The benefits also reduce costs for the two corporations directly. This gives FNMA and FHLMC an unfair advantage over other strictly private competitors. These special advantages and benefits should be eliminated. FNMA and FHLMC should be privatized completely.

Eliminating Wasteful Federal Economic Development Programs

The new Administration should build on the Reagan Administration's record of spurring urban economic development by promoting freer markets and removing government burdens on private initiative and economic activity. The new Administration should also continue to promote greater state and local government responsibility for public services and infrastructure.

The Urban Development Action Grant program is inconsistent with these goals. The program subsidizes business ventures which would not be viable without government assistance. It draws private investment into uneconomic projects, thus diverting capital from more worthy projects, or it adds to the profits of private projects which would have been undertaken without federal money. The program creates neither new jobs nor investment; it merely shifts them from one part of the economy to another. By misallocating resources,

UDAG actually reduces the overall number of jobs. As in fiscal 1989, no new funding should be provided for this program.

The Community Development Block Grant program (CDBG) is also inconsistent with the federal government's proper role in economic development. The program funds local public services and infrastructure, shifting financing responsibilities from the local level. It provides federal funds to virtually every local area in the country, rich or poor. And it does so at a time when the federal government is still deeply in the red, and state and local budgets are generally healthy and enjoying budget surpluses. CDBG consequently should be phased out, with the funds used for more urgent priorities.

The new Administration should move quickly to provide federal incentives for enterprise zones to complement existing state and local incentives. The original aim of the zones was to remove federal, state, and local government burdens on economic activity in distressed areas. This would create the open, free-market climate most conducive to entrepreneurship, investment, job creation, and economic growth. The federal government should at least eliminate capital gains taxes within the zones. It should provide tax credits for the investment of capital and employment of workers within the zones to offset the corporate income tax. And it should provide tax credits to workers themselves to offset their income and payroll tax burdens. HUD should be granted broad authority to waive nonstatutory federal regulatory requirements as long as they do not affect health and safety. And state and local governments should be pressed to remove their own tax and regulatory burdens within the zones.

Empowering the Poor

The new Administration should expand on the Reagan Administration's sound urban policy foundation by introducing a new theme— empowerment of low-income Americans. Housing vouchers deliver economic power directly to the poor to solve their need for housing. Resident management and ownership empower public housing tenants directly to improve their living conditions. Transferring abandoned property to homesteading neighborhood groups and individuals empowers inner-city residents. Enterprise zones empower low-income families to find jobs and increase their incomes.

State and local governments can empower the poor by contracting with neighborhood community groups to provide services. This would create jobs and income for inner-city residents. The National Association of Neighborhoods, a nationwide organization of local community groups, provides information to state and local governments on how this can be done and helps new neighborhood groups get started. HUD could publicize and endorse such activities and provide "how to" information to state and local governments, and to start-up neighborhood groups.

HUD should work to eliminate barriers to inner-city entrepreneurship and risk taking. Occupational licensing, bonding requirements, building codes, zoning ordinances, restrictions on home work, and other regulations discourage entrepreneurship and prevent competition with established interests. Eliminating such barriers would create new opportunities for jobs and economic achievement. It also would allow neighborhood groups to provide adoption services, day care, juvenile delinquency programs, education support, and other services addressing critical needs. Too often groups are prevented from doing this by excessive regulations.

INITIATIVES FOR 1989

1) Substitute vouchers for low income programs. Housing vouchers are the best general method of assisting low income Americans to obtain decent housing. Since a voucher provides a family with a certificate of a given value, which can be supplemented, as desired, by family income, it gives low-income Americans the freedom to choose how much they wish to spend on housing and encourages tenants to shop around for the best available unit. The new Administration should propose funding for 100,000 additional housing vouchers in fiscal 1990, and insist on no more new housing construction except for the elderly, the handicapped, and Indians on reservations. The Administration should propose that Section 8 Existing Housing certificates, up for reauthorization in fiscal 1990, be transferred into full-fledged vouchers.

2) Expand public housing resident management and ownership. Management of public housing by residents has been a stunning success. It has reduced operational costs, boosted employment in the projects, and encouraged residents to tackle social problems such as welfare dependency. The new Administration should promote resident management and ownership of public housing. Its goal: to turn over 20 percent of public housing to resident control within four years. HUD should use regulations and seek legislation to strengthen residents' rights to manage and to buy.

3) Solve the homelessness problem. Homelessness is a tragic but solvable problem. It is caused by federal grant policies that have encouraged cities to tear down low-income housing for development projects and by an unwillingness of states and cities to provide community mental facilities for patients released from mental hospitals. To correct this, the new Administration should provide housing vouchers to homeless families, and seek authorization to withhold economic development funds from state and local governments that do not establish community facilities for homeless individuals suffering from mental illness or chronic drug and alcohol abuse.

4) End rent control. Rent control, like all price controls, creates shortages. Cities with rent control, like New York and Washington, D.C., suffer from chronic shortages of rental accommodations because it is not profitable for developers to construct controlled rental units, nor is it profitable for landlords to rent them. The new Administration should publicize the problems caused by rent control and seek authority to deny federal housing funds to localities that control rents. The federal taxpayer should not be asked to finance housing for cities destroying their existing housing stocks through unjustifiable rent control policies.

5) Reorganize general housing finance programs. Federal housing finance programs increasingly have subsidized middle-class and affluent income buyers, rather than Americans with low and moderate incomes. The new Administration should target Federal Housing Administration insurance on low- and moderate-income homebuyers, and prohibit the Federal Housing Administration from insuring loans for upper-income Americans. The Government National Mortgage Association should leave the secondary market operations for FHA- and VA-insured loans to the Federal National Mortgage Association and Federal Home Loan Mortgage Corporation. The special privileges enjoyed by FNMA and FHLMC should be eliminated, completely privatizing these corporations.

6) Shift funding for Community Development Block Grants to more urgent uses. The Community Development Block Grant program channels federal funds to rich and poor communities across the nation. The program conflicts with federalism principles, since it is the states that should have responsibility for funding and managing development programs; the federal dollars that it costs could be used more effectively elsewhere. These funds should be used instead to expand hous-

ing vouchers for the poor, support public housing resident management
and ownership, and assist neighborhood groups in service delivery.

7) Grant federal tax relief to enterprise zones. Enterprise zones are
poor urban areas where taxes and regulations are reduced to stimulate
job-creating enterprises in blighted neighborhoods. The majority of
states have established such zones and they have proved successful.
However, only state taxes have been reduced because federal enterprise zone legislation does not contain tax provisions. The federal
government should eliminate capital gains taxes within enterprise
zones to stimulate capital investment and rejuvenation in distressed
areas. It should provide tax credits for the investment of funds and
employment of low-income workers within the zones, offsetting most
or all of the corporate income tax within the zones. It should provide
tax credits to workers in the zones themselves, reducing their income
and payroll tax burdens.

15

The Department of the Interior

Gordon S. Jones*
Task Force Chairman

The Department of the Interior manages some of the most important natural resource and environmental assets in the United States. The Department also typifies those agencies that exist to serve politically powerful constituency groups. Its constituencies include farmer recipients of subsidized water, wilderness lovers, livestock grazers, national park visitors, and members of Indian tribes. All find in the Interior Department a source of major benefits for which they have to pay little, or in many cases, nothing at all. Frequently, the true benefits to the nation of the Department's functions are much below the costs to the nation, but since the beneficiaries of Interior services pay few of those costs, they create powerful political support for existing Interior programs.

A direct attempt to cut off the longstanding benefits received by the Interior clienteles would have little chance of political success. Rather than trying simply to eliminate the benefits, the new President should try to create new incentives for the traditional clienteles to improve resource management and generate revenues for the Federal Treasury. The government, for example, could allow farmers to sell their rights to receive subsidized water to nonfarm users, such as municipalities, perhaps recovering some part of the subsidy from the selling price. This way, it might avoid the possible future need to finance expensive new projects to meet urban water needs. Wilderness areas could be put under the management of a board composed of concerned citizens, such as environmental leaders and federal land inholders, who might then raise funds through user fees, management contracts, and other

*Commenting and contributing generously to this chapter were *Mandate III* Task Force Members Daniel Bloom, Kent Jeffreys, Jo Kwong, Perry Pendley, R.J. Smith, and Robert Weidner. They do not necessarily endorse all of its views and recommendations.

BUDGET AND PERSONNEL

Secretaries

Donald P. Hodel	1985–present
William P. Clark	1983–1985
James G. Watt	1981–1983

Personnel

March 1988	70,246
April 1980	81,931
April 1970	69,728

Budget Outlays

Fiscal Year	Total (billions)
1989 Estimate	$ 5.0
1988 Estimate	$ 5.4
1987 Actual	$ 5.1
1986 Actual	$ 4.8
1985 Actual	$ 4.8
1980 Actual	$ 4.5
1970 Actual	$ 1.1

private sources, relieving the federal government of some of the financial burden of managing the land. The government could issue long-term leases to private livestock grazers, enabling Interior to rely more heavily on private incentives to maintain the productivity of the land, thereby eliminating a large, unproductive federal managerial expense by a revenue-producing lease.

Two governing principles are widely accepted across the spectrum of American politics: that government should leave to the private sector those activities that the private sector can perform better, and that government activities that meet mainly state and local needs should be administered by those levels of government. Applying these principles to the Interior Department would prompt the Department to shed a number of its current activities. Past efforts to do so, however, have been undermined by political miscalculations and the resistance of Interior clienteles. Future efforts thus should devote as much attention to crafting a political strategy as to the content of the needed substantive changes.

———————————◇———————————

SUMMARY OF AGENCY FUNCTIONS

The Department of the Interior (DOI), established in 1849, consists of a diverse collection of agencies linked more by history and by their common importance to America's West than by any administrative, economic, or other logic. This geographic aspect of Interior stems in part from the fact that the federal government retained large areas of land in most Western states for years after they achieved statehood. Even today, the federal government owns 85 percent of Nevada, 46 percent of California, and an average of 50 percent of the Rocky Mountain and Western states.

The Interior Department is thus above all a federal property management agency. Its responsibilities extend to the oceans, where Interior manages the leasing of the outer continental shelf for oil and gas development and seeks currently to create a leasing program for ocean mining within 200 miles of the U.S. coastline. As a land manager, the Department controls the access of livestock ranchers, miners, timber harvesters, and other groups to the vast resources of the federal lands. In 1985, for example, production from leases on federal lands yielded 18 percent of U.S. oil, 29 percent of U.S. natural gas, and 19 percent of U.S. coal. Interior also makes federal lands available for extensive recreational use.

The principal offices of the Department are:

◆ *Bureau of Indian Affairs*, which oversees federal policies regarding Indian tribes.

◆ *Fish, Wildlife and Parks*, which includes the U.S. Fish and Wildlife Service, which is responsible for protecting endangered species and administers 89 million acres of preserves. The office also oversees the National Park Service, which administers national parks, monuments, and historic sites.

◆ *Land and Minerals Management*, which manages federal lands and mineral deposits. The office includes the Minerals Management Service, with responsibility for offshore and some onshore minerals; the Office of Surface Mining Reclamation and Enforcement, which oversees federal and state policy regarding coal mining; and the Bureau of Land Management, which controls 341 million acres of public lands used principally for grazing and reserves the mineral rights below an additional 169 million acres of private land.

◆ *Territorial and International Affairs*, which has responsibility for promoting the economic and political interests of American Samoa, Guam, the U.S. Virgin Islands, and the trust territories of the Pacific Islands.

◆ *Water and Science*, which includes the U.S. Geological Survey. which is charged with identifying water, energy, and mineral resources; the Bureau of Mines, which monitors supplies of strategic and critical minerals; and the Bureau of Reclamation, which manages the construction and operation of water projects intended to reclaim arid and semi-arid lands in the West.

―――――――――――――◇―――――――――――――

INSTITUTIONAL CONSTRAINTS

The Department's policy initiatives are constrained by several factors. One is the very age of the Department and most of its bureaus. Most Interior agencies have a long history and hence well-established interests and bureaucracies. The General Land Office (predecessor, with the Grazing Service, to the Bureau of Land Management), for instance, was founded in 1812. A number of Interior agencies by and large have accomplished their original mission or outlived their purpose. Yet the bureaucrats and the interests who depend on these bureaus campaign aggressively to preserve them.

Interior is well known not only for its longstanding pork-barrel politics of public works, such as the irrigation and dam projects of the Bureau of Reclamation, but also for a newer brand of park-barrel politics based on benefits to recreational users of federally administered lands. Ranchers, hunters, farmers, timberers, park visitors, and miners, wilderness buffs, trail bike riders, and boaters are among the millions of Americans who obtain subsidized products and services from Interior, and who fight every attempt to reduce the budgets or functions of the bureaus that reward them.

Another constraint on good Interior policy is the mass of congressional mandates and court-imposed restrictions on the discretion of the secretary. This limits his or her ability to manage the Department and further strengthens the power of interest groups. Because the Energy and Natural Resources Committee in the Senate and the Interior and Insular Affairs Committee in the House have tended, in the past, to be dominated by legislators from Western states and districts, they are particularly sensitive to the local interests whose political support they need for reelection. Thus authorization and appropriations bills dealing with Interior often contain detailed policy prescriptions. Typical is congressional delay or prohibition of outer continental shelf lease sales. Past efforts to raise visitor fees at national parks have been frustrated by congressional prohibitions.

―――――――――◇―――――――――

THE REAGAN ADMINISTRATION RECORD

When Ronald Reagan entered office, the Interior Department had just been the scene of major political and policy confrontations. The Western states, which had provided the President with his widest margin of election victory, had fought Carter to a standstill over water policy and had staved off the worst excesses of wilderness policy and endangered species legislation. The Sagebrush Rebellion, a catchall phrase denoting a desire for greater Western autonomy, was at its peak, and candidate Reagan had declared himself a Sagebrush Rebel.

As the new secretary, James Watt had impressive credentials. Having worked earlier at high levels of Interior, he had more detailed knowledge of Interior policies and operations than any incoming secretary in recent memory. He also possessed considerable administrative skills and a clearer sense of what he wanted to accomplish than most new secretaries. This enabled him to succeed in a number of areas. Interior management of mineral leasing long had been beset by a confusing and unworkable division of responsibility between the Bureau of Land Management (BLM) and the Geological Survey. Under Watt's direction, oil and gas leasing on the outer continental shelf was consolidated in a newly created agency, the Minerals Management Service (MMS). Similarly, the leasing functions for coal and other onshore minerals were then consolidated in the BLM.

Under Watt, the MMS successfully revamped oil and gas leasing on the outer continental shelf (OCS). Total OCS acreage leased rose sharply from 2.3 million acres in 1981 to 6.6 million acres in 1983, allowing the U.S. oil industry to begin exploring in many areas that would not have been available as soon under the old system. And with strong Interior support, the Coastal Barriers Act was enacted in 1982. This prohibited the use of federal loan and other subsidies for the development of the coastal barrier island system (mostly along the East Coast), leaving the development decisions instead to be made by the forces of the marketplace.

Substituting the operation of markets for bureaucratic decisions was the principle that led Watt to require users to pay a greater share of operations, maintenance, and new construction costs of such Interior programs and projects as dams or water delivery systems. He reasoned that as long as federal projects carry a subsidy, and in many cases even pay 100 percent of costs, there is little incentive for local beneficiaries to examine the real worth to them of particular projects. Levying a fee on the users of a project, on the other hand, forces those users to weigh the potential benefits against the cost. Because of Watt's initiative, states and other beneficiaries of water projects today contribute a higher share of the project costs. Similarly, ranchers were asked to pay a greater share of the costs of federal investments in public rangelands.

Perhaps the greatest policy success of the Watt years was to calm the great resentment that had built up in the West during the Carter years. Watt successfully reassured the West that Interior management would be responsive to Western concerns.

The Reagan Administration has made modest progress in introducing market considerations into the pricing and thus allocation of water. During the Reagan years, no new major water projects have been approved or launched into full construction, indicating that the elimination of expensive subsidies has restrained the demand for new facilities. The funding for existing projects has been restructured to give a higher priority to projects closest to completion, thus allowing some real returns from projects to start much earlier than originally anticipated.

In water policy, as in other areas of Interior activity, sound economics often also makes for sound environmental policy. The Western states are increasingly diverse, with growing environmental and tourist-related interests balancing the older timber, farmer, and rancher interests. These divisions may enable the new Administration to reject the construction of uneconomic new projects, and to introduce wider use of market pricing for water without incurring the united wrath of the West.

Watt's problems stemmed mainly from Interior's inherent institutional tensions. Although required on the one hand to assert federal interests that may conflict with Western interests, the Department on the other hand must be a spokesman for the West. The problems created for Watt by Interior's conflicting roles were illustrated well by the privatization episode that contributed significantly to the erosion of his political support. As the incoming Secretary of Interior, he made it clear that he would seek no radical changes in federal land tenure. This meant that Watt was not enthusiastic about Reagan White House proposals to sell off, or "privatize," some Western lands. Not surprisingly, the privatization proposals were as provocative and unsettling to many Westerners as had been many actions of the Carter Administration. When privatization of some federal lands became the official policy of the Reagan Administration, Watt had no choice but to defend it. He was then skewered by both environmentalists and Western interests for a policy he had opposed.

The cloud remaining over Interior following Watt's departure in late 1983 has impeded Interior activities for the remainder of the Reagan Administration. His successors have concluded, as had many previous secretaries, that bold or controversial actions would be so misrepresented and distorted by political opponents that they would be impossible to carry out. Thus the approach of Secretaries William Clark and Donald Hodel has been to carry out policy directions generally similar to those favored by Watt, but in an incremental and low-key way.

Although controversial decisions affecting the environment have provoked the most criticism against the Reagan Administration, the Administration's greatest failing has been its seeming lack of interest in courting environmentalist support for its market-based policies. In many cases, a common objective could have been served by such policies, offering the potential to forge a powerful political coalition. Market incentives often can achieve environmentalist goals more effectively than can bureaucratic control and ownership. A Reagan Administration effort could have built a liberal/conservative coalition similar to those that have deregulated the economy and cut taxes. Indeed, one of the important recent developments in the environmental movement has been the emergence of those who advocate economic tests and market methods to protect the environment. The new Administration should seek a detente with moderate environmentalists to complete the Reagan agenda.

---◇---

THE NEXT FOUR YEARS

The new President must reaffirm the federal government's obligation to protect the nation's natural resources and use them in the best interests of the American people. He must point out that this will be most credibly carried out by decentralizing the ownership of many tracts of public lands, and by introducing market incentives to encourage that resources be used efficiently and with regard to their value. To achieve this, he should support legislation to transfer the ownership of many tracts of public land to the states, or in some instances to private organizations. Similarly, he should press for greater use of markets, rather than political or bureaucratic procedures, to allocate scarce water resources in the West. He should explain that requiring farmers and city planners to consider the real cost of water would protect America's rivers and other water resources from overuse.

The new President should declare that the Interior Department will seek to transform Indian reservations and U.S. overseas territories from economic backwaters, dependent on the federal government, to self-sufficiency. He should stress that well-intentioned policies have suffocated economic growth, and that his Administration is committed to administrative and legislative actions to spur local enterprise. And he must mount a campaign to allow the orderly development of America's energy and mineral resources. Failures by previous Presidents to explain the importance of such development to national security and economic growth have allowed environmental lobbyists to block essential mineral exploration and development.

Improving the Management of Public Lands

Recognizing the importance of its fiduciary duties, the Reagan Administration attempted in the first term to improve federal management of public assets through privatization. It argued correctly that users of land take greater care of it if they own it. Yet the Reagan Administration was inept in dealing with the powerful constituencies involved, particularly ranchers. Privatization should still be Interior's goal. Grazing or other land rights should be privatized by transferring them to the current users. The rights could be sold or leased, and should be freely transferrable, just as any other private property rights. At the same time, the existing rights of hunters, fishermen, and other recreationists to enter on the land could be protected.

The creation of new grazing rights and matching protection of existing recreational users might be accomplished by selling or auctioning grazing leases for, say, fifty years, as has been done in Australia, and would generate greater political support than outright conveyancing of private title, which is always attacked as a giveaway of the nation's patrimony. Yet it still offers those benefits of private ownership that tie individual rewards to successful management practices, offers wide flexibility for managerial initiative, and eliminates the need for a bureaucracy of planners, controllers, and overseers. With a 50-

year lease program, Interior could rely largely on the private interest of the rancher to maintain the grazing land, and the rancher himself would have the ownership incentive to improve the land and to use it with care for its long-term value.

The new President should seek legislation to increase the present ten-year limit on grazing leases, issuing 50-year leases to federal livestock grazing lands that would allow ranchers to assume the major management responsibilities. Such leases would have to guarantee continued open public access for hiking, hunting, and other recreational uses.

Still, a long-term lease policy would lack some advantages of outright sales; since only grazing rights would be leased, leases would not permit the use of marginal public land for alternative, more valuable uses, such as commercial or residential development. Thus, in addition to the lease plan, and as a long-term goal, the new Administration should devise a policy for land sales. These sales could be politically acceptable if certain rules were followed. First, ranchers who have been using the federal lands put up for sale should be given adequate advance notice of the sale and then fully compensated for any losses they might incur in giving up their investments in the land and for any adverse effects on the value of adjoining private ranch property. Second, hunting and other recreational users should be given a pledge that sale proceeds would be placed in a fund for such recreational purposes as improving winter range for antelope or other big game, protecting duck breeding grounds, or improving wilderness and park systems management.

As with any other major change, the Department must launch a vigorous campaign to explain to the public the merits of the new land policy. The opposition to major policy innovations can be expected to charge that creating new private rights would be "giving away" the public lands. To address and rebut such criticisms, the American public must be made aware: 1) that the creation of new private rights in many cases merely would confirm formally a property right that long ago developed informally; 2) that it is misleading to speak of federal ownership of public lands as a public benefit; and 3) that the selling price would be at competitive market levels, established perhaps through an auction process. More accurately, public lands policy is a vehicle for giving substantial government subsidies to major private users of public lands. The new Administration should explain that to transfer new private rights to these groups is not to give away the land, but rather to reduce the huge federal subsidies now being paid to private users.

If partial or full privatization proves politically unachievable, the new Administration could try the alternative of seeking to transfer to the states management responsibility for or ownership of grazing and other lands. It must understand that such a transfer would require the states to bear significant management costs previously assumed by the federal government. Hence, a strategy for transferring federal land or other facilities should offer the states a fiscal carrot; the federal government, for instance, could pay the full state management costs for a fixed period, and then reduce its payments gradually.

Transfers of federal land and facilities to the states could threaten some existing users in the West who have grown accustomed to federal managers and their policies. Ranchers using public lands, for instance, may fear that the states would raise grazing fees to current market rates. Thus, in proposing land transfers to states, the new Administration should seek to mitigate the impact of increasing fees substantially. Similar protective arrangements may be needed with miners, hunters, and other current users of public lands to obtain their political neutrality or support. Putting existing federal lands in state and private hands is likely to spur innovation, better serving the goals of environmental protection and economic efficiency.

The new Administration also should move swiftly to sell the remaining parcels of surplus federal lands in urban areas, in the "checkerboard" (alternating federal and nonfederal square miles left over from the old railroad land grants), in other fragmented ownership areas, and in other places where effective federal management of the land is impractical today. At least 25 million acres of federal land are in these categories, representing a potential sales value of more than $5 billion.

Decentralizing Ownership of Parks and Wilderness Areas

The federal government today manages the National Park System, the fish and wildlife refuge system, and the wilderness system. The public relies on Interior to protect these mountains, deserts, forests, and other lands which, in some cases, are important symbols of the American heritage. These national land systems, however, also include lands and properties of little national importance. Those should be managed by the states, localities, or private organizations. When these lands are transferred from the federal government, such transfers may need to be accompanied initially by federal financial support for the state or private organizations managing these lands.

The states are closer to the users of the lands and facilities than is the federal bureaucracy and thus are more likely to be sensitive to user needs and demands. State management is more flexible than the federal government. States also would differ in their management systems, providing a laboratory to develop different styles and approaches.

Private organization management of parts of the federal domain would offer many of the advantages of state management. The groups would be accountable to their contributors and supporters and would thus have a great incentive to maximize the return for every dollar spent. Volunteers might be willing to contribute their services, thus saving taxpayer dollars. Parts of the Appalachian Trail, for example, are maintained by local trail club volunteers under agreements with the National Park Service. Private managers of publicly owned facilities often adopt a proprietary attitude to the lands and properties for which they hold the management responsibility, thus enlisting strong local support and commitment.

Private management may be particularly appropriate for wilderness areas of critical environmental concern, and other environmentally fragile and sensitive areas. As a demonstration of the management of wilderness areas, the new Administration should seek the creation of one or more regional Wilderness Boards composed of groups of Americans with an interest in sensitive public lands. These would include not only prominent wilderness organizations, but also local government officials, citizens' organizations, and others concerned with access to lands. These Boards would set basic policy directions regarding future recreational and other uses within wilderness areas, and would be permitted to allow limited development. In many instances, this would lead to more carefully monitored oil and gas drilling, because more efficient drilling would produce higher revenues for the Boards. The Audubon Society, for example, long has allowed oil and gas drilling in its Rainey bird sanctuary in Louisiana.

A Wilderness Board program, however, must be subject to two requirements. First, Boards must include representatives from all interested parties. Otherwise radical environmentalists could use the Board to pursue their own agenda at the expense of other Americans. Second, such a Board should be self-financing, with revenues derived from fees, leases, and donations. If the Board could lobby for and obtain federal funds, it would not take a balanced approach to conservation and development.

Short of creating a Wilderness Board, the new Administration should take steps to replace federal funding of lands with more reliance on user fees. Funding national-interest lands, such as Yosemite and Yellowstone National Parks, through the federal budget process produces an erratic pattern of support. Funds ebb and flow according to politics and competing government priorities, rather than on the basis of need. It would be far better to permit the parks to raise much or all of their current unmet funding needs through increased visitor and other user fees. Park managers also should be given wider discretion in determining how to spend the funds they obtain. Raising fees would allow managers to limit the number of visitors to a level that does not harm the environment. Yosemite and other parks are endangered because of too many visitors. This is hardly surprising: the entrance fee at Yosemite is only $5 per carload per week, and many park facilities charge no fee at all.

Interior should also begin transferring Fish and Wildlife Service fish hatcheries to state governments, or sell them to private operators who could supply fish to public agencies and other purchasers.

Improving Access to Federally Owned Minerals

As a rule, the federal government does not extract the minerals from land it owns. Typically, it will lease the land to private industry, which will develop only the minerals and leave the land in public ownership. The federal government's leasing policy for the extraction of minerals on public lands historically has been based on a distrust of market forces. By selecting and limiting the sites to be made available for leasing, Interior also controls the total level and location of mineral extraction.

A substantial federal planning and monitoring apparatus, located within Interior's Bureau of Land Management and Minerals Management Service, has tried to manage this policy. Government planners, however, are poorly equipped to determine the commercial attractiveness of mineral deposits. Historically, government projections of future production demands and prices have proven far off the mark. Rather than continue trying to second-guess the minerals market, Interior should offer for lease a significant number of potential mineral development sites, and then leave it to the marketplace to sort out which of these should be developed and at what price.

The development of federal energy resources raises substantial revenues for the federal government—more than $3.8 billion in 1987 in royalties, bonuses, and rentals, as well as significant additional revenues from corporate income and other tax collections. The market value of offshore oil and gas production alone exceeded $15 billion in 1986. Production from federal leases helps reduce U.S. energy imports. The federal lands also contain such potential sources of strategic nonenergy minerals as platinum group metals and chromium, necessary for energy production, pollution control, and defense weaponry.

It has proven politically difficult to use a free market to organize minerals leasing, including energy resources. Opponents have convinced the courts or Congress to reverse or delay Interior leasing decisions. Overcoming this opposition will require clear and strong assurances that legitimate environmental concerns will be met. It also will require that Interior consult extensively with the states and with other users of the public lands, to try to address major concerns about the social and environmental impact of minerals development at particular sites. Having done this, Interior then must launch an ambitious public education campaign explaining the merits of minerals development leasing. The delays in mineral leasing typify how concentrated local and other parochial interests can override a greater national interest.

To increase access to mineral deposits, the new Administration should press strongly for oil and gas leasing in the Arctic National Wildlife Refuge. The American public can be convinced that these energy resources can be developed without damage to the environment. The prospect of discovering major oil and gas deposits in the Arctic Refuge offers the nation enormous dividends—many billions of dollars to the Federal Treasury and a significant boost in future national energy security. Significant oil and gas deposits are also off California's coast. Since the 1969 oil spill from drilling activities in California's Santa Barbara Channel, California has received uniquely preferential treatment concerning offshore drilling. This drilling should be increased.

Current coal lease policies require that mineral rights on leased land be developed within a specified period (usually five years) or the lease is lost. This requirement of "due diligence" in developing the resource could result in premature development of public lands. The new Administration should revise these rigid due diligence requirements to allow market forces to set the timing of development. It could do this by allowing lessees more time to begin development activities or by allowing mining firms to make payments each year until development begins to compensate the government for lost royalties. These changes would permit firms to respond more to market forces in deciding when to develop the mineral resources.

Introducing Markets for Water

In its publication *Assessment 1987: A New Direction for the Bureau of Reclamation*, Interior acknowledges that the era of large-scale construction of water projects has ended and proposes a new policy to operate and manage Western water resources. The report explains that there are few suitable sites remaining for dam building. In addition, huge new projects are certain to encounter powerful environmental opposition and pressures to reduce federal outlays. The new directions proposed by the study include: transferring operations and maintenance responsibilities for power and water projects to local districts and other local beneficiaries; contracting with the private sector to manage projects retained under federal control; transferring title for some water facilities to local users or other local recipients; obtaining higher contributions from users; and establishing water markets to encourage conservation and more efficient use of water.

The new President should move swiftly and boldly to impose a water policy based on the *Assessment 1987* principles. Immediately upon taking office, the new Administration should issue a policy directive strongly committing the Bureau of Reclamation to support an expanded use of markets for Western water and announce that Bureau projects, rules, and procedures will pursue this goal. The Department should use its administrative powers to encourage the future sale of water rights. The Department, for example, should give local water districts greater freedom to sell water outside their districts.

The new Administration then should propose omnibus water marketing legislation that would include measures to modify reclamation laws that interfere unnecessarily with water sales. Among the modifications: elimination of requirements that water use be tied to land uses; permitting the sale of water to municipalities; elimination or reinterpretation of restrictions on sales of surplus water from an irrigation project; or granting of authority to the Secretary of the Interior to facilitate water sales that comply with state water laws. This is perhaps the first area where a coalition between the new Administration and environmental groups on the issue of market forces and environmental protection could be forged. Already the Environmental Defense Fund supports the principle of permitting agricultural water users to sell excess supplies to municipalities.

Encouraging Greater Self-Reliance for Indians

The Bureau of Indian Affairs (BIA) is Interior's largest agency, in terms of both budget and number of employees. The Department's responsibilities toward American Indians may give the secretary his or her biggest headaches. On the one hand, efforts to improve the dismal conditions of many Indians often are resisted as an example of undesirable infringement on Indian self-determination. On the other hand, hesitation to take action may be denounced as lacking compassion. The secretary also is caught between the roles of spokesman for the non-Indian West and of trustee for the Indians; on occasions, these two roles conflict, such as in the allocation of rights to Western surface water supplies. Indians themselves, of course, disagree on many issues.

Recent Interior secretaries tended to try to avoid the problems inherent in Indian affairs, hoping that matters would stay quiet. Yet given the massive social problems of most Indian reservations, including unemployment, alcoholism, and poverty, this course is unacceptable. The next secretary should master the key issues associated with Indian affairs and try to improve the living condition of American Indians.

He will need to pay attention to three interrelated conditions. First, economic development must quicken on Indian reservations. Growth is retarded on Indian reservations for the same reason it is retarded in Third World countries: private property is not secure, regulations suffocate enterprise, and marginal tax rates are too high. Tribal governments have substantial powers to make economic investment and development attractive to private industry. Yet they have based their policies on massive federal subsidies for so long that they find it difficult to develop their own initiatives to foster Indian enterprise. To make matters worse, the signing of land and mineral leases by local Indian tribes, as well as many other tribal actions, frequently must be approved by the Bureau of Indian Affairs, a process that can take years, making it difficult or impossible for tribes to respond promptly to business and other opportunities.

Second, Indian education must be improved. Indian schools fail for the same reasons that inner-city schools fail: they reflect the interests of administrators, not the needs of parents. Education on Indian reservations should be transferred from the Bureau of Indian Affairs to private educators who could bid on contracts for delivering educational services.

Third, Indian tribes and communities must become more stable and mature in their internal political and judicial processes. Indian reservations are often characterized by corrupt tribal regimes that exercise almost total hegemony over all tribal affairs, and even over the affairs of individual Indians. Bureau of Indian Affairs policy should be directed toward encouraging alternative power centers on reservations, not toward strengthening existing arrangements.

In addition, the new Administration should take action to deal with numerous disputes between tribes and both federal and state governments. These disputes center on treaties between the federal government and the tribes. Government tribal relations are constitutionally and legally murky, and characterized by friction and resentment on both sides. Unsettled claims for compensation, the right of state law enforcement officials to enter reservations, the taxing power, and the right of the tribes to close the borders of their reservations are among the questions ignored from year to year. Since federal treaties are involved, the new secretary should hold discussions with the state governments and should direct his staff to present him with options for settling them, whether it takes administrative action, new legislation, or even constitutional amendments. Among the ideas he should consider would be a lump sum settlement of individual Indian claims against the federal government, and a termination of the trust relationship. Individual Indians should receive title to the land, free and clear, with no restrictions on use or alienation. Until these uncertainties are eliminated, there is no hope for progress on the reservation.

Above all, the new Administration should speak the truth about the situation on the reservations: collectivism is killing the Indian. Whenever possible, the secretary should use his discretion to channel federal benefits to individual Indians, rather than to the tribal governments. Where there is no discretion, the secretary should seek it from Congress. The only way out of subsistence poverty for the American Indian is the development of private property rights, enforced by firm and predictable law.

Streamlining Federal Research

Two Interior agencies deal primarily with scientific research and technological development: the Geological Survey and the Bureau of Mines. The first was created more than 100 years ago and the second more than 75 years ago. Interior secretaries tend to pay little personal attention to these agencies, even though they involve substantial expenditures and personnel.

The Bureau of Mines should be abolished. Its original purpose was to encourage the development of a domestic extraction industry. The industry no longer requires such federal assistance. Those Bureau functions that are proper federal responsibilities, such as the collection and dissemination of minerals information, should be transferred to the Departments of Energy or Commerce. Research on air quality control technology should be transferred to the Environmental Protection Agency. The research and development facilities of the Bureau of Mines should be sold to the private sector. Without a Bureau of Mines, private industry would assume a greater role in mining research and development and do a better job—at no cost to the taxpayer.

The Geological Survey enjoys the reputation of being one of America's leading scientific organizations. It also enjoys a reputation for being unresponsive to the secretary's requests for information needed in making policy. The new Administration should review the Geological Survey to revise the agency's priorities to ensure that they meet the nation's policy information needs.

Igniting Economic Growth in the Territories

The Office of Territorial and International Affairs (TIA) represents within the federal government the economic and political interests of the territories, which include American Samoa, Guam, and the Virgin Islands. For many decades, Washington has provided direct aid, rather than encouraging local enterprise development in the territories. In addition, the mainland U.S. system of regulations and taxes, for the most part, has been applied to the territories, with little regard for local economic conditions. These policies have prevented the territories from competing with nearby countries and has led to excessive economic dependence on the federal government.

The Reagan Administration has taken important steps to unshackle the economic potential of the territories by cutting down on red tape and encouraging the sale to the private sector of some government assets, such as a railroad in American Samoa. The next Administration should build on this. In particular, TIA should use its technical assistance funds for projects designed to strengthen the private sector and should seek ways of encouraging more private investment in the territories' infrastructure. In addition, TIA should continue investigating labor, environmental, immigration, and other onerous regulations that make it difficult for the territories to compete in the international economy.

———————————◇———————————

INITIATIVES FOR 1989

1) **Introduce a market for water.** Western water policy currently provides large subsidies to agricultural users, while discouraging conservation. In addition, the lack of an effective market for water means

that it is not distributed primarily to those users who value it most highly. The new President should take administrative action to allow water to be bought and sold more easily. By permitting easier private sale of water by farmers with access to water reserves, it would be distributed more efficiently. This would provide expanding municipalities with additional supplies, without having to develop new sources of water through expensive federal water projects.

2) Curb federal dam construction, below-cost timber sales, subsidized grazing arrangements, and other environmentally harmful activities. The federal government currently subsidizes many activities that benefit certain constituencies, such as farmers, timber companies, and ranchers, yet can damage the environment. The new Administration should seek environmental legislation to end such subsidy programs.

3) Transfer one or more environmentally sensitive areas to private management. Excessively bureaucratic management of public lands often serves the goal of conservation less than would certain forms of private ownership. The new Administration thus should introduce legislation for a pilot program to test private forms of management and ownership of public lands, such as by nonprofit groups, as an alternative to federal control.

4) Propose legislation to merge the overlapping functions of the Department of Energy and the Department of the Interior. There are many common issues affecting energy and nonfuel minerals that fall under the jurisdiction of both departments. A more rational set of policies could be achieved by merging the two agencies into a single Department of Natural Resources. (See Chapter 11.)

16

The Department of Justice

Marshall J. Breger*
Task Force Chairman

The Department of Justice, the primary federal agency dealing with legal issues, has a wide range of responsibilities from enforcing the nation's civil rights laws to managing federal prisons. During the Reagan years, the Department has been charged with executing many of the most important and controversial aspects of the President's policy agenda. Among its most important successes have been the appointment of a large number of conservative judges to the federal bench and the reform of antitrust enforcement policy. But it has also had failures. For instance, while the Department clearly has articulated the case for a color-blind civil rights policy, it has been losing the battle against the imposition of racial goals and quotas by the courts.

There is much left to be done. Internal reorganization of the Department is needed to free the attorney general from day-to-day management responsibilities, to ensure that the attorney general's policies are uniformly pursued, and to centralize the Department's international affairs activities. The Department must continue litigation to pursue the goal of a colorblind society and strengthen efforts to reduce drug use by introducing tougher penalties for drug use and by centralizing enforcement efforts in a "drug czar." The Department also should reexamine U.S. immigration policy, focusing on the economic impact of sanctions against employers hiring illegal aliens and on easing the plight of refugees. It also should beef up criminal law enforcement, take the lead in expanding the use of private prison construction, and

*Commenting and contributing to this chapter were *Mandate III* Task Force Members Robert Delahunty, Catherine Zacks Gildenhorn, C. Boyden Gray, Patrick McGuigan, and Ronald Robertson. They do not necessarily endorse all of its views and recommendations.

Task Force Deputy Chairman: Heritage McKenna Senior Policy Analyst James Gattuso.

BUDGET AND PERSONNEL

Attorney Generals

Richard L. Thornburgh	1988–present
Edwin Meese, III	1985–1988
William French Smith	1981–1985

Personnel

March 1988	72,687
April 1980	56,244
April 1970	38,039

Budget Outlays

Fiscal Year	Total (billions)
1989 Estimate	$5.8
1988 Estimate	$5.2
1987 Actual	$4.3
1986 Actual	$3.8
1985 Actual	$3.6
1980 Actual	$2.6
1970 Actual	$0.6

---

encourage use of alternative dispute resolution procedures to reduce costly litigation. The Justice Department should continue the Reagan Administration's policy of relaxing antitrust restrictions. And the new Administration should ensure a high standard of ethics in government by streamlining and better enforcing existing ethics statutes and seeking legislation to apply them to all government officials, including members of Congress.

SUMMARY OF AGENCY FUNCTIONS

Established in 1870, the Department of Justice is the primary legal arm of the United States government. Among the major divisions and agencies of the Department are:

◆ *The Civil Rights Division*, which is responsible for enforcing federal civil rights laws.

◆ *The Antitrust Division*, which, along with the Federal Trade Commission, is responsible for enforcing the antitrust laws.

◆ *The Civil Division*, which represents the United States and its departments and agencies in litigation before the courts.

◆ *The Criminal Division*, which enforces federal criminal statutes.

◆ *The Land and Natural Resources Division*, which litigates on behalf of the United States in cases involving land owned or sought by the federal government, and enforces federal pollution laws.

◆ *The Tax Division*, which represents the United States in tax cases.

◆ *The Federal Bureau of Investigation*, which investigates possible violations of federal law for the Department.

◆ *The Drug Enforcement Administration*, which investigates, along with the FBI, possible violations of federal drug laws, and enforces regulations concerning legal drugs.

◆ *The Bureau of Prisons*, which manages the federal prison system.

◆ *The Immigration and Naturalization Service*, which administers federal immigration and naturalization laws.

◆ *The Office of the Solicitor General*, who represents the United States in all cases before the Supreme Court.

◆ *The Executive Office for United States Trustees*, which oversees the activities of U.S. Trustees, who supervise the administration of bankruptcy cases.

INSTITUTIONAL CONSTRAINTS

The policy agenda of the Justice Department is inherently and unavoidably political, as it is inextricably involved in advancing the President's agenda. Yet the Department's processes and deliberations must be among the least politicized. Department attorneys are guardians of the law and the integrity of the legal system, as well as advocates of the Administration's legal policies. Often they are bound by statute and court precedent to enforce policies that differ from their own political agenda. The Department's primary allegiance must therefore be to the integrity—not the outcome—of the legal process. This is often a difficult line to draw, and a harder one to follow. It is, however, inherent in any notion of the rule of law.

The Department's most important client, then, is the system of justice itself. Still, the Department does not operate in a political vacuum. Many outside groups, such as state and local law enforcement agencies and the organized bar, must be taken into account when departmental policy is set. The greatest constraints on policy-making by the Department, however, are imposed by the other branches of government—Congress and the judiciary.

During the Reagan Administration, Congress has exercised increasing power over the Department, using riders on appropriations bills to impose arguably unconstitutional limitations on the Department's powers to litigate. In 1983, for example, Congress prohibited the solicitor general from using any federal funds to make a certain argument regarding antitrust law before the Supreme Court, in effect gagging communication between the executive and judicial branches. Such measures seriously constrain departmental policy-making and threaten the constitutional separation of powers.

The most important constraint on policy formation at Justice comes from the judiciary. Many of the policy goals of any Administration can be achieved only through judicial interpretation of existing law and of the Constitution. The Justice Department is free to articulate its view of the law, but the judiciary is the final arbiter.

———————————————◇———————————————

THE REAGAN ADMINISTRATION RECORD

Under Jimmy Carter the Justice Department advocated a politicized liberal agenda. Justice officials worked to expand racial quotas, enforce rigid antitrust policies, and increase the barriers to putting suspected and convicted criminals in jail. Upon taking office, the Reagan Administration reversed this course. Yet its overall record is mixed. Its most important single achievement has been the appointment of a corps of jurists committed to the philosophy of judicial restraint. In addition to three Supreme Court members, the Reagan Administration has selected 81 of the 168 sitting federal appellate court judges and 275 of the 575 district court judges. With their lifetime appointments, these judges will influence the development of the law for decades.

Another solid achievement has been in antitrust. Building on changes in the intellectual climate, the Department's Antitrust Division rejected the Carter Administration's inflexible, "big is bad" approach to antitrust enforcement. Instead it began to examine the full economic effects of particular business activities before deciding whether to act to stop them. The Supreme Court consistently has affirmed this approach, making it difficult to turn back the clock.

The Department also has begun a national debate on several crucial issues. In constitutional law, it has become a prime advocate of principles of federalism and original intent as well as of stricter application of the separation of powers principle, doctrines which are crucial to ensure that the delicate balance created by the framers of the Constitution is not upset. The Department also has strongly advocated liability reform and a color-blind civil rights policy.

These efforts may lead to long-term success. In the short term, however, little substantive reform has been achieved. The Administration was handed a series of judicial defeats on affirmative action, for instance, placing the goal of a colorblind society out of reach in the near future. Many of the Department's legislative initiatives regarding antitrust, product liability, and other issues went nowhere in Congress. The war on drugs still remains to be won.

––––––––––––––⟡––––––––––––––

THE NEXT FOUR YEARS

The Department of Justice should be helping to create a society that is freer of drugs and safer from crime and terrorism, that is less discriminatory (whether the discrimination be characterized as malevolent or benign), breeds less litigation, and harbors less public corruption.

The Department should be the leading force in two "wars"—on drugs and against dishonest government. In both, it will have to tie its efforts more closely to those of other law enforcement agencies, especially those of the states. The Department also needs to advocate strongly procompetitive and proconsumer policies, including the repeal of obsolete antitrust legislation. It should advocate tort reform, and encourage methods of dispute resolution other than litigation. It should continue to press for a society in which decisions in employment, housing, and education are untainted by racial considerations. And it should urge adoption of immigration measures that would let more "new seed" immigrants into the country.

Perhaps most important, the Department must hold itself to the highest ethical standards. In recent decades, American society has suffered a deepening distrust of authority in all its guises. The Department of Justice has not been spared this obloquy. Heightened suspicion, even when misplaced, calls for heightened self-scrutiny. Thus, the Department must be zealous in purging any trace of racial discrimination from its ranks and must be vigorous in prosecuting public corruption cases—even those involving Justice and other executive branch officials, members of Congress, and federal judges. It must avoid even the appearance of impropriety.

Restructuring the Justice Department

As the Department is now structured, the deputy attorney general, the Department's second highest official, is responsible primarily for the day-to-day operations of the Department, in addition to supervising directly the civil litigation and nonlitigating divisions. The third-ranking official, the associate attorney general, supervises the law enforcement components of the Department. (If the deputy attorney general is an expert in criminal law, the associate attorney general takes on civil law supervisory responsibilities.) Under this structure, the attorney general in theory is freed from many administrative chores to develop the major themes of departmental policy.

To assist the attorney general in fulfilling these responsibilities better, a second associate attorney general position should be created. One of the two associate attorneys general should then supervise civil justice activities, with the other handling criminal justice efforts. Each of the assistant attorneys general in charge of the litigating and policy divisions within the Department then would be responsible to one or the other of these two associate attorneys general, who in turn would report to the deputy. This would allow the deputy attorney general to oversee the Department's central management activity and function as the chief operating officer of the Department. This, in turn, would free the attorney general from hands-on management duties, enable him to concentrate on setting broad policy for the Department, and give him greater opportunity to use his bully pulpit role to engender public debate on key issues.

Restructuring the roles of the attorney general and the deputy also would permit the Department to exercise closer control over the 94 local U.S. attorneys. While these officials now report directly to the deputy, there is often insufficient Department control over their activities. This weakens the government's overall effectiveness. Under the new structure, the deputy's chief responsibilities would include monitoring the U.S. attorneys to ensure that arguments they make before the courts are in line with Department positions. In certain classes of cases, U.S. attorneys could be required to submit pretrial information to the Department, outlining positions they propose to take.

A new office of National Security and International Law, headed by an assistant attorney general, should be created. Responsibility for the international aspects of the Department's activities currently is widely dispersed. For instance, the Criminal Division includes International Affairs and Internal Security sections, and the Civil Division includes a Foreign Litigation Office. The Office of Intelligence Policy Review and the Lands and Natural Resources, Tax, and Antitrust divisions all routinely deal with international matters.

This decentralized approach is no longer adequate. It will not be enough merely to enlarge an existing office within the Department. The Department-wide oversight and management of international legal policy issues and the administration of specific statutes involving international questions are better handled by a separate office dedicated to these tasks.

The new assistant attorney general, moreover, should have expertise in international law issues and the authority to speak to the rest of the federal government, including Congress and the State Department, on Justice's behalf. The resulting combination of expertise and rank should strengthen the Department's hand in the inevitable interagency disputes over international legal policy.

The Office of Legal Policy should be restructured. Although many of its policy recommendations and legislative comments have been of high quality, it has faced an institutional obstacle in transforming its proposals into concrete results: the litigating and counseling divisions give little heed to broad policy suggestions from another office. If the Office of Legal Policy is to remain a "think tank," it must be given additional clout. At present, moreover, while the Office of Legal Policy helps to select judicial and departmental nominees, its responsibility ends when the President makes the nomination. As a result, confirmation often has had low priority. Those who select a candidate ought to be responsible for shepherding the candidate through the Senate confirmation process. The follow-through on a nomination therefore should be transferred from the Office of Legislative Affairs to the Office of Legal Policy.

Creating a Color-Blind Society

The new President should require that the Department of Justice's civil rights work be integrated into a comprehensive strategy involving the White House and other executive agencies, including the Departments of Education and Labor and the Equal Employment Opportunity Commission. This strategy must be rooted in a clear conception of the goal to be achieved: the furtherance of a tolerant, pluralist, capitalist society that offers incentives to individual talent, guarantees substantial protections to racial and religious minorities, and transforms the extraordinary diversity of the American people into a source of dynamism and strength.

The role of the Department of Justice in this is important but limited. It must continue to enforce the legal system's prohibitions against discrimination. Yet even if the Department of Justice gives highest priority to enforcing the laws against racial discrimination, the serious problems of joblessness, crime, drug abuse, illegitimacy, welfare dependency, and urban decay would remain. A strategy for dealing with the problems of minorities thus must combine enforcement of civil rights with other national policies in labor, education, and housing.

Civil rights protection involves a number of specific policy areas. Among them:

◆ *Housing*. The new President should work to end the use of quotas in public housing. Quotas and set-asides are still widely, if mistakenly, assumed to benefit racial minorities. But the second generation of quota cases, already beginning to arise under the Fair Housing Act of 1968, demonstrates that what was designed as a floor soon becomes a ceiling, and that a quota system meant to increase minority numbers in certain areas ultimately may limit them. Example: Starrett City, a New York City housing complex, used a quota system euphemistically described as "integration maintenance" to limit the number of black residents to avoid frightening away white residents. The intent was to preserve a racial balance, capping blacks at about 21 percent of the residents, and whites at about 65 percent. As a direct result of this policy, many blacks were denied decent and affordable housing. The new Administration should continue to press the case against quotas through legal action or legislation as appropriate.

◆ *Employment*. In the 1988 Supreme Court decision in *Watson v. Ft. Worth Bank & Trust*, a plurality of the justices, led by Justice Sandra Day O'Connor, made it more difficult to sue an employer for subjecting prospective employees to tests. As long as the employer has a legitimate business reason for a test, the Court ruled, that employer is not in violation of civil rights statutes, even if the test gives rise to statistical disparities among different racial groups. The next Department of Justice should urge lower courts and other federal agencies to follow Justice O'Connor's opinion when examining employers' testing practices. Moreover, the government's 1978 Uniform Guidelines on Employee Selection Procedures, to which the Justice Department was a signatory, should be overhauled. The revised guidelines should relieve employers of the need to validate their testing procedures.

Winning the War on Drugs

The Reagan Administration's "War on Drugs" cannot be called a success. Still, it probably has prevented the situation from becoming worse. The new President must learn from past mistakes.

One mistake has been lack of coordination. The Customs Service and Drug Enforcement Administration (DEA) often squabble over investigative authority—and thus often have run their separate investigations without telling one another. Customs and the Coast Guard clash. Customs adopted a "zero tolerance" policy of seizing any yachts with drugs, but the Coast Guard pronounced it unenforceable. The CIA and the State Department fail to transmit international data to Justice in a timely fashion.

To resolve these problems requires a central authority, or a drug czar, to lead the antidrug effort. This authority need not be a new office—the attorney general or Vice President, for instance, could fill it. Whoever is selected, however, must make the war on drugs a major piece of his or her agenda and create the necessary chain of command to carry through that effort. No new Cabinet agency, however, should be created, as such action would simply create a new bureaucracy with its own institutionalized imperatives without in any way attenuating the drug problem.

A second mistake has been trying to fight the drug war at the nation's borders. Drugs are not hard to smuggle; U.S. borders are vast and hard to police; and the rewards for successful smugglers far outweigh the risks. Rather than concentrating on the supply side of the drug problem, the new President must emphasize control of the demand side. That means targeting the 23 million Americans who use illegal drugs. Although ultimately the U.S. must rely on deterrence, through use of the criminal law, efforts should continue to reduce drug use through education. Educational programs should be targeted at youths who are most likely to become drug users.

A major part of the effort to control the demand side will involve drug testing. It should become more prevalent in many areas—schools, the transportation industry, workplaces, prisons. Federal agencies should encourage testing whenever a basis for doing so exists. The Department of Transportation already has been energetic in this area. Congress should assist Transportation by requiring random testing for common carrier operators. At the same time, the Justice Department should encourage states to develop their own drug programs. The Department of Justice should work to make federal prisons drug-free.

Sentences for drug use crimes should not be made so unrealistically harsh that juries will fail to convict, or so light that they fail to deter. A measured response is required. Heavy fines may be more appropriate than long prison terms. Loss of federal educational benefits for student users is another possible penalty. Federal employees, especially those in safety-sensitive jobs, should face loss of work or chances of promotion. Where appropriate, professional licenses should be subjected to revocation or suspension.

The Department of Justice brings the big "cases" against the drug suppliers. It also should play a key role in litigating the cases that will decide how widely the tools of enforcement—such as testing—can be used. The Department of Justice also should support legislative efforts aimed at users and suppliers. These should include a death penalty provision for drug kingpins and drug murderers; life sentences for third-time trafficking offenses; a "bounty hunter" statute providing rewards for information leading to the conviction of dealers; and laws making it easier to bar aliens who are traffickers from entering the country, or to deport them if they are here.

The Department, if necessary, should sponsor clarifying legislation to ensure that the National Labor Relations Act, the Rehabilitation Act, and Title VII of the Civil Rights Act are not used to obstruct drug control policy. Under existing law, plaintiffs can argue, for example, that their drug addiction is a "handicap" within the meaning of the Rehabilitation Act, or that an employer's refusal to hire drug users constitutes unlawful discrimination if it has disparate effects on different racial groups. Employers should be allowed to police their own workforces for drug abuse without being hampered by the fear of legal liability under federal labor or civil rights statutes.

Protecting Americans from Crime

The Reagan Administration has presided over the most substantive reform of criminal law in U.S. history. The Comprehensive Crime Control Act of 1984 fashioned sweeping revisions in sentencing, bail, and other aspects of law. Three further reforms should now be undertaken by the new Administration.

The exclusionary rule, under which illegally obtained evidence cannot be used in court, has failed to deter police conduct significantly. Congress thus should explore any constitutionally permissible alternatives that would better serve the deterrent function of the rule. Such alternatives might draw upon the English "judges rules," in which a judge who is made aware of illegal police conduct refers any allegations of such conduct to the police authorities for administrative review, excluding the tainted evidence only in instances of extreme impropriety. Other alternatives might include expansion of tort liability for police misconduct and creation of an administrative review board (civilian or otherwise) to investigate and punish police misconduct. At the same time, current court-made exceptions to the exclusionary rule should be codified in statute, including the "good faith" exception, which precludes operation of the rule when police officers have made a good faith mistake.

Second, legislation should be prepared to limit the filing of habeas corpus petitions, under which prisoners may challenge their incarceration in federal court even if they have already exhausted the normal appeals process. These filings strain the resources of the federal courts, further delaying justice. The Department should introduce legislation to place time limits on a prisoner's access to federal habeas corpus relief and to prohibit the granting of a habeas corpus writ by a federal court when a claim already has been fully and fairly adjudicated in a state proceeding.

Third, the new Administration should compare existing statutes providing for capital punishment for certain federal offenses to ascertain whether existing statutes comply with current case law. If appropriate, new legislation providing for capital punishment should be proposed.

Reforming the Prison System

Vigorous prison reform should be pursued by the next Administration. As part of this effort more prisons must be constructed. Federal prisons now are badly overcrowded on average, operating 50 percent above capacity. According to a 1988 National Institute of Justice study, the cost of building a new cell and maintaining a prisoner in it is $25,000 a year. Yet, according to that same study, new crimes committed by each released prisoner cost society about $430,000 in victim losses. Sentencing 1,000 additional offenders to prison each year thus would require about $25 million in prison construction and maintenance, but would save about $430 million in damages, costs, and private security expenditures.

The fiscal 1988 federal budget for building and modernizing prison facilities is about $200 million. This should be increased. Prison management and construction costs, meanwhile, should be held down by using private-sector firms to build and operate more prisons. Private management can cut operating costs in an average prison by as much as $700,000 per year.

Prison industries, or factories within prisons that manufacture and sell products, such as linens for homeless shelters and public school lockers, should be expanded. While most of these industries are operated by government entities, some are run by private firms. Such industries allow inmates to become productive, acquire good work habits, and earn money which they then can give as compensation to those they have injured. The Bureau of Prisons should continue to encourage expansion of prison industries at the state level by setting up model projects, pilot programs, and other experiments. In addition, the Bureau should encourage increased private financing and management of federal prison industries, proposing legislation to allow this, if necessary.

At the same time, prison overcrowding could be reduced by alternatives to incarceration for less dangerous offenders such as fines, community service, or residential incarceration. Many states have developed programs, such as California's Community Service Alternative program, in which nondangerous offenders serve their sentences by working in public service areas, like hospitals.

The new Administration should support the sentencing guidelines recently developed by the U.S. Sentencing Commission. These guidelines go a long way in ensuring fairness and consistency in the sentencing process. The guidelines are threatened by a pending constitutional challenge to the Sentencing Commission. Should the Commission be found unconstitutional, the new Administration should introduce legislation incorporating the guidelines.

Improving Immigration Policy

America's immigration policies measure the depth of the nation's commitment to an international order that respects individual rights and freedom of movement. They test America's extraordinary commitment to diversity and make a significant impact on the domestic economy and society. Entry regulations can enlarge or restrict U.S. labor markets and affect a wide variety of social and economic factors, including wage rates, inner-city conditions, welfare burdens, crime, and race relations. Immigration policies can alter the age and occupational distribution of the working population, affecting the availability of key skills, the funding of the Social Security system, and a score of other key economic factors.

The 1986 Immigration Reform and Control Act (IRCA) was designed to curb the flow of illegal immigrants to the U.S. The legislation contained two major components: it established an amnesty program for illegal immigrants who lived in the U.S. prior to 1981, thus allowing them to become legal citizens; and it introduced fines and penalties against U.S. employers who hire illegal immigrants.

The sanctions provisions should be critically reviewed by the new Administration. The available evidence suggests that these employer sanctions have had a negligible impact on illegal immigration. Further, the value of using businesses as enforcement agents for the Immigration and Naturalization Service remains to be proved. Sanctions may also have a significant discriminatory impact on legal aliens and American citizens who might be confused with illegals. Clearly, the next Administration should press for cost-effective efforts by the U.S. Border Patrol to apprehend illegal aliens when they cross the border and after they have entered the country. Of far greater importance, more legal channels should be created for workers to come to the U.S. To do this, an expanded guestworker program should be tested. To ensure that guestworkers return to their native country, a portion of their wages could be held in escrow, to be refunded when the workers return home.

The new Administration should seek reform of the preference system that now determines immigration eligibility. Under the current system, about 90 percent of the immigrants legally allowed into the U.S. each year are admitted because they have a family connection here; only 10 percent are admitted on the basis of job skills or similar economically valuable characteristics. Family preferences should be limited to immediate family members, and eliminated for more distant relatives. The allotment for those with economically valuable talents and skills should be tripled, as proposed in legislation sponsored by Senators Edward Kennedy, the Massachusetts Democrat, and Alan Simpson, the Wyoming Republican.

Under the Kennedy-Simpson legislation, a cap of 590,000 per year would be set on the total number of immigrants who could enter the U.S. each year. The next Administration should resist attempts to establish such an overall cap. An overall immigration ceiling would restrict policymakers' ability to adjust immigration levels to correspond with changes in the U.S. labor market and other economic factors. The level of legal immigration should instead be permitted to vary according to economic conditions and the size of the U.S. population.

Providing Asylum to Political and Religious Refugees

The Reagan Administration's reforms of the system granting asylum to refugees from political and religious persecution should be applauded. One Reagan reform is the Asylum Policy and Review Unit (APRU) within the Department of Justice, which reviews asylum cases and can recommend reversal of decisions made by the Immigration and Naturalization Service (INS). A second reform proposal, contained in a set of regulations that has been published for public comment, would transfer the power to make initial asylum decisions from INS district directors to a new corps of asylum officers. INS personnel too frequently emphasize the enforcement role of that agency—keeping people out—rather than its humanitarian role—letting people in. As a result, these officials often are insensitive to the plight of refugees. The proposed new asylum officers would be specially trained in, and deal regularly with, refugee issues. The new Administration should give final approval to these pending regulations.

The new Administration also should focus on the plight of certain classes of political refugees. In particular, those who have fled communist totalitarian regimes in Southeast Asia demand urgent attention. Many refugees from Vietnam and Cambodia have been denied entry into the U.S. because of arbitrary State Department or INS determinations. The next Administration should review these denials, creating a joint State-INS team for this purpose. Also deserving special consideration are refugees who have escaped from Afghanistan, Nicaragua, and other war zones. Many of these refugees have been detained for fear they will disappear into the general American population while their asylum review cases are being considered. A bail system should be considered as a substitute for detention. In addition, religious and other concerned groups should be encouraged to sponsor these refugees to avoid the need for detention.

The refugee admission system needs to be more fluid, more responsive to international contingencies, and more conscious of America's special historical role as a haven for those seeking freedom. Too often the number of refugees recommended by the Justice Department to be allowed into the U.S. is determined by budgetary considerations. If the Soviet Union decides to let more Armenians, Baptists, Jews, or dissidents emigrate, the Department of Justice should be allowed to increase the number of admissions, rather than keep the original numbers by reducing the slots for other deserving refugees.

Promoting Business Competition and Efficiency

The new Administration must oppose legislation to tighten antitrust regulation, and press for legislation to reduce further the harm to consumers from bad antitrust law. In particular, the new Administration should seek legislation to modify section 7 of the Clayton Act to ensure that efficiency enhancing mergers are not blocked. Despite changes in court interpretation and enforcement of the merger laws, the language of the laws has not been changed substantially in a generation. The 1914 Clayton Act should be revised to ensure that in deciding merger cases, courts take into account economic efficiency and consumer welfare, rather than just industry concentration alone. In addition, the new Administration should press Congress to repeal the 1936 Robinson-Patman Act. This law bars firms from offering lower prices on products to certain distributors or retailers unless there is a clear difference in cost. Meant to inhibit the growth of chain stores, the Act now mainly discourages many manufacturers from offering discounts and encourages litigation.

The new Administration should seek passage of legislation to modify "joint and several liability" in antitrust cases. Under current law, a defendant found liable for an antitrust violation is liable for the entire amount of damages due to the plaintiff, even if other parties involved could be found equally, or more, liable. The result is that plaintiffs are able to force many defendants in multiparty cases to settle even meritless cases out of court; the defendants understandably fear that if they are the last to do so, they will be forced to foot the largest bill.

Heading Off a Tort Law Crisis

Tort law—the area of law governing when one person is civilly liable for a wrong done to another—was until recently viewed as a legal backwater, rich in theory but devoid of serious public policy significance. Yet in the past few years, tort law has been thrust into the headlines by the liability insurance crisis. Responding to this problem, the Department of Justice spearheaded the Administration's Tort Policy Working Group, which assessed the national implications of liability law and issued guidelines for federal and state legislatures seeking to improve the tort system. These guidelines include the principles that liability should be based on fault and that damage awards should be reasonable and proportioned among wrongdoers according to their contribution to the injury suffered.

For the most part, tort rules are, and should remain, a matter of state law. One of the few areas where federal action is appropriate, however, is product liability. Because of the interstate nature of manufacturing, states are able to use their product liability laws to benefit their own consumers at the expense of out-of-state manufacturers. The new Administration should thus press for federal legislation to establish national product liability standards.

In addition to product liability, another much publicized aspect of the liability crisis is the dramatic increase in medical liability costs, jeopardizing the availability of specialized medical care for some in certain geographic areas. In response to this problem, the Department of Health and Human Services, in 1987, drafted a Model Health Care Provider Liability Reform Act. This identified reforms for malpractice law, roughly tracking the guidelines of the Administration's Tort Policy Working Group. Adoption of the model act was left to the states, rather than to Congress. The next Administration should work with governors and state legislatures to encourage states to adopt these malpractice reforms.

Ensuring Access to Justice

Any system of laws that is too complex or expensive for participants to understand and use does not deliver justice. This increasingly has become the case with the American legal system. While the Department of Justice is not the cause of this, it can do much to ensure that access to justice is available to all.

The Department should endorse, and wherever possible, assist efforts to seek alternatives to litigation throughout the legal system. Increased use of mediation, conciliation, "minitrials," and (where appropriate) arbitration would make the American legal system faster, simpler, and fairer. To this end, the Department should support legislation requiring pretrial arbitration in selected federal district courts. It also should support training of federal judges in alternative dispute resolution (ADR), including, where appropriate, aggressive settlement techniques at the district and appellate levels

Justice should encourage federal agencies to use ADR in contract dispute cases and similar litigation involving the federal government. In addition, the new Administration should support legislation such as the Administrative Dispute Resolution Act of 1988, sponsored by Senator Charles Grassley, the Iowa Republican, which would simplify procedures and remove obstacles to the use of mediation and other nonlitigation dispute resolution techniques by federal agencies.

In addition to a prompt, reasonably effective dispute resolution process, access to justice requires a legal system that does not create incentives to litigation. The new Administration should propose legislation to clarify statutes providing for the award of attorney fees, such as the Civil Rights Attorney Fee Award Act of 1970. These statutes provide for payment of attorney fees to successful plaintiffs in certain cases. Ambiguities in the statute have spurred substantial litigation over when particular plaintiffs are eligible for such payments, and in what amount. New legislation should define exactly when a party is entitled to an award of attorney fees and how much the award should be. Private attorneys should be required to produce time sheets as documentation of their claimed fees. The legislation should also provide that prevailing defendants, as well as plaintiffs, may receive attorney fee awards.

The new Administration must attempt to revamp legal aid to the poor to ensure that federal resources are expended to help poor persons resolve their legal disputes, rather than to pursue broad social or political goals. The Reagan Administration's initial strategy to reform legal services did not work. In trying to shut down the Legal Services Corporation (LSC) without providing the poor with alternative forms of legal assistance, it merely cut the LSC budget somewhat, but did little to change its structure. To ensure better legal aid to the poor, the new Department should explore new methods of providing legal services. These could include contracting with private attorneys, giving the poor legal services vouchers, and encouraging development of informal neighborhood dispute resolution centers, at which legal problems could be resolved without litigation.

Assuring Ethics in Government

One of the most important attributes of any civil society is a belief in public integrity and ethics in government. The Founding Fathers viewed corruption as a disease that can destroy a republic. It is vital, therefore, that the Justice Department work vigorously to guarantee proper ethical conduct by public employees.

The Justice Department's anticorruption efforts at the national level are made difficult by the deficiencies in much existing law, particularly the Ethics in Government Act of 1978. This law suffers from both overregulation and underenforcement. There are, for example, highly complex and confusing disclosure forms which appointees to senior federal positions are required to complete. These forms make technical violation of the law possible by even the most scrupulous government officials. At the same time, review of these forms is largely limited to detection of obvious conflicts of interest. Little effort is expended in determining the accuracy or completeness of the information submitted. The goal of ethical government would be served better by introducing simpler forms and by a careful audit of the financial information supplied.

Another source of overregulation is the sheer number and complexity of conflict of interest rules that apply to government employees. These regulations are confusing and hard to enforce. The lack of a range of penalties for violations makes a measured response to particular violations difficult. As a result, as found by a 1988 General Accounting Office report, the Public Integrity Section of the Justice Department's Criminal Division prosecutes very few cases of alleged conflict of interest violations referred to it by government agencies. Other agencies are reluctant to pursue administrative sanctions against employees after a matter is dropped by Justice, as they usually defer to Justice's expertise in the area. The new Administration should propose legislation to simplify the Ethics in Government Act's financial disclosure requirements, making them easier to follow and to enforce. At the same time, the number of available civil penalties, such as fines or forfeitures, should be increased, making it practical for ethics officials to prosecute a wider range of offenders.

The Department also should work to end the double standard in the ethics law, whereby executive branch officials are subject to restrictions that are not applied to members of Congress or to legislative branch staff. The Department thus should support legislation to extend the Ethics in Government Act's postemployment restrictions to the legislative branch. The Department also should support proposals to bring uniformity to the rules governing standards of conduct within the two branches. Congress should not place requirements on others that it will not place on itself.

The Department of Justice should make the elimination of public corruption a high priority for the 94 U.S. attorneys across the country. When appropriate, U.S. attorneys' offices should set up public corruption task forces and coordinate their efforts with state and local officials. The Justice Department should provide anticorruption investigation training for state and local prosecutors.

A 1987 Supreme Court decision, *McNally vs. United States*, which narrowed the statutory definition of mail fraud, has limited severely federal prosecutors' efforts to curtail corruption by local officials. That case held that the federal mail fraud statute could no longer be applied to cover the violation of such intangible rights as a citizen's "right to honest government." At least 98 investigations have been disrupted because of the Court's ruling. To plug this hole opened by the Court, the mail fraud statute should be amended to define fraud in a way that enables U.S. attorneys once again to use this statute in their anticorruption arsenal. The legislation should impose criminal sanctions on individuals who corruptly endeavor to deprive or defraud citizens of the honest services of federal, state, or local government officials or to corrupt the election process. Such legislation can be drafted so that it does not violate principles of federalism.

Nearly all state and local prosecutors favor a strong anticorruption involvement by the federal government. Federal substantive laws in this area, for instance, generally are more stringent than state laws, and federal procedural laws, such as investigative grand juries and immunity, favor successful prosecutions. In addition, many state prosecutors lack statewide criminal jurisdiction, which seriously hampers their ability to investigate multicounty corruption schemes.

When investigations focus on the conduct of local officials, moreover, local prosecutors often face the difficult task of investigating members of an agency with whom they routinely work. And in some instances, state or local law enforcement officials themselves are under investigation or may be too corrupt to be effective. Indeed, in many drug-ridden counties in depressed states, corruption is so pervasive that effective action by local law enforcement officials is impossible. Thus, the national interest in ensuring that state and local corruption does not destroy America's democratic institutions is sufficiently great to accept the U.S. attorneys' pleas for these strengthened federal powers.

————————⟡————————

INITIATIVES FOR 1989

1) Create a second associate attorney general position. The current structure of the Justice Department leaves the attorney general with too many administrative duties. With one associate attorney general for criminal matters and another for civil matters, the deputy attorney general would be free to focus on the Department's central management functions. This would free the attorney general to concentrate on setting the broad policy themes for the Department and to exercise his bully pulpit role to lead public debate on fundamental legal issues.

2) Create a new assistant attorney general position for national security and international affairs. Responsibility for such international issues as terrorism and criminal proceedings against foreign officials currently is widely dispersed. A new assistant attorney general position would centralize the oversight and management of international policy issues and the administration of specific statutes involving international questions.

3) Amend the mail fraud statute to make it easier for U.S. attorneys to fight corruption. A 1987 Supreme Court decision, *McNally vs. United States*, limited the use of mail fraud statutes to prosecute cases of corruption by local officials of government. The mail fraud statute should be amended to define fraud in a way that allows U.S. attorneys to fight corruption.

4) Clarify and simplify the ethics laws, including the Ethics in Government Act, to solve problems of overregulation and underenforcement. Deficiencies in the Ethics in Government Act, including complex and confusing provisions, have a chilling effect on the recruitment of talented government officials. The new Administration should simplify the regulations enforcing the Act. The new Administration also should encourage greater use of civil, in contrast to criminal, penalties for violations of the Ethics in Government Act, while extending the reach of the ethics laws to Congress.

5) Detect, prosecute, and punish more drug users. The war against drugs cannot be won by focusing almost exclusively on the supply of drugs. Successfully interrupting the flow of drugs will be almost impossible as long as there is a strong demand for drugs among Americans. The new Administration thus must combine tough action against suppliers with carefully designed penalties more aggressively enforced against users.

17

The Department of Labor and the National Labor Relations Board

William H. Peterson*
Task Force Chairman

The Department of Labor administers federal unemployment and job training programs, enforces federal safety and wage regulations, and in general oversees U.S. labor policy. The National Labor Relations Board is an independent regulatory agency which protects employee rights and deals with labor-management relations.

The new President should improve the free-market environment necessary for creating productive jobs. In particular, labor market flexibility should be expanded. When the factors of production, including labor, can be redistributed quickly by individuals and businesses to areas of greater market demand, overall economic output increases, contributing to higher living standards. The new President therefore should resist congressional attempts to impose on businesses federal requirements for such mandated worker benefits as child care and health insurance. These mandated benefits deter new job creation by adding costs to businesses. When not accompanied by increased business productivity, such costs drive up prices for U.S. goods and leave less funds for improving business efficiency. This makes America less competitive.

Most labor law today has a pro-union bias. This is unfair to the 83

*Commenting and contributing generously to this chapter were *Mandate III* Task Force Members James Bennett, Daniel Heldman, Marvin Kosters, Francis O'Connell, and Robert Rector. They do not necessarily endorse all of its views and recommendations.

Task Force Deputy Chairman: Heritage Center for International Economic Growth Director Edward L. Hudgins.

BUDGET AND PERSONNEL

Secretaries

Ann McLaughlin	1987–present
William E. Brock	1985–1987
Raymond J. Donovan	1981–1985

Personnel

March 1988	18,046
April 1980	23,924
April 1970	10,536

Budget Outlays

Fiscal Year	Total (billions)
1989 Estimate	$23.1
1988 Estimate	$22.0
1987 Actual	$23.5
1986 Actual	$24.1
1985 Actual	$23.9
1980 Actual	$29.7
1970 Actual	$ 5.1

percent of the American work force which does not belong to unions. The National Labor Relations Act of 1935 should be amended to give workers the right not to join or support unions.

A recent Supreme Court decision declared the use of union dues for political purposes against the will of a union member to be unconstitutional. The new Administration should establish guidelines and an enforcement mechanism to enforce this decision. It also should seek to amend the 1934 Hobbs Act to make interstate union violence a federal offense like other forms of interstate violence.

Minimum wage laws, which hinder job creation in inner cities and for low-skilled workers, should be amended or repealed. And government attempts to mandate wage scales for dissimilar jobs through the pseudo-scientific "comparable worth" system of determining wages should be resisted. The new Administration should issue a directive legalizing all work activities performed in the home. Current prohibitions limit the freedom of workers who cannot stay away from home at a regular job.

Federal job training programs still waste money and produce questionable results. Therefore the new Labor secretary should issue a directive requiring that all such programs be subject to controlled experimental tests to determine which programs are most effective. The test results should be used to allocate scarce training resources.

Drug and alcohol abuse costs the American economy billions of dollars each year in lost wages and poor health. The quality of U.S. products suffers. Since unions can influence the habits of their members, the new President should urge them to increase their efforts to eliminate substance abuse among their members.

$$\diamond$$

SUMMARY OF AGENCY FUNCTIONS

The Department of Labor (DOL) enforces some 140 statutes affecting employment. It is one of the government's largest (by some measures the largest) regulatory and rule-making agencies, covering issues from unemployment and disability insurance to mine safety and health.

The five largest DOL offices are:

◆ *The Employment and Training Administration (ETA),* which administers the nation's federal unemployment insurance program. Outlays from the Employment Insurance Trust Fund were $19.8 billion in 1987, over 80 percent of the DOL budget. Another major ETA activity is administration of the Job Training Partnership Act (JTPA) of 1982, the federal government's principal job training program. ETA gives JTPA block grants to the states to develop and administer training programs at state and local levels. The U.S. Employment Service, also part of ETA, seeks to place unemployed workers in new jobs.

◆ *The Employment Standards Administration (ESA),* which administers the 1938 Fair Labor Standards Act that establishes minimum wage and child labor regulations, rules governing commercial work at home, and overtime standards. ESA also administers some aspects of affirmative action plans. The 1932 Davis-Bacon Act, the 1936 Walsh-Healey Act, and the 1965 Service Contract Act, all of which are administered by the ESA, regulate federal contracts with the private sector and empower DOL to set wage scales in federally funded projects.

◆ *The Occupational Safety and Health Administration,* which develops and sets workplace safety and health standards. It requires employers to keep safety and health records, conducts workplace inspections, issues citations for violations—64,000 in fiscal 1986—and imposes penalties on offending employers.

◆ *The Mine Safety and Health Administration (MSHA),* which sets mine health and safety standards, inspects mines, investigates accidents, and assesses civil penalties for violations. Some 130,000 such violations were cited in fiscal 1986. MSHA also conducts educational and training activities on mine health and safety at on-site underground and surface mines.

◆ *The Bureau of Labor Statistics (BLS),* which collects and publishes statistics on the labor force, unemployment, consumer and producer prices, wages, hours worked, employee productivity, and safety and health. It also publishes *Monthly Labor Review* and *Occupational Outlook Quarterly.*

Labor issues are also addressed by *The National Labor Relations Board (NLRB),* which is an independent regulatory agency. The statutory objectives of the NLRB are to protect employee rights and reduce industrial strife, and thereby smooth the flow of commerce and industry. In accordance with regulations established in the National Labor Relations Act of 1935, the Board seeks to do this by conducting secret ballot elections to determine if employees wish to be represented by a union, and by investigating and remedying unfair labor practices on the part of either employers or unions. In fiscal 1986, it conducted 4,520 elections, in which employees voted for union representation in 1,951 cases, or 43 percent of the total.

———————————◇———————————

INSTITUTIONAL CONSTRAINTS

A new Labor secretary seeking to maintain a flexible labor market will run into considerable resistance. At the basis of opposition to a free-market labor policy is the political influence of powerful labor unions.

Organized labor's share of the nation's wage and salaried employees continues to decline in both relative and absolute terms. The number of American workers holding a union card fell from 21 million in 1979 to 17 million in 1987, or from a postwar high of 35.5 percent of the labor force in 1953 to just 17 percent today. In addition, unions continue to lose a majority of NLRB employee representation elections. Faced with this failure to win the hearts of American workers, organized labor has adopted the strategy of putting increased pressure on its traditional friends in Congress. The current push for mandated employee benefits, for instance, is heavily supported by union lobbyists. It reflects an attempt to get by legislation, for both organized and unorganized employees, what it could not win at the bargaining table or through NLRB elections. This approach also has popular appeal. For example, attempts to require all employers to offer health care benefits appear to be a free gift to employees, and one without a cost to the federal treasury.

Part of the mandated benefits strategy of organized labor appeals to Americans' sense of fair play. Most noteworthy was the adoption of legislation requiring businesses to give 60 days notice of layoffs or plant closings involving more than 100 workers. While in the long term, this requirement will hinder job creation, the specter of workers being fired with little notice seems to many an injustice requiring federal remedy. The adverse effects of mandated benefits, moreover, do not always occur immediately. Sometimes, they appear to be the direct result of unwise legislation. Elected officials who oppose such legislation thus must present a sophisticated economic argument to the public, something these officials often feel is too difficult a task.

While job creation has been very strong since 1983, the restructuring of the economy and labor market, combined with more extreme economic changes in some regions of the country, gives organized labor political strength well beyond its numbers. The interests of management and labor in opposing foreign imports, for example, often coincide. In addition, new, growing, dynamic industries which have created millions of jobs during the Reagan years and which generally are not unionized still lack organized political clout. Thus organized labor is able to keep pressure on politicians to support its programs.

Organized labor still has the traditional support of congressmen and senators from states with large union constituencies and older manufacturing industries such as steel and automobiles. In addition, with the liberals in control of Congress and pro-union elected officials chairing the committees dealing with labor issues, the new Labor Secretary will face considerable opposition to furthering free-market labor policies.

Other groups that benefit from organized labor's agenda include labor attorneys who handle labor disputes before the National Labor Relations Board and unionized contractors on federally funded projects who benefit from high government-mandated wages. These groups can be expected to favor the status quo. As in the case of other federal departments, bureaucrats in the Department of Labor have a vested interest in government regulation of labor and the continuation and expansion of the various Labor Department programs. Over one-third of Labor Department employees are union members.

———————————————◇———————————————

THE REAGAN ADMINISTRATION RECORD

The record growth of jobs during the Reagan Administration demonstrates that sound free-market economic policies, such as taxes, deregulation of business, and international free trade serve working Americans better than do particular actions or policies by the Labor Department. When Ronald Reagan entered the White House, the nation was entering a severe recession. Since 1982, however, 17 million new jobs have been created in America.

DOL's role in creating these jobs has been minimal but essential. It has sought to reduce the regulation of the labor market and cut those federal programs that destroy jobs and prevent new jobs from being created. For this reason the Reagan Administration has opposed attempts by Congress to regulate further the freedom of employees and employers to set their own terms of employment. It has opposed, for example, government-mandated wage scales based on a "comparable worth" formula. Under this flawed philosophy, dissimilar jobs, especially those that tend to be dominated by either men or women, would be evaluated according to an arbitrary standard, and a "comparable" wage for each would be established by government bureaucrats. This is not the same as guaranteeing equal pay for equal work, which ensures uniform pay within the same company for the same jobs, something the Reagan Administration has supported. Comparable worth, rather, would evaluate, say, the work of a truck driver and a secretary to determine which deserves a higher salary according to an arbitrary formula. The Reagan Administration has argued that wages should be set by the market and that the comparable worth approach would in fact give employers less incentive to hire women for fear of government wage regulations.

The Administration has sought a two-tiered minimum wage to enable chronically unemployed teenagers, especially in inner cities, to find entry-level jobs. While the Administration has not secured such a wage, it has made important points in the public dialogue concerning incentives for job creation.

The Labor Department has used research to counter myths and unfounded assumptions concerning labor policy and the workforce and to establish a sound empirical base for future labor policy. In 1986, for instance, DOL commissioned the major study *Work Force in the Year 2000*. The report notes, for example, that women and minorities will make up a larger proportion of the future workforce. This indicates that government programs to help women and minorities secure employment are probably unnecessary.

DOL research also has refuted critics who claim that the 17 million new jobs created during the Reagan years consist mostly of low-paying jobs in the service sector, popularly known as "McJobs," and that the nation is becoming "deindustrialized." Critics had based their charges for the most part on flawed studies. DOL corrected the record, documenting that the number of jobs paying only the federal minimum wage has declined between 1981 and 1987 by 3 million. During this period, almost 95 percent of the new jobs were full-time, with the number of jobs paying more than $10 an hour, or more than $20,000 a year full-time, rising by 12 million, or by 50 percent. DOL also has shown that, while the number of manufacturing jobs has been going down as a percentage of total U.S. employment, it has been doing so for the past 40 years. What is more important, manufacturing output as a percentage of total output has been surprisingly constant since World War II—at about 21 percent of gross national product. The Reagan Administration and DOL thus deserve credit for dispelling myths about low-paying jobs and deindustrialization.

The Reagan Administration also deserves credit for eliminating the wasteful Comprehensive Employment and Training Act (CETA). Since 1961, more than a score of federal job training programs have cost more than $100 billion, with $53 billion alone going to CETA. The Reagan Administration's replacement program, the Job Training Partnership Act (JTPA), has been less costly than CETA. JTPA issues block grants that allow states greater freedom to establish and run their own programs. There is, however, little evidence that JPTA is much more effective than CETA in placing workers in productive jobs.

The Reagan DOL also recognized the problem of adult illiteracy and its adverse effects on the workforce. The Administration understood that with an estimated 20 million functional illiterates, the nation is in danger of developing a permanent underclass of marginally employable workers. Labor Secretaries William Brock and Ann McLaughlin, in cooperation with the Department of Education, established Project Literacy U.S., or PLUS, a voluntary effort to enhance literacy in the workplace. This project enlists the talents and facilities of the American Broadcasting Company (ABC) and the Public Broadcasting Service (PBS) to develop documentary programs to raise the national consciousness about the illiteracy problem and to provide instructional programs to help those unable to read with comprehension.

The Department of Labor also teamed up with the Education Department to publish a 1988 report, *The Bottom Line: Basic Skills in the Workforce*. This study focused on the need for a solid educational foundation for future economic growth.

In his first term, Reagan took a strong stand against the illegal Professional Air Traffic Controllers Organization (PATCO) strike, firing 11,500 air controllers. As public employees, PATCO workers pledged not to go on strike. Through its action, the White House sent a message to organized labor that public and private unions are not above the law.

Despite some successes, the Reagan Administration has failed to carry through the principles of its own labor policy. On many key issues, especially after the first few years of the Administration, the White House seemed concerned only to keep things quiet on the labor front, when what was needed was an aggressively reformist approach. For example, the Administration's appointees to DOL had a status quo orientation and seemed to have little interest in aggressively promoting Reagan's free market policies.

At the National Labor Relations Board (NLRB), the White House made mistakes in key appointments. Example: In 1984, the Administration appointed to a four-year term as NLRB General Counsel Rosemary Collyer, who has a record of favoring organized labor. This is an important post, for the general counsel processes labor complaints from businesses or workers and passes them along to the Board itself for adjudication. In essence, the general counsel has the power to choose which issues will be addressed by the Board and which will not.

Another mistake in making appointments was in selecting the 1985 Task Force on Economic Adjustment and Worker Dislocation. The 21–member group's seven labor representatives were all union officials; left out completely were representatives of America's majority—nonunion labor. The Task Force report, issued in 1986, was poorly researched and policies were recommended with little attempt to judge past labor policy failures. Not surprisingly, the recommendations reflected organized labor's agenda, including calls for more government spending for displaced workers, greater government regulation of business, and a forced government/management/labor partnership.

Yielding again to pressure from organized labor, the Administration has failed to press hard to eliminate the 1932 Davis-Bacon Act and other laws mandating high wages for private workers on federal projects. That Act requires that workers on public projects be paid "prevailing" wages, which in practice means the union scale. This Act costs taxpayers $2 billion per year in higher bills for construction projects, according to a General Accounting Office estimate. More serious, the Davis-Bacon Act discriminates against small businesses, many minority-owned, which cannot afford to pay their workers high union wages.

The Reagan Administration should be pressing for fundamental changes in the National Labor Relations Act to prevent it from being used to impose compulsory union membership on unwilling workers and to confer monopoly status on unions. The Administration has not done so. And the Administration deserves further criticism for dropping its opposition to the proposed congressional ban on the use of polygraph tests by employers. Polygraph testing, especially in such sensitive jobs as cashiers, is a prudent business practice. The Administration and DOL have neither exercised leadership nor made a strong public case for such tests.

Under Labor Secretary Ann McLaughlin, DOL has allowed liberals to seize the child care issue to promote their own agenda and argue for more federal day care funds. The DOL's report, *Childcare: A Workfare Issue,* issued in April 1988, documented the extensive government support already provided for day care and refuted the myth that there is a national shortage of day care facilities. Yet the report reinforces the mistaken notion that the traditional family, in which the mother cares for her own preschool children, is a thing of the past. DOL mainly has addressed child care solely as a labor issue, ignoring the thousands of private firms that provide day care centers across the country and the fact that half of America's preschool children do not have working mothers.

In a recent labor policy move, the Justice Department is attempting to seize control of the International Brotherhood of Teamsters, the country's largest union. The Administration alleges that the Teamsters are too corrupt to run themselves. This action undermines the free-market system. Where specific violations of the law occur in local unions or at the national level, the government should act. But to seize the entire national union amounts to an unprecedented government violation of the rights of workers to organize and sell their labor in the market. This move sets a very dangerous precedent. Presumably, an

Administration hostile to business might seize a large defense contractor because of the corrupt actions of a few individuals.

———————————◇———————————

THE NEXT FOUR YEARS

With 17 million jobs added to the United States economy during the Reagan Administration, America's economic expansion has been the envy of the world. The goal of the new Administration therefore is clear. It must improve further the environment necessary for continued creation of productive, highpaying jobs. This will require further liberalization of the labor market and the removal of government regulations. Government will have to avoid placing new financial burdens or restrictions on businesses and workers. Giving maximum choice to the workers themselves concerning the terms of their employment is necessary. In a free society, workers are allowed to seek employment on terms mutually agreed upon with the employer. For the government to force workers to join unions, for example, violates a worker's rights.

Educating the Public on Productivity and Flexibility

The next President must explain to the American public that high wages and increased purchasing power result from increased economic productivity, not from special interest labor laws. New machines, production methods, and business techniques allow enterprises to produce more goods or services, using available capital, raw materials, and—most important—labor. Efficient companies mean high labor productivity. That means high wages. For this reason, labor law must enhance labor efficiency, not lock in inefficient union practices.

The next Administration must point out that a flexible labor market, that is, the ability of business to hire or to lay off workers quickly in light of changing market demand, best insures higher economic output and thus higher wages. The U.S. has the highest turnover rate for jobs and businesses in the industrialized world. Because American labor, as well as capital and other factors of production, can be redistributed quickly to areas of greater need, America's economic output by entrepreneurs grows more rapidly than in countries in which labor rules reduce flexibility. In Western Europe, for instance, restrictions on plant closing, trade protectionism, and huge government subsidies to old industries preserve less productive jobs and hinder the creation of new, higher-paying jobs. In the long run, economic flexibility helps all workers. DOL should take the lead in educating the public as well as policymakers concerning the connection between labor market flexibility, increased business productivity, and higher wages and standards of living.

Blocking Mandated Benefits

To keep labor markets flexible, the new President must avoid the temptation to mandate by government decree special benefits for workers. Requiring businesses to provide benefits not justified on economic grounds discourages businesses from hiring new employees.

Congress has been considering a slew of bills that would mandate such benefits as unpaid parental leave, health insurance, and a higher minimum wage. These would benefit only a minority of workers, while forcing the majority to pay for the benefits with lower salaries. Higher business costs due to mandated benefits, meanwhile, would be passed on to consumers as higher prices for goods and services. In addition, mandated benefits would restrict the right of workers to negotiate their own form of compensation with employers. Many workers might wish higher immediate take-home pay and less nonsalary benefits. Issues of pay and compensation should be decided by employees and employers, not by the government.

Expanding Employee Choice

Expansion of an employee's choice of working conditions would enhance worker freedom and increase labor flexibility. The new President should enhance employee choice by pressing for changes in existing laws and regulations. He should reaffirm an employee's right to join or not to join a labor union. Section 7 of the National Labor Relations Act of 1935 provides that an employee working for a business with a union approved by as little as 20 percent of the workers and by the NLRB cannot join an alternative union. Often the employee is required to join the approved union as a condition of employment. Yet forcing an employee to join or pay dues to an unwanted union deprives the employee of his or her First Amendment guarantee of freedom of association. If a business freely agrees to hire only union labor, that is its right. But if the employer is forced by the government to hire only members of a certain union as provided under the so-called exclusive representation doctrine in the National Labor Relations Act, free choice is restricted. Hence the National Labor Relations Act should be amended to eliminate the doctrine of compulsory unionism.

Legislation also should be introduced by the new Administration to ensure that union dues are not used for political purposes if employees object. Union dues, said the Supreme Court in *Machinists v. Street* (1961) and *Ellis v. Railway Clerks* (1984), are to be used strictly for collective bargaining and contract administration, including grievance adjustment. This doctrine was broadened by the Court in *Communication Workers of America vs. Beck* in 1988 to include all workers. Yet violations have been widespread. The new President should propose an Employees Political Involvement Act to set clear guidelines for union use of political dues and to establish enforcement authority for this Act. The burden of proof should be placed on unions to show that no funds are being diverted into political or ideological purposes without the express written consent of the affected members.

The General Counsel of the National Labor Relations Board has the power to decide which cases the Board should hear and which they should not. This cuts off an important avenue of appeal for workers or businesses that believe that their rights have been violated. The new President should propose amending the National Labor Relations Act to give the Board Chairman the right to overrule the General Counsel and hear cases the Chairman deems important.

Outlawing Labor Violence

Federal authorities need tougher powers to prosecute violence or the threat of violence in labor disputes. Congress enacted the Hobbs Anti-Extortion Act in 1934 to end widespread violence in industrial labor disputes. In 1973, however, the U.S. Supreme Court, in its 5 to 4 decision in *U.S. v. Emmons*, ruled that violence on an industrial site does not constitute a federal crime if it is employed in furtherance of a "legitimate" union objective. This decision has led to a renewed surge of union violence. Federal legislation is needed to reverse the *Emmons* decision. DOL should draft legislation that would make physical intimidation by unions a federal crime, with the states retaining the right to treat labor violence as a crime as well.

Establishing Market Wages

The new President should press for repeal of the Davis-Bacon Act and other measures that enforce minimum wage laws. Economists are near unanimity that such laws destroy jobs. A 1983 General Accounting

Office report entitled *The Davis-Bacon Act Should Be Repealed*, meanwhile, concluded that Davis-Bacon requirements add some $2 billion annually to the cost of federal construction contracts.

Since vested union interests certainly will oppose reform or repeal of Davis-Bacon, the new Administration must develop tactics to promote reform. First, it should emphasize the cost to the federal budget of higher wages on federal projects. Eliminating Davis-Bacon would reduce the budget deficit. Second, the Administration should introduce a Federal Projects Business Opportunity Bill to set aside a certain percentage of federal projects for the lowest bidder, regardless of whether they pay union wages. This would give opportunities to smaller and minority businesses that cannot afford to pay union scale to work on such projects. This appeals to Americans' sense of fairness and would help create a constituency for Davis-Bacon reform or repeal. Setting aside a certain percentage of federal projects for the lowest bidder, moreover, leaves part of Davis-Bacon intact. It would therefore be more difficult for union supporters to argue that this reform would cut them out of federal projects.

Comparable worth legislation would allow the government to determine the "fair" wage for certain types of dissimilar jobs, such as truck drivers and nurses. Comparable worth is not the same as the principle of equal pay for equal work, which is now law. Comparable worth is an attempt to close an alleged wage gap between men and women by raising the wages in traditionally female-dominated professions to the level of wages in "comparable" professions that are dominated by men. Bills in the 100th Congress, H.R. 387 and S. 552, would authorize a commission to study the federal workforce pay structure. In all likelihood, the commission would not question whether the concept of comparable worth itself has any economic validity. If this is the case, the question is likely to be on what basis comparable worth calculations are to be made. Such a study would serve as the basis for legislation on comparable worth and litigation by workers alleging that wages in certain job categories inherently discriminate against women. There is no evidence, however, that the market systematically underpays workers in traditionally female jobs. In fact, as more women become permanent members of the workforce, and as the status of their jobs increases, their wages relative to those of men are rising. In 1980, women earned 64.4 percent as much on average as men; in 1987, the proportion had risen to 70.3 percent.

The new Labor secretary should emphasize the economic progress made by women and at the same time challenge the fallacies underlying the comparable worth argument. He or she should recognize that a federal study of comparable worth, unless it questions the basic assumptions of this approach to wages, is likely to result in a highly distorted view of the labor market that will serve as the basis for comparable worth legislation. The new secretary therefore should attempt to head off such a study and should make certain that free-market economists, who will not compromise their beliefs for the sake of unanimous agreement on the report, participate in such a study if it comes about.

Expanding the Right to Work at Home

The Home Work Rule of the 1938 Fair Labor Standards Act bans the sale of many items made or worked on at home. The reason for this was a fear in the 1930s that unscrupulous businessmen would exploit workers in the home. And as organized labor grew stronger, it wanted to assure that as much work as possible occurred in factories under potential union control. As a result, seven home industries are still prohibited: buttons and buckles, embroidery, gloves and mittens, handkerchiefs, jewelry manufacturing, knitted outerwear, and women's apparel.

This ban abridges individual freedom and makes little economic sense. For one thing, it forces potential workers to remain idle, limiting America's economic output. For another, it violates the basic right of Americans to work as they please in their own homes. Many workers in remote areas, mothers with preschool children requiring supervision, and handicapped and elderly workers who cannot readily commute are penalized by the ban on home work.

In 1984, DOL lifted the ban on home work on knitted outerwear. An employer can now contract with such home workers if he obtains a DOL certificate. In 1986 DOL sought to ease the ban on the other six industries, but was strongly opposed by the International Ladies' Garment Workers Union, other unions, and several manufacturers associations. They recognized that home workers cannot readily be unionized, and argued that home work competes "unfairly" against factory labor.

The new President will not need congressional approval to eliminate remaining restrictions on home work. He can and should act swiftly and unilaterally to free home workers to prosper from their productive efforts. The pleadings of special interest unions should be ignored.

Rethinking Job Training Programs

Over the past quarter century, more than $100 billion has been spent on federal job programs, with very little to show for it. Almost all evidence reveals minimal long-term job placement for trainees, considerable mismatching of trainees with realistic job possibilities, and a general failure of such training programs to instill a work ethic in program participants. To make matters worse, there typically is no systematic objective standard by which to judge the success of such programs.

The most effective job training programs, predictably, are those conducted by businesses, like McDonald's and General Motors. U.S. companies spend some $40 billion annually to educate and train some 8 million workers.

The continuation and proliferation of untested federal training programs wastes U.S. taxpayer money and raises for job trainees a false promise of job success. The new DOL should, through controlled experiments, evaluate existing training programs in order to identify programs that hinder the chances of participants to acquire permanent employment. Such tests will allow DOL to use scarce resources in the most efficient manner—that is, to sponsor only programs that promise to yield results at a reasonable cost.

The new Labor secretary should promote policies within the Administration that encourage private job training and give workers greater control over their own training. Example: all expenditures by individual workers for their own training should be made tax deductible. Workers should be allowed to draw a portion of their unemployment compensation while training for a new job. In many situations, these unemployment benefits are cut off. Predictably, this provides reduced incentive to seek better-paying jobs, since the workers could be without means of support while training. Allowing them to continue to draw a declining portion of their unemployment benefits while they train for new work would encourage displaced workers to seek private-sector training. By shifting retraining to the private sector, moreover, the costs of government training programs will be reduced.

Halting Substance Abuse in the Workplace

Drug and alcohol abuse is devastating the American workplace. The Research Triangle Institute in North Carolina found that added health care payments and lost man-hours due to substance abuse cost American businesses at least $100 billion annually. Such abuse contributes to lower quality and quantity of American output.

The new Labor secretary should launch an educational campaign warning of the harmful effects of drug and alcohol abuse in the workplace. As part of the campaign, the secretary should instruct the Occupational Safety and Health Administration (OSHA), the Bureau of Labor Statistics, and other relevant offices to collect and publish the best statistics available illustrating how drug and alcohol abuse harms the U.S. economy and makes the U.S. less competitive in the world market. The secretary should ask unions for help in the fight against drug and alcohol abuse in the workplace. Unions could educate their members on the danger of substance abuse to family life, as well as to physical and mental health. DOL should support such union efforts indirectly, by providing information and literature for antidrug activities.

———————————◇———————————

INITIATIVES FOR 1989

1) Oppose mandated benefit bills. Some congressional lawmakers are supporting legislation to require corporations to provide certain benefits, such as health insurance for workers and their families. Such government-mandated benefits give workers the illusion they are getting something for nothing. In fact, such benefits are financed out of money the company otherwise would pay to workers, or by reducing total labor costs by cutting employment. In either case the worker ultimately pays. Moreover, such mandated benefits limit the worker's choice regarding the form of compensation he or she will receive. The new President should expose the myth of "free" benefits, and veto all mandated benefits bills.

2) Amend the National Labor Relations Act to prohibit compulsory union membership. Workers should have the right to choose whether or not to belong to a union. If they decide on union membership, they should have the right as individuals to decide which union to join. To uphold these rights, the National Labor Relations Act should be amended to allow workers to join the union of their choice even if the majority of workers in a given firm belong to another union.

3) Amend the federal election campaign legislation with an Employees Political Involvement Act to enforce the 1988 Supreme Court ban on the use of union dues for political purposes against the wishes of union members. Workers have the right as individuals to decide whether or not to contribute to a political candidate or cause. The Supreme Court has ruled that the use of union dues for political purposes against the wishes of a union member violates this right. The new Administration should establish guidelines and an enforcement mechanism to protect the individual's freedom to choose which political candidates or causes he or she will support.

4) Amend the National Labor Relations Act to allow the Chairman of the National Labor Relations Board (NLRB) to override the NLRB general counsel's decisions on whether or not a complaint will be heard by the Board. The general counsel of the NLRB currently has too much power. There is no appeal for this officer's decision on whether or not to hear a case. A right of appeal to the Board chairman should be granted.

5) Amend the 1934 Hobbs Act to make interstate union violence and extortion a federal crime. While other forms of interstate violence are subject to federal prosecution, labor violence is not. The Hobbs Act which covers such violence should be amended to treat interstate labor violence as a federal crime.

6) Amend or repeal the Davis-Bacon, Service Contract, and Walsh-Healey Acts. These acts, which in effect require high union wages on federal construction projects, add $2 billion to the cost of federal government projects and tend to freeze out nonunion workers. They thus should be repealed. As a step toward this, the new President should seek a Federal Projects Business Opportunity Bill, which would set aside a share of federal construction projects for the lowest bidder, even if such firms do not pay high union wages.

7) Oppose comparable worth legislation or a "study" of the federal wage structure. A comparable worth approach to wages would allow government bureaucrats arbitrarily to set salaries for different professions. Salaries should be set by the free market and by mutual agreement by workers and employers. A federal study of this matter that does not question the very soundness of the comparable worth concept would be merely a vehicle for special interest groups to secure higher wages. The Labor secretary should block such a study. Failing this, he should make certain that solid free-market-oriented economists are involved in the study and have the opportunity to include opposition opinions in the final study document.

8) Change the tax code to allow workers to deduct from their income taxes their expenditures for job training. Businesses currently are allowed tax deductions for their expenditures to train workers. Individual workers paying out of their own pockets to train themselves for work in a new field cannot take such a deduction. To put individuals on an equal footing with businesses and to encourage individual advancement, job training expenditures by private individuals should be made deductible from taxes as well.

9) Seek legislation to allow workers to collect a declining proportion of their unemployment benefits while training for a new job. Often displaced workers who enter a training program in preparation for a new job lose their unemployment benefits completely. To give workers an incentive to seek better jobs that require a period of training without pay, a declining proportion of unemployment benefits should be extended to workers during such a period.

18

The Office of Personnel Management

Donald J. Devine *
Task Force Chairman

The Reagan Administration has restrained somewhat the burgeoning
federal payroll and retirement costs. The new President must
continue efforts to contain costs by creating federal pay, retirement,
and benefits systems fair both to employees and the American taxpayer.

While the Reagan Administration has put into effect civil service
reforms that could enhance presidential authority greatly and reduce
bureaucratic inertia, many Reagan appointees have not used available
tools to manage executive branch personnel effectively. The new
Administration should continue reform efforts to increase the efficiency and responsiveness of the federal bureaucracy; the Office of
Personnel Management (OPM) should stress to new appointees the
importance of personnel policy in managing agencies and departments.

To strengthen the ability of the President to control the executive
branch, the new Administration should increase the number of political
appointees and strengthen their role in government management. The
new President should institute the principle of pay for performance
throughout the federal workforce, to promote fairness, responsiveness,
and efficiency in government operations. And in general, he should
redesign the federal pay system so that salaries and wages reflect
market conditions and are more closely linked to private-sector pay
rates. The new OPM also should restore the merit principle in hiring

---

*Commenting and contributing generously to this chapter were *Mandate III* Task
Force Members Robert Moffit, George Nesterczuk, Mary Rose, and George Woloshyn.
They do not necessarily endorse all of its views and recommendations.
Task Force Deputy Chairman: Heritage Policy Analyst Robert Rector.

BUDGET AND PERSONNEL

Directors

Constance Horner	1985–present
Donald Devine	1981–1985

Personnel

March 1988	6,365
April 1980	8,526
April 1970	5,465*

Budget Outlays

Fiscal Year	Total (billions)
1989 Estimate	$30.5
1988 Estimate	$28.5
1987 Actual	$27.0
1986 Actual	$24.0
1985 Actual	$23.7
1980 Actual	$15.1
1970 Actual*	$ 2.7

*OPM was known as the Civil Service Commission until January 1, 1979.

career civil servants, by using objective tests, rather than racial quotas, to determine the ability of job applicants.

The federal retirement system should be restructured to eliminate such examples of overgenerosity, at taxpayers' expense, as allowing federal employees to retire at age 55. OPM also should protect the retirement savings of employees from future political abuse and protect the U.S. economy from a politicized investment market, by urging Congress to repeal provisions of current law that establish a politically appointed "Thrift Board" to invest employee retirement savings. Individual employees should be given a real choice over who controls their personal retirement assets. And finally, OPM should continue to oppose "comparable worth" in the federal work force and in the private sector. Comparable worth wage controls would undermine the foundations of the free market economy and not serve the interests of women workers.

———————◇———————

SUMMARY OF AGENCY FUNCTIONS

The director of the Office of Personnel Management (OPM) plays a key role in carrying out federal policy, overseeing some 2.2 million federal civilian employees, the largest workforce in the free world. OPM manages the policies that control their selection, promotion, transfer, performance, training, conditions of service, tenure, and separation. OPM also develops pay and retirement policy for the federal workforce and plays a central role in managing relations with federal employee unions.

OPM is more than just a larger version of the personnel department of a private-sector corporation. Article II of the U.S. Constitution vests in the President of the United States the "executive power" of government. Indispensable to the President's ability to translate constitutional authority into real control over the executive branch are the roughly 3,000 political appointees selected by the President. They serve as the President's eyes and hands throughout the enormous federal bureaucracy. OPM also provides the rules, information, and guidance necessary for such political appointees to guide and motivate the enormous permanent career staff. It is in the personnel management policies linking the authority of the President to the activities of the career civil service that the President's ability or lack of ability to govern the executive branch ultimately rests.

———————◇———————

INSTITUTIONAL CONSTRAINTS

The ability of the Director of OPM to control the personnel process within the executive branch is limited by a number of factors. One is the federal employee unions, such as the American Federation of Government Employees, the National Treasury Employees Union, and the National Federation of Federal Employees. These unions work to raise federal pay, expand the number of employees, and curtail managerial authority over federal workers. The financial interests of retired employees, meanwhile, are the concern of the National Association of Retired Federal Employees.

Other organizations represent career managers: the Senior Executive Association and the Federal Managers Association. These, together with the National Academy of Public Administration and the American Society for Public Administration, seek to enhance the prestige of the career civil service and to expand its influence within the political process, often at the expense of the President's political appointees. And federal employees themselves, of course, often are vociferous lobbyists in Congress when their financial interests or job security are perceived as threatened.

Another constraint on the power of the OPM director to control personnel policy is the dispersed nature of employee management within the executive branch. The Federal Labor Relations Authority monitors labor-management relations between agencies and federal unions; the Merit Systems Protection Board adjudicates disciplinary actions; and the Equal Employment Opportunity Commission regulates federal sector civil rights. Even within OPM, a separate Office of Government Ethics regulates financial disclosure for top appointees and executives. Personnel offices, moreover, exist in nearly all agencies. Since agency heads are occupied primarily with carrying out their political missions, personnel matters fall invariably to the career staffs. Unless agency heads insist that their assistant secretaries of administration work to execute OPM-directed personnel policies, inertia is almost guaranteed.

Congress, too, of course, imposes restraints on an Administration's personnel policy. In periods in which the presidency and Congress are controlled by different political parties, Congress seeks to undermine presidential power by limiting the ability of the President and his political subordinates to control the tenured bureaucratic workforce. Congressional intervention in the details of personnel and public administration often will have enormous ramifications through every department and arena of public policy.

$$\diamond$$

THE REAGAN ADMINISTRATION RECORD

The Reagan Administration inherited a newly reformed federal personnel system which greatly enhanced the ability of the President's political subordinates to manage the executive branch. The civil service law had been changed dramatically by Jimmy Carter in the Civil Service Reform Act (CSRA) of 1978. This established a personnel system with performance, flexibility, and responsiveness as its goals.

Under the prior civil service law, the 8,000 top career managers had virtual tenure in their jobs; it was nearly impossible to transfer top-level personnel between positions. This made policy change difficult, and in some instances impossible. With CSRA, political supervisors were permitted to reassign top-level career staff, known as Senior Executive Service, as needed. It thus became possible to bring eager new top-level personnel to manage a program and to transfer individuals whose attachment to bureaucratic routine and the status quo impeded innovation. Under the old system, moreover, rewards were given largely for seniority. Under CSRA it became possible for managers to discipline employees who performed their duties poorly or would not follow policy directives, and to give incentive bonuses to senior level employees who were productive and creative in meeting leadership goals.

Recognizing the importance of the act in empowering the Reagan Administration to control the federal bureaucracy, Reagan's incoming OPM moved decisively to make sure that CSRA took full effect as scheduled on October 1, 1981, despite pressures for delay from Congress, the federal unions, and groups representing federal managers. Reagan also moved swiftly to keep his campaign promise to reduce the number of nondefense personnel and immediately froze all federal hiring. New reduction-in-force (RIF) guidelines were issued, stipulating procedures for determining which employees would be dismissed and which retained when an agency was cut in size. Regular coordination meetings also were held throughout the government, to assure effective management of the personnel reductions.

The Reagan Administration has restrained the rate of increase of pay for federal employees, reducing the extent to which federal employees are paid more than their private-sector counterparts. In 1981, the Federal Employees Health Benefits Program was operating millions of dollars in the red, with dwindling reserves. But by adding deductibles and coinsurance features to the health plans, Reagan's OPM put the system in sound financial order within one year. Thanks to this action, taxpayers saved $13 billion over the following five-year budget cycle.

Savings were also achieved in the disability retirement system. For the first time, this system was limited to employees who were actually disabled. Prior to OPM reforms in 1981, one-third of retirements were for disability—an incredible rate for a predominantly white collar workforce. An investigation indicated that the reason for this was that an extremely broad definition of disability was used, and little proof required. By adopting a reasonable definition of disability and by requiring proof, the number of disability retirements was reduced by 40 percent with not one single employee complaint. This reform ultimately saved over $5 billion over the next five years.

The most costly benefit provided to federal employees is the Civil Service Retirement System (CSRS). It is the federal government's fourth largest entitlement program. Here, the Reagan Administration has made only a small dent. At the beginning of the Reagan Administration, the unfunded liability of CSRS was a half trillion dollars and was increasing at a rate of $70,000 per minute. When other federal retirement systems were included in the calculation the figures became even more alarming. In 1981 dollars, the total unfunded liabilities of the federal service, foreign service, and the military retirement system together amounted to over $850 billion.

Specific features of the CSRS system, absent from most private-sector retirement programs, were responsible for driving up costs. Among these: high benefit levels coupled with low fund contribution rates; retirement at full benefits at age 55 after 30 years employment; and full automatic cost-of-living adjustments (COLAs) on a biennial basis. Reagan's budget reductions of 1981 finally replaced the biennial COLA increases with annual adjustments. The savings: $1.1 billion per year.

Yet the Reagan Administration still has not fully tamed the runaway retirement system. CSRS continues to cost more than similar private-sector plans. Sweeping reform proposals for the retirement system were included in the President's 1983 federal budget message to Congress to bring the federal system closer to the typical private-sector plan, but Congress rejected the proposals.

The 1983 Social Security amendments will have some impact on the federal system's future liabilities by placing new federal employees under Social Security. New employees now are enrolled in a "Federal Employees Retirement System" (FERS), which combines a Social Security benefit base with a "thrift plan" styled on Individual Retirement Accounts and funded by employee and agency contributions. Because contributions to the thrift plan will be saved and invested for the employee, rather than spent on current retirees, the long-term unfunded liability of FERS will be less than under the prior system. Moreover, the cost of this retirement program is less than that of the previous plan. The cost of benefits under the older CSRS system was estimated by congressional sources at 25 percent of payroll (internal OPM estimates put the cost at 33 percent). The FERS plan is estimated to cost 23 percent of payroll (still higher than the 18-to-19 percent typical in the private sector). Yet the overall impact of this is limited. Participation in FERS is mandatory only for new employees. Older employees had the option of joining FERS or remaining in the CSRS system. At present, only 29 percent of employees belong to the FERS.

◇

THE NEXT FOUR YEARS

The new President should strive to create a federal bureaucracy that can be counted on to carry out the decisions and policies of the elected executive and legislative branches. To do this, the new President should strengthen the role of political appointees, the critical links in the chain of command through which the President controls the executive branch. The new Director of OPM must ensure that new political appointees serving the President understand the critical role of personnel policy in managing executive branch departments and agencies.

To motivate and reward federal employees, and to base federal pay on market conditions, OPM should eliminate pay practices which result in pay levels that are greater or lower than those needed to attract and maintain a qualified workforce.

Protecting Presidential Authority

The new President should give priority to defending and expanding the managerial role of political appointees within the executive branch. When the authority of these officials is weakened, the President's ability to control the executive branch is challenged. Political appointees are a special breed of policy experts moving in and out of government ranks. Their indispensable contribution to government is their shared policy orientation with the President, which enables them to serve as his link to the permanent bureaucracy, providing policy guidance upward to the White House while communicating presidential priorities down to the nonpolitical career staff.

The Reagan Administration has governed with roughly one political appointee per 800 career civil servants. The experience of Reagan's tenure suggests strongly that this number is insufficient to monitor the permanent government, let alone to develop aggressively new policies. While the number of senior political appointees in Presidential Appointee/Senate Confirmed (PAS) positions and noncareer Senior Exec-

utive Service (SES) slots is limited by law, the number that can be
appointed to lower level "Schedule C" positions is not restricted. The
new President thus should oppose any attempt by Congress to reduce
the number of political appointees within the executive branch. He
should introduce legislation to expand the number of noncareer Senior
Executive Service positions by 25 percent. OPM also should be active
in encouraging agency and department heads to increase the number
of Schedule C appointments by 25 percent above current levels.

Injecting Flexibility into Federal Pay and Benefits Policy

Federal employees are rarely paid at a rate competitive with the
private sector. In some cases, they are paid more than the market rate,
in other cases less. The new Administration's policy should be to pay
enough to attract and retain individuals qualified to perform a given
job while not paying more than necessary.

Two basic pay systems are used in the federal government, one
covering most white collar workers, the other covering most blue
collar workers. Most white collar federal employees are under the
General Schedule, a pay system which covers jobs from clerk-typists
to nuclear physicists. The General Schedule (GS) is divided into 18
grade levels, from a GS–1 paying $9,811 to GS–18 paying $72,500. The
pay scale is set on a nationwide basis each year, with no adjustments
for regional differences in labor market conditions. Thus, a GS–5 typist
currently is paid $15,118 whether working in New York City or Biloxi,
Mississippi.

Surprisingly, this rigid system still enables the government to recruit
adequate federal employees for most positions—but at higher than
necessary cost to the taxpayer. General Schedule salaries for most
occupations are above market rates. In addition, in the few cases
where they are lower than market rates, a statutory special pay rates
program allows OPM to approve agency requests for higher rates to
deal with shortages. But there is no parallel process for downward
adjustments to deal with overpaid jobs. Thus the system assures that
the average employee is paid above the market rate for the job.

The present pay system for all white collar occupations is too rigid
to respond effectively to market conditions. The next Administration
thus should seek legislation to permit variations in pay across different
geographical areas. The statutory special rates program should also be
modified to permit pay reductions for specific occupations which are
currently overpaid.

Unlike the General Schedule, the Federal Wage System (FWS) covering blue collar federal workers does reflect local labor market conditions. The government conducts prevailing wage surveys of key blue collar jobs in 135 survey areas, and determines the market rates for these jobs. The rates for other jobs are pegged to a key job. There are, however, a number of serious flaws in this system. Evidence from contracting out studies, where direct comparisons are made with the private sector, suggests strongly that workers in many nonkey jobs, for which no direct wage survey has been conducted, are considerably overpaid. Federal workers also tend to be paid at higher steps within each grade than is the case in the private sector. The Grace Commission calculated that this technicality alone results in federal workers being paid between 8 percent and 12 percent more than their private-sector counterparts. Moreover, FWS wage surveys in a given area may cover only large private-sector firms. Employees in smaller firms, nonprofit firms, and state and local government may be excluded. This results in an upward bias in the estimation of the market wage in the area.

The new Administration should take regulatory and legislative action to reform the system for establishing rates. It should name a task force to reevaluate the pay rates of nonkey jobs. The new Administration also should reform the pay step system so that the average federal employee at each grade level receives the same pay as the average private-sector worker in that occupation at that level. Pay surveys should include a broader array of employers in survey areas.

The new Administration should overhaul federal employees' benefits policy, including health and life insurance, sick leave, and vacation time. Like other employers, the federal government is under constant pressure to expand benefits. It can respond to this pressure in one of two ways. It can retain its current mix of standard benefits and confront an unceasing demand for increased or additional benefits, from child care to long-term care insurance. Or it can establish a "cafeteria" benefits plan, in which each employee can choose a package of benefits within a general allowance of a fixed dollar value. The latter allows the government to be responsive while carefully controlling costs; the former is bound to be highly expensive. The next Administration thus should establish a cafeteria benefits plan. Many private companies have for years offered such plans to employees. Legislation providing for the new plan should set the value of total benefits allotted to employees as a fixed percentage of overall federal pay at the current level. Employees should then be allowed to choose from a wide range of benefit options including converting some of their benefit allocation into higher pay.

Improving Federal Retirement Policy

The Federal Employees Retirement System (FERS) put into effect for new federal employees in 1986 provides a three-part retirement system. First, like almost all other Americans, new federal employees contribute to Social Security and will receive Social Security benefits. Second, new employees will receive pension benefits from a new "basic benefit" retirement plan funded mainly through government contributions. This is a scaled-down version of the older Civil Service Retirement System (CSRS). And third, employees can enroll in an optional "Thrift Plan" retirement fund, which allows employees to invest up to 7 percent of salary, with an equal match of government funds, in a private Individual Retirement Account-style savings plan.

The most objectionable feature of FERS is that the thrift plan funds will be managed by a politically influenced board. Unlike the CSRS, under which employee retirement contributions are spent almost immediately to cover current retirees' annuities, the FERS thrift plan saves and invests employee and government contributions. But in sharp contrast to normal private pension accounts, such as Individual Retirement Accounts or mutual funds, federal employees will have little choice over how their funds are invested. All investment decisions will be controlled by a five-member Federal Retirement Thrift Investment Board. The assets that it manages soon could reach $100 billion. Three Board members are appointed solely by the President and two are appointed by him in consultation with the House and Senate. The Board's chief function is to establish policies for the investment and management of the funds. The board is to be assisted by a 14-member Employee Thrift Advisery Council, comprised of representatives from federal unions and employee organizations, including postal unions, and management groups, and at least one representative from an organization that "promotes the interests of women in government service." Individual federal employees have no choice but to allow these political boards to control their savings.

The new law does include some restrictions to reduce political interference in the thrift fund. But these controls are inherently inadequate; loopholes in any regulatory system inevitably lead to politicized investment decisions. And even the existing meager restrictions can be abolished by a simple majority vote in Congress. As the size of the thrift fund grows, pressures to use the fund politically surely will grow, too. Example: unions and other special interests will be tempted to urge use of the funds for bailing out particular industries; others will seek to use the fund as a base for a national industrial policy. A large politically controlled investment fund also could be used to intimidate corporate America. If the Thrift Board can buy or sell certain stocks to pursue a political or social strategy, it can force the private sector to accede to policies that have not been passed by Congress. The Thrift Board thus should be abolished, and control of thrift plan funds should be decentralized by allowing federal employees to choose freely among a broad spectrum of investments available through IRAs and similar private pension plans.

Federal early retirement policies also should be reformed. One of the major contributing factors to the high cost of the federal retirement system is that it permits federal employees to retire with high benefits, including cost-of-living adjustments (COLAs), at a relatively young 55 years of age after 30 years of service. Retirement so young is virtually unheard of in the private sector. During the Carter Administration, the President's Commission on Pension Policy called for a gradually phased increase of the retirement age to the normal 65. The Reagan Administration has continued these efforts to bring the federal civil service retirement system into line with private-sector practices but for the most part has been stymied by Congress. Recent congressional "reforms" have raised the retirement age for new employees in FERS to age 57 in the year 2222. But this is token change. The new Administration should urge Congress to increase the federal retirement age to 65, effective no later than 1995.

Recruiting Skilled Personnel

In the late 1800s, the federal government replaced the principle of federal employment based on political patronage with the principle of a nonpolitical civil service. Recruitment to the new professional government was to be based not on political affiliation but on merit—the objective skills and abilities of the applicants. From its onset, the idea of a merit-based, nonpolitical civil service was inherently linked to rigorous and objective testing of job seekers—to determine merit and eliminate bias. In 1980, however, the merit system was replaced by a system of implicit racial and ethnic hiring quotas.

Key to the change introduced under Carter was the abolition of the Professional Administrative Career Exam (PACE), an objective test of math, language, and logic skills for individuals seeking professional and managerial positions in the federal government which did not require specialized academic training. Minority groups had sued the Carter Administration, charging that the PACE exam was discriminatory because the proportion of minorities who passed the exam was lower than that of nonminorities who passed. No effort was made by those suing to demonstrate that minority individuals failing the exam were as qualified as nonminorities who passed.

Signing a court consent decree which affirmed the "discriminatory" nature of the PACE, the Carter Justice Department made a legally binding promise to avoid such "discrimination" in the future. In place of objective testing they erected an ad hoc hiring system centered on racial and gender quotas among applicants with minimal academic qualifications. The use of the court-based consent decree to legitimize the abandonment of objective testing has made it difficult for the Reagan Administration to change the policy.

The new Administration should resuscitate interagency negotiations to revise the Uniform Guidelines on Employee Selection Procedures, which control hiring procedures in both the federal government and the private sector. The guidelines should be reformed to establish equal opportunity in hiring based on the merit of individuals, rather than on racial and ethnic quotas. Reforms should include an overhaul of the statistical procedures by which discrimination in hiring is determined.

The OPM should then seek to reintroduce a PACE-type exam test for entry into administrative and professional positions not requiring special academic preparation. The pass level of the test should be set no lower than necessary to assure that there are enough genuinely qualified applicants for the entry jobs available. "Objective" tests with low passing standards circumvent the principle of objective selection of the best job seekers by permitting a continued emphasis on hiring by quota.

Instituting Pay for Performance Management

Unlike the private sector, the federal government tends to base pay increases and promotions on seniority, rather than on good performance. Making matters worse, poor performance tends to be overlooked, as supervisors choose to avoid the lengthy and cumbersome process of the inevitable employee challenges through union grievances, appeals to the Merit Systems Protection Board or the Equal Employment Opportunity Commission, and suits in federal courts. This makes both workers and managers cynical, discourages top performers, and rewards time-servers.

Pay for performance systems are in place for middle- and senior-level managers in government. These allow for substantial performance awards each year for high performers, and provide bonuses for outstanding senior executives. Despite the value and importance of these programs, Congress has resisted Reagan Administration efforts to extend pay-for-performance to nonmanagerial workers. Admittedly, employees under the General Schedule receive within-grade step increases (worth about 3 percent of salary) at scheduled intervals. Each grade has ten steps, allowing for a 30 percent pay range. But over 98 percent of employees obtain their step increases on a normal schedule, making it clear that these near-automatic increases in fact are rewards for seniority, not performance. The next Administration should seek legislation to deal with this problem by creating a universal pay-for-performance system. It should eliminate all automatic within-grade step increases, using those funds strictly for performance increases. Beyond this, it should seek legislation to permit "pay banding," which would join together several consecutive pay levels, thereby permitting an expanded pay range and greater opportunity for pay-for-performance rewards.

Simplifying the Disciplinary and Appeals Process

The federal employee appeals process is an unnecessarily complex and bewildering array of overlapping procedures for resolving job disputes. The result is that it is difficult or impossible to discipline or dismiss unsatisfactory employees.

The process can be simplified and rationalized by enacting four reforms: First, the Merit System Protection Board (MSPB) and the Federal Labor Relations Authority should be combined into a single federal employee appeals panel. This would resolve the conflict and overlap between adjudicating civil service cases and resolving labor management disputes. One agency can adjudicate these cases more quickly and efficiently than two independent bureaucracies.

Second, the Equal Employment Opportunity Commission's (EEOC) role in adjudicating civil service cases that raise civil rights claims should be merged into the new panel. EEOC was established as an enforcement agency, and its role as an adjudicator under the 1978 CSRA is at odds with that purpose. Civil rights claims should be resolved by the combined federal employee appeals panel, with EEOC enjoying the right to seek administrative reconsideration or judicial review of significant discrimination cases.

Third, the new Administration should abolish the special counsel

and transfer all "whistleblower" protection and Hatch Act prosecuto-
rial authority to agency inspectors general. The Hatch Act requires
civil servants not to engage in political activities. The on-site inspectors general are in a far better position than the special counsel to
police the Hatch Act and protect employees.

Fourth, all judicial reviews of federal employee appeal action should
be concentrated in the U.S. Court of Appeals for the Federal Circuit.
Federal workplace disputes raise none of the traditional federalism
issues that warrant district or regional court review. The law of the
federal workplace should be subject to one coherent, unitary interpretation by the courts. The Federal Circuit has performed that task for
most Merit System Protection Board cases for the past six years and is
therefore best positioned to relieve other federal courts of these highly
specialized cases.

Encouraging More Contracting Out

The new President must revive the stalled federal program of contracting with private firms to provide federal services. The federal
government's contracting out efforts have lagged significantly behind
those of the nation's cities and counties. Los Angeles County, for
example, has authorized over 750 service contracts since 1980, saving
Los Angeles taxpayers over $130 million each year. These successes
are duplicated on a smaller scale in hundreds of American cities and
counties. Contracting out at the local level is a bipartisan, good
government issue.

Contracting out has moved far more slowly in the federal government. The main reason is that public-sector unions, whose members
fear layoffs, have used their clout in Congress to gain prohibitions and
restrictions against contracting out. In addition, senior managers and
even political appointees have dragged their feet on the issue—mainly
to avoid confrontation with federal workers. Yet the potential billions
of dollars of cost savings from an expanded federal contracting out
program are well documented.

Under current laws and regulations, many of these cost comparisons
would not result in increased contracting out, even when the private
sector is less costly, because procedures are so biased against the
private sector. A private contractor typically faces a 30 percent price
handicap because various costs are added to the contractor's bid yet
ignored in the government agency cost estimate. Example: A commercial firm's bid must include an allowance for indirect costs, such as
corporate salaries and rent; the agency's need not, although it too

incurs a variety of indirect expenses. The White House should empower OPM with full authority to revise the cost comparison process.

The next Administration should take steps to ease the fear of employees concerning contracting out. One innovative plan to assist government workers affected by contracting out has been developed by the Reagan Administration, but it has never been fully developed or rigorously supported by the White House. Known as the FED CO-OP, it would allow affected federal employees to become stockholders in firms winning federal contracts or even to start their own companies and receive federal contracts.

To make the plan more attractive to government workers, the Administration should request FED CO-OP legislation which would: 1) allow federal employees to receive full value of their stock at any time, rather than having to wait three-to-five years; 2) allow employees to choose to convert some or all of their stock into cash at any time; 3) permit federal employees to participate in proposals to create a FED CO-OP; and 4) provide technical assistance funds to any federal employees willing to establish their own businesses through FED CO-OP. The Administration also must begin to identify specific categories of workers that would be most receptive to FED CO-OP and provide greater inducements for workers to test the program. For instance, OPM should offer an assurance that if these workers fail in their business venture, they will still be guaranteed a job with the federal government.

Privatization opportunities also should be sought within OPM itself. A prime candidate is the retirement claims system. This determines pension benefits for federal retirees, keeps retirement records, and processes monthly annuity checks. The retirement claims process is similar to operations performed by hundreds of insurance companies across the country and thus affords an ideal opportunity for competitive contracting. These private firms tend to be far more efficient than the OPM system. A reason is that private-sector companies are able to boost efficiency by paying employees on the basis of productivity. The federal government cannot do this.

Exposing the Flaws of "Comparable Worth"

Comparable worth is a controversial doctrine that claims that the free market discriminates against workers in traditional female jobs, systematically underpaying them in comparison with workers in traditional male jobs. The solution to this alleged discrimination, according to comparable worth advocates, is to have bureaucracies and the courts determine the "true value" of jobs and then to force employers to pay wages at this value. In effect, this would establish nationwide wage controls, similar to the arbitrary bureaucratic wage setting used in most East European economies. A comparable worth system would require the largest expansion of government economic regulation in U.S. history and would significantly reduce economic growth, thereby lowering the standard of living of American workers.

Comparable worth advocates have chosen an indirect strategy for advancing their policy. They are seeking to impose the comparable worth doctrine first in the public sector, at the state and federal levels. Once established in the public sector, their aim is to expand comparable worth wage controls throughout the economy. Wages set by comparable worth systems are arbitrary, inefficient, and unfair. Imposing comparable worth on the federal workforce would be unjust both to federal workers and taxpayers. Reform of the federal pay system should focus on strengthening rather than removing linkages to marketplace wages.

OPM already has challenged the notion in a study released in September 1987: *Comparable Worth For Federal Jobs—A Wrong Turn Off The Road Towards Pay Equity and Woman's Career Advancement.* This study speaks of a "silent revolution" already taking place among women in the federal workforce, in which women are moving into nontraditional and higher-paying occupations in dramatic numbers. Contrary to the bleak picture painted by comparable worth advocates, the OPM report makes it clear that women, in and out of government, are not being kept in low-paying jobs and denied advancement opportunities. The report reveals the absurdities of the "science" of comparable worth and demonstrates that instituting comparable worth, in fact, would harm rather than help female workers.

Although current research provides no evidence that the free market underpays traditionally female jobs, OPM should undertake further studies to counter the charges of comparable worth advocates. Such new research, however, requires more information than is now contained in OPM's central personnel data file and similar nongovernmental data sources. OPM thus should survey both the governmental and nongovernmental workforce to collect additional information on the legitimate factors which determine male and female pay differences.

Opposing Changes to the Hatch Act

Over 99 percent of the nonmilitary staff of the executive branch are and should remain in the nonpolitical career civil service. Replacing the older spoils system of the late nineteenth century, the merit-based career civil service has rested on two principles: first, federal employment should not be dependent on the outcome of partisan elections, and second, in exchange for immunity to the electoral process, career civil servants must not engage in partisan political activities.

These principles, embodied in the 1939 Hatch Act, in fact have been central to the operation of the American government for nearly a century. Congressional proposals to remove Hatch Act restrictions on the partisan activity of civil servants would destroy the foundation of the nonpolitical civil service, converting federal employees into a super special interest group intervening in elections on behalf of candidates favoring higher pay and expanded government. As long as voters cannot directly remove civil servants from office, civil servants should in turn be limited in their ability to intervene in the electoral process. The new President should continue the Reagan Administration opposition to a change in the Hatch Act.

INITIATIVES FOR 1989

1) Introduce legislation to increase the number of noncareer Senior Executive Service (SES) slots. Political appointees play a vital role within the executive branch, ensuring that the policy orientation of the elected President is reflected in policy development and implementation. They are an indispensable link in the chain of command through which the President controls the permanent bureaucracy; at present the number of political appointees is insufficient to enable them to carry out their crucial functions. Noncareer SES slots now number about 800; they should be expanded to one thousand.

2) Introduce legislation to abolish the FERS thrift board and decentralize control over investment of employee retirement savings. Politicization of the investment of up to $100 billion of federal employee savings does not serve the interest of federal employees and has dangerous long-term implications for the U.S. free-market economy. Under the present centralized structure, political manipulation of these funds is inevitable; control of these monies should be decentralized by giving employees a full range of IRA options. These funds are the property of individual employees, who should be given a free choice over who controls the investment of their savings.

3) Initiate regulatory and legislative reform of the white collar and blue collar pay systems to bring them in line with true private-sector pay

rates. In a market economy, the pay of specific occupations in particular geographic areas is dynamic, adjusting to the pressures of supply and demand. The federal pay system should be reformed to make it more adaptable to changing market conditions and to eliminate practices which result in specific groups of workers being systematically overpaid.

4) Introduce a "cafeteria" plan of benefit options. Legislation should be prepared limiting overall benefits to federal employees to a specific percentage of total payroll costs. Each employee would then be given a benefit allowance of a fixed dollar value and the freedom to choose among a wide variety of benefit options. Allowing employees to choose benefits to meet their individual needs will provide greater employee satisfaction at no greater cost than the current system.

5) Introduce legislation to perfect the FED CO-OP plan. The FED CO-OP plan proposed by the Reagan Administration promises to reduce employee resistance to contracting out by allowing them to benefit financially from the contracting out process. Present legislative restrictions make it difficult for federal employees to become part owners in a contracting firm or to receive cash in lieu of stock. These restrictions should be eliminated.

6) Help executives govern their bureaucracies. Through instruction, example, and exhortation, the OPM Director must ensure that senior political appointees have the understanding and will needed effectively to govern federal bureaucracies. Many political executives in the Reagan Administration failed to use the personnel controls provided by CSRA for the proper management of their agencies. At the beginning of the next Administration, the Director of OPM should conduct biweekly leadership meetings with the Assistant Secretaries of Administration of all departments and agencies to coordinate federal personnel policies throughout the federal government.

19

The United States Postal Service

Thomas M. Lenard*
Task Force Chairman

The United States Postal Service is an independent federal agency. It is also a $40-billion-a-year business that employs 800,000 workers, making it the nation's second largest overall retailer, behind Sears Roebuck, and the third largest employer, behind General Motors and the Pentagon.

The Postal Service was created under the Postal Reorganization Act of 1970 to replace the now-defunct U.S. Post Office Department. This reorganization was intended to depoliticize the nation's mail delivery system by moving its operations out from under the direct control of Congress and the President. USPS, it was said, would operate as an independent, self-sustaining corporation. The National Postal Policy which established the Postal Service defined the Service's primary responsibilities as "to provide postal services to bind the Nation together through personal, educational, literary, and business correspondence of the people. It shall provide prompt, reliable, and efficient services to patrons in all areas and shall render postal services to all communities."

The quality of mail service provided by USPS has come under criticism in recent years for not living up to the promise of being "prompt, reliable, and efficient." Despite dramatic improvements in the nation's transportation and communications networks, the Postal Service acknowledges that mail delivery is a bit slower today than it was in the late 1960s. The productivity growth of its labor force has consistently lagged behind private-sector worker gains, and even may

*Commenting and contributing generously to this chapter were *Mandate III* Task Force Members Congressman Phillip Crane, John Crutcher, Gene Del Polito, Anna Dixon, and Ruth Peters. They do not necessarily endorse all of its views and recommendations.

Task Force Deputy Chairman: Heritage Grover M. Hermann Fellow Stephen Moore.

BUDGET AND PERSONNEL

Postmaster Generals

Anthony M. Frank	1988–present
Preston R. Tisch	1986–1988
Albert V. Casey	1986–1986
Paul N. Carlin	1985–1986
William F. Bolger	1978–1985

Personnel

March 1988	830,537
April 1980	660,998
April 1970	718,517

Operational Budget

Fiscal Year	Total (billions)
1989 Estimate	$37.2
1988 Estimate	$35.7
1987 Actual	$32.1
1986 Actual	$30.7
1985 Actual	$29.2
1980 Actual	$19.6
1970	N.A.

have fallen in recent years. Moreover, the price of a first class postage stamp has risen from 6 cents in 1970 to 25 cents in 1988—a rate of inflation outpacing the consumer price index by 30 percent. The Postal Service's legal monopoly over all domestic first class mail has been estimated to cost consumers and businesses about $6 billion per year.

This disappointing performance should not be surprising. As a government business, shielded from competitive pressures, the Postal Service lacks the incentives to become more efficient that private firms typically face. The challenge for the new Administration thus is to provide USPS with an incentive structure that promotes better service at lower cost.

Mail delivery is an essential component to the nation's communications network and serves as a cornerstone of national commerce. Indeed, over 90 percent of the 150 billion pieces of mail handled by the Postal Service each year are business-related. Hence, an inefficient postal system impedes the competitiveness of American industry. As such, improving Postal Service operations warrants higher priority from the White House than it has received from recent Administrations.

To be sure, the White House has far less clout with USPS—due to the Service's quasi-independent status—than with executive branch agencies or even the independent regulatory agencies. Yet the new President can impose cost efficiencies indirectly upon the postal bureaucracy. His appointments of Postal Governors and Postal Rate Commissioners are of critical importance. Qualified economy-minded proponents of reform, in contrast to those satisfied with the status quo, as have been many Reagan postal appointees, should be selected to push USPS in a market-oriented direction.

Even with all the right people in place, however, the organizational structure of the Postal Board of Governors hinders its ability to reform postal policy. Because of the limited resources at its disposal and its part-time status, the Postal Board of Governors has become virtually a rubber-stamp for postal management, rather than the tough-minded oversight body that it was intended to be. Moreover, the Board consistently buckles to congressional pressures.

To begin reforming the USPS structure, the new President should appoint a Commission to review how the Postal Reorganization Act is working and how the Board of Governors might be restructured to strengthen its oversight capabilities. The Postal Servce has accumulated almost 20 years experience with its current organizational structure; a major review of all aspects of its performance is now in order.

The White House should assemble and actively promote a package of limited reforms to spur competition for some types of mail—such as third class mail—and certain rural areas. USPS should also be required to expand its program of contracting out with the private sector to perform some Postal Service operations. The purpose of these changes would not be to modify seriously the Private Express Statutes, which confer on the Postal Service a statutory monopoly over the category of mail defined as "letters," but to spur improvements in the quality of USPS services.

Most important, perhaps, White House postal appointees must insure that the Postal Service not expand its monopoly into new high-growth communications areas, such as electronic mail, telecommunications, and retail banking. The Postal Service has flirted with moving into these markets—and in the case of electronic mail unsuccessfully has tested the waters. These USPS ventures would go far beyond the agency's mandate and should be expressly prohibited. Nor should USPS be allowed to regulate markets already well served by the private sector—most notably overnight mail and parcel delivery. Private firms should not have to compete against an entity that has the resources of the government behind it.

————————————◇————————————

SUMMARY OF AGENCY FUNCTIONS

When the Postal Service gained independent agency status in 1970, it was for the first time empowered to prepare its own budget, set its own postage rates with the approval of the Board of Governors, bargain collectively with its employees, and make most of its operating decisions as an independent business. The direct role of the President and Congress in dictating the agency's activities was severely curtailed.

Nonetheless, the Postal Service retains important ties to the federal government. The Postal Service and certain categories of mailers— such as the blind, charitable organizations, and libraries—receive annual federal subsidies which must be approved by Congress. These funding strings give congressional committees substantial powers over Postal Service activities. In 1987, for instance, the federal government spent $2.25 billion to fund postal employee retirement and health benefits. Another $650 million was given to the Postal Service as reimbursement for the cost of subsidized mail. This is the so-called revenue-foregone postal subsidy.

The Office of Management and Budget estimates that because USPS borrows funds from the Federal Treasury rather than the private sector, it receives about a $100 million per year subsidy through below-market financing costs for facilities and equipment. USPS is also exempt from paying income and property taxes.

The policies and performance of the Postal Service are developed and monitored by two bodies. These are:

◆ **The Board of Governors**, which acts as the Postal Service's "board of directors." Nine of the Board's eleven members are chosen, with the Senate's advice and consent, by the President for staggered nine-year terms. These nine members choose the postmaster general and the deputy postmaster general, who then become Board members.

A principal Board function is to accept or reject USPS rate hikes. The governors only rarely have disapproved management rate hike requests. The Board of Governors also has veto power over all USPS capital expenditures of more than $10 million.

As the chief executive and operating officers of USPS, the postmaster general and the deputy postmaster general have been delegated broad powers to dictate the course of the agency's operations. They manage day-to-day Postal Service activities and have the authority to hire and fire USPS management.

◆ **The Postal Rate Commission**, which is a five-member independent agency with USPS oversight responsibilities. The Postal Service is required to submit any proposed rate hike to the Postal Rate Commission (PRC) for its review and recommendations. The PRC's recommendations are final unless the Postal Board of Governors votes unanimously to overturn them. The PRC twice rejected the 20-cent stamp, causing the Postal Service to retain the 18-cent stamp throughout 1981. Later it rejected the 23-cent stamp in favor of a 22-cent stamp.

The PRC is also empowered to review any other "changes in the nature of postal services which will generally affect service on a nationwide or substantially nationwide basis." This confers on the PRC substantial, though as yet untapped, influence in shaping the direction and scope of future postal policy. Any attempt by the Postal Service to enter new markets can be vetoed by the PRC. In 1980, for instance, the PRC rejected a Postal Service proposal to move into the telecommunications business.

———————————◇———————————

INSTITUTIONAL CONSTRAINTS

The ability of an Administration to improve the operations of the Postal Service is limited by several factors. First, although many Americans grumble about poor mail service, there continues to be strong support for the concept of universal mail service. Thus any proposal to change the basic structure of the USPS tends to be resisted by the vast majority of the American people.

A second constraint in promoting a reform agenda is the Private Express Statutes. These statutes, enacted in the 1840s, confer on the USPS a legal monopoly of "letter" mail. Many USPS problems can be tracked to this monopoly power. Overturning these statutes would be desirable, since it would lead to healthy competition; in the current political environment, however, it would be almost impossible. With these laws firmly in place, reform of the Postal Service can only occur incrementally.

A third barrier to reform is that the Postal Service, perhaps more than any other agency, is composed of politically powerful interest groups hostile to change. The agency's 800,000 workers and 25,000 postal managers exert enormous influence on Capitol Hill. Legislators are very hesitant to upset the postal unions, whose members live in every congressional district in the country.

Another obstacle to reform is Congress itself. Although the Postal Reform Act was designed to remove politics from USPS operations, congressional interference has increased steadily. Almost no major management decision is made at USPS without the consent of the House and Senate Postal Service oversight committees.

———————————◇———————————

THE REAGAN ADMINISTRATION RECORD

The Reagan Administration has treated the Postal Service with benign neglect. During the Reagan years, almost nothing has changed at the Postal Service except that it has grown substantially larger. Until about 1986, the White House's primary concern was that the Postal Service's impact on the federal budget be minimized. This narrow focus, which ignored the overall costs to the U.S. economy of an inefficient postal monopoly, remained unaltered until the middle of Reagan's second term, when the Administration began to endorse increased competition in mail delivery.

Making matters worse, Reagan Administration appointees to the Board of Governors routinely and openly have impeded the White House agenda. They have failed to comply with the Administration's request that USPS curtail its debt-financed capital investment plan. They consistently have supported moving USPS off budget, despite the Administration's opposition. And the Postmasters General whom they have appointed routinely testify before congressional committees against the Administration's postal policies.

In defiance of the Reagan Administration's stated priority of finding private firms to provide public services, the USPS has resisted contracting out its services. In fiscal 1987, USPS contracted out only about 10 percent of its activities, or $4.5 billion worth. Almost all of these contracting activities began before Reagan took office.

Most telling, perhaps, is that Postal Service management during this decade has caved in to virtually every demand of the Postal Service unions. Economic studies consistently document that the average postal employee salary exceeds that of equally skilled workers elsewhere by more than 20 percent. With benefits, the typical postal worker makes over $17 an hour. It is no wonder that a postal union official boasted after the last collective bargaining agreement that "We made out like bandits." These hefty pay raises were awarded when USPS worker annual productivity rate gains lagged far behind those of the private-sector, blue-collar labor force.

The Postal Service also has made some very expensive business mistakes in the 1980s. USPS reportedly lost $25 million on its "Zip + 4" program in 1982, because it had not yet purchased the proper sorting equipment. Even worse was the Postal Service's ill-fated 1982 venture into the electronic mail market, or "ECOM." When the experiment was abandoned in 1985, ECOM was losing over $1 for every letter it sent. When private firms make mistakes of this type, their stockholders bear the losses. When the Postal Service errs, mailers absorb the losses.

Only in a few areas has the USPS record been bright during the Reagan years. Most significant is the program of converting surplus USPS buildings in central business districts to their "highest and best use." Since 1981 the Postal Service has leased or sold buildings and air rights in 12 cities, including New Orleans, New York, and San Francisco. In New York's Grand Central Station Office, the Postal Service will occupy 150,000 square feet, while private developers will lease one million square feet of some of the world's most valuable and costly real estate. These ventures earn the Postal Service $60 million annually, with billions of dollars more forecast over the lifetime of these contracts. This sound business practice should be continued and encouraged.

Although the USPS Board of Governors has balked at fundamental postal reforms, other Reagan Administration officials sparked a serious and healthy public debate over the Service's future direction. Office of Management and Budget director James Miller, Federal Trade Commission Chairman Daniel Oliver, and Council of Economic Advisers member Thomas Gale Moore have urged that the Postal Service's monopoly grip on the mail industry be loosened. These efforts, when coupled with rising consumer frustration with USPS, have changed the tone of the debate on the Postal Service. Even the liberal-leaning *New Republic* admitted in April 1988: "This time the Reaganites are right. Monopoly has been a bad thing for the U.S. mail." A *New York Times* editorial took a similar position: "Experience over 15 years, shows

that mail delivery is most efficient where government does the least
and where services are set by competition.''

THE NEXT FOUR YEARS

The American public has grown increasingly frustrated with the
severe problems confronting the nation's mail delivery system.
Postal Service prices have been accelerating 30 percent faster than
inflation for two decades, and the price of a first class stamp is expected
to rise to 30 cents by the end of the decade. Meanwhile, mail delivery
is about 10 percent slower today than it was in the late 1960s.

A White House suggestion to repeal the Private Express Statutes,
however, is sure to mobilize opposition and doom all other achievable
attempts at postal reform. Indeed, pushing even moderate postal
reform likely will ignite fierce political resistance. In particular, the
postal unions and Congress are likely to unite in opposition to any
White House postal policy that would weaken their grip on USPS
activities.

The top Postal Service priority of the new Administration should be
to push for a more competitive, proconsumer market for mail service.
The White House Domestic Policy Council should endorse expanded
competition in mail as a means of spurring improvements in the quality
of USPS's service performance and promoting greater consumer
choice.

Consumers have benefited enormously from competition in limited
service areas, including overnight mail and parcel delivery. This competition has been introduced without ''skimming the cream'' of USPS's
monopolized first class mail service. Moreover, private companies,
such as Federal Express, have demonstrated that, like the Postal
Service, they too will deliver packages anywhere in the U.S. at
affordable prices. Hence, competition has not impaired the universal
system of mail delivery, as is often predicted by the postal bureaucracy, but rather enhanced it.

Recognizing the Importance of Postal Appointments

Past Presidents almost uniformly have overlooked the vital role that
their postal appointees can play in steering USPS policy. Although in
practice postal management has assumed nearly unchecked control
over day-to-day postal decisions in recent years, the Board of Gover-

nors, if it chooses to assert it, has legal oversight responsibilities covering most postal activities.

A number of qualifications should be examined in evaluating prospective appointees for the Board of Governors. Management experience in directing large multiproduct firms is certainly important. Appointees collectively should also understand transportation needs, real estate management, financial management, industrial automation, labor-management relations, collective bargaining, and retail service operations—all of which reflect various aspects of the business of running the nation's postal system. The frustrating experience with Reagan appointees has indicated, however, that although a sound business background is highly desirable, it is not sufficient to ensure that the appointees will be sympathetic to reform. Equally important is that the selected individuals be receptive to procompetitive changes and politically sophisticated, for their job is inherently political.

Restructuring the Board of Governors

The 1970 Postal Reorganization Act envisioned the Postal Board of Governors as an external control over the activities and decisions of postal management. Yet the Board of Governors has proved itself woefully reluctant to exercise oversight. Instead the Board has become a rubber-stamp for postal management decisions, approving over 95 percent of management requests brought before it. The Board's agenda, for example, is set by postal management. The most critical management decisions are typically made by the Postmaster General without even requesting Board approval. For instance, in early 1988, when the Postal Service closed window hours by half a day a week at local post offices and ended Sunday mail collections, the Board was never consulted.

For the Board of Governors seriously to challenge Postal Service policies, the Board's organizational structure must change. One problem is the Board's staff; it is so minuscule that the Board is dependent entirely upon postal management for information and analysis. Another problem is that the Board meets only two half-days a month; Governors thus lack the expertise and resources to challenge postal management decisions effectively.

To remedy this, the Board of Governors should vote itself funds for a full-time professional staff independent of USPS management. The Board should have an independent counsel. It also should create two semipermanent committees. The first should be a Capital Investment Committee to investigate all planned USPS capital purchases and real estate investments. The second should be an Efficiency and Rates Committee to examine all rate requests, labor agreements, productivity changes, and progress on cost control. These committees would enable the Board of Governors to monitor the operations of the postal system and to scrutinize more closely and objectively USPS management.

Forging a New Labor Policy

The 1970 Postal Reorganization Act gives postal workers the right to bargain collectively with postal management. The result: management buys labor peace by offering high wage rates and agreeing to intrusive work rules even though they impede productivity. For instance, after the General Accounting Office reported in 1982 that USPS could save about $100 million per year by contracting out janitorial service, postal management bowed to a union demand that the agency not contract out this activity.

There is, after all, no incentive for management to resist union pressures. Both the unions and management know that higher labor costs can easily be passed through to postal rate payers, who have almost no alternative to using the Postal Service. The problem is that the mailing public is not represented at the bargaining table. As a result, postal managers have no incentive to take a tough stand against the postal unions and thereby reduce operating costs. Management never has been held accountable for its repeated failure to win even minor union concessions. (And in the rare instances when postal management does get tough with the unions, Congress intervenes on behalf of the workers, as it did in 1984 when Postmaster General William Bolger tried to establish lower wages for new hires.)

Postal management now must draw the line on labor policy. Since 80 percent of USPS expenses are labor-related, cutting costs depends mainly on negotiating work rule changes and more reasonable wage rates. This requires the Board of Governors to become involved actively in the bargaining process. It also requires resolve to reject any management-labor agreement that fails to protect the interests of the rate-paying public.

The Postal Service is required by law only to pay wage rates "comparable to the rates and types of compensation paid in the private sector." It is not required to pay workers the 20 percent premium they now receive. While the wages of the current workforce cannot be rolled back, postal management should hold these workers' cost of living adjustments (COLAs) to the inflation rate.

The postal service does not need to pay new workers the excessive existing pay scales in order to attract a sufficient number of new workers. Each year USPS hires about 45,000 new workers. Postal management should negotiate a permanent two-tier wage structure paying new hires wages comparable to those earned by private-sector blue collar workers. In 1984 the Postal Service wisely introduced a form of two-tier wage structure. Under this arrangement, all new hires receive slightly lower wage rates than existing workers; this lower wage scale for new employees is brought up to parity with old hires in about two years of postal employment. Building on this, USPS should negotiate permanently lower wage scales for new hires.

The most severe problem plaguing the Postal Service, however, has not been high wage rates, but worker productivity that continually lags behind the private sector. Several observers, including Postal Rate Commission Vice Chairman Patti Birge Tyson, believe that Postal Service productivity actually has declined in recent years. To provide incentives to reverse these declines in worker output, the Postal Service should build into its wage structure a pay-for-productivity incentive. The annual increase in pay should depend upon the previous year's overall worker productivity gains.

A related problem is Postal management's tendency to bargain away such key managerial prerogatives as the freedom to contract out services and the right to hire part-time workers. USPS is prohibited from hiring more than 5 percent of its workers part time. Yet, pay rates for temporary workers average about $6.00 per hour—less than one-third the hourly wage rate for full-time regular workers. Such work rules drive up USPS costs and should be rescinded during the next round of labor negotiations.

Encouraging Competition in Mail Delivery

Despite the Postal Service's statutory monopoly on the delivery of letters, the agency today faces competition from the private sector in such fringe activities as parcel delivery and overnight mail. Indeed, USPS estimates that more than 40 percent of its overall mail volume and 20 percent of its revenues are subject to competition from private companies. Of course, the first class mail market is controlled entirely by the Postal Service.

Allowing private sector competition in selected areas would benefit consumers through lower prices and improved service, forcing the Postal Service to become more efficient in its own operations as it struggles to retain its market share. The Postal Service's 1988 rate change proposal, for instance, contained price increase requests for its monopolized first and third class mail markets, while suggesting about a 10 percent decrease in prices for its overnight Express Mail, where private alternatives are available. The Postal Service has not reduced the cost of a first class stamp since 1919.

Even in those areas where USPS jealously guards its monopoly status, the agency contracts with private businesses for a wide range of functions. Private truckers, railways, and airlines, for example, carry virtually all interstate mail. Retail functions, such as selling stamps and weighing packages at 4,000 local post offices, are done by private firms under contract to the USPS. Mail on more than 4,500 rural routes is delivered by private "star route carriers." These are private citizens who contract with USPS to pick up mail at the local post office and deliver it to rural homes in their own cars or trucks. Contracting out rural delivery in fact costs the mailing public about 33 percent less than when the Postal Service handles these deliveries itself.

Despite the documented success of private-sector participation in the mail industry, the Postal Service has restricted its growth. This resistance has been so intense that when Congress trimmed the USPS budget slightly in 1988, postal management chose to cut window hours at local post offices and discontinue Sunday collections rather than absorb the cuts, with minimal service disruptions, by expanding its arrangements with private firms.

To begin to expand competition in mail delivery, limits should be set on the scope of the USPS monopoly. The USPS currently construes the meaning of a "letter" broadly enough to include advertising flyers (if they are addressed), posters, and computer tapes. The new President must pressure the Postal Service to adopt a more reasonable definition of a letter. To accomplish this, the White House should issue regulatory briefings to the Postal Rate Commission, or the President could even instruct the attorney general to issue a legal interpretation of the monopoly laws.

A fair definition of a letter surely should cover all first class mail and thus not threaten the core existence of the Postal Service. In other areas, however, the term should be defined nearer to everyday usage. In particular, advertising matter and electronic mail should not be defined as a letter, which would not bar the Postal Service from continuing to deliver this type of mail; it simply would prevent USPS from having a monopoly and would allow private firms to compete in these categories of mail delivery as they do in parcel delivery.

A strong case can be made for exempting advertising matter from the Private Express Statutes. Very few Americans would consider a sale flyer from the local supermarket a letter. More important, the Postal Service has poorly served this market. The Third Class Mail Association has found that about 70 percent of third class mail is delivered late, and between 3 percent and 15 percent is not delivered at all.

USPS is not unalterably opposed to private firms delivering advertising mail. In fact, after Congress cut back federal subsidies to USPS in 1987, the agency threatened to stop accepting third class mail to control costs. Permitting third class mail delivery competition would benefit consumers by freeing up Postal Service resources for its primary task of providing first class service for first class mail.

Restrictions on private delivery of "urgent" or overnight mail should also be loosened. Regulations now require private couriers, such as DHL Worldwide Express and Federal Express Corporation, to charge at least $3 or double the first class postage, whichever is higher, for overnight mail. This ostensibly is to stop the private sector from "skimming the cream" off the first class mail market. Yet the Air Courier Conference of America, a trade association representing private letter carriers, correctly criticizes the double postage requirement as "regulatory overkill." A more reasonable restriction, such as one and a half times the first class postage, should be imposed.

About 40 percent of today's mail volume, some 60 billion pieces a year, is presorted by private firms. This eases the Postal Service work load and lowers business mailing costs. Yet the USPS management has been lobbying to reduce the 4-cent-per-letter discount for presorted mail. Lowering the discount would, of course, reduce the incentive for private firms to sort the mail. As a result, much mail sorting would go back into the agency's hands. Since predating has both lowered business mailing costs while allowing the postal service to devote more of its personnel to delivering the mail on time, the Postal Rate Commission should not allow the Postal Service to lower the presort discount.

Postal Service retail functions encompass all of the window services provided at local post offices. As an experiment, in about 7,000 small towns, USPS should contract with department and convenience stores—such as Sears or Seven-Eleven—to sell stamps, determine postage amounts, accept packages, and collect mail. This would offer greater customer convenience and save the Postal Service an estimated $90 million a year. Postmaster General Anthony Frank wants to expand the USPS program that allows stores to sell postage stamps on consignment. This is a small step in the right direction.

Mail processing too can be handled by the private sector. Rather than spend the hundreds of millions of dollars that it plans on constructing new mail processing centers and automated sorting equipment, the USPS Board of Governors should contract out sorting and processing in these locations.

The extremely successful and venerable program of contracting out with private citizens to deliver mail on rural routes should be expanded. By contracting out with star route carriers to serve an additional 10 percent of rural routes, the Postal Service could save about $50 million per year.

As the Postal Service increases its contracting out initiatives, it should offer Postal Service workers the opportunity to provide functions for the Postal Service under contract by forming their own companies. Postal workers should be given the right to bid on all contracts issued by USPS, and the Postal Service should offer to transfer USPS assets over to the workers forming private companies. USPS should honor the accumulated pension benefits of any postal workers choosing the privatization option.

Under current law, private letter carriers are prohibited from depositing any item in a household's mailbox if it does not have U.S. postage affixed to it. This prohibition inhibits private-sector competition with the Postal Service for the delivery of types of mail not covered by the Private Express Statutes. It also fundamentally infringes on the property rights of citizens, since the mailbox belongs to the property owner, not the Postal Service. If homeowners wish to restrict their mailboxes to USPS, they can do so by posting an appropriate notice. The Justice Department should be requested to rule on this, or the Postal Rate Commission should be urged to challenge its legitimacy.

Controlling Postal Service Debt

Postal Service borrowing for capital expenditures has been rising dramatically. Its outstanding debt has climbed from $1.4 billion in 1983 to over $7 billion expected in 1989. Several members of Congress wish to raise the Postal Service's $10 billion debt ceiling to $30 billion.

This rapid accumulation of Postal Service debt is counter to the interest of mailers and federal taxpayers. Unlike its private-sector rivals, which must borrow from commercial banks at market interest rates, the Postal Service borrows from the federal financing bank at taxpayer-subsidized interest rates. The Office of Management and Budget complains that "postal borrowing competes with other Treasury borrowing and crowds out or raises rates for other private sector borrowers.'' Moreover, about half of all postal borrowing finances the construction of new postal facilities, most of which are unnecessary. USPS should not be acquiring new property and equipment for mail processing, for instance, but rather should contract out this activity.

To restrain the growth of the USPS debt and promote contracting out, the Postal Board of Governors should impose a moratorium on all new USPS capital construction. At a minimum, the Governors should require USPS to conduct a contracting out feasibility study to determine whether it would be more efficient for the Postal Service to contract with a private firm to perform a service, rather than build a new facility to provide the service. The White House should oppose and veto any legislation raising the USPS debt ceiling above its current $10 billion level.

Measuring Postal Service Performance

The Postal Service lacks credible measurement of how long it takes to deliver a letter. Although the Postal Service boasts that it meets its delivery standards 95 percent of the time, virtually every private-sector test of the Postal Service's delivery record, including those conducted by the *New York Times*, the *Miami News*, *Time* magazine, *Readers Digest*, and American Express, has revealed a much less reliable on-time delivery rate. Similarly, the Postal Service consistently claims productivity improvements; most independent assessments find otherwise. The lack of a credible performance measurement system impedes management efforts to improve overall postal efficiency and productivity.

The Postal Service uses an in-house monitoring system called Origin Destination Information System (ODIS) to measure delivery performance. The General Accounting Office has discovered ''weaknesses in ODIS local statistics'' and condemned the overall data as ''questionable.'' At its best, ODIS merely measures the time that mail is in transit between an originating facility where the stamp is canceled and a destination distribution center. ODIS does not measure what mailers are most interested in: the time it takes for a piece of mail to travel from a collection box to the destination mailbox. The Postal Board of Governors should retain a private-sector firm to monitor USPS compliance with its delivery standards.

Unlike most other federal agency inspectors general, the chief postal inspector is not appointed by the President, but rather is selected by and serves at the pleasure of postal management. According to the General Accounting Office, this conflict of interest understandably

"leads to questions about the Inspection Service's independence."
The Postal Board of Governors should request from Congress the
authority to place the Postal Inspection Service under its authority, to
insure that postal management does not interfere with its investigations.

Identifying the Budget Impact of the Postal
Service Subsidies

In fiscal 1987, federal subsidies to USPS totaled $2.9 billion. Over
$2 billion of this went to the postal employees' retirement and health
benefit programs. Given the high wages of the postal workforce,
taxpayer-subsidized fringe benefits are unwarranted. Also unjustified
are "revenue-foregone" subsidies to the Postal Service. These subsidies are ostensibly to allow USPS to charge low rates for the distribution of educational materials. Mass mailings by nonprofit groups should
not be partially paid for with federal tax dollars. The new President's
budget plan should recommend termination of these subsidies.

Efforts by some in Congress to move the Postal Service subsidies
off budget is an attempt to immunize the agency from federal budget
control and cuts. This would be bad public policy. The reason for
moving USPS on budget in 1985 was to give Congress a global view of
the federal budget, thus allowing it to set spending priorities. Moving
agencies off budget interferes with establishing priorities for federal
programs.

Postal Service subsidies have the same impact on the federal budget
deficit as do Pentagon spending and welfare programs. Moving federal
payments to USPS off budget is an accounting gimmick that disguises,
but does not alter, the economic impact of these subsidies. As Congress and the President struggle to control federal spending, they
should be promoting the principle of truth in budgeting. The good
government position therefore is to keep USPS subsidies on budget.

Preparing the Postal Service for the Future

A principal challenge facing the new President and his Postal Service
appointees is to block USPS efforts to expand the boundaries of its
monopoly. USPS should not be permitted to enter new areas of
communications capably handled by the private sector.

The Board of Governors should prohibit USPS from entering intra-
corporate communications, retail banking services, envelope and publications sales, and electronic mail markets. The explosive growth of

electronic communications—including facsimile transmissions and computer-based message services—has created a viable indirect competitor to hard-copy first class mail. These markets' growth potential is sure to be jeopardized if they are brought under the USPS protective monopoly. This can best be prevented by keeping the Postal Service out of such markets entirely.

$$\diamond$$

INITIATIVES FOR 1989

1) Appoint reform-minded postal officials. Both the Postal Rate Commission and, to an even greater degree, the Board of Governors, have failed to exhibit the political skill and determination to force change upon the Postal Service. The new President should begin the process of reform by appointing reform-minded, economically and politically sophisticated Americans to the Board of Governors and the Postal Rate Commission.

2) Appoint a presidential commission to assess postal performance since reorganization. Nearly two decades have passed since the Postal Reorganization Act. The new Postal Service was intended to behave as a business enterprise, free from political constraints. To determine whether the Postal Reorganization Act has accomplished what it intended, the new President should appoint a commission to review USPS performance and suggest structural changes to improve postal service. It should explore such issues as whether postal efficiency has improved or deteriorated since 1970, whether the Postal Board of Governors and the Postal Rate Commission need to be strengthened, and whether congressional meddling in postal affairs—on the rise in recent years—has impeded postal reform.

3) Give the Postal Board of Governors an independent full-time staff. The Postal Board of Governors faces institutional constraints that prevent it from acting as the independent oversight committee it was intended to be. With almost no staff or resources, the Board depends entirely on postal management for information and advice. Not surprisingly, it never says "no" to postal managers. A full-time staff would enable the Board to assess USPS performance and policy objectively and independently.

4) Establish a two-tier wage scale. Postal management must ensure that wage rates offered to all new postal employees are competitive with those of private-sector workers. The Office of Management and Budget has estimated that paying all newly hired workers private-sector wage rates, rather than the 20 percent premium now paid, while paying existing workers at the current scale, would save the Postal Service $300 million a year initially and up to $3.5 billion a year eventually. This two-tier wage structure has become an increasingly common feature of private-sector collective bargaining arrangements. The USPS Board of Governors should press management to negotiate a two-tier wage scale during the next round of labor negotiations.

5) Negotiate fundamental work rule changes. The USPS is riddled with inefficient labor practices that lead to costly inefficiency. One indefensible rule is a tight limit on part-time employees. This means that many full-time workers often must be paid at times of day or year when there is no work for them to do. Private firms would use part-time employees for such positions. Thus the ceiling on USPS use of part-time labor should be raised from 5 percent to 15 percent, saving USPS up to $2 billion per year, or about 2 cents on the cost of mailing a first class letter. Many of the agency's chief rivals, such as United Parcel Service, rely heavily on part-time labor—particularly during peak mailing seasons—to hold down costs to consumers.

6) Experiment with wide use of private carriers in rural areas. The Postal Service subsidizes mail delivery in rural areas through the profits it earns from delivery of mail in high-density geographical areas. Rural delivery is the least profitable portion of the national mail system and yields none of the "cream" that the Postal Service is fearful of losing to competitors. Moreover, the Postal Service already contracts with private carriers on thousands of these rural routes. If private firms can serve this market more efficiently than the Postal Service, they should be allowed to do so. Thus private carriers automatically should be used to deliver mail in rural areas whenever they can do so less expensively than USPS staff.

7) Loosen restrictions on private delivery of advertising mail and urgent mail. Limiting competition in third class mail and urgent mail has benefited consumers. The new Administration should promote the concept of loosening remaining pricing and entry restrictions on these markets.

8) Expand contracting out postal activities to reduce mailing costs. The Postal Board of Governors should press USPS management to expand its reliance on the private sector for such activities as retail services, rural delivery, and mail processing. Past USPS experience with contracting out has cut costs. In mail processing, the Postal Service could contract with private firms to sort mail in a dozen cities in which mail volume is increasing. These "demonstration projects" could test the feasibility of contracting out mail processing on a wide scale.

9) Create an independent mail monitoring system. USPS has a clear conflict of interest in monitoring itself. To end this, the Board of Governors should hire private auditors to monitor mail delivery standards. Several private mail monitoring firms already exist.

10) Keep the Postal Service on budget. The postal unions launched a campaign in 1988 to remove the Postal Service from the unified federal budget. Their aim: make the USPS no longer subject to budget constraints to meet federal deficit reduction targets. Yet, given the monopoly status of the Postal Service, such budget pressure is virtually the only method available to force postal management to trim costs. Removing the USPS from the budget essentially would remove its finances from public scrutiny. Thus the new President should veto any legislation moving USPS subsidies off budget.

11) Prohibit the Postal Service from entering new and developing communications markets. No public interest is served by the USPS expanding the scope of its operations. Indeed, the USPS no doubt would use access to new markets to engage in unfair, subsidized competition at taxpayer expense. The Board of Governors should prohibit new postal service ventures into developing markets that are served well by the private sector. The Governors should insist that Postal Service management expend its resources improving first class mail standards.

20

Independent Regulatory Agencies

Much of the responsibility for administering and enforcing federal regulatory laws falls to agencies outside the orthodox Cabinet departments. Known generically as "independent regulatory agencies," these agencies, although constitutionally part of the executive branch, are not under the direct control of the President. For this reason, they are sometimes referred to as a "fourth branch" of government.

Altogether, there are over a dozen such regulatory agencies in the federal government, ranging from the 100–year-old Interstate Commerce Commission to the Consumer Product Safety Commission, created in 1973. Usually these agencies are administered by several commissioners appointed by the President for fixed terms of office. The chairman of each commission is usually chosen by the President from among the commissioners. The commissioners cannot be removed by the President before their terms expire, except for good cause. And because their terms are staggered, it takes several years for a new President to appoint a majority of a commission's members.

Nevertheless, through the appointment process, a President can affect substantially the policy direction of these agencies. In fact, during the Reagan years, the independent commissions have been among the most dedicated and most successful advocates of the Reagan Administration's free-market agenda.

Because the work of these agencies often overlaps that of executive branch departments, the activities of many of these agencies are briefly discussed elsewhere in this volume. For example, the Interstate Commerce Commission and Federal Maritime Commission are discussed under the Department of Transportation; the Nuclear Regulatory Commission is discussed under the Department of Energy; the National Labor Relations Board under the Department of Labor; and the International Trade Commission under the Commerce Department. Other important commissions include the Federal Communications Commission, the Federal Trade Commission, and the Securities and Exchange Commission, and they are discussed below.

BUDGET AND PERSONNEL

Personnel

Year	FCC	FTC	SEC	TOTAL
1988	1,856	1,036	2,050	4,942
1980	2,228	1,859	2,080	5,167
1970	1,518	1,272	1,386	4,176

Budget Outlays (millions)

Fiscal Year	FCC	FTC	SEC	TOTAL
1989 Estimate	$105	$67	$160	$332
1988 Estimate	$102	$66	$135	$303
1987 Actual	$ 87	$66	$112	$275
1986 Actual	$ 92	$62	$106	$260
1985 Actual	$ 94	$65	$106	$265
1984 Actual	$ 87	$66	$ 94	$247
1983 Actual	$ 82	$65	$ 90	$237
1982 Actual	$ 80	$68	$ 83	$231
1981 Actual	$ 81	$71	$ 89	$241
1980 Actual	$ 76	$69	$ 73	$218
1970 Actual	$ 24	$20	$ 24	$ 64

The Federal Communications Commission

William A. Russell, Jr.*
Task Force Chairman

Although a relatively small agency of the federal government with a budget of only $97 million and a staff of 1,800, the Federal Communications Commission (FCC) regulates the fastest growing industrial and service sector of the U.S. economy. Led by Chairman Mark Fowler until 1987, and then by Dennis Patrick, the FCC has done more than almost any other federal agency or department to translate Reagan principles into policy, substantially deregulating the communications industry—often over vociferous congressional opposition. While much more remains to be done, the FCC is a case study of how policy can be reformed.

---◇---

SUMMARY OF AGENCY FUNCTIONS

Established by the Communications Act of 1934, the FCC is an independent agency charged with regulating interstate and international communications by cable, radio, satellite, television, and wire. This includes allocating spectrum frequencies to various users, regulating the licenses of these frequencies, and regulating interstate rates and service of common carriers, such as telephone companies. The agency is directed by a five-member Commission nominated by the President and confirmed by the Senate for staggered five-year terms. The chairman is designated by the President. FCC's primary operational areas are divided among four bureaus: Mass Media, with authority over broadcast issues; Common Carrier, which covers telephone and other common carrier issues; Private Radio, which regulates activities of licensees in areas such as cellular radio and CB radio; and

---

*Task Force Deputy Chairman: Heritage McKenna Senior Policy Analyst James Gattuso.

Field Operations, which investigates technical problems and enforces Commission operating rules.

———————————◇———————————

INSTITUTIONAL CONSTRAINTS

The Commission regulates some of America's most politically powerful companies—including the national television networks, local broadcasters, movie producers, and local and long-distance telecommunications companies. These client groups frequently compete fiercely with each other and thus try to exert strong pressure on the FCC for favorable rulings and regulation. The competing commercial interests try to influence FCC action through complaints and petitions to the Commission, lobbying Congress, and direct litigation in court. The Senate Commerce, Science, and Transportation Committee and the House Energy and Commerce Committee oversee the FCC and can constrain its decisions through legislative action. The leadership of these committees generally has opposed rigorous deregulation. In addition, the FCC itself often is divided, thanks to the naturally competing interests of five independent commissioners. And under a weak chairman, the Commission staff can be a major factor in the decision-making process. Because of the volume of work and the technical complexity of the issues, the commissioners can often be heavily influenced by the presentation and policy recommendation of the staff, particularly the bureau chiefs.

———————————◇———————————

THE REAGAN ADMINISTRATION RECORD

The FCC consistently and successfully has carried out the Reagan goal of freeing markets through deregulation. This success provides a particularly valuable lesson, not so much because of what has been achieved, as how. From the time he assumed the FCC chairmanship, Mark Fowler had a clear agenda because of his strong personal commitment to free markets and to deregulation. Immediately after being nominated as chairman, Fowler established five general objectives for all FCC actions to serve. They were: 1) creation, to the maximum extent possible, of an unregulated competitive marketplace environment for telecommunications, both to foster industry growth and to improve service to the user; 2) elimination of unnecessary regulations and policies to reduce costs and spur competition; 3) assurance that the public receives service as quickly and efficiently as possible; 4) coordination and planning of international communications to further international commerce and national defense; and 5) elimination of government action infringing on the freedom of speech and the press.

The five Fowler objectives, which were entirely consistent with the Reagan agenda, became the basis for an agency-wide "management by objective" system that directly affected policy and performance. All proposals presented to the commissioners had to include an explanation of how each furthered one or more of the agency objectives. Fowler sought to draw the FCC's career staff into this strategy. He believed wisely that the federal civil servant will carry out a program if it is properly explained and not unfair to the employee and if career rewards are tied directly to fair reviews.

Many of the Commission's decisions, of course, still faced substantial opposition from client groups and Congress. Fowler sought to offset this by encouraging potential beneficiaries to voice their support and by skillfully articulating proposals to the public. While pushing for major changes in policy, moreover, he understood when to compromise to placate opponents and at the same time to make some progress. Through timely compromises, federal communication policies were changed substantially, while potential legislation by Congress to override the Commission and enact stricter rules was forestalled.

Among the FCC's successes: The "fairness doctrine," which discouraged broadcasters from airing controversial programs, was repealed; competition in broadcasting has been heightened by opening the broadcast spectrum for low-power television, direct broadcast satellites, and 700 new FM stations. Government interference in the content of programming was also reduced by removal of many regulations.

The FCC also scored major achievements in the common carrier area. In the wake of the divestiture of local telephone companies from the American Telegraph and Telephone Co. (AT&T), for instance, long-distance telephone rates were restructured, so that local telephone rates would no longer be subsidized by long-distance charges.

───────────────◇───────────────

THE NEXT FOUR YEARS

The challenge for the FCC under the next Administration must be to expand upon the procompetitive, free-market principles of the

Fowler and Patrick years. The FCC must continue to lift the regulatory burden of the communications industry by easing the rules restricting the economic activities of firms and lifting rules on both what and how broadcasters communicate to the public. Some regulation, of course, is necessary in this area—for instance, the FCC must prevent individuals from interfering with the use of particular broadcast frequencies. But to the greatest degree possible, the Commission should strive toward a communications industry in which economic decisions—and decisions on what to broadcast to the public—are made by consumers and citizens, not by the government.

Freeing the Baby Bells

To further increase competition, the FCC should seek legislation to remove the court-imposed restrictions from the regional Bell operating companies (BOCs or Baby Bells). These restrictions, imposed under a federal judge's consent decree breaking up the AT&T Bell system, prevent the BOCs from entering many service areas, such as providing telephone equipment or computer information services. By barring such major U.S. firms from these growing markets, these restrictions limit competition and seriously could threaten U.S. international competitiveness in telecommunications, computer sciences, banking, securities marketing, and other areas. Court-imposed restrictions on telephone company provision of cable television services also should be removed to increase competition.

Increasing Cable TV Options

Current rules bar telephone companies from transmitting cable television signals on the new fiber-optic transmission systems increasingly used by telephone companies. As the use of fiber-optics grows, U.S. households may potentially find themselves deprived of the choice of receiving cable TV via their phone lines. Consumers would be limited to their local cable TV firm, which almost always has a monopoly. The FCC should act to repeal its rules barring this service and urge the courts and Congress, if necessary, to remove the legal bars they have imposed on such activity.

Auctioning Radio Frequencies

One of the FCC's most basic responsibilities is the assignment of radio spectrum frequencies to users. While most such frequencies already have been assigned to licensees, many of importance—including some of those for microwave transmission (used for pay television, among other things), cellular mobile radio (for car phones), and low-power television—remain unassigned. Most unassigned frequencies are assigned through lotteries. This has not worked well. Potential licensees spend thousands of dollars filing numerous applications for more frequencies than they can use, simply to increase their chances of winning the number they want. Worse, many applicants never use the licenses they win; they simply sell the frequencies to the eventual user after they are assigned, gaining an immediate windfall for themselves while the taxpayer receives nothing.

The lottery method should be replaced by auctions, in which frequencies are assigned to the highest bidder and the payments to the U.S. Treasury. This would grant the frequencies to those who value them the most without the need for a lottery, while the federal government could earn as much as $300 million per year.

Simplifying the Renewal Process

The FCC should simplify the renewal process for broadcast licenses. Television broadcasters must apply for renewal of their licenses every five years; radio broadcasters must apply every seven years. While such renewals are almost always granted, the procedure can be long and costly, especially if a challenge is raised by a rival or a member of the public. Because of this, the process has been abused by many organizations and individuals who have used the threat of a renewal challenge and the consequent lengthy delays to gain favors, or even payments, from broadcasters. The FCC should explore methods of discouraging such abuses.

Deregulating Network Television Programming

The Commission should remove its rules that bar television networks from owning or syndicating television programming. These rules exist merely to benefit Hollywood producers. There is no compelling rationale for this government intrusion in the marketplace.

Making Licensing Color-Blind

In assigning and reviewing licenses, the Commission now provides preference to firms owned by racial minorities or women. Not only are these preferences constitutionally suspect, but they usually do not serve their intended purpose of increasing the minority voice in communications, because the licenses can simply be sold to nonminorities after the FCC makes an assignment. This assignment preference may soon be ruled unconstitutional by the federal courts. Whether it is or not, these rules should be repealed by the FCC.

Reconsidering the Independence of the FCC

Serious consideration should be given to abolishing the FCC as an independent agency and transferring its functions to the Department of Commerce, which already has a voice in communications policy through its National Telecommunications and Information Agency. The functions of the International Communications and Information Policy Bureau of the Department of State also should be transferred to Commerce. Because of the importance of telecommunications to the U.S. economy, it needs to be part of a Cabinet-level department and requires a centrally coordinated policy.

———————————————◇———————————————

INITIATIVES FOR 1989

1) Remove unnecessary cross-ownership rules. The FCC currently prohibits telephone companies from operating cable TV systems, and networks, from producing TV programs. These prohibitions are intended to prevent monopolies but in fact reduce competition. The Commission should remove these restrictions. To the extent possible, the FCC also should remove limits on ownership of broadcast stations by newspapers and reexamine the restrictions on newspaper ownership of cable television companies.

2) Introduce legislation to remove restrictions from the Baby Bells. Under the court-imposed AT&T breakup, the Bell operating companies are prevented from entering certain areas of business, such as supplying computer information services. This restricts competition and harms U.S. competitiveness. The Commission will have the opportunity to assist bipartisan congressional efforts to remove the court-imposed restrictions on the Bell operating companies. This should be its major common carrier legislative effort in 1989.

3) Eliminate race and gender preferences. The FCC must deal with the politically volatile question of race and gender preference. Congress has restricted the Commission from repealing these policies through general rule-making. The Commission, however, should refuse to apply these gender preferences in license application and renewal cases, stating its belief that they are unconstitutional.

The Federal Trade Commission

Bruce Yandle*
Task Force Chairman

Created in 1914, the Federal Trade Commission's (FTC) law enforcement and regulatory activities focus on enforcing antitrust laws and consumer protection statutes and conducting major economic studies. In addition, the Commission acts as an advocate for pro-competition policies before other federal, state, and local agencies.

The FTC's antitrust enforcement authority is used in filing and prosecuting cases in federal court dealing with price discrimination, alleged monopolies, and collusion. It shares this responsibility with the Department of Justice.

In the area of consumer protection, the FTC can impose fines and seek court action against firms or individuals violating laws relating to deceptive and unfair advertising, packaging and labeling of products, consumer credit information, and a variety of other areas. The Commission also can promulgate broad trade regulation rules. Typical of these industry-wide rules are those requiring used car dealers to provide certain information to buyers, funeral homes to provide itemized prices and other information to consumers, and food stores to stock advertised items in sufficient quantity to meet expected demand.

Though not related to the enforcement of any particular statute, the production of economic studies is also a major part of the Commission's work. These studies cover a range of economic issues affecting consumers, and in the past few years, have added to the debate in such diverse areas as airline deregulation and fuel economy standards.

Since 1981, the FTC has pursued a fourth mission: participating in hearings and proceedings as an advocate for competition before federal, state, and local regulatory agencies. Through this advocacy program, the FTC has been able to use its expertise in regulatory law and economics to persuade other agencies to adopt more proconsumer, pro-free market policies.

---

*Task Force Deputy Chairman: Heritage McKenna Senior Policy Analyst James Gattuso.

As are most other independent commissions, the FTC is organized as a collegial body with ultimate decision-making by a multimember panel. Its five members are nominated by the President and confirmed by the Senate for seven-year terms; one of these five is designated chairman by the President. Reagan's first FTC chairman was James C. Miller III, who served from 1981 to 1985, when he became Director of the Office of Management and Budget. He was succeeded by Daniel Oliver.

INSTITUTIONAL CONSTRAINTS

The FTC's operations are constrained by its responsibility for enforcing a wide-ranging set of statutes. These include such highly visible activities as reviewing proposed business mergers and taking action on the basis of antitrust laws to delay, modify, deny, or approve these mergers. While the FTC has no choice but to review merger requests, it can exercise considerable discretion in selecting cases to be pursued under other statutes and rules. But in practice, this discretion is limited by the agency's congressional oversight committees. Congress routinely directs the agency to engage in some activities and denies funding for others. Activities declared off limits by Congress in recent years have included actions to prosecute the insurance industry for antitrust violations, regulate children's advertising, study or investigate possible anticonsumer aspects of agricultural cooperatives, and advocate repeal of the laws against resale price maintenance. Because of this, the nominally independent agency is thus actually tightly and continuously controlled by Congress.

Unlike single-purpose regulatory agencies that have jurisdiction over discrete industries, such as the Federal Communications Commission, the FTC can investigate any firm or industry suspected of violating a statute under its jurisdiction. Thus the activities of the FTC attract interest group attention in many quarters. Since FTC actions can have enormous economic consequences, the agency provokes political reactions when it takes action to enforce laws and when it chooses not to do so. The agency also stirs controversy when it advocates pro-competition policies before other governmental bodies. Petitioners seeking tariffs or quotas from the International Trade Commission, for instance, are not pleased when the FTC argues against them. Similarly, new car dealers often are angered when the FTC testifies against state legislative proposals to limit the number and location of additional dealers. As in any bureaucratic political organization, the FTC staff also influences the agency's actions and direction. And contacts between politically active FTC staff and congressional aides affect the congressional reaction to Commission initiatives.

————————◇————————

THE REAGAN ADMINISTRATION RECORD

The FTC has changed dramatically in the 1980s. During the Carter Administration, the FTC was an enthusiastic advocate of regulation. This changed abruptly under the Reagan Administration, as major changes at the FTC began reflecting changes in the American attitude toward economic regulation. In particular, the Carter Administration's emphasis on industry-wide rules and antitrust investigations has been replaced by a case-by-case analysis in which circumstances particular to each case are reviewed. Special attention has been paid to potential consumer benefits from the business activities under review. Before taking formal actions, the FTC has made increasing use of economic analysis to help ensure that the activity being questioned reduces consumer welfare and economic efficiency.

The FTC's new approach has reflected the growing conviction among scholars that "big is not necessarily bad" in industry, that world competition is a powerful force benefiting consumers, even in domestic industries that are highly concentrated, and that economic efficiency should be the overriding concern of antitrust authorities. The anticompetitive effects of rules and the use of regulations by special interest groups to cartelize industries also have been recognized by the FTC in the Reagan years. At the same time, the agency has accelerated its prosecution of cases of fraud against consumers, especially nationwide fraud schemes, supplementing the law enforcement efforts of U.S. attorneys and state and local law enforcement officials.

The program under which the FTC acts as an advocate on behalf of competition and market principles in proceedings before state and other federal agencies was expanded during the Reagan years. Significantly, the advocacy program cuts across bureau lines, has no defined budget, and brings together expert lawyers and economists on a case-by-case basis. The output of the program has included testimony before Congress, state legislatures, and federal regulatory bodies and filings in regulatory proceedings.

This effort has provided enormous benefits to the public. For example, while traditional consumer groups seldom seek to influence the International Trade Commission when it is considering action that could increase consumer prices, the FTC does. The same can be said for countless other federal regulatory actions. In this sense, the FTC has become a genuine consumer advocate.

Not all efforts to focus FTC activities have been successful. It has failed to consolidate and reduce the number of FTC regional offices. As a result, some budget reductions were delayed, as resources intended for use in Washington were distributed less effectively around the country. Similarly, the Reagan Administration has failed in its efforts to obtain clear legislative language from Congress to guide the Commission in interpreting federal statutes affecting such areas as advertising and deceptive practices.

———————————◇———————————

THE NEXT FOUR YEARS

During the new Administration, the FTC should build on the progress of the Reagan years to push for more competition and consumer choice. The premise of the FTC should be that the Commission exists to insure that the marketplace works, not to preempt market processes through regulation. To do this effectively, some statutes must be changed, such as those dealing with antitrust. (See Chapter 16.)

Strengthening Markets to Benefit Consumers

Much can accomplished without legislative action if the Commission focuses its activities and resources on areas where they can best protect and foster market processes. This can be accomplished in several ways. The Commission should continue to make the case for market-oriented policies at federal, state, and local levels through its competition advocacy program and its Bureau of Economics. It can protect consumers by prosecuting fraud, thus ensuring the integrity of the marketplace. At the same time, the Commission should review past actions to eliminate rules or consent decrees that do not help consumers. None of these actions requires legislation.

———————————◇———————————

INITIATIVES FOR 1989

1) Expand the advocacy program. Through its competition program, the FTC urges states and other federal agencies to pursue market-oriented regulatory policies. This program has been successful and should be expanded. More staff time should be allocated to this, although there is no need to establish specific office of advocacy.

2) Establish a National Fraud Center and develop fast track procedures for processing fraud cases. The FTC should increase its efforts to crack down on consumer fraud. Particular emphasis must be placed on the activities of those who operate fraudulent interstate schemes, making investigation and prosecution by any local agency difficult. To do this, the Commission must establish a National Fraud Center. At the same time, it should develop fast track procedures for expediting the processing of fraud cases, which currently cannot be handled effectively by the slow and ponderous procedures of the FTC.

3) Expand the activities of the Bureau of Economics. The FTC should continue joining debates in which competition and consumer interests are at issue. To do this, the new FTC should increase the staff of its Bureau of Economics and instruct the Bureau to analyze and issue reports on all major proposals to increase regulation in the economy or reduce competition in U.S. markets. The reports would be distributed to the media, Congress, academics, and others involved in policy-making.

4) Thoroughly review major FTC actions over the past four years. To improve the criteria by which the FTC chooses its cases, the staffs of the Bureaus of Competition and Consumer Protection should study the major actions of the past four years, identifying their results and comparing them with what was expected. The studies should devote particular attention to merger consent orders, through which the FTC approves a merger while the firm requesting the merger agrees to specified restrictions on its activities. The findings of these reviews should be used to improve agency decision-making criteria and modify existing orders.

5) Review all trade regulation rules more than four years old. Too often, trade rules remain on the books after they have outlived their usefulness. To prevent this, they should be reviewed systematically. Such a review would allow the FTC to reevaluate all trade rules that were adopted without a full economic analysis of their likely effects. Any rules found not beneficial to consumers should then be repealed.

The Securities And Exchange Commission

Henry N. Butler*
Task Force Chairman

The Securities and Exchange Commission (SEC) enforces the nation's securities laws, which regulate the issuance and sale of financial securities. In the short term, the SEC's most important challenge is to fight off new regulatory schemes. The SEC must rethink its assault on insider trading, which has threatened the efficiency of the securities markets by hindering the transfer of information. In the case of corporate takeovers, the SEC needs to return to a neutral position—neither encouraging nor discouraging takeovers, but rather leaving such decisions to the market. And the SEC should support the repeal of the 1933 Glass-Steagall Act, which places a "wall of separation" between commercial and investment banking. Repeal would allow U.S. commercial banks to enter investment banking, spurring competition and thus increasing efficiency and improving service to the investor. This also would enable U.S. banks to compete as equals with large British, Japanese, and West German financial institutions.

$\diamond$

SUMMARY OF AGENCY FUNCTIONS

The Securities and Exchange Commission was created by Congress in 1934. Consisting of five members appointed by the President for five-year terms, the SEC has had two chairmen during the Reagan years, John Shad from 1981 to 1987, and David Ruder since 1987. The chief function of the SEC is to enforce the federal securities laws in order to foster investor confidence and smooth the workings of the securities markets. To do this, the SEC has broad authority to promulgate rules and to investigate and prosecute violations of the federal securities laws and rules. Its regulation of stock exchanges is limited

---

*Task Force Deputy Chairman: Heritage McKenna Senior Policy Analyst James Gattuso.

to overseeing the operations and enforcement of the exchanges' regulations. A substantial amount of SEC resources are devoted to regulating firms in the securities industry, including brokers, dealers, and investment advisors. Using its quasi-legislative powers, the SEC has adopted rules and regulations relating to information that must be furnished to the Commission and provided to potential investors. Through the Office of the Chief Economist, the SEC studies contemporary market issues, including the impact of program trading, corporate takeovers, and insider trading.

INSTITUTIONAL CONSTRAINTS

Like most independent agencies, the SEC is not totally independent of either the executive or legislative branches. Executive branch pressure stems from its need to coordinate policy with other financial policy agencies and organizations, like the Treasury Department, the deposit insurance agencies, and the stock exchanges. SEC policy changes usually require cooperation from one or more of these agencies to be successful.

The legislative branch pressures the SEC because lawmakers invariably desire to "do something" about some real or perceived problem. Corporate takeovers and restructurings, for example, are often seen as such problems; congressional committees thus have been pressuring the SEC to limit takeovers. The SEC's vigorous attack on insider trading violations, in fact, almost surely has been a direct response to congressional pressure on the issue. Similarly, the stock market crash of October 1987 prompted calls for increased regulation of stock exchanges through such devices as higher margins and limits on daily price variations. Fortunately for U.S. capital markets, the SEC has resisted these calls from Congress.

THE REAGAN ADMINISTRATION RECORD

When Ronald Reagan took office, the activities of the SEC were not a major public concern. The agency seemed to be relatively noncontroversial, simply administering well-accepted statutes. The incoming Reagan Administration generally shared this view. But with the record numbers of corporate takeovers, highly publicized insider-trading cases, and a stock market crash, the SEC now finds itself in the center of controversy.

In keeping with the Reagan Administration's goal of freeing financial markets from excessive regulation, the SEC has reduced the regulatory burden on securities firms. Yet it has made little progress toward more far-reaching deregulation of securities. In fact, in the wake of the October 1987 stock market crash, the SEC has done little to blunt pressure for increased regulation. SEC Chairman David Ruder has, in fact, been a vocal advocate of increasing SEC regulatory powers.

Among the SEC's most important accomplishments during the Reagan years has been the integration of the disclosure requirements of the Securities Act of 1933 and the Securities Exchange Act of 1934. Disclosure requires that all material facts pertaining to the transfer of securities be made public. Integration of the disclosure requirements allows the requirements of both acts to be fulfilled in one statement— previously, separate statements were needed. Without weakening the full disclosure requirements, the integrated disclosure program is saving publicly held corporations and their shareholders over $1 billion per year in paperwork, underwriting, and interest costs. The SEC also has improved its operations by establishing the Office of the Chief Economist. Though economic analysis can identify the costs and benefits of changes in regulatory policies, it had been given little weight in past SEC decisions. The new office institutionalizes a voice for economic analysis within the agency.

These achievements are relatively modest, however, compared to the greater task of substantially changing securities regulation. Here the SEC has failed. It has not challenged the premises of government regulation of securities markets. Numerous empirical and theoretical studies now suggest that federal securities regulations impose tremendous costs and generate few, if any, benefits. The case for deregulation is compelling, yet the SEC has not moved to reduce the government role in capital markets.

————————————◇————————————

THE NEXT FOUR YEARS

Despite the October 1987 plunge in share prices, the Reagan era has enjoyed the most sustained bull stock market in U.S. history. This reflects a strong, expanding economy and the widespread expectation that it will continue. To sustain this expanding economy, however, the securities and financial markets must be allowed to operate as efficiently as possible. To help ensure this, the SEC should vigorously oppose increased regulation by Congress.

Resisting New Regulation of Financial Markets

The SEC must resist pressures to increase regulation of the stock markets. Although the steep and abrupt decline in share prices in October 1987 sent tremors through the professional and individual investor communities, the most harmful long-term effects of the crash could come from Washington in the form of greater regulation of securities markets. Many proposals for regulation aim at establishing uniform rules for the different types of U.S. financial markets. To be sure, the markets for stocks, stock index futures, and stock index options are linked closely through electronic technology; marketplace boundaries are crossed to such an extent that these markets are effectively unified. The development of unified markets does not mean, however, that the regulations governing each market should be identical. Each has its distinctive products, procedures, and systems of trading. Unified regulation could threaten the diversity and dynamics of these markets and thus reduce their effectiveness. The SEC should thus resist, rather than support, efforts to consolidate regulatory authority.

Other proposals aim at reducing market volatility. October's events demonstrated that such new technologies and mechanisms as computerized program trading can cause extraordinary volume, which at times overwhelms the capacity of markets and triggers wide price fluctuations. There is, however, little need for the SEC to regulate volatility. There are strong incentives for the exchanges themselves to increase their capacity to handle large trading volumes; traders, after all, profit from handling increased volume. Similarly, competition among exchanges to trade the stocks of particular corporations provides incentives for them to process information efficiently.

The SEC also should be cautious about proposals to control fraud. Technology has opened the door to nonstop worldwide trading, making it much easier for U.S. investors to conduct their business abroad. This increasing internationalization of markets has made it easier to engage in fraudulent conduct. Nevertheless, in its efforts to control fraud in the international markets, the SEC must be careful not to impose unnecessary costs on legitimate activities and thus make U.S. markets uncompetitive with foreign exchanges.

Redefining Insider Trading

Insider trading cases have captured the public's attention, with the SEC leading efforts to crack down on this activity. Yet scholars disagree about the degree to which this ought to be illegal, and if so, how it should be defined. Misuse of confidential and proprietary information, they argue, is simply a breach of contract and is best resolved in a civil suit for damages rather than in a criminal case. In fact, many, such as Henry Manne, Dean of the George Mason University School of Law, see insider trading as essentially a victimless crime. As long as shareholders are informed of the possibility of such insider trading, these activities would not be unfair to any insider.

Yet, rather than reducing the scope of insider trading laws, the SEC in recent years has been pushing to broaden the statutory definition. The SEC argues that the definition must not only be broad enough to include all activities currently prohibited, but flexible enough to apply to a range of other investment activities. While this might make it easier for the SEC to prosecute insider trading cases, it also would penalize many engaging in what most Americans would consider honest business activity. This would chill the securities industry and impose tremendous efficiency costs on the capital markets. The SEC thus should adhere to the narrower traditional definition of illegal insider trading. It should also allow firms to alter their corporate charters to allow for inside trading, if they so desire.

Freeing the "Market for Corporate Control"

The threat of a takeover by noncontrolling investors encourages corporate managers to improve the market value of a corporation's shares by making the firm as profitable and efficient as possible. Known as the "market for corporate control," this often provides benefits for both stockholders and the economy. This market, however, is impeded by the 1968 Williams Act, which regulates tender offers by restricting the timing of making and accepting offers and by forcing bidders to reveal their identity before they can act. By reducing the chances of a successful takeover and its potential rewards, the Williams Act makes it easier for inefficient managers to keep control of companies. The SEC should advocate changes in the Williams Act to minimize the burden that it places on the market for corporate control.

Yet even Williams Act restrictions are minor compared to many state anti-takeover laws enacted in recent years. These directly limit the ability of individuals to gain control of corporations without the consent of the management. Managers, of course, are not the owners of a corporation; they merely work for the shareholders. Many of these state statutes have been enacted specifically to help the management of local firms threatened by takeovers. The SEC should mobilize its resources, using both economic studies and direct advocacy, to discourage enactment of such harmful statutes by states.

───────────────◇───────────────

INITIATIVES FOR 1989

1) Support the repeal of the Glass-Steagall Act. This 1933 act requires the separation of commercial banking and investment banking. (See Chapter 22.) The Act does not promote bank safety and soundness but rather hinders competition in both banking and securities. The new SEC should support the repeal of Glass-Steagall and press for the elimination of other regulatory hurdles that prevent banks from becoming more potent competitors in the domestic and global investment banking industry.

2) Clarify and limit the definitions of insider trading. The insider trading laws, while intended to protect investors, unreasonably restrict legitimate activities and often have been used to hinder takeover efforts. Insider trading also is a vague term, and so the laws lead to confusion and uncertainty in the securities industry. Moreover, it is not clear that insider trading necessarily hurts investors. The SEC should drop its effort to expand the scope of these laws and instead move to clarify and limit their application.

21

The Department of
Transportation

Ralph L. Stanley*
Task Force Chairman

The Department of Transportation (DOT) was a key agency in executing the Reagan Administration's strategy for reinvigorating the United States economy. Building on legislation passed under Jimmy Carter, DOT oversaw the adjustment of the airline, rail, and trucking industries to the new world of deregulation. Under Ronald Reagan, the fruits of deregulation have become more evident to Americans in the form of enormous savings and service improvements. In addition, DOT has begun privatizing government-owned assets by selling Conrail and prodding greater private-sector involvement in urban mass transit.

Yet much remains to be done by the new Administration. To allow the nation's airways to keep up with the deregulated airline system, the air traffic control system must be extracted from the creaking federal bureaucracy. Because the system has difficulty adjusting to rapidly changing market conditions, it holds back expansion and improvement in airline services. In addition, market pricing based on supply and demand of landing slots at U.S. airports should be encouraged. Reforms in railroad, trucking, and maritime shipping rules need to be pursued by the new Administration. The Interstate Commerce Commission should be eliminated, as should federal subsidies to Amtrak. The surface transportation system urgently needs reform. In

---

*Commenting and contributing generously to this chapter were *Mandate III* Task Force Members Dan Campbell, Stephen Moore, Robert Okun, Stan Sender, Fred Smith, and Frank Wilner. They do not necessarily endorse all of its views and recommendations.

Task Force Deputy Chairman: Heritage McKenna Senior Policy Analyst James Gattuso.

BUDGET AND PERSONNEL

Secretaries

James H. Burnley IV	1987–present
Elizabeth H. Dole	1983–1987
Andrew Lewis	1981–1983

Personnel

March 1988	62,302
April 1980	73,134
April 1970	63,563

Budget Outlays

Fiscal Year	Total (billions)
1989 Estimate	$26.4
1988 Estimate	$26.3
1987 Actual	$25.4
1986 Actual	$27.4
1985 Actual	$25.0
1980 Actual	$19.8
1970 Actual	$ 6.7

particular, federal Corporate Average Fuel Efficiency (CAFE) regulations should be lifted, the federal highway program should be transferred to state control, and private-sector involvement in mass transit increased.

SUMMARY OF AGENCY FUNCTIONS

The Department of Transportation was established in 1966 to consolidate transportation functions within one Cabinet-level department. The principal agencies are:

◆ *The Federal Aviation Administration (FAA)*, which operates the air traffic control system, regulates the safety of aviation, and administers federal grants to airports.

◆ *The Federal Railroad Administration (FRA)*, which regulates rail safety and administers rail subsidies, including those to Amtrak, the national passenger railroad system.

◆ *The Federal Highway Administration (FHWA)*, which manages federal highway programs and regulates motor carrier safety.

◆ *The Urban Mass Transportation Administration (UMTA)*, which distributes federal grants and other assistance programs for local transportation.

◆ *The Maritime Administration*, which subsidizes and in other ways assists the U.S. merchant fleet.

◆ *The National Highway Traffic Safety Administration (NHTSA)*, which carries out federal programs relating to automobile safety, fuel economy, and other functions.

◆ *The Coast Guard*, which, among its many functions, rescues boaters, prevents the illegal entry of drugs and other goods into the U.S., and, in time of war, can be mobilized for military use.

◆ *The Saint Lawrence Seaway Corporation*, which manages the Saint Lawrence Seaway between Canada and the U.S.

◆ *The Research and Special Programs Administration*, which regulates the transportation of hazardous material by any type of carrier.

◆ *The Office of Commercial Space Transportation*, which issues licenses for all private commercial space launches. (See Chapter 9.)

U.S. transportation policy also is influenced by a number of independent agencies not under DOT jurisdiction. These include the Interstate Commerce Commission, which administers federal regulation of barges, buses, railroads, and trucks; the Federal Maritime Commission, which exercises a similar role for seagoing vessels; and the National Transportation Safety Board, which investigates all aviation and railroad accidents, and some accidents involving other modes of transportation.

———————————◇———————————

INSTITUTIONAL CONSTRAINTS

While ultimate decision-making authority rests with the DOT secretary, the agencies within DOT have considerable power and independence. For one thing, they control the details of policy, for another, because they have considerable expertise in the technical details of managing transportation programs, they are often essential in formulating new policies. While a secretary, for instance, can propose changes in the air traffic control system, pursuing any credible reform plan is difficult without support from the FAA.

Private interests affected by DOT's programs, ranging from the airlines to the auto clubs, also play a major role in policy formulation. While outright support from these interests is not always necessary in achieving policy goals—airline and trucking deregulation, for example, was achieved over the vociferous opposition of those industries—such support is extremely helpful. Congress, and its committees dealing with transportation, impose another important constraint on policy-making. In addition to its obvious power to pass substantive legislation, Congress can hinder the Department's agenda through specific restrictions contained in appropriations bills. In 1986, for instance, Secretary Dole announced the formation of a commission to study the privatization of Amtrak. But before the commission could get under way, Congress specifically prohibited DOT from spending any money to study privatization, killing the commission before it was born.

————————————◇————————————

THE REAGAN ADMINISTRATION RECORD

When Ronald Reagan took office, the deregulation of America's transportation system, set in motion by legislation passed during the Carter Administration, was just being implemented. Deregulation of airline fares and routes had been enacted in 1978, while legislation partially deregulating the trucking and railroad industries had been signed in 1980. It was Reagan's challenge to build on this legacy. To an extent, he has done so. As important, he has blocked legislation to reregulate transportation. Reagan's Interstate Commerce Commission, moreover, has played a crucial role, through its regulations and rulings, in furthering the deregulation of trucking and railroads.

In the Reagan years, economic deregulation has become one of the great economic success stories of the 20th century. In each of the three deregulated modes of transportation—airlines, trucking, and railroads—consumers now enjoy substantial benefits. The prices they pay for all three major deregulated modes are lower than they would have been without deregulation. Shippers using trucks enjoyed rate reductions ranging from an estimated 25 percent for "truckload" carriers to 12 percent for "less than truckload" carriers between 1977 and 1982. Rail shippers are now paying about 17 percent less (based on overall revenue per ton-mile). And the cost of air travel is some 20 percent to 30 percent lower than before deregulation.

In addition to saving consumers money, reduced airline costs have "democratized" air travel by making it more widely available to the American public. People who ten years ago would have had to travel by bus, or not travel at all, now can afford to fly. While this may be deplored by the businessman traveling on an expense account, who would rather have empty seats next to him than a family on vacation, for the average American, immense new opportunities are now available.

Lower prices have not come at the expense of service quality; in fact, quality has improved. For instance, before deregulation, shippers using truck lines had fewer choices as to the service they received—that was limited by law. Today shippers routinely negotiate for more frequent service, for pickup and delivery at specific locations, or simply for faster service. The result is a more efficient and customer-sensitive industry. Rail shippers have seen even more significant service improvements. With costs rising and revenues declining, railroads before deregulation were strapped for money to maintain their tracks and equipment at acceptable levels. With their new flexibility, railroads now can concentrate on putting resources where they are needed, rather than being forced to spend money on uneconomic lines or costly practices mandated by regulation.

None of these improvements came at the expense of transportation safety. On the contrary, safety has improved. In trucking, for instance, the fatality rate per mile driven is down about 16 percent since deregulation; on railroads, the number of accidents dropped more than 70 percent between 1980 and 1987. Despite widespread claims to the contrary, airline accidents also have decreased. Overall, the total number of airline accidents involving major air carriers and commuters was down about 13 percent in the nine years after deregulation, compared with the nine years before. Even more significant, the accident rate, which takes into account the huge increase in traffic since deregulation, is down by about a third.

The Reagan Administration has won passage of legislation deregulating interstate busing, freight forwarding, and international shipping. Firms in each of these industries have received greater authority to determine their rates and service levels. In addition, the Shipping Act of 1984 lessened antitrust regulation of ocean carriers, allowing U.S. carriers to compete more effectively with foreign vessels. Other important Reagan successes include the sale in 1987 of the federally owned Consolidated Rail Corporation (Conrail) to the private sector, raising almost $2 billion for the Federal Treasury (counting $300 million paid directly out of Conrail's cash reserves).

The Reagan Administration has eased the burden on the taxpayer by introducing more private-sector capital and innovation into mass transit. The Urban Mass Transportation Administration, for instance, as a condition of receiving federal funds, now routinely requires local transit authorities to study the feasibility of using private firms to provide services. Spurred by UMTA, many local transit authorities around the country now contract with private firms, typically at cost savings of 30 percent or more. Federal subsidies to local transit systems, of course, still remain too high—but this DOT initiative has at least created a private-sector presence in this area of transportation. Other Reagan Administration accomplishments have implications far beyond transportation. Reagan's 1981 dismissal of the striking air traffic controllers, for instance, set the principle that the government can enforce a ban on public employee strikes. Establishment of the Office of Commercial Space Transportation in DOT may pave the way for a private space industry. (See Chapter 9.)

Still, the Reagan DOT has failed in several major areas. In some cases, this was because Congress stymied White House proposals. For instance, the Administration has failed to eliminate subsidies to Amtrak, to abolish remaining trucking regulations, or to block enactment of pork-filled highway authorization bills. Even though Congress has been the main culprit, the Administration often shares the blame. At times, for example, it ignored political strategies that could have given its proposals a greater chance of success. Thus, although it proposed eliminating Amtrak's subsidy each year, it was not until late in its second term that the Administration considered privatization, an option which would keep Amtrak operating while eliminating the need for subsidies. This would be less threatening to Amtrak supporters than the simple elimination of Amtrak. By and large, however, the chance of legislative success in most of these areas would have been remote, regardless of the strategy employed, because of the entrenched interests involved, and Reagan's lack of a majority in Congress supportive of his agenda.

Other Reagan Administration failures have been those of missed opportunities. Consider, for example, the debate over airline deregulation. While the Reagan DOT staunchly and tirelessly has defended airline deregulation, until recently, it was generally reluctant to take the offensive on air travel issues. Instead of pointing out areas where reform is needed, such as the air traffic control system and building the case for market-based solutions, DOT generally just defended the status quo. As a result, it failed to capitalize on the understandable anger of air travelers over delays and congestion to push forward structural reform of the air traffic system. Instead, by default, this anger focused on airline deregulation as the culprit. Only in 1987, after James Burnley became secretary, did DOT begin to focus the discussion on air traffic control reform by pointing to the problems inherent in federal control over the system.

———————————◇———————————

THE NEXT FOUR YEARS

The new Administration should work to reduce further the government's role in transportation. While the specific steps required vary widely among different transportation modes, in general the Administration's goal should be: 1) to preserve and further deregulation so that providers of transportation can respond quickly to consumer needs; 2) to privatize, or at least increase the private-sector role in, transportation and thus instill strong incentives to respond to those consumer needs; and 3) to reduce subsidies, so that the costs of transportation services are borne by those receiving the benefits.

Restructuring and Pricing Airport and Airway Services

Since the airlines were largely deregulated in 1978, airline traffic in the U.S. has soared. This growth is one of the most important successes of deregulation, but understandably has created a new set of challenges for American aviation as the nation's airports and airways try to adjust to increased traffic load and changing traffic patterns. The result has been delays and irritation for air travelers. These problems are caused largely by the institutional structure of the airport and airway system, rather than the deregulation of the airlines. While the commercial airline system has been deregulated, airports and airways have not; they are still operated by government and kept virtually immune to market forces. Thus, though the airlines have expanded and redeployed resources to meet the needs of American consumers, the bureaucratic air traffic control and airport systems have adjusted less well to the changes in aviation.

To remedy this, the new President should move swiftly to introduce market incentives into the government-operated parts of the air travel system. In particular, the new Administration should work to reform the air traffic control system and encourage market-based pricing of airport services.

The air traffic control system long has been hamstrung by constraints stemming from its status as part of the federal bureaucracy. For example, by mandating a uniform pay scale nationwide, the federal civil service system has made it difficult for the FAA to keep a sufficient number of controllers in regions with high living costs. In addition, federal procurement rules have delayed the acquisition of up-to-date equipment for the system. And because all expenditures on air traffic control must go through the cumbersome congressional appropriations process, long-term planning is difficult and politicized.

This situation could be remedied in several ways. In the short term, the new Administration should press to streamline the civil service, procurement, and budget rules to make the system more efficient. Then the new Administration should propose comprehensive structural reform to create an independent corporation to manage air traffic control. This new corporation should be free of federal personnel and procurement rules. The corporation also should be financially self-sufficient through revenue raised by charging direct fees to the users. To ensure that this independent air traffic control system be accountable to the needs of its users, it should be placed under the control of those users, with its directors appointed by airlines, private aviators, federal government users, and even air traffic controllers. In this way, the system would have the ability and incentive to respond quickly and fully to aviation consumers' changing needs.

The new Administration also must apply market principles to the allocation of takeoff and landing rights at the major U.S. airports. Most airports still simply allow aircraft to land or depart on a first-come, first-served basis. This leads to delays and angry passengers. Airports do charge fees, but these typically bear no relation to the market demand for landing slots—instead they usually are based on aircraft weight. Thus a jet landing at the busiest hour at O'Hare Airport pays the same fee as one landing at midnight. Further, private planes generally pay very little for landing rights, sometimes only $25, even though they may keep waiting a jumbo jet carrying hundreds of passengers.

Airports could allocate their valuable takeoff and landing rights more sensibly. They could, for instance, auction slots, allowing airlines and other potential users to bid for the right to land or take off at a particular time. In this way, the slots available at each airport could be distributed according to the market value placed on them by users. Example: if two airlines wanted to schedule flights for 4:30 P.M. from a particular airport, the one which values that time the most could bid the most for the slot. Thus, if one expects its 4:30 P.M. flights to be full, and the other can only sell half its seats, the first could bid more for the slot. Airports also could charge fees that vary according to the demand for rights at particular times of the day. Example: an airport could charge more for the right to land at 4:30 P.M., a peak time, than it does at 11:00 P.M.

Such steps should be taken by local airport authorities. Federal law, however, prohibits almost all major airports, because they have received federal aid, from charging fees which are "unreasonable" or "discriminatory." The new Administration immediately should make it clear that its Department of Transportation would not interpret this language to bar market-based methods of landing rights allocation. And if necessary, it should seek changes in the underlying statute to clarify federal policy.

Protecting Airline Computer Reservation Systems from Regulation

An emerging transportation issue relates to the airline travel industry's computer reservation systems (CRSs). These allow travel agents quickly to access desired information about flights and fares, make reservations, write tickets, and issue boarding passes. Because the major CRS systems are owned by airlines, such as the American Airlines "Sabre" system, many claim that these airlines are able to harm consumers by giving preferential treatment to their own flights. In 1984, in response to such claims, the Civil Aeronautics Board promulgated regulations prohibiting such "bias." These rules were later expanded by DOT. Many have suggested even more restrictive regulations limiting the information provided by such systems and the way they do business, and even divesting them from airlines.

The new Administration should examine this issue closely before moving toward more regulation. First, it may be unnecessary. Because the CRS industry is a competitive industry, competition can prevent preferential treatment which harms consumers. Equally important, such regulation would be dangerous. This is a relatively new industry, whose structure and practices are constantly changing. No economist or government bureaucrat can say which is the best form for the industry to take. Enormous future benefits to consumers could be lost if the federal government freezes the development of this dynamic industry and forces it to operate within a rigidly defined set of rules. The DOT instead should consider removing those harmful CRS regulations that already exist.

Improving Railroad Industry Efficiency

To blunt pressure for reregulating the railroad industry, the new President not only should announce his opposition to new controls but vow further reform. As a first step, he should propose reform of the special rules that inflate rail labor costs. These rules force rail management and labor to bargain under circumstances unlike those in any other American industry, retard change and modernization in the industry, and hinder the ability of railroads to compete with other modes of transportation. Moreover, like other restrictive labor laws, these rules destroy jobs. To remedy this, the new Department of Transportation should take action in three areas.

The first is the regulation of the labor-management bargaining system. The Railway Labor Act lays down procedures for amending rail (as well as airline) labor contracts, including the imposition of mandatory "cooling off" periods and various nonbinding arbitration procedures before any strike can begin. In the event of a major rail strike, Congress can, and often does, force the parties to accept binding arbitration of the dispute. While seemingly harmless, this system can impose unnecessary costs on the industry. The procedures for negotiation required under the Act are extremely time-consuming—three or more years can elapse before a contract change can be effected. Thus, railroads needing to move quickly to adjust to changing business conditions often find themselves stymied. If Congress steps in to force arbitration, moreover, the parties are unable to accept the risk of a strike in return for a change they feel is vital. Instead, a solution is forced upon them. Under the old, regulated system, this lack of flexibility had little effect. Competition was muted, and regulators typically protected firms from the consequences of inefficiency. In today's world, where railroads compete intensely for business not only among themselves, but with other modes of transportation, such a lack of flexibility could be disastrous for the industry and the consumers it serves. The new Administration should launch a comprehensive review of this system, and propose reforms to increase the ability of the industry to react to changing market conditions.

The second area of railroad labor law needing urgent reform concerns "labor protection" rules. These rules were first spurred by the massive consolidation of the railroad industry during the 1930s and 1940s, when the industry employed as many as one of every 20 U.S. workers. It was then felt that special rules offering extensive income guarantees to workers affected adversely by railroad restructuring were necessary to avoid labor unrest. These rules, now mandated by statute and Interstate Commerce Commission regulation, require railroads that merge or abandon trackage to pay a salary to any employee displaced by that action for up to six years, or until he or she finds a new job. Experience shows that these rules do not save railroad jobs, but can actually destroy them, particularly on marginal lines. The reason: the risk of paying labor protection increases the cost of acquiring uneconomic lines from other railroads, which often discourages such transactions, even though such acquisitions might increase overall efficiency and preserve jobs. In 1987, the Interstate Commerce Commission refused to apply these labor protection rules to newly formed short-line and regional railroads, making it easier for such firms to buy lines and sparing them from abandonment. This is a step in the right direction. The next Administration should build on this by urging Congress to further curtail these rules or eliminate them altogether.

The third area for reform is the Federal Employers' Liability Act of 1908. It establishes a costly and burdensome compensation system for on-the-job injuries of railroad employees. While based on the principle of fault, the Act imposes extremely high administrative, legal, and other transaction costs on the participants. This means heavier operating expenses for railroads and less money available for injured workers. Repeal of this Act is overdue. In its place, workers and railroads should be freed to agree between themselves on what compensation system will apply in cases of on-the-job injury.

Completing Trucking Deregulation

Partial deregulation of the trucking industry has been a success; further deregulation is needed. Trucking companies now enjoy almost complete freedom to set rates, routes, and their level of service; they remain burdened by immense paperwork, however, because the federal government still requires formal approval of truck rates and routes. This paperwork totals a million or more pages each year, wasting millions of dollars. And the existence of this remnant regulatory structure would make it easier for Congress to restore regulation of the industry. The new Administration, as did the Reagan Administration, should seek to remove these remaining regulatory burdens.

The new Administration, however, should resist efforts to replace regulation with increased antitrust coverage. Currently, the trucking industry is free of many antitrust restrictions. This allows groups of trucking companies to join "rate bureaus" to establish guideline rates for particular types of shipments. These are very different from the cartel agreements which can hurt the consumer. The rates published by trucking "rate bureaus" are not binding. Trucking companies can, and usually do, deviate from them. Competing firms can always enter the market and undercut the guideline rate. In effect, the rates act like the "Kelly Blue Book" used to price cars, giving truckers a starting point for negotiation. This is of particular importance to small trucking companies, which often cannot afford to maintain "in-house" rate departments. If such a service is economically beneficial, as it appears to be, it should not be prohibited by the antitrust laws.

While the federal government has partially deregulated interstate trucking, many states still impose onerous regulations on intrastate traffic, hurting their own economies. The new Administration should use its bully pulpit to encourage states to repeal such regulations. Moreover, where state laws interfere with the interstate movement of goods, the federal government should be prepared to preempt these restrictions.

Abolishing the Interstate Commerce Commission

The Interstate Commerce Commission (ICC), created in 1887, is the nation's oldest regulatory commission. Its 102nd birthday in 1989 should be its last. The partial deregulation of the trucking and railroad industry has reduced the ICC's functions considerably. During the past eight years, its staff has been cut from almost 2,000 to about 700 employees. Complete deregulation of the trucking industry would make many of these remaining employees unnecessary. Thus the new Administration should urge Congress to abolish the ICC. Its functions, such as oversight of railroad regulation, should be transferred to the Department of Transportation.

Elimination of the ICC serves more important goals than mere administrative tidiness. First, it would signal strongly that the era of comprehensive economic regulation of transportation is over. Second, dismantling the apparatus by which this regulation has been administered would make it much more difficult for future Congresses to revive regulation.

Ending Protectionism for the Maritime Industry

The U.S. maritime industry long has been entangled in an extensive net of federal restrictions and subsidies, ranging from statutes to protect U.S. shipping from foreign competition to programs to subsidize the construction and operation of U.S. oceangoing vessels. The explanation for federal involvement in this area long has been national security: in time of war, the U.S. would need a strong domestic merchant marine fleet to transport supplies. Unfortunately, in practice maritime programs too often have become simple attempts to protect the industry against foreign competition.

The Reagan Administration has taken several significant steps to improve this situation. It ended the "construction differential subsidy" program, which provided direct subsidies for the construction of U.S. ships. The Administration also is not renewing contracts for operating subsidies. Through the Shipping Act of 1984, which lessened antitrust regulation of ocean carriers, and legalized contracts between carriers and shippers at rates other than those of the published tariffs, the industry has been freed to compete more effectively against foreign competition through deregulation, without using protectionism or subsidies.

Much more needs to be done by the new Administration. The loan guarantee program for new ship construction should be ended. While this guarantee program was originally to be funded by fees from those receiving the loans, it has required funding from general funds, thus placing the burden on taxpayers. Perhaps more important, the new Administration must seriously challenge various laws protecting U.S. shipping from foreign competition. "Cargo preference" requirements, under which a certain percentage of goods shipped or financed by the U.S. government must be transported on U.S. vessels, should be repealed. These requirements not only raise costs for taxpayers, but can hobble exports. It has been estimated, for instance, that this requirement adds about $35 per metric ton to the cost of U.S. farm exports (which are subject to cargo preference because of federal farm programs).

Of course, it is possible that in a free market and without federal aid, the U.S. merchant marine would be smaller than believed necessary for national security. In such a case, federal expenditures to meet this defense need would be justified. However, such military needs should be addressed through direct expenditures for particular services rather than through protectionist laws and general subsidies.

Restructuring Federal Support for Mass Transit

Federal subsidies for urban mass transit programs began in the early 1960s. Over the past quarter century, the federal Urban Mass Transportation Administration (UMTA) has distributed almost $50 billion in federal subsidies to cities to build new subway systems and purchase new buses and to operate these systems. Despite this massive investment, ridership is actually lower today than before federal assistance was started.

UMTA currently offers about \$3.5 billion each year in transit assistance to U.S. cities. This aid takes two forms: capital grants for new construction and purchases of buses, and operating subsidies to existing systems. With federal capital grants paying up to 80 percent of a new rail or bus system, cities understandably lobby hard for systems, no matter how costly or uneconomic they may be.

Federal operating subsidies provide cities with even more perverse incentives. The larger the operating loss of a transit system, the more federal money the city obtains from DOT. Cities that seek to cut costs and boost efficiency by contracting out operations to the private sector often must forfeit their federal operating assistance, despite evidence that contracting out can reduce operating costs by between 20 percent and 50 percent. Consequently, less than 5 percent of transit services were contracted out through competitive bidding in 1985. The situation has improved only marginally since then.

The objective of federal transit assistance should be to serve the mobility needs of urban commuters, not to fund inefficient multibillion dollar public works projects. If the program cannot be repealed entirely, the new Secretary of Transportation should press Congress to revise the Urban Mass Transportation Administration capital grant formula. The federal match on capital grants should be reduced from its current 80 percent to 50 percent. This would force cities to consider more carefully the costs and benefits of a new system. If city residents are not prepared to finance at least half the cost of a new transit project, it ought not be built. UMTA also should require that all transit projects receiving federal capital grant funds be awarded through competitive bidding to ensure that cities spend federal dollars as economically as possible.

The new Administration also should urge Congress to create an urban transit "block grant." This would end operating subsidies to individual transit systems and replace them with a consolidated grant program for transit with few restrictions on how the funds are used. Each city would receive an annual payment based on such objective criteria as population density, number of transit passengers per week, and the amount of gasoline taxes paid. This block grant would eliminate the current inequities in the disbursement of federal transit funds. Although all cities contribute to the gasoline tax which funds federal transit assistance, a mere 15 large urban areas receive almost three-quarters of the funds. A block grant, moreover, would give cities the incentive to use the money efficiently. By contrast, the current incentives encourage cities to structure their transportation policies not according to need or efficiency, but rather to that which assures them of receiving federal funds.

The new Administration should propose repeal of Section 13(c) of the Urban Mass Transit Act. This provision requires cities receiving federal transit funds 1) to "preserve the rights, privileges, and benefits of existing collective bargaining agreements," and 2) to protect individual transit employees from any reduction in pay or employment as a result of the receipt of federal funds. Thanks to Section 13(c), public transit workers' pay scales are almost 50 percent above those of private transit employees. Moreover, the provision makes it extremely difficult to contract services out to private firms with lower wage scales or fewer employees.

Reducing the Federal Role in Highway Assistance

The primary objective of the postwar federal highway program has been to build the interstate highway system. Today, approximately 97 percent of the system's planned mileage is complete, and about 70 percent of federal highway money now funds local freeways, roads, and bridges. Since the program's goals have been fulfilled, the new President should proclaim the interstate highway system complete and propose reforms to reduce the federal role in local road-building.

In particular, the Administration should define clearly the federal role in highway assistance. In 1914, to reduce pork-barrel highway spending, Congress adopted a rule barring funding for any specific roads. In recent years, Congress has abandoned such self-restraint. The 1982 highway authorization bill, for example, funded ten earmarked projects. The 1987 bill included money for over 100 special projects, including an access ramp to an Ohio amusement park and a $3 million parking garage in Chicago. The new President should declare that he will veto any highway bill that contains such pork-barrel projects or that usurps the proper state role for road construction.

Since the states are prohibited from charging tolls on any road or highway that has received federal funding, regardless of how little, the states are unable to charge users directly for the costs of maintaining the system. This prohibition should be lifted to allow states to charge tolls at least up to the amount necessary to fund extensions and repairs. As a first step, the new Administration should propose lifting this ban on user fees for primary highways (not part of the interstate

system) and secondary and urban roads, which receive 75 percent
federal funding.

Congress also should be pressed by the new Administration to
remove requirements that inflate highway construction costs. Mandates attached to federal highway funds by Congress raise these costs
by approximately 20 percent. These mandates include minority and
small business contract set-aside programs, "Buy America" provisions, and the 1931 Davis-Bacon Act, which effectively requires union
wage scales in federally supported construction projects. The purpose
of federal highway money should be to improve the nation's transportation system, not to pursue social policies or to force union wage
scales on nonunion firms.

For the long run, the new Administration should propose returning
to the states all road-building responsibilities, along with the gasoline
tax funding mechanism. The federal government should reduce the
federal gasoline tax from its current 9 cents per gallon to just 2 cents.
One penny per gallon would finance the urban mass transit block grant,
while the other penny would maintain the interstate highway system.
States then could raise their own gasoline taxes to the level necessary
to finance local transportation needs.

Privatizing Amtrak

Amtrak, or the National Railroad Passenger Corporation, was created in 1970 as a two-year federal experiment to save the nation's
bankrupt passenger railroad service. In fiscal 1988, Amtrak received
approximately $600 million in federal subsidies—or about $30 per
passenger per trip. Most of these passengers are middle- and upper-
income Americans. All of Amtrak's routes currently lose money—
even the heavily traveled Northeast Corridor, which runs from Washington, D.C., to Boston. Although the Reagan Administration has
trimmed Amtrak's subsidy by about 50 percent since 1981, it has fallen
short of its goal of terminating all Amtrak subsidies.

The new President should propose a five-year plan to phase out
federal subsidies to Amtrak. This incremental reduction would give
Amtrak management sufficient opportunity to reorganize, revise its
marketing plan, reduce labor costs, and shed its worst money-losing
lines. To compensate partially for this loss of federal funds to Amtrak,
the federal government should immediately require local commuter
trains in New Jersey and Pennsylvania to reimburse Amtrak fully for
their use of Amtrak's lines in the Northeast Corridor. In addition, as
recommended by President Reagan's Commission on Privatization,

Amtrak's federally protected monopoly over passenger rail service should be repealed during the subsidy phaseout period to allow private companies to reenter the market and serve rail passengers wherever they see an opportunity for commercial services.

During the five-year transition, a task force headed by the Secretary of Transportation, with representatives from private industry, should be formed to determine Amtrak's future. The task force should consider selling potentially profitable routes, along with accompanying capital equipment, to private owners. To encourage Amtrak employees to support such privatization, the task force should consider either the discounted sale or outright transfer of Amtrak to its employees. Such transfers in Britain have proved highly successful in creating political support for money-losing government corporations. In the case of routes that cannot be made profitable, the task force could consider, as an alternative to privatization, requesting that the states served by them assume ownership and control. Routes that are rejected by the states and do not interest private investors should be discontinued.

Eliminating CAFE Fuel Economy Standards

Under the 1975 Corporate Average Fuel Economy regulations—widely known as CAFE—each automobile manufacturer selling in the U.S. must maintain a minimum fuel economy average for the cars it sells. In 1988, for instance, each manufacturer's entire fleet was required to average at least 26 miles per gallon. The standard for model year 1989 vehicles is 26.5 mpg. When gas prices were high, the CAFE rules were unnecessary. Consumers demanded smaller, more fuel efficient cars, raising average fuel economy faster than CAFE required. But in recent years, with falling gasoline prices, CAFE requirements have become increasingly difficult for manufacturers to meet, since consumers have been choosing to purchase better performing and more comfortable cars. These cars tend to use more fuel and thus reduce manufacturers' fleet-wide fuel efficiency averages.

Rigidly enforcing CAFE standards, at best, would save only a small amount of fuel. An improvement of one mile per gallon in fuel economy, for instance, would reduce U.S. gasoline consumption by only 1.2 percent annually. At the same time, the costs of compliance are high. CAFE could shift U.S. auto manufacturing jobs abroad, as U.S. manufacturers move production of larger cars abroad to increase the average fuel efficiency of their domestic fleets. According to a 1988 Federal Trade Commission study, rigidly enforcing CAFE could cost the U.S. tens of thousands of jobs.

CAFE also may cost lives. This is because CAFE regulations will force consumers to buy smaller cars, which generally are less safe than larger cars. According to a 1988 study by economists Robert Crandall of the Brookings Institution and John Graham of the Harvard School of Public Health, CAFE could cause thousands of extra highway deaths; for the 1989 model year cars alone, these analysts estimate CAFE will be responsible for between 2,200 and 3,900 additional deaths.

The new Administration should take action to remove CAFE regulations. First, it should use the discretionary authority granted to it by the CAFE law and order the CAFE standard returned to 26 mpg or lowered even further. It then should urge Congress to repeal this harmful and unnecessary regulation.

—————————————————◇—————————————————

INITIATIVES FOR 1989

1) Investigate potential methods of restructuring the air traffic control system. The current federally operated air traffic control system has been unable to keep up with the changes in air traffic triggered by deregulation. It lacks the ability to do so because, as a federal agency, it is bound by restrictive personnel, procurement, and budget rules. It also lacks incentive to do so because it is accountable to politicians rather than its users. The new Administration must develop a plan to reorganize the system as a separate corporation, while at the same time giving its users direct control over its operation.

2) Firmly oppose all efforts to reregulate the railroad industry, and propose elimination of unfair labor rules which hamper productivity and destroy jobs. The partial deregulation of the railroad industry has been a success, halting the decline of American railroads while improving service and lowering prices for shippers. Efforts to reverse these gains must be firmly opposed by the new Administration. Equally important, the Administration must propose an agenda for further railroad reform, especially of the antiquated labor laws which hamper productivity while destroying jobs.

3) Propose legislation to eliminate remaining rate and route regulation of truckers, without affecting the industry's antitrust status. The partial deregulation of the trucking industry also has succeeded. Deregulation should now be completed through legislation to eliminate remaining rate and route regulations which cost the industry millions of dollars each year. This legislation should not deprive the industry of its current status under the antitrust laws. To address the antitrust issue, the Administration should establish an independent commission to study whether trucking "rate bureaus" have a positive or negative effect on consumer welfare.

4) Continue efforts by the Urban Mass Transportation Administration to encourage private-sector involvement in mass transit and to revise grant programs. UMTA has been encouraging private firms to provide local transit services, saving money for the federal and local governments and improving service. These efforts should be continued. At the same time the new Administration should propose changes in UMTA grants to local transit authorities by decreasing the percentage of federal subsidy available for capital construction, and by replacing varying operating subsidies with unrestricted block grants. This will encourage local authorities to weigh the costs and benefits of particular projects better, and to build systems which meet local needs, rather than federal requirements.

5) Employ DOT's discretionary authority to return the CAFE standard level to 26 mpg or lower. Corporate average fuel economy (CAFE) standards require automobile manufacturers over several years to increase the average fuel efficiency of their cars sold in the U.S. This has forced Americans to buy smaller cars, which are less safe than the larger vehicles many want to buy. In addition it could shift automobile production overseas, costing thousands of American jobs. Current law gives DOT the authority to lower CAFE standards to 26 mpg, if a higher level is not "feasible." This authority had been exercised until the 1989 model year when it allowed the level to rise to 26.5 mpg. The new Administration should act to return the CAFE standard to 26 mpg or lower.

6) Publicize examples of pork-barrel highway projects. The 1987 highway bill was filled with dozens of pork-barrel highway projects, mandating specific highway construction projects. While such projects help get Congressmen reelected, they also illustrate how highway decision-making power has been usurped from local authorities by the federal government. These projects should be well publicized by the Administration, so as to garner support for defederalization of the highway programs when the current authorization expires in 1990.

22

The Department of the Treasury

Thomas M. Humbert*
Task Force Chairman

The Department of the Treasury is principally responsible, according to the *U.S. Government Manual*, for ". . . formulating and recommending economic, financial, tax, and fiscal policies; serving as financial agent to the U.S. Government; enforcing the law; and manufacturing coins and currency." The Secretary of the Treasury generally serves as the President's chief economic adviser and spokesman. The way in which the Treasury Department discharges these responsibilities, particularly its tax and economic policy formulation mandate, can influence significantly the framework within which the U.S. economy operates.

Despite record increases in federal tax revenues as tax rate reductions have stimulated American entrepreneurship and growth in the economy, the budget deficit has increased during the Reagan presidency. This has been the result of record increases in federal spending, caused in large part by congressional resistance to the Administration's budget cut proposals.

Deregulation has helped spur new financial services for Americans. Technological advances, as well as innovative interpretations by bankers and regulators of existing banking laws, have lowered the legal wall separating investment and commercial banking. Nonetheless, the 1933 Glass-Steagall Act, which restricts the activities of both banking sectors, remains to be torn down completely. Deregulation of deposit interest rates and of the activities in which thrifts may participate have allowed many prudent savings and loans to thrive. The failure to deregulate federal deposit insurance, however, has encouraged many

---

*Commenting and contributing generously to this chapter were *Mandate III* Task Force Members Catherine England, Stephen Entin, David Fand, and Richard Rahn. They do not necessarily endorse all of its views and recommendations.
Task Force Deputy Chairman: John Buttarazzi.

439

BUDGET AND PERSONNEL

Secretaries

Nicholas F. Brady	1988–present
James A. Baker, III	1985–1988
Donald Regan	1981–1985

Personnel

March 1988	171,158
April 1980	139,282
April 1970	102,790

Budget Outlays

Fiscal Year	Total (billions)
1989 Estimate	$205.7
1988 Estimate	$198.9
1987 Actual	$180.3
1986 Actual	$179.2
1985 Actual	$164.9
1980 Actual	$ 76.5
1970 Actual	$ 19.3

banks and thrifts to engage in excessively risky activities. Some thrifts, taking advantage of federally insured deposits, engaged in particularly unwise practices and collapsed, leaving the government to pick up the tab.

Inflation has been brought under control, thanks to a policy of general monetary restraint carried out by the Federal Reserve Board and backed by the Administration. Yet, because the international monetary system lacks any anchor or standard of value, exchange rates have fluctuated widely and interest rates remain high compared with their historical levels.

The most important economic policy lesson of the Reagan years is that economic progress is best assured by public policies that least constrain and distort the incentives and initiatives of the private sector's decision-makers and consumers. The excellent performance of the U.S. economy in recent years, however, is not attributable to skillful government management of this or that policy instrument. It is attributable to the capacity of the private market system to mobilize and direct production resources into uses that best satisfy the wants of Americans as determined by the market. For the new President, the central goal of public economic policy should be to identify and remove remaining impediments to the efficient functioning of the free market system.

To this end, budget and spending policy should be formulated with the recognition that virtually every government spending program distorts market signals and impairs market efficiency. The new President should insist that Congress restrain spending growth and new spending initiatives. Tax policy should be geared again to the goal of neutrality—where the spending and saving decisions of individuals and businesses are not distorted by tax considerations. Thus the new President should not attempt to use taxes to redistribute income and wealth. At the same time, the continuing bias of the tax code against families should be ended by restoring the personal exemption for children to a level equivalent to that of 40 years ago.

Regulatory policy should focus on improving market performance, not on dictating how markets are to perform their functions or on overruling market outcomes. Regulatory distinctions among commercial banks, investment banks, and thrift institutions should be eliminated, with the aim of providing consumers of financial services the easiest and most efficient access to them and lowering the cost of capital to American business. Monetary policy should not try to manipulate the short-run course of the economy, but instead should concentrate on providing certainty about the stable course of monetary expansion over time.

A necessary prerequisite for price stability and low interest rates is a currency anchored to a price or price index. Historically, guaranteeing the conversion of the dollar, and eventually every major world currency, into a fixed weight of gold or a basket of commodities has created reasonable price and exchange rate stability over long periods of time.

---◇---

SUMMARY OF AGENCY FUNCTIONS

The Treasury Department is charged with developing economic policy, implementing the tax code, and raising tax revenue. Its bureaus are arranged in three main informal groups:

◆ *Policymaking offices, like the Offices of the Assistant Secretaries for Tax Policy and Economic Policy*, which develop policy proposals.

◆ *Offices with both operating and policy-making roles,* like the Internal Revenue Service, the Assistant Secretary for Domestic Finance, and the Comptroller of the Currency, which manage Treasury functions and promulgate regulations.

◆ *Operating subdivisions with little or no policy-making responsibility*, like the Bureau of Alcohol, Tobacco and Firearms, the U.S. Customs Office, and the U.S. Mint.

Although the Secretary of the Treasury is regarded as the Administration's chief economic spokesman, in practice, economic policy formulation is distributed broadly across the government—Congress, various government agencies, the independent Federal Reserve Board, and the White House itself through its policy groups.

———————————————◇———————————————

INSTITUTIONAL CONSTRAINTS

The Treasury may be the lead agency for economic affairs in an Administration, but in reality it is only one player in setting the course of economic policy. Other government agencies and regulatory bodies, together with the Office of Management and Budget and senior White House officials, also influence policy-making. In addition, congressional committees try to take the lead in many areas of economic policy, particularly tax issues, where key constituents and interests groups are affected. And many major decisions are bound by existing economic conditions or laws. In recent years the federal deficit has been such an influence, as has the Gramm-Rudman-Hollings Act mandating certain deficit targets. Added to this equation is the need to consider Wall Street reaction to government proposals and policies. The bond, foreign exchange, and stock markets can fluctuate wildly on the basis of a remark by the Treasury secretary, let alone a policy proposal. An adverse reaction from these markets can force policy-makers to reevaluate or withdraw proposals.

Special interest groups representing business and taxpayers also constrain economic policy, especially actions requiring legislation. These groups lobby hard and contribute to the political campaigns of the lawmakers who are willing to support these groups or oppose measures considered harmful by the groups. Yet the influence of these interests is limited. When the tax committees of Congress meet behind closed doors, the lobbyists have little clout when basic tax issues are discussed. As the debate over the 1986 Tax Act indicated, prevailing public opinion—in that case, strong support for reduced tax rates—tends to overshadow pressure from individual firms or industries.

In developing policy for financial institutions, the Treasury is constrained by the competing interests of commercial banks, investment banks, thrifts, and "nonbank" banks. Interest group pressure is more influential here than in tax policy because ordinary Americans are affected only indirectly and thus tend not to clamor for particular proposals regarding financial institutions. Treasury policy is also influenced by the Federal Reserve Board, the Federal Home Loan Bank Board, and the Securities and Exchange Commission. In some instances, these quasi-independent bodies will lobby Congress for more money to enforce regulations, or as in the case of some Federal Home Loan Banks, for forbearance from closing thrifts.

Monetary policy is formulated chiefly by an "independent" Federal Reserve Board. Still, statements by the Secretary of the Treasury, as perceived by the financial markets, often carry authority equal to that of the Federal Reserve, and often have an immediate impact on exchange rates. Monetary policy is also constrained by international influences and agreements, chiefly those attempting to stabilize or change the value of exchange rates. As such, the Treasury must anticipate and cooperate with the decisions of foreign governments, who often intervene on their own behalf in currency markets.

---◇---

THE REAGAN ADMINISTRATION RECORD

When Ronald Reagan took office, inflation was 13.5 percent and unemployment 7.5 percent, while the Gross National Product (GNP) was actually declining. The turnaround by mid–1988 has been remarkable, what West Europeans enviously call the "American Miracle." By November 1987, the U.S. economy had been growing longer uninterruptedly than at any time in history, except for periods of war. Growth continued strong into and through 1988. Reagan's most visible success has been the extraordinary cut in marginal tax rates: from a top rate of 70 percent, it was cut to 50 percent and then to 33 percent. Sandwiched between these two commendable cuts, however, was the Administration's unwise support for the so-called Tax Equity and Fiscal Responsibility Act of 1982, which included a $99 billion tax hike.

The Reagan Administration can take pride in the policies and legislation that have helped to ignite the remarkable transformation of the once-tottering U.S. economy by freeing up the wheels of the private sector. The central features of Reagan's economic strategy have been lower tax rates, deregulation, and a stable money supply. Lower tax rates increase incentives to work, save, invest, and take risks. Deregulation enhances competition, resulting in lower prices for consumers, and markets that operate quicker and more smoothly, increasing overall efficiency, and greatly reducing the shortages and surpluses of goods and services which characterized the 1970s.

The Economic Recovery Tax Act of 1981 (ERTA) lowered the top marginal rate from 70 percent to 50 percent and indexed personal exemptions, the standard deduction, and taxable income brackets, essentially eliminating "bracket creep." ERTA also replaced the complex and antiquated depreciation system for U.S. business with a simple and modern capital cost recovery system, the Accelerated Cost Recovery System (ACRS). This system shortened the depreciable life of assets, thus giving business larger tax deductions and increasing cash flows available for reinvestment.

The rapid increase in the deficit in late 1981 and 1982 produced the mislabeled Tax Equity and Fiscal Responsibility Act (TEFRA) of 1982. This significantly reversed several of ERTA's important advances, particularly the capital recovery provisions. Most of the additional revenue expected to be raised by TEFRA came from additional taxes on saving and investment, thus reintroducing a strongly anti-business, antisaving, and anticapital formation bias into the tax code. Moreover, it was a significant move away from the goal of "tax neutrality," a term used by experts to mean that spending and saving decisions are made according to fundamental economic factors, not artificial tax considerations.

Following TEFRA, other revenue-increasing tax measures, including parts of the Tax Reform Act of 1986, have been departures from the theme struck by the initial Reagan economic program.

The 1986 Act, for example, repealed the investment tax credit and modified ACRS; these were major retreats from neutrality. Other measures, such as introduction of an alternative minimum tax for corporations, punitive revisions of the foreign tax provisions, and repeal of the net long-term capital gains exclusion by individuals, also have increased the relative costs of saving and capital, and distorted investment decisions.

At the same time, the 1986 Act removed more than 4 million Americans from the federal income tax rolls by providing very substantial increases in personal exemptions and the standard deduction. While this made sense, the Act unwisely phased out the personal exemption for upper-income individuals in what is an undisguised income redistribution measure. In fact, the 1986 Act will be shifting about $120 billion of income tax liabilities from individuals to corporations between 1987 and 1991. Even with the lower personal and corporate tax rates, certain types of investment and savings probably are taxed higher now than they were before the 1986 Act. Yet dramatically lower tax rates on labor and capital will encourage other types of business investment and entrepreneurship, since lowering the cost of labor reduces a major cost of doing business.

Moreover, only individual Americans pay taxes. Taxes are levied on businesses, but the money to pay those taxes ultimately comes out of the pockets of investors and workers, in received earnings, or consumers in higher prices. Thus the shift in tax liabilities from individuals to corporations is more apparent than real. Nevertheless, further efforts should be made to reduce the role of tax in business and family decision-making. The aim should be to integrate corporate taxation into the individual income tax.

The Reagan Administration has moved swiftly to reduce red tape in the financial industry, enabling banks and other institutions to respond to the needs of a growing economy. Most interest rates paid on deposits have been deregulated. New financial instruments such as "securitized" loans and commercial paper, as well as more liberal interpretation of existing banking law by the courts and federal regulators, have moved commercial banks and investment banks closer together in form and function. Interstate banking, moreover, is rapidly advancing as state lawmakers have opened their borders to out-of-state banks.

This partial deregulation benefits sound institutions and their borrowers and depositors. Deregulation allows banks and thrifts to diversify risks across geographic and product lines as well as to broaden their investment opportunities. For borrowers, deregulation eases access to and lowers the costs of capital as new entrants into the financial industry generally have increased competition resulting in lower borrowing rates. For depositors, the lifting of interest ceilings means that many now earn interest on deposits at rates effectively above that of inflation.

Yet federal banking laws and regulations still have not caught up with the technological and international innovations driving the financial services sector. The Reagan Administration has failed to level the playing field in financial services by winning repeal of Glass-Steagall, the 1933 law which severely restricts commercial banks from engaging in securities business and prevents investment banks from offering deposit facilities to individual Americans. Whereas foreign-owned commercial banks may operate investment banks in America, U.S. law denies U.S.-owned commercial banks the same privilege. U S.-owned banks, however, can maintain investment banking facilities overseas. The result: an increasingly large number of American firms are looking overseas when seeking capital. An unclear and ambivalent response to the thrift crisis, moreover, has left that industry worse off and has brought forth calls by some congressmen for reregulation.

The retreat from the original Reagan tax strategy has been due in large part to the increasing focus by lawmakers and some Reagan Administration officials on the federal deficit. This reveals a misunderstanding of the nature and scale of the deficit. Some critics of the Administration argue that the gap between revenue and spending has been due to supposedly unparalleled levels of defense spending under Ronald Reagan. National defense was about 5 percent of GNP in fiscal 1980, well below the 7-to-9 percent range typical of the 1960s. The early Reagan budgets envisioned defense spending rising to just over 6 percent of real GNP, still below the proportion spent in the 1960s. Defense spending rose to a peak of 6.5 percent in 1986, before slipping to an estimated 6.1 percent in 1988. At most, therefore, defense adds $148 billion to the federal budget in a period when federal revenues are up $337 billion.

Other critics argue that the deficit has been caused by excessive tax cuts. Yet, although tax rates have been reduced, the major tax bills during the Reagan years, together with previously enacted measures, have left total federal revenues virtually unchanged as a share of GNP compared with 1980—and well above 1972 levels. Receipts were 18.0 percent of GNP in fiscal 1972, 19.4 percent in fiscal 1980, and are projected to be 19.3 percent in fiscal 1988 and 19.5 percent in fiscal 1993. Without substantial cuts in individual income tax rates and tax indexing, taxes would have soared to 25 percent of GNP due to bracket creep and rising payroll tax rates, had the economy been able to withstand such punishment. The tax "cuts" of the early Reagan years were, in fact, merely reductions in the rapid increases enacted under prior law.

The cause of the sudden imbalance between taxes and outlays early in the Reagan Administration was a surge in spending caused, in part, by the 1981–1982 recession. This unexpected surge of red ink began panicking many Administration officials and congressional leaders within a year of Reagan's entering the White House. Deficit reduction soon became the driving force behind Administration and congressional budget policy, which yielded such counterproductive policies as the 1982 TEFRA tax increases.

The truth is that the federal deficit is not now nor was it ever out of control. The "cyclical" portion of the deficit, created by recession, peaked in fiscal 1982 and 1983 and amounted to about 3 percent of GNP—well over half the total deficit at that time. This high spending was due to unemployment insurance, welfare, and other costs associated with the recession. This deficit was a reaction to recession, not a threat to the economy, and has declined as the economy has surged toward full employment.

The net interest portion of the deficit is just over $140 billion. This is distorted by inflation, which led to the higher interest rates that show up in the budget as additional outlays. This same inflation, however, reduces the real value of federal debt owed to Americans by the government. The trouble is that this drop in real federal liabilities is not shown in the budget even though it offsets completely the inflation-induced rise in debt service costs.

What measures this distortion is the federal "structural" budget. This budget, which measures noninterest outlays less receipts, generally has been in balance, fluctuating between plus and minus 0.6 percent of GNP in the 1978–83 period, and slipping to a deficit of about 1 percent of GNP in 1984–1986, before climbing back to a deficit of 0.5 percent of GNP in 1987 and near balance in 1988. Counting state and local surpluses of about 1 percent of GNP, this portion of the deficit was in surplus in 1987.

Thus as the economy reaches full employment, it is clear that high real (that is, inflation-adjusted) interest rates are the principal cause of the government deficit. Since 1981, real interest rates have raised the cost of servicing the government debt by almost 200 percent, making interest payments the fastest growing segment of federal spending. If interest rates on government debt could be reduced to the more historical levels of 4 percent or 5 percent, down from current levels of 7 percent or 8 percent, the federal deficit would be slashed by more than half.

The Administration has presided over a period of uncertain monetary policy. Many observers believe that the Federal Reserve Board has vacillated between extreme tightening of the supply of money and hitting the monetary accelerator. These wide fluctuations in monetary policy have whipsawed the economy. Yet despite these shorter-term fluctuations, double-digit inflation seems to have been broken by a long-term policy of strong restraint of monetary growth. The Administration generally has supported the Federal Reserve's tight money policy, even during the depths of the recession, when many argued for a more countercyclical policy.

More recently, the Treasury has sought to exert stronger leadership over monetary affairs by convening a number of international monetary conferences, designed first to urge the Federal Reserve Board to bring the dollar to a more reasonable level through monetary easing, and then to encourage international markets to stabilize the dollar. The dramatic reduction in the dollar's value since the third quarter of 1985 has provoked a healthy surge in U.S. exports and pared down the trade deficit.

Yet there is confusion about the goal of U.S. policy. Neither the Treasury nor the Federal Reserve Board has enunciated clearly its objectives or how they will be achieved. At times, vague statements are made about supporting noninflationary economic growth. At other times, the authorities stress lower interest rates. Yet clearly defined government objectives are fundamental to the efficient operation of free markets, and perhaps nothing is more important to the proper functioning of free markets than a currency of stable purchasing power.

The Administration has failed to reform fundamentally international economic development institutions. While pledged to molding these agencies toward a free market entrepreneurial strategy, the International Monetary Fund (IMF) still remains a bastion of austerity economic advice, recommending tax increases and currency devaluation as the solutions to debt problems. This philosophy is fundamentally out of step with the Reagan economic philosophy of growth and opportunity. (See Chapter 27.)

———————————◇———————————

THE NEXT FOUR YEARS

The central goal of the new President's economic policy should be to identify and remove impediments to the efficient functioning of the free market system. The new President must seek to eliminate regulatory constraints in every market. The guiding and paramount principle in budget and spending policy should be that less is better. And the goal of tax policy should be the flattest and lowest rates possible.

Reorganizing Treasury

The new President should reorganize the Treasury to eliminate two persistent problems that have weakened decision-making during the Reagan years. The first is that tax revenue estimates are made by the Office of Tax Analysis under the Assistant Secretary for Tax Policy. The tax policy division is largely staffed by lawyers—and properly so. But revenue estimates require strong economic skills. Estimating tax revenue thus should be moved to the Assistant Secretary for Economic Policy; more realistic and accurate estimates of tax revenues likely would be obtained. The second problem has been the large number of offices reporting directly to the secretary and deputy secretary. This makes it difficult for these top two officials to control effectively some key Treasury activities. Some officials, meanwhile, find it difficult to obtain proper access to the secretary, so their important activities are not always given sufficient priority by him.

In general, Treasury functions fall into two distinct categories. The first is the financial management of the U.S. government, the production of money, and bank regulatory functions not under the auspices of the Federal Reserve Board. The second group deals with domestic and international fiscal and monetary policy. To improve access to the secretary for those offices charged with formulating economic policy, an "Undersecretary for Tax, Economics, and International Affairs" should be created. Currently there is only an Undersecretary of Finance.

Under this new arrangement, lines of authority would be consolidated. Instead of reporting directly to the Office of the Secretary, the Comptroller of the Currency would report to the finance undersecretary, as would the treasurer, fiscal assistant secretary, and the Assistant Secretary of Domestic Finance. To ensure a high level of coordination among tax policy and domestic and international monetary affairs, the Assistant Secretary for International Affairs, the Assistant Secretary for Tax Policy, and the Assistant Secretary for Economic Policy would be brought together under the new Undersecretary for Tax, Economic and International Affairs.

Constructing a More Neutral Tax System

To be as neutral as possible, the tax system should rely on taxes that least distort the relative prices that the market system would produce in the absence of taxes. This means that economic choices would be altered as little as possible by tax considerations. At the same time, the tax system as a whole should be as effective as possible in making explicit the costs of private activities and government programs.

The mainstay of a tax system meeting these demands would remain an individual income tax, but one configured substantially differently from that in the present code. Such a system would have five fundamental characteristics:

First, it would be imposed only on individuals, recognizing that corporations are inanimate and do not and cannot bear taxes but merely act as conduits supplying taxable income to employees.

Second, it would impose its liabilities on the most uniform possible income tax base. Thus deductions should be limited as far as possible to costs incurred in producing the income included in the tax base. These costs would be treated in the same way, no matter how much income the taxpayer earned. This means that the alternative minimum tax should be eliminated, since a minimum tax imposes different rates of tax on different firms engaged in the same activities. Similarly, only income actually spent would be taxed, while income used to generate more taxable income would not. Thus there should be the broadest and most general possible exclusion of current saving from taxation, and the most complete possible inclusion of all returns on that saving.

Third, it would impose its liabilities at the lowest and flattest possible statutory rates.

Fourth, it would not attempt to disguise its imposition of liabilities. Disguised taxes prevent Americans from assessing whether the activities of government are worth the taxes they pay. Taxes on corporations, for instance, are merely passed on to individual taxpayers through higher prices, yet most Americans assume that imposing taxes on business will mean lower taxes on individuals. Thus the system would eliminate corporate taxation.

And, fifth, it would regard the family as the basic unit of society. As such, tax policy would not discriminate against traditional families, nor favor families in which both spouses are employed over families where a spouse stays home to raise children. Just as tax policy should not discriminate against saving and investment, it is equally as important that it not discriminate against families and children.

Reforming the federal tax system to meet these criteria would be formidable. Several steps must be taken at the outset of the new Administration. The first is to propose legislation to undo the anti-saving, anticapital formation thrust of the 1986 tax law. The real marginal tax rate facing saving and investment decisions is substantially greater than that on income used for current consumption. To reduce the bias against savings and capital formation, the new President should press for at least 60 percent of net long-term capital gains to be excluded from taxation, thereby lowering the top capital gain rate to 13 percent. Eventually, all capital gains and losses should be excluded from the base of the income tax.

In addition to restoring the pre–1986 treatment of capital gains, the new Administration should seek legislation to establish full and effective "expensing" of all capital outlays, irrespective of the type of capital, its owner, or its use, as the standard for a truly neutral capital cost recovery system. Notions of "useful life" and "economic depreciation" should be excised from the Internal Revenue Code. Expensing allows the entire cost of a capital item to be deducted from taxable income in the year of its purchase. To preserve tax neutrality, the business deduction for interest expense should be repealed. This would create a tax code that is neutral between saving and investment.

Renewed emphasis also should be given to removing tax impediments to personal saving. The 1986 law's severe restrictions on Individual Retirement Accounts (IRAs) should be repealed, along with the limits that legislation imposed on 401(K) plans and other employee saving arrangements. This liberalization not only would reduce taxes on savings, but would encourage individuals to assume greater responsibility for setting aside funds for the education of their children, their retirement, and their health care.

The next Administration should seek to roll back other 1986 Tax Act provisions that increase the complexity and punitive impact of the income tax on businesses. Among these: the alternative minimum tax on corporations, which discriminates against rapidly growing firms, and the foreign tax provisions, which not only violate the neutrality principle, but also subject the overseas operations of U.S. firms to heavier tax burdens than are imposed on their foreign competitors.

Designing a Pro-Family Tax Code

A policy designed to end the tax system's bias against the American family by ending the oppressive taxes on children would be, perhaps, the most important new tax policy initiative of the new President. In the last half century, the tax system has become significantly biased against children as the personal exemption has eroded in value. In 1948, a personal exemption of $600 equaled 42 percent of average per capita income. Had the personal exemption kept up with income growth, the exemption in mid–1988 would be worth $6,468. Yet, although the 1986 Tax Reform Act doubled the personal exemption to $2,000, it offset only partially the erosion in the exemption's value. Between 1960 and 1984, the average tax rate, as a proportion of income for single Americans and married couples with no children, did not increase, but for a married couple with two children, it climbed 43 percent; for a family with four children, average tax rates increased 233 percent.

This huge tax increase has forced both spouses in many families to enter the workforce. This, in turn, has provoked demands for federal programs to subsidize day care services, so that mothers can go to work. But rather than provide expensive federal day care, the solution is to address the root of the problem: overtaxation of American families. A pro-family tax policy should restore the value of the personal exemption for young children, repeal the current dependent care credit (which only benefits two-earner couples who use professional day care), and adjust and expand the earned income tax credit (EITC) for family size. The EITC provides low-income Americans with a tax credit that is a fixed percentage of earned income. Therefore, with the EITC, benefits are increased the more the recipient works. Expanding the EITC also would make sound welfare policy. The reason for this is that it is refundable (that is, it is paid to families even if the credit exceeds their tax liability). Hence it is a welfare benefit linked to work effort. (See Welfare section of Chapter 13.)

Proposals also have been made for a "toddler tax credit" of $750 to low-income families for each child under six years of age. While this is far preferable to federally provided day care, the best approach would be to raise the personal exemption for all children, since all families with children have experienced huge increases in federal taxes.

Tackling the Thrift Crisis

The new President must take swift action to deal with the continued weaknesses of the thrift industry and must revive the financial institutions' deregulation momentum. The insolvency of the savings and loan industry and its insurance fund, the Federal Savings and Loan Insurance Corporation (FSLIC), is perhaps the most urgent financial problem facing the new Administration.

A resolution of the current FSLIC crisis is needed to restore confidence and avoid a serious collapse in the savings and loan industry. Although short-term action must defuse the immediate crisis, prudent and fundamental long-term reforms are needed to correct the flaws in the federal deposit insurance and regulatory systems and thus prevent a similar predicament from recurring.

The current weaknesses of the thrift industry stem in large part from certain incentives in the federal insurance system-administered FSLIC. FSLIC assesses a premium at a flat rate percentage of a thrift's deposits without any regard to the risk implied by the loan portfolio. This has encouraged thrifts to act recklessly. Institutions insured by FSLIC are tempted to pursue higher profits through riskier investments because their deposit customers, who have been led to expect government protection, are largely unconcerned about the thrifts' behavior. Moreover, with no more equity at risk and with federally insured deposits to loan, insolvent banks often make riskier yet higher interest-paying loans in gambles which are safe from their perspective alone.

The Federal Deposit Insurance Corporation (FDIC), which insures bank deposits, is in better shape than its thrift industry counterpart, but suffers from the same serious deficiency of charging premiums not based on risk. Cracks are beginning to show at FDIC, as annual bank failures have set postwar records throughout much of this decade.

Insurance premiums for banks and thrifts must be based on the track record of the institution's management and the structure of its loans and deposits. Here premium costs would reflect the stability of the institution, thus discouraging excessively risky loans and restoring health to the financial industry. By charging a flat percentage premium, FDIC and FSLIC have violated a fundamental rule of insurance and thus have invited catastrophe. FDIC and FSLIC thus should be allowed to vary their premiums according to the risks inherent in the practices of the particular bank or thrift. Bank examiners already assign banks to one of the five categories according to the soundness of their operations. There should now be a corresponding set of categories for setting premiums.

The long-term goal of the new President should be to take government out of the business of insuring bank and thrift deposits, leaving that to the private insurance industry. Only this would restore market discipline to the industry and encourage depositors and investors to monitor more closely the activities of institution managers. Since Americans are used to deposit insurance provided by FDIC and FSLIC, however, it would be impossible to move to private insurance for several years. Nevertheless, the next Administration could take important first steps to improve significantly the current situation and prepare the ground for more complete reform.

Federal regulators, for instance, should prevent any federally insured depository institution from continuing in operation once its equity capital fell below established minimums. That would end the current problem of weak institutions threatening the stability of the strong. Undercapitalized institutions should be given the option of raising new capital or accepting a federally arranged merger. The only other alternative should be immediate liquidation.

FDIC and FSLIC should be required to discontinue bailout policies that result in depositors receiving guarantees in excess of the statutory $100,000 limit. Federal insurance protection should never be extended beyond the bank to the holding company or other affiliates. When a bank's losses exceed its equity capital, uninsured bank creditors should bear a part of those losses. Putting large depositors at risk in this way would encourage them to scrutinize management activities more diligently. Even more market discipline, and hence stability, could be enhanced by establishing a five- to ten-year schedule for reducing the size of federally guaranteed deposits from the current $100,000, an amount that clearly goes beyond protecting small depositors, as well as limiting insurance coverage to $100,000 (or less) per individual rather than the current practice of insuring each deposit of an individual, even if that person's total deposits exceed $100,000.

The above steps would help bring stability to the smaller thrifts and banks that are most under pressure. But if America's financial institutions are to be made more secure, federal action to reorganize troubled institutions must be predictable and swift, particularly when large institutions are involved. The federal banking authorities' uncertainty in dealing with the massive 1984 failure of the Continental Illinois National Bank and Trust Company of Chicago sent confused signals to other large financial institutions regarding the way the federal government would act if they ran into trouble. FDIC, FSLIC, and the Federal Reserve Board thus should develop and publicize a plan for handling large failures. This plan should contain a clearly stated policy for handling potential liquidity problems at solvent banks or thrifts linked to troubled institutions. Swift, predictable action by the federal authorities would alleviate unfounded public unease. At the same time, the new President should make it clear that there will be no federal bailouts beyond the terms of the plan.

Given the problems encountered by thrifts, there have been calls to reregulate the industry. This would be a mistake. Although deregulation may have provided thrifts with additional ways in which to take business risks, it also provided sound benefits to its depositors, borrowers, and consumers in the form of improved services and a better return on their savings. The problem is not deregulation. It is allowing managers a free ride on federal insurance and permitting insolvent institutions to continue operating at the expense of sounder thrifts.

Thrifts' basic insurance premium is one-twelfth of one percent of deposits—the same as banks. FSLIC-insured institutions must pay, in addition to the basic premium, a special assessment of one-eighth of one percent, which is used to rescue insolvent thrifts. It is unfair for well-managed thrifts to have to pay FSLIC insurance premiums two and one-half times the rate charged to mutual savings banks with FDIC coverage. Thus if a thrift meets the FDIC's capital requirements, it should be permitted to transfer to the FDIC from the FSLIC. But if they wish to transfer, such thrifts should be required to pay an "exit fee" to FSLIC. While this may appear unfair, successful thrifts have in fact benefited over the years from being able to raise funds at a lower cost than they could have otherwise without federal deposit insurance. Thus they should bear some of the burden of relieving FSLIC's crisis. The fee could equal some reasonable percent (0.5 percent has been suggested) of the firm's average deposits over three years.

Permitting thrifts to transfer to the FDIC, however, ignores the key issue of whether it is necessary to have a separate U.S. thrift industry. Savings and loan associations, encouraged by federal regulators, originally were organized to pool individual savings and provide home mortgages. Permitting thrifts to convert to banks, however, would not dry up mortgage lending, since many sources of home financing exist outside the thrift industry. Home buyers can today finance the purchase of their homes through commercial banks, finance companies, credit unions, insurance companies, and even automobile manufacturers. All of these industries stand on a more solid footing than the shaky saving and loan industry.

Thrifts unable to transfer to the FDIC should be sold or liquidated. Liquidation likely may involve taxpayer funds. While the thrift industry, as any other industry, should survive or fail without taxpayer assistance, Congress has already committed itself to backing federally insured depositories with the full faith and credit of the United States. To renege on this promise would compromise seriously the credibility of the American banking system as well as the value of government securities.

Reforming U.S. Banking Laws

After introducing policies to return both the banking and savings and loan industries to a sound footing, the new President should address the issue of bank powers. The Glass-Steagall Act of 1933 separates financial institutions into investment banks, which underwrite stock offerings and most bond issues, and commercial banks, which lend money and maintain demand deposits. This Depression-era legislation is out of step with today's financial industry and has placed U.S. banks at an increasing disadvantage to foreign competitors.

Giving broader freedom to banks to deal in securities, real estate, insurance, and other financial services would increase competition, thus giving consumers better and more varied services. And by encouraging diversity, it would enhance the stability of the financial industry.

Some critics of such deregulation claim that it would recreate the alleged unstable banking conditions of the 1920s and 1930s. Recent historical research, however, has found that the ability of commercial banks to deal in securities was not the cause of the Depression, nor was the Glass-Steagall Act a proper response to the problems of securities firms and banks.

The goal of the next Administration's policies regarding financial institutions should be to increase market discipline and competition in all financial markets. To do this, Glass-Steagall should be repealed, as should the 1956 Bank Holding Company Act, which restricts bank activities and ownership, and the 1927 McFadden Act, which restricts interstate banking. Anyone should be able to own a bank, and bank holding companies should be able to own any other type of business, as long as the bank is adequately and separately capitalized.

Stabilizing International Finance and Monetary Policy

Monetary policy is complicated by the fact that legal authority in the monetary area rests primarily with the Federal Reserve System, an agency with independent statutory authority. A presidential proposal to change monetary policy would clash with a widely accepted view that monetary policy should be nonpolitical and that the Federal Reserve should not be subject to political pressure.

In practice, monetary policy is highly political and subject to substantial presidential influence and control. Thus the new President and Secretary of the Treasury should encourage the Federal Reserve Board to pursue a monetary policy that would enhance strong economic growth. This requires monetary growth which is stable and predictable over the long term to assure price stability. Similarly, stable exchange rates resulting from consistent monetary policy are needed to encourage trade.

A necessary prerequisite for price stability is a currency "anchored" in some way, to a commodity for instance, so that monetary authorities cannot increase or decrease at will the supply of the currency. Historically, guaranteeing the conversion of the dollar and other currencies into a fixed weight of gold created reasonable price and exchange rate stability over long periods.

Thus the new Administration should give serious consideration to recreating a monetary system that is anchored by gold or some "basket of commodities" including gold; the value of the dollar would be pegged to such a basket. This means that the dollar would be fully convertible into a fixed quantity of these commodities. There cannot be a stable international monetary system with discretionary central bank intervention. A modernized gold standard also would help separate monetary from trade and budget policy, a prerequisite for exchange rate stability.

―――――――――◇―――――――――

INITIATIVES FOR 1989

1) Enact a revenue-neutral tax reform to increase the personal exemption for children to $6,500. The American family is overtaxed. The failure of Congress over the last four decades to keep the personal exemption at the same proportion of family income has imposed an increasing tax burden on lower- and middle-income families. This has forced spouses into the workforce to maintain after-tax family income. Increasing the exemption to $6,500 would restore tax exemption to tax the same proportion of income that prevailed in 1948.

2) Expand and adjust the earned income tax credit (EITC) to account for family size. The EITC is a tax credit for lower-income families based on a fixed percentage of earned income. It grants tax relief to the working poor. Increasing the EITC thus would provide extra income to lower-paid Americans on the verge of poverty. Adjusting it for family size would further reduce the antichild bias of the tax code on lower-income families.

3) Win passage of a Taxpayer's Bill of Rights. A "Taxpayer Bill of Rights" would provide the proper checks on the IRS to ensure that tax enforcement is administered in a fair, judicious, and professional manner. Such a Bill of Rights should, among other things: enable taxpayers to recover damages in court for IRS actions that are reckless or intentionally in disregard of statute; require the IRS substantially to justify its actions or else pay the taxpayer's legal fees; and make the

IRS ombudsman, who represents taxpayer interests, a presidential appointee rather than an IRS civil servant. The burden of proof in tax cases should be shifted from the taxpayer to the IRS.

4) Enact a 1989 Tax Reform Act to remove the antisaving biases of the 1986 Act. The 1986 Tax Act contains numerous provisions which discriminate against savings and investment. The new President should introduce legislation to repeal these discriminatory features. Such legislation should reduce the capital gains rate, restore the tax deductibility of IRAs and 401(k) plans, and permit the immediate expensing of all capital outlays.

5) Block all tax increases. With federal tax revenues as a share of GNP running at historic highs, Americans are not undertaxed. Government spending, on the other hand, has established new records for peacetime. New taxes, moreover, would reduce economic activity, thus reducing revenues. And, if past experience is a guide, Congress will use new revenues for new spending.

6) Develop, with cooperation from the FDIC and Federal Reserve Board, contingency plans to handle large bank failures. The federal response to major bank failures, such as that of the Continental Illinois National Bank in 1984, has been inconsistent. This has created an atmosphere of uncertainty. To end this uncertainty, and thus improve confidence, the federal authorities need a clear and well-publicized plan for dealing with future failures by large banks. The plan should include a procedure for conducting routine business through the failed institution since merger or shutdown arrangements take some time. Large banks often act as correspondent banks for smaller local banks. Correspondent banks receive deposits from smaller banks. Correspondent relationships are established to facilitate check collection, provide increased lending capabilities, and offer other banking services such as foreign exchange services. When a large bank fails, local banks may themselves be jeopardized because of correspondent relationships. Most important, a policy should be established for handling liquidity problems at solvent banks or thrift institutions that might have a correspondent or other business relationship with the troubled institution. A policy statement should be issued eliminating a bailout as a possible response, regardless of the bank's size.

7) Introduce legislation to phase in securities, real estate, and insurance powers for banks. The 1933 Glass-Steagall Act and portions of the 1956

Bank Holding Company Act restrict the ability of banks to provide many services to consumers. This restricts diversification and so makes banks more vulnerable to changes in the economy. The new Administration should propose legislation to remove these restrictions. Expansion of activities for banks should be tied to reform of the federal deposit insurance system. As a first step in deposit insurance reform, the maximum $100,000 limit for all new deposits should be lowered and risk-based premiums introduced.

8) Take steps to merge thrifts into the banking industry. The Federal Savings and Loan Insurance Corporation (FSLIC) is in deep financial trouble, and well-managed thrifts currently have to pay high premiums to cover the costs of bailing out insolvent thrifts. This penalizes solvent thrifts and potentially could undermine their financial soundness. Well-managed thrifts thus should be permitted to obtain lower cost insurance from the Federal Deposit Insurance Corporation (FDIC), which insures banks. The moratorium on thrifts acquiring FDIC insurance should be lifted by the Federal Home Loan Bank Board immediately. All FSLIC-insured thrifts should be given a deadline to transfer to FDIC or find a buyer. Those failing to do so must be closed down.

9) Allow conversion of the dollar into a certain weight of gold, and convene an international monetary conference to develop a strategy to reform the world monetary system on the basis of a gold standard and/ or similar "anchor." Exchange rate stability is needed to maintain orderly and strong international trade. But stability is impossible when currencies are not linked to the value of a commodity, and thus domestic monetary authorities can vary the supply of money—and hence the value of a currency—almost at will. By restoring the dollar to the gold standard, or some similar tangible standard, stability would be reintroduced to the dollar. Moreover, given the strength and dominance of the U.S. economy, the U.S. Treasury can and should take the lead to encourage other major countries to link their currencies to the same standard.

PART THREE

FOREIGN POLICY AND NATIONAL DEFENSE

Foreign Policy and National Defense Overview

by W. Bruce Weinrod

The Reagan Administration took office confronting a decade-long accumulation of foreign and defense policy problems. Reduced military spending, unilateral halts in weapons systems, neoisolationist views, and a reluctance to consider the use of force all contributed to a perception abroad of U.S. retrenchment. Detente, flawed arms control treaties, and loosened restrictions on strategic trade and credit flow to the Soviet bloc were helping shift the military balance away from the West.

At home, Americans seemed demoralized and unwilling to play a global role. Vietnam, Watergate, the leadership failure of the Carter years, and the downplaying of the Soviet challenge by the Nixon, Ford, and Carter Administrations had led some Americans to conclude that: the threat or actual use of U.S. force, except where narrowly defined vital U.S. interests were clearly at stake, was unwise; the U.S. no longer could influence significantly the course of world events; the U.S. was the primary cause of international tensions and conflict, or at least was as much to blame as Moscow; the expansion of U.S. international influence was undesirable; the triumph of leftist or Marxist insurgencies and movements in developing nations was inevitable; and the President's authority to use force overseas should be seriously constrained.

Much of this has changed in the Reagan years. The Kremlin has admitted that it, not the U.S., has been on the wrong track, and has begun a reform program which could transform the Soviet system dramatically. The other communist giant, the People's Republic of China, is pursuing a far-reaching economic restructuring and openly uses free-market mechanisms. And in Eastern Europe, there is unprecedented political and intellectual ferment. Communist ideology, it now is almost universally said, has lost all appeal to the general population.

As important, democratic capitalism is gaining. In Latin America and Asia, transitions from authoritarian rule to democracy have taken place in a dozen nations. Many governments in the developing world are trying free-market economic programs. Many of the Third World elite are rejecting collectivist ideologies and recognizing the connection between democratic capitalism and economic growth. And the anticommunist insurgencies in Afghanistan, Angola, Nicaragua, and elsewhere have prevented at a minimum the full consolidation of any new communist regimes in the developing world; this has led, in Afghanistan, to the first forced withdrawal of Soviet troops since World War II. The global correlation of forces, which shifted alarmingly toward the Soviets in the 1970s, now has swung sharply back toward the U.S.

While many factors, of course, are responsible for such historic developments, a key role has been played by Reagan Administration policies. These have shifted decisively the underlying dynamics of U.S. foreign and defense policies in several important ways:

Enhancing America's role in the world. Reagan has directed and presided over America's reassertion of its active world role. Previously, the U.S. had been drawing inward and seemed unwilling or unable to exert influence even close to its borders. The Sandinista hijacking of the Nicaraguan revolution, for example, was helped greatly by the deliberate 1979 U.S. decision to abstain from influencing the political dynamics of the immediate post-Somoza environment, thus leaving a vacuum which the Sandinistas filled. In contrast, the U.S. moved quickly in 1986 to help genuine democratic forces after the flight of Ferdinand Marcos from the Philippines.

Reestablishing a willingness to use force. U.S. behavior in the 1970s led many observers to wonder aloud whether the U.S. ever would be capable of using force in a situation that did not present an unambiguous direct challenge to vital U.S. interests. The U.S. 1983 intervention in Grenada and the 1986 air strike against Libya changed this. It broke a psychological dam that blocked even the possibility of U.S. action. The result: U.S. adversaries now hesitate to take actions undermining even peripheral U.S. interests.

Changing the dynamics of U.S.-Soviet relations. Moscow has observed and taken into account Reagan's rhetoric and actions. In view of renewed U.S. strength, it is no accident that Moscow has not launched a new overseas adventure since Reagan has taken office. The dynamics of U.S. policy toward the USSR also have changed noticeably under Reagan. He abruptly shifted course from Carter's tentative, guilt-ridden approach which humored the Soviets and ignored their harsh rhetoric. The Reagan Administration also has taken the philosophical dimension of the U.S.-Soviet struggle very seriously. In the 1970s, the U.S. had become a pacifist in the war of ideas. Reagan has changed this, increasing funding for radio broadcasts and, for the first time in recent memory, challenging the ideology of communism itself. In his 1982 speech to Britain's Parliament, he not only called for the spread of democratic pluralism, but also stood Marxism on its head by predicting that communism would "end up on the ash heap of history."

Establishing sound arms control policies. While arms control has assumed a larger role in the final months of his Administration, Reagan generally has sought to make arms control negotiations only one of several key issues in U.S.-Soviet relations. Reagan's approach to arms control, meanwhile, significantly differs from earlier administrations. First, the U.S. has insisted upon negotiating actual reductions in nuclear weapons rather than regulated increases or freezes. Second, it largely has succeeded in shifting the subject of strategic arms reductions from launchers to missiles, warheads, and throwweight; this is important because launcher limits, attempted in the unratified 1979 SALT II strategic arms treaty, did not really hinder the Soviet nuclear buildup. Third, Reagan has forced Moscow to concede the principle of on-site inspection. Fourth, the U.S. has pursued these policies consistently rather than retreat at the first sign of Soviet recalcitrance (as the Carter Administration repeatedly did). Fifth, Reagan has been willing to walk away from an existing arms treaty that did not serve U.S. security interests, as he did with SALT I and II in 1986.

Sixth, Reagan has rejected the 1970s practice of preemptive concessions or "goodwill gestures," where the U.S. would concede an important bargaining point without any equivalent Soviet concession, hoping that the Kremlin would respond magnanimously to such gestures, which in fact it never did. Seventh, Reagan generally has avoided the euphoric excesses of earlier arms negotiations and has continued to remind Americans of the dangers posed by Soviet ideology and behavior, even when negotiations were at a critical stage, while previous administrations severely muted criticism of the Soviets for fear of offending them. Eighth, Reagan publicly and repeatedly has called Moscow to task for its arms treaty violations, while previous Presidents overlooked such violations in the perceived interest of overall U.S.-Soviet relations. Ninth, Reagan has rejected the temptation to buttress his popularity with an arms agreement, even before the 1984 election, demonstrating instead that it is possible to win reelection as President without having an arms agreement in hand.

Finally, and in the long run perhaps most significantly, the Administration has encouraged the development of a new paradigm for thinking about strategic arms control. This paradigm abandons the focus on offensive nuclear forces and the prohibition on defenses against nuclear attack. The new approach perceives strategic stability based primarily upon the ability to deter or defend against nuclear attack through strategic defenses rather than exclusively upon the ability to strike first or successfully retaliate.

Conducting effective alliance management. While supporting a strong North Atlantic Treaty Organization (NATO), the Administration has been willing to risk Alliance disagreement in the successful pursuit of important security interests. In 1982, for example, Reagan ignored warnings that U.S. sanctions imposed on European allies for their support of a Soviet oil pipeline might unravel NATO; he ordered sanctions. After expressing initial ruffled feelings, the allies finally began taking such security issues much more seriously and eventually agreed to reject a new Soviet pipeline proposal which would have made Western Europe significantly dependent on the Soviet energy shipments. Reagan also endorsed the Pentagon's hardline approach of tightly restricting the transfer of militarily useful advanced technologies from NATO to the Soviet bloc. After experiencing initial strong European resistance, this policy also has largely been adopted, and has made it considerably more difficult for Moscow to obtain militarily useful technology. The Administration has persuaded West European nations to agree that they should not subsidize trade with the Soviet Union.

Developing a firm policy toward international organizations. The Reagan Administration, more than any other since the founding of the United Nations in 1945, has changed U.S. policy toward the U.N. Although the U.N. as an institution still is reflexively hostile to U.S. values and interests, the Reagan Administration has made it clear that there are limits to U.S. patience with international organizations, and that continued U.S. support for, or even membership in, such institutions cannot be taken for granted. The Reagan Administration effectively told other nations that the positions they took in the U.N. could have direct consequences on the nature of their bilateral relationship with the U.S.

Shifting policy toward developing nations. The Reagan Administration has shifted policy toward the developing world. Rather than humor anti-Western socialist demagoguery, the Administration has pressured both developing nations and multilateral financial organizations to encourage an environment conducive to private-sector-driven economic growth. As a result, free-market-oriented thinking is permeating the younger generation of leaders and academics in many developing nations. Some governments are introducing such free-market policies as privatization, lower marginal tax rates, and deregulated agriculture, and are welcoming foreign private investment.

Conceptualizing the relationship between democratic pluralism and U.S. security. While the U.S. has always identified itself with freedom and pluralism, the Reagan Administration has linked the fate of democratic pluralism to U.S. security. The Administration's 1982 unveiling of the National Endowment for Democracy (NED) to fund democracy worldwide signaled that U.S. security interests are best served by the spread of democratic forms of government.

As important, the Administration has given this policy sophisticated operational content in three ways: first, it has used the NED to initiate projects that would pay off in the long term by helping to create, strengthen, or consolidate nascent democratic forces and institutions. These forces will be particularly useful as the day for democratic transition from authoritarian regimes arrives in such nations as Paraguay and Chile. Second, the Administration has developed and executed a subtle and calibrated approach to the short-term transitional challenges that have occurred in a number of Latin American nations, the Philippines, and South Korea. Third, the Administration has assisted viable Western-oriented movements seeking to topple Soviet-backed Marxist-Leninist regimes.

Responding to indirect aggression. Moscow and its proxies have understood that democracies—the U.S. in particular—have difficulty responding to subtle, ambiguous forms of aggression such as subversion, weapons infiltration, *coups d'état*, and destabilization through violence and terrorism; and that these democracies have similar difficulties responding to the Soviet use of proxies, such as the Cubans in Angola. As Reagan took office, it appeared that the U.S. could respond, if at all, only to clearcut major security threats. Here the Reagan Administration has charted the new course known as the "Reagan Doctrine." It has done so using two methods: first, targeted, limited military assistance to governments threatened by Marxist-Leninist insurgencies such as El Salvador; second, the provision of moral, political, economic, and even military support for viable movements resisting a Soviet-backed Marxist-Leninist regime as, for example, in Angola and Nicaragua.

While the Administration has achieved much, there understandably have been problems and shortcomings. Among them: 1) confusion and delay in deciding upon a secure basing mode for the new MX intercontinental ballistic missile that would make the MX less vulnerable to destruction by Soviet nuclear attack; 2) bowing to Congress's demands that the development or deployment of military systems, like an Anti-Satellite (ASAT) system, be linked with arms control progress; 3) failure to coordinate adequately policy governing the sale of items with military potential to the Soviet bloc or to give the Department of Defense a clearer role in that process; 4) committing U.S. forces to Lebanon without sufficient evaluation of its implications; and 5) failure to reorganize the U.S. Agency for International Development (AID) and have it pursue vigorous free-market and private-sector-oriented development policies. Sharing much of the blame for some of these shortcomings, of course, is Congress, which often refused to give the Administration the resources needed to carry out its policies.

The Administration also has not conveyed to the American public a complete sense of the goals of U.S. foreign and defense policy. This is necessary to provide guidelines for Administration policymakers, to demonstrate cohesion and purpose to the public, and to sustain public and congressional support for U.S. policies.

---◇---

THE NEXT ADMINISTRATION

While the nation may recover from flawed domestic policies, there is little margin for U.S. error in international politics. The U.S. must maintain not only its own security, but also help protect its allies and friends around the world. In the international arena, the ultimate contest is between the open and the closed society—between democratic pluralism and monolithic totalitarianism.

As did Ronald Reagan, the new President should focus on a few fundamental objectives rather than trying to do everything. Specific policy ideas should be evaluated on the basis of whether they would further such objectives as meeting the Soviet challenge, strengthening America's defense, and responding to changing international dynamics. In applying these principles, the new President will be faced with a global context for its foreign and defense policy that is substantially different from that which the Reagan Administration inherited. This new environment includes:

◆ An America which is more confident and willing to exercise an active international role and which is stronger militarily, yet which faces a shrinking defense budget.

◆ A Soviet Union which presents a new and more sophisticated challenge to the West and is undergoing important and potentially historic domestic changes that, among other things, will make it more difficult for the Kremlin to sustain its overseas empire.

◆ A North Atlantic Treaty Organization (NATO) in which some members seem unwilling to carry their fair share of the common defense burden and in which a reassessment of the role of U.S. ground troops may be required.

◆ A Pacific Basin community which includes an increasingly strong and assertive Japan and other nations becoming independent of the U.S.

◆ Growing challenges and difficulties for the U.S. in retaining access to important overseas bases needed to project U.S. military power.

◆ A People's Republic of China which may be reassessing its relations toward the U.S. and the USSR, as well as its role in Asia, and which may become more capitalist and democratic.

◆ A group of potential regional powers, such as Brazil, India, Indonesia, Iraq, and Nigeria, that are growing in economic and military power and in many cases seeking some distance from both the U.S. and the Soviet Union.

◆ The spread of such high-technology weapons as short- and medium-range missiles, which even smaller nations can use to neutralize somewhat the military advantages of larger nations.

◆ A growing acceptance of democratic capitalism as a development model by many politicians and intellectuals in the Third World.

MEETING THE NEW SOVIET CHALLENGE

The new Soviet challenge is essentially the old Soviet challenge—an expansionist empire whose values and actions represent a serious threat to the West. While there are indications of an ideological and practical reassessment of Moscow's international role by some elements of the Soviet leadership, thus far, Moscow has not altered its ideological commitment to support revolutionary warfare or significantly reduce its assistance to radical insurgencies and regimes. Yet it would be a serious mistake for the new President not to recognize that a new generation of Soviet leaders is seeking change. Whether the change is genuine or is merely designed to lull the West into complacency is unclear. What is clear is that the change sought by Soviet leaders is intended to strengthen the communist system. The new President must devise criteria to evaluate the significance of Soviet change and must scrutinize Kremlin policies for signs of genuine, fundamental, and long-lasting reforms.

In responding to this new Soviet challenge, the new President should:

Hold Moscow accountable for its proclaimed *glasnost'*. The Kremlin boasts a new policy of openness. Thus far, however, this policy has been primarily a method for a new elite to replace the old ruling group. The U.S. should suspend judgment on the "new openness" until real changes begin to occur. Such changes would include development of genuine opposition political parties, a genuine free press and freedom of speech, freedom to practice religion and to emigrate, and an end to domestic passports.

Press for Soviet withdrawal from Afghanistan. The new President should press Moscow to keep its pledge to pull all Soviet troops out of Afghanistan by continuing to supply the Afghan freedom fighters with arms. As important, the U.S. should work for a truly independent Afghanistan with its own political, social, and economic arrangements.

Meet the new Soviet diplomatic challenge. The new Soviet leadership is much more skilled than its predecessor at making policies look reasonable. The new President must give the highest priority to responding to this new Kremlin style. Most important, the new administration must restructure its policy-making process so as to analyze and respond more quickly to Soviet developments. The U.S. must continue to emphasize to Western publics that Soviet actions, not just rhetoric, must change.

Intensify the battle of ideas. The new President should allocate more resources for such projects as research and development on direct-broadcast satellites (DBS) and video cassettes. These are peaceful ways of bringing outside ideas and information to Soviet citizens. If the Soviet system really has changed, Moscow should not object to this peaceful competition of ideas.

$$\diamond$$

STRENGTHENING AMERICA'S DEFENSE

Reagan has done a great deal to strengthen America's defenses. The challenge for the new President is to continue this improvement in the face of budget constraints. It can be done only if the nation's security is placed above bureaucratic, congressional, regional, and other pressure groups. In a democracy, it is inevitable that national security policy will be shaped by considerations other than geopolitics. Congress, the American public, the media, interest groups, and other factors all influence the development of policy. In addition, the U.S. suffers from the breakdown of a bipartisan foreign policy consensus. Nonetheless, the U.S. needs to establish and maintain a comprehensive, integrated and consistent long-term approach to achieving U.S. international objectives.

The new President vigorously must continue the Strategic Defense Initiative (SDI). He should clarify the goals and priorities of strategic defense; upgrade air defenses, since a defensive system also should protect against incoming bombers and cruise missiles; integrate civil defense planning into the SDI; develop short-term options for a ballistic missile defense to increase protection immediately of the vulnerable U.S. retaliatory capability, especially the new MX missile; and make the production of defenses against shorter-range missiles a high priority to provide protection to West European nations, Israel, and South Korea.

The new President must continue modernizing strategic offensive forces, strengthening conventional defense capabilities, and developing new technologies for NATO to offset the Soviet bloc's quantitative advantages. Restrictions on strategic trade with the Soviet bloc should be tightened, while all subsidized credit flows to Moscow and its satellites should be ended. Arms reduction negotiations with Moscow should be approached with caution, not made the centerpiece of U.S.-Soviet relations.

Particular attention should be given to the problems created by the Soviets and their proxies, like Cuba, in the developing world. Low intensity conflict—that is, violence and conflict that do not reach the level of conventional war—is something which democracies fight with great difficulty. The new President should develop a new organizational structure to coordinate U.S. policy and actions regarding low intensity conflict policy. U.S. intelligence capabilities must be improved to enable the U.S. to deal with terrorists before they have acted.

———————————◇———————————

RESPONDING TO A CHANGING
INTERNATIONAL ENVIRONMENT

The overall international environment will continue to change. Many West Europeans seem ambivalent toward U.S. defense policies. While they want U.S. protection, they reject either the conventional or the nuclear component currently necessary to provide such protection. And while the Pacific Basin offers opportunities for increased trade and the growth of democratic institutions in the Philippines, the Republic of China on Taiwan, and South Korea, the region also faces a growing Soviet military presence. Some Latin American nations are becoming reluctant to work closely with the U.S., and the future of both Nicaragua and El Salvador remains uncertain. Iranian fanaticism continues to threaten U.S. interests in the Persian Gulf, and the Middle East in general remains a powder keg. Soviet and Cuban penetration of Africa, along with that continent's own internal instabilities, makes this continent of great concern.

As the new President devises tactics to cope with developing circumstances, he must retain such sound fundamental principles as:

Assuring equitable NATO burden-sharing. The new President should encourage the apparent interests of some European governments, especially France and West Germany, in improved conventional military capabilities and closer military coordination. The U.S. should insist that Western Europe share more equitably the burden for the common defense and investigate whether some of the U.S. ground troops based in Europe could be used more effectively elsewhere. The

U.S. also should encourage NATO to consider such creative ideas as the construction of anti-tank barriers consisting of buried pipelines filled with liquid high explosives.

Solidifying the free Pacific community. The new President must seek to strengthen the Western-oriented Pacific community of nations and maintain and expand businesslike relations with the People's Republic of China. The new President should invite the Republic of China on Taiwan and South Korea to establish a Free Trade Area with the U.S. The democratic transitions in the Philippines and South Korea should be consolidated; special assistance must be provided to Manila to combat the Philippine communist insurgency. The new President should press Japan to carry its weight in the common defense of the West by increasing payments for the U.S. defense of Japan and the U.S. role in the Persian Gulf, and by providing increased aid to such key nations as Turkey, the Philippines, and El Salvador.

Ending communist expansionism in Central America. The presence of a communist base in Central America threatens neighboring nations, including the U.S., and jeopardizes U.S. supply lanes to its allies elsewhere. The new President should seek military aid for the Nicaraguan democratic resistance. The long-term objective must be the replacement of Sandinista rule by a democratic system.

Raising Mexico policy to a high U.S. priority. Mexico's importance to U.S. strategic and economic interests generally has been ignored. The new President must devote more effort than his predecessors to dealing with U.S.-Mexican bilateral issues and do so with great sensitivity. While respecting Mexico's independence, the U.S. should seek improved bilateral trade and financial agreements, with the eventual objective of establishing a U.S.-Mexico Free Trade Area. The new President must seek greater cooperation with the Mexican government on narcotics trafficking and immigration. The new administration delicately should seek ways to convince Mexico that the democratic model of political and economic development—pursued by Guatemala, Uruguay, and Venezuela—would be better for Mexico and its Central American neighbors like Nicaragua than the Marxist model.

Fostering free enterprise in less developed countries: One important reason why the Soviet Union was able to make such inroads in less developed countries (LDCs) after World War II was that socialism appeared to be the LDC road to prosperity and economic justice. After decades of economic stagnation under socialist economic policies, many Third World countries are being forced to admit that these policies are unsound. They look with envy at the remarkable economic successes of countries that took the capitalist road, such as South Korea and the Republic of China on Taiwan. Indeed, even the Soviet Union and the People's Republic of China are taking steps to introduce market mechanisms and limited private ownership. The new President should seek to export capitalism through policies of the Agency for International Development, and by encouraging international lending agencies to focus on strengthening the private sector in LDCs.

―――――――――――――◇―――――――――――――

BUILDING A NEW CONSENSUS

In the 1970s, Secretary of State Henry Kissinger counseled that America no longer had the will to support a strong foreign policy. Therefore, Kissinger suggested that the best that the U.S. could do was to reach a global accommodation with the Soviet Union. A few years later, Jimmy Carter concluded that the natural resources upon which the U.S. global strength depended were very limited and that a national malaise had infected the American people.

Kissinger, Carter, and those who echoed them were clearly wrong. The suggestion that the U.S. inevitably is in decline now seems ill-conceived. Signs of American strength abound. This is a major legacy of Ronald Reagan to his successor. Since 1981, the context for thinking about U.S. foreign and defense policy has shifted from whether the U.S. should take an active role in the world to the extent of that role; from whether the U.S. should have a tough-minded approach to Moscow to how tough; from whether the U.S. should support anti-Marxist insurgencies in developing nations under Soviet domination to the nature of such aid; and from whether the U.S. should pursue strategic defenses to the intensity of such pursuit.

The new President should build on this Reagan legacy. The new President's most important challenge perhaps is to reconstitute the American bipartisan foreign policy consensus. He should bring together liberals and conservatives who share a common perception of the nature of the Soviet challenge to the West and America's proper role in the world. This would require compromises by both liberals and conservatives. The new U.S. foreign policy consensus should share a perception that the Soviet Union is the principal U.S. adversary and appreciate the need for a strong national defense sustained by annual real increases in military spending. This consensus also would understand that it is sometimes necessary for the U.S. to use its military might and also to provide assistance to forces struggling against Soviet-backed communist regimes as in Nicaragua and Angola. Finally, the new consensus would support U.S. efforts to encourage democratic pluralism and free markets in developing nations.

Almost two decades have past since the nadir of American internal divisions over the Vietnam War. These divisions were the fulcrum which shattered the post-World War II U.S. foreign policy consensus. Old wounds now are healing and new generations are entering the political process. This will allow the new President to assemble a new bipartisan foreign policy consensus. And, in the longer run, it will allow America to maintain its security and spread democracy and economic freedom throughout the world.

23

Executive-Legislative Relations and U.S. National Security

Kim R. Holmes and David B. Rivkin, Jr.*
Task Force Chairmen

Throughout United States history, the legislative branch in some measure has been involved in devising U.S. foreign policy. From the early days of the Republic, the Senate provided its "advice and consent" to the treaties negotiated by the Executive. Congress as a whole appropriated money for national defense and foreign policy functions. Congress also participated in some major foreign policy debates, such as those over the U.S. role in Latin America, U.S. entry into World Wars I and II, and U.S. membership in the League of Nations and the United Nations. After World War II, congressional interest and involvement in foreign policy greatly increased. Originally, a strong bipartisanship and shared worldview enabled Congress to work closely with the executive branch in protecting national security and blocking communist-inspired aggression and subversion. This period of relative harmony, however, did not last.

In the past, the executive and legislative branches of the federal government occasionally have disagreed over their respective constitutional prerogatives pertaining to foreign affairs. At no previous time, however, have the disagreements been as numerous and intense, mounting to an acute executive-legislative confrontation, as in the past two decades. The executive-legislative confrontations of the early 1970s originally were limited primarily to issues involving the use of military power; they rapidly spread, however, to the general conduct

---

*Commenting and contributing generously to this chapter were *Mandate III* Task Force Members Gordon Crovitz, Peter Davis, Steven Galbach, C. Boyden Gray, Michael Horowitz, Michael Malbin, John Schmitz, Bretton Sciaroni, and Robert Turner. They do not necessarily endorse all of its views and recommendations.
Task Force Deputy Chairman: Joseph Schmitz.

of diplomacy, oversight and regulation of intelligence operations, negotiation, interpretation and abrogation of treaties, and conditions and
prerequisites to the dispensation of U.S. aid to foreign countries.

Overall, during the 1970s, Congress enacted some 150 separate
statutory provisions restricting the President's ability to control the
conduct of U.S. foreign policy. In the 1980s, dozens of additional
statutory provisions were passed. Meanwhile, the number of congressional committees and subcommittees asserting the right to receive
foreign policy information from the executive branch and to provide
guidance to the Executive has increased many times. As a result, an
"imperial" Congress, aided by massive staffs, now seeks to micromanage virtually every foreign policy activity of the executive branch.

This has made it extremely difficult for the President to conduct
foreign policy. For example, U.S. ability to cooperate with friendly
intelligence services in sensitive intelligence ventures has been undermined by excessive reporting requirements imposed by Congress, and
by the ever-present possibility of congressional leaks. Congressional
micromanagement of such foreign policy operations as the transfer of
military or economic aid makes the U.S. virtually incapable of dealing
in a timely fashion with rapidly evolving developments in the Third
World. Example: During the 1979 Somali-Ethiopian war over the
Ogaden, the U.S. could not respond rapidly to Somalia's request for
assistance and had to solicit help from Saudi Arabia. There was no
opposition to the U.S. assisting Somalia; the problem simply was that
the executive branch, hobbled by congressional restrictions on foreign
aid, could not deliver timely aid. Such enormous obstacles to prompt
U.S. action have made Third World leaders increasingly reluctant to
cooperate with the U.S.

————————————◇————————————

THE REAGAN ADMINISTRATION RECORD

The Reagan Administration took office firmly committed to waging
an assertive foreign policy. As a result, the Administration has
managed to reverse some of the erosion of presidential foreign policy
powers. Reagan, for example, vigorously has resisted congressional
efforts to tie his hands in the conduct of arms control negotiations. He
has fought and defeated numerous congressional resolutions to freeze
nuclear weapons.

He was less successful with the Anti-Apartheid Act of 1986, which
contained specific instructions to the President on how to terminate

existing bilateral agreements with the Republic of South Africa. The detailed instructions contained in the statutory language are almost surely an unconstitutional encroachment by Congress into the executive branch's conduct of diplomacy. The President appropriately adopted a principled constitutional position: his veto statement asserted that the Act constricted U.S. diplomatic freedom and tied the hands of the executive branch in dealing with a crisis gathering in a critical African region. Though the veto was overridden, Reagan's action was a necessary and important statement of constitutional principle.

During the tenure of CIA Director William Casey (1981–1987), the Administration sought to roll back congressional micromanagement of U.S. intelligence operations. It opposed, for example, congressional efforts to stifle U.S. covert paramilitary operations in Central America.

The Administration also has sought to defend executive branch constitutional prerogatives during the debate over the interpretation of the 1972 U.S.-Soviet Anti-Ballistic Missile (ABM) treaty. It has rejected congressional arguments that certain ambiguous testimony, presented by Nixon Administration officials in 1972, determined the treaty's meaning. Rather, the Reagan Administration has argued that, for purposes of both domestic and international law, the treaty's meaning ought to be determined by what the parties to the treaty actually agreed to.

Distressingly, however, the Reagan Administration has lacked tenacity in asserting the executive branch's constitutional right to conduct foreign policy. Thus, the Administration has seen some of its earlier successes transformed into failures. In the intelligence oversight area, for example, the Administration failed to veto continuing resolutions containing the Boland Amendments that restricted U.S. assistance to the Nicaraguan freedom fighters. And then it failed to advise Congress that it had no intention of complying with the more far-fetched interpretations of the most restrictive Boland Amendment.

The Administration also has blundered on occasion in dealing with congressional efforts to expand oversight of intelligence activities. Among other things, Congress has sought to require the President to provide prior notification to Congress of all covert operations, except for extremely sensitive situations in which such a notification could be withheld for no more than 48 hours. In handling this, the Administration has conceded on such matters of principle as admitting that no national security information can be indefinitely withheld from Congress.

With respect to the debate over ABM treaty interpretation, the Administration failed to oppose effectively the addition of the so-called Byrd amendment to the Intermediate-range Nuclear Force (INF) treaty resolution. This amendment states that the treaty should be interpreted on the basis of authoritative testimony provided by the executive branch to the Senate and that, in the future, no reinterpretation of the treaty by the President would be permissible without Senate approval. This amendment erodes executive branch treaty-making powers.

While the Administration has contended that the 1973 War Powers Resolution was unconstitutional, it nevertheless has avoided action that might be construed as a violation of the resolution. It agreed, for example, to provide reports about the deployment of U.S. forces to Lebanon. The Administration has shied away from constitutional confrontation, even when necessary to defend presidential foreign policy prerogatives. In particular, during the Iran-Contra congressional hearing, the Administration indiscriminately released sensitive defense and intelligence information, damaging U.S. national security and undermining the venerable concept of executive privilege.

The most important Reagan Administration failure has been its inability to educate the American people regarding major constitutional issues and to generate political consensus for restoring the proper constitutional balance between the Executive and Congress in making foreign policy decisions.

———————————◇———————————

THE NEXT FOUR YEARS

Congressional micromanagement of foreign affairs usurps the President's constitutional authority and poses a serious long-term threat to U.S. national security. To restore the constitutional separation of powers, the next President must be willing to challenge congressional meddling in foreign affairs. He must pick his battles carefully and be prepared to take his case directly to the U.S. public. Resolute action is needed immediately to halt the dangerous and unconstitutional erosion of the Executive's foreign policy authority.

Adopting a Principled Approach to Executive-Legislative Relations

The new President should order a review of the practical and constitutional principles relevant to the division of responsibility in foreign affairs between the Executive and Congress. Such a review should be conducted by a high-level bipartisan commission, comprised of constitutional scholars, former senior government officials, and retired members of Congress. This commission should produce a comprehensive report on executive-congressional relations. The President personally must focus public attention on the report and make its recommendations part of his legislative and public agenda.

Factors to be considered by the commission should include:

◆ *Congress's role in debating the broad outline of U.S. national security strategy.*

◆ *Supreme Court rulings reaffirming presidential preeminence in the conduct of foreign affairs.*

◆ *The allocation of foreign affairs powers envisioned by the Constitution.* Practical imperatives and the constitutional framework and history clearly demonstrate that the President possesses plenary executive foreign affairs powers. By contrast, Congress has only the specifically enumerated and limited foreign affairs powers: to declare war, to define and punish piracies and offenses against the law of nations, to regulate foreign commerce, and the Senate's power to provide advice and consent to treaties negotiated by the Executive.

◆ *Congressional indirect influence on foreign policy through its appropriations power.* The constitutional framework and context, as well as numerous court cases, clearly indicate that the congressional power of the purse should not be used to undermine the constitutional prerogatives of the President or to micromanage executive branch functions. Thus, Congress cannot constitutionally pass an appropriations bill that, for example, bars the executive branch from spending funds to carry out discussions with a particular country.

Obtaining a Political Mandate for Bolstering Presidential Authority in Foreign Affairs

The new President should seek a political mandate to reestablish the proper structure of government and to recreate the constitutionally mandated balance between the executive and legislative branches in the conduct of foreign affairs. To obtain this mandate, the President should make the executive-legislative relationship in foreign affairs a major electoral issue.

Drawing the Line on Congressional Micromanagement

The new President should adopt a principled stance on all foreign policy issues with constitutional implications. Specifically, if he declares that a congressional enactment dealing with foreign affairs is unconstitutional, he also should indicate that, at least in the absence of a binding judicial determination to the contrary, he will not enforce the act. The President also should publicly declare that Congress should stop acting irresponsibly in labeling as unconstitutional presidential actions that it dislikes merely on policy grounds. Instead, the President should call upon Congress to follow the proper, constitutionally prescribed path of impeachment if it perceives serious misconduct by the President.

Restoring the Role of the Political Process in Resolving Executive-Legislative Confrontation

The new President should declare that he wishes to avoid confrontational or legalistic approaches to interbranch disputes on foreign policy issues. He then should use the political process to resolve major foreign policy differences and interbranch policy disputes. In a major foreign policy controversy, for example, he should take his case directly to the American people to force debate on the merits of the issue. He should not allow Congress to obscure the issue with debates exclusively on legal issues.

Building a Sound Framework for Executive-Legislative Partnership

To establish a constitutionally and practically sound structure for executive/legislative cooperation in making foreign policy, the new President should consult with and brief congressional leaders regularly. Toward this end, the President should indicate his willingness to meet regularly with an informal group of key congressional leaders to exchange views and to solicit advice on foreign policy issues.

———————◇———————

INITIATIVES FOR 1989

1) Redraft the War Powers Resolution. The new President should direct his attorney general, working with the other executive departments, to draft new war powers legislation. The 1973 War Powers Resolution requires the President, among other things, to withdraw within 60 days U.S. troops deployed overseas and engaged in hostilities or facing the imminent threat of hostilities, unless Congress approves their continued presence. The resolution diminishes the President's ability to deal with foreign policy crises and enables Congress, through mere inaction, to interfere with the discharge of the President's inherent constitutional power as commander-in-chief.

New statutory language should make clear the President's inherent authority to respond to attacks on U.S. citizens and property and to armed aggression against the U.S. and its allies. New war powers legislation also should reject the assumption, underlying the 1973 resolution, that any use of U.S. military power invariably amounts to waging war, and that this would require congressional consent.

2) Protect classified information. Congressional leaks of classified information, particularly intelligence data, hurt U.S. intelligence capabilities greatly and undermine cooperation with friendly intelligence services. The new President should submit to Congress a draft statute that imposes stiff criminal penalties on those who leak classified information, particularly pertaining to intelligence. These penalties would be imposed on all parties guilty of leaks, including members of Congress and staff. (See Chapter 25.)

3) Suggest creation of a Joint Intelligence Committee. The existence of an intelligence committee in each House of Congress complicates intelligence oversight, invites congressional leaks, and strains relations between Congress and the Executive. The new President should push for the creation of a single congressional intelligence committee, with membership comprised of an equal number of senators and congressmen from both parties and with a small professional staff. (See Chapter 25.)

4) Impose the same security clearance requirements on members of Congress as on members of the executive branch. Though members of Congress serving on intelligence oversight committees have access to highly sensitive information, they need not submit to security background investigations. As a result, many members feel they are exempt from regular procedures instituted to protect classified data and are virtually above the law. The new President should promulgate regulations requiring members of Congress and congressional staff who have access to classified information to submit to the same security checks that the intelligence organizations require of their own personnel.

5) Seek reforms in congressional handling of defense budgets. There is a broad consensus that congressional handling of defense budgets is

unsatisfactory. During the past decade, for example, Congress typically has failed to pass defense appropriations bills before the beginning of the relevant fiscal year. Most members of Congress, instead of
concentrating on broad defense policy issues, have focused on the
minutiae of defense spending. And the proliferation of congressional
bodies dealing with defense issues has triggered numerous turf battles,
resulting in duplication of reporting requirements imposed on the
Executive. While these problems are largely the fault of Congress, the
new President should suggest solutions and push for their adoption.
Among them:

◆ *Support two-year budgeting for the defense budget.* Biennial budgeting would enable the Pentagon to engage in longer-term planning and
further encourage multiyear procurement contracting, which has
proved a cost-effective method of purchasing weapons systems and
equipment. This would reduce the number of eleventh-hour changes to
the defense budget.

◆ *Request the relevant congressional committees to reduce the number
of reports on defense matters they require of the executive branch.* This
would diminish congressional micromanagement and the time spent by
executive branch officials in responding to myriad congressional requests for reports and testimony.

◆ *Request the relevant congressional committees to reduce the number
of line-item changes they introduce in the defense budget.* This will remove
pork-barrel politicking from the business of strengthening America's
defense.

In keeping with the concept of a biennial budget, the President
should submit a multiyear defense budget to Congress and make its
adoption a top legislative priority. Such a long-term outlook budget
would enable the executive branch to follow a more rational defense
planning process.

6) Protect the integrity of the executive branch activities. While the
President, of course, should hold executive branch officials accountable for their actions and discipline them in appropriate circumstances,
the President also should protect executive branch officials from excessive pressure from Congress. The President must stand by his appointees when they are attacked or challenged by congressional committees. When appropriate, he should invoke executive immunity and
order executive branch officials not to testify before Congress. This
would have been the correct approach in dealing with the congressional
inquiries into certain sensitive aspects of U.S. intelligence operations

that were spawned under the guise of investigating the Iran-Contra affair.

7) Protect the integrity of U.S. intelligence operations. Existing congressional intelligence oversight procedures and relevant legislation allow congressional micromanagement of all aspects of U.S. intelligence activities. This has compromised U.S. intelligence operations, allowed damaging leaks, and discouraged U.S. allies from cooperating with U.S. intelligence agencies. For example, reportedly congressional leaks about joint U.S.-Egyptian-Sudanese efforts to oust Libyan dictator Muamar Qadhafi derailed that effort and hurt future intelligence cooperation between the U.S. and Egypt. The new President should veto congressional efforts to impose additional restrictions on covert operations, if these efforts further erode U.S. intelligence capabilities and handicap U.S. ability to wage an assertive foreign policy. (See Chapter 25.)

24

The Department of State

The Department of State formally represents the President in the conduct of American foreign policy. As a practical matter, other nations' perceptions of U.S. foreign policy are shaped almost entirely by State Department representatives. The Secretary of State officially is the President's principal foreign policy adviser, a member of the National Security Council, and the ranking member of the President's Cabinet. In practice, the influence of the State Department and its secretary varies in different administrations: former Secretary of State William Rogers (1969–1973) was overshadowed by the President's National Security Adviser, Henry Kissinger; other Secretaries of State have come to wield more power, as did John Foster Dulles in the Eisenhower Administration and George Shultz in the second Reagan Administration.

The State Department was founded in 1789 under President George Washington, with Thomas Jefferson as the first Secretary of State. In 1789, Jefferson had a staff of six and a budget of $56,000 to operate diplomatic posts in five European countries. As America's international stature increased, particularly after World War II, the State Department expanded enormously. It now has missions or embassies in about 150 countries.

Years of tinkering with the structure of the State Department have made its organization one of the most complicated of any government department or agency. At the top of the pyramid are the secretary and his principal deputies; next come five geographic bureaus, each covering a region of the world and headed by an assistant secretary with four or five deputies. So-called functional bureaus, meanwhile, handle such areas as intelligence and politico-military affairs.

The State Department's responsibilities cover the entire spectrum of U.S. relations with other countries and such international organizations as the United Nations, including negotiating treaties and economic agreements, overseeing U.S. foreign economic and security assistance, and coordinating international efforts to promote human rights, counter terrorism, and interdict drugs. These functions are

BUDGET AND PERSONNEL

Secretaries

George P. Shultz	1982–present
Alexander M. Haig, Jr.	1981–1982

Personnel

March 1988	25,535
April 1980	23,408
April 1970	41,058

Budget Outlays

Fiscal Year	Total (billions)
1989 Estimate	$3.4
1988 Estimate	$3.3
1987 Actual	$2.8
1986 Actual	$2.9
1985 Actual	$2.6
1980 Actual	$1.9
1970 Actual	$0.4

shared with three independent agencies—the U.S. Information Agency (USIA), the Agency for International Development (AID), and the Arms Control and Disarmament Agency—which work closely with the Department of State.

———————————————◇———————————————

INSTITUTIONAL CONSTRAINTS

Two kinds of constraints affect the State Department's role in the foreign policy process: first, those within the Department that make it difficult to carry out a President's policies; and second, external factors that affect the Department's ability to function effectively.

Often, the State Department, or powerful factions within it, deliberately obstruct executive branch policies. A typical example has been the consistent opposition by State Department careerists to the "Reagan Doctrine" of support for anticommunist freedom fighters. These members of the U.S. Foreign Service are the most powerful impediment to presidential control within the Department. Many of the over 4,000 Foreign Service Officers in the State Department share a strong institutional bias toward compromise and negotiation—useful and necessary at times, but not always helpful in the conduct of a strong foreign policy. State Department careerists also tend to develop what is known as "clientitis," or identification with and sympathy for the policies and culture of the foreign countries in which they have lived and worked. This self-identification, in conjunction with an institutional aversion to confrontation, encourages them to further their own agendas, often at the expense of the President's.

The President's ability to direct U.S. foreign policy is constrained too by Congress, the press, and a growing number of public interest groups. The result has been uncertainty among both allies and adversaries regarding U.S. foreign policy goals and the strength of U.S. commitments.

The pitfalls of congressional micromangement have become obvious in the long-simmering controversy over aid to the Nicaraguan democratic resistance, popularly known as the "Contras." The Congress voted for covert aid in 1981 and 1982, overt aid in 1983, an aid cutoff in 1984, nonmilitary "humanitarian" aid in 1985, military aid in 1986, another cutoff in 1987, and nonmilitary aid again in 1988. This contradictory and restrictive legislation has made it impossible for the President to carry out a consistent foreign policy. Further, congressional involvement on this and other foreign policy issues has become so great that the Secretary of State and other top Department officials spend up to one-fourth of their time responding to congressional requests for testimony.

In the case of Contra aid, congressional opponents coordinated their policy with State Department opponents of the President's policy who worked hard behind the scenes to protect their own turf. This tacit coalition between aid opponents in Congress and the State Department was backed by groups of neoisolationists and self-described "liberal activists," including such left-wing special interests as the Council on Hemispheric Affairs, the Committee in Solidarity with the People of El Salvador, and the Commission on U.S.-Central American Relations. This domestic constituency was joined by an international constituency, which included the InterAmerican Development Bank, the World

Bank, and the International Monetary Fund, all of which favor government control and direction of Latin American economies.

Overcoming this myriad of institutional constraints will be an important challenge for the new President. To succeed, he must act quickly and imaginatively to capture the foreign policy-making process and assert firm control of the State Department. Only this can assure the effective execution of his policies.

U.S.-Soviet Relations

Richard Pipes*
Task Force Chairman

The Soviet Union is the principal foreign policy concern of the United States. U.S. concern is caused by Moscow's domestic repression, which is incompatible with Western values, and Moscow's foreign expansionism and subversion, which threaten security interests of the U.S. and its allies. At the same time, changes are clearly occurring in the Soviet Union, and the U.S. must monitor these developments continuously. These changes include Soviet leader Mikhail Gorbachev's *perestroika* (economic restructuring), *glasnost'* (expansion of public debate within limits defined by the Party), "democratization" (not Western-style democracy but rather carefully regulated lifting of some political controls over citizens' activities), and some doctrinal revisions in foreign and defense policy known as "new thinking" (which includes muted stridency and diminished reliance on crude military intimidation in favor of more sophisticated political means for achieving similar foreign policy and security objectives). Whether these changes will lead to fundamental changes in the Soviet system is uncertain. Though the U.S. will want to keep an open mind about Soviet changes, and when appropriate, give them a chance, U.S. policy must be based upon what the Kremlin actually does, not what it says or what Americans would like it to do. Thus far, the rhetoric of change coexists with the reality of continuity in Soviet policies.

Nothing thus far, for example, has prompted any fundamental or structural, much less irreversible, change in the Soviet political, economic, or social order. Gorbachev has yet to do anything as dramatic as China's returning of land to the peasants. The economic *perestroika*, so far, has remained largely on paper. While new political and social forces have emerged, what has happened thus far is easily reversible,

---

*Commenting and contributing generously to this report were *Mandate III* Task Force Members James Jatras, William Kintner, John Lenczowski, Herbert Meyer, Roger Robinson, and Jiri Valenta. They do not necessarily endorse all of its views and recommendations.

Task Force Deputy Chairman: Heritage Salvatori Fellow in Soviet Studies Leon Aron.

should the leadership so decide. This, in fact, occurred when the Brezhnev regime snuffed out the pockets of pluralism that had emerged during the 1950s "thaw" under Nikita S. Khrushchev. Despite *glasnost'* and *perestroika*, the Soviet Union is and intends to remain a one-party dictatorship, one which systematically denies its citizens human rights, political freedoms, and genuine individual economic initiative. The central role of the Communist Party in political, economic, and social affairs thus has not diminished. Much of what has occurred can be explained plausibly as politics rather than policies—a Gorbachev tactic to push out bureaucrats not loyal to him.

The Kremlin continues to deny the peoples of Eastern Europe the right to national and political self-determination, supports the puppet communist regime in Afghanistan, underwrites Vietnamese occupation of Indochina, and extends massive security, economic, political, and diplomatic assistance to antidemocratic, communist, and terrorist regimes and movements. Despite its widely advertised new thinking, Soviet foreign policy's overriding goal so far appears unchanged: relentless pursuit of tactical and strategic advantages, short of direct military confrontation, in a struggle against Western political and economic interests. As such, neither production and deployment of military weapons nor its nuclear buildup show signs of slowing or ending. And strident, relentlessly anti-Western—and especially anti-U.S.—disinformation campaigns continue virtually unabated in the government-controlled mass media.

The fluidity of the internal situation means that no firm judgment can yet be rendered on the significance of the Gorbachev era. If these positive developments continue and deepen, the limited economic and political liberalization promised by *perestroika* may in the long run prove beneficial to the U.S. by making the Soviet Union a less repressive and less aggressive state. Yet these changes thus far have stopped far short of being comprehensive, structural, or irreversible. The much deeper changes that occurred under the New Economic Policy (NEP) between 1921 and 1928, after all, were reversed completely by Joseph Stalin. The fierce political infighting among the top Soviet leadership, moreover, is far from over, and the West would be extremely unwise to base its policy on the premise that Gorbachev will succeed or even survive.

For a USSR ruled by Gorbachev or his successor, three scenarios are possible: first, the Communist Party may prove itself incapable of maintaining its totalitarian preeminence, and Gorbachev may prove a genuine reformer and a pivotal figure of change in Soviet history;

second, he may be intending a tightly managed and very limited change, which might unleash forces that then do not follow his plan and build a momentum of their own, resulting eventually in dramatic changes in the USSR; third, he may preserve the Soviet system with its repressive mechanisms and expansionist policies intact until the next crisis in the system emerges.

While the U.S. cannot determine the outcome of Soviet developments, at a minimum U.S. policies can encourage or discourage movement toward a more open Soviet society. Open societies or societies preoccupied with domestic economic growth historically have been less interested in aggression and expansionism than closed societies. A more open Soviet society eventually could discard communism as a meaningful element of its worldview. In the interim, it might reach the point where government focuses on economic growth rather than the spread of communism and where, as in China today, state-controlled publications openly state that Marxism-Leninism does not provide all the answers to problems.

A Russia without communism, of course, would not necessarily be a friend of the West. Nor would it necessarily adopt Western values and institutions, particularly if certain strong radical chauvinist elements prevail. But more likely than not, a noncommunist Russia would be a traditional superpower, a country rather than a cause, and as such, would not present a global challenge to the Western world.

These are long-term possibilities. U.S. policy must rest not on hopes and future possibilities but on current realities. If the U.S. prematurely acts as if fundamental changes have occurred in the USSR when they have not, the U.S. risks its own security and that of the West. The U.S. cannot afford to repeat the experience of the late 1970s when President Jimmy Carter proudly declared that U.S. policy was no longer being conducted on the basis of "an inordinate fear of communism." Moscow detected U.S. weakness and indecisiveness and pushed hard, reaping gains in Soviet influence worldwide.

U.S. policy must not tempt the Kremlin to renew its expansionist thrust. Reductions in U.S. defense spending and abandonment of the Strategic Defense Initiative would not provide the Soviets with much incentive for deep nuclear and conventional arms reductions. And U.S acquiescence to paper agreements leaving communist regimes in full control in such countries as Angola, where anticommunist insurgencies exist, would signal to Moscow the freedom to seek new client states in the Third World. If Western transfers of militarily useful technologies or subsidized trade and economic assistance to the Soviet government temporarily resolve Soviet economic problems, they weaken pressures on the Soviet leadership to reallocate the resources from the defense sector to the civilian economy, thereby stifling the forces of democratic reform.

Whatever the final outcome of Gorbachev's policies, he has established a much smoother Soviet international style. Soviet statements now sound less strident, while many Soviet diplomats seem to have attended Western charm school. And Soviet policymakers and advisers know much more about the U.S. than American policymakers and their advisers know about the Soviet Union.

Thus the next four years will be crucial in U.S.-Soviet relations. The new President faces a triple challenge: first, to respond creatively to the newly sophisticated Soviet propaganda and diplomacy; second, to monitor very carefully developments in Soviet domestic and international policies in order to design and execute a coherent, timely, and effective strategy toward the USSR that will encourage Moscow's evolution in a direction desirable for U.S. and Western interests and for world peace; and third, to explain and conduct policy in a way that will gain the sustained support of the American people.

In this period—possibly the first true crossroads for the USSR since Stalin's "revolution from above" in the late 1920s—Gorbachev's *perestroika* must be paralleled by a *perestroika* of the way the U.S. deals with Moscow. The U.S. government policy analysis and decision-making structure must be reshaped to respond quickly and effectively to Soviet developments. These changes must include:

◆ *Restructuring the apparatus for making policy.* There is need for a central office to monitor the Soviet Union and its global activities. Furthermore, the National Security Council and the State and Defense Departments must create new offices to monitor and report on Soviet developments.

◆ *Designing detailed, sophisticated tests to determine the pace and extent of Soviet changes.* The President must request a list of criteria to determine whether apparent changes in Soviet policy are genuine and what they mean for the U.S.

◆ *Defining specific goals for U.S. policy toward the USSR.* The President should commission a report analyzing fundamental U.S. objectives. It should answer such questions as: What does the U.S. hope to achieve? How would success be defined? What is the timetable for U.S. policy?

◆ *Determining the mix of carrots and sticks necessary to move toward these goals.* The new Soviet reality requires a more active and sophisticated U.S. policy offering incentives as well as the threat of sanctions.

◆ *Developing a plan for dealing with the possible collapse of Soviet perestroika*. Gorbachev faces many obstacles in trying to make changes, and he may not succeed. The President should direct that contingency plans be developed to deal with this possibility. He should ask for answers to: What does the U.S. do and how does the U.S. prepare the public if Gorbachev fails and is ousted (or retrenches); if Gorbachev invades Poland or Hungary; if Gorbachev is proved to have deceived the West?

―――――――――――◇―――――――――――

THE REAGAN ADMINISTRATION RECORD

When Ronald Reagan took office, it truly seemed as if Moscow was correct when it boasted that the "global correlation of forces" had shifted from the U.S. to the USSR. During the 1970s, nearly a dozen Third World countries became Soviet client states: Afghanistan, Angola, Cambodia, Ethiopia, Grenada, Laos, Mozambique, Nicaragua, South Vietnam, South Yemen. Combined with the decade-long cuts in the U.S. military budget and unilateral U.S. "restraint," the Soviet strategic buildup—the largest peacetime arms program in world history—dangerously eroded America's ability to deter Soviet aggression and protect U.S. allies. In the last year of the Carter Administration, the string of Soviet victories and the sense of omnipotence that they apparently instilled in the Soviet leadership prompted the USSR to invade Afghanistan.

The greatest achievement of the Reagan years, in perhaps any area, foreign or domestic, has been the reversal of this unfavorable historical trend by restoring the American national will to face and resist the Soviet adversary. Reagan has affirmed an optimistic view of the future of democratic capitalism and the eventual demise of communist totalitarianism, predicting in his June 8, 1982, speech to the British Parliament that communism will be relegated to the "ash heap of history." (See Public Diplomacy section of this chapter.) Reagan's restoration of U.S. military strength reenergized the Western alliance, and the cohesion of the North Atlantic Treaty Organization was strengthened by the deployment of American *Pershing II* and cruise missiles in Western Europe in the face of a massive Soviet campaign of intimidation. (See NATO section of Chapter 28.) The Declaration of the Williamsburg economic summit in 1983 stressed the global nature of the Soviet threat and called for Western strategic cooperation with Japan.

Soviet advances in the Third World were slowed, halted, or reversed by the Reagan Doctrine in Afghanistan, Angola, Grenada, and Nicaragua. In Afghanistan, a major geopolitical victory was won by the U.S.: the Soviet military was defeated on the battlefield by U.S.-backed Afghan Freedom Fighters, and Moscow was forced to begin withdrawing its troops. The result, if the troops are withdrawn completely: Moscow will have been deprived of a strategic stepping-stone to the Persian Gulf; Soviet ability to meddle in Pakistan and Iran will have been greatly diminished; and the Brezhnev Doctrine proclaiming the irreversibility of communist gains will have been discredited. (See Liberation Doctrine section of this chapter.)

The Reagan Administration also has taken measures to reduce the flow of advanced technology and capital to the Soviet Union and its clients. The U.S. convinced its allies to agree not to subsidize interest rates on credits to the Soviet bloc. The Soviet drive to dominate the West European energy market was resisted by establishing a ceiling on Soviet natural gas deliveries to Western Europe. The flow of sensitive Western technology to the Soviet Union has been slowed significantly by the increased effectiveness of the West's Coordinating Committee for Multilateral Export Controls (COCOM). (See Strategic Trade section of this chapter.)

In the important war of ideas, the Reagan Administration has responded to the Soviet ideological offensive by launching the National Endowment for Democracy to help develop, disseminate, and consolidate democratic ideals and institutions. (See Public Diplomacy section of this chapter.) The Administration has used the Helsinki review conferences to publicize Moscow's systematic disregard of the human rights obligation that the Soviet Union assumed by signing the 1975 Helsinki Final Act. (See Public Diplomacy and Human Rights sections of this chapter.)

In arms control, the Reagan Administration has set an important precedent and established a new paradigm of negotiating with the Soviets: patience, refusal to make preemptive concessions, willingness to let the Soviets break off negotiations, insistence on intrusive verification, and insistence that strategic defense not be a bargaining chip. (See Arms Control section of Chapter 28.)

Ironically, but understandably, the Reagan Administration's policies and attitudes might have contributed to Soviet domestic political relaxation and economic reform. By refusing to make unilateral military concessions, by launching the Strategic Defense Initiative (SDI), by confronting the Soviet Union in the Third World, and by refusing to bail out the Soviet economy, the U.S. narrowed Soviet options, thus making reform more likely. In an oversimplified way, Ronald Reagan may have created Mikhail Gorbachev.

Yet huge problems remain unresolved. Arms control again has been allowed to take the center stage in U.S.-Soviet relations at the expense of the much more fundamental issues of Soviet human rights violations and Soviet support of radical antidemocratic and anti-American forces. Rewarding the Soviet Union by returning the Soviet spy Gennady Zakharov in exchange for American journalist Nicholas Daniloff, who was arrested in Moscow in 1986 on trumped-up charges, confused the U.S. public and weakened a very strong public consensus against the Soviet action. (See Terrorism section of this chapter.) And in public diplomacy, the Administration too often has yielded the momentum to the Soviet Union by allowing it to take credit for such arms control initiatives originally proposed by the U.S. as the "zero-zero" option, the principle of weapons reduction, and on-site inspection. (See Public Diplomacy section of this chapter.)

THE NEXT FOUR YEARS[1]

In dealing with the Soviet Union, the new President should be guided by four broad objectives:

◆ Reduce the Soviet military threat to the West by maintaining strategic stability through a powerful and credible deterrence to aggression.

◆ Encourage Moscow and its client states to pursue domestic and foreign policies more compatible with Western security and values.

◆ Prevail in the public diplomacy competition with the Soviet Union for West European public opinion—a contest that the Soviet Union wages daily with the help of its enormous propaganda apparatus, front organizations, and disinformation campaigns (active measures).

◆ Resist Soviet expansion in the Third World.

Establishing an Effective Decision-Making Mechanism

For years, U.S. decision-making machinery for dealing with Moscow had been developed and premised upon a Kremlin led by unimaginative people with few diplomatic skills. U.S. experience had been that important Soviet decisions were made agonizingly slowly. This is no longer the case. U.S. policy machinery now must be changed to deal with a more flexible, faster-moving Kremlin. As yet there has been no single center inside the executive branch that monitors Soviet global policy and seeks to develop an integrated and comprehensive U.S. response. To enable the U.S. to design, execute, and create a flexible policy toward the USSR, the new Administration should create the position of Deputy National Security Adviser for Soviet Global Affairs and an Office of Soviet Global Strategy at the State Department.

Devising Overall Strategy for Dealing with Moscow

The new President needs a comprehensive plan to guide his Administration in dealing with Moscow. The President thus should request that the National Security Council, in consultation with appropriate departments and outside analysts, prepare a National Security Decision Directive (or its equivalent) that specifies:

◆ *Criteria for evaluating change.* Criteria must be established by which changes in Soviet behavior can be assessed. The directive should list these criteria.

◆ *Objectives of U.S. policy toward the Soviet Union.* The directive should state clearly whether the U.S. goal is just to contain Soviet expansionism, to encourage a dissolution of the Soviet empire, to spur a more open society within the USSR, to overturn the Bolshevik revolution itself—or a combination of any of these.

◆ *The assumptions underlying U.S. policy.* Underlying premises are crucial to a coherent policy. Is it assumed, for example, that there is a connection between Soviet domestic reform and a less aggressive Soviet international policy? Is it assumed that domestic reform would lead to reduction in Soviet military spending?

◆ *Priority issues for U.S. policy.* In reality, an approach that pursues all issues in reality pursues none. The directive should spell out the most important Soviet policy issues that the U.S. seeks to resolve, and policymakers then should focus on these priorities.

Setting Criteria for Evaluating Soviet Developments

The U.S. must be able to distinguish between such different types of Soviet changes as: 1) Potemkin village-style artificial changes designed to deceive the West; 2) real changes that are either marginal or can be easily reversed; and 3) fundamental changes that alter the nature of the Soviet system. U.S. policies should be different in each case. In all cases, however, the U.S. should not take actions that would allow Moscow to avoid fundamental reforms in its domestic and foreign policies.

In Soviet foreign and defense policies, the criteria of true change must include: significant reduction in Soviet military and economic support of such aggressive, anti-Western, totalitarian regimes as Angola, Afghanistan, Cuba, Ethiopia, Nicaragua, and Vietnam; unilateral asymmetrical cuts in Soviet conventional forces in Central/Eastern Europe; and, consistent decline in Soviet military appropriations over a period of several years.

In Soviet domestic affairs, the criteria of real change must include: release of all political prisoners; elimination of the Criminal Code articles under which political dissidents have been convicted in the past, such as articles 70 and 190–1 of the Criminal Code of the Russian Republic; unrestricted travel and emigration; de facto, if not formal, decollectivization of agriculture through the transfer of collective farm land to peasants, as has been done in China; creation of an independent judiciary; end of state interference in religious affairs and freedom of religious instruction for children; legalization of independent publishing; and termination of anti-American propaganda in the Soviet media.

Guidelines for the policy should be developed by the Deputy National Security Adviser to the President for Soviet Global Affairs[2] in extensive consultation with the allies and announced by the heads of state of the major industrial democracies at the next economic summit. (See Western Economic Security section of this chapter.)

Reaffirming the Jackson-Vanik and Stevenson Amendments and Creating New Links between U.S.-Soviet Economic Relations and Moscow's Human Rights Policy

The 1974 Jackson-Vanik and Stevenson Amendments tie the tariff treatment received by Soviet goods and U.S. Export-Import Bank credits to freedom of emigration from the USSR. These amendments, which passed Congress by huge majorities, remain symbols of America's commitment to human rights, especially the right to emigrate. These amendments have influenced the emigration policies of the Soviet bloc regimes, including those of the Soviet Union itself.

Building on the success of and bipartisan support for the Jackson-Vanik and Stevenson Amendments, the new Administration should work to extend the list of conditions for expansion of economic relations with Moscow to include compliance with other provisions of the 1975 Helsinki Final Act. The new President should reaffirm publicly the U.S. linkage of human rights and trade with the Soviet Union and make sure that there are no voices in the Administration advocating the weakening or elimination of the amendments. (See Human Rights and Western Economic Security sections of this chapter.)

Devising an Affirmative Forward Strategy on Soviet Nationalities

Like its predecessor, Imperial Russia, the Soviet Union is a multinational empire, of which Great Russians are barely one-half of the population and are likely to become a minority by the year 2000. To win the non-Russian nationalities' support in his bid for power, the Bolshevik leader Vladimir Lenin conceded them the right to secede and form national sovereign states. By 1922, however, Lenin used military force to bring them back into the fold. The problem continues to simmer, as demonstrated by the recent outbursts of nationalist sentiment in Armenia and the increasingly vocal demands for economic, if not political, independence from Moscow in the Baltic republics.

The new Administration must devise a long-term strategy addressing the decolonization of the inner Soviet empire—the Soviet ethnic republics. (See Liberation Doctrine section of this chapter.) The new President should begin by calling the Soviet Union what it is—the last colonial empire in the world. Then he should offer moral and other appropriate support to the anticolonial, national liberation forces inside the Soviet Union. The backing that the U.S. would receive from half of the Soviet population would far outweigh a predictably negative official Soviet reaction. The President should order the Deputy National Security Adviser for Soviet Global Affairs to coordinate the strategy for Soviet nationalities.

Increasing Radio Liberty Funding

Radio Liberty was created by the U.S. government in 1953 to broadcast news about the USSR into the USSR in Russian and other languages of Soviet citizens. Based in Munich, West Germany, Radio Liberty prevents the Soviet Union from isolating its people from the rest of the world, and most important, tells them what is happening in their own country, thereby breaking the Kremlin's information monopoly. Radio Liberty needs $40 million for technical modernization. An additional $10 million is required for the planned expansion of broadcasts in the languages of the Soviet Central Asian Republics (Kazakhstan, Kirghizia, Tadzhikistan, Turkmenia, and Uzbekistan) from the current daily level of one-to-two hours to five-to-six hours. Radio Liberty will require $225 million to build its planned transmitting station in Israel to improve reception in Armenia, Azerbaijan, the Central Asian Republics, and Central Russia. (See Public Diplomacy chapter.) The new President should push for this funding.

Refocusing U.S.-Soviet Summits

Summitry with totalitarian regimes has rarely, if ever, served to enhance Western security. The 1945 Yalta summit gave a green light to Sovietization of Eastern Europe, and the Brezhnev-Nixon summits in 1972, 1973, and 1974 heralded an unprecedented Soviet strategic arms buildup and expansion in the Third World. Whenever a democratically elected leader of the Free World meets with the unelected ruler of the Soviet totalitarian empire, the inevitable outcome is an image of what experts call moral equivalence, that is, treatment of Western democracy and communist totalitarianism as if they were equally legitimate political systems. This confuses the American public, distorts public perception of the USSR, prompts outbursts of euphoria, and weakens the defense consensus in the U.S. and the West in general. As such, the mere occurrence of a summit is a huge public diplomacy victory for Moscow. And since summits effectively impose arbitrary deadlines on negotiating agreements, U.S.-Soviet summits often cause the U.S. to make damaging concessions to meet the deadlines.

Since public pressure for summitry is unlikely to abate, the new Administration must seek ways to avoid possible damage. U.S.-Soviet summits should become low-key and brief annual consultative meetings, convened solely for the purpose of making wide-ranging presentations and reviews of the countries' positions on human rights, regional, bilateral, and arms control issues. The summit should become as routine as the once-riveting but now ordinary semiannual summits of the West German and French leaders and of the seven democratic industrial powers.

———————◇———————

INITIATIVES FOR 1989

1) Create the position of Deputy National Security Adviser to the President for Soviet Global Affairs. U.S. policy toward the Soviet Union has been left largely to the State Department with only occasional pre-summit or crisis-management involvement of the White House. A more forceful and direct White House involvement is necessary. The new President should name a deputy national security adviser to serve as his principal adviser on Soviet affairs. He or she would help develop broad long-term U.S. strategy, coordinate various bureaucracies, and supervise execution of the President's decisions.

2) Create an Office of Soviet Global Strategy at the State Department to be headed by a Counselor to the Secretary of State. Despite abundant evidence that the Soviet Union and its allies and clients constitute a well-coordinated world alliance, the State Department continues to be structured along nineteenth-century geographical lines. As a result, Soviet activities in Afghanistan, Asia, and the Pacific and Soviet links to terrorists or the drug trade fall outside the Soviet desk's range and are handled by many different and uncoordinated regional desk and bureaus. This structure impedes execution of a well-integrated, timely, flexible, and vigorous U.S. policy toward the USSR. The existing Office of Counseler to the Secretary of State should be renamed Office of Soviet Global Strategy; the counseler should become the principal adviser to the Secretary of State on Soviet global foreign policy. The office would follow and analyze trends and patterns of Soviet global behavior and develop and coordinate long-term regional strategies. It would provide the Deputy National Security Adviser to the President for Soviet Affairs with information and recommendations.

3) Respond to Central Eastern European crises. Another period of turmoil in Central Eastern Europe is very likely, given the region's rapidly deteriorating economic situation, the deepening legitimacy crisis of the ruling communist parties, and the confusing signals from Moscow. The situations in Hungary and Poland are especially unstable. The new President should appoint and convene an Interagency Task Force on Central Eastern Europe to be chaired by the Deputy National Security Adviser for Soviet Global Affairs and include representatives of the National Security Council and the Departments of State, Defense, Commerce, and Treasury. As soon as possible, the Task Force should recommend to the President possible U.S. diplomatic, economic, political, and military responses to crises in Central Eastern Europe. Such responses could be: a declaration by the heads of NATO nations condemning a Soviet invasion; coordinated economic sanctions against the Soviet Union in the case of a Soviet intervention; recall of Western ambassadors from the Soviet Union; various degrees of military alert of the NATO forces; and coordinated Western actions at the United Nations. The President should discuss these options with America's allies and establish a mechanism for a swift, coordinated allied response to a crisis in Central Eastern Europe. (See Public Diplomacy, Central/Eastern Europe, and Western Europe sections of this chapter.)

4) Strengthen Western economic security. At the time of activist and imaginative Soviet strategy with respect to Western financial and trade markets, the U.S. should take the lead in strengthening Western economic security. Among possible steps, the U.S. should: focus allied attention on "untied" (i.e., cash) loans to the Soviet Union by Western financial institutions; reaffirm the 1982 Allied Agreement prohibiting government subsidization of loans to the Soviet Union; further reduce transfers of sensitive technology to the Soviet bloc; and maintain Western energy independence by reaffirming the limits of Soviet gas exports to Western Europe. (See Western Economic Security section of this chapter.)

5) End subsidized grain sales to the Soviet Union. The sales of U.S. wheat to the Soviet Union, suspended after the Soviet invasion of Afghanistan, were resumed by the Reagan Administration. While there should be no barriers to commercial grain sales to the USSR, the wheat now sold to the Soviet Union is at prices lower than those paid to farmers by the U.S. government. The difference is made up by U.S. taxpayers, as every 6,000 bushels of grain sold to the Soviet Union costs American taxpayers $4,722. This amount equals the 1987 taxes paid by the average American family of four.

Long-term grain sales contracts are fraught with the danger of creating a sector in the U.S. economy heavily dependent on Soviet trade orders. If continued at all, grain sales to the Soviet Union must be without U.S. government mediation or subsidies. The new President should direct the Secretaries of Agriculture and Commerce to recommend how the U.S. can end all U.S. government subsidies of grain sales to the Soviet Union. (See Western Economic Security section of this chapter.)

6) Enforce the prohibition on importing Soviet goods made with prison labor. Section 307 of the 1930 Smoot-Hawley Act prohibits importation into the U.S. of any product made with prison labor. Determining whether a particular import item is made with prison labor is the responsibility of the U.S. Customs Commissioner. In 1983, the Customs Commissioner ruled that several Soviet products fell into this category. Among them: tea, aluminum, and chocolate. The Customs investigators produced eye witnesses who confirmed the Commissioners' findings. It was established, moreover, that 39 Soviet aluminum mines and manufacturing facilities were within short distances of Soviet prisons and labor camps. During 1986 and 1987, over $45 million worth of aluminum products was imported into the U.S. Proposals to ban these imports were opposed by the State and Treasury Departments. The new President should end this violation of U.S. law by directing the Secretary of Treasury to review the accumulated evidence of Soviet prison labor production and, based on Treasury's recommendations, ban the offending Soviet imports.

7) Oppose new U.S.-Soviet communications agreements unless Moscow stops foreign broadcast jamming. Soviet jamming of Radio Liberty violates the Helsinki Final Act signed by the USSR. Repeated protests by Washington have achieved nothing. The proposed Interagency Committee on U.S.-Soviet Exchanges, or if it is not created, the Director of the Soviet and Eastern European Affairs at the National Security Council, should recommend U.S. sanctions against the Soviet Union if Radio Liberty jamming continues. Sanctions could include reducing the number of official Soviet visitors to the U.S. and denying visas to well-known Soviet propagandists.

8) Create a Foreign Exchange Reserve Fund for Radio Free Europe/ Radio Liberty. Over 70 percent of the RFE/RL's operating expenses are in West German marks. Thus when the value of the dollar relative to the mark decreases, as it has since 1985, RFE/RL requires emergency supplemental appropriations. In 1987, $33 million had to be requested. To avoid the uncertainty of a fluctuating mark and the delay in obtaining funds by emergency appropriations, a permanent Foreign Exchange Reserve Fund of $100 million should be created. (See Public Diplomacy section of this chapter.)

9) Introduce a new weekly program in Voice of America Soviet broadcasts. By using the Soviet media relentlessly to malign U.S. political, social, and economic institutions, the Kremlin seeks to keep instilling in the Soviet people fear and hatred of the U.S. A distorted picture of American reality, moreover, makes the U.S. a less appealing model at a time when many Soviets are calling for real reform. As an antidote to this Soviet disinformation campaign, the Voice of America should launch a weekly program, perhaps entitled "What Soviet Newspapers Are Saying about the United States." It would review articles about the U.S. in major Soviet newspapers and calmly and factually refute the lies and distortions in them. Soviet audiences yearn to hear U.S. truth about social, political, and economic achievements, but they have been disappointed by VOA's inexplicable unwillingness to provide it. The competition provided by this new program might prod Soviet "journalists" to be somewhat more truthful in their portrayal of the U.S. Competition with Western broadcasts, after all, has dramatically improved the accuracy and timeliness of the Soviet media's coverage of Soviet domestic affairs. (See Public Diplomacy section of this chapter.)

10) Set goals for U.S. participation in the so-called Helsinki process. Helsinki review conferences, originally intended to examine how countries had complied with the Helsinki Final Act of 1975, have deteriorated into diplomatic exercises that paper over Helsinki treaty violations by the Soviet bloc in an effort to reach consensus. As a result, the conferences blur the differences between Western democracies and communist dictatorships and strengthen the perception that the two are morally equivalent. The main value of these conferences is the opportunity to publicize the human rights records of the treaty signatories. Whether this justifies continued U.S. participation in these long conferences is something that the new Administration should determine. The Deputy National Security Adviser to the President for Soviet Global Affairs, the Senior Adviser to the President for Public Diplomacy[3], and the Assistant Secretary of State for Human Rights Administration should set criteria by which the benefits of U.S. participation could be assessed. If the U.S. continues attending Helsinki review sessions, it should be only to serve specific goals set by the new Administration. (See Human Rights and Public Diplomacy sections of this chapter.)

11) Place strict conditions on U.S. participation in a "human rights" conference in Moscow. The Soviet Union has been insisting on hosting a human rights conference in Moscow. The aim is clear: to create an image of the Soviet Union similar to that of any other nation that has just a few "routine" human rights problems. Until the USSR substantially stops violating its citizens' human and political rights, U.S. attendance at such a conference without preconditioning would hand the Soviet Union a major propaganda victory and demoralize Soviet bloc human rights activists. (See Human Rights section of this chapter.)

12) Create an interagency summit planning group at the White House.
U.S.-Soviet summits require early and careful public diplomacy planning. In the past, such planning has been hindered by the absence of institutionalized procedures for interagency coordination. The group should include representatives of all foreign policy agencies—Commerce, Defense, State, USIA—and be chaired by the Senior Adviser to the President for Public Diplomacy. The new President should make it clear that the senior adviser, not Cabinet department representatives, is in charge of overall planning. Summit preparation should: 1) establish what objectives the U.S. is trying to achieve by going to the summit; 2) indicate major public diplomacy themes in support of these objectives; 3) gauge Soviet objectives, themes, and tactics; 4) analyze the anticipated public opinion impact of U.S. themes; 5) produce a detailed and extensive plan of public diplomacy actions focused on foreign media and opinion elites; and 6) select, train, and brief U.S. officials to be sent to the summit location before the meeting to provide background information to the press on the U.S. agenda and goals for the media. (See Public Diplomacy section of this chapter.)

13) Create an interagency committee on U.S.-Soviet exchanges. There now is almost no policy or interagency coordination of U.S.-Soviet scientific, technological, educational, or cultural exchanges. No one is responsible for defining what the U.S. seeks to achieve through such exchanges. The new President thus should create an Interagency Committee on U.S.-Soviet Exchanges under the auspices of the National Security Council, comprised of representatives of the Departments of Commerce, Defense, and State, USIA, and the FBI. The Committee should be chaired by the Deputy National Security Adviser to the President for Soviet Global Affairs, or if this position is not created, by the National Security Council's Director of Soviet and Eastern European Affairs.

14) Establish more stringent conditions for new U.S.-Soviet cultural or scientific agreements. U.S.-Soviet cultural and scientific exchanges have done little to correct the glaring imbalances in this area. Americans, for example, have unrestricted access to Soviet newspapers, periodicals, and books; the Soviet people, by contrast, have virtually no access to U.S. publications. Soviet spokesmen appear often on American television and op-ed pages of newspapers; American spokesmen almost never have a similar chance of addressing the Soviet people. In 1987, ten times more Americans visited the Soviet Union than Soviets visited the U.S. Most American scholars who go to Soviet educational institutions work in humanities and social sciences; most Soviet scholars who visit the U.S. specialize in such military-related fields as physics, computers, or engineering. While in the U.S., Soviet scholars enjoy nearly unlimited access to publications and the academic community; U.S. scholars in the USSR are severely restricted in their contacts and movements.

Further exchange agreements with the USSR must correct this imbalance. The proposed U.S. Interagency Committee on U.S.-Soviet Exchanges should recommend to the President how a balance can be established. If an Interagency Committee is not created, U.S.-Soviet exchanges should be reviewed by the Director of the Soviet and Eastern European Affairs of the National Security Council. No new exchange agreements should be signed until the inequities are corrected.

15) Reduce by half the staff in the Soviet Consulate in San Francisco. Such high-level Soviet defectors as Arkady Shevchenko and Stanislav Levchenko confirm that from one-third to one-half of Soviet diplomats are full-time spies. Given the very limited legitimate activities that the USSR's consulate in San Francisco needs to perform, there is no justification for the consulate to have a staff of over fifty. San Francisco is close to some of the sensitive defense-related industries in the Silicon Valley. In 1986, the State Department ordered Moscow to reduce the staff of its U.N. mission from 275 to 170 officials. This was to reduce the number of probable spies in the mission. The new President should follow this precedent and order a 50 percent staff cut in the Soviets' San Francisco consulate. (See Chapter 26.)

16) Give the State Department staff instruction in Soviet global strategy. While the U.S. Foreign Service Institute, attended by Foreign Service officers at various stages in their careers, offers elective courses on the Soviet Union, there is no required course examining the foundations of Soviet foreign policy and its overall objectives. The highly compartmentalized nature of the State Department means that most Foreign Service officers may never study the global nature of U.S.-Soviet competition, even though these officers may deal with aspects of U.S.-Soviet competition in many of their posts. The Secretary of State should order that two required courses in Soviet strategy be added to the Institute's curriculum. A basic course would include the history of Soviet foreign policy, the staffing and activities of the International Department of the Soviet Central Committee, the Soviet proxy network, and examples and analyses of Soviet disinformation campaigns, which should be required of all entry-level Foreign Service Officers. A second, more specialized and advanced course, should be required of mid- and top-level officers as part of their routine continuing career training.

---◇---

NOTES

1. This section is focused largely on the political, diplomatic, economic, and cultural aspects of U.S.-Soviet relationship. The military dimensions of this relationship are examined in detail in Chapter 28.

2. The creation of this position is proposed in this section. In the absence of this position, the task should be undertaken by the Director of Soviet and East European Affairs of the National Security Council.

3. The creation of this position is proposed in the "Public Diplomacy" section of this chapter. If the position is not created, the task shall be given to the Director of Soviet and East European Affairs on the National Security Council.

Central/Eastern Europe

Leon Aron*
Task Force Chairman

The term "Central/Eastern Europe" describes European countries situated between the Federal Republic of Germany and Austria in the West and the Soviet Union in the East: East Germany, Poland, Hungary, Czechoslovakia, Bulgaria, and Romania.[1] The Soviet Union occupied these countries during World War II and imposed Soviet-style regimes against the will of the peoples and in violation of the 1945 Yalta Agreements, which called for free political choice for the peoples of Central/Eastern Europe.

The United States commitment to Central/Eastern Europe rests on important moral and geopolitical imperatives. Rejecting Moscow's claim that Central/Eastern Europe is a Soviet "sphere of influence," the U.S. under eleven Republican and Democratic administrations has insisted on the right of the peoples of Central/Eastern Europe to determine freely their political and economic systems. Geopolitically, the area is crucial to the West both as a potential launching pad for a Soviet invasion of Western Europe and as a very vulnerable part of the Soviet empire where that empire's disintegration is most likely to start.

◇

THE REAGAN ADMINISTRATION RECORD

The Reagan Administration inherited a mixed record of U.S. policies towards Central/Eastern Europe. On the one hand, President Jimmy Carter's Special Assistant for National Security Affairs, Zbigniew Brzezinski, placed a high priority on U.S. policy toward Central/Eastern Europe. The Carter Administration pursued the generally productive policy of "differentiation," whereby the level and content of U.S. diplomatic and economic relations with individual Central/

---

*Commenting and contributing generously to this report were *Mandate III* Task Force Members Michael Ochs, Miklos Radvanyi, Milan Svec, Lucia Swiatkowski, and Vladimir Tismaneanu. They do not necessarily endorse all of its views and recommendations.

Eastern European countries were determined by their record on economic and human rights issues. Example: the 1978 return by the U.S. to Hungary of the Crown of Saint Stephen, one of the most revered Hungarian national artifacts, which had been hidden by the Hungarian patriots from the Nazis during World War II and given to the liberating U.S. troops, was a reward for Hungary's apparent political and economic reforms.

At the same time, Carter Administration policy toward Central/Eastern Europe lacked a coherent, long-term, and publicly articulated strategy and was not coordinated with that of U.S. allies. The U.S. failed to establish criteria by which to evaluate change in Central/Eastern Europe.

The Reagan Administration has brought a much needed clarity and strategic vision to U.S. policy toward Central/Eastern Europe. It has refused unambiguously and publicly to concede that the region is an integral part of the Soviet empire. The American commitment to national self-determination in Central/Eastern Europe has been reflected in the Administration's continuing the tradition of a White House statement on each anniversary of the 1945 Yalta agreements, which condemns the Soviet violations of the agreements' guarantees of freedom to the peoples of Central/Eastern Europe. Furthermore, the Reagan Administration has enhanced the symbolic importance of the Captive Nations Week commemoration through the President's personal participation at the annual reception and signing of the Captive Nations Proclamation. Previous administrations marked the event only with press releases.

After martial law was decreed in Poland in 1981, the Reagan Administration imposed sanctions on the regime headed by General Wojciech Jaruzelski. The U.S. suspended all high technology exports to Poland, including spare parts for the equipment sold earlier, and withdrew Most Favored Nation treatment for Polish imports to the U.S. At U.S. urging, the Western governments suspended debt-rescheduling talks with Poland.

The Administration in 1982 brokered an agreement within the Organization for Economic Cooperation and Development (OECD), which represents Western industrial democracies, barring subsidized interest rates on government-backed credits to Central/Eastern European regimes. In doing so, the West European governments sent the important message to Western financial and business communities and the Soviet bloc that the Western taxpayer should not underwrite Soviet bloc borrowing. The Reagan Administration also virtually has stopped the flow of advanced American technology to Central/Eastern Europe. As a result of U.S. initiative, the allied Coordinating Committee for Multilateral Export Controls (COCOM), created in 1949 to prevent acquisition of defense-applicable technology by the Soviet bloc, has become more efficient. COCOM now has increased resources, streamlined licensing procedures, and improved enforcement capabilities. (See Strategic Trade section of Chapter 28.)

The Administration has established a broad dialogue with dissident communities in Czechoslovakia, Hungary, and Poland. The U.S. also has been aiding Poland's anticommunist underground. Overall, since 1985, the U.S. has provided more than $5 million in cash assistance to the underground labor movement Solidarity and other anticommunist groups. As a result, much of the huge network of underground publications in Poland today is supported by the U.S.

The State Department has conducted regular briefings for representatives of Central/Eastern European ethnic communities on the U.S. policies toward the region. They are designed to win the backing of these groups for U.S. policies.

At the same time, however, the Reagan Administration has been unable to forge a unified Western position that would coordinate Western diplomatic and economic policies toward Central/Eastern Europe. Furthermore, the Administration policies have not always been consistent. Since 1981 the Administration continued to grant Romania Most Favored Nation trade status, despite that country's Stalinist record on political and human rights—one of the worst in the region. Deputy Secretary of State John Whitehead, meanwhile, created enormous confusion by his January 1987 trip to Bulgaria and Czechoslovakia, which, along with Romania, are the area's worst human rights violators. In Central/Eastern Europe such a high-level U.S. visitor traditionally signals U.S. approval of a country's policies.

----------◇----------

THE NEXT FOUR YEARS

Since the region's absorption into the Soviet empire after World War II, U.S. policy toward Central/Eastern Europe has been largely reactive. For decades, the concept of rolling back communism, when it was articulated at all, was confined to rhetoric without serious operational content. That such a rollback can succeed, however, is the lesson of the experience of the Reagan Doctrine in Grenada and, possibly, in Afghanistan, and Nicaragua. The premise and principle of this policy, in appropriately modified form, should be applied to Central/Eastern Europe. The task should be to reinforce what already is an overwhelming repudiation of communism by the population of the region.

The success of U.S. assistance to the Polish underground demonstrates that the U.S. can electively assist the democratic opposition in Central/Eastern Europe. The increasing instability in Central/Eastern Europe resulting from imminent generational changes, economic crises, and confusing signals from Moscow may soon present opportunities for democratic forces in one or several countries of the region.

To achieve the ultimate goal of U.S. policy in Central/Eastern Europe—national self-determination and democratic rule for the peoples of the region—U.S. strategy should include three components. First, the U.S. should aid the emergence of a politically relevant civil society that would be capable of challenging the one-party state. U.S. assistance, overt and covert, to the democratic opposition is the means to advance this challenge.

Second, the U.S. consistently should apply economic and political leverage to influence domestic policies of Central/Eastern European regimes. The U.S. methodically and unambiguously should use its relations with the countries of the region to reward domestic liberalization, increased independence from the Soviet Union, and fundamental economic reform—and to punish resurgence of Stalinism.

Finally, the U.S. should increase to the Soviet Union the costs of its domination of Central/Eastern Europe. Soviet policies in the region should be the key determinant of the level of Western economic and political cooperation with the USSR. Moscow must pay an increasingly greater price for the denial of national self-determination to the peoples of Central/Eastern Europe. (See Liberation Doctrine section of this chapter.)

Coordinating Western Economic Security Strategy toward Central/Eastern Europe

A coordinated Western economic security policy should focus on strengthening and perfecting mechanisms to block transfers of products to the Soviet bloc that could give it a military advantage. The new President should take the lead in calling on America's allies to clarify export guidelines and enhance monitoring and enforcement capabilities. (See Strategic Trade section of Chapter 28.)

The new Administration should press the West European and Japanese allies voluntarily to reduce united general-purpose loans to the

Central/Eastern European regimes by West European and American financial institutions. Such loans are cash that can be used for any purpose by the borrower. Funds obtained through untied loans support the aggression of such anti-Western aggressive totalitarian states as Angola, Nicaragua, and Vietnam. Western cash borrowed by the Central/Eastern European countries can be easily "downstreamed" to Moscow, which uses it for espionage, technology theft, disinformation campaigns ("active measures"), the support of terrorism, and for such front organizations as the World Peace Council. As the Polish experience of the 1970s demonstrates, unrestricted access to Western money eliminates incentives for a genuine economic reform of Soviet economies, in the end leaving countries in a worse economic situation than before.

Long-term coordinated Western strategy in economic relations with Central/Eastern Europe should be based on using Western capital and technology as leverage to make the region's regimes more compatible with the West's moral and military imperatives. The new President should order the Senior Interdepartmental Group on International Economic Policy to produce a comprehensive analysis of long-term Western objectives and means in economic relations with Central/Eastern Europe. The analysis should identify criteria to judge progress in Central/Eastern European domestic policies. (See Western Economic Security section of this chapter.)

"Differentiating" in Relations with Central/Eastern European Nations

A policy of "differentiation" links the level of U.S. diplomatic and economic relations with Central/Eastern European countries to their human rights record. This policy has contributed to political liberalization in Hungary and Poland: expansion of permissible public debate, greater tolerance of political opposition, and less severe punishment for dissidents. While carefully tailoring its tactics to each country of the region, the U.S. should encourage indigenous forces of political liberalization throughout Central/Eastern Europe seeking a reduction of the state's role in the economy and greater national self-determination. Success should be measured by the distance that each of the Central European countries has traveled in pursuit of these objectives. (See Liberation Doctrine section of this chapter.)

Undertaking Long-Term Structural Modernization of Radio Free Europe

From its establishment in 1950, Radio Free Europe (RFE) has provided an independent source of information for tens of millions of

Central/Eastern Europeans. Repeated polling over the years shows that at least half of the adult population of Central/Eastern Europe listens to RFE. In addition, Radio Free Europe Research is the largest center in the West for analytical research on Central/Eastern Europe. RFE *Bulletins* are required reading for Western decision makers, indispensable for analysis of the situation in the region. The importance of Radio Free Europe is underscored by Soviet efforts to silence it: $700 million to $1.2 billion annually. Soviet spokesmen made clear as late as May 1988 that Moscow has no intention of suspending the jamming of RFE and Radio Liberty (RL), a sister station that broadcasts to the Soviet Union. The vehemence of criticism in the official Soviet bloc media is added testimony to the importance of RFE's mission.

RFE will be crucial at the time when Central/Eastern European nations begin a dramatic generational leadership change and possibly enter a period of political turmoil. The greater sophistication and dynamism of Soviet foreign policy toward Central/Eastern Europe under General Secretary Mikhail S. Gorbachev also call for a greater U.S. public diplomacy effort.

To meet these challenges, the new President should seek major increases in funding to expand and modernize RFE/RL. Such funds are needed to counter increased Soviet jamming by refurbishing outmoded transmitting facilities, adding new transmitting sites, and buying new, more powerful transmitters. In the next four years, RFE/RL will need $40 million for technical modernization. Added funding is also needed to restore depleted staff levels. RFE/RL have not recovered fully from budget cuts of the 1970s, which reduced their staffs by nearly 40 percent. Recruitment and training of qualified candidates is also essential to replace 125 programming officers scheduled to retire over the next five years. The new President should require his Deputy National Security Adviser for Soviet Global Affairs and Senior Adviser for Public Diplomacy to prepare an analysis of RFE/RL's needs in view of U.S. public diplomacy objectives in Central/Eastern Europe in a changing international environment. (See Public Diplomacy section of this chapter.)

Using Nongovernment Sources in Monitoring, Analyzing, and Developing Policies for Central/Eastern Europe

The next Administration should continue and expand the practice of augmenting official sources in Central/Eastern European countries with information from such unofficial sources as human rights activists and free trade-unionists. (See Human Rights section of this chapter.) To do this, the State Department needs to choose U.S. diplomats for the region with appropriate educational background and language skills. This is especially important in selecting cultural attaches, who traditionally canvass the attitudes of the society at large. The State Department should provide additional training, especially in languages, for U.S. cultural attaches assigned to the area.

Consulting Americans of Central European Descent

Americans of Central/Eastern European descent are a valuable asset in developing and executing U.S. policy toward Central/Eastern Europe. Leaders of this community should be consulted periodically by the Office of Soviet and Eastern European Affairs of the National Security Council and the State Department's East European country desks. Opinions of these leaders are particularly valuable in deciding which emerging individuals and groups in Central/Eastern Europe may be worthy of active U.S. support.

Tailoring the U.S. Information Agency Activities to Central/Eastern European Countries

Activities of the U.S. Information Agency (USIA), especially Voice of America programs and traveling exhibitions, should portray, where possible, the life of a country's ethnic community in the U.S. Citizens of Central/Eastern European countries are deeply interested in their former countrymen's standard of living, educational and cultural achievements, and freedom to practice their religions. This interest should be used by USIA to counter official Central/Eastern European anti-American propaganda and convey the true picture of freedom and prosperity enjoyed by most Americans. To satisfy this interest as fully as possible, the Director of the USIA should order a review of exhibitions and broadcasts to highlight the lives of Americans of Central/Eastern European descent.

Exploiting Opportunities Offered by New Technologies

New communication technologies, especially direct satellite broadcasts (DSB) in which orbiting satellites, rather than ground transmitters, broadcast radio and television signals, reach broad audiences in Central/Eastern Europe. Unlike regular radio and television broadcasts, satellite-related signals are virtually impossible to jam and are the most cost-effective way of breaking the communist regime's information monopoly. Satellite broadcasts can be received with the help of relatively simple satellite dishes. In Poland, for example, they are already rapidly becoming a new status symbol. The Director of the USIA should order a comprehensive review of the development of DBS technology. At the same time, the new Administration should press Congress to increase funding for new communication technologies.

Similarly, a video recorder boom in Central/Eastern Europe, coupled with a thirst for Western culture, offers USIA an excellent channel of communication with the peoples of Central/Eastern Europe. The USIA should increase the number and availability of video cassettes in U.S. embassies and cultural centers. (See Public Diplomacy section of this chapter.)

Inviting Dissidents to U.S. Embassies

Hosting dissidents in the U.S. embassy has been highly praised by the leaders of human rights and democratic political movements in Central/Eastern Europe, especially in Hungary, Poland, and Czechoslovakia. This sends a powerful and much needed message of American support to the dissident communities. These meetings also are an excellent source of firsthand knowledge about political, social, and cultural developments in the host countries. The Secretary of State should order U.S. embassies in Central/Eastern Europe to initiate or expand the practice of inviting members of political opposition and human rights groups to U.S. embassies.

Including Americans of Central/Eastern European Descent in U.S. Human Rights Delegations

The Secretary of State should direct that U.S. ethnic community leaders be invited routinely by the State Department to join U.S. delegations to European human rights meetings, including Helsinki review conferences. Their presence would increase significantly the expertise and the sense of purpose in the U.S. delegations. It would add authority and prestige to U.S. delegations in the eyes of the Central/Eastern Europeans. (See Human Rights section of this chapter.)

Continuing State Department Briefings on Central/Eastern Europe

Leaders of Central/Eastern European communities in the U.S. find briefings on the region extremely valuable in helping them to explain to other Americans of Central/Eastern European origin U.S. policies toward the region and in securing support for these policies. Such briefings also keep the State Department abreast of the feelings and concerns of an important and engaged domestic constituency. The Assistant Secretary of State for European and Canadian Affairs should ensure that such briefings continue.

———————————◇———————————

INITIATIVES FOR 1989

1) Prepare the U.S. response to a crisis in Central/Eastern Europe. A period of turmoil in Central/Eastern Europe is very likely, given the rapidly deteriorating economic situation, political crisis of the ruling communist parties, imminent leadership changes, and a Kremlin preoccupied with domestic political infighting. The situation is aggravated by the Soviet Union's reluctance, caused by its domestic economic difficulties, to alleviate Central/Eastern European crises through increased economic assistance. In the past such a combination led to explosions, for example in Poland and Hungary in 1956. The situations are especially unstable in Hungary and Poland today. The West must not be surprised again by such events and should prepare for them by developing a crisis management structure to be activated on short notice.

The next Administration should start laying the groundwork for such a structure. The new President should appoint and convene an Interagency Group on Central/Eastern Europe to be chaired by the Deputy National Security Adviser to the President for Global Soviet Affairs.[2] The Group should include representatives of the National Security Council and the Departments of State, Defense, Commerce, and Treasury. Within a few weeks, the Group should recommend to the President a U.S. response to a Central/Eastern European crisis, including a Soviet invasion. The options should include: a declaration of condemnation by the leaders of the countries; coordinated economic sanctions against the Soviet Union in the case of a Soviet invasion; the recall of Western ambassadors from the Soviet Union; appropriate degrees of military alert of NATO forces; and coordinated Western actions at the United Nations. The President should discuss these and other options with the allies during the initial round of traditional postelection consultations and set in place the mechanism for a unified Western response to a Central/Eastern European crisis. (See U.S.-Soviet Relations section of this chapter.)

2) Create a mechanism of support for democratic movements in Central/ Eastern Europe. Based on its experience with the Polish underground, the Administration should create an infrastructure of support for democratic and national liberation forces in Central/Eastern Europe. The President should lobby Congress to appropriate overt and covert funding for such items as short wave radios, ink, printing presses, computers with printers, video recorders, and video cassettes. Simultaneously, the National Endowment for Democracy should begin a search for potential recipients of overt grants, which could be channeled, as was done in the case of Poland, through the Free Trade Union Institute, an arm of the AFL-CIO.

3) Press Bulgaria and Czechoslovakia to stop jamming Radio Free Europe. Bulgaria and Czechoslovakia continue to jam Radio Free Europe. This violates the Final Act of the Helsinki conference. In accordance with the policy of differentiation, cessation of jamming should be explicitly linked by the new President to the extent and nature of U.S. economic or cultural cooperation with these countries.

4) Create a Foreign Exchange Reserve Fund for Radio Free Europe/ Radio Liberty. Over 70 percent of the RFE/RL's operating expenses are paid for in West German marks. Thus when the value of the dollar relative to the mark decreases, as it has since 1985, RFE/RL requires emergency supplemental appropriations. In 1987, to cover massive currency losses, $33 million had to be requested by the U.S. Board for International Broadcasting. To avoid the uncertainty of a fluctuating mark and the delay in obtaining funds by emergency appropriation, a permanent Foreign Exchange Reserve Fund of $100 million should be created. Maintained by Treasury, the Fund would be used by RFE/RL only in case of a dollar decline: when there is no change in the dollar position or the U.S. currency rises, the Fund would not be used. The new President should direct his Senior Adviser on Public Diplomacy and Secretary of the Treasury to seek legislation creating a Foreign Exchange Reserve Fund for RFE/RL.

NOTES

1. These nations are often loosely called "East" European, a term fully applicable only to Bulgaria. Historically, Romania has straddled Eastern and Western Europe, while Czechoslovakia, Hungary and Poland are among the oldest members of the West European community of nations. Although a part of the region, Yugoslavia has been independent from the Soviet Union since 1948 and, for that reason, is not usually included in the Eastern European category.

2. The creation of this position is proposed in the U.S.-Soviet Relations section of this chapter. In the absence of this position, the task of coordination should be given to the Director of Soviet and East European Affairs of the National Security Council.

Western Economic Security

Roger W. Robinson, Jr.*
Task Force Chairman

The United States and the West must defend themselves on a number of fronts. Most obvious is the military. The newest challenge is economic, not in the traditional sense of nations fighting for markets or resources, but in the loans, subsidies, and access to capital that affect the West-East balance of power. American policymakers require a strategy for economic and financial security issues just as they do for other security matters.[1]

The Soviet Union has a financial security strategy of its own; it is to procure Western capital both directly (through loans) and indirectly (through subsidized trade) as flexibly and inexpensively as possible to help prop up its faltering economy and maintain its costly global commitments. Currently, the USSR owes the West over $40 billion, up dramatically from an estimated $25.6 billion gross debt in 1985. Whether and on what terms the U.S. and its allies allow the Soviet Union to obtain even more capital are extremely important strategic issues.

Properly structured alliance trade and financial policies toward the Soviet Union can, over time, be among the West's most effective levers to influence Soviet domestic and foreign policy choices. Such alliance policies should avoid giving Moscow preferential treatment. Instead, the policies should be designed to encourage Moscow to make positive tradeoffs between domestic economic revival and foreign adventurism, and between decentralized economic and political controls on the one hand and a totalitarian state on the other.

---◇---

THE REAGAN ADMINISTRATION RECORD

Jimmy Carter's Assistant for National Security Affairs, Zbigniew K. Brzezinski, deserves credit for identifying economic relations with

*Commenting and contributing generously to this chapter were *Mandate III* Task Force Members Norman Bailey, Raul Fernandez, and Micah Naftalin. They do not necessarily endorse all of its views and recommendations.

Task Force Deputy Chairman: Heritage Salvatori Fellow in Soviet Studies Leon Aron.

the Soviet bloc as a key component of the overall political and military equation. On occasion, he linked these relations to Moscow's domestic and foreign behavior. Yet Carter Administration economic security policy toward the Soviet bloc was conducted as ad hoc, crisis management. It lacked consistency and long-term vision. Above all, it failed to engage America's allies in making East-West economic security an integral part of a unified Western policy toward the Soviet bloc.

The Reagan Administration has corrected some of these shortcomings. In 1982, following a U.S. initiative, the Organization for Economic Cooperation and Development (OECD) agreed to eliminate subsidized interest rates on government-backed credits to the Soviet Union. Again at a Reagan Administration initiative, the allies agreed to limit West European purchases of Soviet natural gas. These alliance understandings are embodied in the 1983 International Energy Agency Agreement and the 1983 North Atlantic Treaty Organization Ministerial Communique and endorsed by the Declaration of the 1983 Williamsburg Economic Summit. In the area of West-East technology transfers, measures have been taken to increase the effectiveness of the Coordinating Committee for Multilateral Export Controls (COCOM), an organization established in 1949 by the U.S. and its NATO allies to prevent the transfer of militarily useful technology to the Soviet bloc.

Yet, the Reagan Administration in 1986 initiated taxpayer-subsidized wheat sales to the USSR, which are estimated to have so far cost the American taxpayer $500 million. The Administration also has not paid sufficient attention to growing bipartisan congressional concern over Western lending to the Soviet bloc that is not tied to a specific trade transaction or project, but can be used by the borrower for any purpose. These are known as "untied" loans.

The Reagan Administration has occasionally sent mixed signals concerning opposition to Soviet membership in the General Agreement on Tariffs and Trade (GATT) and the Asian Development Bank. And the Administration in early 1988 recommended that Hungary be eligible for the insurance and loan guarantee programs of the U.S. Overseas Private Investment Corporation (OPIC). Such a recommendation sets a precedent for rewarding a Soviet bloc nation even if it fails, as does Hungary, to comply fully with the human rights provisions of the 1975 Helsinki Final Act. The Administration also encouraged the formation of a U.S.-Soviet energy working group, which has endorsed a proposed U.S. energy project off the Soviet-held island of Sakhalin. Both actions have contradicted established U.S. policy in the area of energy security.

THE NEXT FOUR YEARS

Generally, international trade and financial activities unfettered by government interference should continue to be one of the principal goals of U.S. international economic policy. Free trade is consistent with the precepts of a free society and economic prosperity. Government should provide no trade subsidies, just as government should impose no restrictions except when there is a threat to national security. At the same time, where national security is involved, some government oversight of international economic and financial transactions may be necessary. It is appropriate, for example, for the U.S. to restrict the export of certain high technology items which could benefit Moscow militarily. (See Strategic Trade section of chapter 28.)

At present, the amounts and flows of West to East credit, and how they could be damaging Western security, have not been explored sufficiently by the alliance. Until these financial security issues are fully clarified, the U.S. and its allies should concentrate on collecting data, assessing the national security dimensions, and educating the allied publics. The U.S. policy goal should be the voluntary cooperation of allies and the Western financial community in acting with greater discipline and openness in their financial dealings with the Soviet bloc and client states.

Forging Allied Consensus on the Strategic Dimensions of Western Lending

By most indicators, the center of gravity of Soviet economic relations with the West is shifting from trade to such financial transactions as joint ventures and even the sale in the West of bonds by the Soviet Bank for Foreign Economic Activities. Trade is declining in importance, of course, because the Soviets produce almost nothing that the West or anyone else wants to buy. Without exporting goods, the Soviets have no hard currency to pay for imports.

As Moscow diversifies its financial strategy toward the West, the West, in turn, needs a strategy for its financial dealings with the Soviet bloc. Western commercial banks, of course, should be able to lend money to the Soviet Union, provided that such lending requires no government subsidies, risk insurance, or guarantees of any sort. In some cases, however, Western capital should be regarded as a strategic asset and used to encourage Soviet domestic and foreign policies to be more compatible with Western security interests. Such cases include the anticipated Soviet attempts at massive, multibillion-dollar government-guaranteed borrowing from groups of Western banks, central banks, or international financial institutions such as the International Monetary Fund or the World Bank.

The new President should work with U.S. allies to craft a strategy for dealing with such situations. Without a comprehensive approach to lending to the USSR, not only is the West likely to jeopardize certain security interests, but it is likely to eliminate or significantly diminish the need for reform of Soviet society. Massive funds borrowed in the West, for instance, may provide short-term relief for the Soviet economy without changing the primacy of military spending.

The new President should task the Deputy National Security Adviser for Soviet Global Affairs[2] to coordinate a comprehensive interagency evaluation of West to East financial flows which could be presented to the Senior Interdepartmental Group-International Economic Policy[3] and finally, the National Security Council itself. The analysis should establish detailed criteria by which Soviet domestic and foreign policy will be judged and upon which the extent and nature of Western economic and financial cooperation should be predicated. The study should consider recommending, for example, that private Western financial institutions return to traditional, specific purpose lending to the Soviet bloc and seek to ensure that the end-uses of borrowed funds are peaceful and commercially productive. The West should exercise caution in its economic and financial dealings and wait for a multiyear track record of cuts in Soviet defense spending, irreversible, market-oriented economic reform, reductions of Soviet conventional forces in Central Europe, and a significant scaling down of Soviet global commitments in such places as Angola, Cuba, Nicaragua, and Vietnam before encouraging increased economic interaction.

At the next economic summit, the new President should share the results of the study with the heads of major Western industrial democracies and use the discussion as a first step toward forging an allied consensus on the strategy of West-East financial interaction. At the summit, the President should propose that the OECD monitor the voluntary Western banking reforms needed to redress the untied loan problem. At the same time, the Secretary of State should raise the issue of undisciplined Western lending to the Soviet bloc at the next Ministerial meeting of the North Atlantic Treaty Organization (NATO) and press for a joint declaration on this subject in the communique.

Collecting Data on West-East Lending Activity

The West does not have an adequate accounting of the Soviet bloc's access to Western financial resources or of how the proceeds of Western credits are used. Example: a portion of the proceeds of Western cash credits to Eastern European countries can be "skimmed" and diverted to Soviet client states or to the Soviet Union itself. Moscow could finance Western equipment for a project through a barter arrangement with Western companies , and at the same time, obtain cash loans for the ostensibly same purpose. Example: in the late 1970s, the Soviet Union paid for the Western imports needed to build the Orenburg gas pipeline (valued at roughly $1.5 billion to $2.2 billion) primarily through natural gas deliveries to the West, while concurrently arranging a series of Western "project" loans (totaling over $2 billion), ostensibly to fund the same pipeline.

A comprehensive Western tracking of Moscow's complex and fungible financial transactions may not be possible. Still, significant improvements can be made through voluntary reporting and compliance procedures. The new President should direct the Senior Interdepartmental Group on Economic Policy of the National Security Council to study the problem and present recommendations. Using the results of the study, the new President at future economic summits should advocate a voluntary policy whereby Western banks and governments demand greater data from Soviet bloc borrowers as a condition for lending. These data should include: estimated Western and Japanese bank deposits in Soviet bloc-owned banks, including those located in the West; Soviet bloc debt to nonbanking institutions, such as securities firms, pension funds, and trading companies; and the quality and terms of the Soviet hard currency loan portfolio to its Third World clients, estimated to total as much as $65 billion. Inter-German financial flows should be reported in full to the Bank for International Settlements.

Focusing Attention on "Untied" General-purpose
Loans to the Soviet Bloc

"Untied" general-purpose loans are cash that can be used by the borrower for any purpose. In recent years, the Soviet bloc has shifted its borrowing away from loans tied to designated trade transactions or projects to untied general purpose loans. Of the estimated $24 billion loaned to the Soviet bloc by Western banks and governments in 1986 (not including short-term credit and interbank deposits), over $19 billion is estimated to have been untied cash credits. (These figures are reduced when exchange rate effects are taken into account.)

Moscow can use the proceeds of untied Western credits in a variety of ways. For example, Moscow could use Western credits as bridge loans in support of Soviet arms shipments worldwide. The Soviets could also use Western cash to acquire militarily relevant Western technology, in violation of existing Western regulations prohibiting its export to the Soviet bloc. Espionage is another costly operation financed largely with hard currency, as is the Kremlin's worldwide disinformation campaign ("active measures") against the West.

Besides obtaining numerous untied loans from the West, the Soviets are, for the first time, moving into Western securities markets. In January 1988, the Soviet Bank for Foreign Economic Affairs, out of its Zurich branch, issued a $75 million bond. Six months later, the Soviet Union floated in West Germany a $270 million bond. Continued sales of such securities represent an inexpensive new avenue for Soviet untied borrowing in the West. Current statistical reporting does not register claims of such nonbanking financial institutions on the USSR as securities firms and pension funds. Moscow also is alert to the political potential of recruiting influential new Western constituencies as lenders to the USSR.

The new President should direct the Senior Interdepartmental Group-International Economic Policy to study whether Western cash underwrites Soviet domestic and global operations. If it is found to do so, the new Administration should draft proposals to alert the U.S. and Western private banking institutions that their loans are being used for purposes that could threaten U.S. and Western security. While the study must not recommend U.S. government controls on private bank lending, it could offer the banking community suggestions on how private banks voluntarily could avoid untied lending to Moscow.

Among the suggestions: banks could lend only in support of specific trade transactions and projects; banks could match loan maturities to the duration of the underlying transactions, which would prevent Soviet bloc borrowers from, in effect, turning a short-term loan into a long-term one; banks could aggregate, monitor, and report interbank deposits in all Soviet bloc-owned banks, including those in the West to bank regulators (that is, these deposits are, in effect, untied loans); banks could employ project lending techniques to ensure that loan proceeds are dedicated only to the project or joint venture for which they are made.

Reaffirming the 1982 OECD Agreement

In 1982, the Organization for Economic Cooperation and Development (OECD) agreed to eliminate subsidized interest rates on government-backed credits to the Soviet Union. The new President should reaffirm U.S. support for the agreement.

Incorporating Economic and Financial Security into Defense Burden-Sharing

The new President should advise the allies that West to East economic and financial transactions that directly or indirectly contribute to Soviet military power and foreign adventurism have to be countered by increases in U.S. defense expenditures. If the Soviets gain a military advantage by using untied funds obtained from a Western country, that country should redress the problem. Example: Japan should reimburse the U.S. for the several billions of dollars that the U.S. Navy must spend on submarines to offset Soviet gains in anti-submarine warfare resulting from the unauthorized sale to the USSR of high technology by the Toshiba Machine Company of Japan.

The new President should direct the Senior Interdepartmental Group-International Economic Policy to develop a set of criteria by which to determine whether, and if so to what extent, specific West-East economic transactions damage Western security interests. Based on these criteria, the Office of Undersecretary of Defense for International Economic Security will then monitor such transactions. (See U.S. and NATO section of Chapter 28.)

Opposing Soviet Membership in International Economic and Financial Institutions

Moscow is pressing for entry into such international economic institutions as the General Agreement on Tariffs and Trade (GATT) and the Asian Development Bank. Down the road, it is expected Moscow will seek membership in the International Monetary Fund or the World Bank. Soviet membership in such organizations should be opposed. First, the Soviets traditionally have used their presence in international organizations to propagandistic purposes. Until there is tangible evidence of substantial change in the aims and conduct of Soviet participation in an organization like the U.N., it would be against long-term Western interests to provide the Kremlin with another arena in which to advance its objectives. Second, the large centrally controlled economy of the USSR is fundamentally incompatible with the market-oriented philosophy underpinning these organizations. Third, the Soviets need to demonstrate broader compliance with the Helsinki Accords as a precondition to observer status or membership in these organizations.

———————————◇———————————

INITIATIVES FOR 1989

1) Reaffirm the International Energy Agency (IEA) agreement on Western energy security. In May 1983, the OECD member countries agreed to limit Western European dependency on Soviet natural gas. This IEA Agreement, in effect, limits Soviet natural gas deliveries to Western Europe to 30 percent of the region's supplies. This alliance action was taken to curtail the Soviet political and military leverage which could result from such dependency. Western Europe's dependence on Soviet gas is already approaching this limit. Moscow could eventually be providing 50 percent to 60 percent of Europe's total natural gas requirements in the early part of the twenty-first century. This development would not only make the West excessively dependent on Moscow for its gas needs, but would provide the Soviet Union with up to $150 billion or more in additional hard-currency earnings over a 25–year period. At the next economic summit, the new President should press for reaffirmation of the International Energy Agency Agreement in the summit's communique.

2) Establish the position of Undersecretary of Defense for International Economic Security. The rapidly increasing importance of international economic and financial security issues and their implications for U.S. defense require a permanent high-level office for monitoring, analysis, and policy recommendations. Accordingly, the Secretary of Defense should ask Congress to create the position of Undersecretary of Defense for International Economic Security.

3) Reestablish a Senior Interdepartmental Group-International Economic Policy (SIG-IEP). During its existence from July 1982 to April 1985, the SIG-IEP integrated the analysis of international economic issues and broader U.S. national security objectives to produce policy recommendations for the President. This gave proper priority to international economic security. The SIG-IEP should be reestablished and the roles played by the National Security Council, the Defense Department, and the CIA should be enhanced.

───────────────◇───────────────

NOTES

1. For a discussion of other aspects of West-East relations, see U.S.-Soviet relations section of this chapter and the U.S. and NATO section of Chapter 28.

2. The creation of this position is in the U.S.-Soviet Relations section of this chapter. In the absence of this position, the task should be carried out by the Senior Director for International Economic Affairs of the National Security Council.

3. The reestablishment of this body, which existed in the Reagan Administration's first term, is recommended in this section. If the Group is not reestablished, the study should be undertaken by the Senior Director for International Economic Affairs of the National Security Council.

☎

Western Europe

Kim R. Holmes*
Task Force Chairman

The free nations of Western Europe are crucial to United States security and economic well-being. They are a bulwark against the military expansion of the Soviet Union and its Warsaw Pact allies in Eastern Europe. They demonstrate to the world the vitality and success of democratic institutions and open markets. The members of the European community are, as a region, one of America's greatest trading partners, buying $60.5 billion of United States goods last year, and are key participants in the financial and trading markets of the world economy. And they are the ancestral homes of many Americans, providing the historical and cultural ties that bind Americans and Europeans in the common heritage of Western democracy and freedom.

While relations between the U.S. and Western Europe remain warm, there are disagreements. The U.S., for example, rightly complains about West European agricultural subsidies and about Western Europe's high tax and slow growth economic policies that hurt U.S. trade with Europe. The U.S. government favors modernization of NATO battlefield nuclear weapons, while West Germany is reluctant to do so. Disagreements exist between the U.S. and the governments of Greece, Portugal, and Spain over American basing rights in Europe. The U.S. has not been pleased by the refusal of some West European governments to support American military action against terrorists, such as when France denied U.S. warplanes the right to fly over her territory during the 1986 U.S. Air Force raid against Libya. Finally, complaints in the U.S. Congress that the West European allies do not carry their fair share of the defense burden have created uncertainty in the minds of some Europeans about the permanence of the U.S. military commitment to Europe.

*Commenting and contributing generously to this report were *Mandate III* Task Force Members Dennis Bark, Gerald Frost, Edward Hudgins, Derek Leebaert, James Phillips, and Paolo Stoppa-Liebl. They do not necessarily endorse all of its views and recommendations.

THE REAGAN ADMINISTRATION RECORD

With the support of Bonn and London, Reagan took the lead in holding the Atlantic Alliance together in the face of Soviet intimidation, seduction, and anti-American demonstrations in Western Europe during the debate over the deployment of NATO's intermediate-range nuclear forces (INF) in Europe. The Administration not only has raised the consciousness of many West Europeans to the importance of free market ideas, limited government, tax cuts, and tax reform, but also has encouraged European interest in human rights abuses in the Soviet Union and Eastern Europe.

During the Reagan years, the U.S. government has encouraged Spain to join the NATO alliance. This strengthens Spanish democratic institutions, broadens Europe's unity, and militarily bolsters the Alliance. Moreover, the Reagan Administration can take some credit for dampening West European criticism of U.S. policies in the Third World. And the Reagan Administration merits credit for cementing closer U.S. ties with Great Britain.

Yet the Reagan Administration has failed to manage adequately the political fallout of the INF Treaty in Europe. Indeed, as a result of the Administration's rush to sign nuclear arms agreements with the Soviets, the West German government has been reluctant to fulfill its commitment to support the modernization of NATO's battlefield nuclear weapons. This modernization is necessary to improve the balance of forces in Europe. The Administration also has not communicated adequately to Western Europe the goals and justifications of U.S. foreign and defense policies. It has failed to explain to its NATO allies the arms control reduction proposals of the 1986 Reykjavik summit and the Strategic Defense Initiative (SDI).

Inconsistencies in the Reagan Administration East-West trade policies, meanwhile, have hampered U.S. efforts to persuade Western Europe to limit trade in strategically important goods with the Eastern bloc. On the one hand, the Administration has pushed the European allies to adopt tighter restrictions on strategic trade and economic ventures with the East. For instance, in the early 1980s, the Administration vehemently opposed Western Europe's long-term agreement to buy Soviet natural gas. On the other hand, the Administration has sold Moscow huge amounts of American grain. Because the Reagan Administration's restrictive East-West strategic trade policy lacked credibility with the West Europeans, it was unable to persuade them to reduce their favorable bank loans to the Eastern bloc.

———————————◇———————————

THE NEXT FOUR YEARS

U.S. policy toward Western Europe should have four goals. The first is to prevent Western Europe from coming under Soviet military domination. The second is to deny Moscow the opportunity to intimidate America's European allies politically or militarily. The third is to prevent European trade with the Soviet bloc from undermining NATO military's strength by transferring strategically significant technologies to the nations of the Warsaw Pact. The fourth is to promote economic growth policies and more open markets in Western Europe to ease the U.S. trade deficit.

Creating a New Atlanticism

A major problem of the Atlantic Alliance is Western Europe's overdependence on the U.S. for security. This often causes West Europeans to underestimate the Soviet threat, overestimate U.S. influence in the world, be overly critical of U.S. policy, and doubt the credibility of the U.S. nuclear deterrent. To produce a more stable alliance, the U.S. needs to do two things at once: reduce European dependence on the U.S. and reaffirm U.S. long-term security guarantees to its European allies.

These aims will require the U.S. to craft a policy that, in effect, is a New Atlanticism. This new approach would accept the traditional Atlanticist premise that a U.S. military presence is needed in Western Europe. It would also accept the premise that the U.S. should retaliate with its nuclear forces against the Soviet Union if Europe is attacked. But the New Atlanticism would not, as traditional Atlanticists want, require the U.S. to invest so much in the conventional defense of Europe. The U.S. now contributes a huge proportion of its own resources—estimated to be around half of its defense budget—to the defense of Europe, and most of this money goes for conventional forces. The U.S. investment in the conventional defense of Europe is far too much for a nation that must in addition carry the burden for defending Western interests worldwide, not only with its nuclear strategic forces, but with conventional forces deployed at sea and on the ground in places like the Philippines and South Korea.

NATO needs a new division of labor. The goal of the new U.S. policy toward NATO should be for the European allies to take more responsibility for the ground defense of Europe. In particular, they should take a greater share of NATO's burden for providing combat reinforcements and firepower. The President and his Secretaries of State and Defense should encourage greater Franco-German military cooperation, in particular the formation of a Franco-German division, the deployment of French tactical nuclear weapons on West German soil, and the formulation of Franco-German war plans. U.S. policy should promote greater U.S.-European cooperation for the development of standardized weapons and military equipment for NATO. At a special NATO summit, the new President should begin serious discussions with the West European allied leaders on the details of a new NATO plan to share the responsibility of defending Western Europe from the Warsaw Pact.

Coordinating Japanese Trade and Defense Policies with the Atlantic Alliance

Though Japan enjoys the protection of the U.S. military and has access to Western European and U.S. markets, it contributes absolutely no military forces to the West's common defense. The new President must devise a policy to put an end to Japan's being a freeloader. Tokyo must do its share to protect the economic viability and military security of the Western political community. Economically, politically, and militarily, Japan is a de facto ally of the U.S. and Western Europe and should be encouraged to act like one.

To spur Japan to cooperate more closely with the U.S. and Western Europe in economic and military matters, the new President should call a summit of U.S., Japanese, and Western European leaders to discuss ways to improve cooperation on defending Western interests. In his first meeting with the Japanese Prime Minister, the new President should urge him to coordinate security and economic planning with the West Europeans and the U.S. The President specifically should press Japan: 1) to increase from $800 million to $2 billion a year its economic aid and assistance to the Philippines, an important U.S. ally; 2) to participate in more U.S. military exercises in the Pacific Ocean; 3) to provide funds to help underwrite such U.S. military operations as those in the Persian Gulf where Japanese interests are directly affected and where U.S. European allies are already involved; and 4) to add to Japanese naval forces a small fleet of helicopter carriers for the maritime defense of the Far East.

The Japanese should be pressed also to send observers to the North Atlantic Assembly in Brussels and to NATO military headquarters in Stuttgart, West Germany. The U.S. Secretaries of State and Commerce should work closely with the West Europeans to press Tokyo to drop trade barriers against American and European goods. (See Asia section of this chapter.)

Explaining U.S. Policy to the Western European Public

The new President should launch a vigorous public diplomacy effort to explain all aspects of U.S. foreign policy to West Europeans. It should stress that Americans and West Europeans have common interests and destinies. It should explain the background and the reasons for the U.S. military presence in Europe, the Strategic Defense Initiative, and such U.S. policies as aid to the Nicaraguan Democratic Resistance. It is in the mutual interest of the U.S. and the West Europeans to undertake a joint public diplomacy effort to correct misunderstandings.

To improve ties between West European and American youth, the U.S. Information Agency (USIA) should expand its grant programs for West European undergraduate students. Bringing many more young West Europeans to the U.S. could build long-term personal ties between them and Americans.

Encouraging the European Community to Pursue Growth-Oriented Economic Policies

Western Europe continues to erect barriers to exports from the U.S. and other countries; this slows world economic growth. Such barriers, for example, keep U.S. agricultural products out of the Common Market, while European subsidies to its industries give them an artificial competitive advantage over American industries. European Community subsidies and price supports to farmers undermine incentive and innovation and cause overproduction that floods the international market with cheap agricultural goods, making it difficult for U.S. farmers to compete. In addition, the domestic policies of most West European countries (Britain being the major exception) dampen economic growth. Example: laws making it nearly impossible to lay off workers in stagnant industries have prevented the restructuring needed to expand West European production and create more jobs.

At the next economic summit, the new President should press the West Europeans to follow such growth-oriented economic policies as lower taxes and economic deregulation. More productive Community economies and more disposable income for European consumers would expand the European market for U.S. goods. The Secretaries of State and Commerce, plus the U.S. Trade Representative, should oppose any new European trade barriers and continue to press the European Community directly though the General Agreement on Tariffs and Trade to end subsidies of agriculture and industry.

Restricting the Transfer of Military Technology to the Soviet Bloc

In 1987, Japanese and Norwegian companies were caught selling restricted technology to the Soviet Union. The Japanese and the Norwegians illegally sold tooling machinery which the Soviets are using to improve the performance of their attack submarines. This has substantially increased the threat to U.S. and allied naval forces. The illegal Japanese and Norwegian sales underscore the importance of coordinating restrictions on the flow of advanced technology to the Soviet bloc. It makes no sense for the U.S. and its allies to spend billions of dollars on advanced technology weapons to offset Soviet bloc conventional force superiority if this technology falls into Soviet military hands.

To prevent this, the Secretaries of State, Defense, and Commerce should develop a plan for better coordination of U.S. and allied restrictions on militarily valuable trade with the Soviet bloc. The U.S. plan should establish stricter procedures for Western customs services to prevent the illegal export and diversion of militarily significant equipment to the Soviet bloc. West European countries should be encouraged to improve and refine their knowledge of Soviet military-technical needs and use this knowledge in devising an effective and practical multilateral export control list. Finally, the U.S. should push for the selective expansion of restricted products on the strategic export list of the Control Coordinating Committee (COCOM) to include items involving microelectronics, computers, telecommunications, and the fabrication of advanced metals, alloys, ceramics, and composite materials. (See Strategic Trade section of Chapter 28.)

Strengthening Turkey's Security Role in Europe

Turkey anchors NATO's eastern flank, providing a formidable barrier to Soviet expansion in the eastern Mediterranean and the Middle East. Approximately 25 percent of NATO's intelligence on Soviet strategic nuclear activities, weapons development, military readiness, and force movements comes from Turkish facilities. Bases in Turkey could be crucial to blocking a Soviet military thrust toward the Persian Gulf.

To strengthen Turkey's role in NATO, the new President should live up to the 1980 U.S. pledge to underwrite Turkey's NATO defense commitments and modernize the Turkish armed forces. The Reagan Administration's fiscal 1988 request for $785 million in military aid is the minimum that the U.S. should be giving to Turkey as a prudent investment in Western security. Aid levels should not be tied to the status of the Cyprus dispute; that thorny problem will be resolved only by compromise between Greece and Turkey, not by U.S. pressure. Nor should aid levels to Turkey be linked with aid levels to Greece in the arbitrary congressionally imposed ten to seven ratio. The 1986 "southern flank" congressional amendment that allows the Administration to transfer surplus military equipment to Turkey, Greece, and Portugal should be invoked by the President to give the greatest benefit to Turkey.

---◇---

INITIATIVES FOR 1989

1) Establish a high-level commission to review U.S. European policy. The new President should establish a commission to recommend ways to update U.S. policy toward Europe. The commission should be comprised of well-known senior policy experts with a broad and intimate knowledge of Western Europe and NATO. The commission should chart a comprehensive long-term policy for U.S. strategy toward Europe in such areas as: 1) giving the European NATO allies more responsibility for the ground defense of Western Europe; 2) updating NATO's strategic and military doctrines in light of the Intermediate-range Nuclear Force (INF) Treaty, the Strategic Defense Initiative, and deep reduction proposals in strategic nuclear offenses; 3) developing a sound policy for conventional arms control agreements and alliance military modernization; 4) improving U.S. public diplomacy in Europe; 5) explaining the relationship between U.S. global policies and West European security; and 6) developing a more coherent concept of how closer political relations with the Soviet Union and Eastern Europe could affect the security of the West.

2) Call a special summit of industrialized democracies to discuss security cooperation with Japan. To encourage greater Japanese coordination of security policies with the Atlantic Alliance, the new President should propose a special summit with the leaders of Canada, Japan, and NATO's European members to discuss ways to increase Japanese participation and cooperation in defending the common interests of the industrialized democracies. To underline Japan's importance to Western solidarity and security, the summit should be held in Tokyo. (See Asia section of this chapter.)

3) Launch a "Project Europe" at the United States Information Agency to explain and discuss U.S. foreign policy with the West European public. To conduct a more effective public diplomacy effort toward Western Europe, the director of the USIA should launch "Project Europe" to expand its media and exchange programs with Western Europe. The purpose of "Project Europe" should be to send the message that West Europeans and Americans continue to have common interests and destinies. The USIA director should request funding for expanded exchange programs for overseas undergraduate students. To reach a wider listening audience, he should ensure that Voice of America broadcasts in Europe are transmitted by the FM system, and not by the current outdated short-wave system. The USIA director should expand the "American Participant" program for Europe by sending greater numbers of American foreign and defense experts to Europe to explain U.S. policies. (See Public Diplomacy section of this chapter.)

4) Seek increased security aid for Turkey. This is needed to strengthen Turkey's capability to contribute more effectively to the security of southern Europe. Turkey now receives $490 million annually in military aid from the U.S. At a minimum, it should be receiving $785 million in military aid to modernize its military forces.

5) Put pressure on Greece. The new President should order the Secretary of State to adopt a tougher policy toward Greece. Since 1981, Greek Prime Minister Andreas Papandreou, a socialist who has taught at U.S. universities, has used shrill anti-American and anti-Western demagoguery to exploit Greek xenophobia. Throughout the early 1980s, he threatened to shut down four major U.S. bases. He also generally balks at cooperating with the U.S. in fighting terrorism. At his first meeting with Papandreou, the new President should make it clear that future Greek anti-Western actions and statements will not be cost-free. He should be informed privately that, if he terminates the U.S. base rights, he will forfeit most of the U.S. aid that his country receives. (This amounted to $344 million in military aid for fiscal 1988.) The Secretary of Defense should order the preparation of detailed contingency plans for transferring the functions performed at Greek bases to bases in Turkey or Italy. The new President should tell the Greek Prime Minister that he expects the Greek government to live up to its NATO defense obligations. And if Greece continues to drag its feet on extraditing to the U.S. terrorists accused of killing Americans, the new President should impose a "travel advisory," which would cut American tourism in Greece.

☎

Mexico, Central America, and the Caribbean

Richard Stone*
Task Force Chairman

United States global strategy is based on a secure southern flank. Central America, the Caribbean, and Mexico, in which 131 million people live, is the most crucial part of this flank. The region includes the Panama Canal which connects the Atlantic and Pacific sea lines of communication. In peacetime, 55 percent of all U.S. crude oil and 45 percent of U.S. exports and imports transit the Caribbean sea lines of communication. During a European crisis, 60 percent of resupplies from the U.S. to the North Atlantic Treaty Organization (NATO) would flow through those sea lines. These U.S. security interests could be put at serious risk by the Sandinista communist regime's consolidation of power in Nicaragua. Also at risk is the stability of the new and still fragile democracies of El Salvador, Guatemala, and Honduras, as well as Costa Rica's well-established democracy. Ultimately, even Mexico could be affected adversely by the prolonged political turmoil and economic stagnation that would accompany a permanent communist regime in Managua.

There is a vast economic potential in the region. If the productive energies of the peoples of the region can be unleashed through imaginative economic policies that provide incentives for individual entrepreneurs and businesses, there may yet emerge a regional equivalent of Singapore or South Korea.

⸻◇⸻

THE REAGAN ADMINISTRATION RECORD

The Reagan Administration has blunted Soviet expansion in Central America and has spurred the spread of democratic institutions. At

*Commenting and contributing generously to this report were *Mandate III* Task Force Members Georges Fauriol, Roger Fontaine, Thomas Glakas, Philip Peters, Max Singer, and Jose Sorzano. They do not necessarily endorse all of its views and recommendations.

Task Force Deputy Chairman: Heritage Policy Analyst Jorge Salaverry.

the start of 1981, Guatemala had an authoritarian government, and the movement to democracy in Honduras and El Salvador was weak. All three countries now enjoy freely elected democratic governments. Freedom and democracy were restored in Grenada by U.S. military action in October 1983. The only remaining dictatorships in the region are Cuba, Haiti, Nicaragua, and Panama.

The Reagan record concerning Nicaragua is mixed. The Administration did succeed in its most fundamental objective—preventing the consolidation of another communist regime in the hemisphere. Reagan also won congressional support, albeit intermittent, for military assistance to the democratic forces fighting the Sandinistas. At the same time, Administration pursuit of its Nicaragua policies left much to be desired. One reason is that the Administration has failed to mobilize the executive branch behind its policy in Nicaragua. Another is that it did not vigorously pursue a well-organized campaign to educate the U.S. public about the importance of Central America to U.S. security. At critical junctures, the Administration submitted insufficient aid requests to Congress and supported them with ineffective campaigns disproportionate to its own definition of the stakes involved in Central America.

The Administration made a major mistake when, on August 5, 1987, it proposed the Reagan-Wright peace plan, which grew out of discussions initiated by House Speaker Jim Wright. The plan listed demands that the Sandinista regime was to meet before the U.S. would sever military aid to the Resistance. The Reagan-Wright plan was ill-timed and ill-considered. It was announced just when the Nicaraguan Resistance was scoring battlefield successes and picking up U.S. public support as a consequence of Lt. Col. Oliver North's July 1987 testimony before the congressional select committee investigating the Iran-Contra matter. The haste with which the Reagan-Wright plan was conceived and its apparent reversal of earlier Reagan policy toward the Sandinistas prompted the presidents of the Central American democracies to sign the flawed plan known as "Esquipulas II" or the "Arias plan" (after its author, President Oscar Arias of Costa Rica). This has failed to bring peace and democracy to Nicaragua.

The termination of U.S. military aid to the Nicaraguan Resistance has lifted the pressure from the Sandinistas to democratize Nicaragua; it also has given the Sandinista regime the time needed to increase its military forces to threaten its neighbors. And it has produced grave risks to the survival of the popular military resistance movement known as the Contras.

In El Salvador, the Reagan Administration's record is also mixed. The Reagan Administration moved quickly to assist the Salvadoran government, whose subsequent military gains against the communist insurgency have enabled democracy to take root. Because of Administration policies, by 1985, El Salvador had a democratic government, human rights violations had been minimized, and the U.S. Congress was sending over $100 million annually in military aid. The insurgents no longer threatened the government's survival. Yet the Administration's economic policies in El Salvador have failed. Despite economic aid totaling over $2 billion, El Salvador's economy remains in terrible shape. Most U.S. economic aid has been consumed by the Salvadoran government and not channeled to productive investment through the private sector. And the policies and spirit of the Salvadoran government have discouraged private investors. This has made the Salvadoran economy highly dependent on U.S. economic assistance.

In Honduras, the Administration has provided economic aid and helped to improve the professionalism and defensive capability of the army. The Administration showed its commitment to Honduras and its determination to deter communist aggression when, in March 1988, it sent the U.S. Army's 82nd Airborne division to Honduras immediately after Sandinista troops invaded Honduran territory.

Among the Reagan Administration's most ambitious foreign policy initiatives has been the Caribbean Basin Initiative (CBI) launched in 1982. Its aim has been to spur Caribbean economic growth by opening U.S. markets to Central American and Caribbean goods. Thus far, however, CBI's results have been disappointing. This is in large part because Congress diluted the Reagan CBI proposal, denying duty-free treatment to many products, which can be produced efficiently in the Caribbean basin, such as textiles and leather goods. Some new trade and investment, nevertheless, has been stimulated by CBI, especially in agribusiness.

After receiving early attention, Mexico has occupied a lower priority for most of the Reagan years. Policies have been made by different Cabinet agencies, depending on the issue, with little coordination. Debt policy, for example, has been conducted by the Treasury and drug policy by the Justice Department's Drug Enforcement Agency. The Administration's economic policy toward Mexico has had modest results. The Reagan Administration was instrumental in helping Mexico get through a financial crisis in 1982 and again in 1986–1987, when Mexico obtained U.S. support for an international financial bailout that included over $10 billion in new loans. Agreements have been negotiated with Mexico to reduce trade barriers between the two countries. Yet the Administration has missed opportunities to condition U.S. financial assistance to Mexico on needed economic structural changes. In fact, periodic financial rescue from Washington has given Mexico the opportunity to delay such changes. The Administration also has failed to condition U.S. financial assistance on changes in Mexico's foreign policy in Central America. More than any other Latin American country, except Cuba, Mexico has openly obstructed U.S. policy goals in Central America and has been helpful to the Sandinista regime.

U.S. policy toward Cuba has had several successes during the later Reagan years. In May 1985 the U.S. launched Radio Marti to broadcast information to Cubans about their government's policies of domestic repression and overseas meddling in Angola and Ethiopia. And in 1988 the U.S. succeeded, in part because it appointed anti-Castro Cuban emigre Armando Valladares as its representative, in convincing the U.N. Human Rights Commission to undertake its first investigation of Cuban violations of human rights.

THE NEXT FOUR YEARS

The U.S. should seek four objectives in its Mexico policy: 1) to devise an appropriate and acceptable means to help Mexico to prevent communist disruption of the Mexican political and social system; 2) to encourage movement toward a more democratic government; 3) to encourage a free-market economic policy, which is fairer to its poor people and spurs economic growth; and 4) to insist quietly that Mexico stop acting as a surrogate for Castro and the Sandinistas in the region. In Central America, the U.S. should seek an open, pluralistic Nicaragua which reduces the size of its military forces, stops aid to antidemocratic Latin American insurgencies, and ends its de facto military alliance with the USSR and Cuba. A second key U.S. goal must be the consolidation of democracy and the stimulation of economic growth in El Salvador, Honduras, and Guatemala.

Although composed primarily of very small island nations, the Caribbean Basin is of substantial importance to the U.S. The principal U.S. objectives there should be to encourage political stability and economic development through an economic common market. As for Cuba, meanwhile, the U.S. should begin planning for the post-Castro era, so that pro-democratic forces are in place with the resources and infrastructure to seek control.

Conditioning U.S. Financial Assistance on Economic Policy Changes

Economic stagnation in the region is largely due to socialist and statist economic policies. In this, the U.S. is a guilty accomplice. Most U.S. economic aid to Central America, even under the Reagan Administration, has reinforced the state's stranglehold on the economy. The bulk of U.S. financial assistance to the region has gone to the public sector. The U.S. Agency for International Development, for example, has given millions of dollars to keep Salvadoran land from being owned by the individuals who are working it.

There is no way that the U.S. or international institutions can restore the economy of Mexico or other countries where citizens are convinced that it is imprudent to invest in their own economies and are moving their money out of the country. If Mexico cannot convince Mexicans to invest in Mexico, the U.S. public and private sectors should not attempt to do so either.

The U.S. thus should link new financial assistance to Central American countries to the introduction of policies that protect private property and allow maximum economic freedom. Such policies are good for the economy and will help convince people that their country is a good place to invest. Such policies must increase the role of the entrepreneur and encourage risk-taking, innovation, and other private-sector behavior. Central American governments should pledge, among other things, that there will be 1) no arbitrary expropriation of private property, 2) measurable privatization of state-owned enterprises, and 3) progressive relaxation of controls on prices, especially of agricultural products.

Reducing the Debt Burden

Servicing Central America's $18.1 billion ($11.9 billion excluding Nicaragua) foreign debt is a heavy financial burden. Plans to deal with the debt so far have been flawed. The Baker plan, proposed by Treasury Secretary James Baker in 1985, for example, focused on debt management rather than debt reduction, and would increase the overall debt. The Bradley plan, proposed by Senator Bill Bradley (D-NJ) in 1986, on the other hand, essentially calls for writing off the debt. Ultimately, the debt crisis can only be solved through economic freedom, which produces economic growth. In a growing economy, more funds are available not only to meet debt payments but also to invest in productive enterprises.

The new President must devise a strategy for Central American states to lighten their debt burdens. This strategy should lead simultaneously to debt reduction and to structural reform in the region's economies, which could be achieved by striking a bargain in which the U.S. would accept a schedule of reduced interest payments in exchange for the debtor country's reducing the state's role in its economy. Government companies could be denationalized, for instance, with their ownership transferred to their employees.

The debt problem is also the responsibility of the U.S. commercial banks that made the loans to the Central American countries. Many of the loans were bad business decisions; the banks, like other industries, must face the consequences of bad decisions. As such, the new President should seek to prevent international lending organizations, such as the World Bank, from lending Central American countries funds to be used to pay interest to commercial banks, unless the banks cooperate in the effort to solve the problem. This would give these banks greater incentive to find ways to reduce the overall debt. For one thing, they could convert a portion of the debt owed them into equity holdings in the industries of the debtor country. For another, the banks could cut their interest rate spreads—the profit margin on their loans—as would any other industry when its market contracts. The banks should be strongly encouraged to continue building up their reserves against these loans. U.S. banks in any event should not be protected through a U.S. government bailout.

Encouraging Privatization of State Companies

In Mexico, Central America, and the Caribbean, the state's strong presence in the economy wastes large amounts of the population's resources and discourages private investment, which is the engine of economic development. Often, Central American governments totally own companies. In Mexico, for example, the government-owned CON-ASUPO agricultural marketing board sets prices of basic agricultural products such as corn, rice, and beans, while the government-owned FERTIMEX prevents any competition in fertilizer supply. State-owned enterprises typically lose enormous sums, which then are covered by government borrowing, which, of course, adds to Third World debts.

The U.S should encourage Central American governments to trans-

fer state-owned companies to the private sector, a process known as
privatization. For privatization to be successful, the new private company must have the freedom to set wages and prices, to hire and fire
workers as it sees fit, to import raw materials or capital goods without
protectionist obstacles, and not to be burdened with high taxes. This
means that privatization must occur in conjunction with other reforms.

The new President should instruct the U.S. Agency for International
Development (AID) to hire privatization experts to assist Central
American nations in the privatization process. In addition, AID should
be instructed not to fund any new government-owned enterprises. The
Secretary of the Treasury should press the World Bank and the Inter-
American Development Bank to link new loans to Central American
countries to measurable privatization progress and to offer technical
and financial assistance to expand the private sector in Central America.

There are a number of techniques that can be used to privatize a
state-owned enterprise, depending on a nation's economic and political
situation. One is to sell a state-owned enterprise to the highest bidder.
Another is known as debt/equity swaps. Under such a transaction, a
Western bank owed money by a debtor country sells the debt for cash,
usually at a discount, to a middleman interested in investing in the
debtor country. The investor then swaps the debt to the government
of the debtor country in exchange for an equity share in a state-owned
enterprise. By this transaction, the country's debt is reduced, while
some ownership in state-owned companies is transferred to private
hands.

In countries where there is suspicion of foreign investors or where
other obstacles to debt/equity swaps exist, a state enterprise could be
privatized by offering stock for part or all of the enterprise to the
general public. In Jamaica, for example, a cement company and a
commercial bank have been privatized in this manner. This spreads
stock ownership, and thus support for private property, to a wider
segment of the general public. (See Chapter 27.)

Allocating Resources for ESOP Projects

The 1986 report of the Presidential task force, *Project Economic
Justice*, chaired by Ambassador J. William Middendorf II, emphasized
the need to broaden the base of ownership of productive resources in
Central America and the Caribbean. A means proposed by the report
to achieve this is the expanded use of employee stock ownership plans,
widely known as ESOPs.

The ESOP financing technique allows workers with little or no savings to invest in the company for which they work. An ESOP in effect is a trust that borrows funds from traditional financial sources such as banks. These loans must meet the same feasibility standards and corporate guarantees as direct loans to the corporation. The loan funds are used by ESOP either to buy stock for the workers from present owners or to finance expansion or modernization of the company. The loan funds received by the trust are wholly secured by, and repaid from, future profits. Workers make no cash payments from payroll deductions or savings, and their present savings are not at risk. Shares of the stock are allocated to individual accounts of workers only as the shares are "earned." This means that the company contributes cash out of future pretax profits to the trust, thus "buying" shares for the workers as part of their benefits. The cash, which is treated as a tax-deductible employee benefit, is used to repay the stock acquisition loan.

ESOPs can be used to refinance existing loans owed by the company, finance the acquisition of new assets, acquire other companies, or buy out existing stockholders. ESOPs broaden ownership of business without forcibly redistributing the wealth of current owners and can be used when state-owned companies are sold to private owners (privatization) to facilitate debt-to-equity swaps.

AID should request $50 million annually to provide loans for the establishment of new employee-owned companies in Central America and the Caribbean. The U.S. representative in the Inter-American Investment Corporation (an affiliate of the Inter-American Development Bank), which is expected to begin operations in late 1988, should be instructed to insist that $10 million of the $51 million U.S. subscription be earmarked for direct equity investments in employee-owned companies in Central America and the Caribbean. (See Chapter 27.)

Improving Economic Relations with Mexico

A stable and prosperous Mexico is important for both Mexican and U.S. security. Mexico's economic growth depends to a large extent on increased exports to the U.S. The new President could spur this by pressing for reduced U.S. barriers to Mexican products, particularly food processing and electronics, which do not have strong U.S. protectionist lobbies. The new President then should seek to reduce U.S. barriers in sectors where protectionism is strong, such as textiles and footwear.

The U.S., meanwhile, should urge Mexico to give much better

protection to U.S. patents, trademarks, and copyrights. Some U.S. agricultural, chemical, and pharmaceutical companies reportedly refuse to introduce new products into Mexico because of the lack of product patent protection. The new President should propose the creation of a U.S.-Mexican commission to explore the possibility of establishing a U.S.-Mexican Free Trade Area (FTA). In an FTA, all tariffs, quota restrictions, and many nontariff barriers are removed. This would give each country the opportunity to concentrate its productive efforts and resources toward making those goods for which it has comparative advantage. (See Chapters 9 and 27.)

Expanding the Caribbean Basin Initiative

The Caribbean Basin Initiative (CBI) was designed in 1982 by the Reagan Administration to help the Central American and Caribbean nations' economies by opening the U.S. markets to their goods. The trouble is that Congress barred the CBI from giving a number of important Caribbean products greater access to the U.S. market. Because of pressure from U.S. special interest groups, stiff quotas limit the import of beef and sugar. Crude and refined petroleum, textiles, leather goods, and canned tuna products, among others, are also excluded from the CBI's duty-free treatment.

The new President should submit to Congress revised CBI legislation. It should open U.S. markets to a broader range of Caribbean products by reducing or eliminating the list of those denied duty-free treatment. In addition, CBI's congressionally imposed 12-year lifespan should be extended to at least 25 years. Growth in export capabilities takes time. This extension would provide an important incentive to local and foreign investors to finance longer-term ventures in the region.

Restructuring Policies toward Cuba

The need for creative thinking on policies toward Cuba is long overdue. The new President should: 1) inform the Soviet Union and Cuba, formally, that because of the Soviet military presence in Cuba and Cuban involvement in Soviet-financed and directed wars and other military activities abroad that violate the 1962 Kennedy-Khrushchev agreement, the U.S. no longer will consider itself bound by that agreement which, in effect, guarantees that the U.S. will not undermine the Castro regime; 2) denounce repeatedly in the United Nations and other international forums Cuba's disruptive international and oppressive domestic policies; 3) discourage Western banks from lending further funds to Cuba; 4) publicize the names of U.S. corporations and their front companies that violate the U.S. embargo on trade with Cuba; 5) support the creation and establishment of a TV station to broadcast to Cuba (TV Marti) to complement the successful transmissions of Radio Marti; and 6) encourage and support the growth of a domestic opposition in Cuba.

Improving Defense Capabilities of Friendly Nations

The best obstacles to communist takeover are democratic institutions and sustained economic growth. Building democratic institutions, however, takes time. In the short run, governments need military aid to defend themselves. The new President should offer friendly Central American armies more grants for education and training in the U.S. The U.S. should be ready to provide each Central American ally with the military equipment it needs to counter internal and external threat.

Honduras, for example, confronts an enormous threat from neighboring Nicaragua's huge army, the region's largest. The U.S. should continue military assistance programs designed to modernize Honduras's armed forces, particularly, replacing aging Honduran *Super Mysteres* war planes with F–5E/F fighters. These aircraft would help maintain the regional balance of power. Guatemala, meanwhile, faces an internal communist insurgency. A congressional ban forbids supplying lethal aid to Guatemala. This ban was imposed when Guatemala was ruled by an authoritarian government. Since Guatemala now has a democratically elected government, the new President should ask Congress to lift that ban. In El Salvador, guerrillas terrorize civilians and sabotage the country's economic, social, and political infrastructure. The new President should request necessary equipment and supplies for the Salvadoran military.

Protecting U.S. Security Interests in the Panama Canal

In the near term, any reopening of issues related to U.S. involvement with the Panama Canal would do a political favor for Panamanian dictator General Manuel Antonio Noriega, who relies on anti-U.S. rhetoric to legitimize his dictatorship. In the long term, however, the U.S. needs to ensure that it can protect the Panama Canal. The new President thus should consider seeking a new U.S. base rights treaty with Panama, similar to those with Italy, Turkey, and other countries. This would reaffirm Washington's commitment to the 1978 Panama

Canal treaties, demonstrate a desire for cooperation with the Panaman-
ians, and dampen "anti-Yanqui" feelings on the part of those who fear
a treaty abrogation. A treaty, however, would have to give the U.S.
the right to keep U.S. troops in Panama beyond the year 2000 and to
take appropriate steps, including military action, to protect the Canal.

As another possibility, the new President could consider renegotiat-
ing provisions of the Panama Canal treaty that deal specifically with
U.S. security interests. Renegotiation should seek to ensure the permanent stationing, beyond the year 2000, of U.S. military forces in
Panama and the right of the U.S. to act independently after the year
2000 to maintain the security of the Canal and guarantee its regular
operation.

Expanding the International Visitors Program of the U.S. Information Agency (USIA)

A small but influential number of Central Americans are anti-American. These include journalists, intellectuals, academics, religious leaders, and leftist politicians who can influence public opinion. Large
numbers of them should be brought to the U.S. by the International
Visitors Program, which is part of the U.S. Information Agency.
Although the program has grown substantially in the past two years, it
still brings only about 122 Central Americans to the U.S. annually for
a visit of approximately 30 days. The new President should at least
double the program. The average cost per visitor is about $5,500.

The USIA has a program to translate books into Spanish. The
director of USIA should require that special priority be placed on
books dealing with democratic capitalism and refutations of "liberation
theology" as well as "dependency theory," concepts that rely heavily
on Marxist analysis and blame the industrialized world for Latin
America's poverty. The U.S. and the Department of Education should
work together to develop a major program, which would furnish
textbooks on politics, history, and economics to the school systems of
Central American and Caribbean nations. (See Public Diplomacy and
South America sections of this chapter.)

Increasing Educational Assistance

Approximately 7,740 Central American students were in U.S. colleges and universities during the academic year 1986–1987, of whom
about 4,000 were receiving some form of U.S. government financial
assistance. As of December 1987, there were 6,150 students from

Central American countries studying in the Soviet Union and Eastern Europe. Although more Central Americans study in the U.S. than in the East bloc, even more should be exposed to the U.S. The next President should seek increased funding from Congress to bring Central American students to the U.S. The U.S. should encourage its allies to increase their scholarship and assistantship programs for Central American students.

Persuading Japan to Support U.S. Policies in the Region

Japan remains dependent on the U.S. for military protection. To the extent that instability mounts in Central America, the U.S. may have to focus more of its attention there and turn it away from other countries, including Japan. Thus the new President should seek Japanese support for common interests in the Central American region. He should press Japan to stop buying sugar from Cuba, increase its purchases from other Caribbean basin countries such as the Dominican Republic and Jamaica, and strongly encourage Japan to increase investment in Central America and the Caribbean. (See Asia section of this chapter.)

―――――――――◇―――――――――

INITIATIVES FOR 1989

1) Make Nicaragua's democratization a top priority. The new President should state explicitly at the start of his Administration that the U.S. objective is to assure the strategic stability of Central America and to prevent the establishment there of a Soviet base that threatens the U.S. Essential to this is a democratic Nicaragua. It would not threaten its neighbors and would observe human rights. A democratic Nicaragua, moreover, would end its de facto military alliance with the Soviet Union and Cuba. The President should demand concrete actions by the Sandinista regime within three months to dismantle the Marxist-Leninist structure of Nicaragua. Significant legislation of December 1987, sponsored by Representatives Beverly B. Byron (D-MD) and Rod Chandler (R-WA), passed the House of Representatives by a large margin. This legislation listed the minimum acceptable actions, including: allowing political parties and the democratic opposition to meet and march publicly without harassment, abolishing the role of the Sandinista Defense Committees (CDS) and other party organizations

in dispensing rationing cards and government services; repealing the
suspension provisions of the Nicaraguan constitution; and separating
the armed forces from any political party. Other actions called for by
the Joint Resolution are to reestablish press and media rights, religious
freedoms, labor rights, and *campesino* (peasant) and ethnic groups
rights.

If concrete steps to dismantle the Marxist-Leninist structure have
not been taken at the end of three months, the new President should
build the American public and political support needed for a sustainable program of U.S. assistance to the Nicaraguan Resistance. Among
other things, the Kissinger Commission on Central America should be
reconvened to make further recommendations. The new President
should be prepared to break diplomatic relations with Nicaragua,
recognize the Nicaraguan Resistance as the legitimate government of
Nicaragua, and immediately seek congressional funding for military
aid to the Resistance. Several Nicaraguan political parties, independent
labor unions, and private sector organizations have united under an
umbrella opposition organization called the Democratic Coordinator.
Its members face government harassment and financial difficulties.
The new President should direct that Nicaragua's internal democratic
opposition be provided with financial resources and such office equipment as computers and photocopy machines.

2) Continue supporting El Salvador's electoral process. The Salvadoran
people have supported democracy and rejected the communist guerrillas by voting in five different elections since 1982. The new President
should seek to help consolidate El Salvador's fragile democracy. He
should urge the Salvadoran government to oppose any nonelectoral
"power sharing" arrangements with the Salvadoran guerrillas. U.S.
military or economic aid should not be tied to the electoral victory of
any particular party in the 1989 presidential elections but rather to
policies based upon democratic capitalism.

3) Protect democracy and U.S. security in Panama. The new President
should request his National Security Adviser to develop a plan for a
turn toward democracy in Panama. Elements of such a plan might
include: 1) strong pressure on Panama by the U.S. and the democratic
nations of Latin America to establish democracy; 2) encouragement
and aid to the democratic opposition forces inside Panama; 3) working
with democratic elements inside the Panamanian military; 4) making a
clear U.S. statement that any Panamanian interference with the operation of the Panama Canal or any harm done to U.S. citizens in Panama

would trigger a strong U.S. response that could include military action; and 5) a plan for how the U.S. and other democracies can help consolidate democracy in Panama once military rule has ended.

4) Discuss differences with Mexico on Central America policy. The Mexican government has chosen to try to protect itself against communist destabilization by acting as a de facto Cuban ally. The new President should make clear that the U.S. will not allow this strategy to be used without a U.S. response and that it is incompatible with close and good relations with the U.S. The new President should meet with the president of Mexico at the earliest opportunity and explain what U.S. security interests are at stake in Central America. He should seek to convince the Mexican president that it is in Mexico's interests for Central America to be democratic and free of Soviet influence.

5) Update legislation dealing with Central America. In the past, most Central American countries were ruled by dictatorships. Most now have democratically elected governments. Some U.S. legislation affecting Central America is therefore anachronistic. The congressional ban on U.S. lethal aid to the Guatemalan army, for example, was passed when Guatemala was ruled by the military. Now that Guatemala is a democracy, the new U.S. President should order a review of Guatemala's military requirements. He also should work with Congress to revise and update existing legislation to reflect current Central American conditions. Legislation, for example, should be revised to allow U.S. training for police forces.

6) Consider reactivating the Central American Defense Council (CONDECA). In 1963, all Central American nations except Costa Rica founded the Central American Defense Council (CONDECA) to ensure the region's collective security. The Council ceased functioning in the mid-1970s. It may be needed again to protect its members from Nicaragua. The new President should appoint a Departments of Defense and State task force to visit the Central American democracies, including Costa Rica, to discuss the advisability of reactivating CONDECA.

☎

South America

David Jordan*
Task Force Chairman

South America has served as an encouraging model for democratic evolution in the developing world. Economically, it has become one of the most important U.S. trading partners. U.S. exports total approximately $15 billion annually to South America and the U.S. serves as a market for nearly 50 percent of South America's goods. In addition, South America owes close to $200 billion to U.S. creditors, while U.S. direct investment in South America is estimated at $30 billion. Geostrategically, the cooperation of South American nations is crucial to halting Soviet bloc expansion or control of vital Southern Hemisphere Pacific and Atlantic ocean sea lanes.

———————◇———————

THE REAGAN ADMINISTRATION RECORD

In 1980, U.S.-South American relations were tense and often unfriendly. The Carter Administration had pushed for human rights improvements in such an aggressive manner that it alienated many governments, without removing authoritarian regimes from power.

The Reagan Administration has reformulated and strengthened U.S. policy toward the Americas. In part as a result of the Administration's support for democratization, Argentina, Bolivia, Brazil, and Uruguay have democratized their political processes since 1981. And in 1984, when a military coup was threatened in Bolivia, U.S. pressure helped prevent a return to authoritarian rule.

The Reagan Administration also has had some success in extraditing South American drug bosses to the U.S. The Medellin Cartel, Colom-

---

*Commenting and contributing generously to this report were *Mandate III* Task Force Members Georges Fauriol, Roger Fontaine, Esther Wilson Hannon, Robert Henderson, William Perry, and Paul Wisgerhof. They do not necessarily endorse all of its views and recommendations.

Task Force Deputy Chairman: Heritage Policy Analyst Michael G. Wilson.

bia's illegal drug mafia, has been the key target. The extradition and subsequent conviction of Carlos Lehder, one of the cartel's key figures, on drug charges in Florida in 1988 has been a major accomplishment. There also has been some reduction in South American narcotics production and shipments. Cocaine production and processing in Ecuador, for example, has been eliminated almost entirely. In Bolivia in 1986, six Army *Black Hawk* helicopters, several transport planes, and about 160 U.S. military personnel participated in a joint U.S.-Bolivian antidrug operation code-named Blast Furnace.

A serious Reagan Administration shortcoming however, has been its failure to push South American countries harder to reform their economies. Despite the opening of their electoral processes, many South American nations continue to allow their economies to be dominated by the state, breeding inefficiency and corruption. The only exceptions are Bolivia and Chile, which have introduced free-market policies. In the case of Chile, the results have been impressive, probably because economic liberalization has been the policy since 1977.

Too often Reagan Administration bilateral aid programs have ignored the root causes of South America's anemic national capital markets: inflation caused by printing money, artificially low interest rates set by South American central banks, state domination of the banking sector, and inadequate protection of private property. Belatedly, in a summer 1988 visit, Secretary of State George Shultz made the case for economic reform directly to the South American public and their officials.

While the Administration deserves credit for trying to push economic reform as a condition for U.S. relief of South American debt, this effort generally has failed. The plan unveiled in 1985 by then-Treasury Secretary James Baker assumed that South American economies must grow if they expect to service their debt. This in turn required liberalized economic policies. As such, the Baker Plan encouraged international lending institutions such as the International Monetary Fund (IMF), the World Bank, and the Inter-American Development Bank (IDB), as well as private banks, to provide additional funds to South American countries in exchange for these governments restructuring their economies along free-market lines. In reality, while multilateral banks have made some new money available, market-oriented economic reform has nevertheless been very limited.

The Administration also has not done enough to pressure Congress to expand military cooperation, training, and aid programs in the Americas. Most of today's South American military leaders support democracy and have helped consolidate democracy in their countries. These officials therefore should be invited to resume military assistance and training programs with the U.S.

The Reagan Administration also has not focused sufficiently on the growing problem of insurgencies against democratically elected governments in Colombia, Ecuador, and Peru. The Administration might have done more to highlight the problem and to help South American governments to defeat insurgent activity as well as narcotics trafficking and terrorism.

THE NEXT FOUR YEARS

Given South America's proximity to the U.S., its economic problems, and growing Soviet efforts to influence the region, the U.S. should adopt a set of objectives for its policies toward the Americas. These objectives should include: the stabilization and consolidation of democracy in nations where it has emerged during the Reagan years, such as Argentina, Bolivia, Brazil, and Uruguay; encouraging stable transitions to democracy in the remaining nondemocratic nations in the region, such as Chile and Paraguay; helping to stimulate economic growth to ameliorate the debt problem and spur further development of a South American middle class; helping to defeat insurgencies which threaten democracy and security in such nations as Colombia and Peru; responding forcefully to the growing danger from narco-terrorism led by the drug cartels and fostered by Cuba's Fidel Castro; and moving toward mature partnerships based upon common adherence to democratic principles, private-sector economic development, and removal of trade barriers. In particular, the U.S. should seek a better relationship with Argentina and Brazil, which have the potential to become world powers.

Encouraging Democratic Pluralism

The U.S. faces two different tasks in encouraging democratic pluralism in South America. The first is to help consolidate still-fragile democratic institutions in Argentina, Bolivia, Brazil, and Uruguay, where transitions from authoritarian regimes to democracy began during the Reagan years. The second task is to encourage and support democratic pluralism in Chile, Guyana, Paraguay, and Suriname. However, the U.S. must be careful that its policies do not weaken pro-U.S. regimes that are threatened by communist subversives.

The primary U.S. objective in these situations should be to strengthen such key independent institutions as political parties, business groups, labor unions, trade associations, and educational institutions. To do this, the new President should seek increased congressional funding for the National Endowment for Democracy (NED), a government-funded private organization designed to assist the growth of democracy in the Third World. (See Public Diplomacy section of this chapter.)

The U.S. should give financial and technical assistance to develop strong independent judicial systems. The U.S. Justice Department and the American Bar Association can provide expertise to South American lawyers, bar associations, judges, and justice ministries. An independent, effective, and honest judicial system is fundamental to the growth of democracy.

Support for democratic pluralism by the South American armed forces also is necessary. Without such support, the long-term prospects for democracy are problematic. The U.S. Department of Defense should use its International Military Education and Training (IMET) programs to foster and reinforce democratic values in South American armed forces by exposing them to the competence and professionalism of the U.S. military. IMET is a U.S. government grant program that provides technical training and personal contact between U.S. and South American military professionals.

Using U.S. Aid to Encourage Long-term Economic Growth

Stable long-term economic growth is crucial in sustaining democracy. Growth requires an environment that encourages investment, borrowing for productive economic enterprises, risk-taking, savings, and hard work. It also requires a free and stable capital market consisting of private banks, legally enforced protection of savings and other assets from nationalization, low inflation, and freedom for investors to move money in and out of a country.

South American governments must be perceived as respecting property rights so that their citizens will feel safe investing in local economies rather than sending their money abroad. When governments inflate their currency or threaten nationalization, people take their money out of the country and deposit it in safer Western banks, thereby depriving their local economy of investment capital. This is a lesson painfully learned recently by nearly bankrupt Peru, with its state-controlled economic system, rampant inflation, and nationalization policies.

The new Administration should press for free-market-oriented economic reform in South America. First, the U.S. should aid debtor nations only if they cease pursuing failed economic policies; new money often removes the incentive for such countries to make hard choices concerning economic reform. Second, the President should highlight the grassroots and informal free market economic activity that is spreading throughout South America. Peruvian economist Hernando de Soto's finding that approximately 50 percent of Peru's economic activity is in the black market indicates that South Americans can become successful entrepreneurs even under conditions of extreme government intervention in the economy. Finally, the new President should link all U.S. foreign aid to a recipient's economic progress as measured by an Index of Economic Freedom. Components of the index would include such factors as tariff levels, rates of taxation, size of the state sector, amount of private banking, and protection of property rights. U.S. economic assistance programs should not force recipient countries to pursue policies that dampen economic growth. For example, in exchange for loans to help meet balance of payments problems, the International Monetary Fund (IMF) requires various economic policy changes by recipient governments. Some IMF conditions call for tax increases or import restrictions. Yet higher taxes penalize the productive private sector, holding down long-term economic growth; and trade barriers help perpetuate inefficient domestic industries by removing competition and raising the cost of goods needed by businesses and citizens of such countries.

The U.S. Agency for International Development (AID) should make available technical assistance and, if absolutely necessary, financial aid to support economic reforms designed to spur growth. Such reforms include privatizing state-owned industries and using employee stock ownership plans (ESOPs). AID should continue to offer information and training on debt/equity swap programs to retire part of the foreign debt. The U.S. also should offer to negotiate Free Trade Area (FTA) agreements with any country interested in complete trade liberalization. In an FTA, two or more countries remove all tariff and many nontariff barriers against each other's goods. (See Chapters 9 and 27.)

Helping Resolve the Foreign Debt Crisis

U.S. policy toward South American debt should be premised upon helping countries that are helping themselves. As such, U.S. support for World Bank, International Monetary Fund (IMF), and "Paris Club" of Western governments assistance to debtor countries should depend on how determinedly these countries are pursuing various free market techniques for reducing their foreign debt. One technique is called debt/equity swaps. This is a private- sector technique for retiring a portion of a country's debt by allowing part of that debt to be swapped for an equity holding or something else of value in the debtor country. For example, a Western creditor bank exchanges some of its bad South American debt for cash, albeit at less than face value. This cash is offered by a business or other investor wishing to invest in the debtor country. This middleman investor then takes the note he is holding to the government of the debtor country and swaps it for something of value. This middleman might acquire equity shares in a government-owned enterprise; he might acquire shares of stock owned by the government in a local joint-venture enterprise with the private sector; or he might acquire local currency, perhaps at a favorable exchange rate, from the government. In Mexico, for instance, a Japanese automobile manufacturer obtained currency to fund expansion of its Mexican plant. In Bolivia, an environmental group acquired from the government a parcel of land to be preserved for ecological reasons. The debtor country, through a debt/equity swap, can retire part of its debt without having to pay out scarce dollars. The creditor bank that had faced the prospect of losing its investment through the default of the debtor country recovers part of this investment. Most important, the capital is more likely to be allocated to a productive enterprise.

Currently, only about half of the highly indebted South American countries targeted for increased assistance under the Baker Plan allow for debt/equity swaps. Only Chile has an institutionalized program to encourage its own citizens—rather than just foreign investors—to take part in the swaps, thereby inducing them to bring home the flight capital they have taken out of the country.

U.S. trade policy should be coordinated with debt policy. It makes no sense for the U.S. to encourage South American countries to grow economically if U.S. markets are then closed to South American exports. This is what happened with Argentina when Washington's rigid enforcement of health regulations kept quality Argentine beef out of the U.S. (See Chapter 27.)

Emphasizing Regional Cooperation

In recent years, the U.S. role and influence in South American multilateral institutions and official conferences have diminished. This is a result both of South American nationalism and the low U.S. priority placed on such institutions. The principal inter-American multilateral organization is the Organization of American States (OAS). The OAS is a regional multinational body created in 1948, designed to complement the United Nations and provide a forum in which the nations of the Americas can air their grievances and settle disputes.

The new President should strengthen U.S. participation in the OAS and seek to make the OAS an effective instrument for the development of democracy and capitalism in the Western Hemisphere. He should also press the OAS to focus on several priority issues including drug trafficking, immigration, terrorism, and the debt.

The new President should pursue these objectives by emphasizing actions requiring multinational cooperation. These could include: expanded U.S. Navy and Coast Guard port call privileges to assist in the war on drugs; the creation of multinational anti-drug/terrorism military forces; and increased inter-American cooperation in removing nontariff trade barriers. Washington could also directly seek to increase its clout within the OAS in several ways: by linking U.S. aid programs to nations supporting U.S. positions in the OAS; by instructing U.S. ambassadors to meet more frequently with South American foreign ministers to urge greater cooperation with the U.S. in the OAS; by augmenting OAS funding; and by increasing the number of senior level U.S. officials attending and addressing OAS meetings.

A key problem facing the OAS has been its lack of resources, data, and information. The U.S. State Department should make available to the OAS information and technical resources on such issues as drug control and antiterrorism warfare. Multinational diplomatic task forces should be developed to meet regularly and discuss these issues. The State Department, meanwhile, should better use the OAS forum to outline clearly U.S. foreign policy objectives in the region.

Expanding Inter-American Military Cooperation

Most of the U.S. legislation creating the framework for U.S.-South American military relations is outdated, formulated when most South American countries still had authoritarian governments. Now that all but four South American countries are democratic, this legislation unwisely limits U.S. programs with the region's governments, armed forces, and police. The new President therefore should propose changes in U.S.-South American military and security relations. He should push Congress to fund U.S. weapon and technical assistance to help South American democracies defend themselves.

Many of the problems facing South America are centered around what is known as "low intensity conflict." This refers to insurgencies, organized terrorism, paramilitary crime, sabotage, and other forms of violence not associated directly with open warfare involving large military units. The use of radar equipment, helicopters, pursuit jets, night vision equipment, surveillance planes, personnel carriers, and other modern weaponry should take priority in combating these problems. U.S. training for South American police forces also should be considered.

The new Administration should expand its International Military and Educational Training (IMET) programs. The bulk of this training should involve low intensity conflict and drug eradication exercises. Expanded military cooperation with South America's armed forces should include: U.S. military, naval, and air training missions assigned to South American capitals; increased South American participation in U.S.-sponsored inter-American military school training programs; and expanded arms sales. In addition, the new Administration should seek to revive the Inter-American Defense Board. Established in 1942, the Defense Board was designed to prepare for the collective security and self-defense of the Western Hemisphere. U.S. goals should be to keep the South American armed forces out of politics, assist friendly democratic governments to maintain effective defenses against externally supported aggression and subversion, strengthen South American alliances, and make military facilities throughout South America accessible to U.S. forces.

Waging War Against Drug and Terrorist Organizations

Narcotics and terrorism can no longer be dealt with as separate issues. Groups involved in one of these activities are almost always involved with the other. The next Administration should negotiate with all South American countries—especially Bolivia, Brazil, Colombia, Ecuador, Peru, and Venezuela—to establish mutual assistance programs and expand coordination of intelligence and drug control agencies throughout the region. The new President, with support from Congress, should seek South American cooperation in creating multinational military antidrug units. When appropriate, these units should combat the drug cartels in the field by raiding refineries, launching attacks against cartel strongholds, and arresting traffickers. This should be combined with crop-substitution and educational awareness programs. The South American peasantry needs to be convinced that they can make a living growing legal crops, as well as to be made aware of the dangers posed by illegal narcotics.

The new President should invite leaders from those countries waging the war on drugs to convene regional summits focusing specifically on the narcotics issue. Such summits should seek, among other things, to strengthen extradition procedures to bring drug bosses to justice in the U.S. The summits also should consider how to coordinate antidrug laws, hot pursuit rights against drug dealers, and technical assistance programs such as arms and radar sales.

Increasing Educational and Cultural Assistance

The Soviets are ahead of the U.S. in providing government-sponsored education programs for South Americans. In 1987, only about 7,000 U.S. government scholarships were offered to South Americans. The Soviet bloc, on the other hand, offered nearly 10,000—up from 2,900 a decade ago. South American students are being educated and trained in Cuba, Eastern Europe, and the USSR. The vast majority are from poor families who otherwise would not have been able to afford any education overseas.

The new President should seek increased funding for the U.S. Information Agency (USIA) to expand cultural, educational, and social ties with democratic South American institutions. The new Administration also should encourage its allies in Western Europe and Asia to increase educational assistance for South Americans.

———————◇———————

INITIATIVES FOR 1989

1) Create a South American presidential advisory team. The President needs a team of advisers from all U.S. government agencies which can focus exclusively on hemisphere issues.

2) Emphasize South America's importance to the U.S. Soon after his inauguration, the new President should address the Organization of American States to outline U.S. foreign policy objectives regarding South America. The President then should visit at least Argentina, Brazil, and Venezuela to articulate U.S. policy objectives and indicate U.S. willingness to help solve the region's problems.

3) Encourage privatization and market-oriented economic policies.
Economies dominated by the state, like those of Argentina and Peru,
have failed to grow sufficiently to raise living standards and expand
individual opportunities. The new President should work to persuade
South American governments to develop programs for turning over
state-owned companies to the private sector, to make them more
efficient and productive. By linking U.S. financial assistance to reforms, the State and Treasury Departments should encourage South
American countries to expand or initiate employee stock ownership
programs (ESOPs). With ESOPs, employees purchase or are given
stock shares in a newly privatized company, thereby granting them
either partial or full ownership. This provides employees with an
incentive to work harder and more effectively, since they share in the
companies' profits. Assistance also should be tied to progress or plans
to expand economic freedom in accordance with an Index of Economic
Freedom devised by AID. (See Chapter 27.)

**4) Coordinate with the South American governments new approaches
toward drug reduction and eradication.** The new Administration,
through the Drug Enforcement Agency (DEA) and the State Department's Bureau for International Narcotics Matters, should increase
pressure on South American governments to cooperate more in the
fight against South America's drug mafias, the Medellin and Cali
cartels. Such cooperation could be linked to expanded U.S. military
and financial assistance. At the same time, the U.S. will have to assume
responsibility for being the world's leading narcotics market and take
tougher actions against drug dealers and drug users.

The new President should create a U.S.-South American multinational drug task force to meet regularly to investigate means of combating the narcotics problem. The new Administration should rush
materiel and technological assistance (helicopters, night vision equipment, radars, speedboats, surveillance planes, and weapons), and
financial support to Bolivia, Brazil, Colombia, Ecuador, Peru, and
Venezuela, for drug interdiction purposes. The State and Justice Departments should take immediate action to improve and enforce extradition agreements with South American governments. These agreements, which bring international drug chieftains to trial in America,
are among the most effective instruments in combating the global
narcotics trade. The Administration should make extradition of the
key Medellin and Cali bosses from Colombia the highest priority.
Finally, the U.S. Justice Department should set up the processes
immediately for confiscating the drug dealer's financial assets in the

U.S., and encouraging South American governments to do the same at home.

5) Expand ties with regional armed forces. The new President should improve ties with South America's armed forces because of the important role they play in politics. U.S. relations with the region's militaries are increasingly strained, however, by abrupt cutoffs of U.S. military aid, sanctions related to previous human rights violations, and a general lack of interest by U.S. policymakers. Access to key figures in South America's armed forces is essential if the U.S. is to influence political struggles in the region effectively. The new President should expand the programs at the U.S. Army School of the Americas at Fort Benning, Georgia, and the Inter-American Defense College in Washington, D.C.

6) Encourage Chile and Paraguay to continue democratizing. The new President should encourage Chile and Paraguay to democratize. He should offer to expand economic and military aid and other forms of cooperation with these countries as their democratization processes continue. Such a process should include a free and open electoral process, competitive opposition parties, independent trade unions, and freedom of the press.

7) Press for increased South American support for prodemocratic forces in Central America. The democratic political elite of several South American nations are currently involved in, or have recently emerged from, struggling with nondemocratic forces. These leaders clearly understand how difficult this struggle can be—yet they have generally remained aloof from the struggles inside Nicaragua and Panama to end authoritarian rule. The new President and other U.S. officials should challenge the democratic leaders of South America to work together to provide moral and even financial assistance to the internal democratic forces in Nicaragua and Panama. The U.S. also should help send leaders of the democratic opposition in these nations to South American capitals to make their cases directly.

8) Expand United States Information Agency (USIA) activities. Through the USIA, the U.S. government in 1989 should at least double the number of scholarships and technical training opportunities for South American secondary school students and teachers and provide low-cost textbooks, books on political and economic theory, training manuals, and other educational tools in Spanish and Portuguese. These materials should include in-depth studies and essays analyzing relationships between economic freedom and both economic development and political pluralism. The USIA also should increase the number of grants it offers to South Americans in its visitor programs. The U.S. Department of Education should seek to expand its contacts with South American education ministries. Such initiatives are needed to counter Marxist ideas and teachings in South America's educational systems.

Asia

Roger A. Brooks*
Task Force Chairman

Strategically and economically, Asia is becoming more important to the United States. In 1987, U.S.-Asian trade totaled about $241 billion; by contrast, trade with Europe was $170 billion. Japan, the Republic of China on Taiwan, and the Republic of Korea, respectively, are America's second, fifth, and seventh largest trading partners.[1] Japanese direct investment in the U.S. alone was $33.36 billion in 1987, while U.S. direct investment in Japan was $14.28 billion. By the next decade, U.S. trade across the Pacific is expected to be twice that of trade across the Atlantic. At the same time, the U.S. has a vital strategic investment in its major military bases in Japan, the Philippines, and South Korea. Recognizing Asia's importance and vast potential, the Reagan Administration has reaffirmed U.S. support of its Asian allies and friends and has helped create an environment conducive to the growth of democratic institutions.

The new President will face an array of challenges to U.S. influence in Asia. Significant among these: continued buildup in the quality and quantity of Soviet military and naval forces; a general waning of Asian popular support for U.S. foreign policy; growing trade friction between the U.S. and its Asian friends and allies; an effort by many Asian nations to seek alternative export markets to those of the U.S.; uncertainty over U.S. tenure of military bases in a crisis-ridden Philippines; increased calls by Vietnam for international aid and trade; incentives offered by Moscow for Asian nations to invest in the development of the Soviet Far East; an increasingly assertive Chinese

*Commenting and contributing generously to this report were *Mandate III* Task Force Members Peter Allgeier, Andrew Brick, Raymond Chang, Robert Downen, Richard Fisher, Brad Gordon, Edward Hudgins, Charles Lichenstein, Shou-hsiang Liu, James Morhard, Larry Niksch, Daryl Plunk, Michael Privitera, Katsuro Sakoh, Thomas Timmons, William Triplett III, and Jong-Ick Shin. They do not necessarily endorse all of its views and recommendations.

Task Force Deputy Chairman: Heritage Asian Studies Center Deputy Director Kenneth Conboy.

foreign policy to give Beijing a higher regional profile; and increased calls, particularly in the U.S. Congress, for defense burden-sharing between the U.S. and its major Asian allies.

The new President must define what he desires in Asia and what he realistically is prepared to offer the Asia/Pacific region. Such a definition should emphasize the important role played by U.S. aid programs and regional defense commitments in contributing toward Asian economic development and political stability. His Asian policy must have short- and long-range goals and should be characterized by consistency and continuity, which U.S. policy toward Asia has lacked since the Vietnam War.

THE REAGAN ADMINISTRATION RECORD

Eight years ago, Asian confidence in the U.S. as a dependable ally probably was at a post-World War II low. South Korea remained shaken after the Carter Administration proposed to call U.S. military forces home from the Korean Peninsula. Pakistan, facing 116,000 Soviet soldiers across its border with Afghanistan, had its U.S. military aid completely cut off in 1977. And the Association of Southeast Asian Nations (ASEAN)[2] faced a Vietnamese occupation army in Cambodia with only a dim hope of U.S. assistance.

The Reagan Administration has restored Asian confidence in the U.S. The Administration has spurred democratization in the Philippines, the Republic of China on Taiwan, and South Korea; helped the growth of Asia's newly industrializing countries (NICs)—Hong Kong, Singapore, South Korea, and Taiwan—and headed off harmful protectionist legislation directed against them; opposed normalization of relations with Hanoi until Vietnamese troops leave Cambodia and Hanoi gives an accurate accounting of Americans still missing from the Vietnam War; balanced U.S. relations between Pakistan and India; shifted the focus of U.S. security planning in Asia from Beijing to Tokyo; and fulfilled the Taiwan Relations Act by selling Taipei the weapons and technology adequate for its defensive needs.

At the same time, however, the Reagan Administration has failed to craft a comprehensive and integrated Asian policy; instead it typically has addressed issues case by case. It also has failed to focus sufficient attention on the Cambodian conflict; to support the Sri Lankan government adequately during its recent internal turmoil; to criticize human rights abuses in the People's Republic of China; to expose Soviet support for the Communist Party of the Philippines; to criticize sufficiently New Zealand's antinuclear policy; to give adequate military assistance to the Philippines, Thailand, and other Southeast Asian friends; and to launch a credible public relations effort in Asia to counter inroads made by Moscow after Mikhail Gorbachev's 1986 speech in Vladivostok.

———————————◇———————————

THE NEXT FOUR YEARS

The new President faces an increasingly powerful and dynamic Asia/Pacific region. In recognition of Asia's overwhelming economic and strategic importance, the new President should formally tilt the primary U.S. focus away from the Atlantic toward the Pacific, ushering in the Pacific Century. Economically, the new Administration must strive for an era of increased and balanced trade with Asia. Key to this goal should be a U.S. policy promoting more free trade, specifically, bilateral Free Trade Areas throughout the Asia/Pacific region.

U.S.-Japan relations have been the cornerstone of U.S. strategy in Asia during the Reagan Administration; they should remain so. The U.S. should strive to reverse the disturbing increase of anti-Americanism and help foster political stability throughout Asia. Central to this goal should be the development of a pan-Pacific strategic relationship with the noncommunist countries of Asia. This relationship should include greater political cooperation, more joint military exercises, and a U.S.-led regional effort to aid the Philippines. The new President also must underscore the continued Soviet threat to the region, despite the recent, benign diplomatic and economic approaches of the Gorbachev era.

Maintaining Consistency in U.S. Asia Policy

The U.S. needs a coherent and consistent Asia policy that addresses trade, foreign assistance, security relationships, and regional cooperation. It must define clearly what the U.S. wants and what the U.S. is realistically prepared to contribute. An appropriate U.S.-Asian policy must state U.S. interests and how these would benefit the interests of the noncommunist nations of the Asia/Pacific region.

Once devised, this U.S. policy must be consistent. Too often Washington has wavered as an ally in Asia. What Asians have seen in the recent past, after all, has been a U.S. retreat from Indochina, an uneven commitment to resettle refugees fleeing Indochina after 1975, uncertain support for Pakistan, and formal derecognition of the Republic of China on Taiwan.

To achieve policy consistency, the new President should direct his National Security Council to issue a National Security Decision Directive (NSDD), outlining the principles of U.S. policy toward Asia. These principles should include: promoting democracy, but in a subtle manner that minimizes public differences with Asia's friends and allies; opposing protectionist legislation at home, while pressing Asian nations to agree to a specific timetable for lowering their barriers to the import of U.S. goods; and pledging not to scale back current U.S. defense obligations in Asia.

To help avoid structural inconsistencies in policy-making that result from lengthy "learning curves" required by new Administrations, the new President should appoint an Asian-U.S. intergovernmental forum to meet regularly to discuss bilateral or regional issues with Asian friends and allies. Under the aegis of the White House, and in cooperation with the U.S. Information Agency, the forum should include officials from the Departments of Commerce, Defense, and State and the Office of the U.S. Trade Representative. Annual meetings could be held in Hawaii and would serve to establish institutional memory for U.S. policy in Asia, provide a framework for settling contentious regional issues, and show heightened U.S. concern for its relations with Asia.

Strengthening the U.S. Security Commitment

Perhaps more than any previous Soviet leader, Mikhail Gorbachev is paying strategic attention to Asia. Gone is the bluster of the Brezhnev years. Now Soviet leaders and diplomats seem moderate and friendly, taking their cue from Gorbachev's 1986 Vladivostok speech offering peace, arms control proposals, and improved relations with Asian countries. At the same time, Moscow has been pursuing its traditional Asian goals of strategically isolating Japan and China; undermining Western alliances and displacing the U.S. as the dominant Asian power; consolidating Vietnamese-Soviet hegemony in Indochina; and creating new client states.

To achieve these goals, the Soviets, despite the Vladivostok speech's soothing rhetoric, have been upgrading the quantity and quality of their military forces in the region. Among them: 57 Soviet tank and motorized rifle divisions—an increase of four divisions since 1985; 100 mobile SS-25 nuclear ballistic missiles; vastly upgraded base facilities at Vietnam's Cam Ranh Bay; fully manned infantry divisions and MIG–23 *Flogger* fighter aircraft stationed on islands immediately north of Japan; and 860 vessels in the Soviet Pacific fleet, an increase of 40 ships and submarines since the end of 1984. These augmented forces dramatically increase Moscow's military capability in Asia compared to a decade ago.

To help U.S. allies and friends confront this mounting danger, the new President must articulate clearly that such a Soviet military buildup threatens Asia's noncommunist nations. Washington must maintain its current troop and aircraft levels in South Korea; increase its air and naval exercises with Japan; increase the Rim of the Pacific (RIMPAC) exercises for the navies of Australia, Canada, Japan, and the U.S.; construct a third aircraft carrier for the U.S. Seventh Fleet to counter the anticipated deployment of a Soviet nuclear-powered aircraft carrier in Asia during the coming decade; sell the necessary defensive weapons to Taipei, as allowed by the Taiwan Relations Act; increase military aid to the Philippines; and deploy a squadron of F– 15E *Eagle* fighter-bombers to Clark Air Base in the Philippines to counter Soviet Tu–16 *Badger* bombers now at Vietnam's Cam Ranh Bay.

Ensuring Democracy in the Philippines

The new President must be committed to helping America's democratic friends in the Philippines defeat the communist insurgency. He must press Manila to pursue a political-military strategy that attacks the Communist Party of the Philippines' (CPP) political strength in the countryside and allows for rural economic growth to undercut CPP's appeal. At the same time, the U.S. must provide Manila with the military and economic aid to fight the CPP, which receives support from the Soviet Union. A free and democratic Philippines will be more likely to renew the current military bases agreement with the U.S. when it expires in 1991. For the U.S. to lose access to Philippines bases would be a greater strategic setback in Asia than the U.S. defeat in Vietnam.

Reassessing U.S. Policy toward China

Few of America's relationships with other countries have exhibited the fragility, confusion, and contradiction of the U.S.-Chinese relationship. Since the beginning of this century, U.S. policy toward China has shifted significantly with each Administration: from the indifference of Theodore Roosevelt to Woodrow Wilson's sacrifice of Chinese sovereignty at Versailles to Franklin Roosevelt's vision of a unified, independent China. For over two decades after the communists won control of the mainland in 1949, U.S. policy sought to contain and isolate the People's Republic of China (PRC). More recently, and more sensibly, the two nations have tried to define a common ground for what should be one of the world's most important bilateral relationships. Considerable progress has been made toward this, despite continued divergent, and at times, contentious U.S.-PRC interests.

China remains important to the U.S. for several reasons. A China with constructive ties to the U.S. has proved, in general, to be a force for stability in Asia and the world. Today, the PRC has the world's ninth largest economy, is the world's third largest producer of energy, fourth largest producer of steel, and possesses the third largest nuclear force. With a population of over one billion, the PRC represents the globe's largest potential market for U.S. products—although the two-centuries-old American dream of turning China into a mass consumer of American goods has remained unfulfilled. Competing with the Soviet Union, England, France, and the U.S. as one of the world's largest arms exporters, the PRC also is a nation increasingly capable of influencing events in Asia and elsewhere.

The PRC apparently views the U.S. as equally important. As before 1949, the PRC now has extensive scientific, technical, and cultural links with the U.S. And access to American technology, skilled manpower, and capital has helped foster China's economic growth and fuel its economic reform efforts—efforts that preceded by nearly a decade the Soviet Union's much publicized and still fledgling *perestroika*. China sends 22,000 students to U.S. universities annually. Most important, Beijing relies upon the U.S. to balance the Soviet threat in Asia.

To build upon the current healthy U.S.-PRC relationship, the new President must avoid the fluctuating relationship with China that characterized much of the past century. An essential premise of a consistent U.S. relationship with China is that it is not in the U.S. interest to have Beijing either allied with or actively hostile toward Moscow. Relations between Washington and Beijing should not be regarded as what strategists call a zero-sum game. Meaning: the U.S. does not necessarily gain if Chinese-Soviet relations cool, nor does the U.S necessarily lose if those relations improve. While Washington need not encourage Beijing to improve its relations with Moscow, Washington need not fear modest improvement.

Still, the new President unambiguously must advise Beijing that a

PRC-Soviet alliance would alarm the U.S. and force the Administration to reappraise the full range of its dealings with China. Although there is little likelihood that this will occur, the importance of the issue should nevertheless be made clear to the Chinese. The mounting Soviet military might in the Pacific and around Asia must worry China as much as it does other Asian nations and the U.S. While the new President thus should expect China to act independently in its foreign policy initiatives, he still should expect Beijing to maintain closer ties to Washington than to Moscow.

The U.S., in cooperation with the PRC and other regional powers friendly to Beijing, should pursue policies aimed at reducing the Soviet threat in Asia. The new President, within months of his inauguration, must make clear to the Chinese that the U.S. military bases in Japan, the Philippines, and South Korea check the Soviets and thus serve PRC interests. As such, the new President should ask Beijing for subtle and appropriate help, particularly in assuring continued use of the Philippine bases by U.S. forces. The next Administration should consult with the PRC in devising a strategy to counter Soviet aggression within and outside Asia.

B eijing should understand, as does Washington, that Soviet expansion anywhere in the world ultimately threatens both the PRC and the U.S. As such, the U.S. should seek Chinese cooperation and support in countering Soviet expansionism in Central America. Just as the U.S. has been helping counter Soviet expansionism in Southeast Asia on China's threshold, Beijing should help keep the Soviets away from U.S. borders. For one thing, at the United Nations and other international organizations, Beijing could vote to censure aggression by the Soviets and their clients in the Third World. For another, Beijing could provide token aid to El Salvador, the Nicaraguan Democratic Resistance (the Contras), and others fighting to halt Soviet expansionism.

The new President must carefully explain to the PRC the strong U.S. commitment to a forward military defense in the Asian region. He should ask Beijing to establish a reciprocal relationship with the U.S. in military intelligence and training. He should request that his Secretary of Defense visit the PRC and that the U.S. Navy increase its calls at China's ports. The next Administration, however, should not establish a formal military alliance with the PRC. This would be viewed as provocative by both the Soviet Union and U.S. friends and allies in Asia.

The new President must be sensitive to America's Asian allies on regional security issues. He should advise the Chinese that tacit or explicit support for certain insurgent groups—such as the Communist Party of Malaysia—complicates U.S. diplomacy. The security and economic concerns of Japan, South Korea, the nations of ANZUS and ASEAN, and Taiwan are vital to U.S. interests and must be taken into account by the Chinese leadership. Moreover, immediately upon taking office, the new President should reaffirm unequivocally that the U.S. will accept only a peaceful resolution of the Taiwan issue. And he should explore with the PRC effective ways to reduce tensions on the Korean peninsula. The U.S. should consult with the PRC on regional refugee affairs and attempt to enlist Chinese support in the United Nations on this and other issues where U.S.-China interests converge.

The U.S. should expand educational and cultural contacts with China through the U.S. Information Agency and the Department of Education by funding programs to sponsor junior and senior American scholars in the sciences, social sciences, and humanities to travel to China and conduct research. In turn, the new Administration should encourage the Chinese to increase their student enrollment in the U.S.

At the same time, the new President must not hesitate to criticize China for its systematic human rights abuses in Tibet and for human rights infractions elsewhere in China. The new President should insist that Beijing keep its word to safeguard democratic rights and freedoms in Hong Kong as that British colony moves toward rejoining China. The President should state publicly that Beijing's treatment of Hong Kong will be weighed in the balance of Sino-American relations.

The next Administration's principal challenge in formulating China policy may be in economic, scientific, and cultural relations. Washington should encourage U.S. private investment in the PRC by sponsoring trade and investment fairs and conferences and arranging for potential American investors to visit China. The best spur to such investment would be effective PRC laws to safeguard U.S. interests and investments in the PRC. The new President should urge improved access for U.S. products to the Chinese domestic market. He should try to convince the Chinese that its confusing licensing, registration, and foreign exchange regulations, tariffs, and taxes discourage American firms from doing business in China. And in cooperation with the West Europeans and Japanese, the U.S. should urge China's financial institutions to clarify their procedures in order to make their services more accessible to U.S. businesses.

Furthermore, the next President should advise Beijing that the U.S.

strongly supports Taipei's membership in international economic organizations. He should assure Beijing that the U.S. will support PRC membership in these organizations when the PRC has made more progress toward establishing a market economy.

Since the PRC has no internationally accepted patent law, the next Administration must urge the Chinese to take action to protect intellectual property rights. The lack of legal protection for U.S. technology may be one of the most enduring problems between the two countries.

Without question, it is the lure of high technology that prompts Chinese business interest in the U.S. The problem is that the Chinese could use the U.S. technology to design weapons for U.S. adversaries in the Middle East and elsewhere. The new President should commission a study to quantify and identify the strategic impact of U.S. technology transfers to the PRC. In addition, the Departments of Commerce, Defense, and State must coordinate their efforts better to determine which U.S. goods and technology can be transferred to the PRC. This list must be based on realistic criteria and not aimed at halting all U.S. technology transfers to the PRC. Technology associated with electronic warfare, nuclear weapons, and delivery systems, of course, should be withheld. Yet it makes little sense to prohibit the export of technologies that the Chinese easily can obtain elsewhere, such as low-level computer software and industrial technology. And strangling a possible transaction with bureaucratic red tape can prompt the Chinese to turn elsewhere for products.

Linked to the issue of technology transfer are PRC requests to purchase U.S. military technology and hardware. The new President should approve the sale of a limited amount of defensive weapons to the PRC; these may include communications and transportation equipment, and perhaps anti-tank and anti-aircraft systems. It is essential, though, that any U.S.-PRC military relationship not undermine U.S. commitments to its allies in the region, particularly the delicate balance in the Taiwan Strait.

Because perceptions of an accelerating U.S. defense relationship with China could send confusing political and diplomatic messages to U.S. friends and adversaries, the new Administration must develop, along with America's friends and allies, guidelines for the forms and methods of military cooperation with China. Until such guidelines are determined, the focus of the U.S.-PRC military relationship should be less on arms sales than on cooperative efforts between the two nations' military establishments. This should include limited intelligence sharing, port calls, and a joint naval exercise in the South China Sea.

The new President should recognize the potential for mutual misunderstanding in the U.S.-China relationship. To prevent this, he should strengthen, where possible, the multitiered and segmented structure that has helped manage the increasingly complex U.S. policy toward China. This includes the President and his principal foreign policy advisers, China specialists in the White House, Departments of State and Defense, CIA, Asia specialists in the Congress, private foundations, academia, and the press. The President and his chief advisers thus not only must devise a coherent and sustainable policy toward China, but they must meet regularly and systematically inform and educate the U.S. communities interested in China about this policy.

Cementing U.S.-Republic of China Relations

The ROC on Taiwan has been a staunch supporter of the U.S. for decades. Taipei shares Washington's belief in individual freedom, has been democratizing its political system, and is an extraordinary example of free-market economic success. In recognition of the importance of Taipei, the new President should reaffirm U.S. friendship with the ROC by declaring the primacy of the Taiwan Relations Act, which passed Congress by huge majorities in 1979. The Act requires that the U.S. defend the ROC and provides for the sale to Taipei of weapons necessary for its defense.

The new Administration should establish a qualitative index to determine the kinds of weapons that the U.S. can sell to Taipei. Currently, an inflationary index is used that reflects adjustments in prices but fails to reflect the changing ROC-PRC balance of power. A qualitative index would provide the new Administration with an objective framework to help decide whether the ROC needs, for example, advanced interceptor aircraft and other modern equipment to defend itself and whether the Taiwan Relations Act allows the U.S. to sell Taipei these systems.

The new President should continue U.S. encouragement of democratization in the ROC and defend the ROC's right to membership in such international organizations as the General Agreement on Tariffs and Trade (GATT), the Organization for Economic Cooperation and Development (OECD), and the Asian Development Bank (ADB). The success of ROC political reform efforts may depend in large measure on the ROC leadership's confidence in its ability to maintain stable and steady external relations. ROC membership in international economic organizations could help achieve such stability.

To expand U.S.-ROC bilateral trade, the new President should launch negotiations for a U.S.-ROC Free Trade Area. This would eliminate, over time, such restrictions as tariffs and certification requirements that inhibit trade between the two countries. In the meantime, the new President should press the ROC to reduce its huge trade surplus with the U.S. The best means of doing this is to pressure Taipei to cut tariffs further on imported farm products. The next Administration should push for greater U.S. access to the Taiwan market for American banking, insurance, and security businesses.

Establishing a System of Free Trade and Opposing Protectionism

Calls in Congress for trade protection threaten the U.S. economy and economic relationships with Asia. Over one-third of U.S. foreign trade in 1987 was with the Far East; for several Asian nations, trade with the U.S. amounted to even more. The new President must resist protectionist pressures in the U.S. Congress. As important, he must press Delhi, Seoul, Taipei, Tokyo, and other key Asian capitals to reduce, by stages, their unwarranted tariff and nontariff barriers to U.S. products.

The new President should encourage exchanges between U.S. legislators and their counterparts in America's major Asian trading partners. By this, Congress could better understand the barriers to free trade that exist in these countries and then find creative ways to remove them. The White House should sponsor seminars and conferences on international trade to which Asian and U.S. legislators would be invited. The Public Liaison Office of the White House should devise a strategy to alert the U.S. consumer to the dangers of protectionism, and the U.S. Information Agency should educate Asian nations about the serious dangers of continued barriers to U.S. access to their markets.

The new President should appoint a commission to explore the steps needed to establish bilateral Free Trade Areas (FTAs) with Asian countries as a means of opening up overseas markets to U.S. goods and services and stimulating more balanced trade relations. The commission, under strong leadership from the President, would help overcome the bureaucratic inertia that characterizes the State Department's approach to the issue. The U.S. already has negotiated FTA agreements with Canada and Israel. (See Chapter 9.) Several Asian nations, including Singapore, Thailand, the Republic of China on Taiwan, and even Japan, have started investigating the possibilities of a FTA with the U.S. The new President should emphasize FTAs at the highest level in bilateral and multilateral contacts.

Increasing Military Burden-Sharing

The new President must press Tokyo to begin contributing to the defense of Free World interests in Asia at a level commensurate with Japan's enormous wealth. Responding to carefully applied pressure by the Reagan Administration, Japan has increased its defense outlays from 1981 to 1987 by 6.4 percent annually and is moving rapidly toward fulfilling its 1981 pledge to defend air and sea lanes up to 1,000 miles from its coast. The new Administration must continue to press Japan to continue to increase its defense spending and quickly fulfill its 1981 pledge.

At the same time, the U.S. must be sensitive to Asian nations' fears of Japanese rearmament and to the Japanese public's potential anger at U.S. pressure. Washington thus should prod Tokyo to increase its commitment to Asian security through means less provocative than expanding Japanese military forces. Tokyo could share the defense burden by supplementing U.S. military and economic aid efforts in Asia. Example: Tokyo could increase foreign assistance to the Philippines as part of an overall package of aid in exchange for U.S. base rights in the Philippines. Tokyo, along with Seoul and Taipei, could join a U.S.-sponsored Foundation for Economic Growth which would promote market-oriented policies for Asia's less developed countries. (See Chapter 27.)

A lack of public support by Filipino and, until recently, South Korean leaders for the U.S. presence in their countries has allowed the opponents of this presence to fan flames of anti-Americanism. The new President should ask Manila and Seoul privately to acknowledge publicly, in appropriate ways, the security and economic benefits they receive from U.S. military bases. Washington should stress to the six members of the Association of Southeast Asian Nations that their public support for the U.S. military bases in Korea and the Philippines is crucial if the U.S. is to remain in the region to deter Soviet adventurism and to counter Beijing's growing military strength.

Expanding Public Diplomacy

Historically, U.S. public diplomacy has given a low priority to Asia, particularly the South Pacific and Korea. This has given Moscow the opportunity that Gorbachev has begun to exploit. To make matters worse, the younger generation of Asia's leaders lack the kind of reflexive good will toward the U.S. that their fathers had from fighting alongside American soldiers against the Japanese, and later North Korean, invaders and benefiting from generous amounts of U.S. reconstruction assistance. The U.S. must recognize these changing attitudes.

To regenerate Asian good will for the U.S., Washington must launch a public diplomacy offensive. The U.S. Information Agency, for instance, could run more cultural exhibits in Asia and organize more U.S.-Asia people-to-people and legislative exchanges, both targets of increased Soviet attention. The U.S. could provide many more inexpensive reading materials, especially in South Asia, where well-made yet cheap Soviet books have been supplied in large quantities.

U.S. public diplomacy should remind Asia of the military threats posed by North Korea, the Soviet Union, and Vietnam. U.S. officials should stress that the U.S. military presence limits Soviet meddling and that recent Soviet diplomatic initiatives contain little substance. The U.S. must react more quickly to such self-serving Soviet initiatives as proposals for antisubmarine warfare and nuclear-free zones, aimed at inhibiting the movement of U.S. forces through the Asia/Pacific region.

Balancing U.S. Relations in South Asia

The next Administration should continue the Reagan policy of avoiding a zero-sum game in South Asia. Better relations with India need not be at the expense of U.S. relations with Pakistan—and vice versa. The U.S. could improve relations with India by sending greater numbers of high-level delegations to Delhi, including a visit by the new President and Secretaries of State and Defense; by reciprocating the 1985 Indian Festival in the U.S. with a U.S. Festival in India; by giving more emphasis to U.S. Information Agency programs in India; by requesting more Indian port calls for U.S. naval vessels; and by exploring ways of increasing U.S. sales of high-technology items with dual civilian/military applications.

Delhi must understand, however, that the U.S. will provide necessary defensive weapons systems to Pakistan. The Reagan Administration already has pledged a $4 billion, six-year (1987–1993) aid package to Islamabad. With the Soviet withdrawal from Afghanistan now becoming a reality, the new President should help foster Pakistani stability by increasing economic aid to Islamabad, especially programs to help Pakistan cope with its more than 3 million Afghan refugees. At the same time, the next Administration quietly should encourage the

Pakistani government to return Pakistan to the path of democratization, made more difficult by the dissolution of Parliament in May 1988.

The U.S. should offer Sri Lanka more international military education and more funds to train officers in Sri Lanka's expanding armed forces. The U.S. should increase substantially economic assistance to build roads and develop a second Sri Lankan Free Trade Zone around the southern port of Galle. The U.S. also should provide low-cost English and Sinhalese language books and periodicals to compete with the inexpensive books from Moscow's Friendship Societies in Sri Lanka.

Reinvigorating the ANZUS Alliance

From 1951 to 1985, the Australia-New Zealand-U.S. (ANZUS) Alliance stood as the South Pacific counterpart to NATO, facilitating defense cooperation and deterring Soviet adventurism. In 1984, however, the newly elected New Zealand labor government chose to pursue strict antinuclear policies that would have forced the U.S. to reveal if specific U.S. ships or aircraft carried nuclear weapons. As a matter of policy, the U.S. refuses to confirm or deny the presence of these weapons. As a result, the U.S. in 1985 suspended formal military cooperation with New Zealand, and in 1986, withdrew its defense obligations to New Zealand under ANZUS. This was the first formal break in the ANZUS alliance since it was founded.

Australia has opposed New Zealand's antinuclear policies, which have weakened ANZUS, and has continued defense cooperation with the U.S. Canberra's Labor government, however, has sought to promote the 1985 South Pacific Nuclear Free Zone Treaty (SPNFZT), which could prevent Australia from providing bases for U.S. forces that may have to leave the Philippines. Washington, London, and Paris have refused to sign protocols to SPNFZT; Moscow and Beijing have signed.

New Zealand's antinuclear policies and the Nuclear Free Zone treaty have been a windfall to the Soviets, who have been actively exploiting anti-Western sentiments and economic and ethnic tensions in the region. The Soviets also are working through such surrogates as trade unions and peace groups to destroy ANZUS and create South Pacific client states.

The new President must invigorate the ANZUS Alliance. He must mount a campaign to explain to the people of New Zealand the damage caused by the Labor government's antinuclear policies and how they have furthered Soviet goals in the South Pacific. He must be ready to offer renewed U.S. cooperation with New Zealand if it changes its policies. Even without New Zealand, the next Administration must increase military cooperation with Australia and seek to dissuade Australia from promoting the flawed SPNFZT. Washington should encourage Canberra to participate in more multilateral naval exercises and also to offer increased economic and military aid to the Philippines.

────────────────◇────────────────

INITIATIVES FOR 1989

1) Deliver a major Asian speech. The new President should make a major speech on U.S. policy toward Asia early in his presidency. It could be delivered from Hawaii or Guam, and it should be designed as a U.S. answer to Soviet leader Gorbachev's successful Vladivostok speech of July 1986.

The new President's speech should underscore the importance the U.S. attaches to Asia, pledge to keep U.S. military forces in the region at their current levels, promise continued support to the Philippines, call for continued democratization in the region, and propose free trade areas between Asia and the U.S. After the speech, the new President should visit India, Indonesia, Japan, South Korea, Pakistan, the Philippines, and Thailand. Other visits should take the Secretaries of Commerce and the Treasury to Hong Kong, Japan, South Korea, Singapore, and Thailand; and the Secretary of Defense to India, Indonesia, South Korea, Pakistan, the Philippines, the PRC, and Thailand. Such visits would offset the recent spate of Soviet delegations calling on Asia.

2) Name a new ambassador to Japan immediately. U.S.-Japanese relations have suffered not only because of continuing trade frictions, but because U.S. policy toward Japan has lacked strong and consistent leadership. The senior U.S. diplomatic presence in Japan, in particular, has lacked firmness in dealing with the Japanese on trade and security issues. To make matters worse, senior U.S. diplomats in Tokyo seem to have discouraged other members of the embassy from sending candid reports to Washington detailing the strains in the U.S.-Japanese relationship.

Tokyo is the most important U.S. diplomatic post in Asia. The new President should treat it as such by making the appointment of a new ambassador to Japan a top priority. The new ambassador should be energetic, have strong private-sector credentials, and have close personal ties to the President. This will acknowledge the importance of U.S.-Japanese relations and give Tokyo a means of communicating directly with the White House.

3) Ensure that U.S. bases remain in the Philippines. The new President must state unequivocally that the U.S. intends to keep its bases in the Philippines to preserve strategic stability in Asia. The next Administration should conclude the current military bases review to ensure continued U.S. access to its bases in the Philippines. The U.S. should offer Manila a bases compensation package of at least $500 million a year in economic and military assistance for fiscal 1990 and 1991. At present, the Philippines receives $299 million a year in aid. The new Administration also should seek to begin negotiations for the next bases agreement or treaty by early 1990.

To help alleviate the Philippines' economic plight and aid government forces in combating the leftist insurgency, the new President should urge other industrialized nations, such as Japan and the Republic of China on Taiwan, to increase economic assistance to Manila. The Japanese have said they will give more aid to the Philippines. The U.S. should begin drawing world attention to the outside threat to the Philippines' fledgling democracy, including the aid from the Soviet Union to the Philippines communists.

4) Reassess U.S. foreign aid policy. Indonesia, Pakistan, the Philippines, Thailand, and others have relied on U.S. aid to help them develop their economies and modernize their armed forces. In recent years, however, U.S. military assistance, especially to the ASEAN nations, has decreased sharply. Between fiscal 1985 and fiscal 1987, U.S. security assistance to Thailand fell from $102 million to $52.3 million; to Indonesia, it dropped from $42 million to $12 million. Only the Philippines saw U.S. security aid increase from $51.3 million to $102.8 million. The cut in aid to ASEAN has reduced U.S. influence and undermined ASEAN security. The new President should restore security aid levels to those of 1985, particularly to Indonesia and Thailand, while increasing aid to the Philippines and Sri Lanka.

The new Administration should review U.S. aid programs in Asia. Though the region is becoming a model of economic development, many countries there face insurgencies or external threats. The new President must recognize that high-visibility U.S. aid projects increase private-sector cooperation and foster goodwill toward the U.S. Such projects should include construction of power plants, schools, training centers, roads, and bridges. The new Administration should increase the number of scholarships and training programs in the U.S. for South and Southeast Asians to develop a core of future Western-educated pro-U.S. business and government leaders. In South Asia, U.S. scholarships are only a fraction of those offered by the East bloc.

5) Promote free trade with Asia. In his 1989 State of the Union address, the new President should pledge that he will use all the available mechanisms of the multilateral trading system, particularly the General Agreement on Tariffs and Trade (GATT) and direct bilateral pressure, to convince America's major Asian trading partners, especially Japan, to open their markets further to U.S. products. Tokyo, in particular, should be put on notice that Washington no longer will tolerate the official and informal Japanese barriers to U.S. goods. The President also should announce a reinvigorated effort to press for improved patent and copyright protection for U.S. manufacturers in Asia, particularly in ASEAN. The new Administration should propose to Taipei that it explore establishing a Free Trade Area with the U.S. Other Asian nations should be invited to discuss creating Free Trade Areas with the U.S. (See Chapter 9.)

6) Demand that Vietnam withdraw all of its forces from Cambodia and Laos. The new President must show his concern for the continued security of noncommunist Southeast Asia by lending greater support to ASEAN's backing of the Coalition Government of Democratic Kampuchea (CGDK) in its opposition to Vietnamese occupation forces in Cambodia. Washington should increase material assistance to the noncommunist Cambodian factions of the CGDK, call for the Vietnamese to participate fully in all further negotiations on Cambodia, and demand that free elections be conducted in Cambodia only after a complete withdrawal of Vietnamese forces.

The U.S. should make no economic or diplomatic concessions to Vietnam until Hanoi removes its forces from Cambodia and Laos and reduces the size of its active and reserve military forces, which are currently the fourth largest in the world. This will reassure ASEAN of Washington's concern for regional security.

7) Reassess relations with the People's Republic of China. The new President should convene meetings of his senior advisers to define a policy toward China that serves U.S. interests and to determine where those interests diverge from Chinese interests. Common interests include Chinese opposition to Soviet expansion in the Far East,

Chinese support for U.S. forward defenses in Asia, and increased U.S.-Chinese trade. The new President must also make clear to the Chinese U.S. concerns over human rights violations in Tibet, possible PRC threats to democracy in Hong Kong, and U.S. insistence on a peaceful resolution of the Taiwan issue. High-ranking U.S. delegations to the PRC should express U.S. concerns over China's growing weapons sales to the Middle East. The new President also should commission a report on the transfer of high technology to the PRC. The new Administration should maintain limited military ties with Beijing and schedule a visit by the Secretary of Defense to discuss future U.S.-PRC military ties. Discussions should explore the possibilities for increased port calls, enhanced intelligence sharing, and arrangements for a joint naval exercise in the South China Sea.

8) Establish a more consistent policy toward the Republic of China on Taiwan. The new President publicly should declare his support for full U.S. compliance with the Taiwan Relations Act. His Administration must continue negotiations on contentious trade issues between the U.S. and the ROC. Most important will be further reductions in the ROC's barriers to the import of U.S. goods and services, including high tariffs on produce and poultry. Adequately to allow the U.S. to comply with the Taiwan Relations Act, the new President should name a commission to prepare a qualitative index for U.S. military sales to the ROC. As part of an effort to assist Taiwan in gaining membership in international organizations, the new Administration should publicly state its support for bringing the ROC into the General Agreement on Tariffs and Trade (GATT).

NOTES

1. Canada, West Germany, Mexico, and Britain are the first, third, fourth, and sixth largest trading partners.
2. Brunei, Indonesia, Malaysia, the Philippines, Singapore, and Thailand.

Afghanistan

H. Joachim Maitre*
Task Force Chairman

The Soviet Union has prosecuted a brutal nine-year war against the Afghan people which has claimed approximately 1 million Afghan lives. The April 14, 1988, Geneva accords on Afghanistan seem to testify to Moscow's failure to score an outright military victory in that war. But the accords do not necessarily spell defeat for the Soviet Union. They may indicate merely that Moscow has changed tactics in an attempt to salvage, not abandon, the $150 billion Soviet investment to subdue Afghanistan. Soviet Communist Party leader Mikhail Gorbachev is using the accords to cut Soviet losses and improve Moscow's image while continuing to prop up the communist puppet regime in Kabul. Most important, Gorbachev may hope to use the Geneva accords diplomatically to isolate the Afghan *mujahideen* freedom fighters and deprive them of external support.

As long as communists hold power in Kabul, Moscow has a strategic steppingstone to the oil-rich Persian Gulf and the Indian subcontinent. Even if Soviet troops withdraw from Afghanistan, Moscow will be capable of intimidating, penetrating, or even dismembering neighboring Pakistan and Iran, both of which will be facing changes of government in the future. The total withdrawal of Soviet troops would be only the first step in the anticommunist *mujahideen*'s uphill struggle for the liberation of all of Afghanistan from communist domination. The war in Afghanistan will continue until the brutal communist dictatorship in Kabul is replaced.

————————————◇————————————

THE REAGAN ADMINISTRATION RECORD

When the Reagan Administration took office in 1981, it found that the Afghan resistance was receiving only a trickle of small arms,

---

*Commenting and contributing generously to this report were *Mandate III* Task Force Members James Hackett, Peter Huessy, David Isby, and Elie Krakowski. They do not necessarily endorse all of its views and recommendations.

Task Force Deputy Chairman: Heritage Senior Policy Analyst James A. Phillips.

obsolete military supplies, and no humanitarian aid from the Carter Administration. Reagan steadily increased the quantity and quality of military aid. Most important, in early 1986 after considerable delays, Reagan ordered the transfer of sophisticated American-made *Stinger* anti-aircraft missiles to the resistance. These missiles enabled the *mujahideen* to blunt the Soviet air-mobile special forces, helicopter gunships, and ground attack warplanes, the cutting edge of Soviet counterinsurgency forces. The *Stingers* helped the *mujahideen* raise the military and economic costs of Soviet occupation. In 1987 alone, approximately 200 Soviet and Afghan government aircraft were destroyed.

Essential for defeating the Soviet troops was the Reagan Administration's restoration of close working relations with Pakistan. Pakistani-American ties had deteriorated enormously under Carter. Improved relations with Pakistan made it easier to aid the Afghan resistance, which has enjoyed sanctuary in western Pakistan. At congressional prodding in 1985, the Reagan Administration began sending humanitarian aid to civilians remaining inside Afghanistan. This saved lives and helped the *mujahideen* hold their base of support and frustrate Soviet scorched-earth tactics designed to depopulate resistance strongholds.

The Administration's policies helped the courageous and tenacious *mujahideen* to outlast Soviet forces in battle, inflicting the first military defeat on Moscow since the 1941 Nazi invasion of Russia. This humiliation will exert a demoralizing influence on the Soviet military. Moreover, it signals to Eastern Europe and the developing world that the Red Army is not invincible.

Despite the great strides in aiding the Afghan resistance, however, the Reagan Administration has failed to provide adequate training in battlefield tactics. And although the Administration has raised the Soviet military costs of the war, it has not done enough to raise Moscow's political costs. The Administration, for example, failed to break relations with the puppet communist regime in Kabul and to recognize the resistance coalition as Afghanistan's legitimate government. It did not withdraw Most Favored Nation trade status from the Kabul regime until Congress forced it to do so in February 1986.

Whether the Soviet military failure in Afghanistan becomes a geostrategic defeat depends on whether the Soviets continue to be kept out of Afghanistan. Here the Reagan Administration has stumbled badly since spring 1988, failing to press the advantage. The U.S. agreed to guarantee the April 1988 Geneva settlement. This permits the Afghan communists to retain power, which strengthens their claim to legitimacy, and fails to recognize the legitimacy of the resistance. Although the Geneva accords ultimately may benefit the *mujahideen* by setting the terms for a complete Soviet military withdrawal by February 15, 1989, the accords in the short run could allow Moscow to gain through diplomacy what it could not win on the battlefield if Pakistan should halt cross-border aid to the resistance. Such aid became more uncertain after the August 17, 1988, death of Pakistani President Mohammed Zia ul-Haq in a suspicious plane crash. Moreover, the accords fail to require the withdrawal of Soviet advisers, which allows Moscow to continue dominating Afghanistan's internal affairs. And although the accords specify the terms for a Soviet withdrawal, they ignore the issue of Afghan self-determination. Furthermore, since the *mujahideen* are excluded from the agreement, there will be no ceasefire, let alone real peace. Continued instability will give Moscow future opportunities to intervene, overtly or covertly, in Afghan affairs and contribute to regional instability.

———————————◇———————————

THE NEXT FOUR YEARS

The U.S. too often has won wars on the battlefield only to lose them in the peace agreements. Now that the U.S. has agreed to act as a guarantor of the Geneva accords, it must make sure that Moscow does not regain by subverting the agreement what it lost on the battlefield. Moscow must be held to every promise it has made. At the same time the U.S. must not lose sight of its own long-term goal: the creation of a free, independent, noncommunist Afghanistan that will contribute to regional stability and be a buffer state between the Soviet Union and Pakistan.

Continuing Aid to the *Mujahideen*

The new President should stand by Ronald Reagan's commitment to continue aiding the *mujahideen* as long as Moscow continues to aid the Afghan communists. The new President should adhere to the February 29, 1988, "sense of the Senate" resolution, approved 77 to 0, that the U.S. "should not cease, suspend, diminish, or otherwise restrict assistance to the Afghan resistance . . . until it is absolutely clear that the Soviets have terminated their military occupation" and the resistance is "well enough equipped to maintain its integrity" during a transition to a new government.

The new President should warn Moscow that, if it violates the accords, especially in regard to withdrawal of Soviet troops, the U.S. will increase military aid to the *mujahideen* immediately. Even if the U.S. and USSR both stop aiding their Afghan clients, the military aid infrastructure built up in Pakistan to channel aid to the resistance must be maintained intact so that U.S. military aid could be resumed quickly in the event of Soviet treaty violations. Military supplies should be prepositioned discreetly in Pakistan for rapid transfer to the resistance at the first sign of Soviet cheating on the agreement. Moscow must be warned that a failure to withdraw from Afghanistan will poison U.S.-Soviet relations and prompt U.S. responses on a wide range of issues. Moscow must not be allowed to follow North Vietnam's example of violating agreements to withdraw from Laos in 1962 and from South Vietnam in 1973.

Achieving Authentic Peace in Afghanistan

No peace is possible in Afghanistan as long as Afghan communists remain in power. The *mujahideen* were fighting the Kabul regime before the Soviet invasion and will continue fighting until the communists are ousted. The U.S. government should not wade into the quagmire of trying to cobble together a coalition government containing communists and noncommunists. Rather, the U.S. should help build a durable resistance alliance that could evolve into a full-fledged government. To give the *mujahideen* groups incentives to maintain solidarity, the President should promise to recognize such a coalition as the legitimate government once it has proved to be a functioning institution inside the liberated areas of Afghanistan. The U.S. should halt aid to resistance groups that undermine *mujahideen* unity; groups that cooperate fully should get increased aid.

Maintaining Close Ties with Pakistan

The best guarantee against a Soviet victory in Afghanistan is a solid U.S.-Pakistani relationship. The six-year $4 billion U.S. military and economic aid program to Pakistan should remain a high priority and be spared from cutbacks prompted by shrinkage in the foreign aid budget. (See Asia section of this chapter.)

Helping the Resistance Expand Press Coverage of the War and Soviet War Crimes

The full details of the war, including the many Soviet atrocities in Afghanistan, are largely unreported and unknown outside Afghanistan.

Although a small number of Afghan journalists have been trained in Pakistan in a U.S.-funded program, much more needs to be done. The new President should request that Congress provide more funds to the Afghan Media Resource Center, a clearinghouse for information on Afghanistan. The new President also should order the U.S. Information Agency to step up coverage of Afghanistan by bolstering its Afghanistan country program, and help increase awareness of events there, especially in developing and Islamic nations. The Voice of America should expand its Dari and Pashto language news services, to let the Afghans know that they have not been forgotten.

Assisting the Long-Term Reconstruction of Afghanistan

Roughly 5 million Afghans, the world's largest refugee group, have been driven into exile in Pakistan and Iran by a systematic Soviet terror campaign designed to depopulate Afghanistan and weaken the resistance. These refugees will need extensive help in returning to and rehabilitating their war-torn homeland. An estimated 15,000 of Afghanistan's 20,000 villages have been destroyed. Minefields must be removed. Houses, roads, bridges, water supplies, irrigation networks, health systems, education programs, and agricultural systems must be rebuilt. When a noncommunist government has been formed in Kabul, the new President should request Congress to appropriate substantial war recovery aid. The new administration also should organize a multilateral effort to rebuild Afghanistan's shattered economy and restore stability. Britain, Egypt, France, Japan, Pakistan, Saudi Arabia, Turkey, and West Germany could contribute financial aid, advisers, or technical expertise to the project. A multinational military effort, similar to that organized to clear the Suez Canal after the 1973 War, should help clear minefields and train Afghans to do so.

————————————◇————————————

INITIATIVES FOR 1989

1) Warn Moscow to fulfill the terms of the Geneva Accords. The new President, through the National Security Council and the U.S. intelligence community, should monitor closely Soviet compliance with the accords. He should warn Moscow that Soviet violations will provoke an immediate U.S. response across the entire spectrum of U.S.-Soviet relations. Such responses should include: an increase of U.S. military aid to the *mujahideen*, particularly *Stinger* missiles, long-range mortars, and mine-clearing equipment; a suspension of U.S.-Soviet arms control negotiations; and the end of the nascent superpower detente. The new President should proclaim that Soviet compliance with its Geneva commitments will be considered a litmus test of Gorbachev's much vaunted "new thinking" in foreign policy.

2) Recognize the *mujahideen coalition* government. The new President immediately should order the State Department to withdraw recognition of the illegitimate Kabul communist regime, shut the U.S. embassy in Kabul, and recognize instead the 28–member interim government proposed by the *mujahideen* coalition in February 1988 as Afghanistan's legitimate government until elections can be held.

3) Channel humanitarian aid through the new coalition government. U.S. humanitarian aid to Afghans living inside Afghanistan should be doubled to $90 million per year. It should be channeled through the provisional government formed by the resistance coalition, once Washington has recognized it. This will encourage unity among the *mujahideen* groups. Absolutely no U.S. aid should be channeled through the Kabul regime; such a mistake would strengthen its hold on power, prolong the war, and allow Kabul to force resettled refugees to accept government control or face starvation.

4) Appoint a high-level official to coordinate policy. The new President should appoint a senior National Security Council official who would be given direct access to the Oval Office to coordinate all U.S. policy on Afghanistan.

5) Strengthen the unity of the *mujahideen coalition*. *Mujahideen* political unity now is more important than ever as the Afghan struggle enters a new phase. To frustrate Moscow's divide and rule tactics, the U.S. should work with Pakistan and Saudi Arabia to encourage greater political unity among the *mujahideen*. Washington should help to broker a power-sharing agreement among all noncommunist Afghan groups. It should not favor one group over the others, but should make it clear that groups that do not cooperate in building a broadly based government will be deprived of American aid. Once a government is formed, all aid should be gradually channeled through it, while direct aid to individual resistance groups should be reduced. This will strengthen centralized authority and give individual resistance leaders added incentive to join the coalition government.

6) Seek Soviet war reparations. The Afghans will suffer the pain of the brutal Soviet aggression and occupation for generations. The U.S. should organize an international effort to form an independent commission to assess war damages and press for Soviet reparations. Moscow also must be pressed to return to Afghanistan thousands of children sent to the Soviet Union for indoctrination during the war and to help remove the millions of land mines it sowed throughout the country.

7) Rule out the forced return of Soviet prisoners of war. The Secretary of State should make certain that all Soviet prisoners of war held by the Afghans who do not wish to go home to the Soviet Union will be welcomed in the U.S. as refugees. It would be tragic to repeat the mistake made after World War II in which thousands of Soviet prisoners of war were forcibly repatriated, only to be treated as traitors and executed or imprisoned in labor camps. Soviet prisoners of war should be given a choice of returning to the Soviet Union or of following the precedent established after the Korean war, when thousands of Chinese and North Korean prisoners chose to remain outside the communist bloc.

The Middle East and Persian Gulf

Daniel Pipes*
Task Force Chairman

The Middle East figures prominently in the superpower rivalry because of its geostrategic and economic importance. It is the center of gravity of world oil production and is crucial to the long-term economic health of the free world. The U.S. imported approximately 1.7 million barrels of oil daily from the Middle East in mid–1988 and is projected to import much more in the 1990s. Politically, the Middle East is the arena where Israel, an embattled democracy closely allied to the U.S., struggles for survival and where the Iran-Iraq conflict and rising fundamentalist Islamic forces exert a destabilizing influence over the region.

THE REAGAN ADMINISTRATION RECORD

When the Reagan Administration entered office, the Middle East/ Persian Gulf region was reeling from the Iranian revolution, the Soviet invasion of Afghanistan, and the start of the Iran-Iraq war. Simmering too were persistent Arab-Israeli tensions, Lebanon's deepening anarchy, and Libya's growing meddling in its neighbors' affairs. Most threatening, perhaps, the Soviet Union was on the move, attempting to encircle the Persian Gulf by overrunning Afghanistan and raising its presence in Ethiopia, South Yemen, and Syria.

The Reagan Administration has helped block the Soviet drive to the Gulf through Afghanistan by strongly supporting Pakistan and the Afghan *mujahideen* resistance. The April 14, 1986, U.S. air strike against Libya reduced Libyan terrorism and isolated Libyan dictator Muammar Qadhafi. The U.S. has led the reassertion of Western

---

*Commenting and contributing generously to this report were *Mandate III* Task Force Members Brad Gordon, Laurie Mylroie, and Darryl Nirenberg. They do not necessarily endorse all of its views and recommendations.

Task Force Deputy Chairman: Heritage Senior Policy Analyst James A. Phillips.

primacy in the Persian Gulf by marshaling Western navies to blunt and deter Iranian aggression in Gulf waters. This action, coupled with "Operation Staunch," an American effort to deny Iran access to foreign arms supplies, appears to have contributed significantly to the Iranian decision to end the Iran-Iraq war.

The Reagan Administration, meanwhile, has executed a consistent policy regarding the Arab-Israeli conflict and convinced Arab states that they cannot drive a wedge between the U.S. and Israel. U.S.-Israel strategic cooperation has been solidified by agreements on intelligence exchanges, military cooperation, and defense procurement. Washington has prodded Israel, and to a lesser extent Egypt, toward free market economic reforms which have fostered economic growth in deregulated sectors of their economies.

The Administration's most painful failure has been the 1984 withdrawal of U.S. Marines from Lebanon and its inability to help the Lebanese restore a national consensus that would deprive terrorists of their Lebanese bases of operations. Although the long-term objective of the Administration's secret Iran initiative—restoration of working relations with post-Khomeini Iran—was necessary and correct, the execution of the initiative was flawed.

———————————◇———————————

THE NEXT FOUR YEARS

The U.S. has four main goals in the region: 1) to block Soviet penetration; 2) to assure the security of Israel; 3) to maintain Western access to Middle Eastern oil; and 4) to maintain good working relations with moderate Arab states while reinforcing such pro-Western trends as democracy. American interests are best served by stability. Therefore, the U.S. must work for negotiated solutions to the Arab-Israeli conflict and the Iran-Iraq war, two of the chief sources of Middle Eastern instability.

Reinforcing the Strategic Alliance with Israel

Israel is a valuable U.S. ally because of its pivotal location, opposition to communism, commitment to Western values, superb military forces, experience in capturing and countering Soviet-made weapons, excellent intelligence network, and creative defense research organizations. The new President must free himself from the zero-sum mentality that, until the Reagan Administration, had led the U.S. to hold Israel at arm's length in a vain effort to gain close strategic cooperation with reluctant Arab states. It is close U.S.-Israeli ties that often have been the incentive for Arab leaders to improve their own relations with the U.S.

The new President should direct the Secretary of Defense to integrate Israel discreetly into the global anti-Soviet defense system in the strategic area between the North Atlantic Treaty Organization's southern flank and the Persian Gulf. This area includes the eastern Mediterranean Sea and its littoral. Joint U.S.-Israeli contingency plans should be drawn up and updated to give American military forces access to Israeli ports, airbases, and medical facilities in a crisis. Heavy weapons, medical supplies, fuel, and ammunition should be prepositioned in Israel for U.S.use in Middle Eastern or NATO southern flank contingencies.

U.S.-Israeli military intelligence liaison and technical cooperation should be organized to promote maximum information exchange in the joint assessment and countering of the Soviet military threat. Israeli innovations in military technology such as Remotely Piloted Vehicles, armor-piercing munitions, radar homing missiles, and fighter aircraft avionics should be adopted when practicable. The Defense Department should encourage exchanges with Israel in defense research, particularly Israeli contributions to the Strategic Defense Initiative. (See Strategic Defense section of Chapter 28.)

Encouraging Direct Bilateral Peace Talks

The historical record shows that only direct talks between Israel and its neighbors produce results. The new Secretary of State thus should not seek an "international conference." This merely would give Arab hardline states a veto over the peace process and enable the Soviet Union to increase its influence by playing to the Arabs while isolating Israel and the U.S. The new Administration should accept a conference only if it is to be a purely ceremonial international event to facilitate bilateral talks.

Minimizing the Soviet Peace Process Role

The new President should block any Soviet role in the peace process until Moscow is willing to prove its constructive commitment by restoring relations with Israel, significantly reducing the flow of weapons to those Arab states at war with Israel, and terminating its support of Middle Eastern terrorist groups.

Containing the Iranian Revolution

The U.S. should work to contain the destabilizing spillover effects of the Iranian revolution. These effects include Iranian-sponsored terrorism, fundamentalist Muslim agitation, and the intimidation of pro-Western states throughout the Middle East. The long-term U.S. goal should be to restore a working relationship with an Iranian government that does not seek to export its brand of revolutionary politics. True rapprochement appears impossible as long as Ayatollah Ruhollah Khomeini dominates Iran.

While leaving the door open to better U.S.-Iran relations, the Secretary of State must realize that Iran's hostility to the U.S. is a function of its ideology and will not be assuaged by American acts of goodwill. Such actions would be interpreted by Tehran as signs of weakness or subterfuge. The regime respects force and weighs carefully the benefits of its anti-American behavior. The new Administration therefore should: maintain efforts to isolate Iran, deprive it of foreign arms supplies, and press allies to ban trade with Iran; be prepared to respond with military force against high-value Iranian military and economic targets (like oil fields) in the event of Iranian-supported attacks on U.S. targets; offer U.S. economic and technical assistance in rebuilding Iran's shattered economy, particularly its oil industry, if Iran negotiates a peace treaty with Iraq and ends its support of terrorists; and offer to recognize the Iranian revolution and limit U.S. support of opposition groups if Iran ends efforts to destabilize pro-Western Middle Eastern governments.

Preventing a Decisive Victory by Either Side in the Iran-Iraq War

An outright victory by either Iran or Iraq would threaten U.S. and Western interests in the Persian Gulf. The continuation of the war, however, is inherently destabilizing and gives Moscow opportunities to expand its influence. Now that Iran has accepted U.N.-brokered peace efforts, the U.S. should seek a negotiated settlement based on the prewar status quo and maintain restraints on arms sales to both Iran and Iraq. The U.S. must maintain a powerful naval presence in the Persian Gulf until Iran makes a firm commitment to restore freedom of navigation and ends its attacks on neutral shipping. The President and Secretary of State should condemn strongly Iraq's use of chemical warfare.

Helping Egypt Reform Its Economy

The new Secretary of State must assure the survival of a stable pro-Western Egypt by helping Egypt salvage its long-term economic future. A swollen bureaucracy mismanages Egypt's dominant public sector while extensive subsidies of food and other essential goods warp economic behavior and exacerbate the huge government deficit. The U.S. must help Cairo maintain acceptable living standards for its poor while instituting the free market economic reforms that will assure Egypt's economic growth. The State Department should use U.S. aid to encourage Egypt to diminish the state's economic role, bolster the private sector, privatize state-run enterprises, gradually eliminate price controls, and move toward a free market economy.

To assist Egypt in making this difficult transition, the U.S. should maintain the current level of $2.1 billion in aid to Egypt while encouraging Western Europe and Japan to increase their aid to Egypt. The Secretary of State should work together with Egypt to encourage other Arab states to follow Egypt's lead in signing the 1979 Egypt-Israel peace treaty. The Secretary of Defense discreetly should seek greater strategic cooperation with Egypt, particularly in blocking Libyan meddling in Chad and the Sudan. To avoid handing fundamentalist Muslims an opportunity to arouse Egyptian anxieties, the Secretary of State should reduce the size and visibility of the official U.S. presence in Egypt.

INITIATIVES FOR 1989

1) Refrain from meddling in the West Bank/Gaza disturbances. Israeli authorities should be allowed to deal with the Palestinian uprising, as they best understand the disturbances and appreciate the risks involved. For the U.S. to advocate Israeli concessions to rioters would reward the violence, perpetuate it, and make the peace process that much more difficult. The new Administration should refrain from giving Israel public advice on how to handle the disturbances.

2) Serve as an honest broker in the Arab-Israeli peace process. The Arabs must negotiate with Jerusalem, not Washington. Overeagerness by the U.S. leads Arab states to believe that Washington will wring concessions from Israel for the Arabs and thus discourage them from making concessions themselves. The Secretary of State should not stake out positions of his own but should push the process ahead when there are signs that both sides are willing to negotiate. Then the Secretary of State should offer his good offices as a mediator. The President should not become involved until it is apparent that there is a reasonable chance for success.

3) Press Iran to stop exporting revolution and terrorism. The Secretary of State should continue to mobilize Western states to isolate Iran. The Secretary of State should warn Iran that, if it continues to support terrorism and threaten the stability of other states, the U.S. will tilt further toward Iraq, providing it economic credits, technical assistance, and possibly even arms.

4) Prepare military options for contingencies concerning Iran. The Secretary of Defense should develop a wide array of possible swift military responses against Iran in the event of Iranian terrorism or Iranian attacks on U.S. ships in the Persian Gulf. Washington should not worry about pushing Iran into the arms of the Soviets because Iran has strong historical, geopolitical, and ideological reasons to fear a Soviet embrace. Iran's hostility to the U.S. is internally generated and will not be assuaged in the short run by sympathetic signals sent by the U.S. Iran responds to firm pressure, not good intentions. Resolute action in the short run may obviate the need in the long run to take far more costly and more risky actions to rein in Iran. The new President thus should order the Defense Department to maintain a strong naval force in the Persian Gulf to deter Iran and be prepared to respond militarily to Iranian provocations.

5) Isolate and maintain pressure on Syria. The Syrian government has feigned interest in participating in the Arab-Israeli peace process and hinted at reducing support for terrorism as a means of breaking out of its isolation and regaining access to Western trade, aid, and investment. The Secretary of State should recognize that these actions are prompted by Syria's internal weaknesses, not by a genuine desire for peace. Therefore, the U.S. must maintain diplomatic pressure on Syria, not relax it. Washington should revert to the tough stance taken in 1986 following revelations of Syrian involvement in a plot to bomb an Israeli airliner. At that time the U.S. Ambassador in Damascus was withdrawn, U.S. oil companies were banned from operating in Syria, restrictions on U.S. exports to Syria were tightened, Export-Import Bank credits to Syria were ended, and an aviation agreement was canceled. The Secretary of State should request Saudi Arabia to reduce its foreign aid to Syria until that nation becomes more helpful in furthering peace between the Arabs and Israel and between Iraq and Iran. If Syria does this and expels Iranian revolutionary guards from Lebanon, then Syria could be rewarded with access to U.S. markets and credits.

6) Codify U.S.-Israel strategic cooperation. Washington should formalize and solidify the 1983 U.S.-Israeli Memorandum of Understanding on strategic cooperation to give the U.S. bureaucracy a vested interest in expanding strategic cooperation with Israel. The President should establish a U.S.-Israel Defense Council, a high-level group co-chaired by the Secretary of Defense and the Israeli Defense Minister, to provide a framework for coordinating the work of the various ad hoc working groups that plan and execute U.S.-Israeli strategic cooperation.

7) Prudently sell arms to Arab states. Pro-Western Persian Gulf Arab states have a legitimate need for arms to counter Iran's larger armed forces. The U.S. thus should sell these states appropriate arms. The $30 billion purchase of British arms by the Saudis, announced in mid–1988, demonstrates that Gulf states can turn elsewhere if the U.S. refuses to sell them weapons. At the same time, the new President must take care that U.S. arms sales to the Arabs do not threaten Israel. A way of dealing with this would be to create a coordinating committee composed of the U.S. and its allies who sell weapons to the Persian Gulf states. This committee would be charged with preventing destabilization of the region through unbridled interallied rivalry in arms sales. Such an arrangement existed in the early 1950s following the Tripartite Declaration in which the U.S., Great Britain, and France pledged to restrain arms sales to the Middle East.

8) Keep pressure on Qadhafi. Libya's mercurial Colonel Qadhafi remains a threat to the stability of states friendly to the U.S. such as Chad, Egypt, Sudan, and Tunisia. The State Department should monitor Qadhafi's activities closely, keep existing economic sanctions on Libya, and press U.S. allies to do likewise. Most important, the U.S. should provide increased military and economic aid to the Chadian government to enable Chad to resist Libyan aggression.

9) Encourage Iraqi moderation. The Gulf war has driven Iraqi policy in a direction that serves U.S. interests—support for U.S. friends, Jordan and Egypt, and opposition to Soviet allies, Syria and Libya.

The Secretary of State should encourage Iraq to support the efforts of moderate Arab states to reach a negotiated settlement of the Arab-Israeli conflict and to halt its support of terrorism. U.S. relations with Iraq should be conducted independently of hopes for improved relations with Iran, just as U.S.- Israeli relations are conducted independently of U.S.-Arab relations.

Africa

Nicholas N. Eberstadt*
Task Force Chairman

Africa's importance to the United States has been well chronicled. Africa's 600 million people provide a potentially huge market for U.S. goods and services, and U.S. firms have invested roughly $4 billion in the continent. The treasure house of southern Africa provides cobalt, manganese, vanadium, and other critical minerals on which the U.S. economy and Western defenses depend. Africa controls the sea lanes around the Horn of Africa and the Cape of Good Hope, through which pass the vast majority of the Free World's oil supplies. Politically, Africa's 40-plus nations comprise almost one-third of the votes in the United Nations, and as such, are an important part of the Third World.

The U.S. also has a humanitarian interest in Africa. In part, though only in part, this is represented by the voluntary donations of millions of Americans to aid for the victims of Africa's natural and man-made disasters. More generally, and in keeping with America's political principles, Americans have a preference that Africans live in a free order under the enlightened and humane rule that can make prosperity possible.

———————————◇———————————

THE REAGAN ADMINISTRATION RECORD

During the Carter Administration, newly established pro-Soviet regimes took root in Angola, Ethiopia, and Mozambique, while the pro-Western Ian Smith government in Rhodesia (now known as Zimbabwe) was replaced by that of a self-proclaimed Marxist, Robert Mugabe. And U.S. influence in South Africa was on the wane. The

---

*Commenting and contributing generously to this report were *Mandate III* Task Force Members Jeffrey Gayner, Joachim Maitre, Grover Norquist, Saul Singer, and Melanie Tammen. They do not necessarily endorse all of its views and recommendations.
Task Force Deputy Chairman: William W. Pascoe.

Reagan Administration, led by Assistant Secretary of State for African Affairs Chester A. Crocker, reformulated U.S. policy toward Africa. The Administration decided that a more assertive approach would yield more positive results. In a few areas it has succeeded. The Reagan Administration, working with France, supplied enough material and intelligence to Chad to defeat Libyan dictator Muamar Qadhafi's attempts to annex the northern part of Chad. The U.S. Agency for International Development (AID) attempted to redesign a few of its programs to tie U.S. assistance to free-market policy reforms in recipient African countries. And after five years of pressure from conservatives, early in 1986, the Reagan Administration finally resumed covert military assistance to Jonas Savimbi's National Union for the Total Independence of Angola (UNITA), the democratic resistance force in Angola. Working with U.S.-supplied *Stinger* anti-aircraft and *TOW* anti-tank missiles, UNITA has turned the tables on the Angolan communist forces and their 50,000 Cuban combat troops, forcing the communist regime to engage in negotiations to remove the Cubans.

Elsewhere in Africa, Reagan Administration policy has not worked so well. For a time, the Administration's most significant policy change from the Carter years was in southern Africa. Reagan sought serious diplomatic engagement with all its governments, believing that conflicts in Angola, Mozambique, Namibia, South Africa, and Zimbabwe could be resolved through international negotiations brokered by the U.S. Known as "constructive engagement," this policy overlooked the deep ideological and political differences among the governments involved.

In Mozambique, constructive engagement has meant that the U.S. seeks to use economic and military aid as inducements to wean the Soviet-backed communist Front for the Liberation of Mozambique (FRELIMO) regime away from its close ties to Moscow. Here Crocker has reasoned that if the U.S. can make FRELIMO feel strong, it would see no need to cozy up to the Soviets. The result: the U.S. has sought to bolster FRELIMO by giving it hundreds of millions of dollars of economic assistance and even small amounts of covert military assistance; the anticommunist insurgents of the Mozambique National Resistance—or RENAMO—meanwhile, have received nothing. National reconciliation has failed to move forward. Crocker's policy directly—and apparently deliberately—has ignored the fact that the FRELIMO regime is composed of long-time, hardline Marxist-Leninists; weaning them away from Moscow is surely impossible. In fact, when challenged, Crocker consistently has been unable to cite any example of a communist regime that has ever been weaned from Moscow.

The most notable failure of constructive engagement has, however, been in South Africa. There the policy offered the most hope, but was undermined by Congress before it was given a fair chance to succeed. As originally conceived, constructive engagement for South Africa meant that the U.S., through quiet diplomacy, would press Pretoria into gradually eradicating apartheid. This effort initially prompted Pretoria to scrap such odious apartheid regulations as the Pass Laws, the Mixed Marriages Act, and the Immorality Act.These reforms received little press, public, or congressional attention in the U.S. What was reported by the American press, however, was the civil unrest in South Africa that began in 1983. As the question of American policy toward South Africa became a U.S. domestic political issue, Congress mandated economic and political sanctions against the Pretoria government. This forced Washington to abandon constructive engagement. With the U.S. no longer effectively pressing for reform, the reformers in Pretoria lost what was probably their most important ally, and the hardliners were strengthened. The result: movement toward a less race-based order in South Africa has slowed significantly.

Even well-meaning but ill-conceived U.S. humanitarian activities in Africa have failed. The $400 million in emergency famine aid given to Ethiopia has not been used by that Marxist regime to prevent mass starvation. Instead, famine has been used as a weapon in the regime's war against resistance forces: food aid has been used as bait to lure peasants into resettlement centers.

Beyond constructive engagement, the Reagan Administration has failed to redefine the debate on Africa. In dealing with Africa, the U.S. has adopted a double standard. A government's geopolitical orientation, rather than its own culture, history, and traditions, has become the barometer by which standards are set. Thus, such U.S. friends and pro-Western governments as Kenya, South Africa, and Zaire are held to the standards to which all industrialized democracies subscribe, while all other black African governments are allowed to be judged by lower, nondemocratic standards.

Further, the word "freedom" in Africa continues to refer only to "freedom from rule by a white minority," instead of freedom as it is generally accepted in the West: freedom of the individual, the rule of law, respect for personal property, freedom to assemble, freedom of the press, freedom to oppose the government, freedom to worship, and the freedom to strike. The rationale for this African definition of freedom is the curious assumption that only whites can oppress blacks; by this deceitful logic, blacks are incapable of repressing other blacks. Thus, once an African nation comes under rule by blacks, it is virtually immune to criticism. Yet repression of blacks by their own black African governments is the rule. Examples include Burundian strongman Michel Micombero's 1972 massacre of 150,000 Hutu tribesmen, the additional massacre in 1988 of several thousand Hutu, Idi Amin's brutal reign in Uganda in the 1970s, Robert Mugabe's suppression of dissidents in the Zimbabwean bush in the early 1980s, and the Mozambican FRELIMO regime's "Operation Production," which forcibly expelled hundreds of thousands of Mozambicans from the urban areas in the early 1980s.

--------------------◇--------------------

THE NEXT FOUR YEARS

U.S. policy toward Africa must rest on the premise that Africa deserves and is capable of much more than to date it has attained. U.S. policy must see Africa as a continent with the manpower and resources to enter the twenty-first century as a region that is dynamic, economically thriving, politically stable, and free. To achieve this, African rulers—and the African peoples who allow them to remain in power—must learn the importance of the free market. Only free enterprise can unlock the rich potential of this resource-laden continent. Africa too must understand that stability comes only with the rule of law, respect for the individual, and self-determination, rule by the consent of the governed. Militarily, Africa must recognize that Moscow's embrace is not easily shed and that it is rarely possible to establish a balanced relationship with the Kremlin. It should be the aim of U.S. policy in Africa to work with, encourage, and aid Africans who understand that their societies can grow only if they become politically and economically free.

Increasing Security Assistance to Africa

U.S. budgetary pressures have severely cut foreign assistance. As such, sub-Saharan Africa has seen U.S. security assistance drop from $150 million in 1985 to $25 million in 1988. By contrast, Moscow has poured over $12 billion in military aid into sub-Saharan Africa since 1980—20 times as much as has the U.S. over the same period. This trend must be reversed. Congressional unwillingness to fund Reagan Administration security assistance requests has sent the wrong signals to African leaders about the reliability of the U.S. as a friend. U.S. Military Assistance Programs (MAPs) would reduce the recipients' dependence on Soviet hardware and advisers, thereby lessening Moscow's influence. MAPs also would increase U.S. diplomats' access to African rulers.

The new Administration should submit to Congress a request for full MAP funding for Africa, most recently estimated by the Department of Defense at about $100 million. Among the recipients should be Kenya, Somalia, and Zaire. If the new Administration fails to obtain full MAP funding, it should shift funds from programs elsewhere to those in Africa.

Reestablishing U.S. Influence in South Africa

U.S. economic sanctions against the government of South Africa, imposed by Congress in 1986 over Ronald Reagan's veto, have reduced dramatically the already limited U.S. influence in South Africa. As Western sanctions against Pretoria have stiffened, the South African government, understandably and predictably, has begun exploring a political relationship with Moscow. A Pretoria-Moscow deal is possible. In exchange for a reduction in Soviet support for the African National Congress (ANC) in South Africa and the South West Africa People's Organization (SWAPO) in South West Africa (or Namibia) and for a withdrawal of Soviet-backed Cuban forces from Angola, Pretoria could promise Moscow to exclude the West from South Africa, a region of vital strategic importance which the West always has seen as its own sphere of influence.

The new Administration should preempt this threat by moving rapidly to reestablish U.S. influence in Pretoria. Steps to do this include: the appointment of a confidant of the new President, known and respected by high South African government officials, as Assistant Secretary of State for African Affairs; a determined presidential drive to repeal sanctions legislation because they have failed to undermine apartheid in South Africa and have hurt mainly South Africa's blacks; continued U.S. vetoes in the United Nations Security Council of resolutions mandating comprehensive sanctions against South Africa; increased assistance to the UNITA democratic resistance forces in Angola; efforts to end South Africa's diplomatic isolation; and pressure on the ANC to negotiate with Pretoria.

Empowering Blacks in South Africa

While the new Administration works to reestablish trust and influence in Pretoria, it should make clear that its goal is a multiracial democratic political and economic structure in South Africa. The U.S. should thus encourage a stable transition to a society where merit, rather than race, becomes the determining factor for achievement. A key premise of the new Administration's approach should be that this transition is most likely if there is economic growth. South Africa's recent vigorous economic growth, after all, led Pretoria to ignore its own discriminatory regulations and restrictions, or to scrap them outright. Conversely, economic stagnation seems to intensify the government's race consciousness, and to strengthen those groups that believe the government should protect white living standards at the expense of nonwhites.

In pursuit of its goals in South Africa, the Administration should make special efforts to assist black Africans. It could do so with a policy of black empowerment, based on the belief that blacks in South Africa—though without a vote—nevertheless wield political power in the form of the essential labor they provide their country's economy. U.S. policy should help blacks win more control over the South African economy. To increase black economic power, U.S. assistance programs should be targeted directly at black economic sectors. Too much of the current U.S. assistance, by contrast, goes to political opposition groups. The Secretary of State should design a program through which the U.S., Western Europe, and Japan assist black education, job training, health care, small business development, and housing.

Relevant U.S. government agencies, meanwhile, should provide their own appropriate assistance to South Africa's blacks. The Department of Education and the Peace Corps, for instance, could send black American teachers into the townships of South Africa. The Department of Health and Human Services could help train blacks to provide basic health care services in the townships, where there are relatively few doctors. The Agency for International Development should work with the Department of Commerce to help blacks in South Africa learn the principles of small business development. Private U.S. organizations should be urged to join the effort. The Secretary of Education, for example, should challenge each president of a U.S. college or university to provide one scholarship per year to a black South African student; this would increase by thirtyfold the number of black South Africans studying in the U.S. at no cost to the U.S.

government. The new President also should request the American Federation of Teachers to send experts to train South African black teachers. The Secretary of Labor should challenge major U.S. labor unions to send union organizers to South Africa to help black laborers organize effective and democratic unions. The Secretary of Commerce should challenge such organizations as the U.S. Chamber of Commerce and the National Federation of Independent Businesses to send experts in small business development to South Africa to assist in nuts-and-bolts educational efforts in black areas of South Africa.

Supporting Resistance Movements in Angola and Mozambique

An important success of the Reagan Administration has been its assistance program to the UNITA freedom fighters in Angola. The new Administration should continue this assistance until the communist regime in Angola and its Soviet and Cuban patrons conclude that the war against UNITA is unwinnable and accept the legitimacy of UNITA as a political actor in Angola. The new Administration then should work closely with UNITA leader Jonas Savimbi to fashion a negotiating strategy that leads to true Angolan national reconciliation. The U.S. should make clear that it will continue to assist UNITA forces until free and fair elections have been held by a coalition government working under international supervision.

In Mozambique, by contrast, the new President should abandon the Reagan Administration's naive attempt, directed by Assistant Secretary of State Crocker, to wean away the communist regime from Moscow. Instead, the U.S. should press the Soviet-backed FRELIMO regime to negotiate with the RENAMO rebels for the formation of a coalition government to hold free elections. If FRELIMO refuses to negotiate seriously, the U.S. should assist RENAMO under terms of the Liberation Doctrine. (See Liberation Doctrine section of this chapter.)

Redefining the Debate on Africa

For too long, guilt has driven U.S. policies toward Africa: guilt about U.S.involvement in the slave trade over a century ago, guilt about the manner in which black Americans were treated after the end of slavery, guilt about the general economic and political success of Western democracies in the face of political instability and economic privation throughout the Third World.

Western governments have allowed themselves to be forced to

respond to an agenda set by radicals who play on this guilt. That agenda calls for never-ending economic assistance from the West to African governments and increasingly shrill demands for writing off the $110 billion in debts owed by African governments to Western banks and governments.

The U.S. must change the nature of this debate. The new Assistant Secretary of State for African Affairs, working with the new administrator of AID, should announce publicly early in the new Administration that new premises will underlie U.S. policy toward Africa. These two officials should use their bully pulpits to focus media and academic attention on this new set of premises. These premises should be: Africa is failing because its own leaders have made serious mistakes by choosing state socialist economic systems over free enterprise; Africa is capable of democracy; Africa is not destined to be poor forever, and it can lift itself out of poverty by changing the policies pursued by its governments; Africa can legitimately be criticized for the economic and political mistakes it has made; Africa cannot delude itself into believing that Western governments will provide vast amounts of unconditional economic assistance in perpetuity; and it is morally wrong to depend forever on the largess of others or to hold one's population hostage for foreign ransom.

Linking U.S. Aid to Free Market Reforms in Africa

The Assistant Secretary of State for African Affairs and the AID administrator should base U.S. aid policy on the promotion of grassroots capitalism. Bankrupt by socialism (a fact that almost all African leaders admit privately and a few publicly), African nations desperately need to return to their free-market heritage. AID should devise an Index of Economic Freedom to judge the incentives created by African governments for their citizens to work, save, and invest. (See Chapter 27.)

African agriculture's decline throughout the 1970s and 1980s is now widely understood to have been caused in large part by the African governments' state marketing boards. These set the official and only price at which farmers may sell their crops. Often this price is far below what the crops would fetch on a free market. Farmers predictably have responded by selling their products in black markets or smuggling them across a border where they can get far higher prices. Often, however, farmers conclude that it does not pay them to produce goods for sale, and as a result, they revert to subsistence agriculture or leave the land entirely to join the urban swell.

With the aid of an Index of Economic Freedom, the AID administrator should announce that the U.S. no longer will assist African governments that continue to block agricultural progress through state-imposed producer prices and government buying monopolies. Nigeria and Senegal, in fact, have eliminated their state marketing boards. Countries continuing to ignore those measures that encourage economic freedom and economic growth should have their aid levels cut. The new Administration together with Washington's European allies should champion truly market-oriented economic reform in an attempt to move the World Bank away from making "policy" loans. Ostensibly, such loans are for the reform of Africa's state-owned agencies and industries, but in fact, they merely perpetuate them. The best market-oriented return that Western countries could provide for Africa, of course, would be to lower their trade barriers against products and services from Africa. (See Chapters 9 and 27.)

Strengthening U.S. Relations with Kenya, Somalia, and Zaire

Kenya, Somalia, and Zaire play an essential role in promoting and defending U.S. interests in Africa: Kenya and Somalia give U.S. naval forces access to strategic facilities, from which U.S. forces patrol the geostrategically vital sea lanes around the Horn of Africa, through which passes most of the Free World's oil; Zaire, it is widely believed, allows U.S. military aid for UNITA in Angola to pass through its territory, thereby making it unnecessary for the U.S. to seek South African cooperation. As open U.S. friends in a continent where this is rare, these governments have come under attack from within and without. The U.S. must recognize the significance of these nations' contributions to U.S. defense operations in the region and take steps to help ease their economic and security problems.

In Kenya, the new Administration should increase military aid to Nairobi to offset the threat posed to the Kenyan government by Libyan dictator Qadhafi and his Ugandan ally, Yoweri Museveni. The new Administration should press for further free market reforms by the Kenyan government to help spur job creation and economic growth.

In Somalia, the new Administration should increase U.S. military assistance to the Siad Barre government, which currently faces a serious challenge from Ethiopian-backed rebels in the north. At the same time, the U.S. should criticize human rights violations if they occur. Military aid should be increased from its current level, $5.5 million, to from $25 million to $30 million. In exchange for this increased assistance, Washington access to naval facilities at Berbera should be extended beyond 1990, when the agreement providing this access expires.

In Zaire, the new Administration should work to ease the government's debt crisis. The new Administration also should press the communist Angolan regime to stop threatening the Mobutu government, if Mobutu continues to aid UNITA; the U.S. should be prepared to come to the aid of Zaire in the event of an attack by communist forces from Angola.

—————————————◇—————————————

INITIATIVES FOR 1989

1) Set new conditions for U.S. emergency famine assistance. Ethiopia and Mozambique deliberately have exacerbated their famines to resettle populations so as to remove local support networks for insurgents. In both cases, the U.S. has provided generous assistance in the hope that it would save lives. The record shows, however, that the deliberate misuse of U.S. famine assistance by Ethiopia and Mozambique actually increased the death toll. To prevent this tragedy from recurring, new conditions should be set for future U.S. emergency famine assistance programs. The AID administrator should announce that to qualify for U.S. assistance: 1) the recipient government must not obstruct relief efforts and should provide all assistance possible to transport the aid to areas where it is needed, including free port docking and unloading; 2) food distribution must be allowed to be handled entirely by international organizations and kept separate from the distribution network of the recipient government; and 3) the recipient government must adhere to the principles of impartiality and nondiscrimination that are expected to guide all disaster relief efforts.

2) Terminate humanitarian assistance to regimes that ignore these conditions. The vast majority of the victims of the Ethiopian famine of 1984–85 actually died of diseases contracted in resettlement centers. Those who survived were forcibly removed to provinces far from their homes. Thus, U.S. famine assistance, though well-intentioned, actually made the U.S. an accomplice to the genocide committed by the Ethiopian regime. This must not happen again. Governments requesting U.S. emergency famine assistance must understand that they will receive aid only under the conditions cited above. To continue to assist a government unwilling to agree to these conditions would again make the U.S. an accomplice to genocide. The Secretary of State and the AID administrator should state these conditions clearly at the start of the new Administration.

3) Upgrade the quality of U.S. intelligence on Africa. For too long, U.S. intelligence agencies have depended for information about Africa on European and South African intelligence organizations. Consequently, U.S. intelligence agencies did not recruit and train sufficient agents of their own in African leadership circles. Now that European influence in Africa is greatly reduced (and hence, European intelligence lacking) and the U.S. is prohibited by law from cooperating with South Africa's intelligence services, there is a severe deficiency in the quantity and quality of U.S. intelligence on the region. To close this intelligence gap, the Central Intelligence Agency, the Defense Intelligence Agency, and the State Department must increase their capabilities, paying particular attention to placing language-certified specialists in the field. Recruitment of black Americans to serve as case officers in Africa should be increased, and incentives provided, for learning important tribal languages and local history. (See Chapter 25.)

4) Toughen U.S. policy toward communist regimes in Africa. The new Administration should abandon the Reagan Administration's policy, designed by Assistant Secretary of State Crocker, of attempting to wean away Mozambique's FRELIMO regime from its close ties to the Soviet Union. The new Administration should pressure FRELIMO to negotiate with RENAMO, the anticommunist rebels. In Angola, the Administration should increase diplomatic and military pressure on the MPLA regime.

5) Block congressional attempts to impose sanctions on South Africa. To reduce damage to black economic fortunes in South Africa, the new President should block new congressional attempts to impose sanctions on South Africa. Blocking new sanctions will make it easier to shift the debate on South Africa from imposing sanctions at all to promoting black empowerment.

The Liberation Doctrine

Jack Wheeler*
Task Force Chairman

The Liberation Doctrine is an action plan to challenge and roll back the Soviet Empire. It builds upon many of Ronald Reagan's policies and actions which collectively have been known as the Reagan Doctrine. The Soviet Empire has been built gradually, over decades, as Soviet leaders patiently and consistently have taken advantage of opportunities for expansion.

In abstract terms, the Soviet Empire is composed of nations in a series of concentric circles, each distinguishable by two variables—chronology and geography—with the circles expanding outward. The smaller circles contain those states closest to the Russian heartland, which have been part of the empire for the longest period of time. Looking at the Soviet Empire in this way, the first circle holds ethnic territories that gained independence after the Bolshevik Revolution but later were annexed by Moscow between 1919 and 1921. These states include the territories now known as the Armenian Republic, the Georgian Republic, and the Ukrainian Republic.

The second circle contains those states over which the USSR gained control as a result of Moscow's 1939 alliance with Adolf Hitler: Estonia, Lithuania, Latvia, and Moldavia.

Moving outward, the third circle of the Soviet Empire contains those nations subjugated by Moscow as a result of Stalin's violations of the Yalta and Potsdam agreements and of the West's refusal to counter his moves, as well as the success of the Cuban revolution in 1959. This third circle forms the core of Moscow's Central/Eastern European empire, and includes Bulgaria, Czechoslovakia, East Germany, Hungary, Poland, and Romania, as well as the Kurile Islands, taken from Japan, and Cuba.

The fourth and outermost circle contains those nations pulled into

---

*Commenting and contributing generously to this report were *Mandate III* Task Force Members Richard Fisher, James Lucier, and Charles Moser. They do not necessarily endorse all of its views and recommendations.
Task Force Deputy Chairman: William W. Pascoe.

the Soviet Empire during the 1970s, when the United States retreat from the world gave Moscow its greatest opportunity for expansion since the 1945–1948 period. In terms of its geographical proximity and importance to Moscow, this fourth circle is the frontier of the Empire. It includes, in the order in which these nations were brought into the Empire, South Yemen, Vietnam, Mozambique, Angola, Laos, Cambodia, Ethiopia, Nicaragua, and Afghanistan. Grenada was inside the circle until liberated by U.S. forces in October 1983.

Though some U.S. leaders, notably Dwight Eisenhower's Secretary of State, John Foster Dulles, at times called for the "rollback" of the Soviet Empire, and others, notably John Kennedy, actually supported freedom fighters seeking to liberate their nations from communist tyranny, Ronald Reagan has been the first U.S. President to proclaim a rationale for worldwide U.S. assistance to resistance movements fighting Soviet-backed communist regimes. This U.S. assistance is what has been called the "Reagan Doctrine," though Reagan himself has not used the term. It is rooted firmly in the Truman Doctrine of the late 1940s, which saved Greece, Turkey, and other European nations from falling under Soviet rule.

The Liberation Doctrine would continue and even expand the Reagan Doctrine. It would offer hope for those nations in each of the Soviet Empire's concentric circles. The means by which the Liberation Doctrine is executed and its immediate goals differ for each circle. What help is realistic and appropriate for the U.S. to offer freedom fighters in Afghanistan, Angola, and Nicaragua is unrealistic for Poland, Latvia, or Armenia. For each circle, however, the U.S. must have an appropriate policy.

Ronald Reagan's policies have changed the nature of struggle in the Third World. Today in Afghanistan, Angola, Cambodia, Ethiopia, Laos, Mozambique, Nicaragua, and Vietnam, anti-Soviet insurgents are fighting repressive Soviet-backed regimes. This is a drastic change in the nature of Third World guerrilla warfare, which for three decades following World War II primarily had seen Soviet-backed communist guerrillas battling against Western-oriented nations and succeeding in creating the Empire's fourth circle.

But the fourth circle is not the only one in which Soviet control today is challenged. Ferment roils the Soviet colonies of Central/Eastern Europe. Never having accepted the legitimacy of the regimes imposed upon them by Moscow, Czechs are protesting for religious freedom, Hungarians for democracy, East Germans for the right to emigrate, and Polish students for academic freedom. These protests take place in an atmosphere of political uncertainty. Soviet control is being challenged even in the second and first circles. Hundreds of thousands of people demonstrate in the Soviet "republics" of Armenia and Azerbaijan over old territorial claims. Muslims in the Central Asian republics have demonstrated for religious freedom. Estonians have created the National Front, the closest thing to a second political party in the Soviet Union since 1917.

The ultimate goal of the Liberation Doctrine should be to dismantle the Soviet Empire, allowing the hundreds of millions of its inhabitants a chance for national self-determination. Two fundamental purposes would be served: bringing self-determination to peoples long denied it, and enhancing Western security.

Strategically, the Liberation Doctrine should aim first to reduce sharply Moscow's ability to exploit many of its geopolitical gains of the 1970s. It challenges one of the central elements of the Soviet belief system, the so-called Brezhnev Doctrine, which proclaimed in 1968 that, once a nation falls under communist domination, it must remain there forever. In the struggle for the allegiance of Third World leaders, the Brezhnev Doctrine seemed to confirm Moscow's boast that the global correlation of forces had shifted toward the USSR. If true, it would mean that Third World societies had little chance of resisting Soviet intimidation and control. The Liberation Doctrine challenge, especially in the case of Grenada and possibly Afghanistan, has refuted the Brezhnev Doctrine. This is of immense geopolitical significance.

―――――――――――◇―――――――――――

THE REAGAN ADMINISTRATION RECORD

When Reagan took office, the U.S. was providing assistance to only one resistance movement: the Afghan *mujahideen*. By 1986, the U.S. was helping armed resistance movements in Afghanistan, Angola, Cambodia, and Nicaragua. With this assistance, which has included sophisticated anti-aircraft and anti-tank missiles, the resistance groups have fought their better-armed opponents to a standstill in Angola and Nicaragua; the Afghan *mujahideen* even have forced Moscow to announce its intention to withdraw the Red Army from Afghanistan—the first time since World War II that Soviet troops were defeated. If Soviet troops complete their withdrawal from Afghanistan as scheduled, and a noncommunist Afghanistan emerges, this will be a tremendous psychological as well as military blow to Moscow.

Further, by creating Radio Marti—the highly successful radio station modeled after Radio Free Europe—the Reagan Administration has encouraged political opposition in Castro's Cuba. Very quietly, the Reagan Administration also has helped another third-circle resistance movement. Since 1985, the Administration has given the outlawed Polish trade union Solidarity and other Polish opposition groups financial aid, as well as assistance in smuggling critical publications, printing machinery, radio equipment, and video cassettes into Poland.

By putting Moscow on the defensive throughout the Third World, the Reagan Administration almost surely has prevented Moscow from bringing any additional states into its Empire.

In Nicaragua, however, U.S. policy has floundered. The on-again, off-again military support provided to the resistance forces as a result of continuing presidential-congressional feuding and the woeful lack of White House leadership beginning in mid–1987, combined with the relatively low sophistication of the military hardware provided by the U.S., has not given the Nicaraguan freedom fighters the means to liberate their nation.

More important than its shortcomings in one country, the Reagan Doctrine's main problem has been the tepid support it has received from most of the State Department. Accustomed to doing business with governments as they are, and always leery of changes in the status quo, the State Department has resisted supporting freedom fighter movements throughout the Third World. This has made it difficult for the Administration to articulate the Doctrine's importance to the American public and to build adequate support for it, which would have yielded more congressional support.

Disappointing too has been the Reagan Administration's failure to assist resistance movements fighting Soviet-backed regimes in such places as Ethiopia and Laos. And the Administration has not designated a single high official with responsibility to execute the Doctrine. Without a principal advocate to push for its implementation by all branches of the government, the Reagan Doctrine became lost in the bureaucratic mazes of Washington.

———————◇———————

THE NEXT FOUR YEARS

A Liberation Doctrine, building on and expanding the Reagan Doctrine, offers hope to the Third World: its very thesis rejects the inevitability of victory by Soviet-style totalitarianism and posits a future where freedom, not communism, reigns throughout the Third

World. The U.S., as the premier defender of liberty in today's world, has an obligation to assist those struggling for freedom and against Soviet domination around the world. Simultaneously, the Liberation Doctrine seeks to deny Moscow the use of the geostrategic assets in its empire, such as access to airfields and naval facilities in Angola, Cuba, Ethiopia, Mozambique, Nicaragua, and South Yemen. The Liberation Doctrine serves the dual ends of enhancing Western security and expanding the boundaries of freedom.

Articulating the Strategic Vision of the Liberation Doctrine

The new President should articulate the strategic vision of the doctrine: the eventual dismantling of the Soviet Empire. Congress, the press, and the American public must be told of how people around the world benefit when the Brezhnev Doctrine's insistence on the irreversibility of communist gains is proved false. Without the mystique of irreversibility, the Soviets will have to compete for influence around the world on the unfamiliar, inhospitable terrain of economic and political systems.

To articulate this strategic vision, the new President and his principal foreign policy advisers should include in all major foreign policy addresses an explanation of the background and significance of the Liberation Doctrine. In all cases, the Soviet Empire should be labeled as such, and all references to Soviet "satellites" should be changed to Soviet "colonies." The Doctrine should be made the principal focus of White House events on the various national days of those states swallowed into the Soviet Empire; representatives of these states living in exile should be invited to meet with the President and then jointly address groups of supporters at the White House. The President's Fourth of July message should cite those struggling for freedom and independence for their own nations, and recommit the U.S. to the expansion of liberty around the world.

Institutionalizing the Liberation Doctrine

A primary problem in executing the Liberation Doctrine had been the unwillingness of the State Department, the CIA, and other key agencies to use the opportunities afforded by resistance movements around the world. To remedy this, the new President should create a Resistance Support Agency (RSA) at sub-Cabinet level with sufficient authority to execute the Liberation Doctrine. Its director should be confirmed by the Senate to ensure a measure of congressional over-sight and should be a close confidant of the President to indicate the seriousness with which the President views this office. The RSA director should be made a statutory member of the National Security Council, and a representative of the RSA should chair meetings of all interagency task forces formed to establish policy for Liberation Doctrine target nations.

Making the Reagan Doctrine a Liberation Doctrine

The U.S. should provide assistance under the terms of the Liberation Doctrine to anti-Soviet insurgencies operating against regimes that are Marxist-Leninist in political structure, de facto or actual military allies of Moscow, or threatening their neighbors. Meeting these criteria are the communist regimes in Ethiopia, Laos, Mozambique, and Nicaragua. As such, the resistance movements fighting them merit U.S. help.

Perhaps more important, the new Administration should begin thinking of extending the Liberation Doctrine toward the inner circles of the Soviet Empire. The new Administration should ask how the U.S. can best encourage political freedom fighters operating in Eastern Europe, or even inside the Soviet Union itself. Genuine liberalization would inevitably begin the unraveling of the Soviet Empire. The new Administration must not assume that it has a monopoly on fresh ideas to support democratic forces. The director of the Resistance Support Agency should encourage the AFL-CIO, U.S. Chamber of Commerce, and Departments of Education and of Labor, among others, to identify ways to aid democratic forces. The AFL-CIO, for instance, could train East European dissident leaders in union organization, while the Department of Education could funnel pamphlets outlining the virtues of self-determination into selected areas.

Clearly, the level and kind of U.S. assistance to armed resistance movements fighting in the fourth circle would not be appropriate to provide in the third or second circle. But there are actions that can be taken by the U.S. Government to encourage political movements fighting for self-determination in the inner circles of the Soviet Empire. In the third circle, the Soviet colonies of Central/Eastern Europe and Cuba, the U.S. should intensify its programs to encourage democracy, national independence, and unreliability among Warsaw Pact armed forces. Over time, this would make it more difficult for Moscow to invade, as it did in Czechoslovakia in 1968, one of its wavering Central/ Eastern European satellites. The U.S. should facilitate communications among dissidents throughout Central/Eastern Europe, enabling them to plan joint activities and act in concert. The U.S. should increase its efforts to establish ties with leaders of the various underground and overt dissident movements and should encourage protests. The U.S. government should make public demands on Moscow further to reduce its control of Central/Eastern Europe. The new Administration should issue statements of support for East European strikers and protesters, even as the President presses Moscow to allow free trade unions, to adhere to human rights standards, and to create democracy.

Within the second circle, containing such nations as Latvia and Lithuania, U.S. policy must be even more circumspect and long-term. Here the Liberation Doctrine should take into account long simmering religious and nationalistic disputes. At the June 1988 All-Union Soviet Party Conference, for instance, delegates from Estonia demanded economic autonomy for their republic. The new U.S. Administration should support this strongly, publicly and privately, and should stress to Moscow the significance of this issue. The new Administration also should press Moscow to allow new political organizations to challenge Communist Party hegemony in the Baltic states.

Recent developments inside the USSR indicate that many of the national groups absorbed inside the Soviet Empire are not permanently reconciled to their fate. Example: at the June 1988 All-Union Soviet Party Conference, delegates from Estonia demanded economic autonomy for their "republic." The tensions between Armenia and Azerbaijan over disputed territory reveal that what is at issue is not simply a dispute between provinces of the same nation (as, say, a squabble over territory between Indiana and Ohio) but a conflict between different nations.

The new President should request his top advisers to develop a comprehensive U.S. response to these important developments inside the USSR. Such a plan should use all appropriate U.S. resources to encourage a full flow of information to nationalistic elements and effective communication between them. The objective should be to encourage decentralization, as well as strengthening of independent national identities.

To erode further Moscow's control, Radio Liberty should increase its native language broadcasts into the first circle of the Soviet Empire. Private and official operatives should smuggle into these captive nations books in their native languages, highlighting the differences between the peoples of these nations and the people of Russia.

The Liberation Doctrine also should take advantage of the religious revival inside the Soviet Union. The new Administration should smuggle Bibles across the Soviet frontier, in at least a dozen languages, to give Soviet believers books long unavailable.

The new Administration also should seek to exploit Muslim fundamentalism in the Central Asian republics of Kazakhstan, Kirghizia, Tadzhikistan, Turkmenia, and Uzbekistan. This could be accomplished by using experienced Afghan *mujahideen* to smuggle millions of *Korans* across the Afghan-Soviet border. These same *mujahideen*, who have fought the Red Army to a standstill, could also assist Soviet citizens in the Central Asian republics in organizing underground political movements.

<hr>

INITIATIVES FOR 1989

1) Support a Freedom Fighter Assistance Bill. The new Administration should work with Congress to enact a Freedom Fighter Assistance Bill mandating: creation of the Resistance Support Agency (RSA), whose responsibility would be to coordinate execution of the Liberation Doctrine by appropriate federal bureaucracies; the Director of the RSA to be a presidential appointee, confirmed by the Senate, who will sit on the National Security Council; and establishment of a Resistance Support Fund of $1 billion per year with which the Administration could support resistance movements. Nothing in this legislation should preclude the extension of overt or covert U.S. assistance to any resistance movement through any other channels deemed more appropriate by the President.

2) Define a clear objective for each resistance movement. The new Administration should immediately define its objectives for each of the resistance movements receiving U.S. aid and then establish and assign tasks to accomplish the objectives.

In Afghanistan, the new Administration should set as its goal the removal of all Red Army troops and the establishment of an independent, noncommunist Afghan government. Toward this end, U.S. military assistance to the Afghan *mujahideen* should continue as long as Soviet assistance to the communist regime in Kabul continues. (See Afghanistan section of this chapter.)

In Nicaragua, the new Administration should set as its goal a genuine peace that brings democracy, military force reduction, and an end to Soviet bloc military involvement in Nicaragua, leading to an independent noncommunist government. Toward this end, the new Administration should seek renewed military funding for the Nicaraguan Democratic Resistance forces to enable them to liberate Nicaragua from the communist Sandinista regime. (See Mexico, Central America, and the Caribbean section of this chapter.)

In Angola, the new Administration should set as its goal the removal of the estimated 50,000 Cuban combat troops and the fulfillment of the 1975 Alvor accords, which promised free elections in Angola. U.S. officials should insist that the current four-party negotiations, which include the U.S., South Africa, Angola, and Cuba, be expanded to include a delegation from the National Union for the Total Independence of Angola (UNITA). The U.S. also should make clear that U.S. military assistance to UNITA will continue until all Cuban troops have left Angola, the communist MPLA regime has stopped receiving weapons from Moscow, and free elections have been held with UNITA as a participant. (See Africa section of this chapter.)

In Cambodia, the new Administration should set as its goal the removal of all 140,000 Vietnamese combat troops and the establishment of an independent, noncommunist Cambodian government. Working with the Southeast Asian nations of ASEAN and with China, the U.S. should increase assistance to noncommunist Cambodian resistance forces. (See Asia section of this chapter.)

In Mozambique, the new Administration should set as its goal direct negotiations between the FRELIMO communist regime and the RENAMO insurgents to end their 12–year conflict and establish an independent, noncommunist Mozambican government. If FRELIMO refuses to negotiate, the new U.S. Administration should consider providing Liberation Doctrine assistance to RENAMO. (See Africa section of this chapter.)

In Central/Eastern Europe, the U.S. strategy of achieving national self-determination and democracy for the peoples of the region should include three components. First, the U.S. should assist overtly and covertly the democratic anticommunist opposition. Second, the U.S. should link its relations with Central/Eastern European regimes to their domestic policies, rewarding political relaxation, independence from the Soviet Union, and economic decentralization and privatization; at the same time, resurgence of Stalinism should be countered and punished. Finally, Moscow must be made to pay an increasingly greater price for its continuing denial of national self-determination to the peoples of Central/Eastern Europe; Soviet policies in the region should be a key determinant of the scope of Western economic and political cooperation. (See Central/Eastern Europe section of this chapter.)

3) Launch a public diplomacy campaign to build support for the Liberation Doctrine. Congress, the press, and the American public must understand the value of the Liberation Doctrine, just as the U.S. came to rally behind the Truman Doctrine. The new President, Secretaries of State and Defense, U.S. Ambassador to the United Nations, and Director of the newly created Resistance Support Agency should coordinate efforts in a public diplomacy campaign. Among other things, this campaign should include an Oval Office meeting between resistance movement leaders and the President and his top advisers, press conferences with these resistance leaders, TV interviews with resistance leaders and Administration officials, meetings of the editorial boards of the nation's top newspapers with these resistance leaders and Administration officials, introduction of U.N. resolutions, and presidential speeches at such symbolic sites as the Jefferson Memorial, New York and San Francisco harbors, Miami, and the U.S.-Mexican border. (See Public Diplomacy section of this chapter.)

4) Demonstrate presidential support for the Liberation Doctrine. To demonstrate his commitment to the Liberation Doctrine, whatever Congress does, the new President could break diplomatic relations with the communist governments of Afghanistan, Ethiopia, Laos, Mozambique, or Nicaragua; recognize resistance governments in Afghanistan, Angola, Ethiopia, or Nicaragua.

Human Rights

Charles H. Fairbanks, Jr.*
Task Force Chairman

The Declaration of Independence is testament to the faith of America's Founding Fathers in the inherent human right to life, liberty, and the pursuit of happiness. Human rights are not limited by national or ethnic boundaries, but are "self-evident" in the universal Rights of Man. Faith in this principle is embodied in the United States Constitution, which recognizes that tyranny, arbitrary by nature, never can provide adequate assurance against the abuse of its own power.

Today, as two centuries ago, tyranny in the world is the principal impediment to universal human rights. Yet tyrannies, in recent decades, have labored to capture the term "human rights." During the 1970s, a loose coalition of Soviet bloc and Third World dictatorships used its United Nations majority to redefine the Rights of Man. New "rights" were invented, and from them a set of political axioms was deduced that justified such human rights abuses as press censorship and repression of religious liberty.

The U.S. was founded for the purpose of advancing human freedom and dignity. These values are grounded in Western political and religious traditions. U.S. policy cannot permit those values to be cut loose from their moorings and redefined by tyrannical regimes seeking to further their own agenda. Totalitarian and dictatorial regimes cannot be considered partners in the struggle for international human rights. They are the source of the problem.

———————◇———————

THE REAGAN ADMINISTRATION RECORD

The Carter Administration policies bolstered attempts by the U.N. and others to redefine human rights. The annual State Department

---

*Commenting and contributing generously to this report were *Mandate III* Task Force Members Gerald Canbee, James Ciccone, Jay Kosminsky, and Joshua Muravchik. They do not necessarily endorse all of its views and recommendations.

Task Force Deputy Chairman: Heritage Salvatori Fellow in Soviet Studies Leon Aron.

Country Reports on Human Rights Practices, initiated by the Carter Administration, stressed the "economic and social rights" criteria of the U.N. more than the civil and political rights that had been the traditional focus of American concern. The Reagan Administration wisely has reversed the Carter emphasis, removing economic and social rights as a category of human rights from the State Department's annual human rights reports, emphasizing instead political and civil rights. Other Reagan Administration changes in the human rights report have included dropping the vague criterion of "political participation," and replacing it with "citizens' right to change their government." "Political participation" is a formulation welcomed by dictatorial regimes because it is open to broad interpretation. The formulation "citizens' right to change their government" is a more exacting standard of true political participation, measuring the ultimate power of individuals against the power of government.

The Reagan Administration has pursued a two-track human rights policy: casework to help individual victims of human rights violations and a larger effort to encourage democracy. It was this second track that Ronald Reagan emphasized in a major 1982 address on human rights to the British Parliament, in which he reaffirmed America's active commitment to the historical struggle for freedom and democracy against the forces of tyranny. In line with its efforts to encourage democracy, the Administration sparked the 1983 creation of the National Endowment for Democracy, which may be one of the Administration's greatest institutional legacies. The NED is an independent corporation established by congressional charter to help further democratic movements worldwide. The Administration also has increased its direct contacts through U.S. embassies with democratic groups in Central/Eastern Europe.

The Administration has pursued human rights in international forums, including the U.N., where U.S. delegates have exposed and condemned human rights violations of totalitarian regimes. Responding to three years of relentless American effort, for example, a U.N. committee decided in 1988 to investigate human rights abuses in Cuba.

The Reagan Administration has avoided what had become the Carter Administration's public handwringing at the expense of effective policy. Thus the Reagan Administration successfully encouraged and helped manage complex transitions to democracy in El Salvador, the Philippines, and South Korea. By working to help create or sustain genuinely democratic opposition forces in countries with pro-American authoritarian regimes, the U.S. has not repeated such costly Carter era blunders as acquiescing to the replacement of authoritarian regimes in Nicaragua and Iran with the brutal Sandinistas and ayatollahs. Understanding that human rights abuses are grounded in the political system, the Reagan Administration has given high priority to preventing communist regimes from coming to power in El Salvador and elsewhere and from keeping power in Afghanistan, Angola, Cambodia, and Nicaragua.

Yet the Administration has missed significant opportunities to help undermine such human rights violators as the regimes in Ethiopia and South Yemen. The Administration too has winked at some human rights abuses in the People's Republic of China, even when Beijing repressed popular demonstrations in Tibet. Nor has the Reagan Administration used much American leverage to expose and oppose the human rights violations of Soviet bloc states, in particular Poland and Romania. Example: the Administration continued until 1988 to grant Most Favored Nation trade status to Romania, which is ruled by Central/Eastern Europe's most brutal dictator, Nicolae Ceausescu. The annual State Department human rights reports, meanwhile, often have failed to cite human rights abuses by such nongovernmental terrorist organizations as the Palestine Liberation Organization, the Irish Republican Army, or the Tamil Tigers in Sri Lanka.

———————————◇———————————

THE NEXT FOUR YEARS

The U.S. needs a sustained, consistent approach to encourage governments to take responsibility for correcting human rights violations and developing democratic institutions of government. This requires weighing several criteria for determining the appropriate level of U.S. response to human rights violations. Criteria should include:

◆ The nature of the violations—systematic and egregious violations of human rights such as mass population transfers or enforced famine may require immediate attention.

◆ The costs to the U.S. of injecting itself into a human rights struggle, with special attention to U.S. security interests.

◆ The domestic situation in the country in question, including the political orientation and viability of opposition groups.

◆ The possibility of a democratic political system taking root.

◆ The likely course of events if the U.S. takes no steps on behalf of human rights or other measures.

◆ American public support for U.S. actions.

Case-by-case decisions should be made with the understanding that U.S. action in support of democratic pluralism and respect for human rights must be approached with prudence and with a realistic assessment of the chances for success. As Iran and Nicaragua painfully demonstrate, chances for democracy and human rights improvements are not always increased by overthrowing an authoritarian ruler, but may at times be better advanced by strategies designed to pressure existing regimes.

Above all, U.S. policy should be guided by an ethic of result, not an ethic of intention. The objective should be to foster concrete improvements in human rights, not to make policymakers feel virtuous.

Developing Strategies for the Transition to Democracy

In cases in which the U.S. does help precipitate the downfall of a nondemocratic government, the U.S. must be prepared to be engaged actively over the long run to encourage the development of democracy. American engagement during and after the fall of Philippine strongman Marcos must be the model, not American renunciation of influence when the Shah and Somoza fell. The Secretary of State should require the Assistant Secretary of State for Human Rights and Humanitarian Affairs to develop a general strategy for such involvement, including such measures as assistance in creating democratic institutions at national and local levels; help in economic reforms, including privatization of state-owned holdings and guaranteeing private property rights; and economic, educational, health, and other assistance carried out, where possible, in conjunction with other democracies.

Renewing the Commitment to the National Endowment for Democracy

The National Endowment for Democracy (NED) was established in 1983 to expand democratic institutions worldwide. While NED now enjoys significant bipartisan support, its funding falls short of its mandate. Its budget has slipped from the $31.3 million authorized in 1983 to a $16.9 million appropriation in 1988.

The new President should direct his Office of Management and Budget to prepare budget requests restoring NED funding to its 1983 level, plus some additional funds to allow NED to continue to test the sincerity of the newly proclaimed policy of *glasnost'* in Central/Eastern Europe and the Soviet Union.

Mobilizing Societal Forces for Reform

In some instances, U.S. human rights efforts have concentrated primarily on state-to-state relations, while neglecting churches, dissident groups, local business communities, and other societal forces that can erode oppressive, antidemocratic practices. U.S. policy for human rights could achieve more than it has by encouraging the action of private forces. Not only the U.S. government, but many diverse elements of American society can work effectively for human rights.

U.S. diplomats, for their part, have had a long-standing policy of contact with reform-minded groups in areas such as Latin America and South Africa. In the Middle East and elsewhere in Africa, U.S. diplomats need greater awareness of opposition currents.

While U.S. diplomats must be circumspect in contacting dissident groups, the U.S. can provide them with material support through other means. For example, last year Congress appropriated $1 million for the banned Polish independent trade union Solidarity. The National Endowment for Democracy also has provided Solidarity with financial support which has been used to provide such items as printing presses and radio equipment. The Assistant Secretary of State for Human Rights should identify other groups that might benefit from such aid. (See Central/Eastern Europe section of this chapter.) The President and other high Administration officials should encourage private U.S. philanthropies to increase their own support to human rights activists and reform-minded groups in nondemocratic countries.

Seizing the Offensive in the Human Rights Debate

Regimes with collectivist ideologies, such as Marxism/Leninism, have sought to control the terms of the human rights debate by focusing on alleged social and economic "rights" to the exclusion of such political rights as freedoms of assembly, speech, and the press. In so doing, they seek to distract attention from their own violations of human rights. Ironically, they continue to do so despite their social and economic failures.

U.S. representatives in the international arena, from the President down, should take the initiative in shaping the terms of the human rights debate. The Secretary of State should direct U.S. ambassadors and negotiators at such international forums as the U.N. to adhere to a standard that holds up individual liberties and political rights as the sine qua non of a government's human rights record. They should stress, for example, that "human rights" in the most fundamental sense refers to the inalienable immunization of an individual against the power of the state. They should reject the argument that alleged "economic and civil and social rights" can compensate for a loss of civil and political rights, counter with the fact that a system based on liberty meets employment, housing, and other human needs better than does a system that denies liberty. Examples: West Germany vs. East Germany, South Korea vs. North Korea, South Vietnam (until 1975) vs. North Vietnam, and the Republic of China on Taiwan vs. the People's Republic of China.

Expanding the Reagan Doctrine

The Reagan Doctrine has promoted human rights in two ways. First, by assisting anticommunist insurgencies, the U.S. directly challenges regimes that have been some of the globe's worst human rights violators. Second, American involvement with anticommunist resistance forces gives the U.S. crucial leverage to influence the human rights practices of resistance groups and their policies once a victory is achieved. (See Liberation Doctrine section of this chapter.) The new President should expand the Reagan Doctrine into a Liberation Doctrine that not only continues to fight repressive regimes in Afghanistan, Angola, Cambodia, and Nicaragua, but remains alert to opportunities to carry the fight to other vulnerable Marxist-Leninist regimes.

————————◇————————

INITIATIVES FOR 1989

1) Publicize criteria to judge short-term policy effectiveness. The American public's support for U.S. human rights policies will depend in large measure on how well the new Administration conveys its objectives and the prospects for their realization. In cases such as South Africa, there is a wide gap between the ultimate American objective— the end of the apartheid system—and the kinds of successes that can be expected in one-to-four years. The Assistant Secretary for Human Rights and Humanitarian Affairs should be asked to prepare, in some cases, a list of short-term human rights objectives to serve as criteria of policy success on the road to the ultimate objective. By establishing criteria by which progress can be judged, American idealism can be engaged in support of realistic strategies of change.

2) Set goals for U.S. participation in the Helsinki process. The final act of the 1975 Helsinki agreement binds its signatories, including the

Soviet Union, to "respect human rights and fundamental freedoms." The results of the Helsinki process thus far have been mixed. Positive change in Soviet bloc human rights practices has been painfully slow. Indeed in some cases nonexistent. Yet the Helsinki Review Conferences have been an important forum for publicizing the human rights records of Soviet bloc nations. On the negative side, the conferences have tended to blur the differences between Western democracies and communist dictatorships, strengthening the perception of moral equivalence between the two.

The new President should convene a task force of individuals from inside and outside the government to assess the Helsinki review process. The task force should consider how further U.S. participation in the process might be more effective in supporting fundamental political change, and if so, under what conditions. The new President should ensure that U.S. representatives at any follow-up conferences continue to expose Soviet bloc human rights violations and insist that the Soviet bloc fulfill its commitments under the 1975 Helsinki accords. These include: facilitating the reunification of families separated by national borders, increasing cultural and educational exchanges, permitting free entry and exit for persons married to citizens of other states, and permitting widespread circulation of Western publications inside the Soviet Union.

3) Place strict conditions on U.S. participation in a "human rights" conference in Moscow. The Soviet Union has been insisting on holding a "human rights" conference in Moscow. Until the USSR substantially stops violating its citizens' human and political rights by adherence to the letter and spirit of the Helsinki accords, it would be a serious mistake for the U.S. to attend such a conference. The U.S. should avoid even preliminary discussion of its participation in a Moscow human rights conference until the Soviet government pledges to release all Soviet political and religious prisoners, places no restrictions whatsoever on foreign, and especially, domestic participation in the conference, and agrees to televise the entire proceeding throughout the USSR.

4) Enforce Section 307 of the Smoot-Hawley Act. Section 307 of the 1930 Smoot-Hawley Tariff Act prohibits the U.S. from importing goods made by prison labor. Although the U.S. Customs Commissioner in 1983 found that several Soviet exports to the U.S. violated Smoot-Hawley, the Reagan Treasury Department refused to prohibit importation of these goods. The new President should require his Treasury secretary to enforce the ban on the importation into the U.S. of products made by prison labor. (See U.S.-Soviet Relations section of this chapter.)

5) Reaffirm Administration support for the Jackson-Vanik amendment. Under the terms of the 1975 Jackson-Vanik amendment, nations cannot qualify for U.S. Most Favored Nation (MFN) trade status unless they grant their citizens freedom of emigration. During the 1970s, when the Soviet Union actively was seeking MFN status, the amendment forced Moscow to increase steadily the number of permits granted to those seeking to emigrate from the USSR; in 1979, a record 51,000 exit permits were granted. As the Soviet Union now resumes its quest for MFN status, Jackson-Vanik could help thousands of other Soviet citizens exercise the basic human right of choosing where to live. The new President should inform Congress of his support for the Jackson-Vanik principles, and of his intention to make emigration for Soviet religious and ethnic groups and dissidents a major human rights tenet of his Administration.

6) Take action against Ethiopia's Mengistu. The dictatorship of Mengistu Haile Mariam in Ethiopia has perhaps the world's worst human rights record. Forced resettlement and collectivization policies, combined with government use of food aid as a weapon, have killed directly or indirectly by famine approximately one million Ethiopians in this decade. (See Africa section of this chapter.) The new President and Secretary of State should pressure Moscow, publicly and privately, to halt its military aid (totaling $5 billion from 1977 to 1988) to the Mengistu regime. If famine again threatens Ethiopians, the U.S. should act to ensure the safe passage of food to stricken areas, considering the use of military force to do so.

7) Help build a democratic alternative in South Africa. Despite some progress, such as the elimination of internal passport controls, blacks and other minorities in South Africa remain victims of systematic human rights violations by the white government. As part of an overall U.S. strategy of working with nongovernmental groups, the Assistant Secretary of State for Human Rights should develop a strategy for using American private activities in South Africa to build a free multiracial civil society outside of apartheid, to present the South African government with hard choices in maintaining apartheid, and ultimately to disintegrate the political structure of apartheid from below. Under this strategy, U.S. private firms and groups would work with South African independent trade unions, businesses, churches, and democratically oriented political organizations. (See Africa section of this chapter.) A policy of vigorously using the private sector to exert pressure for change is undermined by U.S. punitive sanctions, which are opposed by many South African blacks. Sanctions mark a return to the Carter objective of clean hands rather than concrete change.

8) Pressure Polish ruler Jaruzelski. The 1981 imposition of martial law by General Wojciech Jaruzelski's communist regime quelled the incipient Polish revolution, but did not dim the Polish people's desire for freedom. The new President should make the full legalization of the Solidarity trade union a quid pro quo for any further U.S. economic concessions to the Polish leadership. The new President should request congressional funding for increased support to democratic forces in Poland. (See Liberation Doctrine and Central/Eastern Europe sections of this chapter.)

9) Demand repeal of the U.N. resolution on Zionism. In 1975, the U.N. General Assembly passed a resolution declaring that "Zionism is racism." This resolution is an affront to human dignity, singling out the Jewish people and identifying their movement for national self-expression as uniquely illegitimate. Repeal of that resolution would right an injustice. The Secretary of State should appoint a representative to work with the U.S. Ambassador to the U.N. to mobilize other governments to repeal the resolution. The Secretary of State should work with Congress to coordinate a strategy for using American financial leverage at the U.N. toward this end.

State-Sponsored Terrorism

Charles M. Lichenstein*
Task Force Chairman

Terrorism—attacking noncombatant targets or taking hostages for the purpose of advancing or publicizing a political cause—threatens all contemporary societies. Terrorism's fundamental threat is to social stability and, ultimately, to the legitimacy of democratic regimes. Free and open societies are inherently vulnerable to terrorists. Democratic processes, as well as constraints governing the use of force, make it difficult for democracies to organize and sustain effective countermeasures.

The threat from terrorism is growing. Terrorism, with direct state support, has become an integral part of the global power struggle and is a form of low intensity warfare. Terrorists are better organized, better equipped, and more professional than they were a decade ago, and terrorist escalation threatens the future use of chemical, biological, and even nuclear weapons.

The Soviet Union, Cuba, Iran, Libya, North Korea, and Syria—with such accomplices as the Palestine Liberation Organization (PLO), the Red Brigades, and the Japanese Red Army—have used terrorism in an effort to diminish U.S. global influence, humiliate U.S. military forces, drive the U.S. out of strategically important regions, and destabilize governments friendly to the U.S.

Nations, directly or indirectly, sponsor about 90 percent of all terrorism. Terrorist states provide money, weapons, logistics and communications, and false passports and safehouses. The Free World's response to this has been fitful and piecemeal. While there are no quick fixes for transnational state-supported terrorism, multinational collaboration is essential if terrorism is to be checked. Prudent use of both conventional countermeasures (timely sharing of intelli-

*Commenting and contributing generously to this report were *Mandate III* Task Force Members Yonah Alexander, Alvin Bernstein, Christopher Harmon, Joel Lisker, Richard Messick, and Herbert Meyer. They do not necessarily endorse all of its views and recommendations.

Task Force Deputy Chairman: Heritage Senior Policy Analyst James A. Phillips.

gence, police procedures, the use of armed force) and unconventional countermeasures (covert operations and counterterrorist assault teams) is required. And such efforts must be amply funded and sustained.

Both the Reagan and Carter Administrations were the victims of state-sponsored terrorism. The new Administration thus must develop and sustain a coherent national strategy that effectively denies the goals of terrorist groups and punishes the states that sponsor and support them. The costs of terrorist acts against the U.S. and its allies must be raised beyond any intended benefits. Terrorism feeds on its own success: in the absence of effective countermeasures, the terrorist is encouraged to step up the attack.

———————————◇———————————

THE REAGAN ADMINISTRATION RECORD

Although the exact mix of effective measures against terrorism is and must remain secret, some specific successful actions by the Reagan Administration are known. The April 1986 U.S. reprisal air raid against Libya not only punished Libyan dictator Muammar Qadhafi for his support of terrorism, but also prompted West European states to intensify their own antiterrorist activities. The Reagan Administration, meanwhile, has made effective use of travel alerts, forcing such countries as Greece to tighten airport security. These alerts warn U.S. citizens of potential risk, and tend to discourage all but essential travel. There also has been growing cooperation within U.S. executive departments and agencies to counter terrorism and growing cooperation and intelligence exchanges among Free World governments. Important too have been the increased measures to anticipate, preempt, and avert terrorist acts; it is believed that there were nearly 150 such preemptions from 1986 to 1987.

The Reagan Administration, however, has failed to formulate and execute a coherent counterterrorism strategy that could be communicated unequivocally to terrorists, their state sponsors, and the American public. The State Department's official listing of "terrorist states" seems subject to political considerations: the Soviet Union and Iraq, for instance, are missing from the list. The essential ingredients of covert antiterrorist operations, the need for secrecy and effective counterterrorism intelligence, have never been made clear by top Administration officials, including the President. This is important because the U.S. cannot defeat clandestine terrorist groups unless it has the capacity to act secretly. U.S. military and intelligence resources have yet to be coordinated fully; interservice rivalries have yet to be eliminated. (See Chapter 25.) Too often, important intelligence gathered in Washington is not shared quickly enough with officers in the field. There also are too many intelligence leaks.

———————————◇———————————

THE NEXT FOUR YEARS

The new President should make it clear that any state supporting terrorist groups will face diplomatic, economic, and political sanctions imposed by the U.S.—and, to the maximum extent possible, its allies. The Secretary of State should raise the struggle against terrorism to a high priority in bilateral relations with other states. The military option should not be foreclosed. The U.S. must send the unambiguous signal, through legislation and executive orders, that any nation supporting terrorism can count on a strong U.S. response at a time and in a manner of America's choosing.

Maintaining the Military Force Option

The use or threat of military force is essential for punishing and deterring state-sponsored terrorism. The military response should be swift and must raise the cost of promoting terror above the price a state sponsor of terrorism is willing to pay. Example: The April 1986 reprisal against Libya forced Qadhafi's terrorism into remission and strengthened the threat of U.S. retaliation against any other states contemplating supporting terrorism. Future counterterrorist operations, like the Libyan reprisal raid, are likely to take place in hostile environments. Counterterrorist units therefore will have to rely increasingly on conventional forces for support. The Secretary of Defense should order counterterrorist special forces to train in joint exercises with conventional forces to assure smooth coordination in actual counterterrorist operations.

Tilting U.S. Policy Against States
Supporting Terrorism

States that sponsor terrorism should be punished by a tilt in U.S. policy toward their adversaries. Example: U.S. support of Chadian forces in their fight against Libya probably has done a great deal to undermine Qadhafi's support within his own army.

Lowering the Profile of Hostage Taking

The U.S. should not reward terrorism by submitting to hostage-takers' ultimatums or by paying ransoms. Doing otherwise only encourages future acts of terrorism. Making a deal to free one set of hostages puts other Americans at risk. The new President, meanwhile, should avoid "yellow ribbon" policies that raise the profile of hostages without gaining their release. The President should never "confine himself to the Rose Garden" nor appear to be hostage to the hostage-takers. Such actions tend to encourage more taking of American hostages and to play into media-generated pressures to negotiate with terrorists.

To maximize terrorists' nervousness and uncertainty, the U.S. should not rule out any option in dealing with them, including deception and the breaking of promises made under duress to terrorists. The safety of hostages should never be given higher priority than their freedom. Rescue missions should not be ruled out. Nor should reprisal raids. The U.S. should relentlessly hunt and apprehend hostage-takers long after the incidents are concluded.

Organizing to Fight Terrorism

The Secretary of Defense should make sure that the Special Operations Command, created in the 1986 reorganization of the Pentagon's Special Operations Forces, is not allowed to atrophy into just another layer of bureaucracy between high-level officials and special forces in the field. The headquarters of the Special Operations Command should be moved from Florida to Washington, D.C., to integrate it as much as possible with the military chain of command and facilitate coordination with other civilian and military agencies dealing with terrorism. The Secretary of Defense should upgrade the readiness of special operations forces by allocating greater resources to special forces personnel and equipment. Some military officers continue to avoid special operations assignments because they feel that such assignments do not advance careers. The Pentagon must provide greater incentives for officers to make a career of the special forces by creating greater upward mobility and the possibility of achieving senior rank.

Procuring the Necessary Weapons

Special operations forces so far lack sufficient airlift and communications equipment. The Air Force, which is charged with the responsibility for moving special forces into and out of crises, has a fleet of only 14 aging MC–130 *Combat Talon* transports and 19 MH–53 *Pave Low* helicopters. Current plans call for the procurement of 24 new MC–130s and modification of 11 HH–53 helicopters for special operations missions by 1992. These procurement plans should be accelerated. (See Low Intensity Conflict section of Chapter 28.)

Bolstering Counterterrorism Intelligence

A top priority for the U.S. intelligence community must be to improve intelligence relating to terrorism, particularly intelligence derived through U.S. field agents from indigenous foreign sources. The new President should direct U.S. intelligence and counterterrorism agencies to increase the number of intelligence personnel and technological assets specifically dedicated to counterterrorism. These agencies should intensify efforts to infiltrate terrorist groups to gain advance notice of terrorist operations, apprehend terrorists, and disrupt terrorist logistics and communications. (See Chapter 25.)

Mobilizing International Action Against Terrorism

The new President must lead a multinational campaign to fight terrorism. Although terrorism probably can never be eradicated altogether, concerted international action can raise the costs to the terrorists substantially and thereby reduce their threat. Such cooperation could include: multilateral economic sanctions against states that support terrorism, sharing of intelligence on terrorist groups, joint counterterrorist training exercises, and cooperative contingency planning for responding to terrorism.

Creating a NATO Counterterrorist Force

As a first step toward a multinational effort against terrorism, the Secretary of Defense should call on America's NATO allies to set up a NATO coordinating committee for high-level consultations on joint responses to international terrorism. This committee should create a joint NATO counterterrorist force drawn from all member countries. The force would respond to terrorist attacks on NATO military facilities, or at targets in any NATO country. (See U.S. and NATO section of Chapter 28.) Other friendly countries, such as Australia, Israel, Japan, Kenya, Pakistan, the Republic of China, the Republic of Korea, Singapore, and Zaire, should be encouraged to participate in parallel multinational antiterrorist forces in other regions.

Opposing New Protocol Amendments to the Geneva Convention

Additional protocols to the 1949 Geneva Convention on the treatment of prisoners of war were signed by the U.S. in 1977. These new protocols, strongly supported by the Soviet bloc and other states supporting terrorism, would extend "prisoner of war" status to such "national liberation movements" as the PLO and the IRA and to those fighting "racist" or "colonialist" regimes, such as the terrorist African National Congress and the South West Africa People's Organization. Such loopholes could permit terrorists to escape the sanctions of criminal law in those countries that ratify the protocols and thus severely curb counterterrorism operations. These protocols should be repudiated by the new President and withdrawn from Senate consideration.

Issuing Travel Advisories

Many countries that refuse to fight terrorism vigorously have an economic interest in attracting American tourists and maintaining close business and commercial relationships. In 1985, a State Department travel advisory issued for Athens airport after the hijacking of a TWA airliner prompted Greece to tighten its security procedures, after dragging its feet for years. The Secretary of State should use travel advisories to press uncooperative states to assure the safety of American tourists.

―――――――――◇―――――――――

INITIATIVES FOR 1989

1) Relax self-imposed counterterrorism constraints. The new President should reexamine all executive orders that inhibit use of the full arsenal of weapons against terrorist groups that have attacked U.S. citizens. For example, Executive Order 11905, issued in 1976, which imposes restrictions on special operations, needs to be refined so that it does not exclude U.S. commando assaults on terrorists who have killed Americans. U.S. counterterrorist agencies should be free to apprehend terrorists in anarchic areas such as Lebanon, not just in international waters or airspace.

The new President should order the National Security Council to prepare a legal analysis of the 1973 War Powers Resolution and a Senate bill proposed in March 1988 that would require giving notice to Congress at least 48 hours before the initiation of covert action. If necessary, these measures should be amended substantially or repealed. Such requirements slow response to terrorist actions and jeopardize the secrecy of counterterrorist operations.

2) Strengthen existing counterterrorist forces. The new President should order the Secretary of Defense to raise the priority of the training, equipping, and ready deployment of counterterrorist units. These units include Army, Navy, and Air Force special forces units. Rescue/Assault teams should be stationed close to such high-threat areas as the Middle East and South America, to reduce the time needed to mount a response to a terrorist incident.

3) Expand the State Department list of states sponsoring terrorism. The State Department maintains a list of nations sponsoring terrorism. Those on the list are denied access to U.S. aid and trade concessions. In mid–1988, the list included Cuba, Iran, Libya, North Korea, South Yemen, and Syria. The Secretary of State should add Afghanistan, Nicaragua, the Soviet Union, Yugoslavia, and most of Central/Eastern Europe to the list.

4) Modify the "political offense exception" to extradition. The "political offense exception" allows nations to block the extradition of fugitives. This device has been used to prevent the extradition to the U.S. of individuals wanted for the commission of violent crimes. The Secretary of State should propose treaties with America's allies similar to the Supplementary Extradition Treaty with Britain, which provides that crimes of violence will not be considered political offenses and therefore exempt from extradition under the primary U.S.-British extradition treaty. Similar treaties with other states would make it clear that the U.S. and its allies will not grant safe haven to those engaged in violence to overthrow or destabilize democratically elected governments.

5) Urge media self-regulation. Terrorists seek publicity to "advertise" their alleged "causes" and use the mass media as their ally. The new

President should direct his Assistant for National Security Affairs to work with media representatives on drafting guidelines for responsible coverage of terrorism.

6) Launch a public diplomacy offensive. The new President immediately should launch an intensive campaign of public information and education about the nature and dimensions of the terrorist threat and its devastating effects on the stability and legitimacy of democratic governments. It should be a personal effort, with the full weight of presidential prestige and authority. This public diplomacy offensive should be as specific as the protection of classified sources and methods permits: naming the countries that sponsor, support, and tolerate terrorism; spelling out the essential elements of an effective counterattack, including presidential authorization of preemptive "special operations"; and describing case studies of successful U.S. and multinational countermeasures. The new President should request that Congress reestablish a subcommittee on terrorism to provide a congressional focus on terrorism that has been lacking since 1986.

25

Public Diplomacy

Fred Ikle*
Task Force Chairman

In contrast to traditional diplomacy, which deals with government officials, public diplomacy seeks to advance foreign policy objectives by influencing the general public's attitudes toward and perceptions of current world affairs. Always influenced by public opinion, the diplomacy of the United States and its allies is becoming increasingly dependent on public reaction to information. The war for the hearts and minds of entire peoples is increasingly conducted on the pages of newspapers, magazines, and on television screens. This is making public diplomacy one of the most important components of relations between states. Moscow seems to understand this well. Since Mikhail Gorbachev took power in the Kremlin, Soviet diplomacy has been growing in sophistication and scope. Today, more than ever, public diplomacy is a crucial arena of U.S.-Soviet competition.

―――――――――◇―――――――――

THE REAGAN ADMINISTRATION RECORD

When the Reagan presidency began, the U.S. image in the world probably was at a post-World War II nadir. The U.S. abandonment of its South Vietnamese allies and the fall of friendly regimes in Cambodia, Ethiopia, and Iran; the abrupt cancellation of the enhanced-radiation weapon (the neutron bomb) by President Jimmy Carter; U.S. impotence in the face of the kidnapping of American diplomats by

―――――――――――――――――――――――――――――――――――

*Commenting and contributing generously to this report were *Mandate III* Task Force Members Kenneth Adelman, Martin Coleman, John Lenczowski, R. Daniel McMichael, Constantine Menges, Robert Schadler, and General Richard Stilwell. They do not necessarily endorse all of its views and recommendations.

Task Force Deputy Chairman: Heritage Salvatori Fellow in Soviet Studies Leon Aron.

Iran; Carter's "national malaise" speech and the erroneous claim by
his Ambassador to the United Nations that there were thousands of
political prisoners in the U.S.—these are a few of the events that
contributed to the world's perception of the U.S. as a gravely weakened and inept giant, torn by self-doubt, ridden by guilt, and void of
any sense of national purpose, let alone mission, in its conduct of
world affairs.

At the same time, the Soviet Union was in the midst of its historically
unprecedented military buildup. The Kremlin dramatically had expanded its overseas empire, crushed dissent in the Soviet Union and
reform movements in Eastern Europe, and invaded Afghanistan. To
the world, the notorious "global correlation of forces" seemed to be
turning irreversibly in the Soviets' favor.

The Reagan Administration set out to reverse this global perception.
A sense of historic optimism permeated and revitalized U.S. public
diplomacy. The U.S. responded to the Soviet ideological offensive by
launching, in November 1983, the National Endowment for Democracy, a nonprofit organization created to strengthen democratic ideas,
movements, and institutions throughout the world. In 1983 Radio Marti
went on the air beaming 14 hours of daily programs at Fidel Castro's
Cuba. To follow, analyze, and publicly expose Soviet disinformation
campaigns, the Administration created the Interagency Active Measures Working Group. Consisting of representatives of the U.S. Information Agency (USIA), CIA, Arms Control and Disarmament Agency,
and the Departments of Defense and Justice, the Group produces
authoritative and widely disseminated annual reports. At the Helsinki
conferences, the U.S. delegate has publicized systematic violation of
human rights in the Soviet bloc.

The moral basis of U.S. foreign policy was elucidated also in Vice
President George Bush's September 21, 1983, Vienna speech on
U.S. policy toward Central and Eastern Europe. He pointed to the
Soviet denial of national self-determination for the peoples of the
region as the "primary root" of East-West tension, rejected the
permanence of the division of Europe, and declared U.S. support for
"all movements toward the social, humanitarian, and democratic ideals" in Central/Eastern Europe.

Reversing two decades of erosion in funding and staffing, the Reagan
Administration has provided the USIA with new means to fulfill its
public diplomacy mission. A pattern of neglect of the Voice of America
has been arrested and reversed, as increases in its operating budget led
to program expansion and allowed long overdue modernization of

facilities and equipment. In October 1983, VOA resumed daily broadcasts in English to Western Europe, which had been stopped in 1960. In 1982, the President signed a National Security Decision Directive that contained a long-term modernization plan for Radio Free Europe/ Radio Liberty. The *Worldnet* satellite television service was introduced, and favorable financial terms for satellite time in Western Europe were obtained. Interactive press conferences of American policymakers with foreign journalists are now among *Worldnet*'s most popular programs.

At the same time, however, public diplomacy planning has lacked long-range perspective because the Reagan Administration has not carried out fully the President's 1983 National Security Decision Directive (NSDD 77) to coordinate public diplomacy policies of the federal agencies. As a result of this and other planning deficiencies, by 1987, the U.S. had ceded the public diplomacy initiative largely to the Soviet Union. Moscow was able to take credit for Reagan's arms control initiatives, like the principle of weapons elimination (the "zero-zero" option) and intrusive on-site verification. (See U.S.-Soviet Relations and Western Europe sections of this chapter.) And in preparing for the 1988 Moscow summit, the U.S. negotiating team failed to secure for Reagan the same access to the Soviet people that Gorbachev had to Americans during his December 1987 visit to Washington. As a result, some of the best speeches of the Reagan presidency—in Moscow University, the House of Writers, and the Danilov Monastery—remained unknown to the Soviet people, except for the VOA listeners.

———————————◇———————————

THE NEXT FOUR YEARS

The new President should make effective public diplomacy an integral part of his foreign policy agenda. As part of his public diplomacy strategy, he should pursue three basic objectives: 1) tell the world the truth about the U.S. and its foreign policy; 2) convey the advantages of the American political and economic system and democratic capitalism in general; and 3) encourage nations to attain and guard individual liberties, human rights, democratic political institutions, and private free-market economic enterprise. Without being shrill or overbearing, the U.S. should not shy away from fighting, and winning, battles for world public opinion. Having by far the best product to sell, a carefully planned and precisely executed U.S. public diplomacy campaign can defeat the forces of totalitarianism and violence in the contest of ideas.

Expanding Voice of America Modernization

With a $170 million annual operating budget and 2,837 employees, Voice of America is a major component in the U.S. public diplomacy effort. Yet it is dwarfed by other major international radio broadcasters, particularly Radio Moscow, in facilities, equipment, personnel, signal strength, and broadcast hours. VOA broadcasts 1204 hours a week in 44 languages; Radio Moscow broadcasts 2,246 hours weekly in 81 languages.

To improve VOA, the U.S. Information Agency (USIA) has proposed a multiyear $1.8 billion program to build new VOA relay stations and expand and rehabilitate the existing broadcasting facilities. This, however, has been trimmed to $1.3 billion by the Office of Management and Budget (OMB). This cut will prevent VOA from meeting the policy objectives set by Reagan and the National Security Council. The new President should order the OMB, USIA, and the National Security Council to review the VOA modernization program in light of current price estimates, the cost of establishing new transmitting sites, and overall broadcast requirements. A thorough and detailed modernization estimate should then be presented to Congress with the objective of bringing the funding level to at least the original USIA request of $1.8 billion.

Exploiting New Technologies

New communication technologies can enable the U.S. to reach audiences in almost every corner of Central/Eastern Europe. Direct-Broadcast Satellites (DBS), for example, can be received with the help of relatively simple satellite dishes; the proliferation of such dishes in Central/Eastern Europe has created excellent conditions for increased use of DBS by USIA. Unlike regular radio and television broadcasts, satellite-transmitted signals are virtually impossible to jam. DBS presents perhaps the most viable and cost-effective way of further undermining the information monopoly that the communist regimes seek to preserve.

Similarly, the spread of video recorders in Central/Eastern Europe and the Soviet Union and a thirst there for American cultural goods offer USIA the opportunity to present an uncensored view of the Western reality and promote cultural diversity in the region. To do this requires a sharp increase in the number and size of video cassette libraries in U.S. embassies and cultural centers in Central/Eastern Europe and the Soviet Union. (See Central/Eastern Europe section of this chapter.)

To take full advantage of DBS, video recording, and other new communications technologies, the new President should order the Director of USIA, the National Security Council, and the OMB to review the long-term technological modernization needs of the USIA as well as means of increasing the working hours and the number of cassettes offered by existing video libraries. An itemized funding request should then be submitted to Congress for authorization.

Seeking Increased Funding for Radio Free Europe/Radio Liberty

Radio Free Europe (RFE) and Radio Liberty (RL) broadcast to Central/Eastern Europe and the Soviet Union with the emphasis on domestic political developments. For almost four decades, the stations have prevented the Soviet Union and its Central/Eastern European clients from establishing an information monopoly and isolating their peoples from the rest of the world. In the next four years, RFE/RL will need $275 million for technical modernization and program expansion. Of this, $225 million is for a new RL transmitting station in Israel and $40 million is for a new RFE transmitter in Portugal. An additional $10 million is required to expand RL broadcasts in the languages of the Soviet Central Asian republics (Kazakhstan, Kirghizia, Tadzhikistan, Turkmenia, and Uzbekistan) as well as those to Azerbaijan from the current one to two hours daily to five to six hours daily.

To help the Board for International Broadcasting, which governs Radio Liberty/Radio Free Europe, obtain this funding, the new President should direct his Deputy National Security Adviser for Soviet Global Affairs[1] and the Senior Adviser to the President on Public Diplomacy[2] to prepare and present to Congress a long-term detailed blueprint for RFE/RL development. The study should include a section on the strategic importance of the stations in view of the current turmoil in Central/Eastern Europe and the Soviet ethnic republics.

Balancing Security and the Requirements of Effective Public Diplomacy

Increasing terrorism puts overseas U.S. personnel and installations at risk. At the same time, effective public diplomacy requires that the

USIA's libraries, cultural centers, and press offices be accessible to the foreign public. The goals of adequate security and effective public diplomacy must be reconciled. What is optimal for the State Department (for example, moving a U.S. embassy from a vulnerable downtown location in a foreign capital to the more secure suburbs) may greatly diminish foreign public access to USIA's facilities. Flexibility, rather than mechanical application of general security standards, should determine security measures for U.S. public diplomacy facilities.

The new President should order the Director of USIA to recommend security measures that would not jeopardize USIA's ability to carry out its public diplomacy mission. The recommendations could include greater authority for USIA to define its security needs; requiring the State Department to consult with USIA on security standards for USIA installations; and granting the ambassador's country teams (the ambassador's principal advisers and senior embassy personnel) primary responsibility for determining how to secure their facilities.

Resisting Attempts to Weaken the USIA

Proposals are being considered by some members of Congress that would impair seriously USIA's ability to carry out its public diplomacy mandate. Such proposals include making the Voice of America an independent corporation outside USIA and removing the scholarly exchanges, such as the Fulbright program, from USIA jurisdiction. More important, it has been suggested that the USIA's role as the principal tool of U.S. public diplomacy be transferred to the State Department. Yet USIA has been an effective tool of U.S. foreign policy, with an $820 million annual budget, 900 information officers around the world, the Voice of America and a worldwide network of satellite television broadcasts, libraries, culture centers, dozens of foreign language magazines, and cultural and scholarly exchanges. The Agency has amassed unique expertise and personnel resources for telling the U.S. story to the world.

Weakening USIA and transferring its functions to other bureaucracies would diminish the effectiveness of the U.S. public diplomacy effort by duplicating functions, wasting expertise, and creating bureaucratic chaos and turf battles. While there is room for the agency's improvement, the new Administration should prevent the USIA from fading as an institution.

Expanding and Modernizing
American Libraries Abroad

U.S. libraries overseas give millions of foreigners an opportunity to learn about American life, traditions, and values. While there has been an increase in USIA's book programs budget, it is still below the 1960s level in constant dollars. The Soviet Union annually exports more than 70 million cheap, subsidized books: USIA subsidizes only 600,000 books. Books should be chosen with the objective of presenting an accurate and balanced picture of American social, political, and economic life. USIA's library budget—currently around $3.5 million—should be at least doubled. The U.S. libraries abroad need more video cassettes and video equipment and more staff experienced in these technologies. The Director of USIA should propose a multiyear program of library modernization and expansion. Corporations and private individuals should be asked to contribute to the program by donating books and money.

Increasing the Number of USIA Personnel
in the Ambassadorial and Deputy Chief of
Mission (DCM) Positions

To improve the quality and motivation of Foreign Service Officers who choose to specialize in public diplomacy, USIA officers should be given equal consideration with their State Department colleagues for all senior diplomatic positions, including deputy chief of mission (DCM), charge d'affaires, and ambassador.

Improving Public Diplomacy Training for Middle- and
High-Level Foreign Service Personnel

The strategy and tactics of public diplomacy components of U.S. foreign policy are neglected in the training of Foreign Service Officers. The Secretary of State should require a course in media and advocacy skills for U.S. ambassadors and deputy chiefs of mission. The Foreign Service Institute should introduce a required course in public diplomacy for its middle and senior officer programs.

———————————◇———————————

INITIATIVES FOR 1989

1) Create the post of Senior Adviser to the President for Public Diplomacy. U.S. public diplomacy has been headless. No senior member of the Reagan Administration has been in charge of planning, coordination, and fulfillment of public diplomacy goals. To remedy this, the new President should make the Director of USIA his Senior Adviser to the President for Public Diplomacy. The President also should issue an executive order making the Director of USIA a member of the National Security Council.

2) Revive a public diplomacy planning group. The Special Planning Group was established in 1983 by Reagan in a National Security Decision Directive (NSDD 77) to help coordinate public diplomacy activities of the various U.S. foreign affairs bureaucracies and to provide long-term public diplomacy planning. It has not met since mid–1987. The Group should be reconstituted, chaired by the Senior Adviser to the President for Public Diplomacy, and meet periodically to develop and coordinate public diplomacy strategy and report to the President on implementation of his directives.

3) Double funding for the National Endowment for Democracy (NED). The National Endowment for Democracy was established in 1983 by Congress to encourage democratic values and institutions throughout the world. The Endowment supports business organizations, free trade unions, and a variety of other indigenous democratic groups in countries as diverse as Afghanistan, Chile, Nicaragua, Poland, the Philippines, and South Africa. Yet budget cuts, diminishing interest by the second-term Reagan Administration, and the sharp increase in NED's programs have reduced the average per program funding from $90,000 in 1983 to $25,000 in 1988. NED's overall budget for fiscal 1988 is $16.9 million.

A tight budget forces NED to limit its activities to helping democratic forces in only the most pressing cases (Chile, El Salvador, and Poland), virtually ignoring the Islamic world, Africa, Asia, and such important countries as Brazil. And the lack of resources prevents NED from building on its own successes. For example, a Turkish magazine, *Yeni Forum*, established with an NED grant, is now one of Turkey's most influential journals of ideas. It has the potential of becoming a national center for democratic training of young political leaders, yet the Endowment lacks the funds to bring about the creation of such a center.

To enable NED to advance U.S. foreign policy objectives, its budget should be at least doubled to $34 million. The new President should direct his national security adviser and his Senior Adviser for Public

Diplomacy to present to Congress a long-term blueprint for NED activities, justifying the increased outlays.

4) Improve U.S.-Soviet summit planning. In the past, preparation for U.S.-Soviet summits has been hindered by the absence of institutionalized procedures for interagency coordination. The President should direct his Senior Adviser for Public Diplomacy to gather and chair a summit planning group, which would include representatives of the relevant foreign policy bureaucracies. To insure that summit preparation adequately reflects the White House public diplomacy agenda, the President should make clear the senior adviser, and not department representatives, is in charge of overall planning.

5) Prepare a public diplomacy response to a crisis in Central/Eastern Europe. Another political eruption in Central/Eastern Europe is likely, especially in view of the unstable situations in Hungary and Poland. In anticipation of this, a public diplomacy response should be devised by the Senior Adviser to the President for Public Diplomacy and the Deputy National Security Adviser to the President for Soviet Global Affairs or, if these positions are not established, by the Director of Soviet and East European Affairs of the National Security Council. As possible public diplomacy responses to Central/Eastern European upheaval, the new Administration may include: publicizing any Soviet troop movements during the crisis; an emergency session of NATO foreign ministers to affirm Western support for the right of national self-determination for the countries of Central/Eastern Europe; and coordinated U.S. and allied diplomatic actions, such as a United Nations resolution condemning any Soviet aggression and a simultaneous recall of allied ambassadors from the Soviet Union. (See Central/ Eastern Europe section of this chapter.)

6) Introduce a new weekly program in Voice of America Soviet broadcasts. A new weekly VOA program, perhaps entitled "What Soviet Newspapers Are Saying about the United States," would broadcast reviews of articles about the U.S. in major Soviet newspapers and calmly and factually refute the lies and distortions in them. The Soviet audience yearns to hear U.S. truth about social, political, and economic achievements, but has been disappointed repeatedly by VOA's inexplicable failure to provide it. (See U.S.-Soviet Relations section of this chapter.)

7) Assign senior United States Information Agency officers for regular tours of duty at the White House. There is very little day-to-day interaction between those making U.S. foreign policy and those responsible for public diplomacy support of that policy. Participation of senior USIA officers in formulating U.S. foreign policy will add the public diplomacy perspective to the deliberations of the National Security Council.

8) Raise the Central American Program of Undergraduate Scholarships (CAMPUS) to its original level. A direct result of the Kissinger Commission's 1984 recommendations on Central American was CAMPUS, created to bring disadvantaged Central American students to study in the U.S. and to counter expanded Soviet bloc scholarship programs. The original 1985 appropriation of approximately $4.5 million allowed 154 young Central Americans to come to the U.S. The 1988 appropriation, however, is only $3 million, which pays for only 90 students. CAMPUS should be brought back at least to its original level. The President should direct his Senior Adviser for Public Diplomacy to lobby Congress for additional funding. Such an effort should include a careful analysis of expanding the program to the Caribbean, Asia, and Africa.

————————————◇————————————

NOTES

1. The creation of this position is suggested in the U.S.-Soviet Relations section of this chapter.

2. The creation of this position is proposed in this section.

☎

26

The Intelligence Community

Ray S. Cline*
Task Force Chairman

The mission of the United States intelligence community is to assess the capabilities, vulnerabilities, and intentions of other countries, principally those of actual or potential adversaries. Whenever conduct of other nations poses a major threat to U.S. national security, U.S. policymakers, employing intelligence assets, often seek to influence the behavior of such nations. There are various methods for obtaining intelligence. Among them: U.S. operatives, foreign agents, imagery collected from satellites, and other devices capable of intercepting communications and electronic emissions.

High-quality intelligence is especially important for democracies, which, in protecting their national security interests, tend to rely more on the skillful use of political, economic, and diplomatic leverage than on military power. Open societies, moreover, are easy to penetrate; closed societies protect their secrets (and their policymaking processes) resolutely. These asymmetries put democratic countries at a serious disadvantage, which can be only partially ameliorated when democratic countries have intelligence agencies to provide them with timely notice of their adversaries' strategic designs.

The nature of present-day warfare heightens the importance of intelligence. In the nuclear era, the U.S. and its allies are vulnerable to surprise attack, from which recovery may be difficult if not impossible. This makes it imperative to monitor the military capabilities and preparations of America's major adversaries.

In collecting and analyzing information, intelligence agencies must contend with efforts at penetration and deception by hostile intelli-

---

*Commenting and contributing generously to this chapter were *Mandate III* Task Force Members Laughlin Campbell, Charles Lichenstein, Herbert Meyer, and Bretton G. Sciaroni. They do not necessarily endorse all of its views and recommendations.

Task Force Deputy Chairman: David B. Rivkin, Jr.

gence services. The detection and foiling of such efforts is known as counterintelligence.

Simply knowing what may happen, of course, is often not enough. Required also is the ability to influence events, to avert threats to U.S. national security, and to advance U.S. interests. Some of these activities are undertaken overtly, as a part of regular U.S. diplomatic and military operations. Nevertheless, because the U.S. may not want its adversaries to know the precise details of these activities, or because of the political or cultural sensitivities of recipients of U.S. assistance, there is a clear need to take some actions covertly. These covert actions allow the U.S. government at times to act in a way that makes U.S. involvement not apparent, or, at least, plausibly deniable. Covert actions can include: providing economic and military assistance to foreign governments and movements, training foreign personnel, supporting democratic forces and national liberation movements abroad, and countering hostile propaganda. Given the range of threats facing U.S. security and the instabilities and turbulence present in many Third World countries, covert action remains a key instrument of U.S. national security operations. Its role, if anything, has grown in the last decade, and this trend is likely to continue.

———————————◇———————————

THE REAGAN ADMINISTRATION RECORD[1]

The Reagan Administration inherited an intelligence community plagued by deficiencies in such major areas of intelligence operations as collection, analysis, counterintelligence, and covert operations. Specifically, the intelligence community faced a range of problems that, unless properly addressed, threatened to undermine and outstrip U.S. intelligence capabilities. These problems included:

◆ Regional instabilities in such areas as Africa, Central America, the Middle East, and Southeast Asia, which increased the number of targets of urgent interest to U.S. intelligence.

◆ Erosion of the earlier popular and congressional consensus that a robust intelligence capability represents the first line of American defense and merits strong support.

◆ Popular, media, and congressional fascination with covert action operations, which obscured the fact that the principal tasks of an intelligence service are to collect and analyze information.

◆ Increasing congressional efforts to micromanage the intelligence community and impose crippling constraints on intelligence operations.

◆ The demoralization of the intelligence community because of the hostility of many top Carter Administration officials toward the role of intelligence in government.

◆ Leaks and mishandling of classified material, along with failure to enforce security obligations upon former holders of security clearances.

As a consequence, some intelligence professionals were reluctant to support covert action. They feared that exposure of such operations would outrage the public and subject the intelligence community to harsh criticism by Congress and the media. At the same time, some intelligence professionals came to believe that the best solution was to play along with congressional and media critics of the intelligence community.

These worrisome attitudes were addressed by the Reagan Administration's first Director of Central Intelligence, the late William J. Casey. The Administration has bolstered the morale of the intelligence community and has provided badly needed funds for improving collection and analysis. Casey improved the quality of national intelligence estimates and expanded their breadth, enhanced competitive analysis of key issues, and reversed the neglect of the use of human sources of intelligence (HUMINT)[2] to collect data. The Reagan Administration also has restored the concept of covert action as a legitimate instrument of statecraft. Most important, senior officials of the Reagan Administration, including the President, have embraced explicitly the value of timely and accurate intelligence and its contribution to successful U.S. national security decision-making.

Yet deficiencies in U.S. intelligence capabilities persist. Some of the problems are structural, others are attributable to policy failures. In the HUMINT area, for example, such problems as getting well-placed deep-cover sources of intelligence are hard to solve because of past political purges of experienced CIA operational officers and overreliance on technical collection. What foreign officials are thinking and planning for the future can seldom be overheard or photographed. To identify and recruit human beings to provide this kind of information is difficult and time consuming.

Technical collection efforts against the USSR, while successful in many instances, do not always provide appropriate data for analysts to draw firm conclusions. And while national estimates seek objectivity of analysis, they may fail to achieve it because of prevailing political attitudes. During the detente years of the 1970s, for instance, benign feelings toward Moscow prompted the U.S. government to underestimate the Soviet budget commitment to defense programs and weapons systems. An intramural intelligence argument persists over whether faulty estimates come from inadequate raw data or misanalysis of adequate data.

Covert action operations conducted by the U.S. government are usually (and quite properly) shrouded in secrecy. This makes it impossible to provide an informed and detailed scorecard on U.S. covert action successes or failures. Given the fact, moreover, that covert actions are often employed under extremely difficult circumstances, simply demonstrating that specific U.S. covert actions failed does not necessarily indicate an erroneous policy decision or faulty execution by the intelligence community.

While the Reagan Administration has done much to reinvigorate U.S. covert action capabilities, it has failed to obtain popular and congressional support for covert action operations as an essential element within legitimate national security programs. Covert action cannot and should not substitute for a coherent and explainable national security policy. It probably has been a mistake, therefore, for the Reagan Administration to have depended almost exclusively on covert action when the Administration failed to generate sufficient public and congressional support for its Central American policy. This covert effort and its publicized tie-in with the Iran operation resulted in congressional and public outcry and damaged U.S. covert action capability overall and the credibility of the intelligence community itself.

The Reagan Administration also has failed to insulate the intelligence community from the vicissitudes of executive-congressional foreign policy battles and to prevent the enactment of new and harmful statutes that allow meddling in the details of intelligence operations. In fact, intelligence oversight, as practiced by Congress, has harmed the intelligence community, resulting in disclosures of sensitive intelligence data. Congress bears the major blame for this. Yet the Reagan Administration has failed to challenge Congress on the grounds of executive privilege and separation of powers when presented with such constitutionally dubious legislation as the Boland Amendments to appropriations bills. The Reagan Administration also has acquiesced in forcing the retirement of certain government officials, including intelligence officers, criticized by Congress for promoting the policy objectives of the President.

The President, in his National Security Strategy Report of January 1987, announced that a number of steps had been taken to improve U.S. counterintelligence capabilities, and he promised that efforts would continue as a matter of high national priority. Yet U.S. counterintelligence capabilities remain seriously deficient. Elementary arithmetic indicates that the FBI manpower devoted to internal security cannot keep track of the at least 4,250 officials in the U.S. representing Cuba, Eastern Europe, the People's Republic of China, and the Soviet Union. Because of the understandable secrecy, outsiders do not know whether the CIA has recovered from the devastation of its foreign counterintelligence capabilities by the internal purges beginning in 1973. It is assumed, however, that Casey and his successor, Judge William H. Webster, have restored counterintelligence to its vital role. Despite initial pledges, the Reagan Administration has done little to stop leaks of classified information and foster better information security.

———————————————◇———————————————

THE NEXT FOUR YEARS

With a growing diversity of subjects, with the staggering challenge of absorbing the voluminous raw information at hand, and with an increasing number of government users to satisfy, the intelligence community must shore up its traditional capabilities and address new tasks. It therefore must select target priorities carefully, strengthen recruitment of well-trained area experts to build for the future, reform and constrain the congressional oversight structure, and develop more sophisticated counterintelligence and counterespionage processes.

Directing Intelligence Collection

The purpose of collecting information in the field and applying scholarly research and analysis to turn it into intelligence is to provide decision-makers with what they need to formulate policy. The new President has a responsibility to identify those subjects he wants covered—the technical term is "establish requirements." Given the overwhelming masses of information and data, policymakers must establish priorities (including time and money) to get what they want, not just what is readily available.

The Director of Central Intelligence (DCI), assisted by his intelligence community staff, can manage requirements and priorities within the intelligence community. But between the producers and the users of intelligence, there must be better communications. The new President should issue an appropriate decision document establishing specific procedures to improve communications. He should direct, for example, that no decision document be issued without ensuring that the relevant intelligence input has been provided. The DCI should arrange with the executive branch officials to accept more mid-level and senior intelligence analysts into their departments. This would give intelligence analysts a better understanding of the decision-making process, enabling them to communicate more effectively with intelligence users and tailor requirements for collectors.

Improving Language and Area Expertise

Since the primary function of foreign intelligence operations is the recruitment and handling of foreign agents, the new President should stress rebuilding the corps of area and language experts, which has been depleted by the retirement of the World War II generation. Similar language and area expertise is needed by analysts working on country desks. Knowledge in depth of a foreign country and its culture requires some residence in the country and the ability to read and speak its language.

Since U.S. colleges and universities are not providing enough area and language experts, U.S. civilian and military intelligence agencies must expand their own training programs, including temporary residence abroad in situations where the trainee is compelled to speak the local language. Recruiters should not have to consider only fresh crops of college graduates. The U.S. is a multiethnic nation with a broad range of language talent and experience. From this pool, an adequate number of mature candidates can be recruited and trained to operate in foreign cultures where maturity is valued more than youth.

Streamlining Congressional Oversight

Current congressional oversight has harmed U.S. intelligence activities by exposing and leaking classified information and micromanaging covert operations. The new President should press Congress to reform the intelligence oversight process. He should call for a joint House-Senate congressional intelligence committee to replace the current separate House and Senate committees. This committee should be comprised of an equal number of Democrats and Republicans.

Strengthening Counterintelligence

During the Reagan Administration, there has been increased appreciation in the U.S. government of domestic and foreign security and counterintelligence problems. Most of this, however, has been in reaction to specific espionage cases or to security problems such as Marine guard derelictions at the U.S. embassy in Moscow. Rather than reacting incrementally to specific cases, the new Administration must restructure the intelligence system to give a key role to counterintelligence and counterespionage. Counterintelligence studies both what the U.S. has to protect and the actions of hostile services trying to penetrate U.S. protective measures. Counterintelligence accumulates knowledge, devises strategies, and serves as a general staff for collection and counterespionage operations.

Counterespionage operates to catch spies, to "double" them (recruit them to work for the U.S.), or to penetrate hostile intelligence services. The CIA (for foreign intelligence) and the FBI (for domestic counterintelligence) need funds and personnel for counterintelligence work and additional counterespionage operatives to finish reconstituting the professional services, which were reduced to almost nothing in the mid-1970s: the counterintelligence staff at CIA was cut from approximately 300 professionals to a total of about eighty.

During the process of restructuring and training, the new Administration must remove limitations on counterintelligence and security investigations. The Attorney General should propose that the Foreign Intelligence Surveillance Act of 1987 be amended to remove the probable criminal cause requirement that has to be satisfied before surveillance of U.S. citizens or permanent U.S. residents can be initiated. Demanding "probable criminal cause" is inappropriate in intelligence operations. The reason: espionage investigations involve the examination of contacts, payments, and communications such as dead-drops that cannot be designated criminal *per se*, but which may damage national security far more than an ordinary crime. The new President should issue an Executive Order to allow the CIA to work with the FBI on cases in the U.S. involving suspect foreign intelligence officials or agents. The National Security Act of 1947 only bars the CIA from engaging in domestic law enforcement; in the last decade, however, this clause in the 1947 Act has been interpreted as proscribing any CIA involvement in investigations taking place on U.S. soil.

———————◇———————

INITIATIVES FOR 1989

1) Improve language and area capabilities. To bolster the analytical capabilities of the U.S. intelligence community, CIA and military intelligence services should earmark funds and recruit trainees for developing language skills and area expertise.

2) Combat disinformation. Disinformation is false or misleading information deliberately proffered by hostile intelligence services to confuse or mislead the U.S. intelligence community and U.S. decision-makers. To reduce the danger of disinformation, the Director of Central Intelligence should provide guidelines for and mandate that all intelligence producers make a periodic critical review of their sources, human or technical.

3) Bolster counterintelligence. The Director of the FBI should increase FBI manpower and funds dedicated to counterintelligence tasks in coordination with CIA. The Director of Central Intelligence should continue to rebuild staff and field strength to conduct vigorous foreign counterintelligence collection and counterespionage operations.

4) Create an executive-congressional intelligence task force. The new President should seek to resolve the problem of how to balance legitimate congressional oversight of intelligence with constitutionally based executive privilege and separation of powers principles. He should convene a bipartisan special task force, comprised of former senior executive branch and congressional leaders, to determine how the existing system of congressional oversight of intelligence activities can be reformed.

5) Better protect classified information. Intentional and inadvertent release of U.S. classified information has become almost commonplace, particularly on Capitol Hill, and even within the executive branch. The Attorney General, in cooperation with other agencies, should draft statutory language categorically outlawing all unauthorized disclosures of classified data.

—————————◇—————————

NOTES

1. Open discussion of intelligence achievements and failures is inherently difficult, since many intelligence operations and analytical products remain highly classified, even after they have been completed, and cannot be discussed in an open forum. Thus, it only is possible to present an appraisal of broad trends in the intelligence community.

2. The term HUMINT connotes data collected by human operators and agents, as distinct from data collected by satellites and other technical means.

27

The United Nations

Alan L. Keyes*
Task Force Chairman

The United States has a special relationship with the United Nations. There would have been no U.N. founding conference in 1945 in San Francisco without U.S. leadership. The U.N. Charter adopted there reflects the principles of U.S. constitutional democracy, and the U.S. always has been and remains the U.N.'s most generous supporter. Since the U.N.'s founding, the U.S. has contributed some $17 billion to the various U.N. bodies and agencies, roughly 25 percent of the estimated $65 billion spent by the U.N. system through 1987. Even when the U.S. was withholding a portion of its annual payments to the U.N., it was still contributing over $800 million each year, far more than any other country. As it stands now, American taxpayers in 1988 will provide about $1 billion of the approximately $4 billion that will be spent by the U.N. system.

In spite of the strong U.S. commitment to the U.N., Americans have begun to feel that the U.N. has become hostile to legitimate U.S. national interests—and with good reason. In the U.N. General Assembly in 1987, support for U.S. positions fell to an all-time low of 18.7 percent. Since the late 1960s, a working majority of developing countries (often in alliance with the Soviet bloc) has imposed a radical anti-Western and anti-U.S. ideology on the agenda of every U.N. committee and working group. This ideology demands the redistribution of global economic resources and points to the West, particularly the U.S. and Israel, as responsible for international conflict. There is scant reference to worldwide Soviet aggression. For example, U.N. resolutions on

---

*Commenting and contributing generously to this report were *Mandate III* Task Force Members Paul Belford, Roger A. Brooks, Phillip Christenson, Daniel Cohen, Thomas E.L. Dewey, Charles Lichenstein, Juliana Pilon, and Robert Winters. They do not necessarily endorse all of its views and recommendations.
Task Force Deputy Chairman: Heritage Policy Analyst Mark Franz.

Afghanistan never mention the USSR by name; they merely call for the removal of all "foreign troops." Likewise, in its arms control resolutions, the General Assembly completely ignores the Soviet expansionism that is at the root of the so-called "arms race."

Similarly, the U.N. Security Council, whose proposals the U.S. still can veto, has focused obsessively on the real or perceived transgressions of Israel and South Africa but ignored Vietnam's occupation of Cambodia, the Soviet invasion of Afghanistan, Cuban and Nicaraguan support of Central American insurgencies, and scores of other genuine threats to world peace. To varying degrees, U.N. specialized agencies have suffered politicization of their work. The World Health Organization, for instance, has funded numerous studies of alleged psychiatric stress among Palestinian refugees in the "occupied territories" and wages political warfare against multinational corporations which, purportedly, spearhead neocolonialism in the Third World.

A succession of U.S. administrations have considered the U.N. as only marginally relevant to key U.S. political and diplomatic interests, and have used it primarily for political appeasement of developing countries. This was especially the case in the Carter Administration, when U.S. delegates openly sympathized with the extreme political and economic demands of the most radical developing countries and "liberation movements."

The Reagan Administration, by contrast, has moved the U.N. up in priority, significantly changing U.S. policy toward the U.N. Although the U.N. as an institution still is reflexively hostile to U.S. values and interests, the U.S. at the very least has made clear that there are limits to its patience, and that continued U.S. support for, or even membership in, U.N. institutions cannot be taken for granted.

———————◇———————

THE REAGAN ADMINISTRATION RECORD

While representing the U.S. at the U.N. from 1981 to 1985, Ambassador Jeane J. Kirkpatrick repeatedly warned that "business as usual" at the U.N. was not acceptable. It was her view, fully supported by Reagan, that the U.N. had to be taken seriously. As an institution purporting to represent the opinions of the international community on issues ranging from human rights to disarmament, the U.N.—and the behavior of states in the U.N.—was inherently important. Making Americans aware of the U.N's importance was perhaps Kirkpatrick's greatest long-term contribution to a sound U.S. policy towards the U.N.

Kirkpatrick's policies have been diluted since 1985. The U.S. Mission to the U.N. in New York has tended to abdicate its own responsibilities to State Department careerists whose main objective apparently has been to avoid roiling the U.N. waters. However, in the Bureau of International Organization Affairs (I.O.) at the State Department, the Kirkpatrick legacy has been continued. For example, the Office of Multilateral Coordination has been set up within I.O. to ensure that countries that oppose principal U.S. policies and interests at the U.N. and other multilateral forums suffer the consequences of these actions in their bilateral relations with the U.S.

Because of Kirkpatrick's leadership, the previous futile U.S. attempts to appease the Third World majority which controls the U.N. machinery were largely abandoned. So was the "damage limitation" philosophy that had pervaded the U.S. Mission to the U.N. They were replaced by a consistent and principled defense of U.S. national interests at the U.N. From this defense flowed a number of Reagan Administration successes in U.N. organizations.

The Kirkpatrick team, for example, put U.N. members on notice that the U.S. would no longer countenance vicious assaults on its friends. As a result of this overdue U.S. stand, the campaign to delegitimize the State of Israel has lost its momentum. The annual effort to expel Israel from the General Assembly has attracted decreasing numbers of votes in recent years. The U.S., in 1985, left the United Nations Educational, Scientific and Cultural Organization (UNESCO) because the Reagan Administration rightly perceived that UNESCO had become politicized to the extent of violating its own charter. The U.S. has made it clear that it will withdraw from any U.N. organ that excludes Israel. This policy was unanimously confirmed by Senate Concurrent Resolution 68, passed on April 14, 1982, and by House Concurrent Resolution 322, passed by a vote of 401–3 on May 12, 1982.

In the same way, the Reagan Administration has shattered the U.N.'s smug confidence that the U.S. will pay in full its enormous assessed contribution to the U.N. even though the U.N. majority relentlessly attacks and works against the U.S. and its friends and allies. The U.S. has not paid its full U.N. dues since 1986 in an effort to end the U.N.'s budgetary waste and financial mismanagement. These actions have made it clear that U.S. support for the U.N. system cannot be taken for granted.

Similarly, by refusing to sign either the Law of the Sea Treaty (1982) or to vote for the World Health Organization's 1981 resolution approving an infant formula code, the Administration has served notice that the U.S. will not acquiesce to global regulatory schemes that impede economic growth in developing countries. Reagan Administration positions on these and similar issues have slowed the drive by the U.N.'s radical majority for the so-called New International Economic Order (NIEO), which rests on the absurd assertion that Third World poverty is the result of economic growth in the industrialized West. The NIEO would force the developed nations to pay a sort of "reparation" for their success. U.S. action also has helped soften ideological hostility toward the philosophy of free market capitalism by some U.N. member states.

The Reagan Administration, meanwhile, has shown that the U.N. can be used positively as a forum for the affirmation of U.S. values and interests. This is particularly the case in human rights, where U.S. initiatives have highlighted violations of human rights in communist countries, particlularly Cuba, Ethiopia, Nicaragua, and the Soviet Union itself, adding a new element to the terms of U.N. debates on these subjects.

The chief Reagan Administration failing in its policy toward the U.N. has been the reticence and inconsistency with which it has confronted U.N. management and budget problems, particularly within the Secretariat and many U.N. organs and specialized agencies. For example, the Soviet Union and its satellites have used and continue to use the U.N. and its agencies as a base for espionage operations against the U.S. There are some 1,000 Soviet and Soviet bloc personnel serving at the U.N. in New York. About 300 of these are in the U.N. Secretariat, where they assume the guise of "international civil servants" while spying against the U.S.

The Reagan Administration has recognized this problem and taken some steps to deal with it. In 1986, it ordered a 40 percent reduction in the size of the three Soviet missions to the U.N. It also has placed tighter travel restrictions on Soviet bloc personnel associated with the U.N. But more must be done since Soviet bloc intelligence networks in New York are still very much in operation.

Similarly, on the crucial issue of U.N. budget and management reform, the Administration has failed to apply the rules of strict accountability and management efficiency that it proposed at the 1986 U.N. General Assembly. The soaring U.N. budget by the early 1980s had become a powerful symbol of the U.S. inability to influence U.N.

spending, even though the U.S. consistently has provided one-fourth of the U.N. budget. Congress then took strong action in the absence of Administration leadership. In the Kassebaum-Solomon legislation of 1985, Congress stipulated that the U.S. should pay no more than 20 percent of the U.N. budget until weighted voting (voting power roughly equal to share of financial support) was introduced into the U.N. budget process.[1] From 1985 to fall 1988, the U.S. withheld some $500 million from the regular budget of the U.N. and its specialized agencies. The U.N. response has fallen far short of demands made in the Foreign Relations Authorization Act, FY 1988 and 1989. This law calls for reform in three specific areas: abuse of the international civil service, personnel reduction, and consensus voting on budget matters. As of September 1988, however, every Soviet national remains on a short-term, fixed contract at U.N. headquarters. This makes them responsive to pressure from Moscow. This directly violates Article 100 of the U.N. Charter which calls for an independent and "exclusively international" civil service.

The staff reductions at the Secretariat, meanwhile, are not the result of eliminations of positions, but attrition. The posts can, and probably will, be refilled as soon as the money spigot is turned back on. And consensus decision-making on the budget, which would give the U.S. a virtual veto, has been proposed but is untested.

The Reagan Administration has erred too by stressing that its concerns about U.N operations stem solely from the U.N.'s financial and managerial failures. While there were and are legitimate concerns about U.N. management, the U.S., from the outset should have sought enhanced leverage over U.N. programs and activities—not merely better U.N. accounting procedures. The Administration likewise has not recognized the enormous power that the Secretariats of U.N. organizations wield. Secretariat staff influence and sometimes even draft U.N. resolutions, carry out all resolutions, and control U.N. functions from day to day. U.N. Secretariat employees tend to be ideologically hostile to the U.S. and are well positioned to act against U.S. interests. Soviet bloc employees in the U.N. Secretariats continue, in effect, as agents of their own governments and even kick back to their governments a major part of their high salaries (of which the U.S. contributes 25 percent). The Reagan Administration, moreover, has made no systematic effort to recruit and place in the U.N. Secretariat Americans willing to stand up for democratic values and principles.

THE NEXT FOUR YEARS

The United Nations could become a valuable international organization: it could help spur economic growth in developing countries; it could advance human rights; it even could contribute modestly to international stability and peace. So far, it has not.

The new President should devise a clear and consistent policy toward the U.N., which would give the U.N. incentives to fulfill its promise. Some of these incentives would continue Reagan Administration attempts to make the U.N. more accountable for its programs and expenditures and to put the U.N. on notice that it cannot take U.S. support for granted. Other incentives should reward the U.N. for changing its policies and operations. A U.N. program to encourage private-sector growth in the Third World, for example, should be rewarded with generous U.S. support, as should a sincere U.N. effort to halt the conventional arms race among many Third World countries.

On some matters, however, the new President must give the U.N. not incentives but ultimatums. The U.S. should set a deadline, for example, after which it will tolerate no further use of U.N. facilities in the U.S. for spying against the U.S. This is a U.N., not a U.S., responsibility, and it has never been seriously discharged by the U.N. Secretary General. The congressional resolutions stating that the U.S. would leave any U.N. organization that expelled Israel have proved the effectiveness of ultimatums in achieving U.S. goals.

The new President is fortunate that his predecessor has established a foundation of generally sound policies toward the U.N. A bipartisan majority in Congress, moreover, endorses and often has toughened and expanded these policies. The new President should build on this foundation and continue the revision and redefinition of U.S. relations with the U.N. Only through such a redefinition can the U.N. fulfill its important mandate, and the U.S., in good conscience remain its most generous supporter.

Rethinking U.S. Participation in the U.N.

The new President should put the entire U.N. system on clear notice that continued U.S. participation and funding are by no means assured and that future U.S. support will be selective: U.N. agencies that efficiently carry out the mandates of their charters and serve U.S. interests will receive preferential treatment; those that fail to meet such tests will receive lower priority or none at all. U.S. withdrawal from UNESCO in 1985, after repeated warnings about specific deficiencies, provides a model for further actions the U.S. could take in a "worst-case" scenario.

To carry out such a policy, the new President must aggregate the necessary expertise to conduct exhaustive cost-benefit analyses of U.S. participation in the U.N. generally and in its 80 affiliated agencies. Astonishingly, except for occasional congressionally mandated audits of particular U.N. offices or programs—the General Accounting Office study of the U.N. Department of Public Information in 1985–1986 is the most recent case—no recent Administration ever has subjected the U.N system to intensive scrutiny. The State Department's International Organizations Bureau (IO) should be ordered to audit the U.N. system comprehensively with technical support from the Office of Management and Budget. The new President should make future U.S. funding of all U.N. agencies contingent on the completion of such audits, and on a finding that U.S. participation in each agency serves the U.S. national interest.

There should be no sacred cows in future appropriations requests for U.N. agencies. U.S. officials currently know as little about the management and effectiveness of the "good" U.N. agencies—the United Nations Children's Fund (UNICEF), for example, or the High Commissioner for Refugees—as they do about the obvious targets of reform, such as the preparatory commission of the Law of the Sea Treaty (which the U.S. wisely has not signed) or the Department of Public Information (which often acts as a propaganda front for the PLO and for international regulatory schemes that propose to redistribute wealth from industrialized countries to the Third World). It is the responsibility of the President and his senior foreign policy team to present a clear priority list for future U.N. funding in the Administration's initial budget, in which priorities are anchored in a rational calculation of the U.S. national interest.

Raising the State Department's Stake in the U.N.

Dealing with U.N. affairs traditionally has been a low prestige assignment in the career Foreign Service. The new President should raise the profile of multilateral diplomacy generally and of U.N. affairs in particular. Multilateral diplomacy is a unique and valuable arena of diplomatic practice and an excellent training ground for young careerists.

The few Foreign Service officers who have acquired multilateral diplomatic skills from service at the State Department's Bureau for International Organization Affairs or at U.S. missions to international organizations are now routinely rotated to assignments in which these special skills are wasted. To avoid this, multilateral diplomacy should be reorganized as a distinct, high-priority career path ("cone" in State Department jargon) within the Foreign Service, with the prospect of rising within this specialty to the top Foreign Service rank of career ambassador. The creation of such a cone would be an incentive to honing expertise in multilateral diplomacy and, in time, develop a cadre of skilled multilateralists in the career Foreign Service. In this regard, the U.S. would be well advised to emulate the Soviets, who are masters of the multilateral diplomatic game.

Most important, the State Department must end its opposition to congressional efforts to ensure U.N. reform. State consistently has positioned itself as the defender of the U.N. at the cost of U.S. national interest. The new President must insist that the Secretary of State work in cooperation with Congress on U.N. reform. In fact, State should be encouraged to come up with its own ideas for improving the U.N.

Halting U.N.-Based Soviet Espionage

For 40 years, the Soviets' systematic and pervasive use of the U.N. system, particularly at U.N. Headquarters in Manhattan, as a base for espionage against the U.S. has been amply documented. The FBI estimates that at least 35 percent of the approximately 1,000 Soviet and Soviet bloc nationals at U.N. missions and within the U.N. Secretariat engage in espionage. Yet this always has been treated as a U.S. problem, and the burden shouldered by FBI counterintelligence agents and local and state law enforcement officers.

The new President, of course, should continue the initiatives of the Reagan presidency in rebuilding and strengthening the FBI's counterintelligence capabilities, imposing and policing tight travel restrictions on Soviet and Soviet bloc personnel at U.N. missions and within the U.N. Secretariat, and ordering reductions in the number of Soviets permitted to staff these missions. Just as important, the new President should demand that the U.N. itself share the burden of controlling U.N.-based Soviet espionage. It is a U.N. as well as a U.S. problem and a flagrant violation of the U.N. Charter's provision for a neutral and professionally competent international civil service. This espionage imposes enormous financial and security costs on the U.S. And it is unfair, for it results simply from U.S. generosity in hosting the U.N. headquarters in Manhattan.

Among the conditions attached to full U.S. funding of its U.N. assessments, none is more critical than an end to Soviet abuse of the practice of "secondment," by which more than 99 percent of Soviet and Soviet bloc U.N. Secretariat employees are on fixed, short-term, noncareer contracts and, as such, are subject to Moscow's control. Calling a halt to this violation of the U.N. Charter is fully within the power of the U.N. Secretary-General. The U.S. must insist that this power be exercised. Moreover, the U.S. should call for regular rotation of top-level Secretariat assignments among nationals of all the U.N.'s regional blocs. This would break the Soviet lock on such key posts as head of the U.N. Library and chief of document distribution to the U.N.'s worldwide Information Centers.

Achieving U.N. Budget Reform

The centerpiece of the much heralded U.N. Reform Resolution (41/ 213) adopted by the U.N. General Assembly in 1986 was a consensus procedure for reviewing and adopting the U.N.'s biennial administrative budget (which funds the Headquarters operations, some peacekeeping operations, and several specialized agencies). The new budget procedure was anchored in an "enhanced" Committee for Program and Coordination (CPC), in which the U.S. and other major U.N. funders would have a commanding position. Already, less than two years into the era of U.N. reform, this arrangement has been revised in a way that dilutes, rather than strengthens, U.S. influence. The CPC has been expanded from 21 to 34 members, giving the Soviet bloc/ Third World coalition an effective working majority. Rule by consensus, moreover, which was to have been the core of effective reform and would have given the U.S. a veto on runaway U.N. spending, is not mandatory; it simply is "encouraged."

The new President should mount a concerted effort with U.S. allies (including almost all of the U.N.'s major funders) to revive a genuine U.N. reform process and give the CPC real veto power over the U.N. budget. More important, the U.S. must take the lead in the CPC in reviewing U.N. programs that have long since outlived their usefulness. Prime candidates would include: the Committee on Decolonization, which spends most of its energies attacking U.S. "imperialism" in Guam, Micronesia, and Puerto Rico); the Center on Transnational Corporations, which attributes Third World poverty largely to the machinations of U.S.- and European-based multinational corporations;

and the Committee on the Inalienable Rights of the Palestinian People, which is little more than a PLO propaganda arm against what it calls Zionist aggression). The U.N. budget itself is only the surface manifestation of what ails the organization. Expensive, useless, and often counterproductive U.N. programs are the root of the problem, and any genuine U.N. reform effort has to start there.

$$\diamond$$

INITIATIVES FOR 1989

1) Set forth the U.S. agenda in a September 1989 U.N. speech. In the U.S. speech that opens the annual session of the U.N. General Assembly in September 1989, the new President personally should spell out the U.S. agenda for fundamental U.N. reform as the precondition for any future resumption of full U.S. funding of its U.N. assessments. This agenda should be: effective control by the major U.N. funders, including the U.S., of the U.N. budget and program review process; an end to the abuse of secondment, by which the Soviet Union maintains a lock on key positions in the U.N. Secretariat; U.S.-U.N. collaboration in cracking down on U.N.based espionage directed against U.S. national security; and intensive program, management, and budgetary audits of U.N. specialized agencies to assure that they are adhering to their respective mandates of social, economic, and humanitarian activities.

2) Demand an end to espionage. The new President should issue an ultimatum to the U.N. Secretary-General demanding that the U.N. institute effective measures for eliminating espionage activities by its employees. If the Secretary-General fails to demonstrate progress in curbing this criminal activity, the Administration should begin withholding from the U.S. contributions to the U.N. budget the amount of money it costs the U.S. to counter spying by U.N.-based agents.

3) Advance U.S. foreign policy goals at U.N. forums. The new President should continue the initiative of the Reagan years of using U.N. forums—such as the annual session of the U.N. Human Rights Commission in Geneva—to promote major objectives of U.S. foreign policy. Among these objectives are highlighting human rights abuses in the Soviet bloc and in such Soviet satellites as Cuba and Nicaragua, promoting free market processes as the model for Third World economic development, and exposing the existence of low intensity conflict (that is, state-sponsored terrorism, insurgencies, and national liberation movements) as the preferred vehicle for global Soviet aggression.

―――――――――――――◇―――――――――――――

NOTES

1. In addition to the regular U.N. budget, the 20 percent limit applied to those specialized agencies that are financed through mandatory assessments.

28

International Economic Development

J. William Middendorf, II*
Task Force Chairman

Poverty in less developed countries (LDCs) is a tragedy for those countries and a threat to America's economic and security interests. Improvement in the LDCs' economic condition is good for the United States. Recognizing this, the U.S. tries to spur LDC economic development through two sets of institutions. The first is the U.S. Agency for International Development (AID), which is responsible for handing out most of America's foreign aid. The second set are such multilateral agencies as the International Monetary Fund and the World Bank.

During the Carter Administration, many U.S. policymakers seemed to endorse the erroneous proposition that Western economic success is responsible for poverty elsewhere in the world. Thus it was felt that massive transfers of wealth from rich to poor countries not only could eliminate poverty but were essential morally as a kind of reparations. This ignored the real cause of poverty in the LDCs—flawed economic policies. State-sponsored monopolies and ownership of industries, accompanied by massive state subsidies, regulation of wages, prices, and production, trade protectionism, high taxes, impenetrable red tape, and the threat of expropriation have resulted in corruption and economic stagnation, undermining the efforts of ordinary LDC citizens

---

*Commenting and contributing generously to this chapter were *Mandate III* Task Force Members Stanley Armstrong, Doug Bandow, Richard Bissell, John Bolton, David Luft, Paul Craig Roberts, Eric Russi, Gabriel Roth, David Smoot, and Heritage Research Associate Melanie Tammen. They do not necessarily endorse all of its views and recommendations.

Task Force Deputy Chairman: Heritage Center For International Economic Growth Director Edward L. Hudgins.

to improve their own condition. Foreign loans and "expert" advice from the West, meanwhile, typically have caused those countries to sink deeper into debt and have allowed ruling elites to continue pursuing economically destructive policies.

The Reagan Administration repudiated the premises of Carter-era aid programs and has changed the development policy debate, focusing attention on the need for LDCs to invigorate their own private sectors. AID under Reagan has been urging LDC governments to privatize state-owned industries, cut taxes, reduce trade protection, allow wages and prices to be set by the market, promote economic freedom, and protect the right of private property.

But real reform in the less developed world has been slow in coming. This is due in part to the sheer scale of the task. In greater part, however, it is because the Reagan Administration has not gone far enough, failing to exercise sufficient leadership with AID and the multilateral agencies. Talking about market reform, while allowing AID to continue to promote an array of LDC public sector projects and programs, sends mixed signals to developing countries. The new President thus must give new momentum to the changed direction in development policy. In particular, he must make a central point of his arguments that a silent grassroots, free enterprise revolution is underway in the LDCs. The proof of this, he should say, lies in the hundreds of millions of poor LDC citizens who avoid repressive government taxes and regulations by working in the black market or informal sector. He should support these entrepreneurs and small businessmen by pressing Third World governments and international agencies to remove economic controls that force LDC entrepreneurs into a black market.

To enable AID energetically to support this LDC silent economic revolution, the new President should call for a revision of the 1961 Foreign Assistance Act, which governs AID, to eliminate conflicting internal goals and give priority to growth-oriented development strategies. AID should devise an Index of Economic Freedom to guide AID officials in devising programs and to measure the success of various development policies. AID personnel should be given training and incentives to push policies to promote privatization in LDCs. And no new U.S. funds should be given to such multilateral organizations as the International Monetary Fund and the World Bank until they demonstrate that their loans exclusively promote free-market economics.

SUMMARY OF AGENCY FUNCTIONS

After World War II, the U.S. expanded greatly its foreign aid efforts to promote economic growth, first in war-torn Europe and Japan, and then in the rest of the world. Various programs to advance this objective were consolidated in 1961 into AID, which today conducts programs in some 118 countries. Technically, AID reports to the President through the International Development Cooperation Agency (IDCA), a little-used organizational mechanism for establishing U.S. development policy and ensuring intergovernmental coordination on specific development issues. The Administrator of AID currently is also the Director of IDCA. IDCA directs two other organizations: the Overseas Private Investment Corporation (OPIC), which helps insure U.S. overseas investment against losses caused by nationalization or other political harm, and the Trade and Development Program, which studies the feasibility of projects that might be financed by developing countries and then undertaken by private U.S. firms. While they have a direct line to the President, both IDCA and AID are expected to operate under the foreign policy guidance of the Department of State.

The main forms of AID assistance are:

◆ *Economic support funds (ESFs)*, which totaled $3.3 billion in fiscal 1988, given mainly to Israel ($1.2 billion), Egypt ($820 million), Pakistan ($220 million), El Salvador ($215 million), and the Philippines ($189 million).

◆ *Development assistance funds*, which totaled $1.81 billion in fiscal 1988, are intended as genuine economic development aid and are channeled through specific development projects.

◆ *The PL–480 food assistance program*, or "Food for Peace," which totaled $1.1 billion in fiscal 1988, is jointly administered by AID and the Department of Agriculture.

◆ *Disaster relief assistance*, for temporary disasters like floods, earthquakes, or famines.

A number of international organizations also play a central role in economic development efforts. The U.S. is a member of these bodies and provides a substantial proportion of their funds. Among the most important:

◆ *The International Monetary Fund (IMF)*, which was established in 1944 to administer a system of fixed exchange rates for the world's currencies, and in the early 1970s, shifted its focus to inducing private banks to loan money to LDC governments by providing implicit IMF loan guarantees.

◆ **The International Bank for Reconstruction and Development (World Bank)**, which also was established in 1944, initially as a vehicle for providing capital to rebuild Europe and Japan after World War II, and later turning its attention increasingly to the less developed world.

————————————◇————————————

INSTITUTIONAL CONSTRAINTS

International and domestic constraints have weakened the Reagan Administration's ability to expand the LDC private sector as a means of triggering rapid LDC economic development. The greatest resistance to such reforms comes from Third World political leaders and bureaucrats themselves. Thanks to their academic training, and very often, the advice they receive from Western technical experts, many are philosophically hostile to the ideas of deregulation and decentralization. More important is their personal stake in the status quo. Their jobs, salaries, and political power depend on their near-absolute control over the economies of their countries. Real economic reform would remove economic control and decision-making power from government officials and return it to private citizens and businesses. As the Reagan Administration has discovered, while the rulers of many countries will agree to reforms to obtain aid, they often balk at making the changes after they have received their funds.

U.S. AID bureaucrats also hinder effective LDC economic development policies. Many still are steeped in now-discredited economic development theories based on centralization and a dominant public sector. Many of these AID officials accept a static view of wealth and capital. They assume that only through massive transfers of wealth can LDCs become industrialized. They ignore the potential of Third World peoples to create capital themselves if freed from repressive economic policies. These AID officials do not understand that economic freedom is the primary ingredient for economic growth. This is hardly surprising because, in most instances, they have spent their entire AID careers distributing foreign aid funds for public-sector projects. They are comfortable dealing with governments and state officials, but have had little contact with the private sector, especially small-scale businesses.

Many of AID's primary programs, meanwhile, work at cross purposes. Senior State Department officials generally view U.S. foreign aid as a kind of inducement (read: bribe) to keep countries on friendly terms with the U.S. Often this aid undermines conditions for sustained growth. The funds going to Israel and Egypt, for example, may achieve their geopolitical objectives but harm these countries economically. Similarly, food aid under the P.L. 480 program certainly helps U.S. farmers, but depresses LDC food production by undercutting LDC farmers.

Congress, meanwhile, doles out economic aid to its own favorite projects, earmarking funds for various countries and functions. In fiscal 1989, some 97 percent of AID's $3.3 billion economic support fund budget is earmarked. Congress also requires that AID-financed projects in LDCs use a certain amount of U.S. goods or products, even if such products are too costly or inappropriate for the projects. Such congressional micromanagement makes AID's policies uncoordinated, contradictory, and ill-suited to promoting economic growth.

The IMF, World Bank, Inter-American Development Bank, and other multilateral development institutions also constrain U.S. policy. Conditions attached to IMF loans sometimes promote higher taxes and have promoted trade protectionism. These conditions may help in the short run with balance of payments problems, but they can torpedo economic growth. The World Bank lends almost exclusively to government enterprises. This strengthens the state sector at the expense of the private sector and removes incentives for LDC governments to reduce wasteful public spending. Thus officials, even Americans, with these agencies often pursue policies which blunt the effectiveness of AID.

Another constraint on effective development policy is, ironically, the private voluntary organizations (PVOs) that try to alleviate world poverty. Many PVOs are to be praised for their intentions. This surely is the case with CARE and Catholic Relief Services. The trouble is that most PVOs are more interested in dealing with poverty's effects and manifestations than with its underlying causes. Further, few of these organizations are genuinely either private or voluntary. Most PVOs receive most of their funds from AID. Thus they have a strong institutional interest in pressing for humanitarian assistance programs, which ignore the fact that high life expectancy, health care, education, and low levels of infant mortality require strong economic growth. There is, meanwhile, no strong or widespread organized political constituency in the U.S. intent on promoting general economic growth in the Third World. Thus members of Congress tend to be most responsive to the PVOs and to businesses in their districts, such as farming and international construction firms, that benefit from AID projects.

THE REAGAN ADMINISTRATION RECORD

During the Carter Administration, U.S. foreign aid policymakers accepted the premise that the West is to blame for LDC poverty. Transfers of wealth to the governments of poorer countries thus were seen as a kind of moral obligation of the West—a way to absolve collective Western guilt. By ignoring the need for economic freedom, the Carter Administration unwittingly laid the foundations for an economic crisis in the Third World.

By 1981, many LDCs, especially in Latin America, were at the brink of economic collapse. In late 1982, Mexico announced that it could not meet even interest payments on its debts, setting off a debt crisis in much of the less developed world. The root cause was the economic policies of most LDCs. State-owned or -controlled industries were moneylosers and required billions of dollars in government subsidies. Overregulation made private LDC industries inefficient and deterred the creation of new businesses. Trade protectionism deprived LDC consumers of numerous products and drove up prices for those on the market, thus depressing living standards. Businesses were deprived of the capital goods necessary to increase their efficiency. Wage and price controls distorted markets, diverting capital and labor from more profitable to less profitable enterprises. High taxes penalized productive activity. And the threat or reality of government expropriation of private property demonstrated to all citizens that the state itself was the main threat to prosperity. Reacting rationally to these disastrous policies, citizens in LDCs whisked much of their capital to American and West European banks, depriving their own countries of billions of dollars in foreign exchange.

The Reagan Administration has approached the problem of LDC poverty on several fronts. On the first, it has pushed for political freedom and emphasized that left-wing dictatorships invariably pursue policies exacerbating poverty and use economic and humanitarian aid for political objectives. On the second front, the Administration has set a powerful example of free market policies that has helped trigger a remarkable change in economic thinking throughout the world, including LDCs from Jamaica to the People's Republic of China.

The Reagan Administration also has changed the nature of the dialogue between the industrialized and developing countries. Beginning with his tough speech to the 1981 economic development meeting of Western and LDC leaders in Cancun, Mexico, Ronald Reagan at every opportunity has told LDCs that they will prosper only when their people are economically free. The talk now in the LDCs is of privatization, deregulation, and trade liberalization, not of more central planning and international welfare payments. While actual reform is still too slow in coming, the intellectual foundation for a sustained attack on the causes of worldwide poverty is being laid.

Reagan also has emphasized that widespread ownership of capital helps create political stability in Latin America. In 1985, he launched the *Project Economic Justice* task force, which examined opportunities to promote democratic capitalism in Latin America through expanded ownership of capital.[1] The Task Force report issued in 1986, recommends employee stock ownership plans (ESOPs) as a means of privatizing state-owned industries and expanding support for private property rights in LDCs. AID has hosted important conferences for LDC officials. A 1986 conference on privatization in Washington, for instance, examined how the private sector could provide many services and functions now delivered by LDC governments. The following year, an AID conference in Washington dealt with the informal economic sectors, or black markets, in LDCs. The conference generally concluded that harsh government economic regulations force LDC citizens to take economic matters into their own hands.

Despite the changing nature of the debate, real reform often has been elusive. Example: bowing to pressure from U.S. Treasury Secretary James Baker, international lending organizations and private banks provided additional funds for LDC debtors in exchange for LDC promises to restructure their economies along free-market lines. While the money was advanced to LDCs, there has been almost no restructuring. More serious has been the Reagan Administration's failure to gain sufficient control over the AID bureaucracy to be sure that it promotes free enterprise strategies. Though changes have been made at the top of AID, at the bottom it has been business as usual. A Private Enterprise Bureau, for example, was established as an experimental unit within AID to provide expertise to overseas AID missions and other AID bureaus on private enterprise and to suggest projects to promote private sector activity. Yet the Bureau has been almost universally ignored within AID. Further, AID bureaucrats still are locked into a 1960s development mindset. AID even gave extensive financial and technical support for the collectivization of agriculture in El Salvador, a policy that has devastated that country's economy.

Free-market advocates in the World Bank now contend that Reagan's 1986 appointee as World Bank president, former New York

Congressman Barber Conable, has busied himself with shuffling Bank personnel with little effect on the Bank's overall lending policies. While these critics concede that Conable means well, they maintain nevertheless that he has made little attempt to prod the Bank into adopting policies designed to solve the LDCs' long-term economic problems. Example: In 1988, the World Bank extended a $400 million loan to Mexico to retool its state steel sector. Instead, the Bank should have insisted upon privatization of the ailing state industry. To make matters worse, critics add, Conable's countless "policy-based" loans are devoid of sound policy and are used by their recipients mainly to resuscitate failing state enterprises that depress economic growth.

Finally, the Reagan Administration has failed to follow through on its development ideas and strategies. Worker ownership, through Employee Stock Ownership Plans and other mechanisms, should have been the centerpiece of a strategy of democratic or popular capitalism to empower workers with private property. But AID bureaucrats have given a cold shoulder to this approach, and the Administration has done little to force the issue.

———————————◇———————————

THE NEXT FOUR YEARS

Worldwide prosperity is in the economic, political, and moral interest of the U.S. Prosperous countries can purchase more goods from the U.S. and provide valuable products in return. Prosperous countries are less susceptible to communist subversion. And prosperous countries give their citizens the opportunity to develop and enjoy their full human potential.

Each sovereign country, of course, is free to adopt its own economic policies, for good or ill. The U.S. cannot force countries against their will to be smart and adopt growth-oriented policies. Washington and the West in general therefore need not take the blame for continuing world poverty. Yet Western and U.S. economic policies through AID and such institutions as the IMF and World Bank often have fostered irresponsible practices in less developed countries. America thus can help promote worldwide prosperity by removing the obstacles to free-market policies that the U.S. has helped create and replacing them with powerful incentives to promote reforms.

U.S. development policy for nearly three decades has emphasized direct aid handouts to foreign governments and state enterprises, and it promoted LDC economic planning and centralized control of their economies. While these programs have been well-intentioned, history has judged them failures. The new President must accept these failures and reexamine thoroughly U.S. aid policies. Development success now must be measured not by how much money the U.S. gives away but by the actual results of U.S. aid—by how many more Taiwans and Singapores emerge, by rising levels of per capita income, and by rising and sustainable levels of health care and education.

Redefining the Development Debate

The new President must move from the welcome rhetoric of the Reagan Administration in the development debate to tangible policy changes. This will require a strong public definition and discussion of the nature of the free market solution and resolute action within AID and on Capitol Hill.

The new President should place the U.S. government on the side of the economically repressed throughout the world. The theme of his development policy should be popular or democratic capitalism in the less developed countries. He should emphasize liberating the informal sector—entrepreneurs who survive through their own hard work and efforts by avoiding excessive government regulations. To outflank Marxists and other repressive central planners who pretend to speak for the people, the new Administration should raise the class consciousness of the LDC informal sector by pointing out that the U.S., by virtue of its own democratic traditions and economic success, stands behind the struggle of citizens in less developed countries to gain private property rights and economic freedom. In international forums, such as the U.N., the U.S. should condemn the deprivation of such rights by political elites for hindering economic development. The new President should proclaim, "Property rights are human rights."

The annual economic summits of the seven leading industrial democracies provide an opportunity for the U.S. to enlist its allies in this effort. The U.S. Information Agency and the Voice of America can broadcast these arguments directly to the LDCs.

Spurring Growth by Enhancing Economic Freedom

The debate over economic development policy has been transformed in recent years by the growing recognition that many ostensibly stagnant countries in fact possess a vigorous underground economy, in which small entrepreneurs battle government red tape and provide many basic goods and services for the economy. Peruvian economist

Hernando de Soto, in 1986, published the first extensive empirical study on the informal sector or black market in his country. He shows that over one-third of Peru's gross national product is produced by ordinary citizens seeking to avoid repressive government regulations and controls by operating in the informal sector.

The new President, in his first State of the Union speech and in speeches on the world economy, should highlight the silent grassroots revolution for economic freedom spreading across the less developed world. He should explain to the public as well as to policy and opinion makers that the poor of the world are seeking economic freedom and that only repressive government policies keep the poor from prospering. The new President should use visits to the U.S. by the leaders of LDCs to explain to them the nature of their problems and point out that, as the booming informal sector demonstrates, their own people reject their government's policies. The new President should make the silent free-market revolution a major topic of discussion at economic summits with leaders of other industrialized countries. The new Administration's rhetoric as well as policies should focus on the need to free people from government economic control, to allow them to help themselves.

Encouraging Employee Ownership

Employee ownership should form an important element of the new President's private sector strategy for LDCs. By selling or giving workers shares in a newly privatized state enterprise, workers gain a direct ownership stake in free enterprise. There is already strong bipartisan support for Employee Stock Ownership Plans (ESOPs) in the U.S. Congress, and solid political success and economic success around the world. The new Administration should instruct the administrator of AID to promote ESOPs as a means to privatize state-owned enterprises in LDCs.

Rewriting the Foreign Assistance Act

Currently a special bipartisan task force of the House of Representatives and AID itself are investigating independently the reform of America's foreign aid policy. Central to this must be a rewriting of the 1961 Foreign Assistance Act, which has become a confusing and conflicting document. A new Act should make AID's clear and overriding goal the promotion of indigenously generated, self-sustaining growth in LDCs.

◆ *Policy Coordination.* A new Foreign Assistance Act should take account of the need for coordination of development policies between the administrator of America's foreign aid program and other federal agencies that affect economic growth.

Section 640B of the current Foreign Assistance Act and existing Executive Orders allow the President to create a Development Coordinating Committee (DCC) and appropriate subcommittees to hammer out detailed U.S. foreign assistance policies and positions and to strike a balance among foreign policy, development, and U.S. commercial interests. Another existing Executive Order makes the director of the International Development Cooperation Agency (IDCA), currently the administrator of AID, the chairman of the DCC and the President's principal adviser on development programs and policies. The DCC includes the Secretaries of such executive branches as Agriculture, Commerce, Defense, and State. This mechanism has not been used. A new Foreign Assistance Act should preserve and strengthen the DCC, making its use mandatory to coordinate better development policy within the Administration. This could be done in part by requiring the Chairman of the DCC to report to Congress annually on attempts to coordinate economic development policy.

A new Foreign Assistance Act also must recognize AID's three separate functions: assistance to meet short-term humanitarian needs created by famines and other natural disasters; payments to countries for political reasons, as to Egypt and Israel as part of the Camp David peace accord, or to countries for the right to maintain U.S. military installations; and funds and other forms of assistance to promote economic development. One problem is that these functions often work at cross purposes. Another is that it often is not clear which function a particular program is supposed to promote or how. A new Foreign Assistance Act therefore should separate these functions into individual units of AID or the International Development Coordination Administration. Or these functions should be performed by separate agencies or turned over to other branches of government. Aid motivated by geopolitical concerns, for example, could be handled by the State Department, the advantage being that AID outlays no longer would be misunderstood by the American public; funds given to countries in exchange for political favors should not be mixed with funds for economic development.

◆ *Free Market Principles.* The new Foreign Assistance Act should set as its essential goal the promotion of self-sustaining economic growth in less developed countries through a market-oriented economy. Economic growth is necessary for other forms of social progress, democracy, and respect for basic human rights.

The new Foreign Assistance Act must establish clear foreign assistance objectives for the U.S. government as a whole—AID, the Overseas Private Investment Corporation (OPIC), the Export-Import Bank, the Departments of Agriculture, Commerce, State, and Treasury, the White House Science Adviser's Office, the U.S. Trade Representative, and other agencies that have an important impact on economic growth in LDCs. Policy coordination in the Development Coordinating Committee would be guided by the principles of the new Act.

◆ *Index of Economic Freedom.* Economic development assistance should not be extended automatically to every developing country. Years of experience have shown that foreign aid does not quickly buy change in a country mired in socialist rhetoric, committed to state planning, and uninterested in changing. Since U.S. foreign assistance resources are limited, they should be used only where there is real promise of progress and reform. Criteria for providing economic growth assistance thus are needed. Only countries meeting these standards should receive assistance for development. The criteria should be codified in an Index of Economic Freedom.

This Index would gauge the performance of LDC governments and act as a benchmark for the policies of AID, the International Monetary Fund, the World Bank, and other multilateral organizations. The new Administration should begin devising the Index immediately. It would have exposed as repressive and economically useless such policies as AID's collectivization of agriculture in El Salvador, IMF-backed tax increases and import restrictions, and World Bank support for government agricultural marketing boards. The Index would measure economic freedom as the sum of several indicators. Among them:

1) Taxation. How high are the top rates and at what income levels do they become effective? Studies such as those by Alvin Rabushka of the Hoover Institution show a strong correlation between high tax rates and economic stagnation as well as between low tax rates and economic growth. This indicates how free a citizen is to keep income or property and thus determines the incentives to be productive.

2) Size of the state sector. What percentage of the gross national product, of agricultural production, and of manufacturing is owned by the state? This indicates whether citizens are barred from certain economic activities and therefore are forced to compete with their own government.

3) Private banking. Are citizens allowed to deposit their money safely in private banks or does the government control the banks? How dependent are entrepreneurs on exclusive state sources of credit? How safe are a citizen's savings from government abuse? How much available credit is taken by the government? IMF data indicate that a strong correlation exists between high levels of economic growth, high levels of savings, and high percentages of credit consumed by the private sector.

4) Regulations. How difficult and costly is it to secure a business license? What sort of red tape do businessmen face? What regulations favor established business at the expense of newcomers? When regulations limit the freedom of citizens to establish businesses or add prohibitive costs to maintaining them, economic output is restricted.

5) Wages and prices. How many workers have their wages mandated by the government, and how many goods and services prices are set by the government? Are workers, merchants, and consumers free to buy and sell based on mutual consent, or does the government prohibit certain terms of trade? Division of labor can occur only if wages and prices reflect the relative market efficiencies of the various producers. By prohibiting people from buying and selling on mutually agreed-on terms and by setting wages and prices by arbitrary whim, governments assure that workers and businesses will not benefit by working or producing in those sectors in which they are most efficient.

6) Trade. What are tariff levels? What is the value of goods controlled by quotas or other import restrictions? Are there export controls? These indicate whether citizens are free to buy and sell across national boundaries based on mutual consent.

7) Capital flows and investment. Are there restrictions on foreign investment? Do businessmen have access to foreign capital? Can money be removed from the country freely? Governments often restrict the freedom of citizens to bring money into the country from an irrational fear of foreign domination, thereby depriving the country of capital necessary for economic growth. Restricting the removal of money from a country usually is an attempt to stop citizens from taking their money out of a failing economy. Funds are then usually smuggled out of the country or used in the black market.

8) Protection of property rights. Has the government expropriated or nationalized private property? Are there restrictions on what citi-

zens may own? All other economic freedom is based on the right to own property. If people are allowed to own property, their survival and prosperity is dependent on their own efforts.

An Index of Economic Freedom would set a clear standard for U.S. international economic development policy. It would parallel indices of human rights and political freedom. Economic growth assistance should be given only to countries that show progress on the Index.

Abolishing OPIC

The Overseas Private Investment Corporation (OPIC), like the World Bank's new Multilateral Investment Guarantee Agency, insures investments in LDCs against government confiscation or other harmful acts. While this may reassure U.S. investors, it is unwise development policy because it removes incentives from LDC leaders to act responsibly and protect private property. It also shifts the risks of investing in unstable countries from the businessman to the American taxpayer. OPIC primarily provides a subsidy to U.S. businesses. As such, OPIC should be abolished. At the least, it should be transferred to the Commerce Department, which deals more with U.S. business than with foreign development.

Promoting a Free Market Philosophy within AID

Under a new Foreign Assistance Act that makes economic freedom and growth the central goal of U.S. foreign assistance, AID as a whole would become in effect a private enterprise bureau. A separate Private Enterprise Bureau thus would not be necessary. In the interim, the Private Enterprise Bureau could expand its efforts within AID to conduct seminars on free market issues to AID personnel.

Another step the new Administration should take would be to establish incentives for AID staff to adopt free-market approaches in their work. As a regular part of their duties, AID field officers in LDCs should submit annual reports on the economic freedom in the country to which they are assigned, based on the Index of Economic Freedom. They also should submit regular reports on the extent of the informal sector in their assigned countries and identify the regulations that cause such activity. Reports should be submitted on which enterprises are likely candidates for privatization. These reports should be used to measure an LDC government's efforts to promote free enterprise and as the basis for negotiating the conditions of future U.S. assistance. The regular evaluations and promotions of AID officials should be based in part on their success in providing information to the AID administrator on LDCs in accordance with the Index of Economic Freedom.

AID should provide generous financial assistance and leave to AID officers who wish to train for these tasks; such training might occur outside of the agency or inside. The AID administrator should see that instruction in the task of evaluating economic freedom and informal sector activity is along strict free-market lines. This instruction should include analysis of the problems of past development policies and the nature of economic growth in free societies. The administrator should ensure that, when outside training is involved, university courses or instructors are market-oriented so that AID officials will receive training appropriate to their tasks.

AID officials also would have a greater incentive to promote free market strategies if they were held accountable for the failed projects they have approved. The inspector general who audits AID accounts issues periodic reviews that often reveal flaws in AID projects. He has found, for example, that AID has given ice cream makers to Egyptian schools where no ice is available and ovens to schools that cannot use the only available heating gas. The inspector general should name the AID officers who approve such projects; a copy of this citation should be placed in the officers' personnel files.

Curbing the Excesses of Private
Voluntary Organizations

AID programs frequently are carried out by private voluntary organizations (PVOs). Better control of PVO funding and policies is necessary if AID is to promote economic reform effectively. To do this, the new Foreign Assistance Act should raise the current 20 percent minimum level of private-sector support that a PVO must have to qualify for federal funds; AID should rigorously enforce this minimum. Because many PVOs are private in name only, receiving most of their operating funds from the U.S. government, they have a strong incentive to lobby for the continuation of programs that keep them in business, even though they help little or even hinder economic growth. AID also should take action against PVOs that are found through audits or other means to be involved in extensive waste, fraud, and abuse. For example, future contracts could be denied to such PVOs. Grants to PVOs should be made strictly as a means to advance economic freedom and growth. Spending on PVOs, as with all other AID projects, should be evaluated for efficiency.

Demanding a New Mandate for
International Lending Agencies

The new President should use U.S. membership and clout in international lending agencies to pursue U.S. objectives more aggressively. The U.S. controls about 20 percent of the vote in the IMF and World Bank. Yet their policies bolstering state-controlled economies undermine AID efforts to spur LDC economic growth. The World Bank is seeking $75 billion in new loans and guarantees from its member governments, while the IMF is soon to make a similar appeal for new funds. The U.S. share will be approximately 19 percent of the total. The new President should refuse to grant these organizations more money unless they meet some conditions.

First, the IMF and World Bank must agree to lend no new money to such repressive dictatorships or terrorist states as Ethiopia, Laos, South Yemen, and Syria.

Second, the IMF, World Bank, and other development banks must open their records more to the public. The veil of secrecy makes it difficult to discover the cause of failed policies or wasteful lending. The U.S. should require the World Bank to make public all project papers, which define the amounts, uses, and conditions of loans. The U.S. should require the World Bank to make public the internal evaluations of its loans and lending policies made by the Bank's Operations Evaluation Department. Similarly, IMF loan agreements, including the conditions attached to loans, should be open to public scrutiny.

Third, the IMF, World Bank, and other development organizations should spend no further funds bailing out LDC state-owned enterprises. Such enterprises are a major cause of continuing poverty and debt. Funds for new projects should go only for such infrastructure development as roads. Such funds should be extended only if no private funding of the project, from either domestic or overseas suppliers, is available. Thus, if there is a possibility for private operators to provide bus transportation, no funds would go for a state-owned bus line. In cases where projects built at public expense could be privately managed or even privatized completely, plans for such private involvement should be a prerequisite to new loan money. In the case of IMF loans to help countries meet debt obligations, an estimate should be made of the losses incurred by a country's state-owned industries or subsidies paid to cover the losses of nominally private enterprises. IMF loans should encourage and monitor progress in eliminating such self-inflicted losses by LDC governments.

Fourth, the World Bank must abolish its lending targets. Currently, the Bank sets five-year targets for how much is to be lent to various countries. The targets are always met. This constitutes a quota system for loans by which all countries get their cut, regardless of whether the loans represent the best allocation of World Bank resources. Targets should be abolished and loans only made for projects based on their merits.

Fifth, the World Bank's International Financial Corporation (IFC) should make no new loans until it completely revamps its lending practices. The IFC was created in 1956 to promote private-sector activities via loans to private enterprises in LDCs. Most of its loans, however, go to enterprises owned in part or in whole by governments. IFC even recently has been lending to such communist countries as Poland and Yugoslavia. Until the IFC can assure that its loans will go to private-sector operations, no new loans should be made.

Mastering the Debt Crisis

In tackling the huge LDC foreign debt, the new President must move beyond the Baker Plan. Issued in 1985 by then-Treasury Secretary James Baker, the plan advocates providing more funds to LDCs in exchange for promises from their governments to restructure their economies along free-market lines. The Baker Plan's goal is laudable. But rather than lend more money to debtor countries, adding to their debt burdens, the U.S. should aim at strengthening capital formation within these countries and accelerating economic growth. Currently, billions of dollars are smuggled out of LDCs and deposited in safe foreign banks by the LDC's own citizens for fear of inflation, high taxes, and nationalization. U.S. aid to LDCs should be linked to policies that will coax this flight capital back into LDC economies. In particular, the LDC governments should guarantee strictly the rights of bank depositors to their funds.

The U.S. should insist that aid recipients strengthen their capital markets. They could be encouraged, for example, to arrange more debt for equity swaps. Under such arrangements, an LDC's debt is forgiven by third-party businesses who purchase the debt from the creditor banks in exchange for stock in businesses and enterprises owned in part or in whole by the LDC government. Such swaps allow LDCs to eliminate part of their debts at a discount while bringing potential new investors into the economy. Swaps also prod governments to consider improving their investment climates. Finally, these swaps could offer opportunities for LDCs to attract back into the country capital taken out by their own citizens.

———————————◇———————————

INITIATIVES FOR 1989

1) Rewrite the Foreign Assistance Act. The Foreign Assistance Act establishes conflicting and overlapping goals for AID and micromanages AID activities. The result is that AID faces enormous constraints in pursuing its goal of promoting economic development. The new Administration thus should propose legislation to rewrite the Act. A new Act should give priority to promoting economic growth. In contrast to the existing Act, the legislation should separate aid for economic development from humanitarian assistance and payments for political reasons. If necessary, AID and the International Development Cooperation Agency should be merged. This would allow America's foreign assistance program to be administered more efficiently and would help eliminate conflicting program goals.

2) Devise an Index of Economic Freedom. Currently, there is no standard by which to measure LDC's economic development progress. There is also no set of criteria by which AID can determine if a country is promoting economic freedom. The new administrator of AID should develop an objective index to measure an LDC's progress toward economic freedom and expanded opportunity. This index should be used to determine which countries should receive development aid and for what purposes.

3) Require AID officials to report on the degree of economic freedom in Third World countries. While the Index of Economic Freedom is being developed, the new AID administrator should instruct the agency's officers stationed in LDCs to submit reports on economic freedom, informal sector activities, and industries that are likely candidates for privatization. This will provide the AID administrator and other AID officials with information necessary to make foreign assistance decisions. Further, since economic freedom is the necessary condition for economic growth, this requirement will focus the activities and attention of all AID personnel on the best means by which to eliminate worldwide poverty.

4) Train AID staff in free market economics. Currently few AID officials have technical knowledge of free market approaches to development.

Thus, for AID to promote free enterprise and economic freedom in the LDCs, its staff must receive training in free market strategies. The new Administration should develop a comprehensive training program, perhaps in cooperation with academic institutions, for all AID development officials.

5) Abolish the Private Enterprise Bureau of AID and integrate its development approach into the entire AID structure. The creation in 1981 of the Private Enterprise Bureau of AID reflected an important recognition that economic development and growth must come ultimately from private individuals and enterprises in an LDC, not from the government. The trouble is that establishment of this minor and underfunded bureau relegated private enterprise to sideline status. Spurring private enterprise growth strategies should be the central goal of AID. As such, the new Foreign Assistance Act should disband the Private Enterprise Bureau and should integrate its functions into the entire AID bureaucracy.

6) Abolish the Overseas Private Investment Corporation (OPIC) or transfer it to the Commerce Department. OPIC provides subsidies to U.S. firms doing business overseas. This agency has little or nothing to do with development policy nor can it be justified on general economic grounds. It should be abolished. If this is politically impossible, it should be transferred from the nominal supervision of the International Development Cooperation Agency to the Commerce Department.

7) Enforce tighter standards on private voluntary organizations. The current requirement that PVOs receive 20 percent of their funds from private sources is far too low. Because the vast majority of PVO funds come from the government, they have a vested interest in continuing foreign aid policies that bring them funding, even though such policies might contribute little to LDC economic growth. The standard should be increased to approximately 50 percent. This would lessen the incentive for PVOs to lobby for counterproductive programs.

8) Invite the Republic of China on Taiwan and other countries that are launching their own foreign aid programs to join a U.S.-sponsored Foundation for Economic Growth. The assumption in many LDCs and international development organizations is that economic growth requires large infusions of assistance. Rather than more money, the LDCs need advice and help in pursuing market-oriented policies.

Several of the very successful newly industrialized countries, such as the Republic of China on Taiwan and the Republic of Korea, are starting their own foreign assistance programs. They should not make the mistakes made by the U.S., other older industrial nations, and international lending agencies, of giving money to LDCs without insisting on policy changes that trigger growth. The new AID administrator should invite the top development officials from these newly industrialized countries to a conference to form a Foundation for Economic Growth. The purpose of this Foundation would be to provide technical assistance to LDCs on such issues as promoting domestic capital formation, land reform, privatization, and other growth-oriented policies. The Index of Economic Freedom adopted by the U.S. should be used as a development guideline for the Foundation's activities.

9) Require the World Bank, IMF, and other international lending institutions to make public their loan agreements and internal evaluations. Because of World Bank and IMF restrictions on releasing information, it is difficult for U.S. policymakers and public to judge in detail why the policies of international lending institutions have failed. Congress should require that loan agreements and evaluation of these institutions be made available to the public.

———————◇———————

NOTES

1. This is widely known as The Middendorf Plan, named after the author of this chapter (ed.).

29

The Department of Defense

The Department of Defense is responsible for protecting the United States against foreign military threats. The Department was created by the National Security Act of 1947, which united the Navy Department, the Army's War Department, and the newly independent Air Force. From its headquarters in the Pentagon, the Defense Department raises, trains, and equips U.S. armed forces in peacetime. In wartime, it is responsible for using these forces at the direction of the President.

The President is the Commander in Chief of the U.S. armed forces. Presidential authority over the Defense Department is exercised by the Secretary of Defense, who manages the Army, Navy and Air Force departments through civilian secretaries (the Marine corps is a separate service under the jurisdiction of the Navy Department). The President and Secretary of Defense are advised on military matters by the Chairman of the Joint Chiefs of Staff. The Joint Chiefs consists of the senior military officers of the military services. The chain of military command runs from the President to the Secretary of Defense and through the Joint Chiefs of Staff to military commanders, who have operational command over the forces assigned to them.

◇

INSTITUTIONAL CONSTRAINTS

The Department of Defense, because of its immense bureaucracy, can be a stubborn impediment to the efficient execution of national defense policies.

Such legendary interservice rivalries as the post-World War II showdown between the Air Force and Navy can paralyze defense planning for years. In that debate, each service sought funds for an expensive program to deliver atomic weapons. The Air Force backed its long-range B–36 bomber and the Navy its "supercarrier" *United States*; the nation could not afford both. Even after Truman resolved the

---

BUDGET AND PERSONNEL

Secretaries

Frank C. Carlucci, III   1987–present
Caspar Weinberger   1981–1987

Personnel	Military	Civilian	Total
March 1988	2,113,000	1,073,900	3,285,100
April 1980	2,050,000	969,200	3,019,200
April 1970	3,066,200	1,218,900	4,285,100

Budget Outlays

Fiscal Year	Total (billions)	Military	Civilian
1989 Estimate	$309.2	$285.5	$23.7
1988 Estimate	$299.6	$277.3	$22.3
1987 Actual	$294.7	$274.0	$20.7
1986 Actual	$285.7	$265.5	$20.3
1985 Actual	$263.9	$245.2	$18.8
1980 Actual	$146.1	$130.9	$15.2
1970 Actual	$ 84.2	$ 80.1	$ 4.1

---

debate in favor of the Air Force in 1949, Navy admirals continued to defend their turf, arguing to Congress that the Air Force program would "invite war." Services continue to protect their turf at the expense of Administration policies. For example, from 1985 to 1986 the Army lobbied hard to prevent the transfer of *Stinger* anti-aircraft missiles to the Afghan rebels because the Army leadership did not want to draw down its own war stocks. The Pentagon also probably receives greater scrutiny from the press, interest groups, and the public at large than any other federal department. Congress also has expanded its involvement in defense issues. Increasingly, the congressional budgeting process is used to exercise detailed control over defense programs. This process, known as "micromanagement," often impedes effective Pentagon planning and program management.

Indeed, the history of Ronald Reagan's Strategic Defense Initiative (SDI) attests to the intense pressures that can be brought to bear on a presidential defense proposal, from within and outside the government:

DEFENSE BUDGETS IN 1982 DOLLARS

Total Budget

Fiscal Year	Total (billions)
1989 Estimate	$245.4
1988 Estimate	$246.8
1987 Actual	$252.1
1986 Actual	$249.8
1985 Actual	$236.5
1984 Actual	$222.4
1983 Actual	$213.0
1982 Actual	$198.6
1981 Actual	$192.6
1980 Actual	$172.8

Military Only

Fiscal Year	Total (billions)
1989 Estimate	$226.6
1988 Estimate	$228.4
1987 Actual	$234.4
1986 Actual	$232.1
1985 Actual	$219.7
1984 Actual	$204.4
1983 Actual	$195.9
1982 Actual	$180.7
1981 Actual	$164.9
1980 Actual	$154.9

Civilian Only

Fiscal Year	Total (billions)
1989 Estimate	$18.8
1988 Estimate	$18.4
1987 Actual	$17.7
1986 Actual	$17.7
1985 Actual	$16.8
1984 Actual	$18.0
1983 Actual	$18.1
1982 Actual	$17.9
1981 Actual	$18.1
1980 Actual	$18.0

He unveiled his proposal for strategic defense in a March 15, 1983, speech. The following year, a Strategic Defense Initiative Office was established within the Pentagon to run the program. This ignited bureaucratic turf battles between the Pentagon's SDI proponents and adversaries. The Air Force high command, for example, feared that SDI would drain funds from manned aircraft programs. Then a tacit interdepartmental coalition developed between Pentagon SDI opponents and the State Department, which was pressing the White House to trade SDI for arms control concessions from Moscow. Advocates on both sides lobbied behind the scenes with the Congress, which gradually chipped away at the program despite continuing strong public support and unexpectedly rapid technological progress.

Both sides sought to bolster their arguments with technical data. At the instigation of congressional SDI opponents, Congress's Office of Technology Assessment was commissioned to study the feasibility of strategic defenses. The resulting report was highly critical of SDI, and its conclusions starkly at variance with those of Pentagon researchers and officials at U.S. national laboratories. The OTA report was widely publicized in the media and influenced public opinion, even though the report later was discredited.

Joining the anti-SDI forces within the government were myriad and well-organized groups from the academic and scientific communities, such as the Union of Concerned Scientists and American Federation of Scientists, many of which had been actively involved in the late 1960s debate over missile defenses. They were joined by other interest groups, including the fading nuclear freeze movement, which shifted its focus to SDI after the Administration's success in arms control effectively eliminated the nuclear freeze as a public issue.

The story of SDI illustrates in microcosm the impediments facing any major new weapons system or program. The process cannot be circumvented, but strong presidential leadership can salvage at least part of a program, such as SDI, even in the face of powerful political and institutional constraints.

Strategic Offensive Forces

William Schneider, Jr., and Kim R. Holmes*
Task Force Chairmen

Since the end of World War II, the United States has relied on offensive nuclear weapons to deter war with the Soviet Union. The U.S. capability to deter war requires what has been called the "Triad": land-based missiles, sea-based missiles, and bombers armed with gravity bombs and cruise missiles. Diversifying the ways U.S. nuclear forces are deployed on land, at sea, and in the air is believed to make these forces more survivable against a Soviet nuclear strike. The capability to survive a nuclear attack and to retaliate has been the key to deterrence; it puts Moscow on notice that aggression will be punished by nuclear counterattacks on the Soviet Union. Equally as important, the threat of nuclear retaliation posed by a survivable U.S. nuclear Triad also serves to deter, in conjunction with the North Atlantic Treaty Organization's conventional forces, Soviet conventional or nonnuclear attacks on Western Europe.

◇

THE REAGAN ADMINISTRATION RECORD

Upon taking office, the Reagan Administration found the U.S. falling behind the Soviet Union in strategic offensive forces. In 1981, Moscow had a nearly four-to-one advantage in deployed intercontinental ballistic missile (ICBM) throwweight, a measure of the total destructive explosive power that missiles can deliver to their targets. Throwweight is considered one of the best measures of an arsenal's potential destructiveness. Moreover, while the Soviet Union was adding new ICBMs each year, the U.S. had shut down its only active ICBM production line in 1977, with no plans to deploy a new ICBM until 1986. As a result, land-based U.S. strategic offensive

---

*Commenting and contributing generously to this report were *Mandate III* Task Force Members Mark Albrecht, James T. Hackett, Christopher Lay, Joseph Mayer, and David B. Rivkin, Jr. They do not necessarily endorse all of its views and recommendations.

forces, bombers, as well as ICBMs, were becoming increasingly vulnerable to a disarming surprise Soviet nuclear attack. Similarly, the U.S. was facing the prospect of falling behind Moscow in the quantity and quality of its sea-launched ballistic missiles and long-range strategic bombers.

The Reagan Administration has reversed the decline of the U.S. strategic offensive nuclear arsenal. It has deployed the MX ICBM, the B-1B strategic bomber, and ground-, sea-, and air-launched cruise missiles. The MX missile improves U.S. ability to target Soviet missiles and command posts buried in steel and concrete bunkers. The B-1B bomber and cruise missiles strengthen U.S. ability to evade the formidable Soviet air defenses and strike deep inside the USSR. The development of the Advance Cruise Missile (ACM), which will become operational early next decade, will provide the U.S. air-launched cruise missile force with longer range and greater capabilities to foil Soviet air defense radars. The Reagan Administration also has accelerated development of the radar-evading B-2 Stealth bomber, which can target the extremely valuable military installations that the Soviets choose to protect with their most effective air defenses. The Reagan Administration has continued deployment of the *Trident I* sea-launched ballistic missile and development of the *Trident II* (D-5) missile, which has greater accuracy and payload than any other sea-based ballistic missile in the world. The Administration has begun development of the short-range attack missile (SRAM-II) for strategic bombers, which will be safer, more reliable, and better able to attack against hardened targets and will carry more payload than older models. The Reagan Administration also has improved the command, control, communication, and intelligence systems for U.S. strategic forces. This has included making strategic radio relay stations resistant to the electromagnetic pulse effects of nuclear blasts, improving very low-frequency communication systems with ballistic missile submarines, developing the *Milstar* satellite command and control system to provide a survivable and jam-resistant communication system for U.S. strategic forces, and developing a satellite system capable of detecting nuclear detonations and relaying precise information about the scale of a nuclear attack on the U.S.

Despite this strategic force modernization, however, the Reagan Administration has failed to deploy a land-based missile that, employing either mobility or active strategic defenses, could survive a Soviet nuclear strike. The original goal for the MX, developed during the Carter Administration, was to deploy 200 missiles in a survivable basing mode. Primarily because of congressional opposition to the MX, the Reagan Administration was forced to cut the goal to 100 MX missiles to be placed both in fixed silos and on railroad cars stored in garrisons. However, only 50 MXs, all in vulnerable fixed silos, have been approved for deployment by Congress. The failure to deploy all 100 MXs in a survivable basing mode is a setback to the U.S. deterrent.

Another setback has been the Reagan Administration's failure to articulate a sound strategic doctrine to guide the development, deployment, and operations of offensive and defensive strategic forces. To be sure, the Administration merits enormous credit for launching the Strategic Defense Initiative (SDI) program. But a major obstacle to SDI was the reluctance of the military services and the Joint Chiefs of Staff to appreciate the political and long-term need to move toward a strategic defense posture. Unless U.S. strategic doctrine, which is currently designed to accommodate only offensive nuclear forces, is revised to provide guidance on how offensive forces (missiles, bombers, and cruise missiles) and defensive forces (ground- and space-based interceptors and supporting systems) can work together to enhance deterrence, the promise of SDI may go unfulfilled.

THE NEXT FOUR YEARS

To deter nuclear war, U.S. offensive strategic forces must be able to survive nuclear strikes and then be launched in a devastating counterattack. Strategic forces can be made more survivable by placing them on submarines where they are difficult to detect, in concrete-and-steel-hardened missile silos, and on such mobile platforms as railroad cars or trucks, or by protecting them with strategic defenses. For strategic forces to deter attack, they must be able to threaten the Soviet leadership with the loss of what it holds most dear: its military forces and its ability to exercise political and military authority over the Soviet Union. As such, U.S. offensive strategic forces should have very long-range capabilities, high accuracy, and sufficient destructive capability to attack Soviet nuclear forces and their command and control support facilities.

The Soviet strategic arms buildup, however, is threatening U.S. deterrence. Moscow's deployment of new and highly survivable mobile ballistic missiles such as the SS-24 and SS-25 gives the Soviets a one-two punch of offensive nuclear power. These new Soviet mobile land-based missiles, along with mobile strategic command, control, and communication posts, potentially undermine U.S. deterrence by making it more difficult for U.S. strategic forces to target Soviet missiles in a retaliatory strike.

The growing Soviet ability to launch aerial attacks on the U.S. and its allies with *Bear* and *Blackjack* strategic bombers, long-range AS-15 air-launched cruise missiles, and SS-NX-21 sea-launched cruise missiles poses a growing threat to U.S. land-based missiles, bombers, and missile submarine bases. Undercutting deterrence too is the emerging Soviet capability to build a nationwide anti-ballistic missile system faster than the U.S. can. Soviet gains in this area include the production of new *Galosh* interceptors and a large network of warhead-tracking large phased-array radars (LPARs).

Modernizing U.S. Land-Based Nuclear Forces

To meet the mounting Soviet strategic threat, the new President should direct the Secretary of Defense to devise a nuclear modernization program that creates: 1) a survivable U.S. nuclear force and a command and control system capable of responding flexibly against Soviet military targets; 2) offensive nuclear forces deployed on land, at sea, and in the air so that a Soviet technological breakthrough in one area, such as anti-submarine warfare, would not suddenly jeopardize the bulk of U.S. nuclear forces; and 3) new bombers, cruise missiles, warheads, and penetration aids capable of tracking and destroying mobile Soviet missiles and command and control posts.

Alternatives for modernizing U.S. nuclear land-based ballistic missile forces should be judged according to the degree to which they satisfy three key criteria:

◆ *Cost-effective survivability.* A strong deterrent force requires that enough U.S. land-based missiles survive a Soviet nuclear first strike to retaliate against the Soviet Union. This means that the U.S. land-based missile forces must be more survivable and cost-effective than they now are. Options for improving survivability include active strategic defenses, overland mobility on trucks or railroad cars, new kinds of passive defenses that bury missiles inside mountains, and new deceptive techniques. Deception includes communication practices, hiding missiles in the field under camouflaged cover, or moving missiles about among a large number of "dummy" silos to keep the enemy guessing about the real location of missiles, thus multiplying the number of targets the enemy must attack.

◆ *Providing a credible response to the increasingly diversified Soviet nuclear force.* The U.S. nuclear modernization program must take the emerging Soviet nuclear capabilities into consideration. Moscow is making its nuclear forces increasingly mobile and better protected. Thus, U.S. nuclear forces must be able to destroy Soviet missiles and command and control posts that are mobile or protected by concrete-and-steel-hardened silos buried deep underground. To do this, the U.S. should develop new ballistic missile warheads that burrow into the earth upon impact to destroy Soviet underground missile silos and command and control posts and new maneuverable warheads that change course upon reentering the atmosphere to evade interception and strike at Soviet mobile missiles such as the SS-25 and SS-24.

◆ **Compatibility with arms control agreements.** The U.S. and the Soviet Union are currently considering an agreement that would reduce each side's forces by roughly 50 percent. Under such an agreement, it makes sense for the U.S. to have a land-based ICBM force that allows the deployment of its warheads on a large number of missiles, rather than concentrating them on a small number of missiles, which could be easily targeted by the USSR. The MX missile has ten warheads, while the *Midgetman* has only one.

Deploying Trident Submarines Armed with *Trident II* (D-5) Missiles

Submarine-based ballistic missile forces are the most survivable of all U.S. strategic forces. Since they are difficult to track, they are difficult to destroy. As such, the U.S. should maintain production of *Trident* (*Ohio* class) ballistic missile submarines at the current rate of one per year until twenty are produced; by the end of 1988, nine submarines will have been manufactured. By 1996, seventeen more will have been built. The U.S. should place the newer and more accurate *Trident II* (D-5) missile on all *Trident* missile submarines. This missile's greater payload offsets the decline in total payload of the U.S. submarine force as the U.S. shifts from the numerous *Polaris* and *Poseidon* systems to the less numerous *Ohio* class submarines. The *Trident II* missile's greater accuracy permits deterrence to be maintained with fewer deployed warheads.

Developing and Deploying a Penetrating Strategic Bomber

The U.S. needs a new long-range strategic bomber to penetrate Soviet air defenses that are impassable for the B-52 and difficult for the B-1. The B-52, America's only current cruise missile-carrying bomber, must remain outside Soviet defenses when firing cruise missiles at Soviet targets. A penetrating bomber with stealth radar-foiling capabilities would have the flexibility of striking at such targets of opportunity as mobile missiles and mobile command and control posts. A penetrating bomber, moreover, would force the Soviet Union to continue spending great sums of money on air defenses rather than on such offensive forces as nuclear ballistic missiles and tanks.

If its flight tests are successful, the U.S. should continue developing and eventually deploy the B-2 Stealth strategic bomber until all 132 are in the arsenal. This bomber's innovative design and new materials are believed capable of foiling Soviet air defense radars. Pentagon research should focus on new kinds of surveillance and targeting technologies, such as laser guidance systems and infrared and optical sensors. New remotely piloted vehicles (RPVs), for example, could be equipped with sensors and launched by bombers to scan vast amounts of territory for mobile missiles. Satellites could be used to find mobile missiles and relay such information to U.S. bombers seeking mobile targets. By the end of the century, up to 50 percent of all Soviet targets, including missiles and command and control posts, will be mobile.

Improving Existing Weapons Designs

Too often the Pentagon builds weapons of an entirely new design rather than improving existing weapons. The result is that existing weapons generally do not benefit from the latest technology. Typical is the Air Force decision not to upgrade the current air-launched cruise missile; instead the Air Force is developing a totally new Advanced Cruise Missile (ACM). Yet the current class of air-launched cruise missiles could be given better guidance systems and longer-range capabilities based on existing or near-term technologies. While the ACM should be developed, it must not be at the expense of modest improvements in the basic design of the currently deployed air-launched cruise missiles.

Whenever possible, the Pentagon should upgrade existing strategic forces with modest cost-effective improvements. Near-term technology, for instance, could increase the accuracy, range, and performance of the current class of cruise missiles for conventional purposes. A superhard steel nose, meanwhile, possibly could replace the current perishable, thin-steel noses on nuclear air-launched cruise missiles to enable them to burrow underground upon impact and destroy missile silos buried in concrete-and-steel-reinforced bunkers.

Enhancing the "Eyes" and "Brains" of Ships and Aircraft Carrying Strategic Weapons

Cruise missiles and other stand-off nuclear weapons such as short-range attack missiles are fashioned to attack command and control posts, missiles, air defense sites, airfields, bridges, and other militarily significant targets. To maximize the effectiveness of such weapons, the Pentagon should upgrade the command, control, communication, and sensor capabilities of the ships and bombers that will carry them. Sensors and command and control systems are the "eyes" and "brains" of the ships and planes armed with strategic weapons. Full funding should be provided for the Air Force's *Navstar*/Global Positioning System (GPS), a space-based satellite system to be used by ships for communication and navigation.

Applying New Technologies

Many new technologies being researched and developed by the Strategic Defense Initiative Organization (SDIO) and other government agencies will have applications for offensive strategic forces as well. Examples: optical devices, infrared or heat-seeking sensors, acoustic sensors, new signal processors, lasers, and faster computers. These hold enormous promise for improving the capability of nuclear missiles to locate, identify, track, destroy, and assess the damage inflicted on military targets. Greater missile accuracy also allows the U.S. to deploy less powerful nuclear warheads, which could minimize the collateral range of destruction caused by nuclear explosions to civilian populations.

The Pentagon should establish a program to identify and analyze the potential applications of advanced technologies to offensive strategic systems. Special emphasis should be given to improving the accuracy of missiles. The Pentagon should investigate strategic arms technologies with the help of the National Aeronautics and Space Administration and the Department of Energy. New technologies should be used as soon as possible, whether in existing systems or new ones. New technologies should not be made to wait for the development of entirely new strategic weapon systems.

Building a Survivable and Effective Strategic Command, Control, and Communication System

A nuclear deterrent is worthless if systems that enable the military authorities to control the deterrent can be destroyed by either Soviet nuclear strikes or their anti-satellite (ASAT) weapons. In particular, the U.S. needs ASAT weapons of its own to deter the Soviet use of ASATs against U.S. communication satellites. The Pentagon should request full funding for an accelerated *Milstar* strategic command, control, and communications satellite program for better control of strategic forces and at the same time should increase funding levels for the *Navstar*/Global Positioning System (GPS), a space-based navigation and communication system deployed by the U.S. Air Force. The *Milstar* satellite program should be reviewed continually to ensure that it will be survivable against Soviet ASAT attacks. The Strategic Defense Initiative Organization should continue vigorous research into developing active and passive defensive and other protective measures for satellites against Soviet ASAT weapons and jamming devices.

Fulfilling the Military Potential of Cruise Missiles

To ensure that cruise missiles best serve U.S. defense, the Joint Chiefs of Staff should establish a formal military requirement for a conventionally armed air-launched cruise missile with a range of over 1,000 miles. A formal military requirement is an official military document mandating the development of a weapon system to perform a specific military task. Such a missile could be armed with a conventional warhead for long-range, high-accuracy strikes against terrorist command posts, bridges, airfields, railroad depots, and other militarily important targets deep in enemy territory.

The Pentagon and Congress should work together to provide adequate funding for programs to increase the accuracy and overall performance of cruise missiles, including such improvements as the use of modest radar-evading stealth technologies and the development of a better targeting intelligence data base and processing capability to help mission planning. In particular, the Pentagon should seek funds for accelerating advanced guidance systems programs (the Cruise Missile Advanced Guidance system program, among others) for all cruise missiles, conventional and nuclear, to improve their accuracy.

The Secretaries of Defense, Navy, and Air Force should work with Congress to provide adequate funding for the aircraft and ships needed to deploy conventional and nuclear long-range cruise missiles. These include B-1B bombers, B-52H bombers modified to carry cruise missiles, and attack submarines, destroyers, cruisers, and other sea-launched cruise missile platforms. The Pentagon should emphasize research and development of new surveillance and targeting technologies and command and control systems to improve the way aircraft and ships can employ cruise missiles in combat. It should also consider developing a replacement for the F-111 medium-range bomber to carry not only gravity bombs and short-range "fire and forget" missiles, but also long-range air-launched cruise missiles.

Coordinating Strategic Doctrine for Offensive and Defensive Forces

To accommodate deployment of strategic defenses, the U.S. needs a new strategic doctrine to govern the planning and operations of offensive and defensive strategic forces. The study should be conducted by an outside panel of experts, with input from the Strategic Defense Initiative Organization, the Strategic Air Command, the Office of Net Assessment in the Office of the Secretary of Defense, the Army's Strategic Defense Command, and the U.S. Space Command. The study should address the kind and quantity of offensive and defensive forces needed to provide an effective and survivable strategic deterrent. The study should set operational guidelines for how these forces would work together during wartime. To accommodate deployment of SDI, the Joint Chiefs of Staff and the military services need to accept the evolution of strategic doctrine toward a greater emphasis on defense.

Devising New Strategic Operational Concepts for Advanced Technology Systems

The emergence of new technologies for strategic weapons will require new ways of thinking about how these weapons are to be used in wartime. Future strategic systems, such as hypersonic boost-glide vehicles (a maneuverable launch vehicle that can be launched either by a rocket booster or from an aircraft) and super long-range cruise missiles, will require changing U.S. strategic force tactics. A bomber armed with a hypersonic boost-glide vehicle can remain safely over Alaska, for example, but the warhead carried by the vehicle could strike the Soviet Union. This new capability will require new Strategic Air Command tactics and doctrines for bombers that, for the first time in history, can strike almost as quickly as ballistic missiles do today. If these new missiles are very accurate, they could be used against Soviet mobile missiles and other targets, which can be relocated while under attack. Advancing technology will also create very long-range and accurate conventionally armed air-launched cruise missiles, which could attack targets that can now be destroyed only with nuclear weapons.

To prepare for the coming revolution in strategic doctrine and operational concepts, the Secretary of Defense should task a select blue-ribbon panel of outside experts to study the impact of new technologies on the future of U.S. strategic doctrine and operations.

————————————◇————————————

INITIATIVES FOR 1989

1) Review the land-based ICBM program. The new President should order a review of the role and the need for land-based missiles and the contribution of active and passive defenses to their long-term survivability against nuclear attack. The study should consider the strategic need for a cost-effective land-based deterrent capable of surviving a Soviet attack and analyze the impact of deep arms reductions on the ICBM force. The study should be completed in time for the President to make decisions for the fiscal 1990 defense budget.

2) Accelerate the Advanced Strategic Missile Program. The Advanced Strategic Missile Program (ASMP) is America's only project to develop future technology for U.S. strategic offensive forces. This program is needed as a hedge against the possibility of the Soviet Union's deploying a nationwide strategic defense system faster than the U.S. can. If the Soviets have strategic defenses before the U.S., American strategic offensive forces would have to have greater capability than currently to penetrate Moscow's defensive shield. The U.S. must develop such penetration aids for ballistic missiles as chaff decoys to foil Soviet ground-defense radars and maneuverable warheads to evade Soviet interceptors fired from ground-based launchers. The Secretary of Defense should seek funding to accelerate research on missile penetration aids in the Advanced Strategic Missile Program. Funding should also be increased for research on advanced targeting technologies and concepts to help U.S. nuclear forces find and destroy Soviet mobile missiles. Such programs already exist in the U.S. Air Force's Ballistic Missile Office, the Defense Nuclear Agency, and particularly in the Pentagon's Defense Advanced Research Projects Agency (DARPA).

3) Accelerate cruise missile advanced guidance programs. To fulfill the military potential of advanced cruise missiles, the U.S. must accelerate cruise missile research and development programs. Funding programs for advanced guidance and inflight refueling systems will be a critical first step.

4) Seek full funding for modernizing KC-135R strategic tankers. To retaliate against the Soviet Union, U.S. strategic bombers must be refueled in flight as they head toward their targets. Because the Air Force does not have enough tankers for U.S. bombers, it has been modernizing the KC-135 tanker with new CFM-56 engines to increase range. Adding new engines will increase the KC-135 fleet's refueling capability by around 50 percent. The Secretary of Defense should request full funding for the KC-135 modernization program. This would modernize the entire force of 639 KC-135 tankers by 1996.

5) Accelerate development of the *Milstar* communications satellite and deployment of the *Navstar*/Global Positioning System. This is an important first step in developing a survivable and effective space-based command, control, and communication system for U.S. strategic forces. Such a system will be critical to coordinating U.S. forces around the globe. The survivability of *Milstar*, however, should be continually reviewed, while preparations should be made to develop and deploy backup space-based systems as quickly as possible in time of war. (See Navy section of this chapter.)

Strategic Defense

Kim R. Holmes and Francis P. Hoeber*
Task Force Chairmen

The Strategic Defense Initiative (SDI) is a research and development program launched by Ronald Reagan in 1983 to devise weapon systems that will protect the United States and its allies from nuclear ballistic missile attack by the Soviet Union and other hostile nations. SDI would shift U.S. strategic doctrine away from Mutual Assured Destruction (MAD), which has made offensive nuclear retaliation the only basis of deterrence. MAD would be replaced by a defensive strategy of deterrence based on offensive and defensive forces that places the highest priority on defending the U.S. and its allies against attack and mitigating damage caused by nuclear weapons.

Launching SDI may be the Reagan Administration's most important legacy. Since the program began, enormous technological breakthroughs have been made. Examples: kinetic-kill rockets that destroy objects by crashing into them; surveillance and tracking technologies; antimissile guidance systems; directed-energy weapons (like X-ray lasers, free-electron lasers, and neutral particle beams); and electromagnetic rail guns that fire projectiles at super high speeds. Successful tests of SDI technologies and systems, such as the Delta 181 experiment, which gathered data on missile exhaust plumes in space, have demonstrated repeatedly that concepts and technologies developed by the Pentagon's Strategic Defense Initiative Organization (SDIO) are valid and workable.

SDI's fundamental goal of giving the U.S. and its allies a means to defend against nuclear attack has been demonstrated as technologically achievable at reasonable cost. Soundly based estimates for a near-term strategic defense have placed the cost of a three-layered strategic defense at about $7 billion annually for a decade, or about 2

*Commenting and contributing generously to this report were *Mandate III* Task Force Members Mark Albrecht, Gen. Daniel O. Graham, John Kwapisz, Joseph Mayer, Keith Payne, and David B. Rivkin, Jr. They do not necessarily endorse all of its views and recommendations.

percent of the annual defense budget. In comparison, the U.S. has spent approximately \$17.3 billion per year from 1980 to 1987 on its strategic offensive forces.

—————————◇—————————

THE REAGAN ADMINISTRATION RECORD

When Ronald Reagan took office, U.S. strategic doctrine rested on the premise that the best defense was offense. Accepting the assumptions of Mutual Assured Destruction (MAD) since the signing of the Anti-Ballistic Missile (ABM) treaty in 1972, America's presidents had maintained that total U.S. vulnerability to nuclear attack was not only inevitable, but strategically desirable. It was believed that strategic stability could best be served by deploying offensive nuclear forces such as ballistic missiles and bombers that could survive a nuclear attack and then retaliate. There were no serious plans to develop a strategic defense system, nor was there any commitment to the concept that deterrence of nuclear war required a ballistic missile defense in addition to offensive forces.

The Reagan Administration has changed U.S. strategic policy dramatically. By launching the SDI, it has pulled together the Pentagon's disparate anti-ballistic missile research efforts into a single program. Through presidential speeches and discussions of the SDI concept, the Administration initiated a critical review of the U.S. offense-dominant nuclear strategy and began shifting away from the tenets of MAD. In 1987, the Administration advanced the SDI program into what Pentagon specialists call the "Milestone I" phase of development, where key technologies for tracking and surveillance of ballistic missiles and for space- and ground-based interceptor rockets were approved for further development. Other SDI successes have included the President's wise refusal to bargain away SDI for reductions in U.S.-Soviet offensive nuclear arms, and his winning the support and participation of many U.S. allies in the program.

Yet the Reagan Administration has not provided a coherent set of goals or a deployment schedule for strategic defenses, despite strong public support for the concept of strategic defense. Many of the funding problems SDI has been facing in Congress are due to the Administration's failure to articulate consistently and coherently SDI's strategic and political goals, and a timetable for deployment. Furthermore, although SDI has been an issue in every U.S.-Soviet arms control negotiation since 1983, the role of SDI in arms control has never been made clear. The Administration has never seriously made the case that an arms control agreement with the Soviet Union should not only reduce strategic offensive nuclear forces but also establish a timetable for deployment of strategic defenses. An arms agreement could synchronize U.S.-Soviet offensive reductions with defense deployments to make the transition toward a defense-dominant strategic environment between the U.S. and USSR as smooth as possible.

———————————◇———————————

THE NEXT FOUR YEARS

Strategic defense will make the world safer. Deterrence now rests only on the threat of offensive nuclear retaliation. It should rest increasingly on the capability to defend against an attack, not simply to avenge one after it has happened. SDI would strengthen deterrence and reduce the risk of war by denying the Soviets an easy victory with a nuclear first strike. A strategic defense system also would provide virtually complete protection against accidental nuclear launches, by either the Soviet Union or some other nuclear power.

Achieving Near-Term Deployment of Strategic Defenses

If SDI is to become a reality, work must progress quickly on those technologies and systems that are ready for deployment in Phase I of SDI in the 1990s. Phase I systems include the Boost Surveillance and Tracking System (BSTS), a satellite system that will detect missile launches and track enemy booster rockets; the Exoatmospheric Reentry Interceptor System (ERIS), a ground-based missile interceptor capable of knocking down enemy nuclear warheads outside the atmosphere; the Ground-based Surveillance and Tracking System (GSTS), a ground-based sensor system for tracking warheads in space and discriminating between warheads and decoys; the Space-Based Interceptor (SBI), a small rocket carried on orbiting satellites that is the only system capable of performing the important mission of destroying enemy missiles as they leave the atmosphere, as well as individual warheads in space; and Battle Management/Command and Control, and Communication (BM/C³) systems to ensure that all elements of SDI work together properly.

The Secretary of Defense and the Director of the Strategic Defense Initiative Organization should ensure that these systems receive top priority for funding. Since they show the most promise, they should be developed and deployed as quickly as possible.

A promising new SDI system, the High Endoatmospheric Defense Interceptor (HEDI), should be included in the Strategic Defense Initiative Organization's plan for Phase I deployment of SDI. HEDI is a ground-based interceptor capable of destroying incoming warheads inside the atmosphere. As part of an SDI system, HEDI would provide an extra layer of protection against incoming warheads that "leak" through the space defenses. It could also provide protection against sea-launched ballistic missiles fired at U.S. air bases and command and control posts along the coasts. HEDI should be developed for deployment as early as possible. It uses the same basic technologies as ERIS and could be ready for deployment in the mid–1990s.

According top priority to developing technologies and systems for near-term deployment should not jeopardize basic research on advanced technologies that one day could give the U.S. a comprehensive strategic defense. Among the most promising long-term SDI technologies is the space-based neutral particle beam weapon. This would destroy enemy booster rockets and discriminate between real warheads and decoys in space. Promising too are space-based lasers for disabling missiles and anti-satellite weapons shortly after they are launched, ground-based lasers for destroying boosters, an electromagnetic railgun for shooting down incoming warheads in space, and the Airborne Optical System (AOS) for tracking warheads in space.

To prevent uncertainty about the long-term goals of SDI, the new President should state unequivocally that he is committed to developing these long-term SDI technologies. To this end, the Pentagon should continue research on the X-ray laser, the free-electron laser, neutral particle beams, advanced radars, microwave lasers, hypervelocity guns, airborne optical sensors, and heat-seeking sensors for tracking missiles, rockets, and warheads.

Accelerating Development of a Heavy Launch Vehicle

It has been estimated that deploying a strategic defense system would require lifting 11 million pounds of equipment into space. Because of the 1986 *Challenger* Space Shuttle disaster and other problems with its space program, the U.S. does not now have the launch capability to put 11 million pounds of equipment into space. To obtain this capability, the new President should direct the U.S. Air Force to develop, within five years, a launch vehicle capable of lifting up to 150,000 pounds into space. Such lift capacity is essential for such large SDI components as chemical lasers and neutral particle beams. A large space payload lifter also will be necessary to construct, maintain, and repair many of the elements of the space-based SDI, including space-based sensors and interceptors placed on orbiting satellite platforms. (See Military Space section of this chapter.)

Developing Anti-Tactical Ballistic Missile Defenses

Western Europe is threatened by over 1,000 Soviet SS–21, SS–1c/ *SCUD* B, and *Frog* 7 ballistic missiles with ranges of less than 300 miles. These missiles are not banned by the 1988 U.S.-Soviet Treaty on Intermediate-range Nuclear Forces (INF). The Soviet missiles carry conventional, chemical, and nuclear warheads and pose a significant danger to the Western Alliance. (See NATO section of Chapter ZP2 and Arms Control section of this chapter.) The short-range SS–21 ballistic missiles being supplied by Moscow to Syria, meantime, seriously threaten Israel. So does the *Eastwind* missile sold to Saudi Arabia by the Chinese. Finally, the Soviets have introduced nuclear-capable *Frog* missiles on the southern Kurile Islands in the Pacific, within range of Japan.

To counter these dangers, the Secretary of Defense should encourage the development and deployment of anti-tactical ballistic missiles (ATBMs) to defend Western Europe, Israel, and other regions where U.S. allies are threatened by Soviet short-range ballistic missiles. The ATBM system for Europe should be seen as enhancing NATO's air defenses. It would not constitute a violation of the 1972 Anti-Ballistic Missile treaty between the U.S. and the Soviet Union limiting deployment of defenses against intercontinental ballistic missiles.

The Secretary of Defense should support allied research efforts already directed at developing these ATBMs and support allied efforts to develop their own ATBM programs, such as the Israeli *Arrow* anti-tactical ballistic missile, which shows considerable promise and already has been approved for joint development by Israel and the U.S. The secretary should seek adequate funding for accelerated research, development, and testing of promising U.S. ATBM technologies and systems which could be shared with or sold to U.S. allies.

Promising U.S. systems include the Navy's *Aegis* radar system paired with a two-stage hypervelocity missile; a modified U.S. Army *Patriot* air defense missile; the U.S. Army's *Flage* interceptor, which could demolish warheads inside the atmosphere; and some version of SDI's High Endoatmospheric Defense Interceptor (HEDI) which could knock down warheads inside the atmosphere.

The new President and his Secretary of Defense should strongly oppose congressional attempts to restrict allied participation in U.S.

SDI research. The allies are not likely to support SDI unless they are involved in the program and perceive it as a Western defense rather than simply a defense of the continental U.S.

◇

INITIATIVES FOR 1989

1) Commit to deploying SDI systems as they become technologically available. The new President should direct the Secretary of Defense to deploy strategic defenses as soon as technologically feasible. Deployment should take place in phases, with each phase enhancing deterrence and reducing the risk of war. Deployment of the first phase, which could begin in the mid–1990s, should consist of ground-launched kinetic-kill systems such as HEDI and ERIS; a space-based boost surveillance and tracking system, a ground-based surveillance and tracking system for detecting and tracking enemy warheads as they fly through space, and for distinguishing decoys from actual warheads; computers for commanding, controlling, and managing the SDI system; a space-based interceptor or orbiting satellite armed with rockets for disabling warheads in space; and a space-based surveillance and tracking system for identifying and tracking booster rockets and warheads in space.

As a first step toward Phase I, the new President should order the construction of a single anti-ballistic missile site consisting of 100 ERIS interceptors at Grand Forks, North Dakota, which will begin in 1995 to protect against accidental nuclear launches or small attacks. This system is allowed by the U.S.Soviet 1972 Anti-Ballistic Missile treaty, which permits the construction of one ABM site.

Phase II of SDI deployment should be to improve and expand upon the Phase I system. Phase II would consist of more advanced systems such as neutral particle beams for discriminating between decoys and real warheads in space, more advanced radars, lasers for destroying booster rockets and warheads in space, airborne sensors better able to distinguish between decoys and real warheads, and ground-based hypervelocity guns capable of shooting projectiles at super speed as warheads fall toward missile silos in the ground.

A decision to begin full deployment of SDI in the 1990s will require that the U.S. repudiate the 1972 Anti-Ballistic Missile treaty. Such a withdrawal is justified because of the necessity to enhance deterrence and defend American lives from nuclear attack. The deployment of the single anti-ballistic missile site of 100 interceptors, however, will not require withdrawal from the ABM treaty.

2) Coordinate SDI, nuclear strategy, and arms control policy. The U.S. has no policy on how best to coordinate arms control with plans for deployment of offensive nuclear forces and strategic defenses. U.S. strategic policy lacks a framework in which arms reduction, nuclear modernization, and strategic defenses can work together to strengthen deterrence and reduce the risk of nuclear war.

To correct this, the new President should direct his Secretaries of State and Defense to coordinate SDI's technical requirements, strategic premises, and defense-based doctrine with U.S. arms control and nuclear policy. Arms control policy must be adjusted to emphasize negotiated timetables synchronizing offensive arms reductions and strategic defense deployment. An arms control proposal should be developed that reduces offensive forces while permitting deployment of SDI. The aim of arms control should be to make strategic defenses more effective. U.S. arms control policy should, for example, aim at discouraging development of Soviet weapons designed to counteract SDI, such as so-called fast burn boosters which shoot missiles very quickly into space to avoid destruction by space-based defenses. U.S. policy also should be to make defense easier by reducing the number of Soviet ballistic missiles. (See Arms Control section of this chapter.)

3) Increase funding for SDI. A critical issue will be whether SDI will receive the funds necessary to develop strategic defenses as quickly as technically possible. Congress has cut over $10 billion from the Reagan Administration's SDI budgets between 1984 and 1989. This has slowed research and development, eliminated promising research projects, and forced decisions about future systems to be made without adequate information and analysis. The new President should request at least $6 billion for SDI funding for fiscal 1990. This is the minimum required to maintain a research, development, and testing program that is balanced between the goals of providing near- and long-term options for strategic defenses. In this budget, top priority should be given to near-term technologies and systems that can be deployed in the mid-to-late 1990s. The second priority should be for research and development of the most promising long-term SDI technologies, such as certain directed energy weapons.

4) Establish a public affairs office within SDIO. The Strategic Defense Initiative Organization inside the Pentagon does not have a public affairs office to help it explain the importance of SDI to Congress and the public. They deserve accurate information, timely reports on the program's technical progress, and authoritative explanations of the concepts and strategies of SDI. The Secretary of Defense should reestablish a public affairs office inside the SDIO to counter public misperceptions of the program and to offer corrections of errors about SDI that often appear in the press.

Arms Control

James T. Hackett*
Task Force Chairman

United States arms protect American security and freedoms and those of the Western Alliance by deterring war or threats of war. Political pressures to reduce nuclear weapons led to the Anti-Ballistic Missile (ABM) and SALT I agreements of 1972, followed by the SALT II agreement signed in 1979 but never ratified because of major flaws. These agreements did not reduce or even control nuclear weapons, as they were supposed to do, and have been violated by the Soviet Union.

Moscow, meanwhile, has undermined the basic goals of the agreements by greatly increasing its offensive nuclear power throughout the 1970s and into the 1980s. At the same time, the U.S. showed considerable restraint by deactivating its ballistic missile defenses and building no new ICBMs from 1975 to 1986. Yet Moscow continues to deploy the largest military force in the world, including a massive nuclear missile arsenal capable of destroying most of the U.S. retaliatory force in a first strike. This continuing threat requires the U.S. to modernize its deterrent forces and build strategic defenses.

This does not, however, rule out the pursuit of realistic arms control goals, such as reduced levels of armaments with increased stability. Nor does it preclude arms control initiatives that are in the interest of both sides, such as improvements in the Washington-Moscow hotline and the recent agreement to give advance warning of missile tests. Yet, care must be taken to have an effective compliance policy, to avoid unverifiable agreements, and to assure that arms control agreements increase stability and security.

Advances in missile defense technology have now made strategic defenses feasible. As a result, the U.S. goal in arms control negotiations should be not just to reduce weapons, but to move toward an era in which a combination of strategic defenses and reduced levels of offenses will produce a more secure world.

---

*Commenting and contributing generously to this report were *Mandate III* Task Force Members James George, Sven Kraemer, Michael Mobbs, Robin Ranger, and David J. Smith. They do not necessarily endorse all of its views and recommendations.

THE REAGAN ADMINISTRATION RECORD

When the Reagan Administration took office, U.S. arms control policy was in a shambles. The Carter Administration had engaged the Soviets in a number of arms control negotiations, concluding at the 1979 Vienna Summit when Jimmy Carter and Soviet General Secretary Leonid Brezhnev signed SALT II. That agreement was never ratified by the Senate. By 1981, it was clear that the Soviets were not complying with SALT II, but were continuing to build up offensive nuclear forces, and that U.S. strategic forces had seriously deteriorated during the reduced defense budgets and anti-military sentiment that followed the Vietnam War.

In 1981, the Reagan Administration began modernizing U.S. defenses, deferring arms control talks with Moscow until the U.S. was able to negotiate from strength. When the Strategic Arms Reduction Talks (START) began, some 18 months after Reagan took office, they were based on sensible arms control criteria: real reductions, equality of forces, strategic stability, and effective verification.

The Reagan Administration, meanwhile, pursued the NATO program of deploying *Pershing II* ballistic and ground-launched cruise missiles in Western Europe to counter Soviet SS–20 mobile missile deployments. When deployment of the U.S. missiles began in Europe, the Soviets protested by walking out of the U.S.-Soviet Intermediate-range Nuclear Forces (INF) talks and the START negotiations. Moscow apparently assumed that this would stop the U.S. from sending the new weapons to Western Europe. But the Western Alliance stood firm, the deployments continued, and just days after Reagan's reelection victory in November 1984, the Soviets agreed to return to the bargaining table.

In the meantime, in March 1983, Reagan had announced what may stand as the most important achievement of his Administration—the Strategic Defense Initiative (SDI). This signaled a sea-change in U.S. strategic doctrine, seriously disrupting Soviet military planning and offering the possibility of genuine reductions in offensive nuclear missiles. The Soviet effort to kill SDI probably reached its climax at the October 1986 Reykjavik summit, when Reagan rejected Soviet leader Gorbachev's insistence that the U.S. abandon SDI as the price for reductions in offensive weapons. The Soviets since then have adopted a more sophisticated approach, arguing that the U.S. must agree to continue complying with a restrictive version of the Anti-

Ballistic Missile (ABM) treaty, which would limit the testing and prevent the deployment of most ballistic missile defenses. Knowing that this would kill the SDI program, the President has steadfastly refused to bow to Moscow's demands.

In late 1983, the President's General Advisory Committee on Arms Control and Disarmament issued a report documenting extensive and continuing Soviet violations of arms control agreements. In January 1984, Reagan released his own report of Soviet violations; since then, five more White House reports have been released. This unprecedented public revelation of Soviet violations of agreements opens a new chapter in U.S.-Soviet relations, in which Soviet arms control violations are acknowledged and discussed publicly by the U.S. government.

In 1986, after exhausting every reasonable hope that the Soviets might begin complying, Reagan finally withdrew the U.S. from the expired and Soviet-violated SALT I and SALT II agreements. He declared that the U.S. would base its future strategic force structure decisions on the Soviet threat and not on SALT standards that had been undermined by Soviet noncompliance. Though the State Department warned of a crisis in the NATO Alliance if the U.S. withdrew from SALT, the U.S. action caused barely a ripple. On the contrary, Reagan's bold stand enhanced American prestige and strengthened the Alliance.

Similarly, the Administration has not bowed to a global propaganda campaign directed by Moscow to pressure the U.S. to stop underground nuclear testing. Western security depends on nuclear weapons, Reagan has said. Testing assures operational confidence in the U.S. nuclear stockpile, develops safe and improved nuclear weapons, and tests the effects of nuclear blast on military equipment and communications.

The Administration has pressed Moscow to improve the verification of compliance with the Threshold Test Ban Treaty (TTBT) and the Peaceful Nuclear Explosions Treaty (PNET), which were signed by the U.S. and the USSR in the mid-1970s, but have not been ratified because of apparent Soviet violations. In September 1987, in a major policy change, the U.S. agreed to discuss further limitations on nuclear testing beyond the TTBT and PNET, retreating from the position held earlier by the Reagan Administration, in which it refused to negotiate toward a comprehensive nuclear test ban (CTB) as long as nuclear weapons are needed for the defense of the West.

The Reagan Administration has refused to negotiate limits on anti-satellite weapons tests on the sound grounds that any such agreement would be unverifiable. The Administration also has rejected Soviet efforts to limit tests in space of SDI components, which is part of the Soviet effort to delay or kill SDI.

The U.S. refusal to negotiate about weapons or systems that are essential to the West's defense is an important policy position. The reason: once negotiations begin, there is likely to be pressure from the State Department, elements in Congress, U.S. allies, and "peace" groups to make concessions. Negotiators and other officials typically become seized with the desire to reach an agreement for its own sake, often forgetting national security considerations.

The main arms control failure of the Reagan Administration has been its lost opportunity to be candid with the American people about the limitations of arms control. Reagan edged in that direction when he ordered the preparation and release of the reports on Soviet violations of arms control agreements. But then he took no compensatory measures to induce Soviet compliance or offset Soviet gains from their violations, except to withdraw from SALT I and SALT II, and to insist on full funding for the planned modernization of U.S. strategic forces, which Congress refused to provide. By moving enthusiastically toward new arms control agreements in his second term without requiring Soviet compliance with existing agreements, Reagan has undermined much of the effect of his Administration's reports of Soviet violations.

In its second term, the Administration has seemed eager for arms control agreements with Moscow, discarding the caution that characterized the first term. To have an agreement on Intermediate-range Nuclear Forces (INF) ready to sign at the December 1987 Washington summit, Reagan set a deadline for the negotiations. This forced U.S. negotiators, as many experts had warned, to make unwise concessions as the deadline neared. The result is a verification system that allows U.S. inspectors to inspect only the specific medium-range missile sites and facilities agreed to in advance by both sides, leaving the rest of the Soviet Union off limits to inspectors. The INF agreement thus is a poor precedent for the more stringent verification procedures that will be needed for the proposed START agreement.

THE NEXT FOUR YEARS

The aim of arms control is to improve the security of the U.S. and its allies. The new President should return to the sound principles declared by Ronald Reagan in 1980 and establish an arms control policy that is an integral part of U.S. national security policy, a relatively minor component of U.S.-Soviet relations, and not an end in itself. Arms control policy should be directed by the President through his National Security adviser. The President should use arms control policy to support the Strategic Defense Initiative, to facilitate the transition from offensive to defensive weapons, and to improve U.S. and allied security.

Enthusiasm for arms control as a cheap substitute for national defense is unwise and could encourage Congress and the allies to make dangerous reductions in defense appropriations and readiness, returning the U.S. to the debilitating weakness of the 1970s. Arms are not the problem; they are a symptom. Thus, the new President should look to the security of the nation and the Western Alliance through the development and deployment of effective defenses, instead of seeking solutions to threats to national security through arms control.

Abstaining from Negotiations Not in the U.S. Interest

The new Administration should reject arms control negotiations that are not in the U.S. national interest. Examples: comprehensive test ban talks (as long as nuclear weapons are needed to defend the West, the U.S. must continue to test); discussions of limits on anti-satellite weapons or tests (the U.S. cannot allow the Soviet Union to have a unilateral advantage in anti-satellite weapons capabilities and a safe haven in space for military satellites in a crisis); limits on tests in space (tests are needed for SDI); limits on defensive weapons (limits could prevent the U.S. from developing weapons to protect itself from a nuclear attack by the Soviet Union or any other nation); limits on battlefield nuclear weapons in Europe (this would leave NATO more vulnerable to the Red Army); limits on air- and sea-launched cruise missiles (this technology, in which the U.S. has a considerable lead, should not be bargained away); and talks aimed at banning chemical weapons stocks and production (which is unverifiable).

Halting Congressional Intrusions into
Presidential Authority

The new Administration should oppose strenuously any effort by Congress to constrain controls on U.S. weapons programs or national security policy for "arms control" purposes. This includes any legislation to limit or prevent the testing of anti-satellite weapons, underground nuclear weapons, or weapons in space. It also includes legislation requiring the President to comply with provisions of expired agreements or agreements the Soviets are violating. Such legislation should be vetoed by the new President as an intrusion on his constitutional authority to conduct foreign policy and to provide for the national defense as Commander-in-Chief. (See Chapter 23.)

Reducing Soviet Forces in Europe

The dangerous imbalance of military forces in Europe gives the Warsaw Pact the capability of launching a surprise attack on the West. Warsaw Pact superiority in offensive weaponry ranges from two-to-one to more than three-to-one, and these forces are constantly being improved. With over 50,000 main battle tanks, over 60,000 other armored vehicles, and more than 40,000 artillery pieces, the Warsaw Pact armies are clearly designed for offense. If Gorbachev really wants to reallocate military spending to meet civilian needs, this is where he can realize significant savings.

The long-running negotiations between NATO and the Warsaw Pact on Mutual and Balanced Force Reductions (MBFR) in Europe are being reconstituted as the Conventional Stability Talks. These discussions have been stalled for years by the Soviet refusal to provide accurate data on the number of Warsaw Pact troops. Therefore, the U.S. should try to move these negotiations away from troop numbers and toward a discussion of reductions in offensive conventional weapons. Warsaw Pact superiority means that there must be greater reductions in Soviet tanks, artillery, and other offensive weapons than in similar NATO forces. The goal should be reductions to equal military capabilities in Europe. Those Soviet forces that are reduced must be removed entirely from the Soviet force structure and dismantled, not merely withdrawn from Eastern Europe. To achieve a stable balance, NATO also should insist on numerical or other advantages to offset the greater distance Western reinforcements must travel in a time of crisis.

Improving NATO Defenses

The new Administration should lead the NATO allies in rejecting Soviet efforts to block NATO force improvements through arms control agreements, as Moscow is trying to do through the noncircumvention clause of the INF treaty. This clause, which states simply that nothing will be done that conflicts with the agreement, was added late in the negotiations at Soviet insistence. It is so broad that it gives

Moscow a legal provision with which to attack all NATO force improvements on the grounds that they are inconsistent with the INF treaty.

NATO should reject these Soviet objections and develop and deploy the weapons it needs to defend effectively against the Soviet threat. Such weapons include an improved *Lance* battlefield missile, long-range air-to-surface missiles, an anti-tactical ballistic missile designed to protect NATO against the substantial Soviet force of battlefield missiles not affected by the INF agreement, and such high technology nonnuclear weapons as lasers and new types of explosives. The elimination of NATO's *Pershing II* and ground-launched cruise missiles under the INF agreement makes these improvements more urgent. (See NATO section of this chapter.)

Trying a New Approach to Chemical Weapons Arms Control

Currently, the main problem concerning chemical weapons is their use in the Third World. While it is generally agreed that it would be impossible to verify compliance effectively with a ban on the production or storage of chemical weapons, it may be feasible to develop controls on their international transfer or on the transfer of the technology and equipment to build them. Therefore, the current emphasis on banning U.S. and Soviet chemical weapons should be redirected to the urgent problem of controlling the transfer of dual purpose chemical plants or chemical weapons components from the industrialized nations to Third World countries that may use them in regional conflicts.

The U.S. should lead an effort to negotiate an international agreement by producer and supplier nations to prevent the spread of chemical weapons and components, perhaps comparable to the treaty on the nonproliferation of nuclear weapons and including sanctions on both the suppliers and users of chemical weapons. This will require the cooperation of all industrialized nations of both East and West.

The best defense against chemical weapons is a modern chemical weapons capability that would deter their use. Therefore, so long as the Soviet Union maintains an offensive chemical weapons capability, the U.S. must maintain a modern chemical weapons deterrent.

Developing a New START Proposal

In the Strategic Arms Reduction Talks (START), there has been considerable progress in proposed reductions in nuclear weapons, but the Soviets have continued to insist that the U.S. agree not to deploy defensive weapons in space as a prerequisite for any agreement on reductions in offensive forces. The Soviets also insist on severe constraints on U.S. sea-launched cruise missiles, and Moscow has declined to negotiate a stable transition from offensive to defensive weapons. These Soviet positions are unacceptable.

The present U.S. START proposal seeks deep reductions of nearly 50 percent in the U.S. and Soviet offensive strategic arsenals. There would be a ceiling of 6,000 nuclear warheads, of which no more than 4,900 could be on ballistic missiles. U.S. military strategy is based on multiple warhead missiles, such as the MX and *Trident*, on large submarines with 24 missile tubes each, and on strategic bombers carrying up to 20 air-launched cruise missiles. This means that, under the proposed START agreement, most of the U.S. nuclear deterrent force would be concentrated in a relatively few systems: about 13 ballistic missile submarines at sea, 200-to-300 *Minuteman III* missiles in vulnerable fixed silos, 50 rail-mobile MX missiles in silos, 50 MX missiles in seven rail garrisons, 100 B–1 bombers, and fewer than 100 B–52 bombers equipped with cruise missiles.

These START reductions would leave the Soviets with 6,000 strategic warheads with which to attack the fewer than 600 targets that house nearly all of the U.S. nuclear deterrent. This is a less favorable ratio than at present; thus, the current START proposal would leave the U.S. deterrent more vulnerable to a Soviet attack.

The new President should review the START proposal carefully and revise it in a way that strengthens U.S. security and reduces U.S. strategic vulnerability. The new President should assure that his modified U.S. START proposal supports U.S. strategic policy, preserves the U.S. right to deploy strategic defenses and air- and sea-launched cruise missiles, leaves the U.S. with sufficient forces to defend the nation and protect American global interests, and that the verification procedures do not compromise U.S. security.

Deploying Defenses As Offenses Are Reduced

Arms control should enhance, not diminish, the survivability of the U.S. deterrence. As such, the U.S. START proposal should be redrafted to provide for the reduction of offensive nuclear forces only as strategic defenses are deployed. Such a proposal would recognize the interaction of offensive and defensive strategic forces as the key element of a new nuclear strategy. The first step should be to seek: major protection against an accidental or limited missile launch, deterrence of and some protection against a first strike, reduced levels of offensive forces, improved strategic stability, and greater national security.

Integrating Arms Control with Military Planning

Current U.S. arms control proposals, particularly in the START negotiations, have not been integrated effectively with U.S. military strategy, military modernization plans, military purchasing schedules, or other defense activities. Example: the Defense Department is seeking more multiple-warhead MX missiles and *Trident* submarines, and is opposing small mobile missiles and smaller submarines, even as the State Department pursues a START agreement that would put a premium on weapons smaller than the MX and *Trident* and with fewer warheads per missile.

Allowing the Secretaries of State and Defense to pursue the separate interests of their departments without effective control by the White House has contributed to this problem. Allowing the military chiefs largely to control weapons purchases for their services, with little regard for overall national strategy or arms control policy, is another factor. Greater control of national security strategy by the new President, including his directing the departments and agencies that comprise the National Security Council to support that strategy, would more effectively integrate the nation's arms control and military policies.

Educating the Public on the Realities of Arms Control

The President and his senior advisers should educate the public, Congress, and America's allies on the limitations of the arms control process by speaking out frequently on the dangers and risks of unverifiable arms control agreements, the need to respond promptly to Soviet violations of agreements, and the risk of unwarranted arms control euphoria leading to reduced levels of U.S. and allied defenses. The new Administration should explain how the nation would be more secure than at present with a combination of defensive weapons and more accurate, more survivable offensive arms. A major effort should be made by the Arms Control and Disarmament Agency to identify for declassification and then encourage the declassification of information that reveals the nature and extent of Soviet arms control violations. This information then should be used by the White House and other government agencies to describe the damage to national security caused by Soviet violations of agreements and to explain the rationale for U.S. defense strategy and budgets.

––––––––––––––––––––◇––––––––––––––––––––

INITIATIVES FOR 1989

1) Delay arms control and press Moscow on other issues. The new President should put arms control negotiations with the Soviet Union on hold for at least his first year, while he conducts a thorough review of all U.S. negotiating positions. The President should not resume START negotiations until he is assured of congressional support for a strategic modernization program to develop and deploy strategic defenses and more mobile and survivable strategic offenses. Instead of stressing arms control, the new Administration should press the Soviets on matters important to the West, such as: ending Soviet military support for the communist regimes in Afghanistan, Angola, Ethiopia, Mozambique, Nicaragua, and North Vietnam; stopping Soviet violations of human rights and other provisions of the Helsinki Act; and easing substantially Soviet restrictions on their people's travel and emigration.

2) Direct arms control policy through the National Security Council. The new President should coordinate and direct the arms control activities of the government through the National Security Council to assure that his policies are faithfully executed, that no single agency dominates the arms control process, and that interagency disagreements are promptly and decisively resolved. This can be done by directing the Assistant to the President for National Security or a senior official of the National Security Council Staff to chair all interagency committees dealing with national security and arms control. These important interagency committees, in which policy is made and coordinated, must not be chaired by officials of any specific department or agency, each of which has its own parochial view of policy issues. Only the White House can effectively direct policy to support the broad national interest.

3) Withdraw from the ABM Treaty and order the deployment of strategic defenses. The 1972 Anti-Ballistic Missile (ABM) treaty, as amended, limits ballistic missile defenses to one site each in the U.S. and USSR. This prevents deployment of more than a minimal ballistic missile defense of the U.S. Furthermore, the Soviets have persistently vio-

lated the ABM treaty, most notably with the construction of a major
ABM radar at Krasnoyarsk in the central Soviet Union, a key component of a rapidly deployable nationwide ABM system. In view of this
material breach of the agreement, the new President should provide
effectively for the national defense by giving the Soviets six months
notice of U.S. intention to withdraw from the ABM treaty, as the
treaty itself provides. The President should then begin protecting
America by ordering unlimited tests in space of SDI components and
the development of plans for the early deployment of defenses against
Soviet ballistic missiles. Because of likely political opposition, these
steps should be taken in the first 100 days of the new Administration.

4) Issue a new compliance report. The new President should direct the
National Security Council to prepare an updated report of Soviet
violations of arms control agreements. Then he should make it clear to
Moscow that the U.S. will engage in no new arms control negotiations
until the USSR complies fully with existing agreements.

5) Develop a compliance policy. A compliance policy is needed for
existing and future arms control agreements. The new President should
direct his National Security Adviser to develop a compliance policy
and program, with input from the Defense Department and elsewhere,
that will enable the U.S. to act promptly when Soviet violations are
confirmed. The program should include proposed responses designed
either to induce Soviet compliance or to offset any Soviet gains from
their violations. To give proper attention to the complex problems of
arms control compliance, the new President should establish an Office
of Arms Control Compliance in the White House, perhaps as part of
or associated with the National Security Council staff. The President
also should direct the Secretary of Defense to prepare specific military
responses to Soviet cheating.

Provisions of a compliance policy could include: 1) suspending U.S.
compliance with the violated accord and reversing any withdrawal of
weapons that might be under way; 2) taking steps to position or deploy
forces, conduct weapons tests, or build additional weapons to offset
Soviet gains; 3) applying diplomatic and economic pressures to try to
induce Moscow to stop violating its agreements; 4) funding defense
programs not related to Soviet violations, which will either encourage
Soviet compliance or enhance U.S. security; and 5) declaring the
violated treaty null and void.

The Senate should establish a select committee to monitor Soviet
compliance with existing and future U.S.-Soviet arms control agree-

ments. In addition, Congress should require the President, in his annual report to Congress on Soviet arms control compliance, either to certify that the Soviets are complying in full or, if they are not, to submit proposals for compensatory action, together with requests for the needed funding.

6) Establish a clear position on nuclear testing. The new President should withdraw the U.S. offer to negotiate with the Soviet Union on the complete cessation of nuclear testing. He must declare that it is U.S. policy to continue testing as long as nuclear weapons are important to Western security.

7) Request funds for all-weather, wide-area-search intelligence satellites. The new President should ask Congress to provide funds to increase the number of U.S. intelligence-gathering satellites, especially the new generation of all-weather, wide-area-search reconnaissance satellites. These are needed to verify the INF Treaty ban on Moscow's SS–20 and SS–23 mobile missiles and any START limits that may be reached on Soviet SS–24 and SS–25 mobile missiles.(See Military Space section of this chapter.)

8) Press Moscow to cooperate in managing the transition to strategic defenses. The new President should press the Soviet Union to cooperate in managing the transition from the current reliance on offensive nuclear weapons to a new emphasis on strategic defenses. This should be the major topic of future arms control negotiations between the U.S. and the USSR. Security in the nuclear age can be assured best through a combination of strategic defenses and mobile, survivable offensive forces. U.S. arms control policy should lead Soviet policy toward a stable balance of offenses and defenses. If this country remains defenseless to the Soviet Union's offensive nuclear forces, reductions in those forces by themselves will have little meaning, and could lead to strategic instabilities that might increase, rather than reduce, the nuclear threat to the United States. Thus, the main U.S. goal in the START negotiations should be to seek reductions in offensive forces that go hand-in-hand with the deployment of strategic defenses.

Military Space Policy

Robin R. Ranger*
Task Force Chairman

The United States has become increasingly dependent on space-based systems, mainly satellites, to support its military operations in the areas of command, control, and communications (C³), electronic warfare, early warning of a Soviet ballistic missile attack, navigation, reconnaissance, and targeting. All four U.S. military services, for example, rely on satellite navigation systems to locate the positions of their units. If the Soviets disabled some, or all, of these satellites, they could render the U.S. military blind, deaf, and speechless—unable to see or hear what the Soviet military machine is doing and unable to communicate with U.S. forces. The U.S., meanwhile, depends much more heavily than does Moscow on reconnaissance satellites for arms control verification because, despite claims of *glasnost'*, the Soviet Union remains a tightly closed, secretive society regarding military activities. Indeed, U.S. dependence on space-based systems is such that Moscow may be tempted to start an attack on the U.S. in space.

To prevent this, the new Administration must develop and deploy space-based systems adequate to support U.S. conventional and nuclear force operations, gather intelligence, deter or defeat Soviet attempts to deny U.S. access to space, and verify Soviet compliance with arms control agreements in peacetime. The new Administration also should deploy space-based subsystems of a Strategic Defense, such as space-based interceptors to destroy Soviet ballistic missiles.

THE REAGAN ADMINISTRATION RECORD

The Reagan Administration inherited a U.S. military space policy and a space launch program headed for disaster. For one thing, the

*Commenting and contributing generously to this report were *Mandate III* Task Force Members Thomas Blau, Milton Copulos, Francis P. Hoeber, Kim Holmes, Christopher Lay, and Grant Loebs. They do not necessarily endorse all of its views and recommendations.

Carter Administration actively sought a U.S.-Soviet agreement banning anti-satellite (ASAT) systems. In effect, this would have banned only the development of U.S. ASAT systems, since the Soviets would have retained their operational ASAT. For another thing, the Carter space program was making the mistake of planning to rely on the National Aeronautics and Space Agency's (NASA) manned Space Shuttle for space launches once the shuttle came into service. The Carter Administration did so because it wanted to avoid "militarizing" space, even though the Soviets had long been using space for military purposes. To keep military systems out of space, the Carter Administration resisted using the U.S. Air Force to launch even military payloads.

From 1981 to 1985, the Reagan Administration made considerable progress in reversing the Carter Administration's neglect of military space programs. The Administration balked at heavy Soviet pressure to reopen the negotiations on an ASAT ban, which had been terminated by Moscow's 1979 invasion of Afghanistan. The Administration also stressed the U.S. need for an American ASAT system to deter Soviet ASAT use. The Department of Defense was given the responsibility for designing and executing space programs that met U.S. national security needs. Major improvements were made in space-based systems providing command, control, and communications (C³) support for conventional and nuclear military activities. After Reagan's March 23, 1983, speech announcing the Strategic Defense Initiative, research and development started on the space-based components of strategic defense systems.

But Administration attempts to reduce an inherited dependence on the manned Space Shuttle were frustrated by NASA and its powerful political supporters. They made their case strongly, particularly after the shuttle's successful flights began in 1981. The situation changed abruptly, of course, with the January 28, 1986, explosion of the Space Shuttle *Challenger*.

The *Challenger* loss left the U.S. with a seriously weakened ability to launch into space the military payloads needed to support military operations, to gather intelligence, and to verify Soviet compliance with arms control agreements. Because of the shortage of space-based systems, it has been difficult to communicate with U.S. military forces. They have lacked needed information on the location of potentially hostile military forces, and the U.S. has lacked the information to determine whether Moscow is complying with arms control agreements.

The Administration authorized construction of a new shuttle to replace the lost *Challenger* and restore the manned shuttle fleet to the full strength required to launch into orbit such heavy military payloads as the new KH–12 reconnaissance satellite. In addition, it restarted the Expendable Launch Vehicle (ELV) program, which uses unmanned rockets as space launchers.

The Administration also authorized development of the X–30, an experimental prototype for the National Aerospace Plane. This plane will be able to fly up to 75 miles above the earth, but it will be able to take off from and land on airfields. It will be able to launch military payloads into orbit and perform other military space missions, such as short-notice reconnaissance over a crisis area. The Administration further authorized construction of a large manned space station and a small unmanned space facility on which the U.S. will conduct scientific research on such new products as improved ball bearings to make ballistic missiles more accurate.

In 1988, the Administration established a National Space Policy. Its accompanying presidential directive has restored some cohesion to such fragmented U.S. military and mixed civilian/military space programs as the shuttle. Finally, the Reagan Administration's privatization of commercial space launches should have significant long-term benefits for the military space program. A private sector capability to launch civilian satellites will provide emergency backup for U.S. military space launches.

Some aspects of the Reagan defense space policy have been less successful. After the *Challenger* loss, the Reagan Administration failed to exploit available technologies to launch sufficient payloads for military and intelligence programs. It has not resolved jurisdictional and policy disputes regarding a National Space Policy. Nor has the Administration reformed the NASA organizational structure that contributed to the *Challenger* loss. And it has not always opposed as actively as it should congressional limitations on testing the only U.S. anti-satellite program near operational capability, the F–15 fighter-launched Miniature Homing Vehicle.

———————————————◇———————————————

THE NEXT FOUR YEARS

The next President[1] should issue a directive establishing a comprehensive U.S. space strategy to include military and civilian as well as offensive and defensive uses of space. This directive should instruct the Secretary of Defense to develop the doctrine—the specific goals and the technical means of achieving them—to fulfill this strategy. It should address such questions as: 1) In wartime or crisis, what are the U.S. strategies to deny the Soviets access to space and to assure U.S. access to and control over space? 2) Does the U.S. require nearly exclusive control of space, in the same way that it requires nearly exclusive control of the sea? 3) What space-based systems and space launch capabilities will be required to achieve U.S. objectives? 4) What is the most effective use of these systems?

Providing Military Space Support for SDI

Essential to the Strategic Defense Initiative is the U.S. ability to launch payloads large or heavy enough to test and subsequently deploy SDI components. Payloads will include space-based systems placed on satellites to intercept Soviet intercontinental and submarine-launched ballistic missiles, when they are launched or once they have left the atmosphere (known as boost and mid-course interceptions). The lack of an adequate U.S. capability to place such payloads in space could cripple the SDI program. Thus, the next President must ensure that the U.S. has a space launch capability for heavy payloads. (See Strategic Defense section of this chapter.)

Transferring the Space Launch Mission to the Air Force

The National Aeronautics and Space Administration's monopoly of manned and scientific space launches is the biggest obstacle to an effective U.S. military space policy. NASA should be returned to one of its original missions, basic research; this it always has performed well. NASA must be removed from the space launch mission, which it has performed poorly and at excessive cost. A presidential directive should give the U.S. Air Force jurisdiction over all U.S. government space launches and the relevant budgets and personnel.

Procuring and Deploying Expendable Launch Vehicles (ELVs)

Expendable Launch Vehicles are unmanned rocket boosters that, after launching their payloads into space, are destroyed on reentering the earth's atmosphere. ELVs can lift large loads, and they can be procured in quantities and at costs to provide for most U.S. peacetime launch needs. The manned shuttle, by contrast, is too expensive and too liable to suffer a catastrophic failure to be used for anything except missions requiring the unique capabilities of human operators. Unmanned ELV space launches cost only one-tenth that of manned shuttle launches. Only ELV systems can give the U.S. an adequate reserve of individual space launch vehicles and total launch capabilities. This includes the ability to launch a large total weight of payloads into space in a short period of time—perhaps one week. This reserve is needed to replace rapidly the crucial space systems that could be lost through malfunction or, in major crises, to attacks by Soviet anti-satellite systems.

Current and projected U.S. ELVs fall into three categories: light ELV, the *Delta 2* and *Atlas-Centaur* systems, which can place into low earth orbit (200 to 1,000 miles from earth) payloads from 2,800 to 5,200 pounds; medium ELV, the *Titan* series (*Titan* 2, 3, 34D, and 4), which can place into low orbit payloads of about 30,000 pounds; and heavy ELV, the Advanced Launch System family of launch vehicles, which by the end of the century could put into low earth orbit payloads of over 150,000 pounds.

The new President should direct the Secretary of Defense, the Central Intelligence Agency, and the U.S. Air Force Space Command to review the planned procurement of ELV systems to ensure it is sufficient to meet U.S. military and arms control verification needs, including the replacement of satellites lost in crises or conflicts to attacks by Soviet ASAT systems. The new President should direct the U.S. Air Force, the primary manager of the Advanced Launch System heavy ELV program, to accelerate deployment. The Advanced Launch System family of ELVs could provide space launches at an estimated 10 percent of the cost of existing ELVs by using new technologies and designs and through mass production economies of scale.

Finding Alternatives to the Shuttle

The next Administration should direct the U. S. Air Force Space Command to investigate how existing technologies can substitute for lost manned shuttle capabilities. One alternative to be considered is the "Service" space capsule, a reusable reentry vehicle that originally was employed in recovering data and film from military satellites. After each use, its rockets and heat shields are replaced, and it is ready for up to 100 flights. Another alternative is the *Saturn* V heavy ELV; if rebuilt in an updated version, it could put 250,000 pounds into low earth orbit.

Building and Launching Survivable
Space-Based Military Systems

The new President should direct the Secretary of Defense to assess U.S. requirements for military space systems that can survive and continue to perform during attack by Soviet anti-satellite systems. Current U.S. military space systems, such as the very costly KH–12 reconnaissance satellite, are designed to function mainly in peacetime and are vulnerable to Soviet ASAT attacks. The Secretary of Defense's assessment should consider what the new Electromagnetic Launch (ELM) systems can add to U.S. space launch capabilities. Existing U.S. space launch systems use rocket engines that burn chemical fuels. ELM systems would use a combination of electrical and magnetic (electromagnetic) energy to propel payloads into space from ground stations. These ELM systems probably would be limited to launching very small satellites. However, a dispersed network of many small, inexpensive satellites (known as *Lightsats*) could not be disabled easily by the Soviets and would be relatively easy to replace if attacked.

Defending and Destroying Satellites

ASAT weapons attack satellites to disable or destroy them. Moscow has the world's only operational ASAT, called a co-orbital kinetic-kill vehicle. This vehicle is launched into the same orbit as the satellite it is attacking, tracks its target until sufficiently close, and then explodes destroying it by the impact (kinetic energy) of the resulting cloud of fragments. Moscow is also developing ground-based lasers that could be used as ASATs, such as the massive Dushanbe facility. All of these systems could threaten U.S. satellites.

Satellite defense systems protect satellites against attack. Protection measures include maneuvering to avoid an attacking ASAT and armoring (hardening) the satellite against the effects of an attack. A special problem is the difficulty in determining that an attack on a satellite has taken place. It may be impossible, for example, to tell whether a satellite has been disabled by a Soviet laser or is merely malfunctioning.

The new President must determine what the U.S. must do to counter Soviet ASAT and satellite defense capabilities. The U.S. may not have to replicate Soviet systems exactly. For example, the U.S. may be able to deter, or defeat if deterrence fails, Soviet ASAT use by a combination of ASAT and satellite defense capabilities. In addition, the U.S.

will require an adequate reserve space launch capability to replace systems lost to Soviet attacks. The U.S. is unlikely to be able to deter or defeat Soviet ASAT use in crises or conflicts unless it has an ASAT capability of its own.

Given widespread belief in the U.S. that U.S.-Soviet agreements can prevent competition in ASAT and satellite defense systems, the new President should direct the Department of Defense and the Arms Control and Disarmament Agency (ACDA) to update the 1984 review, which considered whether an effective, verifiable, and enforceable ASAT and satellite defense agreement is possible. The new President also should require the Pentagon and ACDA (see Arms Control section of this chapter) to help the U.S. Information Agency develop a public diplomacy campaign to counter Soviet charges that the U.S. is responsible for the "militarization" of space. The fact is that space was "militarized" long ago by Moscow. (See Public Diplomacy section of Chapter 24.)

Meeting U.S. Intelligence and Arms Control Needs

U.S. satellites cannot adequately track and target Soviet mobile missiles (such as the rail-mobile SS–24 and road-mobile SS–25 intercontinental ballistic missiles), support U.S. military operations, and verify arms control agreements. Arms control verification itself could use all existing U.S. intelligence-gathering assets in space plus newly created assets. The new Secretary of Defense thus should develop a plan to ensure that the U.S. has enough space-based surveillance systems. He also should develop, as required by the provision added to the fiscal 1989 defense budget by Senator Dan Quayle (R-IN), a five-year plan for improving U.S. ground- and space-based surveillance systems including those needed to locate Soviet space systems. Priority should be given to those systems needed to support U.S. military operations, especially naval activities like those in the Persian Gulf. The importance of space-based systems for the support of such U.S. conventional military activities was dramatically demonstrated by Reagan's use of space communications systems to authorize the April 18, 1988, sinking of Iranian naval vessels attacking U.S. naval ships thousands of miles away.

Establishing a National Space Technology
Investment Program (NSTIP)

Military space research in the U.S. is seriously fragmented with significant gaps in some areas of space technology and considerable overlap in others. The new President should establish a National Space Technology Investment Program to pull these activities together and provide coherence and direction to them. The NSTIP would establish goals, timetables, priorities, and agency responsibility for space-related technology research programs of the U.S. government. The NSTIP would be administered by a new Assistant Director for National Space Policy and Technology in the White House Office of Science and Technology Policy.

Accelerating the Manned Space Station Program

The large, manned space station that NASA has been authorized to build has been independently estimated to cost $21 billion in 1984 dollars and is to be operational by 1997. The Pentagon will fund a large part of this because the space station will enable it to carry out a wide range of defense activities, including experiments in space surveillance.

The costs and complexity of this project, plus its dependence on the shuttle, make it vulnerable to delays and congressional cuts in funding. The new President thus should develop a vigorous public information program to explain the importance of the manned space station. He should stress three points; first, this station will be an essential part of the infrastructure that the U.S. will need in using space for military, commercial, and scientific purposes; second, U.S. failure to develop this infrastructure would allow the Soviets to use their enormous space capabilities to enhance their global standing and to gain political, economic, and military advantages; and third, because manned space projects have always attracted greater U.S. popular and political support than unmanned projects, the manned space station can symbolize the American determination once again to become first in space.

The new President thus should direct NASA and the Pentagon to review ways of accelerating the manned space station program. In particular, heavy-lift Expendable Launch Vehicle systems would permit accelerated construction of the manned space station at much lower costs.

Building the National Aerospace Plane (NASP) by 1996

The NASP could bridge the gap between aircraft and space orbital systems; it would take off and land at airfields but would fly outside the atmosphere at speeds up to Mach 25—twenty-five times the speed of sound. This aircraft, known as the *Orient Express* in its civilian version, would have such military applications as launching satellites into orbit, repairing damaged satellites, and retrieving payloads from space. A modified NASP could fly into a low earth orbit with a very heavy surveillance payload for arms control verification or crisis management purposes. The NASP's ability to take off and land from ordinary airfields would give the U.S. multiple satellite launching bases. Today only Cape Kennedy in Florida and Vandenberg Air Force Base in California can be used to launch satellites using ELV, while only Cape Kennedy can launch the shuttle. Reliance on these two bases only invites Soviet attack, including by clandestine means. Furthermore, the NASP program involves basic technology developments that are applicable to other vital military systems.

The next Secretary of Defense should oppose efforts, including those within the Pentagon, to cut the NASP program, making sure that it remains on schedule for a first flight no later than 1996. To achieve this goal will require the annual funding to be maintained at a projected total cost level of roughly $3 billion.

———————————◇———————————

INITIATIVES FOR 1989

1) Establish a National Space Council. The new President should issue an Executive Order creating a National Space Council. This would be a new Cabinet-level group, chaired by the President, to provide firm, coherent leadership for U.S. military and civilian space policy. This should confirm the 1988 National Space Policy's principle of giving the Department of Defense the primary responsibility for military space policy. Existing funding levels, personnel, and technologies are generally adequate to support an effective, affordable military space policy.

The National Space Council should include the President, his National Security and Science Advisers, the Secretaries of Defense and Transportation, the Director of the Central Intelligence Agency, and the Administrator of NASA. Compliance with National Space Council directives would be monitored by the National Security and Science Advisers' staffs.

2) Give the U.S. Air Force responsibility and control of all space launches. As a result of the *Challenger* loss and the privatization of commercial space launches, the majority of future government space launches will be military. These launches require strict security and the ability to operate under attack or threat of attack. Accordingly, the

National Space Council should designate the Air Force Space Command as the sole agency for conducting government space launches. Other government agencies, such as NASA, that want to put payloads in space could purchase launch facilities from the private sector or the Air Force, whichever is cheaper and more convenient. Government agencies and private companies needing to launch heavy loads, including those carried on the manned shuttle, would be able to purchase Air Force launches, but only after priority military payloads were put into space.

3) Accelerate procurement of Expendable Launch Vehicles (ELVs). The Secretary of Defense should appoint a senior special assistant in charge of an accelerated ELV program under the Air Force Space Command. This special assistant must have regular access to the Secretary of Defense to assure the program sufficient budgetary and bureaucratic support.

4) Make contingency plans for shuttle program delays. Despite safety improvements, the shuttle remains so complex that it has an inherently high probability of failure involving further loss of a shuttle and possibly its crew. The damage to the U.S. military space program of another shuttle loss would be so great, in psychological and technical terms, that contingency plans for it need to be made. The new President should acknowledge explicitly the great inherent risk of the manned Space Shuttle in all public discussions of this system. The next Administration should ensure that the U.S. have sufficient spare space launch capabilities to launch essential military payloads and to service them as required, as in the case of the KH–12 reconnaissance satellites.

NOTES

1. Since it is recommended herein that the next President immediately establish a National Space Council, it is assumed that this Council will be responsible for establishing and overseeing the proposed U.S. military space policy. If such a Council were not established, this policy could be executed through other means, such as presidential directives.

The Military Services

Dov S. Zakheim*
Task Force Chairman

Issues concerning the future of the United States military often are
reduced to a question of alternatives:

◆ Should the U.S. focus its efforts on protecting its European allies,
or on providing forces more suitable for fulfilling other global responsibilities?

◆ Should resources be concentrated on development and procurement of new weapons systems, or on improving the preparedness and
battlefield sustainability of existing forces?

◆ Should the Army consist primarily of powerful, heavily armored
troops, or of less capable but more easily transported lightly armored
forces?

The new President will have to make these choices within the
context of adverse budgetary and demographic trends that could affect
the military's ability to recruit sufficient numbers of qualified men and
women. Failure to do so could compel sharp cuts in authorized forces,
reduce standards for accepting volunteers, and increase pay and benefits at the expense of procurement, readiness, and sustainability.
Budgetary and political factors, meanwhile, are converging in a way
that questions how long the U.S. can keep its large Army contingent
in Europe.

Given these factors, all services will have to use available resources
more efficiently and divide responsibilities effectively among themselves and with America's allies. Research, development, and procurement policies will have to be focused more explicitly on areas in which
the U.S. and its allies have a clear competitive advantage over the
Soviet Union. If applied consistently, this "competitive strategies"
approach can enable the U.S. to exploit technological and other
advantages in ways that cannot easily or cheaply be countered by
Moscow. The following sections address the various programmatic

---

*The author served as Chairman of the six *Mandate III* Task Forces that produced the
following reports on the Army, Navy, Air Force, Marines, NATO, and Low Intensity
Conflict.

aspects of each of the critical elements of U.S. defense posture. All are based on a series of common defense principles:

1) The U.S. defense budget must grow steadily in real terms. This is crucial if America is to remain the West's primary guarantor of peace. These defense recommendations thus assume a defense budget increase of 3.25 percent annually. Between fiscal 1981 and fiscal 1987, the defense budget grew an average of 5.5 percent annually, in real terms.

2) Force will remain an essential tool of diplomacy. Accordingly, the Administration must ensure that highest priority among conventional forces be assigned to flexible units that can respond to unforeseen contingencies promptly and in force. As such, budget priority should go to: the Navy, for a forward and flexible maritime strategy; the Marine Corps, as a critical adjunct to the Navy's operations; and tactical air forces, which need planes with longer range and endurance to contribute (as demonstrated by the 1986 strike on Libya) to sea-based flexible forces.

3) The U.S. no longer can avoid reexamining its force commitments to NATO. While the U.S. commitment to NATO remains strong, Washington has failed to persuade its NATO allies to do more to protect themselves, such as providing more firepower, more operational reserves for reinforcements, increased air base protection, close air defenses, and chemical and static anti-tank defenses. The U.S. must focus its efforts on areas in which it has not only a competitive advantage over the USSR but also a comparative advantage over its allies. These include: the highest technology aircraft; precision-guided, long-range cruise missile systems; airborne and ground command and control capabilities; and short-range nuclear systems. Manpower, by contrast, is not an area of U.S. advantage. It may make more sense to rely on the NATO allies to provide a greater share of the added manpower in a crisis. The U.S. should concentrate its resources on ground-based and airborne missiles, munitions, and mines that can strike at enemy bridges, railroad depots, airfields, and tanks. And the U.S. must redistribute NATO's financial burden—though the allies contribute much, they can do more.

4) The U.S. must maintain the momentum of its Low Intensity Conflict/Special Operations Forces (LIC/SOF) program. This program, which saw a revival in the first Reagan Administration, has languished as a result of internal Pentagon bureaucratic politics.

The recommendations that follow respond directly to the long-standing national security policies that have defined the U.S. role in the world since the end of World War II: a defensive orientation, a continuing commitment to allies and friends, a need to demonstrate strength and resolve through forward deployments worldwide, and acceptance of the awesome responsibility of nuclear guarantor of Western security.

The Army*

The Army provides the United States with most of the ground forces necessary to execute its national military strategy. Unlike the Navy or Air Force, the Army can hold or seize territory, an irreplaceable requirement for deterring aggression or defeating an aggressor should deterrence fail. Defending members of the North Atlantic Treaty Organization against Soviet aggression is the Army's primary mission abroad. Over 215,000 U.S. Army troops are stationed in Europe for this purpose. An Army contingent of nearly 30,000 is in South Korea, and smaller contingents are deployed around the globe providing front-line defense of America's other vital security interests. Army forces based in the U.S. can deploy rapidly to areas of conflict, as they did in early 1988 to deter a large-scale Nicaraguan intervention in Honduras.

———————————◇———————————

THE REAGAN ADMINISTRATION RECORD

A decline in military spending dating from the end of the Vietnam War had, by 1980, left the U.S. Army inadequately trained and critically short of supplies. Perhaps more disturbing, years of political and budgetary neglect had taken a serious toll of Army morale and self-esteem. In the last year of the Carter Administration, and much more so in the Reagan years, the Army's readiness to meet aggression and sustain itself in battle has improved substantially. Every year since 1979, the Army has met its recruitment goals. Adequate funding in the past eight years has improved the quality and amount of realistic combat training for Army troops. It also has increased the spare parts and ammunition available for training and wartime reserves. While some shortages persist, particularly in skilled technical and medical

---

*Commenting and contributing generously to this report were *Mandate III* Task Force Members Steven Canby, Kim R. Holmes, Alan Sabrosky, and Heritage Policy Analyst Jay P. Kosminsky. They do not necessarily endorse all of its views and recommendations.

Task Force Deputy Chairman: Jeffrey Record.

personnel, attracting high-quality recruits to the Army and other military services may be one of the most underrated achievements of the Reagan Administration and perhaps its most valuable long-run contribution to American security.

The Army during the Reagan years has deployed and is operating new and modernized versions of critical weapons, including: The M–1 *Abrams* main battle tank, which is roughly comparable to the most advanced Soviet tanks and which has replaced the outmoded M–60 as the mainstay of America's European-deployed units; The *Bradley* Infantry fighting vehicle, capable of transporting troops on the battle-field and providing them a measure of protection with guns and anti-tank weapons; and the *Apache* (AH–64) attack helicopter, capable of night and all-weather operations against enemy tanks and infantry.

Taken together, improvements in manpower and materiel under the Reagan Administration have increased the Army's morale and battle-field effectiveness. Certain problems, however, have persisted. After many false starts, the Reagan Administration has yet to develop an air defense system to protect vulnerable forward Army troops from air attack, or an effective hand-held anti-tank weapon to help offset the Soviet armor advantage in Europe. In the former case, after canceling the problem-ridden Division Air Defense (DIVAD) system, the Defense Department chose to develop a new Forward Area Air Defense System (FAADS). This was a mistake, inviting new delays in fielding a complex weapons system. Instead, the Army should have filled its need for forward air defense by purchasing highly capable systems already fielded by U.S. allies, including France and West Germany. Similarly, the U.S. has continued to field the DRAGON anti-tank system when far more effective systems are available from NATO allies.

Another problem is the Reagan Administration's decision to field five Light Infantry Divisions (LID). A LID consists of roughly 10,000 easily transportable and lightly armed infantrymen. LIDs are to be used primarily for rapid deployment of American Army forces; for example, to seize territory and meet the first wave of Soviet forces in the event of a Soviet push to the Persian Gulf through Iran. But a LID does not have much overall firepower and lacks the supplies to sustain itself in battle. While the U.S. needed to augment the light forces it already had in the Marine Corps and such other Army units as the 25th Infantry Division based in Hawaii (since converted into a LID), the Light Infantry Division has not been a wise and efficient way of doing so.

THE NEXT FOUR YEARS

Eliminating Two Active Heavy Army Divisions

Declining public support for defense expenditures in the face of expanding global commitments requires the U.S. to shift military priorities from maintaining force levels toward increasing the preparedness and quality of active and reserve divisions. To do this, the Secretary of Defense should seek congressional support to eliminate from the active force structure two of the Army's thirteen heavy divisions, totaling approximately 34,000 troops, based in the U.S. and slated for rapid NATO reinforcement. The Secretary should consider keeping the divisions active if the allies agree to pay at least one-half of the costs required to airlift the troops to Europe on schedule.

Obtaining the Close Air Support (CAS) Mission from the Air Force

Providing air support to Army troops engaged directly in combat can be done more effectively by the Army, which is in direct command of the troops, than by the Air Force, which must coordinate close air support through a separate chain of command. The experience of the Marine Corps, which provides close air support for its own troops, has proven the value of such an arrangement. The Secretary of Defense should direct the Joint Chiefs of Staff to develop plans and a schedule transferring the Air Force's close air support mission to the Army. This should be reflected in the respective armed services budget requests.

Improving Mechanized Infantry

New anti-armor technology calls into question the survivability of mechanized infantry, which uses armored personnel carriers (APC) and infantry fighting vehicles (IFV) to transport troops to and around the battlefield. Recent Middle East conflicts, particularly the 1982 Israeli-Syrian war, have demonstrated the acute vulnerability of these vehicles to anti-tank guided missiles and to a wide variety of relatively inexpensive, often hand-held, anti-armor weapons. The Secretary of the Army and the Army Chief of Staff should seek tactical and technological solutions to this vulnerability. These should include greater protection for mechanized infantry by such means as the development of heavily armored tanks capable of transporting infantry, along the lines of the Israeli *Merkava* tank.

Eliminating the Distinction between Armored and Mechanized Divisions

Changes in battlefield tactics and capabilities have led to a convergence in the organization and equipment of armored and mechanized infantry divisions, each of which consists of a mix of tanks and mechanized infantry. Armored divisions have about 20 percent more tanks than mechanized divisions. The Secretary of the Army should do away with the increasingly anachronistic distinction between armored and mechanized divisions, and their different logistics structures, and instead create a single heavy division type.

Restructuring Light Infantry

Light Infantry Divisions (LIDs) are composed of lightly armed and easily transportable troops to be used for rapid response to an international crisis. These divisions, however, would not necessarily possess sufficient firepower to meet Soviet forces, or even some potential Third World adversaries, such as Iran or Libya, that field heavy tank and mechanized infantry divisions. The Secretary of the Army and the Army Chief of Staff should develop plans for restructuring three of the Army's LIDs, currently with roughly 10,000 soldiers each, into a light infantry corps, composed of about ten light infantry brigades of about 3,000 to 3,500 soldiers. These brigades would be trained in general light infantry tactics, and each would specialize in one form of combat, such as mountain, tundra, or jungle warfare. By restructuring light infantry into smaller, more specialized aggregations of troops, forces will be better able to cope with a wide range of contingencies.

———————————◇———————————

INITIATIVES FOR 1989

1) Reject activation of the 6th and 10th Light Infantry Divisions. The Army currently is forming and activating two Light Infantry Divisions (LIDs), the 6th and 10th, in addition to the three already existing. This would give the U.S. excess and redundant infantry capabilities. Accordingly, the Secretary of Defense should seek authorization to change the status of the 6th and 10th LIDs from active to National Guard. Along with the shift to reserve status of two heavy divisions, this change will free resources to increase the readiness and sustainability of existing forces.

2) Expand the Unit Manning System. The army's Unit Manning System instituted in 1982 (as the New Manning System) was designed to keep units together from training to deployment, rather than reassigning individuals to new units after training. The objective was to increase unit cohesion, and ultimately battlefield effectiveness. The program still has not been put into place throughout the Army. The Secretary of the Army and the Army Chief of Staff should ensure that the Unit Manning System is fully implemented throughout the Army.

3) Cancel proposed Forward Area Air Defense System (FAADS) and purchase available allied divisional air defense systems. The Army cannot afford to wait until the early to mid–1990s for the Air Defense Anti-Tank System (ADATS), designed to provide air cover for forces close to the battlefront (Forward Air Defense, or FAADS). Testing has shown that neither ADATS nor such alternatives as a modified Franco-German *Roland* or British *Rapier* can entirely fulfill the FAADS mission. Unlike the unproved and undeployed ADATS, however, which now is not expected to reach operational capacity until 1992, these European alternatives at least are available and fully tested. The Secretary of Defense should request funding for the purchase of an available European system as an interim solution to the U.S. forward air defense mission. Meanwhile, development should continue on advanced FAAD technologies, such as fiber optic guided and hypervelocity projectiles.

4) Consider immediate purchase of an available allied infantry anti-tank weapon. For half a century, the U.S. infantry has lacked a portable hand-held anti-tank weapon as effective as those fielded by European allies and adversaries. Such weapons, to be carried by infantrymen and deployed in great quantity, are needed to offset Soviet numerical advantages in tanks and other armored vehicles. The Secretary of the Army should request funding for the replacement of the currently deployed U.S.-made *Dragon* anti-tank weapon with a more capable system, such as the Franco-German *Milan*.

5) Retrofit the AH–1 *Cobra* attack helicopter with modern anti-tank munitions and keep the *Apache* production line open. With the LHX (experimental light helicopter) no longer envisioned in a ground-attack role, the Army must rely on the new *Apache* and on the *Cobra*, which first was introduced in the mid–1960s. The *Cobra* must be upgraded with modern anti-tank weapons to increase its effectiveness against new Soviet armor, and the full *Apache* program should be completed. The Secretary of Defense should submit a request for budgetary authority to retrofit the *Cobra* with modern anti-tank weapons and to procure the additional 675 *Apache* attack helicopters called for by Army planners.

6) Acquire a low-cost remotely piloted vehicle (RPV). RPVs are small and generally inexpensive pilotless aircraft that carry a television camera and therefore can be guided from a remote (and defended) base. RPVs can be used for reconnaissance and are being studied for an attack role. RPVs were used very effectively in combat by the Israelis to obtain reconnaissance information critical to destroying Syrian air defense missile sites in 1982. RPVs could be used by the U.S. Army to provide intelligence on battlefield actions as they unfold and to identify targets for highly accurate long-range weapons launched by troops, planes, or ships far from the battle lines. The Secretary of Defense should request funds to purchase foreign RPVs, such as the Israeli Mazlat series.

7) Maintain the viability of the All-Volunteer Force. The diminishing U.S. young adult pool, expanding U.S. economy, and persistent shortages of skilled technical personnel in the Army make steps to improve recruitment imperative. The Secretary of the Army should initiate a study of ways in which the Army could increase its appeal to a wider, higher-quality manpower pool, particularly college-bound men and women. The study should consider, for example, flexible enlistment options, such as offering a relatively short period of service with lower pay and benefits, but with substantial postservice educational aid. The Army also should look into selectively targeting recruits with skills in short supply, such as medical technicians, offering them higher reenlistment bonuses or other inducements such as more leave time.

The Navy*

Given America's geopolitical position astride two oceans, sea power is the chief guarantor of the United States' ability to protect its trade lifeline, to secure access to scarce resources and markets, and to support its military forces around the world. The Navy accomplishes these missions with a mix of seaborne assets, comprised of surface ships, submarines, and ship-based aircraft. The Navy also makes a key contribution to the maintenance of nuclear deterrence through its fleet of ballistic-missile-carrying submarines (SSBNs) and its sea-launched cruise missiles (SLCM), carried by surface ships and attack submarines. (See Strategic Offensive Forces section of this chapter.)

The Navy plays a major part in sustaining America's alliance system, which includes the members of the North Atlantic Treaty Organization (NATO), the Rio Pact, Japan, Australia, and other countries, by projecting American power in the Atlantic, Pacific, and Indian Oceans, and in adjacent seas and geopolitical choke points. The Navy is an important U.S. military instrument for potential use in a panoply of Third World contingencies, ranging from indigenous regional instabilities, subversion, and state-sponsored terrorism to small- and large-scale military conflicts involving regional powers.

U.S. naval forces also must contend with the increasing quality of Soviet naval forces and growing sophistication of Soviet naval operations. In particular, the new quietness of Soviet submarines (largely attributable to stolen Western technology) poses significant implications for American naval strategy. Central to the role of the U.S. Navy is what is known as a forward maritime strategy. This calls for the Navy to engage an enemy as far away as possible from U.S. shores, and to maintain undisputed control of the seas.

———————————————◇———————————————

THE REAGAN ADMINISTRATION RECORD

When the Reagan Administration took office, the Navy virtually was unprepared for battle: ships were undermanned, war re-

---

*Commenting and contributing generously to this report were *Mandate III* Task Force Members Roger Barnett, Seth Cropsey, Norman Friedman, James George, Robert Hanks, and Heritage Policy Analyst Jay P. Kosminsky. They do not necessarily endorse all of its views and recommendations.

Task Force Deputy Chairman: David B. Rivkin, Jr.

serves and supplies were lacking, personnel quality had plunged, and crews were not receiving adequate training. The Administration has developed a robust naval force of nearly 600 ships, including 15 aircraft carrier battle groups (CVBGs) and four battleships. Aircraft carriers are the mainstay of the Navy, each fielding an air wing capable of land attack, air-to-air combat, and anti-submarine warfare, among other missions. Battleships, meanwhile, are critical in providing sea-based firepower at distances over 25 miles in support of operations at sea and on shore.

The Administration has improved Navy combat readiness enormously. Between 1981 and 1987, there was a 61 percent decrease in down time, the period during which surface ships are unprepared for combat due to equipment problems. During the Reagan years, aircraft mission capability rates improved by 66 percent. The capability of Navy Reserve forces also has improved dramatically, primarily as a result of providing them up-to-date equipment and of "horizontal integration," a program in which reserve units train and operate with their active-duty counterparts.

The Reagan Administration has emphasized contractor competition for Navy vessels and supplies. From 1982 to 1986, the annual value of competitively awarded contracts rose from $8.1 billion to $23.2 billion. As a result, for example, the costs of the *Tomahawk* missile program dropped from $11 billion to $9.2 billion. Personnel quality also has improved dramatically.

Yet, the Administration has not done so well on some other issues. Most importantly, investment in new naval technologies has lagged behind procurement of weapon systems that incorporate existing technologies. Over the past six years, for example, the Navy's Research, Development, Testing, and Evaluation (RDT&E) budget has grown only 2 percent annually in real terms, while the Navy's overall budget has grown by 3.1 percent per year. Total RDT&E investment constitutes 10 percent of the Navy's fiscal 1989 budget request, a figure proportionally about 50 percent lower than the Air Force, although the Navy is at least as dependent on high technology systems as the Air Force. A relative decline in RDT&E spending adversely affects the Navy's ability to sustain its present qualitative edge over potential adversaries.

The Navy also has not paid sufficient attention to developing less costly alternatives to expensive submarines (including the *Ohio*-class nuclear missile-carrying submarine and the *Seawolf* attack submarine), designed to attack land targets, other submarines, and surface ships.

As a result of the high price tag of these submarine programs, total ballistic missile submarine and attack submarine expenditures have cut heavily into the Navy's operational, maintenance, and ship-building funds.

Toward the end of the Reagan Administration, meanwhile, Congress and the Administration have failed to sustain the naval ship-building program, jeopardizing the 15–carrier naval force structure. Navy aircraft production also has not been sustained at requisite rates. Most seriously affected have been procurement of the Navy's versatile strike-fighter, the F/A–18 *Hornet* (capable of both air-to-air combat and ground attack), and the vertical/short take-off and landing (VSTOL) *Harrier* AV–8B, used to support Marine operations. To keep up with fleet requirements, both of these aircraft should have been produced at rates at least 25 percent higher than has been the case.

THE NEXT FOUR YEARS

Clarifying U.S. Naval Strategy and Its Contribution to National Strategy

Current U.S. maritime strategy envisions attacks by the U.S. Navy early in a conflict against Soviet maritime forces and forces located on the Kola Peninsula, the North Sea, the Norwegian Sea, the Northern Atlantic Ocean, the Sea of Okhotsk, and the Pacific Ocean. The early destruction of key elements of the Soviet fleet, including ballistic missile submarines, could be crucial to the success of NATO's efforts in a conflict with the Soviet Union.

This maritime strategy has been at the center of a long-simmering controversy. Some argue that it is dangerous and provocative to plan for wartime attacks against Soviet ballistic missile submarines and naval bases. Yet the strategy is defensive, for strikes against Soviet territory would be carried out only in the context of a Soviet invasion of U.S. allies or the U.S. It also is argued that a maritime strategy is militarily unfeasible. This is not true if sufficient resources are devoted to building naval power. To do so, some resources will have to be redirected from land forces, a tradeoff that also has been fuel for debate.

The new President should issue a National Security Decision Directive reaffirming the importance of maritime strategy within U.S. national strategy. The directive should instruct the Joint Chiefs of Staff and Chief of Naval Operations to develop the plans and training exercises necessary to execute this strategy under various conflict scenarios, notably against Soviet bases in Asia and the Kola Peninsula in the Arctic.

Improving Interservice Cooperation

An effective forward maritime strategy will require close interservice cooperation. The Secretary of Defense should require the Secretaries of the Navy and Air Force to devise plans for improved interservice cooperation and to conduct regular interservice exercises. The Navy should study the feasibility of conducting joint operations with the Air Force's long-range strike/surveillance aircraft and missile force which would be used in attacks on Soviet naval bases and ships in Soviet waters. Cooperation also should be explored in anti-satellite capability, since both the Navy and the Air Force depend heavily on satellites for surveillance, navigation, and communications. (See Military Space section of this chapter.)

Maintaining Access to Overseas Bases

Given the rising opposition to the presence of U.S. overseas facilities such as the base at Subic Bay in the Philippines, the existence of these bases no longer can be taken for granted. Yet, they enable the U.S. Navy to maintain large, forward-based naval formations, such as aircraft carrier battle groups (CVBGs). The new President should seek to retain and, to the extent possible, augment America's present overseas base structure. At the same time, it is essential for the U.S. to develop alternatives to the bases in locations such as Guam, Saipan, and the Marianas, which are more remote from likely areas of conflict, but are American controlled.

Establishing Naval Force Configuration
for the 1990s and Beyond

The Navy should reach and maintain the minimum requirement established by the Reagan Administration of 15 aircraft carriers and other key elements of the naval force mix including no fewer than four battleships with supporting escorts, 90 attack submarines (there are 100 operating today), and transport ships capable of moving the troops and equipment for at least one Marine Expeditionary Force (MEF) and an entire Marine Expeditionary Brigade (MEB). (See Marine Corps section of this chapter.)

Increasing Naval Aircraft Production

To ensure an adequate naval aircraft inventory, the Secretary of Defense should request funding for increasing the production rates planned for such aircraft as the F/A–18 *Hornet* and AV–8B *Harrier* vertical/short take-off and landing aircraft, both of which have air combat and ground combat roles, and for upgrading the A–6 *Intruder* ground attack aircraft. Higher production rates would enable the Navy to maintain required force levels while lowering unit costs of each aircraft type. The Secretary of Defense also should request sufficient RDT&E funding for the next generation of aircraft, particularly the Advanced Tactical Aircraft (ATA), which eventually will replace the A–6 as the Navy's primary attack aircraft. These measures can ensure that the Navy maintains its qualitative edge over the Soviet Union into the next century.

Reviewing the Navy Escort Mission

The Navy could save money by deemphasizing its mission to escort ships involved in the wartime resupply of Europe, and requiring U.S. allies to fulfill more of the resupply escort mission. (See NATO section of this chapter.) As such, the Navy would need less escort capabilities than it now has. Accordingly, in considering U.S. escort requirements, the Secretary of the Navy should emphasize Third World operations, such as Persian Gulf deployments, rather than a U.S.-Soviet confrontation in Europe.

Enhancing Offensive Capabilities

New technologies make possible precision nonnuclear attacks on naval and land targets. The Navy thus should develop new, highly accurate munitions for its shipborne guns and missiles, which would enable them more effectively to attack such targets as command posts and communications sites now requiring attacks by manned aircraft. The Secretary of Defense should seek extended-range 16–inch shells for U.S. battleships, modification of guided 5–inch shells for gun mounts on cruisers and destroyers and programs to make anti-ship, anti-aircraft, and anti-shore missiles more accurate and more resilient to electronic jamming.

Improving Rapid Reaction Capability

To respond rapidly in those areas of the world where the U.S. lacks adequate forward deployment, the Secretary of Defense should request funding to increase the stockpiles of equipment positioned on ships overseas. This "prepositioning" now takes place on specially configured ships operating in the Atlantic, Pacific, and Indian Oceans. The U.S. should have enough prepositioned ships to support putting ashore a force of at least four Marine expeditionary brigades of about 5,000 Marines each, and necessary equipment anywhere in the world. Current capability can support three Marine brigades. To support the additional brigade, the Navy needs at least six more maritime prepositioning ships (MPS) than presently planned. (See Marine Corps section of this chapter.)

Funding Special Operations Capabilities

Given the expectation of increased threats to American interests in the Third World, the Navy's capabilities to conduct "low intensity" warfare should be bolstered. Specifically, the Secretary of Defense should request increased funding for naval special operations forces. Navy special operations Sea-Air-Land (SEAL) forces are capable of commando raids and special missions against well-defended enemy targets. The numbers of SEAL officers and enlisted personnel should be increased from today's 348 officers and 1,496 enlisted personnel to about 500 officers and 1,700 enlisted personnel. Investment in the specialized equipment required to support the SEALs should also be increased. This includes the Special Warfare Craft Medium (SWCM), used to deploy SEAL forces, and the Advanced Seal Delivery System (ASDS) used to infiltrate SEAL forces ashore.

Strengthening Nuclear Deterrence

The Soviet leadership apparently believes that using nuclear weapons at sea may not lead to nuclear escalation. As such, the U.S. Navy must anticipate the possibility of Soviet nuclear attacks in a naval conflict. To counter this, the U.S. could increase hardening of shipboard systems to enable them better to withstand the blast and electromagnetic effects of nuclear explosions. The U.S. also should improve the ability of U.S. ships to operate in a nuclear-contaminated environment. The Secretary of the Navy should initiate a study of naval nuclear contingencies and possible U.S. responses.

Developing a New Attack Submarine (SSN)

The Navy's attack submarines (SSNs) are designed to track and, if necessary, destroy Soviet ballistic missile submarines, attack submarines, and surface ships. To do this, the U.S. needs an SSN force of at least 90 units into the twenty-first century. Presently, the Navy has over 100 SSNs; however, by the late–1990s, *Los Angeles* (688–class) submarines, the mainstay of the SSN force, will approach block obsolescence; they were first deployed in 1972. The Secretary of Defense should request funding for the higher submarine production rates to maintain the force of 90 SSNs into the twenty-first century.

Because of budget constraints, maintenance of the SSN fleet will require a submarine less expensive than the soon-to-be-deployed *Seawolf* SSN–21 which costs over $1 billion each. To trim unit costs, the Navy should examine whether it needs all of the sophisticated combat systems planned for the *Seawolf*. The Secretary of Defense should request funding for development of a less expensive attack submarine (taking into account procurement and life-cycle costs), to be deployed along with the *Seawolf*.

Bolstering Anti-Air Warfare

In a future conflict, U.S surface ships may be vulnerable to massed attacks by high-performance missile-firing Soviet and Third World aircraft. The Secretary of the Navy should initiate a study of how U.S. ships could improve their anti-air warfare (AAW) capability. Possible solutions to this problem include deployment of additional and improved *Aegis* cruisers (which carry sophisticated radar and missiles to protect U.S. carrier battle groups), and additional investment in electronic countermeasures (ECM) and counterelectronic countermeasures (CECM).

Developing a High/Low Carrier Force Mix

To be prepared better for the inevitable attrition in a major war, the Secretary of Defense should request funding for a "high-low" force mix of expensive, highly capable ships and less expensive ships that can be produced in large numbers in the event of war. Such a force mix, for example, would permit expensive capital ships, such as aircraft carriers, built in peacetime, to be rapidly augmented in wartime by ships capable of accommodating vertical/short take-off and landing (VSTOL) aircraft. Also, a Variable Load Ship (VLS) (featuring a common hull capable of housing such different weapons packages as those for anti-aircraft and anti-submarine warfare), would be particularly useful if a rapid wartime naval expansion is necessary. The Secretary of Defense should request funding for the development and eventual procurement of VSTOL carriers and VLS ships. (See Defense Industrial Preparedness section of this chapter.)

Improving Airborne Surveillance Capability

Locating an enemy force before being located by it has always been essential to success in naval warfare. To ensure that the U.S. can do this, the Secretary of Defense should devote resources to bolster airborne surveillance capability. The Navy needs additional radars, such as the Inverse Synthetic Aperture Radar (ISAR), capable of seeing farther and with greater acuity than existing radars. New satellites should be developed, with capabilities that go beyond the existing *Navstar*/Global Positioning System (GPS), a satellite system used by ships and planes to determine their own precise position, information that can be important for properly programming and targeting precision munitions.

Enhancing Anti-Submarine Warfare Capabilities

New technology, much of it stolen from the West or given to the Soviets by Japanese and Norwegian firms, has made Soviet submarines more difficult to track and harder to destroy once found. The Secretary of Defense should request funding for new anti-submarine capabilities and for new anti-submarine munitions capable of outrunning new Soviet submarines and penetrating their titanium hulls. Research into more advanced munitions and sensors should be pursued by the Navy.

———————————◇———————————

INITIATIVES FOR 1989

1) **Increase authorized end strength.** The present strength of the Navy is 593,200 active-duty forces and 152,600 reserves. It is anticipated that an additional 6,000 active-duty sailors will be required to man fully a balanced Navy of around 600 ships in the 1990s and beyond. The Secretary of Defense should seek funding to maintain and, if possible, increase present levels of naval personnel, and provide addi-

tional incentives for the reenlistment of highly trained technical specialists.

2) Restore shipbuilding rates. To maintain a balanced Navy capable of carrying out a successful maritime strategy, the Secretary of Defense should request funding to build at least 20 ships per year.

3) Improve the reserve force. While the capabilities of the naval reserves have improved, the reserve forces still do not receive adequate training. The Navy should upgrade its reserve forces through more frequent exercises, coordinated with active-duty naval forces. The new President should request Congress to require all merchant ships of U.S. registry to be available for a period each year for joint exercises with the U.S. Navy to be better prepared to undertake resupply or other operations during wartime.

4) Accelerate procurement of minesweepers. Events in the Persian Gulf in 1987 and 1988 reveal the vulnerability of the U.S. Navy to even relatively primitive mine warfare. The Secretary of Defense should request funding to increase U.S. mine warfare capability, both offensive and defensive.

The Air Force*

In war, the Air Force must seize and exploit control of the air. The Air Force consists of four commands, each wth a distinct mission. The Tactical Air Command (TAC) trains to attack enemy air forces in the air and on the ground, destroy such military ground targets as bases and ammunition depots, provide firepower for troops in combat (close air support), and conduct electronic warfare. The Military Airlift Command (MAC) transports troops and equipment from their bases to the scene of battle. The Strategic Air Command (SAC) is responsible for strategic nuclear weapons. (See Strategic Offensive Forces section of this chapter.) And the United States Space Command and Air Force Space Command have primary responsibility for U.S. space activities and space launches. (See Military Space section of this chapter.)

$$\diamond$$

THE REAGAN ADMINISTRATION RECORD

When the Reagan Administration took office, the Air Force had a limited supply of modern planes, munitions, and equipment, and its personnel were insufficiently trained. It was a "hollow force," lacking combat capability. Since then, however, much of the Air Force's fighting ability has been restored. The numbers of F-16 *Fighting Falcon* and F-15 *Eagle* tactical fighters (aircraft designed primarily for air-to-air combat and also to attack ground targets) had risen from about 300 and 580 to 1300 and 800, respectively, by mid–1988. Along with the Navy's F-14 *Tomcat* and F-18 *Hornet*, the F-15 and F-16 are arguably the world's best tactical fighters.

Critical deficiencies in the Air Force's airlift capability (the ability to transport troops and equipment by plane) have been alleviated partially by the addition of 19 C-5B *Galaxy* and 51 KC-10A *Extender* tankers. Airlift also has benefited from the Civil Reserve Air Fleet enhancement program, under which DC10 and Boeing 747, 757, and 767 passenger

---

*Commenting and contributing generously to this report were *Mandate III* Task Force Members David Isby, John Wildfong, and Heritage Policy Analyst Jay P. Kosminsky. They do not necessarily endorse all of its views and recommendations.
Task Force Deputy Chairman: Brian Green.

aircraft are modified to serve as military freighters in the event of a national emergency.

Perhaps most important, Air Force combat readiness has been improved through expanded flying time and more realistic and extensive training exercises, such as the successful "Red Flag" training exercises against aircraft simulating Soviet fighters.

These improvements have increased Air Force combat capability significantly. Example: Tactical forces are now ready to fly 80 percent more combat missions than they could in 1981. Example: Airlift capacity has nearly doubled since 1981, to approximately 47 million ton-miles per day, greatly enhancing the ability of the United States to reinforce NATO allies with troops and equipment and respond to other global contingencies. (Ton-miles per day is the accepted measure of airlift capacity, arrived at by multiplying the number of tons moved by the number of miles they were transported.)

Yet despite these advances, problems remain. Foremost among these is the 18 percent decline in the Air Force budget since fiscal 1985, which has reduced the size of the tactical air force. Early in the 1980s, the Air Force determined that it required 40 tactical wings (each wing normally consists of 72 planes such as F-15s and F-16s) to fulfill its missions worldwide. The Air Force currently has 38 wings; however, the Pentagon plans to reduce this to 35 by 1990, in anticipation of future tight budgets. Declining budgets also have constrained military compensation. Since pay has not kept pace with the private sector, the Air Force has been losing pilots and engineers to commercial aviation at an alarming rate. Budget strictures also threaten modernization. The latest deployed U.S. tactical and airlift aircraft are based on twenty-year-old designs, and will require engineering and avionics upgrading to keep pace with the latest Soviet interceptors and fighters, such as the SU-27 *Flanker* and MIG-29 *Fulcrum*.

———————◇———————

THE NEXT FOUR YEARS

Improving Personnel Retention Rates

Retaining pilots, engineers, and key technological specialists is critical to the Air Force. Yet military pay now is 11 percent behind private-sector pay for similar tasks. A shortage of aviators already has affected combat readiness in the Navy, and could soon jeopardize Air Force combat readiness. Competitive pay traditionally has been the key to retaining skilled personnel in the armed services. Given expected budget limitations, other means of manpower retention must be explored. As such, the Secretary of the Air Force should give priority to studying and instituting such "quality of life" programs as improved family housing through an expanded home improvement loan program, medical and dental care, child care, and dependent education. The Secretary of Defense also should ensure that Air Force budget requests maintain salary levels for critical personnel comparable to those in the private sector.

Exploiting New Technologies

New technology can revolutionize air and space warfare in such fields as remote sensing, high energy weapons, and targeting. The Air Force at times has been reluctant to pursue technologically promising projects because they compete for funds with programs traditionally favored by strong constituencies within the Air Force. The Strategic Defense Initiative (SDI), for instance, has not received Air Force support commensurate with its potential.

A concept the Air Force should explore more fully is "lightsat," a system of lightweight satellites launched from dispersed sites to reinforce or reconstitute U.S. space capabilities during an emergency. The Air Force and Congress also should give more attention to conventional (nonnuclear) air-launched cruise missiles with a range of over 1,000 miles; a cruise missile is a highly accurate jet-powered missile capable of sustained flight close to the ground. Conventionally armed cruise missiles such as the Navy's *Tomahawk* can strike bridges, troop mobilization centers, and airfields deep behind enemy lines during a major conflict. The Secretary of the Air Force should define the missions and determine the potential cost-effectiveness of such promising concepts as "lightsat" and long-range conventional cruise missiles.

Protecting Readiness Gains

Air Force readiness to fight at a peak level of performance and to remain effective during battle depends on a number of factors, including extensive training and the ready availability of spare parts and munitions. The readiness gains of the Reagan years must be sustained during the new Administration. The Secretary of Defense should request Congress to fund fully ongoing readiness programs, particularly those geared toward maintaining adequate munitions stocks and programs to give pilots more actual flight training time, which has declined slightly over the past two years.

Establishing Efficient Procurement Rates

Given budget limitations, the Air Force has tended to stretch out procurement programs, buying a given number of systems over a longer period of time to lessen annual costs. While this cuts outlays in the very short run, it sharply boosts unit costs and thus ultimately the cost of the program as a whole. With modest increases in near-term annual budgets, the Air Force could produce some aircraft and other weapons at a somewhat faster and far more efficient rate, resulting in significant long-term savings. Programs that could benefit immediately this way include the Advanced Medium-Range Air-to-Air Missile (AM-RAAM), and the F-15 *Eagle* fighter. The Secretary of the Air Force should identify additional programs that will contribute most to overall cost savings through more efficient production rates, and the Secretary of Defense should prepare the Defense Department budget request accordingly.

Increasing the Number of Tactical Air Wings

Tactical forces include such planes as the F–15 and F–16, which are designed to gain air superiority over the battlefield and provide firepower in support of ground forces. The Air Force should have 40 tactical wings, each consisting of about 3 squadrons of approximately 24 aircraft to fulfill U.S. military requirements. Currently the Air Force has 38 wings; the cutback to 35 programed for 1990 is considered the bare minimum to carry out essential missions. Maintaining a modern force even at these minimal levels will require the Air Force to purchase about 220 planes annually. The Secretary of Defense should press for funds for at least a 35-wing Air Force.

Emphasizing Force Multipliers

Force multipliers are assets that greatly increase the value and effectiveness of existing forces. Radar, for example, can identify hostile aircraft at great distances and guide intercepting aircraft directly to their targets, vastly improving the effectiveness of each interceptor. Radar thus is a force multiplier.

Since NATO forces are numerically inferior to Warsaw Pact forces, NATO needs force multipliers. The Air Force fields, or is planning to field, a number of potential multipliers. One is the Joint Surveillance and Target Attack Radar System (JSTARS), which will detect, identify, and track moving ground targets deep behind enemy lines. Another is *Tacit Rainbow*, a drone designed to knock out enemy air defense radars. Other multipliers include the Low-Altitude Night Targeting Infrared Navigation system (LANTIRN) to facilitate all-weather low-level ground attacks night or day, and long-range munitions capable of attacking several targets simultaneously. The Secretary of Defense should stress force multipliers in upcoming Department of Defense budget requests.

Fully Funding the Advanced Tactical Fighter

The Advanced Tactical Fighter (ATF), currently under development, should begin to supplement the F–15 *Eagle* in the Air Force inventory in the 1990s. The ATF incorporates stealth technology, improved maneuverability, advanced electronics, and increased reliability and maintainability. Since technology is NATO's ultimate force multiplier, the ATF program is essential to maintaining air superiority against expected Soviet advances in fighter technology. The Secretary of Defense should request full funding for the ATF and oppose program cutbacks that would compromise its technological edge. The Navy's Advanced Tactical Aircraft (ATA), now under development, also will serve as the Air Force's follow-on to the F–111 long-range fighter bomber. The Secretary of Defense should request full funding for both programs.

Developing a Close Air Support/Battlefield
Air Interdiction Plane

Whether the Air Force retains its close air support role in supporting ground forces engaged in battle or whether this role is transferred to the Army (as recommended in the Army section of this chapter), a plane is needed to supplement the aging A-7 *Corsair* and A-10 *Thunderbolt* ground attack planes. Further, new Army doctrine calls for operations deep behind enemy lines. Such operations will blur the distinction between two previously separate Air Force missions: close air support and battlefield interdiction. This confluence of missions, along with expected budget restrictions, raises questions about the expensive research and development for a new close air support plane. Instead, an existing plane already suited to battlefield air interdiction, such as the Air Force F-16 *Fighting Falcon*, could be modified at reasonable cost to give it more close air support capability.

The Secretary of Defense should request funding to develop an upgraded F–16 or other existing plane to be equipped better for close air support and eliminate research and development funding for a new plane for this purpose.

Developing Short-Range Air-to-Air Missile Alternatives

The U.S. and NATO need an advanced short-range air-to-air missile that will be more effective and less susceptible to countermeasures than the current versions of the AIM-9 *Sidewinder*, which was first deployed in the mid–1970s. NATO nations agreed in 1980 that the U.S. would develop an advanced medium-range air-to-air missile (AMRAAM) and that a West European consortium would develop an advanced short-range air-to-air missile (ASRAAM). AMRAAM, a radar-guided "smart" successor to the AIM-7 *Sparrow*, is now in early production. By contrast, ASRAAM has not yet begun full-scale development. If the West Europeans cannot provide, in timely fashion, a short-range air-to-air missile superior to those it is intended to replace, the Air Force should explore its own alternatives. The new President should press his West European counterparts to increase ASRAAM funding, and if that fails, he should request congressional funding for an American alternative.

Assuring Access to Space

The Air Force must fund existing programs to build expendable launch vehicles (ELV) as an alternative to the Space Shuttle. Without ELVs, the Air Force would lack space systems providing intelligence gathering, communications, arms control verification, and projects related to the Strategic Defense Initiative. The Secretary of Defense also should seek continued development funding for the ELV. (See Military Space Section of this Chapter.)

———————◇———————

INITIATIVES FOR 1989

1) Raise pay for key personnel. Because of problems of retaining pilots, engineers, and other highly trained Air Force personnel, the Secretary of Defense should request a pay raise to bring Air Force pay scales closer to civilian pay scales for specialized personnel. He should require the Deputy Secretary for Manpower rapidly to conclude ongoing studies of other means of increasing pilot and engineer retention rates.

2) Fully fund readiness programs. U.S. pilot training programs give U.S. military pilots a critical edge over their Soviet counterparts. Reductions in flying time below the current 18 hours per month would cut into this advantage. The Secretary of Defense's budget request should include full funding for the peacetime flying hour and peacetime operating stock programs. The Secretary of Defense should seek to stockpile spare parts sufficient to permit the Air Force to operate for extended periods during wartime.

3) Increase production of F-15Es to an efficient rate. The F-15E *Eagle*, with advanced electronics and weapons systems, can attack such ground targets as enemy airfields, while remaining the world's best air-to-air combat plane. To bring F-15Es into the tactical air fleet more quickly, and to reduce total program costs, the Secretary of Defense should seek funding to produce 48 F-15Es annually, instead of the current level of 42 and planned level of 36 for fiscal 1989. F-16 *Fighting Falcon* procurement rates should be maintained at current levels of 180 annually.

4) Explore B–1B conventional strike options. The B-1B bomber, designed primarily for a strategic nuclear attack mission, has the range and armament capacity to penetrate heavily defended airspace. These qualities give the B-1B a potential conventional long-range strike role. In view of the mounting uncertainty of U.S. access to bases abroad, an ability to strike worldwide from bases in the U.S. is essential to fulfilling America's global responsibilities. During some Middle East crises, for example, the U.S. has been barred from using some of its West European airbases or even flying through some West European allies' airspace. The Secretary of the Air Force should determine the steps necessary to use the B-1B in a long-range conventional strike role, and the Secretary of Defense should then request the necessary funding.

5) Assess additional tanker requirements. American long-range bombers and transports cannot fulfill their missions without midair refueling from tanker aircraft such as the KC-135 and KC-10A *Extender*. A round-trip bombing run into Soviet territory is a flight of over 12,000 miles; the unrefueled range of a B-1B bomber is about 7,500 miles. The Secretary of the Air Force should investigate whether new tanker assets may be required to support U.S. bomber fleets. The study should focus on how many tankers would be required to keep U.S. strategic forces in the air on alert during a crisis.

The Marine Corps*

The Marine Corps is America's principal expeditionary force. It can fight its way ashore and sustain itself in hostile territory. Marine Corps ground, air, and logistics forces operate in concert with ships at sea to seize and defend advanced bases and territory in a naval campaign. Although its mission superficially resembles that of the classic Pacific naval battles of World War II, the Marines today are much more versatile, using high technology and superior maneuverability to achieve tactical advantage in a wide variety of missions.

In coordination with other naval forces, the Marine Corps allows the President to take quick and decisive action. This ability to project power abroad rapidly is particularly important in low intensity conflict (see Low Intensity Conflict section of this chapter), which poses an increasing threat to United States global interests. The Marines also would play an important role in carrying out the Navy's maritime strategy in a major conflict, securing forward bases in Norway, for example, where they have prepositioned equipment, and elsewhere as required.

◇

THE REAGAN ADMINISTRATION RECORD

When the Reagan Administration took office, the Marine Corps lacked a clearly focused mission, adequate air and sea transportation to potential theaters of combat, and sufficient modern equipment to fight effectively. The Reagan Administration has given high priority to maritime forces in general, and obtained funds to modernize the Marine Corps. This has included: 1) obtaining amphibious ships, such as the LHD and LSD–41 transports to move troops and equipment to areas of conflict and serve as carriers for helicopters and Vertical/Short Takeoff and Landing (VSTOL) aircraft; 2) procuring a new type of assault craft, the Landing Craft-Air Cushion (LCAC), a fast, long-

---

*Commenting and contributing generously to this report were *Mandate III* Task Force Members Jack Grace, Jeffrey Record, Alan Sabrosky, and Heritage Policy Analyst Jay P. Kosminsky. They do not necessarily endorse all of its views and recommendations.
Task Force Deputy Chairman: Mackubin T. Owens, Jr.

range hovercraft used to transport Marines from ship to shore; 3) buying the Light Armored Vehicle (LAV), a wheeled troop transport armed with an anti-tank weapon to provide mobility and firepower to forces ashore; 4) developing the V-22 *Osprey*, a transport and gunship able to take off like a helicopter and then tilt its rotors forward to fly with the speed and range of an airplane, and; 5) deploying the Maritime Prepositioning Force (MPF), consisting of 13 ships organized in three squadrons (one each in the Atlantic, Pacific, and Indian Oceans). Each squadron is a "floating base," carrying 30 days of supplies and equipment for three Marine Expeditionary Brigades (about 15,000 Marines), which can be moved rapidly to link up with airlifted Marines. Finally, the morale and fighting ability of the Marines have been increased by significant improvements in training and readiness.

---◇---

THE NEXT FOUR YEARS

Completing Key Modernization Programs

The Marine Corps is in the midst of several key modernization programs, including the LHD-1 transport, Landing Craft–Air Cushion (LCAC), Light Armored Vehicle (LAV), and V-22 *Osprey*. All must be fielded in sufficient quantities to provide the Marines with the range, speed, and mobility to conduct successful amphibious and battlefield operations. The Secretary of Defense should request the funding necessary to complete these programs.

Clarifying Marine Doctrine and Materiel Requirements

While the Marines have developed innovative new weapons to meet the requirements of modern combat, their introduction raises many doctrinal issues that have yet to be addressed. Examples: Should the Marines consider operating farther inland, given the capabilities of the V–22 and LAV, or should they retain their traditional mission of establishing themselves within about 50 miles of a coast and relying on the army to fight farther inland? What is the role of naval gunfire in an attack launched "over the horizon," beyond the range of naval guns? What will be the role of helicopters once the V–22 becomes available? The Commandant of the Marine Corps should undertake a study to clarify Marine doctrine and tactics in light of new technology, and to make precise recommendations on the mix of forces needed to meet these new requirements.

Augmenting the Maritime Prepositioning Force

Maritime Prepositioning Force (MPF) "floating bases" currently are deployed to provide airlifted Marines with supplies and equipment in areas where they are most likely to be needed. An additional squadron should be activated by 1992 to reinforce existing capabilities in the Atlantic/Mediterranean area, and to enable the Marines to respond better to multiple threats. The Secretary of Defense should request funding for an additional Maritime Prepositioning Squadron.

Increasing Forward Deployments

The Marine Corps presently maintains two Marine Expeditionary Units (reinforced battalions of about 1,900 Marines) in the Mediterranean and the Western Pacific; other Units occasionally are deployed elsewhere for limited periods. Given the competing demands for airlift and sealift likely during a crisis, the Chief of Naval Operations and Marine Corps Commandant should develop plans to deploy at least one additional Marine Expeditionary Unit on station in the Indian Ocean by 1992, as new Marine sealift ("amphibious lift") capabilities become available. The Secretary of Defense should request the funding necessary to deploy this additional Marine Expeditionary Unit.

Expanding Amphibious Lift Capability

The Marine Corps currently has the sealift capability to transport somewhat more than one Marine Expeditionary Force (MEF), about 50,000 Marines and associated equipment. To execute the naval missions associated with a forward maritime strategy, the Marines should have the capability to move at least one Marine Expeditionary Force plus an entire Marine Expeditionary Brigade (MEB) of 15,000 Marines and associated equipment. This will require procurement of eight-to-ten Marine sealift and support ships, such as the LSD-41, LHD-1, and LST, in addition to those currently planned. The Secretary of the Navy and Marine Corps Commandant should determine the precise shipping requirements for transporting one MEF and one MEB, and the Secretary of Defense should request the funding necessary to procure additional ships.

INITIATIVES FOR 1989

1) Establish a joint Army/Marine acquisition program for the V-22 *Osprey* **aircraft.** The Marine Corps has been a pioneer in the development and employment of Vertical/Short Take-off and Landing (VSTOL) aircraft, from the helicopter in the 1950s to the V-22 *Osprey*. As the smallest military service, however, the Marine Corps depends on the aircraft procurement policies of other services and cannot by itself sustain such expensive new technology programs such as the *Osprey*. The Secretary of Defense should require the Army to reverse its decision to withdraw from significant participation in the VSTOL program for fiscal 1989, and then should establish a joint Marine Corps/ Army acquisition program for the V-22 *Osprey*.

2) Cancel heavy weapons and buy light weapons. The Marine Corps has acquired, or is acquiring, "heavy" weapons such as the M1A1 *Abrams* tank and M198 towed 155mm howitzer. Both are capable weapon systems, but better suited to the Army, which has heavy divisions to face a major adversary in a sustained campaign. The Marine Corps' role primarily is to meet lesser contingencies on short notice. This requires light, rapidly transportable forces. The Secretary of Defense should reverse the *Abrams* and MI98 procurement decisions and require the Marine Corps Commandant to review such alternatives as substituting the British-designed M119 towed 105mm howitzer for the M198 and procuring new light tracked vehicle, such as the Belgian *Cobra,* instead of the M1A1.

3) Begin Phasing Out "Fixed Wing" Aircraft. Vertical/short take-off and landing (VSTOL) aircraft, such as the currently deployed AV-8 *Harrier* light attack jet and the V-22 *Osprey,* will be the mainstay of Marine aviation in the 1990s. The *Osprey* acquisition program will be one of the most expensive ever undertaken by the Marines (roughly $12-to-$15 billion for about 550 aircraft). Given expected budgetary constraints, the Secretary of Defense should require the Marine Corps Commandant to develop plans for phasing out "fixed wing" aviation, such as the F/A 18, in favor of VSTOL aircraft.

The U.S. and the North Atlantic Treaty Organization (NATO)*

The North Atlantic Treaty, signed by the United States, Canada, and most of the free nations of Western Europe on April 4, 1949, gave birth to an alliance dedicated to defending the common beliefs and interests of its member nations. The administrative body charged by alliance members with achieving the goals of the Treaty is the North Atlantic Treaty Organization, or NATO, which is governed by the North Atlantic Council. U.S. leaders believed in 1949, as they still do, that the U.S. could not afford to repeat the mistake, made in the first half of this century, of disengaging from Europe and thus encouraging aggression. The U.S. could not and cannot allow the economic wealth and the territory of Western Europe to become dominated by the USSR. The strength of the NATO Alliance always has rested on its unity in the face of the Soviet threat. There are, however, a number of recent developments that endanger this NATO unity. Recent arms control treaties and negotiations, differing U.S. and West European perceptions of the Soviet threat, defense budget constraints, Soviet policies aimed at dividing the U.S. and Western Europe, and renewed calls by members of Congress for U.S. troop withdrawals from Europe have undermined consensus in the Western Alliance.

———————◇———————

THE REAGAN ADMINISTRATION RECORD

At the start of 1981, the NATO Alliance was on the verge of crisis. Hundreds of thousands of demonstrators were filling the streets of Western Europe protesting the proposed introduction into Europe of U.S. intermediate-range nuclear forces (INF). NATO was in bad military shape as well. Ammunition stockpiles in Europe were so low that

---

*Commenting and contributing generously to this report were *Mandate III* Task Force Members Ian Butterfield, Donald Cotter, David B. Rivkin, Jr., Jed Snyder, Henry Sokolski, and Paolo Stoppa-Liebl. They do not necessarily endorse all of its views and recommendations.

Task Force Deputy Chairman: Heritage Defense Policy Studies Deputy Director Kim R. Holmes.

experts feared NATO forces would run out of ammunition in a matter of days if the Warsaw Pact attacked. Other military problems included insufficient airlift capability to rush U.S. troops to Europe in time of war, and the growing capability of Soviet armed forces to launch a *blitzkrieg* attack on Western Europe.

The Reagan Administration has scored a number of successes in strengthening the NATO Alliance. It has been mainly responsible for deploying *Pershing II* and cruise missiles in Europe. It also has increased allied cooperation by promoting such projects as the Conventional Defense Improvements (CDI) program, a nine-point plan adopted by NATO in 1987 to eliminate critical deficiencies in force posture and military capabilities. The Reagan Administration and NATO also have improved the Alliance's capability to reinforce and sustain Europe rapidly in time of war by deploying more long-range cargo planes, prepositioning more military equipment in Europe for use by U.S. soldiers in time of war, and enlarging U.S. ammunition stockpiles. Important as well has been the Administration's key role in improving NATO's anti-aircraft defenses.

Yet many of NATO's problems remain. The Administration and NATO have not eliminated the long-standing vulnerability of NATO air bases, command and control sites, nuclear storage sites, and other key military targets to Warsaw Pact fighter aircraft and conventionally armed ballistic missiles. The Administration also has been unable to reduce substantially Warsaw Pact superiority in tanks and artillery firepower. To make matters worse, NATO has no adequate anti-tank barrier defenses along the inter-German border and too few long-range aircraft and missiles for striking behind enemy lines. As such, NATO remains vulnerable to Warsaw Pact armored assaults along the central front in the Fulda Gap and north German plain.

———————————◇———————————

THE NEXT FOUR YEARS

The goal of U.S. NATO policy must be to maintain the strength, cohesion, and vitality of the Alliance in the face of a growing Warsaw Pact military threat. To do this, the U.S. must remain NATO's leading member to balance the superior power of the Soviet Union. Although NATO has served the interests of the U.S. well, and the U.S. commitment to the defense of Western Europe should be permanent, some changes in the Alliance may be necessary. The new Administration must negotiate deftly with NATO members to update the division of responsibilities in the Alliance.

Sharing NATO Responsibilities

The U.S. is responsible for a disproportionate share of the conventional defense burden in Europe. The U.S. provides around 42 percent of NATO's entire, fully reinforced combat capability on the central front in West Germany. It supplies around 39 percent of NATO's firepower. France, by comparison, provides only 6 percent, and West Germany, 12 percent. The U.S. now spends around half of its defense budget on Europe. Most of this money goes for conventional forces. This U.S. investment in the conventional defense of Europe is far too great for a nation that also carries the obligation of defending Western interests worldwide. The U.S. share of the Western defense burden clearly is too large. To lighten this burden, the new President should call for a special NATO summit to discuss new ways to share responsibility for the common defense.

The summit should be held in Europe. There, the President should deliver a major address before the North Atlantic Assembly, NATO's parliamentary body, declaring that the stability of the Alliance and the permanence of the U.S. security commitment to Western Europe require changes in the Alliance's division of labor. The President should state that, because of the need to concentrate scarce U.S. defense resources on defending Western interests outside Europe, the U.S. cannot afford to increase investment in American ground forces based in Europe. NATO conventional forces need to be strengthened, and this must be the responsibility of the European allies themselves, including the French. They should assume a greater share of NATO's responsibility for providing combat reinforcements and firepower. Meanwhile, the U.S. should continue to retain responsibility for improving nuclear deterrence, and such high-technology missions as deep strike air operations and command, control, communications, and intelligence. To calm European fears about a U.S. troop withdrawal, the new President should pledge not to withdraw large numbers of U.S. troops in the near term, seeing such reductions only in the context of an arms agreement with the Warsaw Pact.

At the NATO summit the President should also request that the European allies pay for at least half of the total cost of the U.S. Air Force's C-17 long-range cargo plane. This is a $38 billion program dedicated extensively (albeit not exclusively) to the mission of rushing U.S. troops to Europe in time of crisis. Since much of the C-17 program redounds to the benefit of the European allies, they should be required to pay for at least part of it. If the Europeans refuse, the

President should order the Secretary of Defense to launch a study of the pros and cons of deactivating (putting into the reserves) two active Army divisions stationed in the U.S. but committed to reinforcing Europe during wartime. Without European funding of part of the C-17 program, budgetary constraints may cause the U.S. to fall short of meeting the goal of building over 100 C-17 aircraft. Without those C-17s, the U.S. may not have the airlift capacity to move those two divisions quickly to Europe in time of war.

Using Competitive Strategies
to Guide Buildup of NATO's Weapons

Strategy is defined as a plan for developing and utilizing national resources for the purpose of implementing foreign and defense policy. A good strategy is one that uses national resources wisely and efficiently. A new concept developed by the Reagan Administration, called "competitive strategies," promises to provide the U.S. and its NATO allies with such a stragegy for developing military forces. The doctrine of competitive strategies holds that the development and deployment of forces and weapons should conform to criteria that capitalize on the relative advantages and strengths of the U.S. and NATO while exploiting the disadvantages and weaknesses of the Soviet bloc. For example, one of the weaknesses in Moscow's plans for a quick invasion of Western Europe is the vulnerability of its rear area forces to NATO attacks. One of NATO's advantages is advanced technology that can support highly accurate missiles supported by very effective command and control systems that could be used to disrupt Soviet and other Warsaw Pact rear area forces before they get to the front.

To take advantage of this Soviet weakness, the doctrine of competitive stragegies would suggest that the U.S. and its NATO allies develop and deploy very accurate and long-range missiles armed with conventional warheads to strike at and disrupt the movements of rear area Warsaw Pact forces. This idea of "deep strikes" is fully compatible with the already established U.S. military operational doctrine of Airland Battle and the NATO Follow-on Forces Attack (FOFA) plan for attacking the enemy in its rear before it can be engaged directly in battle. To ensure that U.S. weapons adequately support the Airland Battle doctrine and the FOFA plan, and meet the criterion of competitive strategies doctrine as well, the Secretary of Defense should accord high priority to those weapons and systems that exploit U.S. advantages in advanced technology. For example, the Secretary should request full funding for the rapid deployment of the Multiple Launch

Rocket System (MLRS), a highly mobile automatic rocket system, whose massive firepower can strike enemy artillery, air defense sites, and armored personnel carriers beyond cannon range. High priority also should be accorded to developing such short-range systems as the Army Tactical Missile (ATACMs) and the *Tacit Rainbow* missile to destroy short-range ballistic missiles and air defense radars deep in enemy territory. To ensure that military commanders can effectively operate these deep strike weapons in combat, the Secretary should request full funding for the Joint Surveillance and Target Attack Radar System (JSTARS), an airborne detection system being developed by the Army and the Air Force to monitor and assist U.S. forces in attacking moving targets well before they reach the main battlefield. To supplement these weapons, the Pentagon should develop conventionally armed air-launched cruise missiles (ALCM) and sea-launched cruise missiles (SLCM) with a range of at least 1,000 miles for deep strike missions against Warsaw Pact bridges, command and control posts, and railroad depots. The Army tactical missile, *Tacit Rainbow,* and long-range ALCMs and SLCMs could, in conjunction with fighter aircraft, strike at Warsaw Pact air bases before they deploy their planes against NATO forces in Western Europe.

Other U.S. systems that could be used for deep strike missions in Europe, and thus deserve full funding from Congress, include advanced missile and rocket munitions such as anti-tank and airfield destroying mines placed on the tips of MLRS rockets, terminal-guided "smart" air-to-surface missiles such as the Air Force's *Maverick* (AGM-65D/G) and AMRAAM (AIM-120A) missiles for pinpoint attacks against enemy bunkers and other ground targets, remotely piloted "drones" for conducting aerial reconnaissance behind enemy lines, and the radar-evading stealth fighter currently being developed by the U.S. Air Force for intercepting Warsaw Pact fighter planes. To the extent possible, the Secretary of Defense should encourage joint development of advanced technology weapons with the European allies according to the criteria established by the competitive strategies doctrine.

Building a Flexible Covering Force

NATO is vulnerable to a surprise attack by the Warsaw Pact with armored and other mobile forces. There are too many troops held in reserve in Belgium and the Netherlands and not enough frontline troops deployed across likely invasion routes in West Germany, particularly the northern plain and the Fulda Gap area. Increasing the vulnerability to a surprise attack are NATO's lack of adequate operational reserves for sustaining combat in a war's early days and incompatible communications and other equipment of the various national military forces that will have to fight side by side.

To prepare NATO for a Warsaw Pact surprise attack, the new President should propose at the special NATO summit that the Alliance create a large Flexible Covering Force (FCF) to defend weak spots at the front during the early hours or days of an attack. Up to 50 percent of all NATO top priority active brigades should be reorganized into the FCF. In time of war they should come under the direct command of the Supreme Allied Commander Europe (SACEUR). The overall end strength of NATO forces need not change. The FCF would be highly mobile for making quick counterattacks and fully ready for combat at all times in terms of manning, equipment, and stockpiles.

Modernizing Short-Range Nuclear Weapons Stockpiles

The Atlantic Alliance needs to modernize its short-range nuclear forces-ballistic missiles and nuclear artillery shells with ranges less than 300 miles—to strengthen nuclear deterrence and, in time of war, to force Warsaw Pact forces to disperse their formations to avoid destruction by NATO nuclear attacks. (The U.S.-Soviet INF Treaty permits missiles with ranges up to about 300 miles.) At the special NATO summit, the President should seek NATO's agreement to develop a replacement for the aging *Lance* missile first deployed in 1972. This new missile should be capable of carrying conventional and nuclear warheads. The missile should have greater range, reliability, and safety than the *Lance* with its 80–mile range. The President should ask Congress for increased funding to accelerate modernization of the U.S. nuclear artillery arsenal to enhance U.S. capabilities to stop massive Soviet armored attacks against Western Europe.

Improving NATO's Defenses against Surprise Attacks

NATO's ability to block a Warsaw Pact attack has been eroded by the growing capability of Soviet armor and artillery forces to launch a surprise attack. To cope with this, the Secretary of Defense should propose that NATO:

◆ *Erect anti-armor defenses along the inter-German border.* To stop or slow Soviet armored offensives, NATO should build relatively inexpensive anti-armor barriers along the inter-German border. A pipeline buried in critical sectors of the central and northern NATO fronts, for

example, could be filled with liquid high explosives upon warning of
an impending Warsaw Pact attack. If detonated, these pipelines would
create impassable ditches that would halt advancing columns of armored vehicles. Other tank barriers would be ditches, mines, and steep
slopes planted with trees.

◆ *Enhance active air defenses.* NATO air bases are vulnerable to
attacks by Warsaw Pact fighter aircraft and short-range ballistic missiles armed with conventional, nuclear, and chemical warheads. To
protect NATO air bases, command and control sites, and other military
installations from preemptive missile attacks, the Secretary of Defense
should propose that NATO's Defense Planning Committee call for the
near-term deployment of an anti-tactical missile (ATM) system to
counter Soviet short-range ballistic missiles. An ATM should be seen
as part of an overall effort to enhance NATO's air defenses.

Improving the Sustainability of U.S. Forces in Europe

Warsaw Pact central front forces have enough ammunition, fuel, and
supplies to support military operations for 60 to 90 days. By contrast,
NATO is far short of its objective of having enough ammunition on
hand to sustain combat for at least 30 days. The Secretary of Defense
should propose that NATO's Defense Planning Committee call for
meeting the 30–day munitions objective by 1994, which will require
additional expenditures by both the U.S. and the European allied
nations. The U.S. already has met this objective for some systems, but
shortfalls still remain, particularly in "smart" or self-guided munitions. Five years is sufficient time to manufacture and deploy munitions. To help meet this objective, the Department of Defense should
request additional funding for U.S. Army smart munitions.

Replenishing NATO Chemical Warfare Resources

The chemical warfare capability of NATO's member nations is
woefully inadequate. The Soviet Union, meanwhile, boasts the world's
most extensive chemical warfare capability, including 60,000 chemical
troops and special brigades to defend Soviet troops from chemical
warfare agents. Moscow could use chemical weapons to shut down
NATO airfields, demoralize NATO troops, and slow efforts to mobilize
NATO reserves and supplies for combat.

To meet this Soviet chemical warfare threat, NATO nations should
accelerate their purchases of improved protection, detection, and
decontamination equipment. The U.S. should continue to modernize

its obsolete chemical arsenal with the new 155 mm shell. Chemical weapons on long-range air-launched cruise missiles could shut down Soviet air operations by attacking airfields deep in Eastern European territory. The Secretary of Defense should urge that at least one European ally deploy the new 155 mm binary chemical shell on its own soil in peacetime. Modernized chemical weapons are needed to deter Soviet use of chemical weapons and to force the Soviets and their Warsaw Pact allies to undertake the costly and cumbersome preparations for chemical warfare that NATO countries now must undergo.

Revitalizing the Conventional Defense Improvements (CDI) Program

In 1987 NATO ministers launched the CDI program to correct nine critical deficiencies in the Alliance's conventional forces. Since then, CDI has stalled. The program has no action plan, milestones, or priorities. To correct this, the new President should make revitalizing the CDI a major priority of U.S. NATO policy. He should urge the Defense Planning Committee to draw up an action plan for correcting the deficiencies identified in the CDI program within five years. The Secretary of Defense should consolidate all U.S. NATO defense programs under a single program manager to ensure that they are adequately represented in the Pentagon budgeting process.

Protecting Nuclear Storage Sites from Soviet Special Forces

Soviet military doctrine calls for extensive use of special forces, known as *spetznaz*, to conduct sabotage and other operations behind NATO lines in the early stages of a war in Europe. NATO air bases and U.S. nuclear storage sites would be the primary targets of these forces. Defense experts believe that NATO nuclear storage sites are particularly vulnerable to Soviet sneak attacks with undercover Soviet *spetznaz* agents already placed in the West. West German politics have dictated that U.S. nuclear weapons be kept at a small number of sites (about 50). During wartime, the weapons in theory would be dispersed, but dispersal would be a politically difficult decision and *spetznaz* could strike first. The Secretary of Defense should ask the Army to review security procedures for U.S. air base and nuclear storage sites against the Soviet special forces threat. The Army should conduct regular spot inspections of site security and devise special teams to simulate *spetznaz* attacks. These simulated attacks would test the effectiveness of the security systems and sharpen the skills of the troops protecting the sites.

---◇---

INITIATIVES FOR 1989

1) Call a NATO summit to discuss burden-sharing, allied cooperation, and force improvements. This should be the new President's first step in updating U.S. policy toward NATO. The agenda of this NATO summit should include such items as new divisions of labor, nuclear modernization, arms control, operations outside of Europe, and revitalizing the Conventional Defense Improvements program.

2) Launch a study of NATO's crisis management system and NATO headquarters exercises. To ensure that NATO's forces are mobilized quickly, effectively, and efficiently upon receiving warning of a Warsaw Pact attack, the new President should propose at the special NATO summit that a one-year assessment of NATO's crisis management and contingency planning systems be conducted. NATO headquarters exercises should be examined, for example, to ensure that Alliance forces could respond quickly and effectively to contingencies other than a massive attack along the central front in Germany. The study should test existing planning assumptions and procedures for managing crises and mobilizing.

3) Fund rocket launchers and long-range missiles. To ensure that NATO can defend against massive Warsaw Pact attacks, the Secretary of Defense should press for rocket launchers and long-range missile systems. The Secretary of Defense should request full funding from Congress for the Multiple Launch Rocket System (MLRS) program to strike at targets beyond cannon range. Special terminally guided munitions also should be developed and deployed on the MLRS. The Secretary should request full funding for the Army Tactical Missile (ATACM) and the *Tacit Rainbow* missile for destroying enemy air defense sites and Soviet short-range ballistic missiles deep in enemy territory and for the Joint Surveillance and Target Attack Radar System (JSTARS) for monitoring and assisting U.S. forces in attacking moving targets behind enemy lines. The Secretary of Defense should ask the Joint Chiefs of Staff to prepare a formal military requirement, certifying the need for new conventionally armed air- and sea-launched cruise missiles with a range of at least 1,000 miles.

Low Intensity Conflict*

Since the end of World War II, United States armed forces have been organized, trained, and equipped primarily to prepare for a major conflict with the Soviet Union. In part because the U.S. has been ill-prepared politically and militarily to cope with limited threats, it has faced an increasing number of challenges below the threshold of major war, what is now called "low intensity conflict" (LIC). Low intensity conflict takes disparate forms: terrorism, insurgency, or direct military challenges in the Third World. It can be brief or extend for long periods of time. Low intensity conflict provides adversaries with relatively low-cost opportunities for undermining the international stability upon which the security and prosperity of America and its allies ultimately rest.

Actions in which the U.S. may have to engage in response to low-intensity threats include: military and other assistance to friendly regimes facing insurgency, civil war, or the threat of coup d'etat; support for national liberation movements, like the Afghan *mujahideen*, fighting Soviet occupation or Soviet-backed Marxist/Leninist regimes; measured, direct use of American military forces, as in the 1983 Grenada operation; and counterterrorist actions.

—————◇—————

THE REAGAN ADMINISTRATION RECORD

The Reagan Administration took office in a global political and military situation that vividly illustrated the dangers of an ineffectual LIC policy: a hostile government in Tehran holding 52 American hostages; a Marxist-Leninist regime in Nicaragua consolidating its power and exporting revolution to El Salvador; Soviet-backed Vietnamese forces occupying Cambodia; and Soviet troops rampaging through Afghanistan. The Administration responded to this with the Reagan Doctrine, which commits the U.S. to providing military and

*Commenting and contributing generously to this report were *Mandate III* Task Force Members Kim Holmes, Peter Huessy, Noel Koch, Lynn Rylander, George Talbot, and Hugh Tovar. They do not necessarily endorse all of its views and recommendations.

Task Force Deputy Chairman: Heritage Policy Analyst Jay P. Kosminsky.

other support for anticommunist national liberation and resistance movements. This has created a conceptual rationale for dealing with that form of LIC. (See Liberation Doctrine section of Chapter 24.)

The Administration has upgraded the effectiveness of Special Operations Forces which, among other missions, can be used to combat low intensity threats and to supply and train foreign military forces. It has supported such Special Operations Forces as the Army's Rangers and the Navy's Sea-Air-Land forces (SEALs). Budgets for these forces have increased from $440 million in 1981 to over $2.7 billion in 1988. Special operations improvements have included:

◆ *Increasing force structure.* Two active duty Special Forces groups, with 1,300 men each, have been added to three existing groups. The Administration has created a fourth Psychological Operations battalion of 150 highly trained experts. These battalions engage primarily in activities designed to demoralize an adversary, such as offering amnesty or rewards for guerrillas who surrender.

◆ *Improving capability to transport Special Operations Forces.* The Administration has funded 32 additional MH–53 *Pave Low* helicopters (a modified HH–53 *Super Jolly Green Giant*), which will bring the fleet to 41, once all have been acquired. The *Pave Low* is specially equipped with advanced navigation and radar systems for night and adverse weather operations, including troop transport and search and rescue.

◆ *Improving Special Operations Forces fighting ability.* Individual units are larger, receive more extensive and realistic training, and generally have adequate spare parts for specialized equipment.

The Administration successfully has fostered a greater degree of international cooperation in countering terrorism worldwide. On occasion, the Administration has gone to the source in attacking terrorism, as in the 1986 raid on Libya. (See Terrorism section of Chapter 24.)

The Administration, however, has failed to articulate a counterinsurgency strategy or improve significantly the government's organization for counterinsurgency and other LIC operations. The Administration developed an initially effective model for counterinsurgency strategy in its handling of El Salvador, where in 1981 it helped save a government on the brink of defeat by a communist insurgency and begin a difficult transition to democracy. That effort began to fall apart, however, in 1984 when communist guerrillas switched tactics.

Until 1986, efforts to coordinate LIC activities throughout the government were ad hoc. In 1986, Congress created a new National Security Council post, Deputy Assistant to the President for National Security Affairs for LIC, and a Cabinet-level Advisory Board for LIC.

This would have established a single channel for strategy and policy development and the integration of LIC efforts by such departments and agencies as the Pentagon, State, CIA, Agency for International Development, and U.S. Information Agency. The LIC Board, however, never was convened. Interagency groups were established to coordinate LIC activities, but they have met only infrequently at a high level. Some agencies, most notably the CIA, have refused to participate at all in the interagency process.

The Reagan Administration also has not done enough to press the armed services to stop dragging their feet on LIC. The White House took until July 1988 to fill the position of Assistant Secretary of Defense for Special Operations and Low Intensity Conflict, created by Congress in 1986. Further, the Pentagon largely ignored the Joint Special Operations Agency (JSOA), established by Congress in 1984 as a Special Operations advocate in the Office of the Joint Chiefs of Staff and at times has neglected JSOA's successor, the U.S. Special Operations Command (USSOCOM). The command was established by Congress in 1986 as a full-fledged unified command comprising 40,000 Army, Navy, and Air Force troops under a four-star Commander-in-Chief, known as CINCUSSOCOM.

In practice, CINCUSSOCOM has been denied authority. The Air Force, for example, was permitted by the Secretary of Defense to slow spending for procurement of the MC–130 *Combat Talon*, a specially equipped aircraft used for clandestine troop transport to and from distant operations. This overruled CINCUSSOCOM, who had identified *Combat Talon* as a priority. As a result, in mid–1988 the U.S had no more *Combat Talon*s in its inventory than at the time of the catastrophic 1980 "Desert One" mission to rescue American hostages in Iran.

Further, while the Administration must be credited for its willingness to commit American forces selectively in support of U.S. interests, political and operational mistakes unnecessarily have lost American lives and materiel. The operational deficiencies of the Grenada action, the downing of Navy attack planes in 1983 by Syrian missiles, the loss of U.S. ships to Iranian mines in the Persian Gulf, and the death of 241 Marines in a single terrorist attack in Beirut in 1983, were caused less by the lack of available superior firepower or quality soldiers than by failures of senior political and military decision-making.

THE NEXT FOUR YEARS

Low intensity conflict is fought in the shadows between peace and war, where politics in its traditional form gives way to armed combat. Such conflicts take diverse forms, from terrorism to insurgency warfare to small-scale fighting between national military forces. To cope with these varied contingencies, the U.S. requires a range of capabilities, effective strategies, and intragovernment coordination. Where U.S. forces are not directly involved in low intensity combat, the U.S. should be capable of helping friendly governments stay in power, or conversely, of helping resistance groups overthrow illegitimate regimes. This can involve training troops, delivering appropriate weaponry, or providing medical, nutritional, and other aid. For those instances in which the U.S. commits troops directly to low intensity conflict, the U.S. requires highly trained and well-equipped forces able to move on short notice.

Constructing and Coordinating a
Low Intensity Conflict Strategy

In large measure, the U.S. has the resources to deal effectively with low intensity conflict. These, however, are spread among too many agencies and the four armed services. There is no doctrine or government machinery to apply them as part of a coordinated policy. The Pentagon's bureaucratic and interservice rivalries that prevent coordination are deeply entrenched.

The congressionally mandated Board for LIC should be convened by the President under the chairmanship of the Assistant to the President for National Security Affairs and should meet regularly. The Board should be a Cabinet-level forum of the heads of departments and agencies involved in LIC. These include the Pentagon, State, CIA, U.S. Agency for International Development, and U.S. Information Agency.

The Board for LIC should assign to the Assistant to the President for LIC the task of creating a national LIC strategy. This strategy should recognize the need to coordinate military programs with appropriate political, economic, and social programs generally known as "civic action." The interdepartmental coordination necessary to carry out the strategy should be conducted by interdepartmental groups under the chairmanship of the Special Assistant for LIC. Strong bureaucratic backing from the Cabinet-level Board for LIC will be required to ensure the effectiveness of these interdepartmental groups.

Ensuring Armed Services Support
for Special Operations Forces

Given the low priority traditionally accorded Special Operations Forces by the armed services and the importance of Special Operations Forces to many LIC operations, the Secretary of Defense and Service secretaries must ensure that the Service chiefs give adequate support to Special Operations Forces. The Secretary of Defense should require regular reports on LIC priorities from the Assistant Secretary of Defense for Special Operations and Low Intensity Conflict and from the Commander in Chief of the Special Operations Command (CIN-CUSSOCOM). After review, the Secretary of Defense should direct the Service chiefs to incorporate these priorities in their budget requests.

Allocating Budgetary Support for
Special Operations Forces

The Secretary of Defense should request funds to allow Special Operations Forces to complete procurement and readiness programs begun under the Reagan Administration. With less than 1 percent of the Defense budget allocated to Special Operations Forces, this should add no serious new strains to available Defense Department resources.

Using Adequate Firepower in LIC

Counterinsurgency warfare and anti-Marxist wars of national liberation are fought primarily by foreign troops with U.S. support. Sometimes, however, U.S. forces can be directly engaged in LIC against well-armed adversaries. Too often, policymakers have underestimated the threat in LIC situations to American lives. For example, a failure to employ advanced air-to-ground missiles or up-to-date tactics contributed to the loss of American A–7 *Corsair* attack planes to Syrian missiles over Lebanon in 1983.

The Secretary of Defense should require the Assistant Secretary of Defense for Special Operations and Low Intensity conflict to draw up guidelines to: employ sufficient firepower in LIC situations; take better advantage of high technology weaponry when feasible; and ensure that

U.S. forces always are operating at high enough readiness and under sufficiently flexible rules of engagement to protect themselves and defeat an adversary with minimum loss of American life.

———————————◇———————————

INITIATIVES FOR 1989

1) Quickly fill the post of Deputy Assistant to the President for LIC. In 1986, Congress created the position of Deputy Assistant to the President for LIC within the National Security Council. The President should fill the position quickly and make the individual the President's chief spokesman for LIC issues and an advocate of programs important to LIC throughout the government. The deputy assistant should have direct access to the President and enjoy highly visible presidential support. The President also should quickly fill the post of Assistant Secretary of Defense for Special Operations and Low-Intensity Conflict to serve as an advocate for LIC within the Pentagon.

2) Define Special Operations Command (USSOCOM) missions. As a step toward eliminating confusion and overlap with other military commands and agencies, the President should issue a National Security Decision Directive explicitly assigning to the Commander-in-Chief of Special Operations Command the responsibility of providing support to resistance movements, except where deemed inappropriate by the President due to foreign policy or national security considerations.

3) Propose changes in the Foreign Assistance Act of 1968. Provisions of the Foreign Assistance Act of 1968 impede supply to friendly governments of sufficient and appropriate resources. A presidential message to Congress should recommend amending the Act. One amendment should permit the U.S. to develop and produce military hardware to be provided as security assistance to friends and allies. Another amendment should relax restrictions that prevent non-American equipment from being provided by the U.S. as foreign assistance. In a number of cases, foreign products are cheaper and easier to maintain than American products.

4) Increase security assistance. Currently, 86 percent of U.S. foreign aid goes to Egypt, Greece, Israel, Pakistan, and Turkey. While Congress should continue to ensure that sufficient aid is directed to such close U.S. allies as Israel, increased funds should be available for countries facing insurgency such as El Salvador and the Philippines. The President should request increased security assistance for these countries.

5) Give priority to Special Operations procurement programs. Special Operations proponents in the Pentagon consistently have sought accelerated funding for the MC–130 *Combat Talon* aircraft. This is a modified Lockheed C–130 cargo plane, equipped with advanced radar, electronic jamming, and navigational systems that enable it to airlift Special Forces clandestinely into and out of distant operations and perform such missions as search and rescue. The *Combat Talon* is essential to improving overall Special Operations Command performance. As part of his effort to enforce Special Operations priorities, the Secretary of Defense should request multiyear procurement of *Combat Talon*s to reach a total force of 38, the minimum military requirement established by CINCUSSOCOM, by the end of fiscal 1991. The U.S. currently has 13 *Combat Talon*s. Other important procurement programs include the Army's MH–47E Special Operations modified helicopter and the CV–22 *Osprey*, a vertical take-off and landing (VTOL) aircraft currently nearing production. The Secretary of Defense should request multiyear procurement of 17 Army MH–47Es by the end of fiscal 1991 and 55 Air Force CV–22 *Osprey*s to meet Special Operations mission requirements.

6) Increase language and area training. Security assistance programs, by which the U.S. provides training and other military support to friendly governments, continue to be plagued by a shortage of well-trained specialists in foreign languages and cultures. CINCUSSOCOM should develop programs to increase language and area training (particularly for Latin America, the Middle East, and East Asia) for relevant special operations, psychological operations, and civil affairs units. Service secretaries should prepare their budget requests accordingly.

Strategic Trade

Wayne A. Abernathy*
Task Force Chairman

The acquisition of Western goods and technology has long been a principal objective of Soviet foreign policy and intelligence efforts. Without infusions of Western technology, it would be far more difficult, if not impossible, for the Soviet Union to maintain modern military forces. As the Soviet economy has fallen farther behind those of the industrial democracies, trade in items with potential military value, known as strategic trade, has become an increasingly high priority for the Kremlin leadership. Accordingly, it has become a top national security priority for the United States and its allies to ensure that such technology does not fall into Soviet hands.

―――――――――◇―――――――――

THE REAGAN ADMINISTRATION RECORD

Strategic trade controls are America's principal policy means for restricting the transfer of militarily significant technology to the Soviet Union. When the Reagan Administration took office, the U.S. strategic trade control system was moribund and neglected. Technology with military utility was being shipped directly from the U.S. to the Soviet Union. In one case, highly polished laser mirrors were being sent to the Soviet Union. Thanks to Reagan Administration enforcement efforts, those responsible were prosecuted and convicted.

The Reagan Administration has revitalized the strategic trade control system and has made strategic trade a high national priority. As a result, the U.S. has greatly complicated Soviet efforts to obtain militarily significant technology, including advanced computer and robotics technology, from the U.S. or other Western allies. At the same

---

*Commenting and contributing generously to this report were *Mandate III* Task Force Members Sumner Benson, Geoffrey Gleason, and Jennifer White. They do not necessarily endorse all of its views and recommendations.

Task Force Deputy Chairman: Heritage Policy Analyst Jay P. Kosminsky.

time, Reagan export control enforcement has increased public and industry awareness of the problem and has stimulated private sector cooperation. These efforts effectively have placed some Western goods and technology out of Soviet reach and, at a minimum, have increased the time and cost to Moscow of obtaining what sensitive goods and technology it does acquire. This has helped to preserve the technological advantage that provides the margin of security in Western defense systems.

A key element in the Administration's success has been increased Defense Department participation in administering export controls at all levels. This reflects the Administration's position that export controls are a national security matter, not just a commercial issue. The Pentagon has established the Defense Technology Security Administration, increasing staff devoted to strategic trade activities from 10 to 135. The Pentagon also has organized the Security and Technical Experts Meeting, a forum in which military experts from Western countries meet to discuss the requirements for export controls on new technologies with potential military significance. Following the Pentagon's lead, the Commerce Department has boosted its export control staff from 203 to 480. And the Customs Service, moreover, has initiated Operation Exodus, involving 290 persons in export control enforcement activities.

During the Reagan years the number of criminal and civil actions against violators of export control laws has climbed dramatically. In cooperation with Congress, legal penalties were toughened in 1985, with forfeiture of goods and import controls added to the list of sanctions available for use against export control violators.

Nearly as important, the Reagan Administration has prodded America's allies to enforce their controls on strategic exports. The Western allies' Coordinating Committee for Multilateral Export Controls, widely known as COCOM, has been reinvigorated. The list of controlled goods has been updated after a decade of neglect. In 1982, the U.S. convened COCOM's first high-level meeting in a quarter century, attended by U.S. Undersecretaries of Defense and comparable-ranking officials from other COCOM countries. As a result of the Reagan Administration's prodding, the allies have improved efforts, increased resources, apprehended offenders, and expelled many of the technology spies employed by Soviet bloc embassies and agencies. The Reagan Administration too has obtained better export control cooperation from such non-COCOM countries as Austria, India, Pakistan, Singapore, South Korea, Sweden, and Switzerland.

The major shortcoming of Reagan Administration efforts in strategic trade has been its allowing the main responsibility for export controls to remain with the Commerce Department, an agency institutionally antagonistic to effective controls. Commerce has failed, for example, to consult regularly with the Pentagon in licensing goods with military applications directly to the Soviet Union. The Administration also has failed to give strategic trade issues a high priority within the National Security Council. Intraadministration disputes thus have festered, frustrating control and making it more difficult for legitimate exporters to get approval for their shipments. As serious, the Administration has not updated the list of "controlled countries" to include Afghanistan, Angola, Ethiopia, Iran, Mozambique, or Nicaragua. Sensitive items sold to these countries undoubtedly have been shipped to the Soviet bloc or China.

Since 1987, the White House has seemed to tire of vigilance on strategic trade issues, effectively taking away the Pentagon's unofficial veto over important strategic trade questions and strengthening the hand of the Commerce Department in interagency disputes. Waning White House export control efforts have led to regulatory and congressional action that has eroded many of the Administration's earlier gains. This has made detection of illegal transfers to the Soviet bloc more difficult and adequate safeguards on legal exports less likely.

———————◇———————

THE NEXT FOUR YEARS

The U.S. and other advanced Western industrial democracies hold a five-to-ten-year lead over the Soviet Union in militarily applicable technology. Maintaining this margin is essential to Western security. The objective of U.S. strategic trade policy is to prevent advanced technology with military applications from reaching Western adversaries, particularly the Soviet Union, either directly or through third parties. This requires strict control measures and effective enforcement by the U.S. and COCOM. Export controls on advanced technologies are an exception to the rule of free trade made necessary by the requirements of national security. Accordingly, control procedures should be enforced consistently and carried out expeditiously to interfere as little as possible with nonstrategic trade.

Renegotiating Extradition Treaties

While the actions of technology smugglers harm U.S. national security and threaten the welfare of American citizens, it is often difficult to bring export control offenders to justice because they are outside of the U.S. Many countries, including U.S. allies, will refuse to extradite those who have violated export controls. To facilitate extradition, the new Administration should renegotiate extradition treaties to make export control violations extraditable offenses.

Improving Enforcement

As licensing burdens decrease because of improved license processing and increased international cooperation, the U.S. Secretary of Commerce should shift manpower from licensing of sensitive exports to enforcement of compliance with U.S. export control policies. A licensing system serves primarily as an incentive to the scrupulous to remain scrupulous. The unscrupulous do what they can to circumvent it. There is no substitute, therefore, for an adequately staffed and effectively managed enforcement and intelligence effort to combat determined smugglers operating outside of the licensing system.

Strengthening Interagency Cooperation

The Secretary of Commerce and the Commissioner of Customs should request that career military and intelligence officers be assigned to the Commerce Department's export licensing and enforcement operations. This would promote information exchange among agencies, thereby facilitating the Commerce Department's access to military expertise and intelligence information, and improving the intelligence community's understanding of the administration of strategic trade controls.

Scrutinizing Exchange Programs

In relations with the Soviet Union and with the People's Republic of China, the new President should avoid repeating the flawed East-West trade policies of the 1970s detente era. These assumed that increased trade links, particularly technology exports, would tie the Soviet Union more closely to the West, making the Kremlin less likely to threaten Western security or exert a disruptive force in international relations. By 1980 it became clear that this premise was false. Moscow simply used the relaxation of strategic trade restrictions to increase the Soviet military threat to the West. The quality of Soviet weapon systems was improved, often incorporating goods and technology obtained from NATO countries without alteration.

To avoid the mistakes of the 1970s, the new President should instruct the National Security Council to ensure that U.S. science and technology exchange agreements with Soviet bloc countries are negotiated and executed in a way that prevents the loss of strategic technology. U.S. intelligence reports detail how the Soviets use such exchanges to acquire technology. Officials with export control experience should be involved in planning and administering these exchanges.

◇

INITIATIVES FOR 1989

1) Designate an officer responsible for strategic trade. Current federal bureaucratic organization for strategic trade issues involves at least seven departments and agencies. Policy coordination is complicated by interagency tension, particularly between the Defense Department, which is concerned primarily with national security issues, and the Commerce Department, which is largely concerned with trade and commercial issues. Without direction and coordination from the government's highest policy levels, interagency disputes will continue to hamper U.S. control efforts. The new President should assign to the Assistant to the President for National Security Affairs responsibility for coordinating strategic trade policy.

2) Revise the list of controlled countries. The Commerce Department divides potential U.S. trading partners into various "Country Groups," which designates the type of strategic trade controls to which each is subject. Currently, the Warsaw Pact countries, plus Albania, Cuba, North Korea, and Vietnam, are in groups that require tight controls. (China also is subject to controls, but by virtue of a bureaucratic quirk, it technically is not listed in a controlled group.)

Such Soviet allies as Angola, Cambodia, Ethiopia, Mozambique, and Nicaragua are not subject to controls and are listed in the same group as U.S. allies including Britain, France, and West Germany. The Secretary of Commerce, in consultation with the Secretary of Defense, should add these Soviet bloc countries to Country Groups subject to strict strategic trade controls.

Further, the current system does not adequately provide controls for countries that are not Soviet bloc states, but nonetheless pose a potential threat to U.S. interests. There exists a category for such countries, "Country Group S," but only Libya presently is in that group. Such other countries as Iran, Syria, and China should be placed in Country Group S, and examined closely on a case-by-case basis. Yugoslavia should be placed in this Country Group if it does not fully live up to a memorandum of understanding with the U.S. to cooperate with COCOM. The Secretary of Commerce, in consultation with the Secretary of Defense, should expand Country Group S and propose new Commerce Department regulations to revise the criteria for assignment to this group as necessary.

3) Publicize export control deficiencies of U.S. allies. The Toshiba/ Kongsberg case, in which technologically very advanced equipment used to grind propellers for submarines and aircraft carriers was sold directly to the Soviet Union by Japanese and Norwegian companies, powerfully illustrates the danger to U.S. national security when U.S. allies fail to fulfill their export- control responsibilities. The deficiencies of Japanese and Norwegian export control efforts were widely known within the U.S. government for years. Congressional leaders and the public, however, should be made aware of allied export control deficiencies before there are major technology losses. The new President should order the Secretary of Commerce, in consultation with the Secretary of Defense, to prepare an annual public report to Congress that compares the export control efforts of COCOM countries, including enforcement efforts, resources, license volume, and processing time.

4) Create a Strategic Trade Administration. The President should recommend that Congress create a Strategic Trade Administration as an independent agency of government. The new agency would assume the export control functions of the Department of Commerce, which has a strong institutional bias against trade restrictions. The new agency would coordinate all U.S. strategic trade policies and be the chief enforcement agency for export control laws.

5) Remove the Export Administration Act sunset provision. The periodic need to renew the Export Administration Act, first passed in 1945 as the Export Control Act, has created a permanent export decontrol lobby. Starting in 1969, each renewal of the Act has been followed by preparations for further weakening of export controls in the next renewal round. These frequent changes throw the U.S. export control system into constant turmoil. There is no sunset provision in the Arms Export Control Act. Similarly, there should be none in the Export Administration Act. The new President should propose legislation to repeal the sunset provision.

6) Establish a national security impact statement. The process of evaluating proposed revisions of Export Administration Act regulations currently is dominated by the Commerce Department, which focuses on commercial considerations. The new President should require the Department of Defense to prepare a national security impact statement to accompany any proposed revision of Export Administration Act regulations and propose legislation to codify the requirement. The new President also should require that the annual presidential report to Congress required by the Export Administration Act include an analysis, prepared by the Pentagon, of the impact on defense costs and the military balance of sensitive goods and technology that have been transferred to controlled countries. Exporters frequently complain about the sales they lose due to export controls. These costs of control should be evaluated in light of the costs to national security of technology transfer to U.S. adversaries. The President should propose to Congress that the Export Administration Act be amended to require this Defense Department analysis.

Defense Management and Acquisitions

Jay P. Kosminsky*
Task Force Chairman

Efforts to trim the federal budget deficit will put continuing pressure on United States defense spending at a time when America's international commitments remain demanding. To fulfill these commitments within the budget's constraints, the Pentagon must become a more efficient and effective manager. The principal management tasks facing the Defense Department are the financial management of its own bureaucracy (health programs, payrolls) and management of acquisition programs (developing and buying weapons and other war materiel). Reforming acquisition holds particularly significant potential for improving military effectiveness and saving money. Every year, the Pentagon spends over $100 billion on developing and buying new weapons. Yet, according to a 1986 report by the President's blue-ribbon panel on defense management (known as the Packard Commission), weapons still "take too long [and] cost too much to produce, . . . often they do not perform as promised or expected."

───────────◇───────────

THE REAGAN ADMINISTRATION RECORD

The Reagan Administration inherited Defense Department financial and acquisitions management systems that were archaic by any private-sector standards: rigidly hierarchical, lacking in competitive practices, and ineffectively audited. The Administration has made some headway in reducing inefficiency. There are new auditing procedures and improved data processing and inventory management. Acquisition reform has received serious attention from both the Reagan Administration and Congress.

The most important milestone was the 1986 Packard Commission

*Commenting and contributing generously to this report were *Mandate III* Task Force Members James L. Wolbarsht and Dov S. Zackheim. They do not necessarily endorse all of its views and recommendations.

Report. In April 1986, the President issued a National Security Decision Directive (NSDD), putting into place the key Packard Commission recommendations. These were intended primarily to create a more cost-effective acquisition system by clarifying lines of authority and communication, improving personnel quality, and stabilizing planning and funding processes. Key legislation putting these changes into law has included the Goldwater-Nichols Department of Defense Reorganization Act of 1986, the Department of Defense Acquisition Improvement Acts of 1986, and the Department of Defense Authorization Act for 1987.

Potentially, the most wide-reaching innovation was the establishment of an Undersecretary of Defense for Acquisition—known in Pentagonese as USD(A)—to oversee all Pentagon procurement. Previously, the Army, Navy, and Air Force each had handled its own acquisitions with little central direction. As part of his mandate, the USD(A) has been given broad authority to set overall Defense Department policy for weapons research and development, procurement, and contract management. Pursuant to the Defense Reorganization Act of 1986, the recommendations of the USD(A) are meant to take precedence over the service secretaries on these and all other acquisition matters.

The Pentagon has adopted a two-year defense budgeting cycle, as recommended by the Packard Commission, with the objective of reducing total program costs by increasing stability in planning and budgeting. Multiyear planning and budgeting can reduce costs, for instance, by permitting firm development schedules and steady production rates. Though Congress wisely has required two-year budgets from the Pentagon, Congress continues to pass Defense Department budgets on a yearly basis. The Administration also has made the acquisition process more cost-effective through improved auditing and increased use of commercially available "off-the-shelf" items instead of designing whole new systems. Each of these programs could have been taken farther.

Despite changes in the Pentagon's management structure and the new programs, questions remain regarding how much these innovations actually improved overall acquisitions cost efficiency. The Undersecretary of Defense for Acquisition has received inconsistent high-level support inside the Pentagon. Many changes streamlining management have come late in the Administration's tenure, and their impact will not be known for some time. Such other programs as multiyear procurement have been instituted only on a limited basis, largely because of congressional hesitance.

Investigations by the FBI and Naval Investigative Service during the final year of the Reagan Administration, meanwhile, have revealed apparent corruption and fraud among some high-level Pentagon procurement personnel and defense contractors. Fraud subverts an acquisition process designed in theory to produce the best weapons at the best price. Taxpayers as a result do not get the defenses they paid for, and the unscrupulous get money they do not deserve.

———————————— ◇ ————————————

THE NEXT FOUR YEARS

Maintaining High-level Support for Management Reform

In reforming bureaucracies, stamina is as important as initiative. The new President and Secretary of Defense must persist in their efforts to reform defense management, particularly the acquisition process, along the lines recommended by the Packard Commission. If they do not, political and bureaucratic pressures quickly will erode any progress.

The intent of reform should be a Pentagon acquisition system characterized by short, unambiguous lines of authority, personnel professionalism, openness to innovation, and program stability. To achieve this, the Secretary of Defense should give strong public and bureaucratic backing to the Undersecretary of Defense for Acquisition, designating him the chief Administration spokesman on Defense management reform. The Secretary of Defense should enforce the authority of the USD(A) over the Service secretaries on acquisition matters. The Secretary of Defense should require the USD(A) to develop a plan for establishing a single direct chain of authority from his office to Service acquisition executives, program executive officers, and program managers in each of the military services. The Secretary of Defense should give the necessary bureaucratic backing to the USD(A) to carry out the plan.

Reducing Corruption and Fraud

The huge sums spent on weapons make Pentagon procurement an attractive target for the corrupt. Making the Pentagon particularly vulnerable to corruption in procurement are program instability, poorly trained acquisition staffs, and cumbersome lines of communication. The best defense against corruption is effective enforcement of existing laws and strong action against companies involved in bribery, fraud, or other criminal actions. The Secretary of Defense should deter illegal activity by punishing violators through such means as exclusion from future contracts and taking legal steps to recover profits from contracts tainted by fraud. Outright contract cancellation should be considered a last resort when contracts vital to national security are at stake.

Crime also can be reduced by eliminating flaws in the acquisition process. Improved personnel quality would reduce the Pentagon's need to use outside consultants, some of whom have illegally sold their knowledge and influence. Improved program stability through multi-year contracting or biennial budgeting would reduce the number of times that contracts have to be rebid or renewed, each a potential opportunity for illegal influence. A streamlined procurement system would make auditing easier.

Hiring and Retaining Skilled Acquisition Personnel

While the Defense Department has made some progress in improving the quality of its civilian and military procurement personnel, the military still does not offer adequate career incentives for military officers to specialize in acquisition. The Packard Commission concluded that the military should continue to handle its own procurement and rejected turning over the process to the civil service or a civilian procurement agency. This recommendation makes sense, mainly because of the generally high integrity of uniformed officers (few ever have been implicated in fraud or corruption) and the inherent advantage of having individuals with direct military experience involved in the weapons acquisition process.

If the military is to keep its lead role in acquisition, however, the professionalism of acquisition officers must be improved. Turnover in procurement positions remains high; officers managing procurement programs often lack experience and training. The Joint Chiefs of Staff should study incentives, including changes in promotion criteria, for attracting qualified officers into extended procurement training programs and tours of duty. Options to be studied should include creating an elite corps of procurement officers, who would be rewarded through promotion for effectiveness in their area of expertise, as would any field commander.

INITIATIVES FOR 1989

1) Establish an outside management advisory board to provide independent advice. The Pentagon's rigid and hierarchical management structure and outdated accounting, auditing, and information management systems impede effective personnel and program management. The Secretary of Defense should establish a permanent advisory board composed of experienced managers from the private and public sectors to identify advanced private-sector management, accounting, and information processing tools and to make recommendations to the Secretary of Defense regarding their applicability to Pentagon financial and acquisitions management. The board should be free to set its own agenda, which would complement the work of the Defense Department's internal Council on Integrity and Management Improvement, which would continue to focus on microlevel management issues.

2) Request two-year Pentagon budgets from Congress. Greater program stability was identified by the Packard Commission as a principal objective of Pentagon procurement reform. The new President thus should request Congress to pass two-year defense budgets. With this, program officials, contractors, and congressional staff would spend less time on cumbersome budgeting procedures; programs would not be subject to jarring and inefficient yearly ups and downs in funding; and opportunities would be reduced for contract-related fraud.

3) Increase multiyear procurement. Multiyear procurement is another means of providing greater funding stability to Pentagon acquisition programs. Under multiyear procurement, Congress authorizes funds, and the Defense Department signs contracts, for the acquisition of weapons systems or components over a period of years, rather than one year at a time. Multiyear procurement reduces costs by permitting materials to be purchased and stockpiled in greater quantity. Though not all defense programs are suitable for multiyear procurement (weapons undergoing major modifications, for instance), this technique should be the rule in Pentagon acquisition. The Secretary of Defense should charge the Undersecretary of Defense for Acquisition with preparing plans to expand multiyear procurement to include all major weapons programs that are not otherwise disqualified by existing Defense Department criteria. The new President should publicly challenge Congress to approve the expanded program, making public the estimated cost savings.

4) Expand enterprise programs. Enterprise programs permit small teams of highly qualified Pentagon managers to develop new weapons. Each team is given autonomy and exceptional leeway in determining how funds are to be spent and how the program is organized. Enterprise programs work best when funds are authorized for the entire development stage of the project, rather than on a yearly basis. This requires congressional cooperation. Some of the most successful past programs, such as the *Polaris* submarine and *Minuteman* missile, were run by similar rules. If full evaluations of existing enterprise programs, such as the *Trident* D5 missile and Army Advanced Tactical Missile System (ATACMS), bear out initial reports, the use of enterprise programs should be expanded to include such projects as the Air Force's Medium Launch Vehicle space booster. The USD(A) should develop plans for expanded use of enterprise programs, and the new President should challenge Congress to authorize and appropriate funds for them.

5) Use competition effectively. The Pentagon has expanded competition in procurement since 1984. The goals of increased competition are to reduce costs and increase quality. Certain factors limit competition's feasibility in the defense industry. For large-scale projects, for example, the market generally is dominated by a few companies: only three aviation contractors are capable of bidding on a strategic bomber, five or so might attempt a fighter aircraft, and only two shipyards can build nuclear submarines. Further, the kinds of items on which companies bid often push the limits of science and engineering, making cost estimates far more speculative than in more traditional industries.

Within these limitations, however, there is room for competition, particularly for purchasing less complex systems and components. Because of the uncertainties involved in developing new technologies, cost should not be the only factor in competitive bidding. Real defense "bargains" are rare. A firm's past performance and its ability to provide support and services must be considered; new criteria to take such factors into account should be developed by the USD(A). Higher quality personnel will help make the more sophisticated bidding process work.

When feasible, the USD(A) should request funding for multiple prototypes of new systems and pit them against each other. This has worked successfully for such projects as the Advanced Warning and

Control System (AWACS) radar and F–16 *Falcon* fighter aircraft, and it is currently being used for the Air Force's new Advanced Technology Fighter. Prototyping is more expensive in the early stages of a program, but it usually produces higher quality and reduced costs in the long run. Contractors should be expected to share some research and development costs of prototypes.

To date, competitive bidding for contracts has been used mainly in the development phase of a new weapons project; it remains the exception during the production phase. Competition during the production phase is known as "dual sourcing." In this situation, companies compete for contracts to continue production of a weapons system after an initial contract has been awarded. In some cases, two companies might produce the same weapons system and compete for the major share of production. Without dual sourcing, companies have little incentive to keep down production costs because they are in no danger of losing the contract. The USD(A) should plan on dual sourcing for all new tactical missiles once they reach production, if there is a reasonable expectation of reducing costs. Combining dual sourcing and multiyear procurement, where feasible, would realize considerable savings for the Pentagon.

6) Improve cost estimates and cost control. Initial underestimation of weapons systems' costs undermines the entire planning and budgeting process by allowing approval of more weapons programs than ultimately can be bought. Recent studies reveal that, on average, major weapons systems cost some 40 percent more than original estimates, a figure that is comparable to other large-scale government projects. One measure to improve cost estimates is baseline planning. Baselining locks in weapons specifications, costs, and schedules for an entire acquisition phase, such as full-scale development. Any deviations from baseline parameters triggers a review of the program. About 90 programs now employ baselining, including most major weapons programs. The USD(A) should expand baseline planning.

7) Expand use of commercial products. It is estimated that $1 billion could be saved annually if the Pentagon regularly substituted commercial products for new designs when practical. Instead of spending millions of taxpayer dollars to develop new field rations, for example, the Pentagon could buy rations from commercial companies that have developed food for backpackers that is cheaper and tastes better than anything the military has produced. The USD(A) should direct service acquisition executives to consult private industry specifications before designing new items. Where feasible, military specifications should be written to allow purchase of commercially available products. The USD(A) should revise Pentagon regulations that require commercial suppliers to relinquish proprietary information about their products. This obviously discourages them from selling their products to the Pentagon.

☎

Defense Industrial Preparedness

Jay P. Kosminsky and Mackubin T. Owens, Jr.*
Task Force Chairmen

United States security requires a U.S. industrial base able to maintain technological superiority over potential adversaries and to expand rapidly in case of war. Realization that the full strength of American industry can be mobilized readily for defense reassures allies, helps deter aggressors, and would be crucial to victory in the event of war.

———————————◇———————————

THE REAGAN ADMINISTRATION RECORD

The Reagan Administration's most important contribution to industrial military preparedness has been the restoration of America's basic economic health and productivity. In addition, the Administration took several steps to put defense industrial preparedness on the national security agenda after decades of neglect. In 1981 it created the Emergency Mobilization Preparedness Board (EMPB), which began developing plans for harnessing the defense industrial mobilization potential of the U.S. economy. In January 1985, EMPB functions were transferred to the National Security Council. By this, the Administration has made mobilization planning a high national security priority. Interagency groups convened under National Security Council auspices have been addressing such military industrial base issues as mobilization and energy vulnerability.

The Administration also has focused attention on "surge capability," the ability to increase U.S. production to meet the demands of war. During wartime, combat attrition would draw down inventories of weapons and ammunition, and American industry would have to gear up to replace them.

---

*Commenting and contributing generously to this report were *Mandate III* Task Force Members Ed Badolato, Richard Donnelly, and Thomas Etzold. They do not necessarily endorse all of its views and recommendations.

In 1988, the Reagan Administration released the Graduated Mobilization Response Plan. This would give the President options for gradually increasing U.S. military industrial preparedness in response to increasing international tension. At the first sign of trouble, for example, the President might choose to increase stockpiles of military components or increase federal investment in military production capacity. Such steps may help avert a crisis by signaling U.S. resolve and would enable the U.S. to surge more quickly to full wartime production should the crisis deepen.

A 1988 Pentagon report, "Bolstering U.S. Industrial Competitiveness," makes recommendations to strengthen U.S. technological and industrial capacity for producing modern weapons systems and to provide the government with a more accurate assessment of the U.S. industrial base. The government currently tracks 480 industrial sectors, using census data that is updated only at seven-year intervals. By comparison, during World War II, the U.S. managed to update its information on 400 industries every six months—without the aid of computers.

A problem is that the Administration waited until its final year to produce the industrial competitiveness report and the Graduated Mobilization Response Plan. Further, such earlier initiatives as increasing the National Security Council role in mobilization planning were not given the political attention necessary to make them effective; of the three intergovernmental groups on mobilization issues, only the group on energy mobilization was consistently effective.

———————————◇———————————

THE NEXT FOUR YEARS

Creating a Readily Mobilizable Force Structure

In war, the U.S. may not be able to afford the long lead times and high unit costs of existing weaponry; the U.S. probably will need to produce enormous quantities of weapons rapidly. To ensure this, the Undersecretary of Defense for Acquisition should require that, when feasible, new weapons systems should be so designed that less sophisticated versions could be produced quickly and easily during wartime. He also should recommend development of versatile weapon platforms, such as the Variable Load Ship (VLS), which would be useful if rapid military expansion were necessary. (See Navy section of this chapter.)

Investing in Surge Capacity

Since the mid–1950s, U.S. wartime contingency planning has assumed that a major war would be short and probably nuclear. The outcome of such a war would be determined by the forces in place when fighting began. Yet, in a protracted war fought with conventional weapons, or even a limited nuclear war, the difference between victory and defeat could be surge capacity, the ability to rapidly expand the production of military equipment after the onset of war.

Surge capacity deficiencies are particularly evident in U.S. sub-tier industries that make components for manufacturing. Examples: electronics, bearings, machine tools, microchips, and materials processing. Here rising civilian demand has diverted resources from defense production, resulting in increased lead times, rising costs, and bottlenecks. There also has been a shift to suppliers in such countries as Japan, South Korea, and Taiwan.

The new President should instruct his National Security Adviser, working with the Undersecretary of Defense for Acquisition, to develop criteria for a limited but increased federal investment to ensure that the government can fulfill all phases of the 1988 Graduated Mobilization Response Plan. Title III of the Defense Production Act authorizes the President to make loans and provide for direct government construction of industrial facilities essential to the wartime expansion of defense production. Investment should be limited to cases in which ordinary market mechanisms cannot meet national defense needs.

Cooperating with Industry

Few voluntary or contractual agreements exist for defense industrial consortia or government-industry joint ventures. Such agreements would speed conversion of industrial capacity to wartime requirements and identify bottlenecks in advance. The President's National Security Adviser and the Secretary of Defense should seek industry cooperation in developing new standby emergency agreements between government and industry and among industries to improve U.S. defense industrial preparedness.

Protecting Supply Lines

The dependence of the U.S. and its allies on foreign energy sources and the transfer abroad of critical U.S. industries require that sea lanes to the U.S. be open in wartime. For this, the U.S. needs the services of the Navy. (See Navy section of this chapter.)

---◇---

INITIATIVES FOR 1989

1) Improve industrial base assessment. Defense mobilization planning requires an accurate and up-to-date picture of the defense industrial base. Defense Department planners currently work with a production base model that divides industry into roughly 480 categories. The database is updated every seven years. Effective planning requires a more refined model along the lines of what the Japanese now do, with some 2,000 industry classifications, updated every six months. The Department of Commerce is responsible for assessing the industrial base. The new President should direct the Secretary of Commerce to upgrade industrial base assessment capabilities to meet the requirements of Defense Department mobilization planners. Preparation of the industrial base model should be coordinated with the Pentagon and other relevant agencies through the National Security Council.

2) Establish an Interdepartmental Group to facilitate defense preparedness planning. Defense mobilization planning involves the Pentagon, the Departments of Commerce, Energy, Transportation, Treasury, and the Federal Emergency Management Agency. The new President should direct his National Security Adviser to convene an Interdepartmental Group for National Security Emergency Preparedness. To be effective, the group will require a clear mandate to coordinate defense preparedness efforts of relevant agencies; develop standby legal and procedural mechanisms to remove barriers (health and safety regulations, for example) to expanded production during wartime or national emergency; prepare standby budget and other legislation to speed transition to wartime production; and determine desirable levels of government investment in "rolling inventory."

3) Revive the National Security Resources Board to oversee mobilization planning. The National Security Resources Board, provided for by the National Security Act of 1947 but abolished in the mid–1950s, was composed of Cabinet secretaries whose departments had a role in defense mobilization. Since then, no forum with sufficient political clout has existed to expedite peacetime, interagency mobilization planning or to oversee wartime mobilization. The new President should reestablish the National Security Resources Board by executive order and require that it meet periodically to review interdepartmental mobilization planning.

4) Revive Pentagon preparedness capabilities. The 1988 Pentagon report, "Bolstering Defense Industrial Competitiveness," made a series of important recommendations that should be adopted immediately by the new President and Secretary of Defense. These include: creation of a liaison, reporting to the Undersecretary of Defense for Acquisition, to serve as an intermediary between industry and the military on manufacturing issues; development of an industrial base action plan specifying short- and long-term Pentagon requirements for technology and manufacturing capability; and development of more effective systems for assessing and disseminating production base information within the Pentagon.

5) Develop a component stockpile plan. Stockpiling such strategic materials as cobalt, petroleum, titanium, and other critical minerals solves only part of the U.S. stockpile problem. Raw materials must go through several processing stages before they can be put to militarily useful purpose. The U.S. therefore should stockpile the components made from these raw materials. Instead of just stockpiling tungsten ore, for example, the U.S. should stockpile penetrators for shells. The Undersecretary of Defense for Planning should initiate a study of U.S. component stockpiling requirements.

6) Extend duration of the Defense Production Act. The Defense Production Act of 1950 (DPA), as amended, is designed primarily to enable defense-related programs to be expanded in a national emergency. These include programs for government purchase of minerals, metals, and other raw materials. Under the DPA's sunset provision, the Act must be reauthorized every three years. This makes long-term planning difficult and creates uncertainty about government policy among defense-related industries. The new President should propose an amendment to Congress to eliminate or extend to ten years or more the sunset provision of the DPA.

PART FOUR

AGENCY MANAGEMENT OF POLICY INITIATIVES

Agency Management of
Policy Initiatives

by
George Nesterczuk

Political managers in government have a natural and understandable predilection to focus their attention and energies on the formulation and direction of policy. This is an expression of the perspective acquired during pre-election activities in campaigns, public policy institutes, and various other policy-oriented organizations. On the other hand, there exists a second category of political appointees who are recruited from the private sector on the basis of specialized program knowledge and management expertise. These individuals enter government straight out of the professional or corporate environment where mission and objectives are well defined by the organization and performance is easily measured in a profit-and-loss statement. Characteristically, this latter group tends to focus on management issues with little or no attention devoted to policy or agenda definition. Neither of these approaches is entirely adequate for the task of effective management of government agencies and programs.

The process of governing for a *conservative* Administration is a much more tedious and laborious venture than for the more liberal counterpart. This is because much of the federal structure represents the institutionalization of liberalism's social and political agenda. The "iron triangle" relationships among congressional committees, federal agencies, and interest group "clients" are very effective in protecting the advantages they derive from existing programs and policies. In this environment, the Administration's agenda represents *change*, which inevitably engenders resistance and opposition.

The laws, regulations, and administrative procedures that establish the framework for agency operations have been generated by the political coalitions that support the programs. After eight years of the Reagan Administration, despite some remarkable successes, it is clear that the conservative agenda has not yet been institutionalized at the day-to-day level of government operations. Much of what was accomplished was achieved through painstaking effort in identifying those elements of statutes, regulations, and procedures which are subject to interpretation and thus provided chinks in an otherwise rigid framework. Unfortunately, such advances are vulnerable to reversal, for future administrations have the same latitude to reinterpret the rules. *Lasting change* can come only through the same route that created the programs and their regulations in the first place—the legislative process, which is to say, through political success.

This does not mean that in the interim the field of battle should be ceded to the left. On the contrary, the struggle for change must be waged not only in Congress but in the executive branch of government. The Reagan experience has provided the conservative movement with a trained cadre of political operatives experienced in the many facets of policy implementation through administrative management.

Many of the veteran company commanders and field lieutenants of these recent policy wars (and some of the colonels as well) have generously contributed both time and effort to the preparation of the following eight chapters of this book. The contributions were made in order to share their collective experience and advice with the new members of an incoming Administration. It is their hope that the knowledge they impart will allow the new cadre to promote the policy agenda more effectively "in the trenches."

This concluding section addresses policy implementation from the perspective of an executive branch agency, which is where policy meets the real world. Two frail links connect the agency to the White House: the appointment powers of the President and the appointees' commitment to the President's agenda. The agenda is initially derived from campaign speeches, issue papers, and the party platform. As the agenda crystallizes and is further refined in the course of the President's tenure, it must of necessity be clearly communicated to agency heads in order to establish the basis for accountability in policy implementation.

The opening chapter, "The Role of the Agency Head," emphasizes the importance the agency head must place on setting an agenda in concert with the President. Of equal importance is the responsibility to recruit and lead a management team which subscribes to the President's policies. Subsequent chapters discuss the interaction with Congress and the interest groups and some of the more important administrative functions and processes of agency management. These include organizational systems, budget, personnel, the regulatory process, policy-making by litigation, disbursement of funds (grants and contracts), financial asset management, and program management (oversight and evaluation).

Each chapter presents a distinct aspect of an agency's operations, focusing on the relevance of the function or process to the implementation of policy. Four recurring themes provide the linkage between the eight chapters: leadership, accountability, agenda setting, and management of detail.

Leadership is required not only of an agency head but of all political managers. Leadership must be manifested in setting and articulating the agenda, in dealing with committees of Congress and the agency's interest groups, and in aggressively promoting the agenda. To maintain effective leadership, political appointees must develop a sense of identity and cohesion. They must believe that they are members not only of an agency team, but of a larger presidential team throughout the government. Agency heads must instill this sense of identity and cohesion because political appointees, though few in number, are collectively the front-line troops of the new coalition dedicated to supplanting the existing "iron triangle."

Aggressive leadership in the policy arena must be complemented with vigorous coalition building. Coalitions are particularly important when program goals and priorities must be redefined. Constituent groups can often provide support for new program performance standards and evaluation criteria that are needed for effective program management.

Personal integrity and scrupulous conduct are indispensable to leadership. Without them credibility is lost, and with it, the ability to lead. Personal integrity includes not only avoiding the usual temptations thrown in the path of government policymakers—which are discussed at some length in Chapter 37. Personal integrity also means loyalty to the team, hard work, honesty in dealing with colleagues, and showing exemplary conduct in carrying out professional duties.

The scope of responsibility vested in political appointees can be extremely broad, at times overwhelming, and calls for the judicious use of delegation. In reality, responsibility can at best be shared, it cannot be delegated. In public administration it will be policy officials, individually and collectively, who are held responsible for process as well as results.

Sharing some of the responsibility through delegation can only be achieved by enforcing a system of *accountability*. A mechanism to enforce accountability exists in the government's Performance Management System. The Performance Management System (PMS) requires the communication of goals and objectives and establishes the concept of reward and punishment as a means of maintaining accountability. The complementary concepts of performance evaluation and accountability apply equally to career civil servants vis-à-vis political management and to political appointees vis-à-vis the agency head.

Agenda setting is indispensable to political management. The policy agenda serves as the compass by which political appointees steer the course. Agenda setting applies to the administrative process as well. Without an administrative agenda (within *each* program area) the management of the agency is vested—by default—in the career staff. Decision-making is then inevitably oriented to maintaining the status quo.

The President's agenda is disseminated through an agency in conjunction with program priorities. Program and administrative priorities are established in the budget through the allocating of funds and staff levels. Thus, the budget process is an integral part of the policy process and is developed in the context of the policy agenda: policy directs the budget, not the other way around, even when the main policy issues are the budget levels of various programs. This is not an academic point; it is vital to policy advocacy. When budget levels rather than policy goals become the focus of policy debate and advocacy by political appointees, the Administration is invariably put on the defensive.

The fourth theme found in these discussions of agency management is the need for *management of detail*. Management of administrative process calls for attention to detail. Attaining fiscal responsibility by avoiding fraud, waste, and abuse requires attention to details. Political survival itself may well lie in attention to detail—in avoiding ethics pitfalls, in giving loyal service 24 hours a day, and in asking questions instead of accepting easy answers. In the private sector detail is less important, for the stakes are different, and thus the rules are different. Private-sector managers are taught to avoid involvement in administrative detail. Career public servants are taught to avoid detail by delegating responsibility. However, political managers cannot escape the detail: public accountability will not permit it.

Attention to detail is not merely a defensive necessity. Given the present rules of the game (the limited arena of policy change allowed by the framework of laws, regulations, and procedures), it is often in the administrative and regulatory details of a program that one can promote the policy agenda. An appointee must be willing to roll up his sleeves and get into the nitty-gritty of agency operations to find the levers of policy change that exist in every program.

Chapters 35 and 36 serve as useful illustrations of the interplay of leadership, accountability, and the need to manage details. These two chapters address subject matter seldom discussed in treatises on political management in the governmental environment, i.e., financial management, credit management, grants, and the procurement process. The interdependence and linkage of the functions to policy initiatives is clearly presented and developed.

As an overview of agency management, the chapters in this section are not definitive treatises on the subject matter, but they do serve several purposes. They provide a concise overview of key management issues which serves as a guide for more detailed inquiries by the political appointee. The presentations also expose the first-time manager to relevant terminology. Finally, this section provides some useful suggestions for effective strategy development and agenda implementation. These suggestions are based on reviews of successful and deflected Reagan Administration management reform initiatives, and should help in establishing a base for the new Administration to build upon.

30

The Role of the Agency Head

by
Donald J. Devine and Jim Burnley*

THE PRESIDENT'S TEAM

Among the most important decisions a President-elect makes are the ones that will visit him frequently in the Cabinet Room and the Oval Office: his appointment of agency heads. In government, policy is people, and the President's government, his Administration, will be his people. If he makes the right appointments, he will maximize his chances for success. If he puts the wrong person in charge of an agency, he and his White House staff will spend a lot of time dealing with problems that flow from that mistake.

Most Presidents-elect spend very little time making these threshold decisions. Suddenly immersed in the ceremonial and policy aspects of the office, and eager to "hit the ground running" after the long ordeal of a presidential campaign, they seldom spend adequate time or devote adequate attention to this most fundamental of leadership tasks: choosing a team. The President's personnel choices are far more important than any comparable decisions in the private sector. The federal government is so large and complex that the Chief Executive must rely upon the judgment of scores of subordinates for the overwhelming number of decisions made during his tenure. The selection of the men and women who will run the vast network of bureaucracies and serve as his representatives to thousands of organizations and to the American people—these crucial decisions must be afforded the time and attention commensurate to their importance.

*The authors are grateful for the ideas and suggestions provided by Gerald Carmen, Daniel Oliver, Terrence Scanlon, and Clarence Thomas in the preparation of this chapter. The views expressed here are, however, solely the responsibility of the authors.

Character, Loyalty, and Competence

In considering candidates for executive departments and agencies, the President-elect need look for only three characteristics and rank them in the proper order. First, does the individual have the character, toughness, and reliability to handle this difficult assignment? The dean of presidential advisors, the late Bryce Harlow, has said that character ranks "number one to ten" in choosing a political leader. Nothing is more important, for the person will be tested, and tested again and again in Washington's trench warfare.

The second test the President should apply is, will this individual be loyal to me and my agenda? It is impossible for the President to specify the detailed agenda for all of the complex issues in the national government. For this, he must delegate responsibility to his top appointees and rely on their judgment. Even the Reagan Administration—which, as David Broder correctly noted, came to office with a more complete agenda than any he had seen in his time covering Washington—set the specific agenda for relatively few policies. Loyalty is the cement which binds a team together. This can be tested by questioning whether the individual knows what the President has said he wants; whether the applicant for agency head has, in general, agreed with the President's positions in the past; and whether he has a reputation for sticking by his friends.

Third, the President must ask whether the individual has the proper mix of leadership ability, management skills, and program knowledge. He must guard against falling into the trap of appointing someone who has gained program knowledge by spending many years in an industry or field with which the agency has a close relationship. Often such people are the worst appointees, because they cannot subordinate loyalty to a special interest group to the loyalty they owe the President. The selection should not be based primarily on technical qualifications, but rather on *who is the most qualified of those who meet the first two criteria, character and loyalty.*

If the President takes the time to find the answers to these three questions for his top appointees, he will have laid the foundation on which to build a successful administration.

———————————◇———————————

THE AGENCY HEAD'S ENVIRONMENT

Being the head of a federal agency is among the world's toughest jobs. Presidents may have "teflon coatings," but the "grease" will stick to the agency head who does his job. This is inevitable, since a significant part of his job is to deflect the heat from the President. And the heat will come. While the President can play the lion, the agency head must be the fox: he must not only know how to avoid trouble, but also when to confront it in order to persevere.

To perform properly as a presidential appointee, the agency head must know the President's agenda. That means he must study the President's speeches and writings, the party platform, and the campaign promises. This is time consuming, but it is impossible to follow the agenda when one does not know it. Attempts will be made to foist other agendas upon the agency head—his agency's institutional prejudices, what the congressional overseers want, what the interest groups desire, what "enlightened opinion" as shaped and interpreted by the media requires. The President's agenda should always be kept in the forefront and other agendas looked upon as distractions and obstacles, never as substitutes. Then, as the agency head is buffeted by his environment, he will have the knowledge necessary to keep score. What must be kept uppermost in his mind is: what percentage of the President's agenda have I achieved, or have I set in motion? This is the standard by which the agency head should measure his success in this once-in-a-lifetime opportunity to make a difference.

The White House

The first institution which will test the agency head's mettle is the White House. In light of the priority placed on following the President's agenda and given the instinctive response of any executive to the headquarters chain of command, one would think that a loyal agency head should take direction from the White House. Yet, as with many things in the topsyturvy world of Washington, the correct approach is counterintuitive, for the White House staff is not always in tune with the President.

The correct relationship to pursue is the bond between the President and the agency head. The President's staff at times pursues its own interests, not necessarily the President's. That is why all good management practice emphasizes line over staff; in this case, the line is from the President to the agency head. If that works, everything else works. All the Executive Office of the President can effectively do is correct errors made in the original selection of agency heads; it is never the optimal control device. *So the answer for the agency head is: if he is loyal to the President, he should never be dictated to by the White House staff.* Otherwise, every clerk in the White House will feel at liberty to call him and tell him the President wants this or that. Obviously, the wise agency head will remain open to the advice of various assistants to the President, but the final decision is his or the President's to make, not the White House bureaucracy's.

Congress

Congress is, if anything, an even more difficult puzzle to solve. Everyone will advise the agency head of the necessity of having good relations with the members of his congressional oversight authorizing and appropriating committees. The problem is that Congress typically has a different agenda from the President's. That is why *he* was elected President, and *they* were elected to Congress. Never was it more truly said that one cannot serve two masters. Of course, the agency head must court these most critical centers of power—be nice to them, do what favors he can, answer their letters promptly, generally pay attention to their often prickly personalities. But the President is the agency head's boss and his interests will sooner or later come into conflict with theirs. Therefore, a comfortable distance should be maintained in the relationship with Congress. There must be cordiality, but there will also be inevitable confrontations.

The best defense against Congress is simple: be prepared. Congressmen have almost no time to learn the details of policy; this is their Achilles' heel. If the agency head knows the details, he can use the often-dreaded committee hearing to advance his reputation and his agenda. He should answer courteously, but never back down. The main reason many agency heads are buffeted in hearings, or even worse, choose to stay away and send cowed subordinates as surrogates, is that they are uninformed (or perhaps just cowardly). Good congressional relations, even grudging respect from the strongest opposition, can only be won by being better informed, well prepared, and having the strength of character to face the opposition.

The Media

Every businessman has been taught how to deal with the media. The standard advice is keep a low profile, tend to your knitting, and stay out of trouble. While this works in the private sector, the "knitting" in the public sector *is* the media. Government is essentially a communication business. Ruled and ruler communicate, one nation communicates to another, interests communicate to centers of power, etc. In government, truly the medium is the message. Keeping a low profile as a government executive means giving up your most important asset, the opportunity to persuade. To be able to be heard in Washington, an agency head must develop a public personality which will help him achieve his agenda. If he becomes a nonperson, Congress and even his own bureaucracy will run his agency for him.

Unfortunately, in Washington's "fishbowl," being a public personality necessarily means that the publicity will be mixed. A media story must have good and bad things to say about its characters, or it does not read well. That is show-biz. This means the bad things will distress one's family, friends, and former business associates. That is why the businessman, as business executive, is correctly advised to stay out of the public's eye. But a government executive must swim in the sea of media or become powerless. If the agency head allows his family's and friends' concerns over this bad publicity to dissuade him from action, he might as well go home.

The Bureaucracy

The textbooks advise the agency head to build a close, personal relationship with the employees of his agency. Yet, in government, they are not really his employees. They are members of a permanent bureaucracy who were there before he came and will be there after he leaves. They were selected by Civil Service examinations, not by the agency head. The head needs to befriend those who can be befriended, of course, but he must lead them, maintain a respectful distance and be somewhat aloof, if he is to motivate these independent agents of the bureaucracy into doing what *he* wants rather than what *they* want.

Many political scientists believe that the agency bureaucracies themselves are formidable lobbying groups for the interests they regulate, more so than any outside group. Since the bureaucracy has an agenda, its primary function is to win over the new agency head to its point of view. The agency head then becomes a symbolic figure, who is manipulated in the interests of the status quo. It is a test of leadership and management acumen for the agency head to get the career sector in the agency to implement his policies rather than vice-versa.

The Interest Groups

All interest groups—the agency's bureaucracy, those regulated by the agency, potential customers and suppliers, and ideological groups—should be courted by the agency head as potential allies. He must not, however, allow himself to be drawn into their rivalries and

petty conflicts, but rather remain above the fray and cast himself in the
role of a judge rather than a player. He must reserve his limited
political capital to deal with the primary issues rather than accommodating secondary concerns in building his coalitions. Moreover, interest groups are the most likely to extend perks, gifts, and other favors,
which should be avoided like the plague. The agency head must behave
like Caesar's wife, even if only for the practical reason that anything
he does—or says, writes or jokes about—may appear on the front page
of the *Washington Post* the next morning. In the Washington game of
trial-by-leak, there are no secrets, no confidences. Integrity, sound
judgment, and prudence call for scrupulous actions and a judicial
demeanor in the face of all these environmental forces.

Temptations

Particular attention should be paid to certain details which may seem
relatively mundane when compared with policy decisions affecting
millions of people or billions of dollars. Experience has shown that
small matters have tripped up the best intentioned political executives,
causing unnecessary embarrassment and personal hardship. Examples
include using official vehicles for personal purposes, asking employees
to do personal chores or errands, expensive or unnecessary refurnish-
ing of office suites, combining personal and official travel, or misusing
the perks of office leading to the appearance of personal gain. It is
advisable for the agency head to set up a review and counseling session
with his general counsel or designated agency ethics officer to familiar-
ize himself and his management team on the potential pitfalls. This
may be somewhat time consuming, but in comparison to the time spent
defending or explaining the appearance of wrongdoing, it is a worthwhile investment. These problems can be terribly debilitating and
demoralizing, and serve only to detract from the primary goal of
implementing the President's agenda.

————————————◇————————————

ESSENTIALS OF SUCCESSFUL AGENCY
MANAGEMENT

Creating the Management Team

In the same way that the President must rely upon the agency head
as his principal subordinate, the agency head must rely upon his

political appointees, since he cannot rely upon accounting and budget tools any more than can the President. He must create a loyal team, assign accountability (through such tools as performance agreements), and then reward those who do the job well. This means that the head must *personally*, like the President, select his top leaders, both political and career. He must be willing to work with the Presidential Personnel Office (PPO) to select individuals who are *mutually acceptable* in terms of competence, commitment and character. But the bottom line in personnel selection is that the agency head should never accept a prospective appointee who does not meet his standards and in whom he cannot have complete confidence.

The White House has every right to monitor how well the agency team performs under the President's criteria, and the agency head should be open to high-level objections from PPO. If the subordinates are not doing their job, ultimately the White House should come after the boss—he is accountable for their performance. All of this is peripheral, however. The essential point is to be *personally involved* in selecting a loyal team of subordinates who can accomplish the President's agenda.

Once the agency's team is in place it is important to create and maintain an esprit de corps among the team through regular meetings, briefings and training programs. The agency head should meet with his entire political team at least once each quarter and with his personal staff at least weekly. The larger the agency and the more numerous its divisions and fiefdoms, the more important such meetings are. Policy briefings by the agency head or senior staff are effective in keeping everyone up to speed and "in the loop." Training programs aimed at improving management skills and effectiveness should be developed around generic themes such as the regulatory process, personnel management, contracts, and public affairs.

Setting the Agenda

As soon as he is selected, the agency head should begin to assimilate the President's agenda and the agency's own institutional point of view. Both must be understood if the latter is to be brought into line with the former. Here, it is wise to learn from President Reagan. Rather than trying to sort through and follow a great multiplicity of government issues, as did Jimmy Carter, Reagan focused on a few important policies. If the agency head identifies a few very important issues in his area, and uses all his resolve and every available weapon (without transgressing the law or ethical canons), he just might be as successful as President Reagan.

The fact that there is no bottom line, however, means that the agency head must *pay much more attention to detail* than he did in the private sector. In the private sector, he could keep track of subordinates by looking at cost centers; in government, he must evaluate people in the context of policy (rather than profit-or-loss), and this is often made more difficult by the fact that the real policy is hidden in the minutiae of administering a program, or in the wording of a few phrases in a regulation.

While he must concentrate on relatively few issues, he must know them thoroughly and, in addition, keep a watchful eye on developing policy areas which might become future problems. Public-sector management is much more difficult than private-sector management because it demands a much greater mastery of detail, provides less objective measures of success, tends to focus on a few very complicated issues rather than the agency as a whole, and requires an ability to see behind one's back while looking at a shifting policy horizon.

Managing

Primary reliance should be upon personnel management, rather than pursuing overly abstract or objective measures of efficiency. Cost-benefit analysis might be useful on occasion (in fact, it is required in regulatory matters), but the essential task is to comprehend the problem in its entirety, study the political environment, and understand the people involved in the process. To do this, the agency head must talk to those people, even down several levels into the organization, motivate and coordinate those who will help, and maneuver around those who pose a problem. Former Secretary of the Interior James Watt used what he called the "rule of three" to set his staffing policy for a subordinate unit. First, appoint a real leader as the head of the major subunit, one who can inspire and motivate. Then, appoint as his subordinate a deputy who has the administrative skills to get the job done. Finally, appoint a third person, who need not possess great technical expertise, whose primary job is to remind the other two why they were appointed: to carry out the President's agenda.

The critical issue for most agency heads is whether they will strive to manage effectively or give in to the environment and just enjoy the perks of office. Of course, this is not unique to government. Andrew Grove, when president of Intel, used to say that managers are paid to elicit better performance, and there is no other way to do so than to assess what good personnel performance is and to measure progress towards that goal. "We managers need to stop rationalizing [how difficult this is] and stiffen our resolve and do what we are paid to do, and that is to manage." Fortunately, Jimmy Carter's one real legacy to government was his Civil Service Reform Act, which provided a technically sound performance appraisal system for the entire Civil Service and a pay-for-performance system for managers and executives.

A successful public-sector executive must rely upon these systems—he does not have that private-sector bottom line—and therefore, must give more attention to these less than optimal but nevertheless critical tools. For if such management tools are as critical as Andrew Grove believes in a private sector which has measurable cost centers, they are even more so in a process-oriented environment like government.

The fundamental fact about government management is that it is different from private-sector management in some very basic ways. Decentralized management works in the private sector only because there is a bottom line, a quantifiable profit-and-loss, under which top management can evaluate progress. The underlying problem in government administration is that there is no equivalent, universally recognized measure of performance. Budgets and accounting statements, for example, cannot be relied on as indicators of success by managers of an agency. In fact, they at times give counterindications and can mislead management. A government budget basically shows how much was spent last year and therefore how much more is "needed" this year because the problem remains unsolved. In other words, budgets are just the instrument by which the permanent bureaucracies in Congress and in the executive branch justify increased funding, no matter how ineffectively the funds may be spent. The only way to redirect the bureaucracy and its self-serving accounting is to build a loyal team which will establish more suitable evaluation systems and criteria to assess progress within the agency, using standards approved by the agency head.

Two noteworthy examples of effective management are ACTION during President Reagan's first term and the Urban Mass Transit Administration (UMTA) during his second. In the former case, Tom Pauken became director of an agency which had been the plaything of the extreme left wing of the Democratic Party. Funds had been distributed with abandon to fringe political action groups, and no attempt had been made to assure that expenditures met either program or legal requirements. By the end of Pauken's first year, he and his team had established and implemented strict criteria, and ACTION's programs had been put back on track.

UMTA had no systems in place when the Reagan Administration took office to require accountability by its grantees. While progress was made during the first term, dramatic improvements began to occur when Alfred DelliBovi became deputy administrator and ultimately administrator. Over the protests of many local transit authorities, he refused to disburse additional grants until monies previously made available to grantees were properly accounted for.

The essence of agency management is personnel management through delegation to a loyal team. A corollary to management through delegation is accountability. With the team in place, and the agenda, goals, and evaluation criteria established, people must be held accountable for progress or lack of it. This is achieved through periodic reviews and critical assessments of the environment on an issue by issue basis. The frequency of reviews will of course depend on the nature of the issue and will vary from daily monitoring to weekly assessments or monthly evaluations. The essential point is to hold individuals accountable in exchange for the authority delegated, taking corrective actions as necessary. A high level of competence should be expected from every member of the management team, and poor performance should be dealt with forthrightly.

Issue Priorities

With a team and management system in place, the agency head can move towards implementation of his agenda. Necessarily, management methods in the public sector will differ from those in the private sector. In the private sector, goals, strategy, and tactics can normally be kept in the family until the desired moment. In Washington's fishbowl, one should assume that everything will be prematurely disclosed unless special steps are taken to prevent it. Priorities should remain confidential until they are ready to be announced. Only the minimum number of people necessary should be involved, and one should not assume the issues which the internal bureaucracy says are the most critical are necessarily the ones the Administration should be pursuing. The bureaucratic perspective may be statistically valid, but the analysis frequently lacks political sensitivity or insight. The agency head must therefore personally set the major priorities and be involved in the creation of the secondary ones. Then, he needs to establish the strategy of when to go public, and periodically revisit his priorities possibly to take advantage of opportunities which may present themselves as the environment changes.

Survival

Since the agency head is the President's most valuable asset, it is important to protect that resource. The most important fact to remember is that everything is public, and much of what is public is based on rumor and gossip. A great deal of information is traded on the cocktail circuit, at the ubiquitous "Washington reception," and other informal gatherings which all feed the rumor mill. Character assassinations are rampant, and everyone plays Washington's "gotcha" game.

Political executives will find an army of sycophants and hangers-on (some with powerful friends) but, unfortunately, few trustworthy allies. Even the President will demand much and give little, for he too has a job to do and cannot afford for the "teflon" to be chipped away. This is all part of the job. Given this reality, it becomes clear why an agency head must pick loyal people to reinforce and project his own leadership.

Unfortunately, the burden on the political executive is increased by the problematic nature of the neutrality assumed to reside in the professional career service. Genuinely "neutral" instruments of government are very hard to find. Everyone is directly or indirectly affected by the government and has a point of view and an identifiable interest at stake. This is especially the case with federal agencies that are under fire for excesses or are targeted for budget cuts. But it also applies to supposedly neutral or nonpolitical institutions—including the General Accounting Office, the Congressional Budget Office, the FBI, CIA, and even that paragon of professionalism and neutral competence, the career staff at OMB.

Nominally it is OMB's job to help the President (and his surrogates—the agency heads) cut or control agency budgets. Through the budget process OMB has tremendous impact on agency programs and thereby an agency head's policy agenda. OMB can be an ally on some budget battles with Congress and with a sometimes recalcitrant agency bureaucracy. But OMB is also the agency which will review and "clear" the agency's regulations and all congressional testimony and proposed legislation—"in the name of the President." There will be times when its views will reflect not the Administration's position but its own historical prejudices and past experiences. After all, OMB is a bureaucratic institution itself, with institutional memory, and its employees may have scores to settle with an agency. The agency head may therefore find himself caught up in a conflict between governmental institutions each protecting its authority or "turf."

Since OMB is administratively a part of the Executive Office of the President, disagreeing with it can easily lead to being accused of opposing "the President's position." It takes political astuteness and strength of character to identify the key policy elements involved in the issue and challenge OMB. The agency head must be able to defend his position in terms of the President's policies—which means knowing the President's position better than the OMB staff. When an agency head experiences a serious policy disagreement with OMB, he should take the issue first to the OMB director, then to the President's chief of staff, and as a last resort to the President himself.

CONCLUSION

In the final analysis the measures of success in Washington are as varied as the number of power centers and interest groups. Congress, the media, the bureaucracy, the special interests, even the White House each has its own standards and expectations. There is no safe haven for the agency head in such an environment and the only fallback is personal integrity and strength of character. It is imperative therefore that the President select people with these attributes, not only for policy reasons, but for the sake of those he asks to make the tremendous sacrifices that come with public service.

31

Congressional Relations and Public Affairs

by
Robert E. Moffit and Richard Teske*

CONGRESSIONAL RELATIONS

The basis of the sometimes strange and baffling business of "congressional relations" is constitutional. It is an essential element of the unique legal tension of the separated powers established by the Philadelphia Convention of 1787. The business of congressional relations is not "public affairs," nor is it ingratiating oneself with members of Congress with the idea of emerging victorious among executive branch colleagues in a Capitol Hill popularity contest. In a political sense, the business of congressional relations is developing and maintaining working relations with members of Congress and key congressional staff for the furtherance of the Administration's—and *only* the Administration's—legislative agenda.

The Institutional Setting

The structure and powers of Congress were among the chief preoccupations of the framers of the Constitution. The Congress was understood to be the "first branch" in a tripartite system of government, ordained really as the first among equals, the equals being the executive and the judiciary.

The founders, and James Madison of Virginia in particular, generally saw the politics of a free society as an open competition of interests,

*The authors wish to thank Bruce Navarro, Miss Eugenie Bauman and Dr. Harold Griffin for their valuable advice and comments. The views expressed in this paper are, however, entirely the responsibility of the authors.

interests that Madison defined as "factions." When Madison spoke of "factions," he referred to groups or associations motivated largely by the economic interests of their members. In Madison's description of democratic politics, it is not the idealized, well-intentioned and well-informed citizen that decisively influences the course of legislation. Rather, it is individuals in groups, well organized and primed for concerted action, who pressure the national legislature to attain those ends most materially beneficial to them. Madison himself did not idolize the process of interest group struggle. He says only that if one labors to establish and maintain a republican or "free" government, one necessarily accepts the free play of men grouped together pursuing their interests as an ineluctable element of political life.

"Factions" or "special interests" are good and serve a benign purpose if they are "controlled"; and the very purpose of the federal Constitution, as outlined in *The Federalist Papers*, is to control them. In both its classical conception among the Federalists and in its modern operations, the Congress is indeed the crucible of interest group politics.

The contrast with the executive is striking. In the executive branch, fewer than 3,000 out of a universe of over two million federal civilian employees (about two-tenths of one percent) are "political" appointees. In contrast, *every* employee in *every* congressional office is a "political" appointee. Unlike policy development in the executive branch with its broad layers of administration and specialization, its virtual army of career policy specialists and budget analysts, and its elaborate and sometimes agonizingly slow "clearance" process, decision-making in a congressional office (or in the staff office of a congressional committee) can be comparatively quick and decisive. Congressional policy is usually flexible in execution, and often a sound barometric reading of the ever-changing intensity of a variety of competing political pressures. Overwhelming crosspressures, however, often delay the legislative process or, in some instances, bring it to a grinding halt.

This is the unforgiving political climate that awaits the new Administration. In fulfilling his political trust, it is the President himself who sets the tone, as well as the political agenda of his Administration.

A forceful presidential personality is important in setting the tone, but it is not enough, especially in dealing with the Congress or the interest groups that energize it. A President's success will depend to a large degree on the steadfast loyalty and cooperation of his senior appointees, the Cabinet secretaries and the agency heads who run his

Administration. In terms of management, he must rely on a complex set of communications offices centered in the White House Office of Legislative Affairs and complemented through the daily operations of various legislative and congressional relations offices in every department and agency of the federal government.

The Agency Setting

The role of the agency's legislative relations officer is often misunderstood. Contrary to conventional wisdom, the legislative affairs officer does not always enjoy a "glamorous" job. It is most often a labor intensive business of making endless rounds of telephone calls; gathering and analyzing pieces of disjointed information; rushing to prepare appropriate briefing papers; rewriting material phrased in the unintelligible jargon of the bureaucracy so that Hill people can understand it; checking and rechecking vote counts; briefing friendly and hostile congressional staff; sitting for hours across a mahogany negotiating table from intense partisan opponents, while keeping congressional allies well informed of the progress of the talks; tracking down late correspondence to and from the Hill; finding a constituent's missing check, contract, or grant award; clearing up inevitable mistakes or misunderstandings, "taking the heat" by apologizing for them on behalf of the agency.

For an agency head, a key management decision is the organization and staffing of the agency's legislative affairs office. Most importantly, the Assistant Secretary for Legislation should not be burdened by "going through" any other agency official. For managerial reasons, such a direct reporting relationship is most desirable because it affords the agency head direct, functional control over the legislative operations of the agency, something that is intrinsically desirable. But more importantly it facilitates an agency head's political responsibilities to the President. The agency's legislative chief cannot afford the luxury of a bureaucratic "clearance" process, or a round of extended "second guessing" among other senior officials. Congressional schedules are not fashioned with any regard to the convenience of senior officials in the executive branch. To the extent that a legislative officer has to play "catch up," he is isolated from the legislative playing field and his influence on the outcome is proportionately diminished. The legislative officer speaks for the agency head directly to Congress or its senior staff; he must be seen as speaking for the agency head and no one else. The credibility of an agency head rests with the perception in Congress that he does indeed speak for his President; likewise the

credibility of the congressional relations officer rests on the critical
fact that he does indeed speak for the agency head and that his
communications are thus genuine statements of Administration policy.

Aside from direct access to the agency head, it is well to assure that
all of the agency's legislative relations are centralized in the agency's
legislative affairs office. From a management standpoint, this could
prove to be the agency head's most difficult task. In any case, it is
always an unfinished task. Both career and noncareer program staff
could harbor their own agenda, and being plugged into the Hill is
tantamount to tapping into an independent power source. Congressional staff also find it convenient to have direct access to a program
office—it gives them a direct pipeline into the bowels of the agency.
So, the new agency head should be aware that there is an informal
complex of preexisting "congressional relations," based on long-time
professional acquaintance or personal friendship, in every agency, well
outside of formal channels. This is especially true in a large department, where resistance to such a centralization among career or noncareer policy staff can be expected. Such resistance is invariably based
upon the technical expertise and program of the career staff. But all
such arrangements are tantamount to having the proverbial tail wag
the dog.

The preeminent need for centralized control over the legislative
operations of an agency is political. Any institutional decentralization of legislative affairs inevitably results in "mixed" or contradictory
signals. This may have nothing to do with "career subversion" of the
agenda; it may have everything to do with institutional tradition or
procedural efficiency. What a program office might, for historical
reasons, consider good public policy may directly contradict the Administration's electoral mandate.

The need for centralization is not confined to the agency. It is also
in the interest of the White House that an agency's legislative program
be centralized, coherent, and well coordinated. The White House and
OMB need a department or an agency speaking unequivocally to
Congress with only one voice.

After establishing clear lines of authority and clarifying managerial
responsibilities, nothing is more important than staffing the Legislative
Office itself. The job of a legislative affairs officer is not the job of a
public affairs expert or a generalist blessed with an abstract or academic knowledge of the thing called the "legislative process." It is the
job best suited to one who knows and understands the workings of
Capitol Hill, who is sensitive to its formalities and respectful of its

political culture. It is the vocation of one who understands, most of all, that the Hill is an utterly hectic and thoroughly political environment.

Much of this might seem obvious, except that it is so often disregarded in the actual practice of governing. Political intelligence is often shabby. Political sensitivities are often cavalierly dismissed. Political realities are often overlooked. The consequences are not only failure in achieving legislative objectives or preventing legislative disasters, but also painful and avoidable embarrassments to the Administration.

Problems of political insensitivity frequently manifest themselves in the area of legislative strategy. To the extent that legislative strategy is elemental to the broader political strategy of the Administration, it is one of a number of functions that should be the exclusive preserve of political appointees. The agency strategy group should be small and include the agency head, his public affairs officer, the relevant program officer, and his legislative officer; when necessary, it can be expanded to include the appropriate political authorities at OMB, the White House Office of Policy Development, or the White House legislative office. In effect, the strategic planning should be the province of those who are daily engaged in the hurly-burly of the legislative process, who have to appear before congressional committees on behalf of the President. It is not, in other words, a task best suited to those who prefer to operate at "very high altitudes," or who crave anonymity or wish to forgo personal accountability.

Understanding the Players

In formulating strategy, assessing options, and pressing the agenda, sound political intelligence is always the cornerstone of legislative success. Right at the start of the session, the agency's legislative office should conduct a survey of relevant congressional interests and concerns. Political imagination is no substitute for sound political intelligence. It is always a mistake at the outset to assume what the Congress will or will not find acceptable; such impressionistic "wisdom" from "old hands" around the department is something that a Secretary or an agency head can do without very nicely. This is especially true if the agency head has every intention of pressing a bold or ambitious legislative agenda. But there is absolutely no excuse for pressing a bold agenda, or for that matter a timid one, in darkest ignorance.

On a personal level, the agency head should become well educated on the members of Congress who are professionally occupied or fascinated with his agency. Likewise, the legislative officer's effectiveness is enhanced the more he deals directly with members of the House or the Senate, though his normal business will be conducted with senior staff, especially the professional staff of congressional committees. It is not enough that the agency head and his legislative officer know the most important members; it is more important that the members know *them*. Positive and regular contact is the only way to build a working relationship; strong congressional relations are cumulative.

The personal background of members, their bases of support (e.g., organized labor, small business, farming or manufacturing interests), their ideological inclinations, voting records, areas of expertise, and current interests are all vital elements in gathering legislative intelligence. The most important function of such intelligence gathering, however, is that it enables the agency head to enlist the right "champion" for the agency's legislative agenda, a "horse to ride" in the vernacular of the Hill. Ideally, the legislative affairs team should be able to identify a member whose personal interest and commitment on an issue of importance to the Administration are well matched by professional background, knowledge, and strategic position on a committee or subcommittee having jurisdiction over the agency's issue. If, in the rare instance, both the senior Republican and the senior Democrat share the same enthusiasm for the issue, the Administration's position is enviable. If that kind of relationship can be replicated in the Senate, the Administration has reached a celestial plane "beyond the dreams of avarice." But such a confluence of personal, political, and jurisdictional interests and enthusiasm is extraordinarily rare. As a practical matter, it does not exist. As a practical matter, the agency's legislative staff must diligently "work" the Hill.

The Legislative Process

With its bicameral structure and organizational lacework of committees and subcommittees, the legislative process is indeed an obstacle course. That is precisely what the Framers of the Constitution intended: a system to force deliberation on public law. But the process is devised to open up new avenues of legislative opportunity, as well as to set up roadblocks to legislative success. If the Administration, through its energetic congressional champion, fails in a subcommittee, he can always try to get the measure of the amendment enacted in full committee. If he should fail in full committee, he can try to secure a rule making his amendment in order on the floor of the House. If he fails on the floor of the House, the Administration has the option of pursuing the same process in the Senate. But in the Senate, he has an even greater advantage, for the rules of the Senate are not nearly as restrictive, particularly on germaneness, and the opportunities for amendment are richer. If the Administration should have the good fortune (as the Reagan Administration did for six years) to enjoy partisan control of the Senate, and thus the Senate agenda and schedule, then the opportunities for controlling the legislative outcome are greatly expanded. It enables the Administration to press for even bolder initiatives in the House, knowing that inevitable rejection will force an acceptable compromise in the Senate.

The Administration's legislative team enjoys the luxury of practicing the craft of influencing Congress through more than one legislative process; for, in Congress, there are legislative processes within legislative processes. Committees that change federal law and reorganize priorities within the executive branch are the authorizing committees; but then there are committees that provide the funding for government operations, the powerful appropriations committees of the House and Senate. While it is absolutely necessary to work the authorizing committees early and often, it is always advisable to maintain regular communications with friends and allies on the appropriations committees and subcommittees. While the rules of the House and Senate generally prohibit authorizing legislation in appropriations bills, the appropriations process can be used to change existing policies or programs simply by denying funds for certain purposes through spending restrictions, most commonly called "appropriations riders."

Beyond the appropriations process, there is the much maligned budget process. The Annual Budget Resolution, passed by the budget committees and both chambers of Congress, sets annual spending targets for the federal government. If the Administration's legislative agenda is stymied in the authorizing or the appropriations committees, there is always the option of "reconciliation" in the budget process. While reconciliation only permits "cuts," it does allow changes in law. It is in the yearly budget reconciliation legislation, reconciling spending allocations with program operations, that real and far-reaching changes in federal law are effectuated. The budget process was the engine for the revolutionary Reagan cuts in domestic spending in the summer of 1981.

With a sound knowledge of the political terrain, the legislative affairs staff should be in a strong position to present the Administration's case. The first formal opportunity to do this, of course, is through testimony of the agency head at congressional hearings.

Hearings—Capitalizing on Opportunity

Hearings are a forum, sometimes an enjoyable spectacle, and almost always an opportunity. The legislative affairs team should, in consultation with the agency head, determine what it is that it wants to accomplish at a hearing. It may very well be that little or nothing positive can be accomplished at the hearing, given either the format, or the topic of the inquiry, or the way in which the issues are being framed. In such a situation, the optimal result is for the agency head or his representative to bé able to get through it in one piece, dignity and reputation intact. But there are other times when the hearing presents an excellent opportunity for the Administration to make its case.

Solid preparation for a congressional hearing requires an immense amount of "leg work." The legislative staff should exercise diligent oversight over the preparation of testimony, gather intelligence on the interests and likely questions of the members of the committee, determining the specific political interests that will surface in the hearing, and enlisting friendly members of the committee to emphasize certain issues or ask questions that can serve to dramatize the points being made by the Administration witness.

Preparation of testimony is usually time-consuming, because of the level of clearances and corrections that it must pass before being transmitted to the Hill. The most effective testimony is generated top-down, rather than bottom-up. When an invitation to testify before Congress arrives on the agency head's desk, it is advisable for the agency head to meet immediately with his legislative and public affairs officers and the appropriate program officers. They should then decide the approach they want to take, what they would like to accomplish, and what issues they want highlighted. The testimony, in other words, should be given its political direction up front, and the first draft should be crafted quickly.

The legislative office should also have *final* clearance over testimony. Program offices and the General Counsel's Office will often have a heavy role in fashioning the final product. But neither the General Counsel's Office nor the program office will have to follow through on the Hill on the basis of that final product.

During the preparation of testimony, the legislative office is usually engaged in developing quality intelligence on what the committee members are likely to ask: what issues trouble them, or what agency actions are likely to win plaudits. As a matter of course, good groundwork should be laid with a friendly staff director, as well as the "personal" staff of "friendly" members, to discern likely reactions or how Administration allies can be helpful. More challenging is working with the senior congressional staff of the Administration's opponents. But opposition senior staff on congressional committees are often surprisingly frank about their interests and expectations and those of their superiors. This is especially the case if the issues are fairly "cut and dried," and the arguments are painfully obvious. They are likely to be reticent only when the committee leadership has a political agenda clearly incompatible with a strong performance by the Administration's witness at the hearing.

STRATEGIC PRINCIPLES

Basic Principles—When to Compromise

Writing of parliamentary politics in Britain, the great English writer G.K. Chesterton remarked: "Compromise used to mean that half a loaf was better than no bread. Among modern statesmen it really seems to mean that a half a loaf is better than a whole loaf."

One does not enter into negotiations with the congressional opposition on any principle other than the desirability of the whole loaf. After the first round of subcommittee hearings, in the initial stages of the legislative process, the agency head can actually lose very little by presenting an ambitious program.

Ironically enough, it is in the very early stages of the process, when a gratuitous concession or two might be offered "to move the process along," that he is in danger of losing the substance of the Administration's agenda. The temptation is to resort to "preemptive compromise." Indulgence of the temptation often takes the form of a "bipartisan compromise" before the legislative battle is even joined; often the "compromise" negates the efforts or the commitments that a stalwart congressional champion may have made at the outset, either in subcommittee or full committee. The temptation is often born of a passion for popularity, a passion usually counterproductive personally as well as politically. The agency head will temporarily thrill to the warm glow of congressional approval; an approval shortly followed by polite requests for further weakening of the Administration's resolve. And, during the course of this unhappy political commerce, the initiative will invariably shift from the Administration to Capitol Hill. The more responsive the agency head becomes to new demands from the congressional opposition, the less effective the agency head becomes as a spokesman for the Administration, ensuring that any respect he or she might have earned among members of Congress as a politician of conviction or intellectual integrity is permanently lost.

Legislative politics, like all politics, is an art. There are indeed times when it is an excellent idea to compromise early and often. There are times when the congressional sentiment, on both sides of the aisle, is running overwhelmingly against the Administration position, when a "bad bill" is, according to the best available vote counts, inevitable— and by wide, veto-proof margins in both houses of Congress. Or times when Administration intransigence on a "bad bill" is sapping congressional "good will" on a "good bill," a top agenda item that is politically feasible and that the Administration really wants or needs. Making a bad bill "better" may be a distasteful task, but, the alternative is worse.

The delicate enterprise of congressional negotiation is most successful when the agency head and his legislative staff are clear, from the outset, about their own policy objectives and reasonably knowledgeable of those of the congressional opposition.

If the objectives of Congress and the Administration are indeed compatible, that compatibility will surface through the process of talking out differences. This can be a tedious task; it is often one of finding the common ground that is buried under a clutter of side issues that rank low on a scale of relative importance, and may only be peripheral to the genuine policy interests of the Administration.

Occasionally, the objectives of Congress and the Administration are simply incompatible. The respective philosophical positions may be mutually exclusive. In that case, the course of action is simple; it is a matter of counting votes, educating actual or potential allies to the inherent virtue of the Administration's position with clear and concise talking points, statistics, or briefing materials, and allowing the democratic process to work its will on the floor of the House and Senate. Head counts may, in such instances, indicate that the votes are simply not there, that the Administration cannot win. Then the question becomes a fundamental political question: Is a legislative loss tantamount to a political loss? The House or Senate vote may be a tough vote for the White House or the agency head in particular, but simply because it is a tough vote for the White House does not mean that it is an easy vote for the congressional opposition. Losing a vote on the floor of Congress may dramatize the issue for the President; winning a vote on the House or Senate floor could conceivably be costly to the President's opponents.

Remember Your Friends

Before a final decision is made to pursue a strategy that incurs political risk to the President, the agency head should not only consult with the White House, but also the congressional champions of the Administration. If the agency head is on the verge of "cutting a deal" in the Senate, the agency head should not finalize it without consultation with allies in the House. If the agency head has asked House Republicans to "hang tough" or go through with a losing vote on the House floor for the sake of principle, he should not cut the ground out from under them by making concessions to Senate opponents on the very issues they battled for on the House floor.

In any case, win or lose, allies should be rewarded in some fashion, at the very least with letters of appreciation from the President or the agency head. Such letters should highlight the basic issues and clearly articulate the wisdom of supporting the Administration's position. These communications are politically useful to members of Congress and their staffs in responding to press or constituent inquiries on the agenda item. The critical point is that congressional relations are cumulative; it is an ongoing process of building on past support, reinforcing and reaching out to new congressional allies, and laying the groundwork for future cooperation.

Seizing the Initiative

We have discussed the business of congressional relations in terms of the personality of the President, the forcefulness and loyalty of his appointees, the managerial responsibilities of the Office of Legislative Affairs, and the articulation of a consistent theme or themes in the Administration's legislative agenda. But legislative success depends primarily upon how these various elements are combined and used.

The first principle of legislative success is to seize and hold the initiative. In practical terms that means that the Administration must define the legislative agenda, not Congress. It is the agency that is to define the issues. It is the agency that is to set the terms of the debate. Beyond the passage or defeat of any particular legislative measure, if the Congress is responding to the Administration in terms that are basically set by the Administration, the Administration has already achieved a large measure of political success. In practice, the core agenda is the Administration's and the negotiation and debate centers on how to best achieve the agenda. During the Reagan Administration, perhaps the single best example of seizing and holding the legislative agenda has been in the arena of national economic policy. After the President's inauguration, his key political and legislative advisers decided to concentrate their efforts on revitalizing the economy through a dramatic set of tax and spending cuts. In the summer of 1981, after appealing to the nation directly, the President and his White House team stunned official Washington in a series of close votes on the floor of the House of Representatives in an historical reversal of national policy.

Likewise, at Reagan's Office of Personnel Management, civil service reform took on a new meaning. The Reagan Administration seized the policy initiative; the House Committee on Post Office and Civil Service had to respond to a steady stream of legislative initiatives, regulations, proposals and guidelines from OPM. The major thrust of the OPM effort was to make the civil service more comparable to the private sector. With a few exceptions, all of the changes promoted by OPM were bitterly opposed by federal employee interest groups, particularly employee unions. In virtually every case, however, Congress found itself responding to the Administration, negotiating down from the politically high "mark-up" price set by Reagan's OPM.

Mobilizing Support

Controlling the agenda and framing the debate are necessary, but not sufficient, for legislative success. A second element of any sound strategy is to mobilize congressional allies, supplying them with useful and effective information.

The issue papers must be clear, succinct, and timely in their delivery. It is an insult to a member of Congress to ask him or her to do battle on behalf of the agency on a moment's notice, without sufficient preparation or ample opportunity to assimilate useful information. It is too often done. Unfortunately, members of Congress who would like to assist the President and his officers are sometimes unable to do so, because position papers are not "cleared" in an agency, or interagency conflicts among officials who have no "feel" for the Hill prevent a timely resolution of the position to be taken for committee action or floor debate. Such delays only serve to benefit the congressional opposition.

While winning by handsome margins or negotiating a successful compromise marks the public record of an agency head, in truth, some of his greatest legislative successes may be the bills that never pass. Controlling the agenda, mobilizing the Administration's bases of congressional support and committing resources early and often will enhance the legislative success of the new Administration.

— ◇ —

PUBLIC AFFAIRS
AND THE INTEREST GROUPS

With anxiety and a touch of fear the new agency public affairs officer approached the department's Assistant Secretary for Public Affairs. The *New York Times* had run this day—his first day—a devastating article on a new Administration policy, based on a leak. He thought he was being summoned for an explanation.

"How dare you talk to the press about this policy."

"But I didn't leak the regulation, this is my first day."

"That doesn't matter, what matters is that you talked to the *Times*."

"But only after the article appeared. As the agency's spokesperson, I thought this was my job."

"You discussed one of the Secretary's prime initiatives. That's the job of this office."

"But I didn't know that was a secretarial initiative . . . "

"That's not the issue."

" . . . And they said you refused to return calls . . . "

"No matter. That's my decision. All you need to know is that you've committed a huge mistake."

Realizing that reason was received as argument, and that his job was in the balance, he not so courageously changed tactics.

"Okay, whatever you say. I swear that I will never again talk on a secretarial initiative. I've got pen and paper. You just tell me what those initiatives are, and I promise from the bottom of my heart, never to talk to the press again."

Finally the assistant secretary responded coldly:

"You aren't high enough in the organization to be told what those initiatives are."

This "Catch 22" story sadly can be retold with minor variation by a great number of political appointees. It illustrates almost every conceivable mistake that can be made handling public affairs. Here are a few simple maxims to follow:

1) Every appointee, every civil servant, every member of the media should know what the crucial policy goals and initiatives are.

2) Leaks happen. Fixing blame is less important in the short run than fixing the problem generated by an inaccurate story.

3) If you ever wish to succeed, you should realize the other appointees are the closest things to allies you have.

4) Clear lines of organization are a must—you can delegate authority, not responsibility.

5) Not to return media calls implies that a story is true. If you wish to limit the spread of untrue allegations, you can't retreat into a shell of silence.

These points may strike some readers as self-evident. They aren't. They are ignored or violated every day somewhere in town. One reason may be because the public affairs position is sometimes filled with a "must hire" or "deadwood." There is a misconception that "anyone can do public affairs." This is possibly derivative of its role in the private sector, where public affairs is a staff office and an expense rather than a line operation and producer of income. In public life, however, it should be obvious that public affairs is crucial. A truth of politics: He who can't communicate well will rarely shape public policy.

The public has an insatiable appetite for "inside information" and the media has an institutional interest in satisfying that appetite. The public wants policy to be made in public and policy processes to be amenable to public scrutiny. Anyone who believes government decision-making can be kept out of the media spotlight probably doesn't belong in a public affairs position.

There are a few items that must remain private. Almost unique in the world, the federal government has defined them by law. Since 1974 the Freedom of Information Act defines only nine areas that can remain private. *Everything else is public.* The agency's public affairs officer should acquaint himself immediately with these nine exceptions and continually remind his fellow political appointees of this so-called "Information Bill of Rights."

Defining the Agenda

It has become almost a cliche: In 1980 Ronald Reagan ran on a strong platform and the first term was a huge success. In 1984, he ran an issueless campaign, and because there was no mandate, the measure of success of the second term was cast in doubt. The same lesson applies to every appointee: without an agenda for change, there will be no change. How a political executive forms and presents this agenda is equally important.

The chief challenge is how to have a specific and meaningful agenda without abdicating the control to outside pressure groups. It starts at the top. If the boss has no idea where he wants to go, his appointees will remain adrift.

When appointed to HHS in 1986, Secretary Otis Bowen identified 28 separate areas he would like to see changed. Those 28 ideas were eventually refined and concentrated into a few specific initiatives. After weeks of negotiation, the Public Affairs office published "the Bowen Agenda." There were four major initiatives, in no special order: AIDS, the Crusade against Drugs, Protecting the Family, and Promoting Quality Health Care. Two special initiatives were reserved for the Secretary's office: Catastrophic Health Care and Medical Malpractice Reform.

Each of these initiatives was broken into subinitiatives and each subinitiative was assigned to a specific member of the Department's senior staff. This "lead" person had authority over all aspects of the issue: timetable, public affairs plan, speeches, personnel, etc.

In this way, each political executive knew what was deemed important. Every person knew who had the authority to lead on each initiative. Every person knew that the ultimate responsibility remained with the Secretary. It was thus possible to measure success. It wasn't the number of speeches, articles, or press releases that mattered—it was the attainment of these specific objectives. It became the tool by which the Department's Policy and Management Councils measured success.

The "special interests" would help in the formation of details, but the overall plan, the political agenda, was set. Budget numbers, full-time equivalent employees, Department resources, and scheduling all flowed from this document. It was a strategic plan in the best sense.

The Interest Groups and Their Goals

Once a strategic plan is established, the agency head must educate his appointees on how to handle the press and special interest groups.

Again, albeit common sense, he needs to remind them of a few basic things:

1) Special interests and the press are not your "friends," nor are they your enemies. They have their jobs and you have yours; the goals are different, so the jobs are different.

2) It's best always to expect that anything you say (including comments at cocktail receptions) will or could be on the front page of the *New York Times*.

3) Like the Legislative Affairs director, the Public Affairs chief is not a "fireman" who puts out controversies. His office is a strategic communications center that must be part of every policy initiative.

When should the agency listen to the special interests? The best guide is to examine how they register their concerns. If they do it in such a way as to be confrontational, they probably do not want or expect change. If they register their concerns constructively, they do expect change and should be receptive to Administration overtures. Establishing an atmosphere of mutual respect through "open communications" can, in fact, serve the agency head's interests, so long as the policy objective is not compromised in the quest for "friendly relations."

In a democracy, ideas come from the people. They do not reside in the exclusive province of certain federal government offices in Washington. Thus, special interests should be viewed more as specialized sources of information.

A prime responsibility for the public affairs executive is to assure that agency officials are exposed to valid and balanced representative opinions of the special interests—*before* the final decision is made. These predecision meetings with outside interests are critical. First, you just might get a good idea. Second, if access is denied, the interest groups' very raison d'être is being challenged. They will undoubtedly call upon their congressional allies and force the agency to open the process. Usually, the agency will pay dearly through concessions in the legislative arena afterwards. Third, by participating in the process the special interests acquire "ownership" of some part of the initiative. This can mean turning an enemy into an ally or possibly blunting or neutralizing the opposition.

Whom should you invite to the meetings? Everybody. Let the "players" define themselves. After a few meetings, those who don't belong won't waste their time coming. Don't waste valuable political capital trying to control who attends.

The agency doesn't have to let outside groups have the actual policy papers. The agency head should share with them his policy goals and let them voice their ideas. Give them photo opportunities; speak at their meetings; don't fear input or access. The power to make the ultimate decision still lies with the agency.

The Mechanics of the System

The Public Affairs office has some basic institutional functions. To a greater or lesser extent, each public affairs office must have provisions for handling the following:

1) News Room—Taking press calls, writing press releases, organizing press conferences, scheduling press briefings, the press secretary role.

2) Freedom of Information—Experienced appointees know that this function provides crucial leverage in public policy debates.

3) Production—Public service announcements, publications, clearinghouses, studios, radio and television programs, artwork, layout, photography, etc.

4) Speech and Editorial—All speeches, articles, testimony, slide shows, tapings, radio and television scripts, etc.

5) Scheduling and Speakers Bureau—Coordinating all initiatives, timing and activities.

6) Public Liaison—Maintaining regular and ongoing contact.

7) Briefings—For internal staff and information flow.

All of these functions may be handled by a few people or by hundreds. What is emphasized and how resources are apportioned is determined by the policy agenda and the strengths of employees.

Established organizational procedures, press releases, speeches, publications, etc., must be totally integrated throughout the department. Someone can't accept an interview with a Sunday talk show without approval and coordination with higher levels. Most agencies have established practices for clearances. These usually have been (or should be) compiled in some form of Public Affairs handbook available to all employees.

Challenges

Many obstacles have been outlined in this discussion. The major one is simple: for the public affairs officer to be taken seriously as a player—not as a public relations flak. He must bring forth the "outside" opinions to the inner counsels. He must articulate inner decisions to the outside. He must do this while retaining the trust of others and his own integrity—no small task.

Then there is the White House. One must remember that the White House Public Affairs office, like the White House congressional relations office, provides an alternative route of information for the agencies. This can be viewed either as a threat or a bonus for the agency head. It is up to the Public Affairs executive to convince the agency head that it is the latter not the former.

One professional challenge deserves special attention: relations with the press. The press does not expect the public affairs officer to know minute policy or program details. Nor do they expect the officer to leak. They realize that because of the very nature of his job, he can't be known as a leaker.

It's up to the public affairs officer to establish the ground rules. If the interview is on the record, or off the record, or on deep background, this *must* be established at the beginning of the phone call, meeting or press conference. Once something is said, it can not be expected for the reporter to ignore it. Again it sounds simple, yet it is the safest way: If you don't want it said, don't say it.

The press does expect the officer to be knowledgeable about policy decisions. He must understand the "who, what, when, where, why and how" that journalists are trained to seek. His role is to articulate the public policy decisions of the Administration and provide the rationale for these decisions. It is not his role to provide "the other side," nor to provide misleading information, nor to admit—even off the record—that the Administration's policy is folly. If he does, at heart he is disagreeing with policy and should consider resigning.

It is correct, at times even wise, to refer the press to people who may oppose your initiatives. The wisdom lies in helping identify your "loyal opposition" rather than having the press wrongly discover a fringe movement. The chief danger is an opposition that remains hidden in damp and dark territory reserved for half-truths, rumors, and prejudice obscured from the general public's view.

Strategy and Tactics: A Case Study

Putting all these lessons together, let's examine a case study: the adoption of Medicare Prospective Payment in 1983. Coupled with Social Security reform, it was arguably the largest domestic policy reform in the first term of the Reagan Administration.

Upon the election of President Reagan, the Department of Health and Human Services undertook as its central policy the construction of a health care system based on a competitive rather than a federal regulatory model. Everyone agreed that the top-down federally planned and regulated health system wasn't working: costs were rising 20 percent per year for a decade and a half. The new Reagan team at HHS believed that the introduction of market place incentives and competition would be the answer.

In 1981, public affairs officers were asked to draft a speech defining "competition" for the new Health Care Financing Administrator. After much frustration, they concluded that there was no agreement as to the specific meaning of "competition." Rarely, but sometimes, the very process of writing a speech drives the policy process. This was such a time.

Competition was defined broadly as three major policy goals:

1) Reform of the Financing Mechanism (targeted at controlling *government* health costs).

2) Development of Alternative Delivery Systems (targeted at *providers*).

3) Emphasis on Information and Choice (targeted at *consumers*).

These three points emphasized that three groups of people—government, providers, and consumers—each had a stake in reform. It also emphasized for each their role: government to control costs, providers to be innovative, consumers to become informed and have a stake in their choices. For two years, in every speech, these three points were emphasized.

From December of 1982, when Secretary Schweiker approved the proposals, to March 1983, at time of adoption by Congress, over 1,000 groups, state offices, organizations, and companies were briefed in ten different cities. This scale of outreach was unprecedented.

Prospective Payment for Medicare hospitals was passed as a "logical rider" to the Social Security Reform Act of 1983. The Administration stressed "market place reforms," "incentives for cost-effective behavior," and "competition." In five years, the reforms have controlled costs, not diminished quality or access, and have been as much a success as anyone could have hoped.

The lessons for all:

—Define the issues early and simply.
—Make sure everyone has a "piece" of the policy.

—Move quickly when opportunity arises.

—Brief everyone and make sure that throughout, the message remains consistent in substance and in harmony with the Administration's overall philosophy.

––––––––––––––––––––––◇––––––––––––––––––––––

CONCLUSION

There is no cook book of guaranteed recipes for effective congressional relations or public affairs. We have examined the practice of these skills by a master communicator. He is clear. He is honest. He is persuasive. The strength and sincerity with which he presents his case is a model for legislative and public affairs. If the officers of the new Administration continue in this tradition, then they will be successful. And both the authors and readers will have Ronald Reagan to thank for the lesson.

32

Personnel Management

by
George Nesterczuk*

In order to lead effectively, the new appointee must not only learn the rules which regulate his environment, he must also understand them in sufficient detail to gain control of the decision-making process. The necessity to deal with detail is what most distinguishes government management from private-sector management. Clearly, there are limits to an individual's span of control and to the amount of detail which he can absorb. Beyond these limits, the executive must rely on performance management systems, which allow him to hold his organization accountable for meeting stated goals, objectives, and priorities. Individual accountability for meeting performance standards at every level of the organization is the key to controlling successively lower levels of the bureaucracy.

It is beyond the scope of this chapter to make the incoming executive fluent or expert in the vagaries of the Civil Service personnel system. Instead the focus will be on those portions of the personnel process most essential to managerial effectiveness. Some of the technical terminology relevant to the federal personnel system is also introduced. Knowledge of the terminology may help the new executive communicate more effectively with the personnel specialists in the organization. Asking the right question is half the battle to getting the right answer; the quality of the answer, however, will depend on the care and attention devoted to the selection of the management team.

*The author wishes to thank the following contributors for their helpful suggestions in the preparation of this chapter: Becky Norton Dunlop, Scott Gordon, Charles Grizzle, Timothy Hunter, Pat Pizzella, Mary Rose, John Schrote, and Jeanne Sclater. The views expressed here are, however, entirely the responsibility of the author.

ESTABLISHING A PERSONNEL AGENDA

There is a natural tendency for all political executives to focus exclusively on policy issues, frequently relegating the attendant resource questions to secondary status. The budget process serves as a rude reminder that policy decisions are inseparable from resource questions, and these in turn have a direct impact on the executive's organization and its ability to implement those policies. It is one of the challenges for political managers to lead and motivate their career staffs, in particular the senior executive corps, to implement program changes which may be perceived as running counter to their professional career interests. Happily there are career executives that are up to the challenge, and it is incumbent on the political executive to find them and assign them an appropriate role on the management team.

Small government serves the taxpayer not only in reduced intrusion but also in better service through increased efficiency and lowered expenditures. Some of these benefits are quantifiable and can be readily monitored to gauge progress. In the personnel area, for example, data are available on full-time permanent positions (FTP), staff year utilization (FTE-Full Time Equivalent), employee turnover (accessions and separations), average grade and number of employees by grade, supervisor to employee ratios, and payroll cost.

Reducing the size of government immediately conjures up the dreaded specter of RIFs (Reductions in Force), but this need not be. Turnover in the federal government is lower than it is in the private sector, but it does take place. Separations run at about 10 percent, which equates to approximately 180,000 positions per year. Every year over 120,000 people are added to the payroll as new hires. An additional 200,000 federal employees change jobs every year via reassignments, and 30,000 transfer from one agency to another. With almost 20 percent of the federal workforce involved in these changes the environment is clearly dynamic. Normal turnover alone therefore provides the executive with many opportunities to change leadership and workload to reflect new policy priorities. RIFs are usually a management option of last resort because of their cost and impact well beyond the immediate organization. When called for, RIFS are always exercised in concert with other actions including hiring freezes, expedited (early) retirement, furloughs, delayed promotions, abolition of vacant positions, etc. RIFs may be unavoidable when entire programs are abolished or in the face of significant budgetary reductions, but even then steps to reduce other spending must also be taken (reduction in travel, training, furniture and equipment purchases, cash awards, etc.).

The political executive needs to establish a workforce plan, not as an end in itself nor as an independent policy item, but as an integral part of the policy- and budget-planning cycle. If a policy change calls for reducing activity and workload in one part of an executive's organization, he should ascertain that attrition will thin out the ranks or take steps to reassign or transfer employees to higher priority areas. Otherwise he faces the prospect of being accused of "wasting" resources by not putting people to work or, even worse, having his organization fill the vacuum with new, equally undesirable activity. "Idle hands are the devil's workshop" is a maxim with real meaning in Washington's political arena.

The political executive will face many obstacles in implementing a personnel agenda, not only from his own bureaucracy, but from external agents as well. They may include other executive branch agencies and interest groups with a vested interest in the programs he administers: OMB, OPM, and of course Congress, with its insatiable appetite to micromanage the executive branch. The executive should therefore be prepared to seize every opportunity which presents itself to further his agenda.

THE PERSONNEL SYSTEM

In 1978, Congress passed the Civil Service Reform Act (CSRA) in an attempt to modernize the system and introduce some much needed management flexibilities. The most significant achievements of the CSRA were the establishment of the Senior Executive Service and the introduction of a meaningful pay-for-performance system. These innovations have allowed political managers to take charge more directly and lead the higher levels of the career bureaucracy.

Structure of the Civil Service

The Civil Service system is built around two fundamental concepts, one of classifying jobs in a hierarchical order of positions, and the other of establishing a series of appointing authorities to fill those jobs. Figure 1 is a graphic, though highly simplified, illustration of the basic structure of the Civil Service.

Figure 1.   Structure of Federal Civil Service *(Simplified)*
Total Executive Branch Employment (Excluding Postal Service):
1,990,000 Full-Time Employees

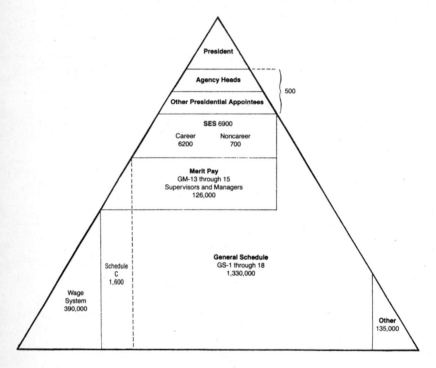

Types of Positions

Executive Schedule (EL I-V)—These positions include Cabinet secretaries, agency heads, sub-Cabinet undersecretaries and assistant secretaries, and members of boards and commissions. They are all presidential appointments subject to Senate confirmation and are usually referred to as "PAS" appointments.

Senior Executive Service (SES)—These are policy setting and program administrative positions classifiable from super-grade level GS-16 through Executive Level IV. Since its inception in 1979, allocated slots in the SES have numbered about 8,000. SES positions are of two types, general and career reserved. General positions may be filled by career or noncareer (political) appointees, or by special temporary appointments. Career reserved positions may only be filled by career executives and are defined in law as being positions necessary "to ensure impartiality, or the public's confidence of impartiality of government."

Merit Pay Managers—Senior management and supervisory positions whose incumbents are subject to a pay-for-performance system similar in nature to the SES Performance Appraisal System. Annual pay adjustments and additional performance awards for these individuals are based in large part on the results of their performance evaluations.

General Schedule—White collar professional, administrative, technical, and clerical (PATC) positions covering over 400 occupations classified from GS–1 to GS–15.

Wage Grade Schedule—Blue collar positions in over 400 occupations classified from WG–1 to WG–13.

Other Schedules—Approximately 135,000 additional positions fall under various other schedules including Foreign Service schedules, Public Health Service, VA doctors and nurses, etc.

Classification of Positions

Positions are classified at specific levels (or grades) in various schedules according to job content, duties, responsibilities, and knowledge requirements. Classification standards are established by the Office of Personnel Management (OPM), and a point scoring system (FES-Factor Evaluation System) is used to assign a grade to any position. New executives are frequently frustrated by this personnel system when trying to recruit staff for their management team.

The key to sustaining the salary levels necessary to accommodate staff lies in using the proper terminology and key words in the Position Description (PD) to drive the FES to the desired result. Otherwise the PD will not "support the grade" you seek, hence the entry level pay you negotiated.

Furthermore, new entrants are usually restricted to the first "step" of each grade (each grade is subdivided into ten pay steps differentiated by approximately 3 percent of base pay). Advanced In-Hire Authority (entry above the first step of a grade) requires special exception and justification which is very difficult to obtain. It is often easier to reclassify a position to a higher grade than it is to obtain such an exception.

Types of Appointments

For clarity and brevity the discussion of appointing authorities will be limited to SES, Merit Pay, and relevant General Schedule positions. The filling of the Executive Schedule is coordinated by the Office of Presidential Personnel (OPP) in the Executive Office of the President (EOP).

SES Appointments—Four types of appointments are available: career, noncareer (political), limited term (career or political), limited emergency (career or political). Career appointments are effected following a competitive recruitment and selection process run by the agency, and submission to OPM for approval by a Qualifications Review Board (QRB). Noncareer appointments are noncompetitive appointments executed by the agency head. During the Reagan Administration a procedure was introduced requiring each noncareer selection to be routed to OPM for authorization. This allowed the Office of Presidential Personnel in the White House to review the selections in a policy version of the QRB. *It is strongly recommended that such a coordinating process on noncareer appointments continue in the next Administration as a way of insuring policy competence and consistency among policy personnel.* Limited Term Appointments are nonrenewable appointments for a term up to three years to a general SES position which will expire because of the nature of the work (e.g., a special project). Limited Emergency appointments are nonrenewable appointments for a period of up to 18 months.

The number of noncareer positions is limited by statute to no more than 10 percent of SES positions government-wide, but the ceiling in any agency can be as high as 25 percent of the agency's SES complement. During the Reagan Administration, noncareer SES appointees varied from approximately 5 percent of the SES in the Defense Department to 25 percent in the Department of Education. Other agencies typically ranged from 10-to-15 percent with a government-wide average just below the allowed 10 percent limit.

Merit Pay and General Schedule Appointments—The appointing authorities for these positions are the same, and fall into Competitive Service appointments (i.e., career) and Excepted Service appointments (i.e., noncareer or tenured with limited protection). Career status appointment requires individuals to be selected from competitive registers maintained by OPM or through delegated authority by the agencies. The process is at best tedious and well beyond the scope of this exposition. Of more immediate relevance to the political executive are the excepted appointments which fall into three schedules as follows:

Schedule A—positions for which it is impractical to hold any examinations. Attorneys form the largest single block of excepted appointments in the Civil Service (approximately 100,000), because it is forbidden by law to "examine" attorneys.

Schedule B—positions for which competitive examinations are impractical because of the lack of competition (e.g., remoteness or isolation of the duty station) but for which a "noncompetitive" examination is required, i.e., verification of a candidate's qualifications against established standards and requirements for the position.

Schedule C—positions which are policy determining or involve a close personal and confidential relationship between the individual and a key policy-making official. These are the "political" appointments used by the political executive to hire policy advisors, special assistants, secretaries, and clerical staff. Schedule Cs do not require examinations but positions (PDs) which they fill must contain descriptive language identifying the job as confidential in nature or having policy-sensitive or determining duties. As in the case of noncareer SES appointments, a variant on the selection process for Schedule Cs was implemented in the Reagan Administration. The variant required Schedule C to be reauthorized by OPM each time they were filled, thus allowing the Office of Presidential Personnel to review the policy sensitivity of the proposed incumbent. *It is strongly recommended that this variant be reestablished by the next Administration to ensure policy competence and consistency among policy personnel.* During the tenure of the Reagan Administration there were typically 1,600 Schedule Cs on board. Together with the 700 noncareer SES and 500 PAS appointees they represented a complement of less than 3,000 political personnel. Possibly because of the smallness of this total, there were many instances of congressional appropriations riders which further limited or reduced this number on an agency-by-agency basis. When engaged in this type of trench warfare vis-à-vis the legislative branch it is all the more important for appointees to choose their political staff carefully and well.

Other Types of Appointments—other occasionally useful types of appointments are Consultants, Experts, Intergovernmental Personnel

Act (IPA) mobility assignments, and temporary or term appointments. The IPAs provide a useful vehicle for hiring state and local government employees for a period not exceeding four years. A final noteworthy appointing authority applies to former congressional staff and White House staff. Under the rules of this authority, employees with three years of service (two years for White House staff) who are terminated for other than cause (e.g., election loss, death in office, staff reductions) are eligible for career status employment in the executive branch, thus by-passing the normal Civil Service competitive selection process. The next Administration will therefore be able to hire current Reagan White House employees as career employees without need of competition or selection from employment registers, *provided they have no break in service.*

It would require several volumes to describe the full details of the personnel process which includes job definition, recruiting, staffing, training, evaluating. Our discussion will focus on those aspects of the process which enhance workforce accountability and responsiveness.

Procedural Aspects

All authority to take action is delegated from the agency head down to various levels in the organization. "Delegations of Authority" (whether they be with respect to issuance of regulations, correspondence control, contract or grant-making authority, furniture and equipment purchases, office assignments, training expenditures, budget approval, personnel actions, travel authorizations, etc.) are documented in great detail in every agency's Administrative Manual or Manual of Administrative Procedures or some like titled document. It is important for every new appointee to obtain this document as soon after taking office as possible, in order to identify who in his organization currently wields the decision-making authority which the executive may want to redelegate to himself. *Withdrawing delegations is a simple and routine matter to effect and it may at times be essential in order to regain control of certain aspects of your operations.*

In the personnel area, delegations address the ability to assign, reassign or transfer individuals from one position to another. Such actions can be initiated to reward individuals, to reflect management priorities, or as punitive measures for poor performance. Reward mechanisms should almost always be implemented in conjunction with superior performance reviews. They include promotion, incentive awards, cash awards and bonuses, special details and choice assignments, and approval for education and training.

Corrective measures include reassignments, specific job-related training, demotions, and ultimately removal. The basis for taking these actions must be carefully documented and must of necessity be backed by unfavorable performance reviews. Experience has shown that, due to a lax enforcement of the performance appraisal process, even the worst performers in government have employment files replete with fully successful performance reviews. To maintain the integrity and the authority of your management system, subordinate supervisors and managers must be encouraged to identify the problem employee and take the appropriate steps to rectify the situation. Corrective actions are invariably subject to appeal and the filing of grievances, and must therefore be managed systematically and with care.

Achieving and Maintaining Accountability

Political executives face the issue of personal accountability every day of their tenure in office. Political appointees are held accountable for their actions, not only to their chain of command, but by Congress, interest groups, the media, as well as their political peers in the Administration. Fortunately a mechanism exists at least to *share* some of the burden of accountability with subordinate members of the executive's organization. The mechanism is the Performance Management System which entails an annual performance agreement against which individual performance is rated. A very important postscript to the process requires that consequences stem from the rating. These are the previously mentioned rewards for good performance and corrective actions for poor performance. *It cannot be sufficiently emphasized that consequences must stem from the performance appraisal process or else it will lose its credibility and utility.*

The standards of performance you expect should be clearly enunciated to your subordinate so that he can then generate a performance agreement. Following an initial meeting during which the workload and priorities for the coming year are communicated, that agreement is then submitted for your review and approval. A mid-term review should be held to assess progress and modify the standard as may be necessary. *The performance agreement is subject to modification at any time during the performance period.* At the end of the performance period an assessment is provided in a meeting with the subordinate. This close out session can also serve as the meeting which establishes the performance standard for the following year. The procedures apply equally to Senior Executives and Merit Pay managers.

Rating levels in the government are not yet standardized, but a five-level system is recommended, as follows: Outstanding, Superior, Fully Successful (FS), Marginal, and Unsatisfactory. There is a historical tendency to overrate employee performance to such an extent that during the Reagan Administration many departments and agencies rated 80 percent of management in the top two categories, 20 percent at Fully Successful, and barely 1 percent below Fully Successful. Such a rating distribution lacks credibility. It is difficult to follow up with any meaningful rewards when 80 percent of a very well paid workforce is found to be eligible.

The first rule in rating employees is to redefine the norm for acceptable performance. A good performer should be told that he has performed well, that you are very pleased with his performance, and that, therefore, you take pleasure in awarding him a Fully Successful rating. This approach takes the stigma off the FS rating and will reasonably redistribute the ratings to capture 50-to-60 percent of subordinates at the FS level. It then becomes possible to rate 10-to-15 percent of the very best performers at the Outstanding level (on occasion this can be stretched to 20 percent) and to compensate them appropriately for their performance. The balance of your managers will fall between the easily identifiable outstanding performers and the much larger bulk of satisfactory performers.

Problem employees need to be dealt with on a separate track. The Marginal level of performance is used to place an employee on probation status working under closer supervision. Corrective measures must be taken such as training assignments or reassignment to another position for a second chance. Two Marginal ratings within a three-year period or one Unsatisfactory rating are grounds for more severe measures including removal.

Mandated or predetermined rating distributions (e.g., a bell curve) are not allowed in the federal personnel management system. However, through the medium of second, level review it is possible to change obviously distorted performance ratings. Subordinate managers should be held fully responsible in their own performance agreements, and in the ratings they receive, for unrealistic or irresponsible rating of their personnel. Second level reviewers should be designated at the beginning of the performance period and they should be made clearly aware of their key role in maintaining the integrity of the performance management system. The second, level reviewer is authorized to change ratings if in his judgment they are in error or if they distort the performance assessment of the organization. The best time to do that is before the first-level official meets with the employee to assign even a preliminary rating.

Finally, *performance standards should be short and to the point* or else they contribute to the management morass and become part of the problem rather than the solution. Early in the Reagan Administration a generic management standard was developed and promulgated for the Senior Executive Service, and, with only minor modifications, it is readily applicable to Merit Pay managers. It is contained on only two sheets of paper and stresses quality, responsiveness, and timeliness in performance as opposed to quantitative factors. The generic standard is supplemented by a one-to-two page work plan tailored to reflect the individual duties, responsibilities and priorities of each executive or manager. The work plan lists specific projects, deadlines, timetables, goals and priorities for which an executive is held responsible. It is a clear, concise document which can be easily updated and maintained. The generic standard meets all the requirements established in statute and is readily available from OPM and most agency personnel offices.

Managing the System

The Senior Executive Service

The key to management resides in the senior executives, making decisions in your name, with the most direct authority over the employees of the agency. The legal entity upon whom control of the agency's SES is vested, is the Executive Resources Board (ERB). The members of the ERB are designated by the agency head who should serve as the chairman. The function is so important that it should not be relegated to lower levels in the organization. The Senior Executive Service is a very flexible executive personnel system that has benefited from the policy of the Reagan Administration's OPM to minimize the number of "clarifications," "guidance," and other regulatory issuances addressing the SES. A great deal of discretion was left to each agency's ERB in interpreting the basic rules of the game for the SES. These include: pay setting policy, establishment of position descriptions, assignment of positions, awarding of bonuses and cash awards, recruitment and staffing procedures, RIF procedures, training programs, and establishment of sabbatical programs. There is no limit on the number or types of appointees which can belong to the ERB. In fact, some ERBs consist entirely of political appointees. Membership on the ERB is discretionary and should reflect the philosophy and management style of the agency head. It is highly recommended that the ERB be kept small, three-to-seven members depending on the size of the agency.

A second body involved in the management of the SES is the agency Performance Review Board (PRB) which can either report to the agency head or be subordinated to the ERB. The PRB, by law, must be constituted of a majority of career executives and its most important function is to make recommendations concerning the awarding of Presidential Rank Award stipends and bonuses. It is the agency head, however, who makes the final determination on bonuses and Rank Awards. The review and recommendation process should be established by *the agency head or the ERB* in such a way as to allow the agency head *full flexibility* to make final changes in numbers of awards or size of awards. SES Bonuses, for which only career executives qualify, are awarded annually and vary from a minimum of 5 percent of base pay to a maximum of 20 percent. The size of the bonus is related to the level of performance, and a payout is mandatory for Outstanding performance. As a control against rating inflation, total bonus payments in an agency are limited to 3 percent of the aggregate SES payroll. With this cap, if there are too many Outstanding ratings, bonus payments become small and less meaningful.

One of the lasting legacies of an Administration can be the quality and management philosophy of the career senior executives it leaves behind. That responsibility rests entirely with the ERB. It is the ERB which manages the career SES recruitment and selection process. The ERB has the option of empaneling itself in reviewing applicants for SES vacancies or it can select a subcommittee to perform that task. The ERB makes the decision on whether to limit a vacancy announcement only to government applicants, or open it to all sources, which then allows recruitment from the private sector. This little-publicized authority allows an Administration the opportunity to leave a lasting imprint on career government. With SES turnover rates of 10 percent per year, a simple calculation indicates that in a four-year period 40 percent of the top career civil servants will have been subject to the selection review of the incumbent Administration.

Reassignments and transfers of senior executives are also controlled by the ERB. The process to reassign and transfer a senior executive is surprisingly efficient and uncomplicated. A senior executive may be reassigned to any SES position in the same agency with only 15 days advance notice. If the reassignment is to a position beyond his geographic "commuting area" the notice period extends to 60 days, but can be effected more quickly at the executive's discretion. The only constraints regarding reassignments and transfers are (1) executives may not be transferred involuntarily to another agency, and (2) *no involuntary reassignments of career appointees may take place during the first 120 days of appointment of a new agency head.* This so-called "cooling off" period during transitions has proven not to pose any undue management burden for new political appointees. It simply provides an opportunity to focus on policy issues and organizational structure before addressing reassignments of career management.

Merit Pay Managers

The performance management system for Merit Pay (GM) managers is very similar to that in force for senior executives, and now includes certain enhancements and improvements deriving from the passage of the 1984 Merit Pay bill. The 1984 Merit Pay bill was the result of an intensive effort on the part of the Reagan Administration to strengthen the linkages between appraisals of performance and consequences stemming therefrom. The Performance Management System for the GM Schedule requires the use of five rating levels including Fully Successful (FS), two levels above FS and two levels below FS. Performance standards must be developed in consultation (consultation, *not* negotiation) with employees, and higher level reviews of standards and ratings are encouraged. Forced or predetermined distributions of ratings are prohibited by law.

Mandatory linkages to performance ratings now exist in determining managers' base pay, monetary performance awards, retention status in RIFs, and in requiring corrective actions in the event of unsatisfactory performance.

In addition to the annual government-wide "comparability" salary increase, GM managers receive a pay adjustment which is graduated according to performance rating (approximately 3 percent if rated Outstanding). Outstanding performers also receive a mandatory one-time performance award not to exceed 20 percent of base pay. The performance awards are funded from a Merit Pay pool containing a percentage of the agency's GM payroll. Performance awards for ratings of Exceeds FS are optional but can be made mandatory at agency discretion. In the event of a RIF, a manager's rating is converted to a numerical score to be added to his years of service in determining his retention status. Unsatisfactory ratings (two levels below FS) result in mandatory reduction in grade or removal.

Merit Pay pools need to be managed carefully because of the direct relationship between ratings and monetary awards. Too many ratings of Outstanding or Exceeds FS can cause an organization to exceed the financial limitations for its pool, thus violating the law. On the other hand, if the size of each award is reduced in order to accommodate an unreasonable number of high ratings, then the value of the award loses its meaning and effectiveness as an incentive. Although rating distributions cannot be forced or predetermined, the limitations on GM pools and the mandatory payments for Outstanding ratings together provide the justification, if necessary, to adjust the final distribution of ratings. Merit Pay pools are managed from the outset of each performance period by holding each pool manager accountable, through his or her own rating, for the reasonableness of ratings in his or her organizational component.

Organizational Structures and Reorganizations

The organization should be structured so as to allow control and ensure responsiveness to the executive in charge. Upon assuming office, the new executive inherits someone else's organizational design, which was set up to reflect that individual's goals, priorities, preferred channels of communication and means of control. It may suffice simply to reassign people and put the right person in charge, but in some instances more wholesale restructuring may be necessary in order to break up policy-formulating monopolies and coalitions in the organization. In general, reorganizations are procedurally straightforward to implement. However, one must always be prepared for potential congressional intervention when a particularly sensitive program is involved. In some cases, it may be wise to proceed with a piecemeal reorganization under the cover of a larger agency-wide restructuring so as not to give the appearance of having singled out a congressman's or an interest group's favorite program.

The simplest reorganization merely changes line reporting relationships, i.e., "rewiring" the organization. This type of reorganization involves block movement of managers, supervisors, and employees using personnel procedures called the "transfer of function." Reorganizations become more complicated, however, when program functions are broken up and redistributed to other organizational components. In these cases individual PDs may need to be rewritten, a much more labor intensive effort for the personnel office. In the most complex scenario, when positions are abolished, classifications are changed, or grades are reduced, standard RIF rules must be applied before the reorganization can take place. At this level of impact the reorganization will take several months to implement. The executive will need to consult with his Management/Administrative Office and his Personnel Office before instituting a reorganization, but he should never be intimidated or put off by the process. The choice of options (from simple reassignments—two weeks to effect, to rewiring the organization, to restructuring functions) should reflect the executive's immediate needs and comport with the schedule of the long-range policy agenda. It may not be possible to reach one's goal without changing the vehicle one is driving, and in such cases it is best simply to "bite the bullet."

It is also wise to prepare a workforce plan in the context of reorganizations. Workforce planning involves the integration of policy, structure, and staffing needs. It is important for the executive to establish some sort of workforce agenda in order to avoid having personnel issues raised as obstacles to achieving policy goals. Among others these obstacles will include "understaffing," "overloading," "critical vacancies that must be filled," "overdue promotions," "inadequate grades," "non-competitive salaries," etc. These issues can and should be dealt with in the context of an overall workforce agenda if it has been established. Otherwise, subordinates will invariably raise these issues in the context of policy decisions and the executive will fall into the trap of trading policy initiatives in exchange for personnel favors. Personnel and budget resources are the executive's to allocate during conveyance of his policy agenda, and the rules for the utilization of these resources must be established at the outset to avoid being "blackmailed" during critical policy confrontations. The main purpose of developing a workforce agenda is to establish those rules. A properly developed workforce agenda will guide hiring and promotions along lines that reflect the executive's priorities, making full use of the normal employee attrition process to facilitate organizational change. Problems such as underutilization of personnel, endemic overgrading, and overstaffing at the midmanagement levels can then be systematically addressed. To regain control of recalcitrant managers or uncooperative organizational units, selective hiring or promotion freezes can be applied, work can be reassigned, or various authorities withdrawn or redelegated, all under the blanket of an agency-wide or program-wide "workforce" or "management" initiative. Administrative budgets can be revised to curtail acquisition of furniture and equipment, travel, training, performance awards, etc.

---◇---

STRATEGIES FOR SUCCESS

Manage the People

The performance management system is designed to convey goals and objectives and provide a means of holding the organization accountable for meeting those goals and objectives. Managing the details of the process of government is accomplished by holding the people involved in the process responsible for desired results. Accountability is achieved when the performance rating is linked to appropriate rewards for exemplary performance and suitable punitive measures for unacceptable performance.

Be creative in making full use of the SES mobility and reassignment flexibilities. Encourage your agency/department to establish a Career Development/Executive Mobility Program to rotate executives into new positions on a periodic basis. This serves to broaden the executives' experience, making them more effective and valuable, and it furthers the Administration's agenda in breaking up existing policy-controlling monopolies in the agency.

Control the Workforce

The organizational structure should reflect the executive's policy goals and priorities, ensure responsiveness and proper access to information for decision-making, and allow control of policy and process via appropriate review and oversight procedures. Functions should be consolidated to reduce overhead and eliminate unnecessary duplication. Field organizations should be particularly scrutinized for opportunities to centralize administrative services.

A corresponding workforce agenda should be developed. Employee turnover and attrition should be utilized to maximum advantage to facilitate organizational change. Uncooperative organizational components should not be allowed to go unchecked and especially not rewarded with budget/personnel increases. Use of patronage plums should be judiciously applied to reinforce good performance. Explore alternative means of implementing organizational mission objectives, including:

◆ contracting out of nongovernmental functions, or of those services having commercial counterparts

◆ maximal use of contractors to deliver services in newly created programs, thereby preventing the creation and entrenchment of a bureaucratic constituency

◆ wholesale privatization of entire governmental programs

The contracting out and privatization options are listed in this section to alert the executive to the need for their consideration in the course of workforce planning. Privatization of government services was a major initiative of the Reagan Administration and it will continue to be a policy initiative unto itself of greater import and significance than the administrative aspects of personnel management. It is an issue better treated in the context of domestic policy and will not be further developed at this point.

Understanding the Career "Patronage" System

The career "patronage" system is in reality a control mechanism in the hands of a key nonpolitical individual in the organization. The authority delegated to this individual can be traced in the agency's Administrative Manual. The political executive can regain control by redelegating to himself or other subordinates authority to approve those patronage plums most sought after by the career bureaucracy. These patronage plums include:

◆ "career ladder" promotions (mistakenly believed to be "automatic" promotions)

◆ competitive promotions (GS–13, GS–14, and GS–15)

◆ selection of employees for choice assignments to boards, commissions, international organizations

◆ details and temporary promotions to more responsible positions

◆ IPA assignments to state and local governments

◆ travel requests above a certain threshold ($500, $1,000, $2,000) to participate in conferences, meetings, field reviews, research projects, etc.

◆ leave requests for short periods (days), long periods (weeks or months), or leave without pay

◆ requests for training or educational programs (a few days to several months costing from hundreds of dollars to thousands of dollars)

◆ bonuses, performance awards, and other forms of monetary incentives and recognition (hundreds of dollars to thousands of dollars)

◆ locations and sizes of offices

◆ purchases of furniture and equipment

◆ allocation of parking spaces

Whoever approves or grants these plums commands a great deal of attention and respect in the organization. New executives are always advised by career staff not to get involved in some of these "administrative" details. The price for taking such advice is loss of control. Through the Delegations of Authority the executive has the opportunity to select any or all of these items for his personal review. He has the option to change the threshhold levels above which documents will require his signature should the volume of transactions prove to be too great. Some of this may be delving into minutia, but it is an investment of time which is well worth the return in increased responsiveness and control. At a later time thresholds can again be changed and authorities redelegated to selected individuals to symbolize trust and transfer of power.

The above provides some basic information a new executive should know to function effectively from the start. For additional information on some of the subjects covered, as well as the many not covered, the reader is referred to three readily accessible publications:

1. *The Federal Personnel Guide*, published annually by Federal Personnel Publications, a division of USA, Inc. (a private firm not connected with the federal government).

2. *The Senior Executives Service*, published by the U.S. Office of Personnel Management.

3. *Manager's Handbook*, published by U.S. Office of Personnel Management.

33

Policy, Budget, and Program Evaluation

by
Kenneth X. Lynch*

Control of the policy process aims at defining program priorities and determining the allocation of resources. As such, the policy process is another name for the decision-making system of the government. In that broad sense, control of policy is synonymous with the control of government. However, control of policy is more complex than it first appears because government itself is complex.

Policy has many facets—statutory, regulatory, budgetary, and administrative—and political executives in an agency need to be involved in all of them, from the launching of new policy concepts through legislative or budgetary initiatives to the rewriting of administrative procedures for loan applications or contract performance monitoring. Looking at the policy process as a continuum—from authorizing statute to the delivery of the service or financial benefit to the agency's "clients"—will open up new horizons for policy intervention frequently overlooked in the preoccupation with the budget process and the constraints imposed by congressional micromanagement.

The broad conservative agenda given a mandate in the presidential election of 1980 and a solid reaffirmation in the election of 1988 should move toward implementation along an equally broad front, from the hearing rooms of Congress to the computer rooms of an agency's disbursement center. This chapter focuses on the tasks of further developing and implementing that broad conservative agenda within federal agencies.

---

*Kenneth X. Lynch is a pseudonym representing the collective contributions of five principal co-authors: Kenneth Clarkson, Scott W. Gordon, Charles W. Jarvis, Edward J. Lynch, and Rick Ventura. Richard B. Abell, Robert B. Carleson, Jeffrey A. Eisenach, John Schrote, and Jeanne Sclater contributed ideas and helpful suggestions.

ESTABLISHING THE AGENDA

Political appointees do not enter office with an opportunity to rewrite their agency's mission statements. Each agency exists to run specific programs, and each program has its own authorizing statutes, regulations, and budget levels. Also inherited by the appointees are the agency's well-defined and well-organized constituencies, which may count some of the appointees among their friends and allies. Strong candidates for appointive positions are likely to be those who have a knowledge of and stake in existing programs—from work on congressional staffs developing them, from work with affected groups lobbying on behalf of them, or from previous executive branch experience. During the course of confirmation, Senate committees may extract promises from nominees about program direction and budget levels. And through authorization and appropriations hearings, members of Congress retain powers to enforce those promises and sustain their influence over priorities within programs nominally administered by the executive branch.

Most importantly, new appointees inherit the authorizing statutes defining legal powers and limitations of office. Career civil servants working in federal agencies—their nominal subordinates—all take oaths to execute the laws "without any mental reservations or purpose of evasion." (This is the same oath taken by political appointees.) Until the Administration gets its priorities enacted into law, the scope of change within federal agencies will be limited, and will depend entirely on the ability of political management to identify the elements of statute and regulation which allow discretionary action. For example, an important element of discretion is the relative priority of programs competing for resources from the same limited pool. This allows an agency head and his appointees to emphasize those programs which are in concert with the Administration's agenda while de-emphasizing those which are not.

These constraints highlight the importance of building legislative and constituent support for program changes and the need to delve into governmental process in much greater detail than might otherwise be expected. Moreover, the increasingly frequent "micromanagement" practices of Congress will ensure that some of the resources essential to support proposals for programmatic changes—for example, studies reviewing alternative methods of program implementation such as privatization—will continue to be blocked.

Lasting change within government must therefore build upon the existing laws, reshaping legal and administrative foundations to advance the President's agenda while efforts at more fundamental changes are waged. Success in these efforts requires a policy process that stresses the primacy of the President's agenda, and transforms administrative functions—budget, personnel, procurement, and related managerial services—so that they support the Administration's policy priorities.

The greatest challenge in this process of policy implementation is to coordinate the budget process with appropriate policy priorities. Many administrations succumb to the temptation to review policy options in terms of available resources, rebuffing many policy initiatives with the retort: "This is a good idea, but the American people can't afford it." Conservative administrations are especially vulnerable to this temptation because they tend to attract skilled economists and accountants who are more likely to emphasize these factors in establishing policy priorities. The frequent result of such budgetary dominance of the policy process is to cede programmatic ground to the guardians of current or expanded programs, with opposition explained primarily in terms of cost. In balancing budgetary goals and policy priorities, responsible policy officials should use the budget process to raise critical questions about spending priorities. The budget is an expression of policy priorities, not their master. If this relationship were kept clearly in mind by Administration policymakers, the public would be treated less frequently to the spectacle of the President signing authorizing legislation one month, cultivating constituents by endorsing a "good" program, only to recommend zeroing it out in the subsequent budget message.

Subordinating budget to policy would also correct the mistaken notion that all policy initiatives should be tied to the "budget cycle." Each major spending program comes up for reauthorization every three-to-five years. If the White House does not interject its policy proposals in that reauthorization process, it forfeits a major opportunity to reshape the program. (The excuse often given—that the Administration has more control over the budget than it has over the reauthorization process and can work "trade-offs" with congressional adversaries within the budget package—has some merit but is not a valid reason for not pursuing *all* opportunities for legislative change.) This "green eyeshade government"—where budget questions come to dominate policy debates—invariably damages the credibility of the President by leaving the impression that the Administration's policy and budget arms are working at cross purposes. Budgetary issues of program cost and burden on the taxpayer are legitimate issues in their own right, but they should be incorporated as strategic elements of the overall policy agenda. It is not "the budget" that is the source of the problem of budget deficits – it is federal spending. Unless the agency's budget proposals are presented and explained in terms of *spending priorities*, it will never engender a policy debate among the public.

The Administration's budget process can also be used tactically to establish a framework within which to force a policy change by constraining policy choices. However, this works best at the macro level of the agency's budget, not at the micro level of individual programs. The standard reaction of program managers faced with a directive to cut back program services to meet a pre-determined budget target is the "Washington Monument Syndrome," where the program manager proposes to cut the most popular part of the program, knowing that public reaction will doom the cuts. A strong agency head can deal with this tactic by sending the program staff back to the drawing boards again and again until real cuts materialize. However, this approach has its limits, and one year's cuts can always be put back in by a friendly appropriations subcommittee next year.

In developing a policy agenda, great care should be taken to define objectives and goals as specific *results*, measured either qualitatively or quantitatively. These results may be programmatically oriented, such as reduction of the incidence of malnutrition among U.S. citizens, or institutionally oriented, such as transfer of the scope of power and control of resources to less-coercive organizational units—for example, the transfer of a discretionary program from federal to state control, from state to local control, or complete privatization. The results sought could also be managerial in nature—increased use of contractor support through the A–76 contracting-out process, or implementation of management improvements, such as better safeguards against waste, fraud, and abuse.

At times the goal may be limited to modifying the menu of policy choices. In those cases achievement may consist in altering the types of questions and public debate arising from a particular issue. One may not succeed in revising or eliminating a poorly functioning government program. But, if one establishes new evaluation criteria or opens new perspectives or facets of the program which allow it to be evaluated against different standards, the potential for responsible solutions or modifications to the program increases significantly. Similarly, if the questions or issues debated within the government agency change, then another victory may be claimed. For example, by proposing radical program and budget reductions in 1981, the Reagan Administration changed the debate from the rate of increase of the budget to how much could be cut and which programs eliminated; from how much to increase staff to how deep a cut can be sustained.

While the nature of the specific policies or questions debated will vary from agency to agency, certain criteria for successful policy implementation are common to all government functions. Success may be measured in the transfer of authority from federal to state governments or to other organizational levels more closely associated with achieving the specific objectives of the program.

---◇---

COORDINATING POLICY AND PROGRAMS

The coordination of policy and administration must begin at the top if it is to be effective. Properly implemented, it will require the President and his senior policy officials to articulate policy goals, then coordinate the budget to channel essential fiscal resources to the programs. Also needed are the public affairs function to cultivate public support for the policy applications of the President's priorities; the legislative liaison functions to develop support for the program within the Congress; legal functions to ensure consistency with other areas of law; the personnel and training functions to ensure that civil servants understand and are capable of implementing the programs; and the managerial systems essential to monitor and evaluate program performance as defined by law, regulation, and program priorities.

Integration of these functions can be done most effectively through conscious organization of institutional operations. Within individual agencies, the senior official responsible for policy must be a "first among equals," with immediate access to the agency head and clear authority to provide supporting direction on policy matters.

During the transition and the first weeks of the new Administration, these senior policy officials should develop statements of the President's priorities in all major policy areas. During interviews for major appointive positions, care should be taken to ensure that candidates for key positions support those policy priorities—not merely in a general sense, but with an ability to apply the principles underlying those policies—as the President understands them—to the offices that they will occupy. Each major agency head and senior policy official should be assigned responsibility to incorporate the President's priorities in developing a policy statement for their agency. These statements should include priorities for changing current programs, estimates of budgetary requirements for the agency, and a reflection of the environment—attentive publics, congressional committees, and judicial constraints—in which the agency operates.

Leading policy officials will develop methods of using appropriate civil service procedures, budgetary powers, and managerial tools to support policy priorities. The more systematic the implementation procedures, the more likely that others will understand the policy priorities, and the less likely that agenda deflection—through accident or malice—will result.

Step one must be agenda definition. Where the President has clearly articulated policy priorities, responsible personnel must be informed of what they are—not merely through policy statements, but through a management-by-objectives system for implementation, complete with defined task assignments, completion schedules, and incentives for exceptional performance. The clearest place to begin policy articulation is with the position descriptions of the people responsible for implementing the policies. If, for example, government policy is that commercial functions will not be performed by government agencies, administrative officials must be accountable for ensuring that all new commercial functions are provided through contracts and that commercial functions currently performed within the government are contracted with private firms. Unless these officials have deadlines in performance standards for conducting inventories of current commercial functions, other activities—the ones that *are* included in performance standards—will receive priority.

Agency statements of objectives must include interim progress charts, with deadlines for accomplishing intermediate goals. Budget, management, personnel and procurement procedures all can help the appointee to advance the agenda more effectively—to frame the discussion—through the deployment of resources and the structuring of responsibilities to set the priorities. Monitoring budget execution through the appropriate use of technology, i.e., information resource management (IRM), will best provide for the successful evaluation of the budget process and deployment of resources.

Establishing a strict Management-by-Objectives (MBO) process to monitor programs towards the goals and objectives of the Administration is crucial. From the agency head down it must be clearly understood that responsibility and accountability for agency management is vested in the political leadership. The understandable tendency for political appointees to focus exclusively on programmatic issues and overlook agency management plays directly into the hands of those who would thwart the achievement of the Administration's agenda.

The collection of data, the conduct of audits, reports, reviews and other resources for analysis, internally as well as by outside groups and think tanks, can be particularly helpful to the appointee. Information from a variety of sources can strengthen program reviews, adding new perspectives that enhance the appointee's ability to ask pointed questions, communicate new sets of priorities, and develop new performance measures.

Even working through sound administrative practices, the process of change requires persistent attention to details as reviews are conducted. Without the concentrated focus of the appointee on agency management; without developing a thorough understanding of the budget process; without a thorough knowledge of the congressional appropriations process; and without an understanding of the appropriate use of information from program monitoring, the likelihood of achieving the Administration's policy objectives is small.

Periodic rewards for exceptional performance—promotions, bonuses, honors, and other recognition—must be available to those who perform in accord with Administration policies. Allowances can be incorporated for shortcomings when factors are beyond the control of the responsible official—for example, when a congressional committee refuses to schedule hearings and/or votes on needed legislative changes. By the same logic, deviation from the Administration's established policy priorities must be rebuked appropriately—with admonitions where reform is possible, with dismissal when the official appears unwilling to comply with Administration priorities. As with rewards, rationale for replacing those who resist Administration initiatives should be well understood by those who accede to the position.

———————◇———————

BUDGET AS AN INSTRUMENT OF POLICY

The budget of any government agency is the most public reflection of its policy priorities. Effective officials will use policy priorities to guide decisions about fiscal resources. Because costs will always be a constraining factor, public officials invariably face strong competition for the funds needed to make the budget reflect the President's priorities. A policy official who has control of the budget office, and has aligned position descriptions and job task responsibilities with policy priorities, will be several steps ahead of the game in making the budget consistent with policy goals. At a minimum, the official will accustom others to using policy to guide resource allocation, rather than having available resources constrict policy—the operating mode of green eyeshade government.

The government's managerial support agencies—the Office of Management and Budget, the Office of Personnel Management, and the General Services Administration—are intended to support political managers in the implementation of policies. When these agencies are functioning properly, they should be led by officials who share the President's priorities and who view their mission as assisting in implementation, not directing the overall government agenda.

Despite the major support role accorded these agencies, they have only a small cadre of political leadership. The Office of Management and Budget, in particular, has approximately fifteen political managers to supervise more than 600 career personnel. The examiners who review agency submissions and impose managerial controls through the budget process are frequently career officials who have never faced a constituency or gained support through the affected interest groups. More than a few political appointees have been astonished when they first heard a GS–14 budget examiner inform them that policy priorities established by agency leadership, in coordination with the White House Office of Policy Development, "are not the President's policies."

Although it is a major statement of resource allocation, the budget should not be the primary determinant of government policy. Rather than an end-in-itself, the budget is an integral instrument of policy formulation, implementation, review, and refinement. The Office of Management and Budget provides valuable service when it enhances policy development; but it is viewed with great suspicion when it impairs faithful execution of the Administration's policy priorities by a fixation on "number-crunching," i.e., squeezing every possible dollar out of an agency budget without regard to the realism of the cut or the impact on new and promising policy initiatives.

The congressional budget process has earned well-deserved ridicule as it has degenerated to a series of continuing resolutions and supplementals—all coming as an end-of-year monolith that will sustain all abuses if signed or shut down the government if rejected.

Unfortunately, budgeting within the executive branch often falls into a disturbing parallel course as the cycle moves toward the January submission of the President's budget for the fiscal year that will begin the next October. When a new Administration enters office January 20, 1989, nearly half of the year's budget will have been spent during the current fiscal year. A budget for fiscal year 1990—controlling expenditures until September 30, 1990—will be nearly in final form, with many decisions made by the current Administration and few opportunities for serious review of programs and priorities. Only after the Administration has managed with a predecessor's budget for a few months will a call-for-estimates for the FY 1991 budget be sent to agencies. In short, the length of the budget process exposes vulnerable agency heads to a year and a half of planning before implementing the first budget that will be wholly their own.[1]

That planning period should be spent well. By making the budget review process within the agency a comprehensive review of programs, new appointees can have the greatest possible policy as well as fiscal impact. With budget officials properly subordinate to political appointees, and with coordination among the legal, legislative, public affairs, and administrative arms of the agency, appointed officials can use the budgetary process to reshape programs in accord with Administration priorities. No part of the budget should be accepted as a "given." Personnel involved in the budget review should be instructed to chart their course on the basis of policy priorities and principles of effective program management, then develop strategies to achieve the essential changes. Effective program management will use the budget reviews to consider alternative arrangements—program changes, contracting for suitable functions, asset sales where these will serve the public interest, elimination of programs where they no longer serve the common good, and institution of new measures with higher priority than existing functions.

Following the agency's internal April call-for-estimates, the Office of Management and Budget will deliver a set of budget "targets" to the agency during June. The budget targets will reflect presidential priorities and provide a set of goals to form the agency's first full submission, in September. If there is a serious conflict between presidential priorities as understood by the Office of Management and Budget and the priorities understood by the appointed head of the agency, it should be worked out in accord with the first set of targets. Negotiating room shrinks later in the budget process.

In late November, OMB will return the submission—a "passback"—reflecting discussions between senior agency officials and OMB leadership. After review by the agency and discussion with OMB, a resubmission will become the basis for the President's January submission to Congress.

OMB plays an important role serving the President in coordinating policy and available resources. Although resources should not drive policy, no effective policy can develop without regard for allocation of resources. Inevitably, at some point, responsible officials must consider whether the public service provided by a program justifies the costs involved. Moreover, with a perspective on the programs of all agencies, OMB is in a unique position to evaluate some of the policy claims of competing departments—whether, for example, there really is a justifiable requirement for distinct map-making facilities within the Departments of Transportation, Interior, Commerce, and Defense, or whether these functions might well be included among the commercial activities best served through the private sector. At a minimum, it might make recommendations about aggregate savings that could be achieved through cooperative interagency agreements, rather than additional personnel at all affected organizations.

With the budget serving as an agent of policy development, all involved in the process can be strengthened in support of larger policy priorities. Provided with a coherent policy rationale derived from the President's priorities, OMB's coordinating role within the budgetary process can enhance presidential control of the executive branch. Where proper policy guidelines have been developed, agency heads will be strengthened in dealings with OMB, directing allocation of resources in line with genuine public needs. In turn, coordinated policy and budget development will strengthen the executive branch in dealing with Congress.

Early involvement in coordinating policy and budget among key political appointees can overcome or at least reduce traditional road blocks and miscommunication. These result from the perspective in the agencies that the initial budget directives are OMB's and not necessarily the President's. From OMB's perspective, agencies are vested interests whose budgets reflect their own (bureaucratic) priorities rather than the President's. It is the responsibility of the President to make clear to his agency heads how they are to interpret OMB's budget targets and what the process will be for resolving differences amiably and efficiently. Honest differences will exist at various stages and appeals of OMB decisions can be made. Yet when the President makes his decisions on the budget, it is imperative that agency heads and their appointees accept the President's budget as their own and support it totally and persuasively.

The agency head has a responsibility to guide agency compliance with the budget decisions. In the course of deliberations within the agency, appointed officials should not fall victim to claims that personnel levels cannot be reduced, or programs not achieved, within the funding levels decided during budget deliberations. Civil service professionals should have among their performance standards requirements to examine alternative methods of providing services, including technological innovations, streamlining management, delegation of authority to state or local governments, and other alternatives to improve service while reducing costs. When told, "That's not the way it's been done around here," appointees must develop enough perception to recognize when settled ways of doing business must be changed in the public interest.

———————————◇———————————

NOTES

1. This comment should not be taken to indicate acceptance of the budget inherited from predecessors. It merely recognizes that time will require any action to be relatively swift, and to go forward without coordination among operating offices, affected interest groups, or congressional committees. Unless these constituencies are prepared to accept the change being implemented through the budget, they have strong institutional capabilities to resist. Prospects for success increase as they are educated about the reasons for implementing a new course of action, and, perhaps, even convinced to assist with needed legislative changes to make the change enduring.

34

Policy-Making by Regulation and Government-by-Lawsuit

by
Joseph A. Morris*

Rebellion against George III was justified in a bill of particulars, our Declaration of Independence, that enumerated the grievous injuries that the King had visited upon the people of America. Among the indictments was this charge:

> He has erected a Multitude of new Offices, and sent hither Swarms of Officers to harrass our People, and eat out their Substance.[1]

British monarchs no longer play the role of villain. But the rise of the modern administrative state has brought with it patterns of regulation and litigiousness that are far more pervasive than their eighteenth-century antecedents; they are all the more destructive because they are *not* imposed by foreign rulers. The modern "Swarms" were sent hither by our own elected rulers.

A generation ago one thoughtful member of the United States Supreme Court, writing from the bench, was already alarmed:

> The rise of administrative bodies probably has been the most significant legal trend of the last century and perhaps more values today are affected by their decisions than by those of all the courts, review of administrative decisions apart. They also have begun to have important consequences on personal rights. . . . They have become a veritable fourth branch of

*The author is indebted to several individuals for advice and suggestions in the preparation of this paper: Mark Disler, Jeffrey Eisenach, Bruce Fein, Mark S. Fowler, Patrick S. Korten, Daniel R. Levinson, Deborah Owens Morris, Daniel J. Popeo, Clifford J. White III, and Michael Uhlmann. The opinions expressed are, however, entirely the responsibility of the author.

the Government, which has deranged our three branch legal theories as much as the concept of a fourth dimension unsettles our three-dimensional thinking.[2]

So wrote Justice Robert H. Jackson. His qualms about the administrative state are all the more remarkable in view of his origins as Franklin D. Roosevelt's attorney general and as a Roosevelt appointee to the Court. Eight Presidents, three chief justices, and one Reagan Revolution later, it seems fair to report that the derangement that Justice Jackson observed has now spread from the realm of legal theory to the entire governmental landscape.

We have erected many new offices. Apart from the thirteen executive departments, the federal government today includes 58 independent establishments and government corporations—one of which, the Veterans Administration, appears to be on its way to becoming the fourteenth Cabinet agency. The government also contains 68 boards, committees, and commissions which were established by congressional or presidential action and whose functions are not strictly limited to the internal operations of a parent department or agency.[3] Many of the best known and most visible arms of the federal government are not counted at all in these enumerations because they are contained within larger governmental units, such as the Cabinet departments; among them are the Air Force, the Army, the Border Patrol, the Federal Bureau of Investigation, the Internal Revenue Service, the Marine Corps, the National Park Service, the National Weather Service, and the Social Security Administration. The operating divisions and subdivisions of the federal government, each with its own legal standing and rule-making authority, are truly legion. Even the Executive Office of the President is today divided into nine "agencies."

In 1987 these federal agencies filled 49,653 pages of the *Federal Register*.[4] The Code of Federal Regulations for 1988, consisting of 50 titles, with most titles requiring more than one volume, easily occupied 15 feet of shelving.

In Fiscal 1986 the federal government as plaintiff commenced 60,779 lawsuits in the United States District Courts; it was named as the defendant in another 31,051 cases filed in district courts.[5] Meanwhile, 4,846 civil appeals in which the government was a party were filed in the United States Courts of Appeals in 1986, and an additional 3,187 appeals were taken to the courts of appeals in federal administrative proceedings.[6] These statistics do not begin to account for the tens of thousands of administrative proceedings brought each year before such regulatory tribunals as the Commodities Futures Trading Commission, Federal Communications Commission, the Federal Labor Relations Authority, the Federal Trade Commission, the Interstate Commerce Commission, the International Trade Commission, the Merit Systems Protection Board, the National Labor Relations Board, or the Securities and Exchange Commission.

An example of the staggering annual load of administrative adjudication is the Social Security Appeals Council, a 20–member body chaired by the Associate Commissioner of Social Security for Hearings and Appeals. The Council sits atop a four-level pyramid of decisions and review, which includes hearings before administrative law judges at the third stage. After all the dispositions of claims at lower levels that winnow out matters before they reach the Council, the Council itself nonetheless decides 50,000 cases each year.[7]

These statistics disclose that a highly decentralized and fragmented federal government is doing a great deal of regulating and an extraordinary amount of litigating. Recent lawsuits—such as the Supreme Court's decision in *Morrison* v. *Olson*[8] upholding the constitutionality of the independent counsel provisions of the Ethics in Government Act[9]—suggest that fundamental principles such as the separation of powers doctrine are in peril and in need of reinforcement.

This chapter offers some insights into how the challenges and problems presented by this litigation maze can be viewed as opportunities for advancing the Administration's policy agenda.

———————◇———————

THE POLICYMAKER AS REGULATOR

Policymakers can influence public policy choices through several mechanisms:

◆ Use of the platform of public office to influence popular sentiment and inform public opinion. Examples range from speech-making to the conduct of administrative hearings presided over by the policymaker, whether or not the hearings are tied to a formal rule-making or decisional process.
◆ Formulation and advocacy of legislative changes.
◆ Decisions on the day-to-day discharge of business.
◆ Litigation, both offensive and defensive.
◆ Informal administrative action, such as the development of guidelines for operations or interpretations of statutes and agency rules.
◆ Formal rule-making.

Formal rule-making—the authority to make regulations that may bind the conduct not just of a government itself, but also of private persons and organizations—is among the most powerful tools that a policymaker can wield.

Basic principles of federal administrative law hold that an agency's rule, if promulgated within the scope of its substantive powers and if issued in accordance with requisite procedures, has the force and effect of law. "It is, as a legal matter, of essentially the same significance as a statute."[10]

The legislative powers of the federal government were conferred by the Constitution upon Congress.[11] It was Congress, and not the President, executive departments, administrative agencies, independent establishments, or government corporations, to whom the Constitution gave the powers to regulate commerce and the value of money; to tax and spend; to prevent the states from depriving persons of life, liberty, or property without due process of law; or to secure from the states the equal protection of the law for all persons subject to their respective jurisdictions. There can be no question that today these powers, even after eight years of the Reagan Revolution, are being exercised as never before. Vast schemes of federal regulation and monumental governmental enterprises abound. Many of them have been called into being, or substantially enlarged, since 1964. All of them have significant consequences, good or ill, for the American people.

But what is remarkable is that proportionately few decisions regarding the exercise of these powers are today made by Congress in the manner prescribed by the Constitution—that is, by the process of open and on-the-record lawmaking for which the voters can hold congressmen accountable. Rather, for every act of Congress imposing an obligation on employers to guarantee their workforces at least 60 days' pay for no work in the event of a plant closing, there are myriad decisions of comparable magnitude that are made by regulatory agencies: to require cars to be outfitted with air bags and eye-level brake lights; to decide whether two newspapers may agree to share printing facilities; or to specify the racial, ethnic, and sexual quotas with which private companies selling goods to the government must assemble their workforces. Such decisions will almost certainly be made through the regulatory process.

Question after question that is considered important by many Americans has been federalized by Congress and then dispatched for actual decision to an entity, administrative or judicial, that is far removed from democratic accountability. It is not true, as is often claimed, that courts and bureaucracies have seized power. Rather, Congress has bequeathed it to them.[12] In an earlier work on this theme, the author offered the following diagnosis of the political motivations behind this recent expansion of the authority of regulatory bodies:

> Politics, . . . rather than a breakdown in the American common legal system, explains these trends. In particular, Congress, as an institution, has found the electoral benefits of the politicization of private problems to outweigh the social costs realized in terms of freedom and productivity. Congress has found that the federalization of public and private problems brings political accountability [which, in the interests of assuring re-election, can be avoided] through a variety of insulating mechanisms. Chief among those mechanisms are the deliberate enactment of ambiguous statutes and the erection of purposefully delaying and complicating machinery of administrative procedure. Provision for federal judicial review is a further device for the insulation of Congress from the political consequences of popular dissatisfaction with the public policy decisions made by the executive officials, administrative agencies, and courts to whom Congress has delegated such decisional authority.[13]

The regulatory power that thus grows in the hands of executive policymakers presents both opportunities and burdens. Opportunities come in the authority to make, interpret, apply, and enforce rules addressing public policy concerns—and, as needed, to trigger adjudications under those rules that serve to vindicate policy choices.

Burdens are of very different kinds. Some are legal, in that they invite persons and organizations aggrieved by regulatory action to bring lawsuits to challenge the policymaker's decisions. Others are political, tied directly to the etiology of the growth of regulatory power. Congress has delegated its lawmaking power precisely so that it can criticize those who wield it. Congress's institutional objective, after all, is to appear to its constituents to be concerned about problems and to be taking constructive action regarding them, while at the same time distancing itself from the actual responsibility for decision-making.

Congressional criticism takes many forms. Benchmarks on the spectrum of congressional pressure include:

1) Mildly intrusive requests by congressional staff for information regarding policy decisions and program management.

2) Highly intrusive demands by members or staff for information or action.

3) Regularly-scheduled oversight hearings orchestrated to induce pressure to conform to demands for information or action.

4) Specially scheduled oversight hearings designed to embarrass or

condemn the policymaker whose public policy goals vary from those of aggressive congressional interests.

5) Deferrals of confirmation proceedings or threats to deny confirmation absent concessions demanded by members or staff.

6) Appropriations riders or other opportunistic legislation intended to force action (or inaction) contrary to executive branch preferences.

7) Orchestration of events intended to force executive assertions of privilege, to result in contempt proceedings, demands for criminal prosecution, or other extraordinary confrontations between Congress and the executive branch, perhaps requiring judicial resolution.

8) Commencement of impeachment proceedings.

Eventualities (1), (2), (3), and (4) are fairly common; (5) and (6) are less common, and depend on the existence of opportunities that congressional interests can exploit; and (7) and (8) have occurred only with great infrequency, although in recent times Congress has resorted to (7) often enough to raise grave concerns about the continuing viability of the constitutional separation of powers. Substantive legislation, publicly and decisively resolving a public policy dispute—the high road—is too honorable to be classified as "pressure" and altogether too rare.

An important factor in the political environment surrounding a particular public policy choice is the steady entrenchment of "iron triangles," a useful metaphor for the political alliance formed by an agency's bureaucracy, the congressional committees having oversight and appropriations authority over the agency, and the interest groups served by its operations. These powerful networks can significantly influence congressional responses to regulatory initiatives that threaten the *status quo*. A policymaker's ability to overcome these obstacles will turn on the courage to act decisively. Success will also demand solid knowledge of the regulatory process. Access to reliable legal advice is indispensable.

———————————◇———————————

THE REGULATORY PROCESS

The exercise of regulatory authority is controlled by a complex body of administrative law, primarily statutory, but with substantial interstices filled by judge-made rules. Prescribed formalities must be observed in making a rule; they must be carefully followed, as well, if a regulation is to be amended or revoked.

The basic charter of modern administrative law is the Administrative Procedure Act (APA) of 1946.[14] Prompted by President Franklin D. Roosevelt, the attorney general appointed a committee in 1939 to inquire into the need for procedural reform in the field of administrative law. The Act reflects enthusiasms of the New Deal era: faith in such notions as scientific administration, professional management, and government by experts; the blending, rather than separation, of powers; and the restructuring of executive action along increasingly legal procedural models. The last point implies both the circumscription, to varying degrees, of the exercise of discretion and the introduction of adversary procedures to the conduct of internal executive branch business.

Subsequent amendments to the APA over the years added the Administrative Conference Act[15] in 1964; the Freedom of Information Act (FOIA)[16] in 1966 (revised in 1974); the Federal Advisory Committee Act[17] in 1972; the Privacy Act[18] in 1974; and the Government in the Sunshine Act[19] in 1976.

The philosophical underpinnings of administrative law are weak. Nonetheless, the theoretical groundwork of administrative law in general, and the APA in particular, is not *necessarily* inimical to liberty and the rule of law. Indeed, one of the leading authorities in the field, Professor Kenneth Culp Davis, discerns a special virtue in the APA in that it strengthens the rule of law as applied to the exercise of government power. For his purposes, Professor Davis understands the idea of "rule of law" to mean the following:

> The rule of law (1) forbids unnecessary discretionary power; (2) allows necessary discretionary power, especially for needed individualizing for changing law, for new programs for which rules are not yet developed, and for determinations which cannot be governed or guided by rules; (3) requires guiding rules or standards, as far as feasible, when governing rules are not feasible; (4) requires structuring and checking of necessary discretion, including, as far as feasible, (5) open standards, (6) open findings, (7) open reasons, and (8) open precedents; (9) requires striving for consistency without requiring consistency, and (10) requires reasoned explanations, as far as feasible, for departures from precedents; (11) requires that every officer who exercises discretionary power be appropriately supervised or reviewed as far as feasible; and (12) requires as much confining, structuring, and checking of the exercise of discretionary power as feasible.[20]

The Davis definition may not be one around which a conservative would rally without reservation; his recurring phrase of qualification, "as far as feasible," demands some explanation, and the limitations he would place upon judicial power are ambiguous. But key concepts are present: there are limits upon legitimate governmental power; those who govern are themselves to be governed; arbitrary exercises of power may be checked by an appeal to a judicially enforceable higher law; and the power of the judiciary, like the power of government in general, is subject to certain well-defined limits.

For the policymaker as regulator, the APA's most important features are those specified for rule-making. Three kinds of rule-making are contemplated by the Act:

1) *Rule-making on notice and comment.* Largely governed by 5 U.S.C. § 553, this category of rule-making reaches most substantive (or "legislative") rules.[21] It is the form of regulation that most broadly affects major government programs. The APA imposes a procedure that consists generally of two exertions by the rule-making agency: first, the publication—in the *Federal Register*—of a "proposed rule" coupled with an invitation to the public to comment upon it; and, second, following the agency's receipt and consideration of the public's comments, the publication of notice of a "final rule" in advance of the rule's effective date.

2) *Rule-making through a trial-type procedure.* Also known as rule-making "on the record," this category of regulation is controlled by 5 U.S.C. 556 and 557. It applies to rate-makings and other kinds of determinations that derive from contested proceedings. Few rules of general applicability are made in this way today; most rules made "on the record" apply to narrow fields of regulated conduct, such as the issuance of specific licenses, the granting of particular transportation routes, or the authorization of rates or prices in controlled markets.

3) *Interpretive and procedural rule-making.* Quantitatively the most common form of rule-making, these exercises are those with minimal participation by parties outside the agency. The rules involved are typically those spelling out an agency's procedures for handling its business and those announcing its interpretations of the statutes committed to it for execution. Agencies may also use this form of rule-making to announce its interpretations of the "notice and comment" rules that it has adopted pursuant to 5 U.S.C. 553.

Just as most rules of importance to policymakers will be those of the "notice and comment" variety, so most legal and political challenges will be to rules of that kind, as well. Experience shows that five crucial problems frequently afflict Section 553 regulation.

First, challengers to a rule-making will frequently contend that the proposed rule is seriously at variance with the statute authorizing it. The policymaker is well advised, therefore, to make sure that the record of the rule-making reflects a clear understanding of its fidelity to the underlying legislative command. The rule-maker generally controls the timing and substance of the analysis and discussion of proposed and final rules that appear with the regulatory texts themselves in the *Federal Register*. Those companion statements should be taken seriously by policymakers, for they will constitute an extremely important part of the record on review in the event that judicial scrutiny is given to the exercise. They provide excellent opportunities to lay out the case not only for the statutory validity of a regulatory course but for its overall merits.

Second, those who seek to compel, rather than oppose, regulation will often contend that a statute requires, rather than permits, rule-making. The policymaker who seeks to resist unnecessary or harmful regulation should avail himself of the public notice and comment process to state his case. He should build the strongest and clearest possible record as to why he construes the statute either to permit the rescission of a rule or to countenance the minimal level of regulation that he proposes to impose. Because statutes assertedly compelling regulation are often fact-driven, the marshaling of facts to show changed conditions in the interval since enactment of the statutory command to regulate can be decisive in winning judicial vindication of a decision not to regulate or to regulate only lightly.

Third, challenges to rule-makings often aver that inadequate attention was given by the agency to comments submitted by the public. An ample discussion of received comments in the *Federal Register* statement on the rule will generally rebut such a contention. Public comments not infrequently achieve precisely what the APA contemplated they would contribute to the rule-making process: commenters have been known to offer suggestions that improve the rule. In any event, the prudent policymaker will want to monitor the flow of comments—especially those that are hostile—so as to anticipate the challenges and criticisms with which he must deal.

Fourth, there are occasions on which the policymaker is moved to change a contemplated rule significantly, subsequent to the publication of notice of the proposed rule-making. It may be, for example, that public commenters have been so convincing in their submissions that the policymaker is persuaded to make substantial changes in the rule before approving it for publication as notice of a final rule. Under such circumstances, so that it can properly be maintained that the public was given a fair and reasonable opportunity to comment on the rule essentially in the form in which it was ultimately promulgated, it may be wise to publish it—as revised—in the *Federal Register* for a second time as the notice of a proposed rule-making. If even subsequent republications are warranted they can be well worth the investment of time and energy. It is not necessary that rules be published in proposed form exactly as they eventually appear in final form; but the failure to accord the public an opportunity to comment on a truly significant provision of the rule can lead to its invalidation by a court. The time thus lost in litigation and subsequent revival of rule-making procedures can vastly exceed the time that would be required to effect a prophy-lactic republication the first time around.

Fifth, challengers most frequently charge that inadequate time was given for comment on a proposed rule or as notice of the effectuation of a final rule. The APA is flexible on timing, and will admit of speedy rule-makings if circumstances justify it. If speed is necessary and appropriate, the policymaker would do well to document the need and to do so publicly. If the time for comment has been demonstrably adequate, then the regulator should also prepare to document the flow of comments over time or the other indicia of the reasonableness of his conduct. As a practical matter, the burden of such a demonstration is not great if the agency has established an efficient mechanism for the receipt, logging-in, and consideration of public comments.

———————◇———————

THE POLICYMAKER AS LITIGANT

As the preceding reflections on the regulatory process make clear, the prudent policymaker keeps one eye fixed on the possibilities of litigation. Litigation has become an intended consequence of the operation of our domestic policy-making system. This is so because an institutional interest of Congress is served by this system's dependence upon formalized contests as to the meanings of congressional enact-ments; that is, litigation is a highly convenient vehicle in which to transfer a thorny public-policy problem from the halls of Congress to the chambers of the executive and the judiciary.

There are two crucial points regarding litigation that cannot be stressed too strongly:

> *Litigation defense can be policy-making offense.* A responsible federal executive will be sued and sued often. One's natural instinct, when made a defendant in a federal lawsuit, is to think that one has done something

wrong. On the contrary, when the conscientious federal executive is sued, chances are that he has done something right. Litigation should be viewed as an opportunity to explain and to defend the Administration's policy choices. The loss of a single lawsuit does not necessarily spell defeat for an entire policy; but victory in a lawsuit can often strengthen a policy and encourage the trend of policy-making from which it emerges.

Losing a lawsuit is not necessarily losing the policy war. Bad cases can make good policy, by informing public sentiment and thereby setting the stage for policy change in Congress, in the executive branch, at the polls, and even at higher levels of the judiciary. Loss of a case can give rise to an opportunity to appeal. It can serve as a stimulus to continued litigation, in both the same court and other courts, at both the same level and above. It can also create opportunities to explain a policy and a controversy to the public.

The point is a simple but all important one: litigation can be a threat, but it can also be an opportunity.[22] Making the most of that opportunity requires the skillful blending of policy vision and legal strategy. This is typically the responsibility of an agency's general counsel.[23] In a litigious age, the role of the general counsel is vital to the success of an agency's mission. Selection of the general counsel, therefore, is among the most important personnel decisions likely to be made in any department.

Complete understanding of the legal environment surrounding a policy dispute cannot be had unless an evaluation of it is obtained from a lawyer who shares the policymaker's fundamental values and commitment to policy change. Policy-making and the proper administration of government entail risk; some risks are political, others are legal. Identifying, evaluating, weighing, and balancing risks are elements of the art that a lawyer must practice when counseling in support of policy change.

There are moments when government's proper role is that of peacemaker and conciliator. But occasions also arise when sober public officials must willingly enter the lists of litigation to assert, defend, and vindicate serious policy judgments. That can be true whether the policy decision at issue was made by Congress, by the President, or by the policymaker's agency itself. Litigation should never be courted unnecessarily, but policy judgments should not be abandoned nor should agency operations be distorted for the sole purpose of avoiding lawsuits.

The policymaker must have the candid advice of one who understands both his goals and his obligations. Such work demands a lawyer who is faithful both to the policy mandate of the Administration of the day and to the underlying system of justice. The job description is that of the politically appointed general counsel. Career lawyers in government agencies tend to counsel the avoidance of risk. Their instincts are to preserve the *status quo* and they are therefore likely to be unsympathetic, at least initially, to policy change. Successful management of policy change requires the careful assessment of risk from a perspective that is both politically sensitive and legally informed.

The Department of Justice holds, by statute, a virtual monopoly[24] on most litigation on behalf of the government in the "Article III" courts—that is, the Federal District Courts, Courts of Appeals, and Supreme Court—and in the courts of the several states.[25] Agencies are generally responsible for supplying their own legal advice and for carrying on the legal activities associated with regulatory processes. They are also typically authorized to conduct their own proceedings before administrative tribunals. But they must work closely with the Justice Department when the forum for resolving disputes shifts to the courthouse. Vital agency interests are often at stake in the cases that the Justice Department steps in to conduct; supervising the work of the Justice Department in those cases is a crucial dimension of the agency general counsel's portfolio.

The Department of Justice generally has a good reputation for absorbing and advocating the policy goals of its client agencies. But Justice Department lawyers cannot be expected to have any better understanding of those goals than the agencies impart to it. Articulation of agency goals and operational needs is a key task of the general counsel, and success plainly demands that the general counsel be keenly sensitive to policy considerations.

───────────────◇───────────────

CHECKLIST FOR DAY ONE

The prudent and effective policymaker needs to be the informed client of key advisers, legal, policy, and otherwise. Under ideal circumstances the conservative leader, upon installation as a federal policymaker, would be able to answer the following questions and garner the following information immediately:

◆ What is the bedrock conservative agenda for my office?
◆ Who are the key personnel in my chain of command?
   ◆ noncareer?
   ◆ career?

- ◆ Who is my legal adviser?
- ◆ What are my legal powers, duties, and constraints? Obtain the following from counsel, in a written compilation accompanied by an oral briefing:
  - ◆ controlling statutes
  - ◆ applicable regulations
  - ◆ internal rules and delegations of authority
  - ◆ live court orders, including consent decrees
  - ◆ an inventory of pending litigation
  - ◆ a statement of what can be changed, and how one can change it
- ◆ What are the decisional paths and procedures within my agency?
- ◆ What is the path to publication in the *Federal Register* and other mechanisms of formal policy-making and rule-making?
- ◆ Who are the key contacts elsewhere in my agency?
- ◆ Who are my key contacts at the central management and representation agencies—the people who will help advance policy agenda, and will give a "second opinion" on a policy, legal, personnel, budget, or administrative matter, when needed:
  - ◆ at the White House?
  - ◆ at the Office of Management and Budget?
  - ◆ at the Office of Personnel Management?
  - ◆ at the General Services Administration?
  - ◆ at the Department of Justice?
- ◆ Who are my key contacts in the agency's field structure? (Field operations can be central to a policymaker's success; after all, about 90 percent of the federal workforce—and almost 100 percent of the American people—will be found *outside* the Washington Beltway.)
- ◆ What issues can be foreseen arising in the near-term?
- ◆ Is there a calendar of important events and other foreseeable external demands?

A crucial dimension of a policymaker's early efforts is the identification of resources. It is important to understand that the policymaker's environment in 1989 will be markedly different from the world of 1980 and 1981. The conservative movement has been anchored by strong intellectual centers undertaking useful and timely policy research, including the American Enterprise Institute, the CATO Institute, the Free Congress Foundation, and The Heritage Foundation. A nationwide network of conservative public interest law firms has finally come of age, among them the Mid-America Legal Foundation, the

Mountain States Legal Foundation, the Pacific Legal Foundation, and the Washington Legal Foundation. From the first day on the job, therefore, a conservative policymaker can be assured of finding sources of information and advice, both within and without the Administration. There can be no substitutes, however, for the moral and policy gyroscopes that are furnished by the law, the President, and the policymaker himself. The agenda of policy change is the touchstone of preparation and the ultimate yardstick of success.

———————————◇———————————

MEASURING SUCCESS

Establishing a checklist for one's first day on the job can be considerably easier than furnishing a yardstick for the last day. Part of the problem, of course, is that defining the "last day" is not necessarily obvious. Given the external constraints of confirmation hearings and delays, congressional calendars, and election cycles, a four-year term of office arguably equates to a two-year window of regulatory opportunity. Timing is vital; speed is essential.

In searching for the indicia of success it may be helpful to identify considerations that are *not* true measurements of accomplishment. One should beware of quantitative tests of regulatory achievement. Numbers of pages in the *Federal Register* do not reveal whether regulatory burdens are being aggravated or eased; the revocation of 20,000 pages of regulatory follies would probably consume at least 40,000 pages of proposed rules, final rules, notices, analyses, and discussion. Counting cases settled does not disclose the merits of the settlements. Staying out of court—whatever the wisdom of such a course may be in private life—is not necessarily a virtue in public office. It will be a rare federal policymaker who can be aggressive and effective and still avoid litigation, either as a plaintiff or a defendant.

Perhaps the best indicia of success are political and qualitative: How well has one defined one's agenda? How well has that agenda been articulated? How many of one's priority goals for legislation, rules, and operations changes have been accomplished? Above all, who has one gathered as one's enemies?

The Reagan Administration achieved many successes, but dramatic changes in the black letter law of legislation was ultimately not among them. Legislative initiatives were pursued primarily at the margins, and even then, with conspicuous exceptions such as tax reform, the Administration was often not the principal proponent of change. The task of pruning the statute books remains to be done. Sorely needed, it may prove as arduous as the cleaning of the Augean stables.

Solid judicial precedents are powerful contributions that conservative policymakers can make. As the left learned long ago, litigation is a battleground with many advantages, among them timing. A plaintiff can commence a lawsuit at the time of his choosing. Moreover, by his choice of forum the plaintiff can pick the battlefield as well. There are limiting factors, to be sure, but the power of initiative is virtually always and everywhere the power to define the terms of debate.

Coordination of regulatory, legislative, and litigation decisions with an agency's public outreach program can be an extraordinarily effective way of achieving public understanding of a policymaker's goals and perceptions. Conservatives must never be reluctant to commence debate and to force the opposition to join. The left is never so successful as when it can mask its ideology and intentions behind veneers of moderation, technical competence, and personal charm. It must be denied that strategy. In the end, the stripping away of masks and the pouring in of sunshine is the only way to gather up the Swarms and send them buzzing thither.

―――――――――――――◇―――――――――――――

NOTES

1. *American Declaration of Independence,* July 4, 1776. (Spelling and capitalization original.)

2. *Federal Trade Commission* v. *Ruberoid Co.,* 343 U.S. 470, 487 (1952) (Jackson, J., dissenting).

3. 737–741. Among these entities are the Architectural and Transportation Barriers Compliance Board; the Committee for the Implementation of Textile Agreements; the Export Administration Review Board; the Federal Financing Bank; the Federal Mine Safety and Health Commission; the Federal Retirement Thrift Investment Board; the Marine Mammal Commission; the Mississippi River Commission; the Navajo and Hopi Indian Relocation Commission; the Physician Payment Review Commission; the President's Foreign Intelligence Advisory Board; and the United States Sentencing Commission.

4. This is the number of pages published in Volume 52 of the *Federal Register,* which opened on January 1 and closed on December 31, 1987. The pace for 1988 is slightly faster: as of June 30, 1988, Volume 53 had already attained 24,919 pages.

5. *Annual Report of the Director of the Administrative Office of the United States Courts* (1986), 175, Table C-2.

6. *Id.* at 138, Table B-1.

7. 1 Administrative Conference of the United States, *1987 Recommendations and Reports* 36 (Recommendation No. 87-7).

8. _____ U.S. _____, 56 U.S.L.W. 4835 (June 29, 1988). *See especially* the dissent of Justice Scalia, _____U.S. at _____, 56 U.S.L.W. at 4847.

9. 28 U.S.C. §§ 591–599.

10. *Chrysler Corp.* v. *Brown,* 441 U.S. 281, 295 (1979); *United States* v. *Mersky,* 361 U.S. 431, 438 (1960); *Atchison, Topeka & Santa Fe Railway* v. *Scarlett,* 300 U.S. 471, 474 (1937).

11. *See, e.g.,* U.S. Const., Art. I, Sec. 8; Amendment XIV, Sec. 5; Amendment XV, Sec. 2.

12. Morris, "Congressional Cowardice: An Inquiry into the Causes of the Public Law Explosion," in 2 National Legal Center for the Public Interest, *The Legal Assault on the Economy* (1986), at 9.

13. *Id.* at 14.

14. 5 U.S.C. §§ 551–559, 701–706, 1305, 3105, 3344, 6362, 7562.

15. 5 U.S.C. § 571–575.

16. 5 U.S.C. § 552.

17. 5 U.S.C. App. I.

18. 5 U.S.C. § 552a.

19. 5 U.S.C. § 552b.

20. 1 Davis, *Administrative Law Treatise* § 2:16, at 130 (2d ed. 1978).

21. "Legislative" rules, in this context, are those promulgated by administrative agencies exercising delegated legislative powers. They are distinguished from merely interpretive, procedural, or internal agency rules.

22. For a fuller treatment of this topic, see Morris, "Clausewitz Updated: Litigation as the Continuation of Policy Making by Other Means," in Rector, ed., *Steering the Elephant* 75 (1987).

23. By *general counsel* I mean, in context, a policymaker's principal legal adviser. In most cases this will be the official who is an agency's chief lawyer, responsible for its legal advice and representation. The precise title by which this official is known varies. In most federal departments and agencies the chief legal officer is, indeed, called the "general counsel," but other appellations—*e.g.,* "chief counsel," "solicitor," and "legal adviser"—are frequently found. In the Department of Justice the official whose duties most closely approximate those of the general counsel in other agencies is the Assistant Attorney General in charge of the Office of Legal Counsel. The Office of Legal Counsel also has responsibility for assisting the Attorney General in the preparation of the Attorney General's legal opinions of government-wide applicability.

24. Although the Justice Department has primary responsibility for the conduct of the Government's courtroom litigation, there are a few highly limited exceptions— carved out by explicit acts of Congress—that confer independent litigating authority on certain agencies.

25. There are occasional instances when the federal government litigates in state courts. The United states might be a party, for example, to proceedings involving real estate or decedents' estates that fall within a state court's jurisdiction. Federal prosecutors, acting under delegations of authority from state district attorneys, sometimes bring criminal actions in state courts. (Except for the anomalous independent counsels dangerously erected by the Ethics in Government Act, the power to prosecute crime at the federal level is vested entirely in the Attorney General, which he in turn delegates to his subordinates in the Department of Justice.)

35

Grants and Contracts Management

by
Carol P. Whitten and Timothy N. Hunter*

Policy implementation is achieved through various means, some simple, some complex. Previous chapters have addressed the process of policy development, and policy as it relates to budget, personnel management, and the regulatory process. This chapter will discuss that aspect of policy implementation associated with the disbursement of funds, specifically through the awards of grants and contracts. Grant and contract expenditures make up the majority of many departmental and agency budgets. Numerous federal programs require some degree of grant and contract support in order to operate effectively. The grant and contracting processes are thought by most political executives to be administrative functions best delegated to career managers. There are, however, substantial policy implications associated with the disbursement of funds, and political appointees need some understanding of the process involved and where to insert policy considerations.

Establishing a grant program is a favorite means for Congress to distribute revenues because of the ability to target the funding to specific groups or segments of the population. Many organizational components in the executive branch have been established solely for the purpose of awarding and processing grants.

Contracting dollars are more difficult to target because of the highly restrictive statutory requirements which regulate the contracting process. These rules and regulations have been propagated to insure fair

*The authors wish to thank the following contributors for their helpful suggestions in the preparation of this chapter: Ampara Bouchey, Kenneth Butler, Elaine Chao, Bob Collins, Bill Hansen, David Kirker, Linda Rule, Kenneth Whitehead, Susan Zagame, and Jerry Vance. The views expressed in this chapter are, however, entirely the responsibility of the authors.

and open competition in the awarding of contracts, thereby protecting the interests of the government (i.e., the taxpayer) and the prospective bidders. Nevertheless there are numerous instances of congressional intervention and micromanagement in both the grant and contract processes. These incursions vary in intensity and scope from written inquiries and telephone calls, to full-scale hearings, or even legislative language directing the award of a grant or contract to a specific recipient.

In light of these political realities and because financial disbursements reflect agency policy, political appointees must learn some of the technical details of disbursement and procurement in order to manage them in a manner consistent with an Administration's goals and objectives. This familiarity can protect the political appointee from becoming uncomfortably lodged between an Administration seeking to reduce federal outlays or redirect spending, and highly energized, well-guided members of Congress (or their staff) eager to advance parochial interests.

Grant and contract functions are almost exclusively relegated to the career sector of government but this need not be and in many instances should not be. There are steps in the process which are best suited to career civil service management and oversight and others which allow or require discretionary decision-making more appropriately left to policy officials.

———————◇———————

GRANTS

Grants are the basic vehicle for providing assistance (usually money) to a recipient to accomplish a public policy purpose. Grants are authorized by federal statute and are usually awarded to states, local governments, educational institutions, and nonprofit organizations, but can also be directed to other groups and organizations, as well as to individuals. Grants can be broken down into two types— discretionary and nondiscretionary. Discretionary grants are usually awarded competitively and allow the selecting official (either the political executive or his designee) some discretion in selecting grantees. Nondiscretionary grants (called formula or block grants) are distributed according to congressional instruction or formula and allow less discretion. However, many types of grant programs are more efficiently distributed by formula since it eliminates lobbying of federal officials by putting program responsibility at the state or local level.

To implement the statutory requirement for establishing a grant program, the agency must first establish a set of procedures by which grants are to be evaluated and awarded. This is done through the issuance of regulations. Regulation development is the most critical area of policy decision-making in the grant process. Although legally rigorous and procedurally bureaucratic, it must be understood by all appointees. Grant programs are controlled primarily by the program legislation, but they are administered by regulations issued by the agency. During the regulatory process, the appointee can exercise discretion in the selection of program priorities (consistent with agency priorities), and in interpreting congressional intent. As a first step, the appointee should review existing regulations and the program's legislative history to determine how best to incorporate an Administration's goals and objectives. The typical response from staff about why something is being done in a certain way will be, "We have always done it this way!" This usually identifies an area where the political appointee may have discretion to introduce new Administration policies.

Once the grant governing regulations are developed, they appear in the *Federal Register* as a Notice of Proposed Rulemaking. The program will receive public comments on the new regulations, ranging anywhere from interest groups opposing any change to concerned individuals offering constructive ideas. Following review of the comments, the regulations are rewritten, incorporating those comments the program chooses to adopt. Grant application packages are then printed and mailed to eligible applicants that have requested an application.

The Closing Date Notice, which is published after the regulations are completed, affords the appointee an opportunity to publicize priorities and solicit proposals in specific areas of interest. This notice usually provides a response period of up to 90 days to submit proposals. Although the application package is controlled by the regulations, the senior political executive should ensure that the package does not contain anything that might be contrary to statute, regulation, or agency policies.

At this point the process shifts to the agency's application review/ evaluation procedure. The specifics of the evaluation procedures may vary from agency to agency but the process is basically the same. An illustrative example follows. The program prepares field reader evaluation criteria and forms and selects field readers that will serve in panels to review proposals. After the closing date, the field panels review proposals and their results are statistically normalized to arrive at a funding list. This rank order list serves as a guideline for funding. The selecting officials then apply additional, previously published criteria (such as geographical distribution), to insure that selections meet program needs and objectives.

After the staff completes a summary of each proposal, slate rankings and priority points are applied. At this point the grant funding slate goes to the grant selecting official for approval. The grant official must take serious note of the slate, since grants funded in his tenure are ultimately his responsibility and it is not unusual for congressional oversight hearings to include questions about a specific grant. Upon approval of the slate, the Grants Office begins negotiations with grantees. After the government ascertains that only allowable and necessary costs have been included in the proposal, the grant is formally awarded and Congress is notified. Congressional notification is a courtesy which allows members of Congress formally to notify constituents that they have received a federal grant. After award, grant administration becomes the responsibility of either the grants program or grants management offices.

Cooperative Agreements are a second method used to provide assistance. They differ from grants in that a grant anticipates no substantial involvement between the grantee and the agency. In a cooperative agreement there is substantial involvement between the grantee and the agency, the extent of which varies with each agreement. The degree of "substantial involvement" is stipulated by the program's legislation, but its interpretation may afford the political executive some discretion.

———————◇———————

CONTRACTS

Contracting is an essential element of federal management providing the opportunity to buy goods in a competitive environment and acquire services not otherwise available from the federal workforce. During the Reagan Administration, the purchase of services was aggressively extended to include some services traditionally performed by government employees. The concept of "contracting-out" was not new to government and had been encouraged by OMB in its circular A–76. Under the rules of A–76, the cost of government services must be compared against the cost of similar, commercially available services. If the cost comparison provides a ten percent or greater savings to the government, the activity is to be "contracted out." Purchase of services in the competitive market is particularly advantageous to the public because it shifts the burdens and risks of internal, agency managed operations away from dependence upon the government's institutional organization. Contracting, in effect, means to transfer these risks from the taxpayers onto private contractors who, through payment and performance provisions, guarantee that a service or product will be provided according to legally binding terms.

Contracts are the vehicle by which the government can procure any item or service from individuals or organizations (for example: office supplies, transportation services, maintenance services, conferences, opinion surveys, printing and publication of books, computers, facility construction, military hardware, research and development). The Federal Acquisition Regulations (FAR) list thirteen types of contracts and three forms of agreements. The most common are fixed price contracts (where the government purchases something for a predetermined price and places the burden of delivery on the contractor) or cost-reimbursement contracts (which are used when it is impractical to assess the price of the service before it is provided). Contracts are controlled by, and require contractors to adhere to, many diverse federal statutes and regulations, such as the Buy American Act, the Small Business Act, various labor laws, affirmative action and EEO requirements, environmental regulations, accounting standards, preference clauses, and federal property management regulations.

A fundamental principle underlying the contracting process is the promotion of fair and open competition. The Reagan Administration placed a heavy emphasis on enforcing this concept and promoted the passage of the Competition In Contracting Act (CICA) in 1984. Among other reforms CICA further restricted the use of "sole source" contracts (noncompetitive award to a specific contractor) and established and defined the role of Competition Advocates in executive branch agencies. One of the chief functions of the agency Competition Advocate is to discourage the use of sole source contracts and to force the review and recompetition of long-standing arrangements with contractors to assure an ethical and objective government/contractor relationship. Since the needs for goods and services vary, agency preference for certain types of contracting instruments varies accordingly. However, all agency procurement and acquisition processes are governed by the same set of complex rules, codified in the Federal Acquisition Regulations (FAR).

Contracts, as disbursement instruments, should be viewed from two perspectives. On one hand, they support or complement government operations, allowing programs to run effectively. On the other, they also represent a mechanism to transfer funds between legislated groups of beneficiaries in the economy. Depending upon the scope and effect of a particular contract the appointee will find either intense public interest and congressional scrutiny in a given contracting program or minimal interest. When this interest manifests itself, it is the appointee who will be held accountable for the outcome of a contract competition, regardless of degree of involvement. Pleading ignorance of the process affords no defense.

As is true of every managerial function, contracting authority within an agency is the ultimate responsibility of the agency head—who initiates the internal delegations of contracting authority. These delegations should be reviewed carefully by all political appointees with procurement authority or responsibility. After consultation with the agency's Procurement Executive and Competition Advocate, they should consider changing the delegations as appropriate.

In broad terms federal contracting can be described in four phases: policy/planning; contract design and solicitation; proposal evaluation and award; contract execution.

The *policy/planning* phase involves the identification of organizational contract requirements. These are detailed in the agency's annual procurement plan which specifies areas of interest, project priorities, estimated cost, and expected duration. It is at this point in the planning cycle that Administration priorities must be inserted. The procurement cycle can be very long (from several months to several years) and early scheduling is critical to successful implementation within an appointee's limited political lifetime.

The second phase, *contract design and solicitation*, relies heavily on input from both program and procurement offices. Decisions are made on the most appropriate contracting instrument to use (fixed price, cost reimbursable, fixed fee, performance clauses, etc.) and a Statement of Work is prepared describing the scope of the effort. During this phase a key decision regarding the Statement of Work concerns the use of design specifications versus performance criteria. Political appointees should encourage staff to specify performance criteria which require bidders to propose original solutions to the problem (i.e., define the outcomes which are sought rather than the means to achieve the outcomes). This affords the government the opportunity to review a variety of potentially innovative solutions to existing problems. Too often government employees design their own solutions, thereby straight-jacketing bidders with overly restrictive specifications which only serve to drive up proposed costs.

Once the Statement of Work and contract package are prepared and approved, a solicitation announcement (synopsis) is published in the Commerce Business Daily notifying potential bidders of the availability of the RFP (Request for Proposal) and of the deadlines for submissions.

The *proposal evaluation/award* phase will be controlled by the selection criteria established in the previous phase and by the quality of personnel assigned to the evaluation panels (known as Source Selection Boards or Source Evaluation Boards). The key individual in charge of this process is the Source Selection Official, who should be chosen carefully. Separate evaluations and numerical scores are developed for the proposed technical solution and for proposed price.

The final phase, *contract execution*, is self-explanatory and deals with monitoring progress and performance over the life of the contract.

The political appointee has a large role to play in the first phase by defining organizational requirements in the context of Administration priorities. In the second phase the appointee's role lies in ensuring that the proposal evaluation criteria are rational and consistent with Administration goals and objectives. In the third phase the appointee should ascertain that the Source Selection Official and the members of the evaluation panel are supportive of Administration programs. In the final phase, an appointee's responsibility lies in making certain that contracts are closely monitored for performance.

———————◇———————

MANAGEMENT INITIATIVES AND REFORMS

During the eight years of the Reagan Administration much was done to improve program management, advance policy goals administratively, and reduce waste, fraud, and abuse. Some of the major initiatives included:

◆ Implementation of many of the recommendations of the Grace Commission, which identified many examples of wasteful practices in government with a potential for saving billions of dollars (for example, offsetting and collecting the income-tax refunds of defaulters on student loans; garnishing salaries of federal employees who were student loan defaulters; referring such defaulters to collection agencies, credit bureaus, and ultimately to the Department of Justice for prosecution).

◆ Consolidation of family support programs under the Family Support Administration, which allowed the Department of Health and Human Services to develop uniform strategies to encourage self-sufficiency, reduce staffing levels, and eliminate duplication of effort in travel and contracts for services.

◆ Establishment of the President's Council on Management Improvement (1984) to develop and implement improved management and administrative systems, identify successful practices in agencies for government-wide implementation, and resolve interagency management problems.

◆ Promulgation of OMB Circular A–122, forbidding federal contractors and grantees from lobbying with federal dollars.

◆ Promulgation of OMB Circular A–123, calling for an annual vulnerability assessment of agency management systems, to identify program areas vulnerable to fraud, waste, and abuse.

◆ Issuance of Executive Order 12354 (1982) on Procurement Reform, which required centralized agency procurement responsibility and the designation of agency Procurement Executives.

◆ Passage of the Competition in Contracting Act (1984) establishing agency Competition Advocates and expanding competitive practices in contracting.

◆ Enactment of the Federal Manager Financial Integrity Act, establishing broad mandates for all federal managers and specific reporting procedures.

The degree of implementation of these management initiatives has varied from agency to agency, and continued follow-up will remain a fertile area of management improvement for future Administrations.

The Grant Review Process

Discretionary grants and competitive contracts are awarded with help from a panel of experts in the field. This process is called "Peer Review" or "Field Reader Panels." These panels vary in composition from all nonfederal reviewers to all federal employees, and this is usually an area where the political executive has discretion to change panel compositions. The Reagan Administration found that during previous administrations, appointees had deferred to the "Iron-Triangle" (Congress, the bureaucracy, and special interest groups) to provide like-minded readers. This allowed programs to remain in the hands of the special interest and professional grant proposal writers. For this reason, the Reagan Administration made peer review reform a major initiative. For the first time, "objective" professionals with expertise in the necessary fields were recruited from the general public, from universities, and from other diverse groups. A bank of new field readers was created in many agencies. In many cases, this move was resisted by the career bureaucracy, while in others peer review reform was ignored by political executives who saw the issue as bureaucratic. Peer review reform proved successful only where political executives took a direct interest in the process, used readers from the new pool, and insisted on final selection approval of all readers.

Proposal Evaluation Review Panels

Competitive contracts are awarded on the basis of scores compiled according to predetermined evaluation criteria. The proposal evaluation criteria are established by evaluation boards or panels made up of agency employees. Selection of panelists is important and the political executive must ensure that the integrity of the process is maintained at all times. Ultimately, it is the political appointee that is held accountable for any transgressions, improprieties, or failings in the system. It behooves the appointee to manage the process (be it grants or contracts) at the discretionary points to (1) minimize vulnerability to fraud and abuse, and (2) ensure policy goals and objectives are met.

Awards to "High-Risk" Grantees and Contractors

During the first years of the Reagan Administration, many political executives found that after one year of a grant or contract cycle, some contractors and grantees had not lived up to the terms of their agreements. It was discovered that many of these people had performed poorly on previous federal obligations. However, there was often no warning mechanism in place to inform agencies of past performance history. This issue became one of the elements of the Administration's management reform agenda in fighting fraud, waste and abuse. As a result, there now exists a government-wide process of tracking contractors who are found to violate contracting laws. For example, if a contractor is debarred by one agency, that is grounds for debarment by any other agency. Debarment precludes receiving a government contract for a specified period of time. Debarment procedures are instituted against a contractor if he is found to be guilty of fraud or other serious violations. This process is now being expanded to apply to federal grants and other nonprocurement transactions, including subcontracts under grants.

Although there are no government-wide "contractor performance" lists, many agencies now have "High Risk" regulations. In many cases, authority was found in existing administrative regulations which only needed updating and implementation. For example, at the Department of Education, a grantee or contractor is considered "High Risk" if:

1) Its financial statements show poor financial stability.

2) It is a newly formed organization or one that does not have prior experience with the federal government.

3) There are serious deficiencies in programs or business management systems.

4) There is a history of unsatisfactory performance, material violations of the terms and conditions, or large cost disallowances on previous federal awards.

5) Financial statements show excessive dependence on federal support (only in the case of grantees).

Once a grantee or contractor is determined to be in this "High Risk" category, the Selecting Official can consider the risks and choose an alternate proposal.

Grants Management

Administration of discretionary grants tends to be a gray area in many agencies, with authority delegated from agency heads, through political subordinates, to career managers. In many cases this is due to the perception by some appointees that management is a low priority. The following are suggestions to improve appointee efficiency, thereby giving the appointee more discretion and authority. As a guide, a new executive might pose the following questions:

1) Are there agency-wide standards regarding the monitoring of grants and contracts? Are there guidelines for establishing effective monitoring procedures, and are program managers held accountable for the quality of their program oversight?

2) Is there cooperation among the agency's political executives in using innovative oversight procedures such as cross-program site visits (in a cross-program site visit, a program officer reviews all the federal programs funded in the agency at the site, not just those in his program)?

3) Are all program requirements being enforced? Grant and contract

files can be randomly selected and reviewed for proper documentation (quarterly reports, end of year reports), with evidence of the responsible official's notes on monitoring and technical assistance.

4) Are grants awarded for a limited term? Since one purpose of discretionary grants is to develop, over a short period, the capacity of the grantee to be self-sufficient, grants made for two or more years should have declining federal involvement. In the case of multiyear awards, have the objectives for the first year been accomplished?

5) Is information about the existence of particular grant programs being disseminated more widely than to the "traditional" grantees?

Small Business Set-Aside

An area suitable for experimentation in expanded competition is the 8(a) "Set Aside Program" (referring to Public Law 95–507, October 24, 1978, Section 8(a) of the U.S. Small Business Administration Act), which provides assistance to small and disadvantaged companies to enable them to become independently competitive. The SBA has the power to enter into contracts with any federal office having procurement powers. SBA can then use its financial, technical and management resources to contract with other federal departments and agencies to supply their goods, services, and construction requirements, and then to subcontract the actual work performance to 8(a) companies. The firms covered by 8(a) come under the "Business Development Program" and have been previously determined to be eligible by SBA to participate. Current rules do not allow price competition among 8(a) firms, i.e., 8(a) contracts are not awarded to low bidders. This policy should be changed to instill among 8(a) contractors the spirit of competition which truly prepares them for graduation into the broader competitive business environment. Political appointees should also review agency policies and procedures to ensure that the widest use is being made of firms from outside the usual agency contracting orbits.

Contracting Out (A–76)

The Reagan Administration's A–76 initiatives enjoyed some marked successes despite congressional interventions to the contrary. Frequently the last areas of management to be considered for possible contracting-out are those that are administrative in nature. Federal administrative management functions are eminently transferable through the contracting process: record keeping, library services, warehousing, information resources operations, personnel, financial management, security, auditing, and program evaluation. These areas should receive renewed and continued consideration for contracting-out in a new Administration.

Privatization

The privatization of government services should be aggressively pursued in the next Administration. Privatization is not a contracting issue per se, although contracting with the private sector can be an important element in the privatization strategy. Privatization in its broadest sense is distinct from "contracting-out," though the latter is considered by some to be a subset of the privatization initiative. Successful privatization in its ultimate form results in complete substitution of private sector sources for traditional government suppliers of the same services. Short of this entirely free market goal for service delivery, it is possible to subsidize private sector sources through the use of government grants and contracts to serve as substitutes or surrogates for governmental organizations. Economies can be realized simply by removing the delivering entity from the overly restrictive and inefficient government environment. Regardless of the degree of privatization ultimately achieved, the next Administration should aggressively pursue every opportunity to further the conservative privatization agenda.

───────────────────◇───────────────────

CONCLUSION

The above presentation is intended to serve as a primer for the government's grant and contract processes. The intent is not to oversimplify what are technically rigorous and complex procedures, but to provide an overview for the new appointee to help in establishing policy and management priorities. The appointee can develop a sufficiently detailed working knowledge of the field and its extensive rules and regulations with diligence and the helpful advice of a trusted career employee.

Above all, a new appointee should obtain, as soon as practicable after taking office, the agency Delegations of Authority to ascertain the level of delegated grant and contracting responsibility of various individuals in the organization. The Delegations should be reviewed and changed as necessary.

36

Financial Management

by
John Marshall and Jeffrey Pahre*

Among the greatest challenges facing any new appointee is that of managing the financial performance of his or her agency. The task is formidable enough, given the vast sums and program complexities involved. But the problem is compounded by the pervasive pressures working against attention to financial performance. The program development, budget and disbursement processes, geared as they are to sustaining the symbiotic "iron triangle" relationships linking the administrative bureaucracy, constituent groups, and their congressional benefactors, receive far greater, if not disproportionate, attention. Consequently, the manager who finds time to focus on the efficiency and effectiveness of financial performance is rare, and, if effective, is a potential threat to the status quo. Moreover, he or she is often frustrated by the narrow limits of real discretionary authority within which one can manage for results. This is compounded by the inherent perverse incentives for poor performance and the inadequacy of tools and resources often inherited after years of neglect. Nevertheless, the cause is not hopeless, only arduous and requiring constant attention, patience, and a long-term view.

This chapter discusses generic financial management strategies and tools that can be useful in laying the groundwork for major policy initiatives while also improving the performance of government financial assistance programs, whether the assistance is in the form of credit, insurance, income assistance, or any other. It then focuses in greater depth on credit program management since these programs

---

*The authors wish to thank the following for their valuable suggestions and comments: Vance L. Clark, Hon. Dorcas R. Hardy, Charles O. Sethness, Mrs. Kathleen Lawrence, Richard Hastings, John Lordan, Arlene Triplett, Gerald R. Riso, Timothy N. Hunter, and Hal Steinberg. The views expressed in this chapter are, however, entirely the responsibility of the authors.

account for by far the largest share of controllable outlays and have the greatest potential for improving financial performance.

———————————————◇———————————————

FINANCIAL MANAGEMENT

Financial management has long been an overlooked and underdeveloped function within the federal government. Whereas its upstream cousin, the budget process, drives policy and resource allocation, and therein commands glamour and respect, the downstream financial management and accounting functions are often perceived as little more than clean-up details after policy decisions have been made, and as professional backwaters. They receive far less management attention, tend to attract lesser talents, and are sometimes understaffed. Systems and procedures tend to be antiquated. Processing backlogs are common, rendering information in financial statements often incomplete, stale, and unreliable. There is no strong constituency in Washington for strong financial management, and there are few rewards. Subpar financial management can often cover, if not reward, questionable program management. Nevertheless, financial management is vital to the public interest, which requires that the appointee effectively control the financial performance of his or her program or agency. It holds the key to revealing, through financial reports, how programs are performing, and more importantly, can provide additional tools to help an appointee shape or justify policy initiatives.

In the early 1980s, the work of the Grace Commission and of other management experts summoned by the Reagan Administration was made immeasurably more difficult when they were largely unable to get answers to some very basic questions about the government's financial performance due to the inadequacy of systems and information. They found, for example, that previous administrations had allowed hundreds of different financial and administrative systems to proliferate, in the absence of common standards, terms, and definitions. This made cost and productivity comparisons impossible. Government loan portfolios were found to be woefully inadequate. Loan files did not always exist or were missing basic documentation. Systems did not exist to age accounts, bill for delinquencies, or permit cross-screening. No one knew exactly how much money was owed the government, how much was delinquent, how much was collectible, or how much was hopelessly in default.

Following years of neglect, OMB launched "Reform 88," an ambitious program to improve internal controls, upgrade and standardize financial and administrative systems, and strengthen management government-wide. Legislative catch-up complemented it, including the Federal Managers' Financial Integrity Act, the Debt Collection Act, and others. President Reagan's OMB instituted formalized management reviews of executive agency progress that were linked to the budget process, and later established a nonstatutory chief financial officer for the executive branch to spearhead financial management reform.

In 1989, new agency appointees will enter a vastly improved financial management environment compared to what appointees encountered in 1981. Although implementation of many of the reform initiatives has been inconsistent, the benefits of the following improvements will be in evidence in most, if not all, agencies:

◆ Cash management and prompt payment practices such as lock-boxes, electronic funds disbursement and collections, credit card applications, and others have been put in place and are yielding interest savings of over $1 billion per year (according to OMB).

◆ Over 300 different financial systems have been restructured, consolidated, and standardized around a new U.S. Government Standard General Ledger and chart of accounts.

◆ Internal Control Reviews to identify areas of high vulnerability to fraud, waste, and abuse have been institutionalized in an annual review cycle, with responsibilities incorporated as critical elements in most manager performance standards.

Although there has been considerable progress, there remains a lengthy agenda of unfinished business facing a new appointee. It will include sharpening some of the tools already in place, and augmenting them with others. Moreover, the appointee can expect prodding from the central financial management agencies, OMB and Treasury, as well as occasional stimuli from GAO and departmental inspectors general, towards the objectives of ensuring that:

◆ Government-wide standardization and consolidation of financial statements, the general ledger, accounting practices and financial information systems are completed for all programs and agencies.

◆ Accounting principles, internal control standards, FMFIA requirements, etc., are fully and consistently implemented.

◆ Cash management is expanded and further enhanced through such innovations as credit cards, preauthorized debits, "smart card"

technology, progress towards a checkless society for domestic and
international payments, and the expanded use of Automated Clearing
Houses.

◆ Cross-servicing arrangements for sharing expertise and administrative workload among agencies gain greater use and acceptance.

◆ Annual audits of agency financial statements are strengthened to
ensure greater accountability and systems integrity.

These initiatives can, and should, be pursued as aggressively as
possible from the start. And with good reason, for there is also a
political dimension to sound financial management that goes beyond
the "good government" issue. The new appointee should view financial management as an important complement to policy implementation. Financial management initiatives can usually be instituted immediately without much debate, resistance, controversy, or downside risk
while simultaneously providing the groundwork or justification for
bolder policy initiatives.

Cleaning up government loan portfolios, servicing systems, and
documentation was an "apple pie" financial management initiative of
the Reagan Administration's Reform 88. It was also a prerequisite to
contracting out servicing and debt collection and portfolio sales to the
private sector. Moreover, financial management can yield immediate
pay-offs, for example, by pinpointing vulnerabilities to fraud, waste
and abuse. By so doing, questions of program and policy effectiveness
may legitimately be raised, and public opinion may be influenced to
support more ambitious policy aims, such as alternative delivery
systems or privatization.

The new appointee cannot overlook the severe downside potential
from neglecting financial management that could be revealed through
routine GAO or inspector general reviews or through politically motivated "hit squads" operating as special audits or investigations. These
can provide the appointee's opposition with ammunition to undermine
otherwise flawless policy initiatives.

A good illustration is the privatization initiative at the Federal Crop
Insurance Corporation in the early 1980s. The Reagan Administration
turned over hundreds of millions of dollars of insurance business to
private sector insurance companies, without establishing adequate
financial controls and compliance mechanisms. Investigations
prompted by critics of the Administration's program discovered millions of tax dollars paid out in erroneous and excessive claims. The
political heat from these revelations substantially thwarted an otherwise laudable, achievable, and generally well-executed effort which

should have served as a privatization milestone in the Department of Agriculture.

Merely implementing the tools of financial management cannot ensure improved performance of a program or agency; it is up to the new appointee to use them to manage for desired results.

Essential to any conservative management strategy is the need to redefine system performance in ways that are consistent with agenda objectives. Reform 88 scored a major breakthrough in instituting reporting on loan delinquencies, write-offs, interest savings, etc., in routine reports, reports that had previously reflected more on constituency servicing indicators—e.g., numbers of loans and dollar value of loans or grants processed, etc. As a result, delinquencies, write-offs, and program costs were ignored or de-emphasized for political expediency. Under Reform 88, cost-consciousness was immediately heightened, and a new, more realistic dimension was added to the policy debate on program performance. New definitions of performance indicators and reporting have progressed fairly consistently through Reform 88.

The next step in the management strategy is to ensure that performance indicators are captured in the relevant managers' performance standards. The federal government's performance management system is one of the few tools available effectively to assign accountability and ensure that the appointee's highest priorities become those of his or her agency. It should be used assertively to move the policy agenda forward. The use of this system is discussed in more detail in an earlier chapter of this section.

In summary, the new appointee's financial management agenda should include, at a minimum, the following elements:

◆ Defining financial performance indicators that are consistent with conservative goals and objectives and communication of expectations for financial performance to employees through performance management systems.

◆ Development of state-of-the-art financial and accounting systems to meet government-wide standards, including audited financial statements based on generally accepted accounting principles. Off-the-shelf packages may be readily available from contractors or other government agencies. In the latter case, cross-servicing arrangements could be explored. The systems may require modification also to provide agency or program specific financial performance reports. The development of appropriate performance indicators and system modifications may require contractor expertise.

◆ Review and strengthening of existing internal controls programs, with special attention to training of in-house personnel and follow-up through performance management systems.

---◇---

CREDIT MANAGEMENT

Management of the government's credit programs is one of its most significant financial responsibilities. The only budget items greater than the government's credit portfolio are defense spending and interest on the government debt. At the end of fiscal 1987, the government's credit obligations included $234 billion of direct loans, $507 billion of guaranteed loans, and $581 billion of credit extended by government-sponsored enterprises, totalling $1,322 billion.

The government extends credit to nearly every sector of the economy and society, including farmers, homeowners, students, small businesses, exporters, utilities, and state and local governments. The credit responsibility is managed by nearly every federal department and agency. At the end of fiscal 1987, the government's credit portfolio included $1,003 billion for housing, $140 billion for business, $122 billion for agriculture, $53 billion for education, and $4 billion for other purposes. The borrowers generally are unable to secure credit from private-sector lenders, because of insufficient collateral or projected inability to repay at current market rates of interest.

The Reagan Administration was the first seriously to question the role of government as a lender, let alone the lender of last resort to poor risk borrowers. Following a vigorous debate, the Administration succeeded in establishing the following principles:

◆ Government lending should be considered only when it adds a unique value not available from the private sector.

◆ Government lending could be rationalized in support of: broad national goals, such as education; development of uneconomic market segments that would ultimately be able to attract private-sector lending, such as small farms and businesses; recovery from cyclical natural disasters, such as dry spells and water shortages, when they impact farmers, water transporters, and others dependent on a natural abundance of water to support their businesses.

◆ Government guarantees should be limited to 70 percent to 80 percent, leaving borrower and lender with enough risk to insure both parties' best efforts at satisfying the initial credit agreement.

◆ Interest rates should be close to and fluctuate with market rates, terms should be short, to encourage early graduation to private-sector lending, and should reflect the degree of risk.

◆ Loan servicing and collection should be performed by the private sector whenever possible, taking advantage of private sector expertise and eliminating the inherent conflict of interest and political liability for agencies caught between representing constituent interests while simultaneously trying to collect debts. Servicing and collecting loans can be passed on to the private sector by guaranteeing loans instead of issuing direct loans, by selling direct loans to the private sector, and by contracting out servicing and collections.

The Reagan Administration also raised, for the first time, the issue of identifying the hidden long-term credit cost of government credit programs. This cost is transferred by Congress from special interests to the taxpayers, and is in effect a subsidy. It consists of: (1) the cost differential between private sector and government terms and interest rates, plus (2) the expected costs of late repayments and defaults on direct loans, plus (3) the costs of claims on guaranteed loans. The subsidy needs to be estimated at the time of budget enactment, and the actual subsidy should be calculated regularly to monitor agency management performance and to provide data for future budgeting. The most direct approach to measuring a subsidy is to sell direct loans to private sector investors as soon as they are created, thereby determining the actual difference between the face amount of the loan and the real market value to nongovernment investors. The Administration initiated a three-year pilot program to sell or prepay direct loans in 1987, generating proceeds of $3.1 billion on face amounts of $5.1 billion from loan sales, and $2.5 billion of proceeds on face amounts of $2.8 billion from loan prepayments. The Administration also proposed legislation to provide separate funding for subsidies, thereby providing explicit estimates of and record-keeping for subsidies.

To implement this credit agenda, the Administration launched an ambitious, government-wide management reform designed to shatter the established mindset that the major government responsibility was to extend credit on favorable terms to favored constituencies. It instituted aggressive legislative and administrative initiatives to emphasize downstream management responsibilities, including:

◆ Prescreening of borrowers
◆ Upgrading automated account-servicing systems
◆ Aggressive debt collection techniques

◆ Writing off uncollectible accounts
◆ Reporting of program performance

The full implementation of these management reforms will provide the next Administration with great opportunities to improve the government's credit management.

The primary task of a new appointee dealing with a credit program should be to insure implementation of the various credit management tools that are prescribed for each of the four stages of the credit life cycle:

◆ Credit Extension
◆ Account Servicing
◆ Debt Collection
◆ Write-Off

The appointees' objective in the first phase of the credit cycle, *credit extension*, should be to assure that the risk of extending credit is consistent with the program objectives.

A new appointee will find that in general qualification, screening, and documentation processes are established and only need monitoring. Some agencies have established procedures to evaluate repayment capability, but essentially none has determined appropriate risk standards to guide actual credit extension.

The second phase of the credit cycle, *account servicing*, addresses routine collection of payments from borrowers and strengthens routine management reporting.

Most agencies have implemented documentation, aging, invoicing, and credit bureau reporting requirements. Automation is improving for the larger credit programs, but many need further development. Management reporting is inconsistent, and management reviews of program performance (subsidies, delinquencies, repayments, and write-offs) are infrequent.

The last two phases of the credit cycle are to *resolve delinquent accounts*.

Generally, the procedures are in place for these initiatives, but compliance is mixed depending on the agency. Foreclosing on collateral and claiming borrower guarantees is unusual. The collection function should be independent from the credit extension function wherever possible to avoid conflicts between effective collection and representing constituencies.

For loan guarantee programs, management is responsible for insuring that the direct lender meets program objectives by:

◆ Determining that the government's risk is appropriate, usually 70 percent to 80 percent, so that the borrower and the lender both extend their best efforts to satisfy their commitments.

◆ Determining that the lender is using the government's screening criteria in extending credit, and is complying with the government's servicing and collection requirements.

◆ Determining that guarantees are not paid until the lender has complied with all collection procedures.

◆ Reviewing lender performance regularly and discontinuing support for lenders with unsatisfactory performance.

An active management review process must be imposed over the agencies' credit cycle responsibilities. Agency management must determine an acceptable risk for credit extension and then monitor performance against that risk. Risk expectation and performance can be measured by subsidy amounts, delinquent and rescheduled amounts, write-off amounts, and direct lender claims on government guarantees. Amounts expressed as percentages will add perspective. Regular review of expectations and performance will:

◆ Determine the compliance of each program with its objectives.

◆ Provide the basis for program changes.

◆ Provide insight on the need for procedural changes or staff training.

◆ Provide a basis for reviewing personnel performance.

◆ Provide data for future budgeting of credit programs.

◆ Provide the necessary data for reporting to OMB, Treasury, the White House, and the Congress.

In most agencies, accountability for performance of credit programs is directed at financial or administrative officials. This is wrong since these executives are basically bookkeepers for the credit programs and merely track the results of decisions made by the credit manager. Accountability for achieving the goals and objectives of the Administration must be redirected to line managers of credit programs using the available Performance Management System for Senior Executives and Merit Pay Managers.

UNDERSTANDING THE ENVIRONMENT

New appointees will find mixed concurrence within the institutions of government on the credit management policies and procedures presented above. The policies and procedures will not be well received by members of Congress who have close ties to the special interests, nor by trade groups and associations protecting their vested interests. Leadership in a conservative Administration will be supportive, but traditionally credit management does not rate high on the spectrum of political priorities. Career employees at the agencies can be motivated to support some of the initiatives, but they will be reluctant to embrace full credit cycle responsibility, particularly the debt collection aspect. They recognize the political difficulty of foreclosing on bad loans and prefer to concentrate on the more welcomed credit extension phase.

Managing credit effectively and representing an agency's constituencies on political and economic issues will generate conflict. Congress enacts poorly crafted legislation promising benefits to various special interests, and it rests with the agencies to implement that legislation. Congressional intent often is vague, frequently purposefully so, and always requires administrative interpretation by the agencies for proper implementation. Rarely, for example, does the budgeting process offer guidance to agencies on acceptable long-term costs of credit programs. As economic conditions change, so do Administration credit collection attitudes. Trade associations will pressure Congress for the most lenient interpretation on legislation, particularly when their constituencies are experiencing economic distress. Appointees spend time defending their actions in congressional hearings, often turned into harangues depicting collection activity in harsh and unsympathetic terms. During the early 1980s Department of Agriculture officials regularly found themselves defending foreclosure of agriculture loans before Congress, in court challenges, and during visits to their friends and families in farming communities. When the Reagan Administration proposed selling Economic Development Administration (Department of Commerce) loans to private sector investors, Congress intervened by enacting the McDade Amendment requiring borrower approval for each sale: what borrower would willingly approve the sale of his loan from a traditionally lenient lender to a tougher private sector investor?

To guide him through this thicket, the appointee should keep in mind that most taxpayers are borrowers in the private-sector marketplace. They must of necessity abide by all the credit management standards and practices enumerated above. They deserve no less than to have their government conduct its business in a fiscally responsible fashion. In a democratic society government is arguably merely a caretaker for that portion of the national wealth which it collects through the instrument of taxation. Accordingly government is ultimately accountable to its citizens for the administration of those funds and political appointees bear the burden of ensuring that government's programs, processes, and procedures are not inherently flawed and subject to fraud, waste, or abuse.

Ultimately, in light of the inherent political difficulties associated with credit management in the government environment, the optimal course is to prevent the government from serving as a lender. This may not be feasible in the foreseeable future but it is a principle and a goal worthy of pursuit. The credit function is better suited to the private market place where rational criteria will guide its execution, rather than to the much more volatile political arena.

—————————◇—————————

ESTABLISHING A FRAMEWORK FOR NEW POLICY INITIATIVES

The legitimacy of government as lender may be subject to debate, but as long as Congress sees fit to enact credit legislation, it is the appointee's responsibility to protect the taxpayer's interests. Therefore, new Administration appointees with credit management responsibility should adopt a strong philosophical base to guide their decision-making:

◆ As long as credit legislation is passed it should be implemented in a tough, business-like manner. Lenient credit practices benefit only the special interest borrower who already is enjoying favorable terms and conditions at the expense of the taxpayer.

◆ Establishing incentives that encourage government borrowers to graduate to private-sector borrowing is an essential policy element that reduces perpetual borrowing from the government.

◆ Selling direct government loans immediately, reducing the share of the government guarantees, and hiring private sector contractors to service and collect loans are sound management initiatives that reduce the overall cost of credit programs to taxpayers.

◆ Most of the high cost of government credit programs is established at the time of budget enactment and the responsibility of agencies is to insure that the subsidy is minimized with effective credit extension, servicing, and collection.

◆ Establishing forecasts and actual reporting of subsidies and credit management performance allows the political executive to shape the policy debate more realistically according to how much current credit programs are costing, and how much future credit programs are expected to cost.

The focus during the first few weeks should be on developing a working framework for each appointee's credit management responsibility, using the above philosophical base. The new appointee should identify available financial data and use it to advantage in redefining the measures of program performance. For example, if a program manager claims that a program is performing well, is he aware that the program has a current delinquency rate of 22 percent, and does he have a plan for improvement?

Finally, the new appointee must understand and accept that management in government is far more ambiguous and complex than in the private sector. Decisions tend to be based more on short-term compromise than on rational, long-term goal setting. The best political decision does not necessarily equate to the best business decision. Astute coalition building will be important in steering a course between program necessities and political realities, and it should begin on the first day with his fellow political appointees in the agencies.

37

Integrity and Accountability

by
James R. Richards and David H. Martin

Each new Administration brings with it a number of newly appointed political executives who will be expected to carry out the mandate, develop the policies and implement the programs of a newly elected President. It is critical that these executives should recognize early the importance of becoming well acquainted with the ethics laws and regulations applicable to them, as well as gaining a clear understanding of their accountability for managing their assigned programs, activities and operations. A quick grasp of these matters will directly affect the ability of the new Administration to gain the momentum it needs to carry out its mandate during the traditional window of opportunity afforded a newly elected President.

———————◇———————

MANAGEMENT ACCOUNTABILITY

Many new appointees may have an erroneous or incomplete vision of how they will take advantage of this all too brief opportunity. They may believe that they will spend their days (and nights) formulating new policies, reorganizing, testifying before congressional committees, mixing with constituents of their programs, and blending into the political/social milieu of Washington, D.C. All of this will come in good time, and some of it, such as testifying before a maze of congressional committees, will come all too soon. Nevertheless, these executives need first to prepare themselves for these time-consuming chores by planning how to avoid the many disasters that can befall the programs for which they are accountable. Fortunately, there are systems, procedures, and even laws which, if properly understood and utilized, can increase the chances successfully to implement and manage a federal program.

First, the new executive must learn the history of his or her program. For those who are appointed by the President and who must undergo Senate confirmation, the learning process seems more like a college cram course as the confirmation hearing approaches. Most of the teachers are top career staff who have been associated with the program in the past. Naturally, these people want to portray the program in its most positive light. If time permits, it might be wise for the new executive to call for the most recent audits or reviews of the program done by independent organizations like the inspector general of an agency, if it has one, or the General Accounting Office. Another excellent source of information would be the most recent (annual) vulnerability assessment or internal control review performed under the Federal Managers Financial Integrity Act. Also, the appointee should not neglect to review recent budget submissions and testimony of predecessors before congressional oversight committees. After the confirmation hearing (and assuming Senate confirmation) a more detailed review of the program and its history should be undertaken.

The Inspector General

During the past decade "fraud, waste, and abuse (or mismanagement)" have become code words to describe a program, activity, operation, or entire agency that is in trouble and may be headed for failure. It is important that political executives be aware of these signals and understand the procedures and systems that are available to prevent fraud, waste, and abuse. One of the key figures in this prevention effort is the inspector general (IG) of the department or agency. Nineteen departments or agencies now have by statute presidentially appointed IGs intended to report only to the head of the agency, although they have the authority to refer criminal matters directly to the attorney general. They carry out their mission using auditors and criminal investigators, and have the power of subpoena to assist them. The IGs file semi-annual reports with the Congress describing significant problems, abuses, and deficiencies in programs and they provide summaries of prosecutions and convictions obtained as a result of their efforts.

The IG audit process is a detailed review of financial and management systems and other agency operations designed to find and recommend ways that these programs, systems, or operations may be managed more economically and efficiently and protected from fraud and waste. The audit reports, although advisory in nature, are discussed at the draft stage with program managers and are then finalized and sent to the head of the agency and key congressional committees. These reports then may be obtained by the press or others under the Freedom of Information Act. Experience has shown that most waste has resulted from inadequate management. For example, audits of automated systems used to distribute benefits such as social security payments or food stamps have revealed problems or lack of controls that have cumulatively allowed multimillion dollar payments to ineligible recipients. Other audits have revealed faulty procurement practices, bid rigging, mispricing, or overcharging and receipt of defective products, which can result in the wasting of many millions of dollars. Knowledgeable managers use the audit report as a tool to improve management of their programs, thus preventing fraud and waste and keeping them off the front pages of the newspapers.

The General Accounting Office

The General Accounting Office (GAO) is a large agency which functions as the auditing arm of Congress. GAO audits can be initiated at the request of congressional committees or even individual members. The GAO performs program reviews and financial audits, and sets the standards under which IG audits are performed. GAO reviews are often more broad and general in scope than those performed by the IG, but they can also be targeted by a member of Congress at a very specific and narrow program area. The GAO, like the IG, usually allows management to respond to a draft audit before issuing a final report. However, the GAO is often directed by Congress not to show a draft to the audited organization for comments and discussion. Thus, the managers of programs reviewed under these circumstances may first read about the results in a congressional report or in the morning newspaper, especially if the results do not cast the manager, the agency, or the Administration in a favorable light. GAO has access to virtually all records in the executive branch, and the head of an agency is required to respond to recommendations made in GAO reports (though he may disagree with them in whole or in part).

The IGs and the GAO each have a number of criteria that they use to determine which program, operation, or activity will be audited or reviewed. For instance, in considering whether to perform an audit or review of a particular program or operation, they will consider the prior audit coverage, the statutory or regulatory deadlines and requirements, the dollar magnitude, the vulnerability, and any other factors which make a program or operation ripe for review. OMB has charged agencies to set up audit follow-up systems under a high level official responsible for resolving audit recommendations when disagreements arise between program managers and the auditors (whether IG or GAO), in order to ensure that corrective actions are promptly taken. Managers of highly visible or controversial programs can find themselves in political turmoil as a result of an audit report, or for refusing to correct glaring weaknesses or taking too long to implement corrective actions.

Internal Controls/OMB Circular A–123

The Federal Managers Financial Integrity Act (Integrity Act) establishes another process which, if properly implemented, may guard a program or operation from fraud and waste. The Integrity Act is implemented by OMB Circular A–123 which provides:

> Agencies shall establish and maintain a cost-effective system of internal controls to provide reasonable assurance that Government resources are protected against fraud, waste, mismanagement or misappropriation and that both existing and new program and administrative activities are effectively and efficiently managed to achieve the goals of the Agency.

This law requires attention not only to financial systems but to administrative systems as well. It requires an annual assessment of the vulnerability to fraud and waste of an agency's programs and activities and should be accompanied with more comprehensive internal control reviews of the components rated highly vulnerable. It then requires the head of the agency to certify to the President and the Congress that there is "reasonable assurance" that all costs and obligations are lawful, that funds and assets are safeguarded from fraud and waste, and that revenues and expenses are accurately accounted for. The agency head must also identify material weaknesses in internal accounting and administrative systems and submit schedules for corrective actions. The term "internal controls" is an accounting term, but in plain language it calls for:

—clear and available documentation for all significant events and transactions;
—prompt recording and classification of all transactions and significant events;

—only authorized personnel acting within the scope of their authority are executing the transactions;

—sufficient separation of duties between personnel authorizing, processing, recording and reviewing the transactions;

—qualified and adequate supervision;

—resources are accounted for and accessible.

The "Helpful" Congress

Life is made more difficult for managers of federal programs when Congress writes directive language into committee reports (or even into laws) which serves to impede effective and efficient management. Some of these directives are designed to inhibit cost-effective approaches to program implementation. New political executives coming from the private sector must remember that the government has no profit and loss statement against which to weigh decision-making, and instead of a board of directors composed of experienced and knowledgeable business managers, the board is composed of 535 members of the House or Senate who, on any given day, can and will tell you exactly how to do your job.

Some of this intervention can be justified through Congress's oversight responsibilities, but the issue of congressional micromanagement goes to the root of the separation of powers between the legislative and executive branches, as envisioned by the framers of the Constitution. Congress clearly has the right to create or abolish a program (i.e., your job) through the legislative process. But the actual execution of the program (i.e., doing your job) was intended to be the purview of the executive branch. Many today believe that Congress is overstepping its bounds when it micromanages the executive branch. This issue is likely to remain a source of controversy for the foreseeable future and is an irritation new appointees must learn to cope with in order to survive on the job.

As a final thought, in the absence of a bottom line against which to measure success, "good" job performance can be difficult to define or quantify. As a result, job performance becomes a highly subjective concept, and in the politically charged atmosphere of Washington, D.C., performance evaluation for a political executive can be based entirely on perceptions rather than substance or facts. The wise executive should therefore take precautions to guard against unnecessarily providing political opponents the ammunition which can undermine his or her effectiveness or credibility. High on the list of precautionary measures to be taken are activities related to personal conduct or ethics.

———————————◇———————————

ETHICS

Executive Order 11222, which sets forth the Standards of Conduct for federal employees of the executive branch, was promulgated by President Johnson in 1965. After 20 years of use and interpretation, it has become pretty much a permanent fixture in the overall conduct of executive branch employees. The Executive Order provides that federal employees shall avoid any action which might result in or create the appearance of:

1) Using public office for private gain.
2) Giving preferential treatment to any person.
3) Impeding government efficiency or economy.
4) Losing complete independence or impartiality.
5) Making a government decision outside official channels.
6) Affecting adversely the confidence of the public in the integrity of the government.

The Executive Order also sets forth the concept of a prohibited source which is basically any entity or person who is doing business with a particular agency or is regulated by an agency. The prohibited source concept has been interpreted very broadly and the basic rule is that executive branch employees may not accept gifts from prohibited sources. There are a series of exceptions to the prohibited source concept which have been a source of trouble, both for those who have to interpret the Executive Order and those who have to hazard a decision as to whether or not a certain gift is prohibited or not in the traditional "grey" area. The Executive Order also limits outside employment and other activities which either would appear to conflict with an official's duties or which might impair his ability to perform his job. It deals with misuse of information, misuse of government property and contains cautionary standards for such traditional things as paying one's debts, not gambling, betting and placing lotteries on government-owned or -leased property and a general prohibition on engaging in conduct prejudicial to the government.

When first written, the Standards of Conduct were designed to be a broad management tool for the executive branch to allow particular agencies to fashion standards of conduct based on the Executive Order which were particularly suitable to that agency. Unfortunately, most agencies simply copied the Executive Order verbatim using little imagination to make the regulations agency specific.

In addition to the Executive Order, there are certain criminal statutes that apply government-wide to all employees. Some of the more significant statutes provide that no employee may:

1) Directly or indirectly receive or solicit compensation for any services rendered by the employee or another person before a government agency in connection with a particular matter in which the U.S. is a party or has an interest, except as authorized by law.

2) Except in the discharge of his or her official duties, represent anyone else before a court or government agency in a particular matter in which the U.S. is a party or has an interest. This prohibition applies to both paid and unpaid representation of another. (18 U.S.C. 203)

3) Participate personally and substantially in his or her government capacity in any matter in which (i) he or she, (ii) his or her spouse, (iii) minor child, (iv) outside business associate, (v) organization in which he or she is serving as an officer, trustee, partner or employee or (vi) any person or organization with whom he or she is negotiating for employment has a financial interest. (18 U.S.C. 208)

4) Receive any salary, or any contribution to or supplementation of salary, as compensation for services he or she is expected to perform as an officer in the executive branch of the U.S. government, from any source other than the government of the U.S., except as may be contributed out of the treasury of any state, county, or municipality. (18 U.S.C. 209)

As mentioned previously, newly appointed political executives who are Presidentially Appointed with Senate confirmation (PAS) will have already been made aware of the contents of the Executive Order and some of the financial reporting requirements of the Ethics in Government Act (Ethics Act). It is necessary for a PAS to file a financial report disclosing assets, income, liabilities and certain other financial matters prior to a confirmation hearing. This report must be reviewed by the Designated Agency Ethics Official and then is reviewed by the Office of Government Ethics and the appropriate congressional committee. Those who do not fall in this category should seek an ethics briefing before taking office or immediately thereafter. At each agency there is a Designated Agency Ethics Official whose function it is to provide education and counseling programs to all employees, including those who are PAS or otherwise politically appointed. Under this official, there are usually subordinates with similar duties in each major component of the agency.

Since ethics has become so politicized in the last four years, it is important to avoid standards and laws which deal in generalities, which present vague standards, and which rely on appearances more than reality.

Recommendation:

Recognizing that the appearance of impropriety may well be as damaging as an actual conflict of interest or an ethical impropriety, the Standards of Conduct Executive Order 11222 should be revised so as to provide, where possible, a clear line for conduct which is not proper and for conduct which is proper. There are many problems with the interpretation of the present Executive Order, not the least of which is the "appearances" standard which, in many cases, is used politically without regard to the underlying facts being fully developed. Simply stated, specific rules should be the goal while avoiding generalities.

Financial Reporting

Public financial reporting has been successful under the Ethics in Government Act. It is essential for the confidence of the public in the government that it understand that the policymakers at the highest levels of government operate in a fair and impartial fashion. Decisions of the government must be made with integrity and without bias based on a person's personal financial holdings. Preparing a financial report for public scrutiny has three beneficial results. First, it raises the ethical, legal, and moral consciousness of the filer. Second, it raises one's awareness of the potential for conflicts of interest. And third, it allows the reviewer to assist the filer in avoiding conflicts of interest. Unfortunately, public financial reporting has also been politicized. Some political activists have elevated financial reporting to the unhealthy position of claiming that ethical violations exist when a filer has merely misreported or not reported finances accurately. That is unfortunate because, according to recent experience, approximately 75 percent of all financial reports received by the Office of Government Ethics have some mistake or inaccuracy. Furthermore, the media and those inclined to politicize ethics view financial reporting as an opportunity to compile a detailed financial biography of an individual and then to publicize or attempt to publicize a nominee's or appointee's net worth. Since the reporting deadline annually is May 15 of each year, we have become accustomed to seeing the President, the Vice President and prominent senators' and appointees' millionaire status publicized in the media. We need to get away from the net worth aspect and to view the financial reporting for purposes of conflict of interest analysis solely.

Recommendation:

The law regarding financial reporting should be streamlined and simplified to eliminate all categories of value for assets and income. There should also be only one category for reporting assets—those valued at more than $1,000—rather than the complicated and confusing threshholding device currently in use. Of course, filers would still provide sources of income and liabilities. Moreover, in view of the need to coordinate the nomination process with Senate confirming committees, the reporting requirement should be standardized among the committees and the executive branch so that one form would suffice for all financial reporting purposes. That would simplify the nomination process, simplify the review process and require fewer personnel at the committee level, in the Office of Government Ethics, and at the White House.

Public financial reporting is an invasion of privacy but arguably for the good of democratic government.

Recommendation:

Public reporting should be limited to high-ranking officials, political appointees as well as those SES career employees who serve in policy-making positions. Again, a confidential, nonpublic reporting system is considerably simpler and easier to review and prepare, therefore, saving many labor hours in preparation and review time at the agency level.

In some instances, it is necessary for a nominee to an executive branch position to sell an asset in order to cure a conflict of interest, where a blind trust or other recusal agreements would not satisfy either a conflict standard or an appearance standard. In those few instances, we think it is proper to provide a tax deferred sale and rollover of the asset into a mutual fund or other equity that will not present a conflict position, the theory being that a person should not be punished based on a taxable event to the later ultimate sale.

Recommendation:

In all of the conflicts of interest areas, especially financial reporting, the use of civil sanctions are much preferable to criminal sanctions.

The specter of a criminal prosecution for a conflicts problem simply invigorates the politicization of the process. Civil sanctions are more effective from the standpoint of administrative enforcement and in the standard of proof required. A provision for high fines and penalties would have as great a deterrent value as criminal penalties.

Ethics training and education is essential in order to avoid conflicts problems and to prevent inadvertent and unnecessary allegations being raised in the newspapers.

Recommendation:

As part of the orientation process, all PASs should receive mandatory training and education before they report for duty at their particular agency. In no case should a political appointee confirmed by the Senate not receive ethics training and education within two months of assuming the particular position. Under present circumstances with so many rules and regulations falling into what is called the grey area, it is a preventive measure that far outweighs the cost of any cure.

Further, annual training should be required at the agency for all employees and for all PASs, with the agency head not only endorsing the program, but attending. There should also be an annual ethics briefing at the Cabinet level conducted by the Chairman of the President's Council on Integrity and Efficiency and that this briefing cover not only ethics and accountability, but fraud, waste, and mismanagement.

Finally, at the White House level some form of sanction should be instituted for those violations of the Standards of Conduct or the Conflict of Interest laws where pursuit of civil or criminal matter has not been warranted by either the Office of Government Ethics or the Department of Justice. It is essential, for any ethics program to have meaning, that the Chief Executive set the tone at his level and that this heightened sensitivity be made a part of management throughout the White House and each executive branch agency. The only way to achieve that is through training, education, and ultimately through some form of sanctions.

Index